THE CONCISE ENCYCLOPEDIA OF THE GREAT RECESSION 2007–2012

Revised and Expanded Edition

Jerry M. Rosenberg

The Scarecrow Press, Inc.
Lanham • Toronto • Plymouth, UK
2012

Published by Scarecrow Press, Inc.
A wholly owned subsidiary of The Rowman & Littlefield Publishing Group, Inc.
4501 Forbes Boulevard, Suite 200, Lanham, Maryland 20706
www.rowman.com

10 Thornbury Road, Plymouth PL6 7PP, United Kingdom

British Library Cataloguing in Publication Information Available

Library of Congress Cataloging-in-Publication Data

Rosenberg, Jerry Martin.
  The concise encyclopedia of the great recession 2007–2012 / Jerry M. Rosenberg. —
Rev. and expanded ed., 2nd ed.
     p. cm.
  Includes index.
  ISBN 978-0-8108-8340-6 (cloth : alk. paper) — ISBN 978-0-8108-8341-3 (ebook)
  1. Financial crises—United States—History—21st century—Dictionaries. 2.
Recessions—United States—History—21st century—Dictionaries. 3. Financial
institutions—United States—History—21st century—Dictionaries. I. Title.
  HB3743.R67 2012
  330.9'051103—dc23
                                                              2012008495

♾™ The paper used in this publication meets the minimum requirements of
American National Standard for Information Sciences—Permanence of Paper
for Printed Library Materials, ANSI/NISO Z39.48-1992.

Printed in the United States of America

For Ellen

Celebrating fifty-one years of love and adventure.
She is my primary motivation. As a lifelong partner,
Ellen keeps me spirited and vibrant.

"Listen less to those whose judgments brought us this crisis. Listen less to those who told us all they were the masters of noble financial innovation and sophisticated risk management. Listen less to those who complain about the burdens of living with smarter regulation or who oppose having to pay a few for the costs of this or future crisis. . . . Risk will build up again . . . and future governments will have to act again to socialize private losses in the interest of preventing catastrophic damage."

—Timothy Geithner, U.S. Treasury Secretary

CONTENTS

PREFACE TO THE REVISED
AND EXPANDED EDITION

The most telling of statistics appeared in mid-September 2011 when the U.S. Census Bureau reported that the number of citizens living in poverty swelled by 2.6 million between 2009 and 2010 to 46.2 million. That is a shocking 15.1 percent of the population, the highest since 1993. Continuing the disturbing numbers, in 2010 income of the typical household dropped 2.3 percent to $49,445, its third consecutive annual fall. Median household income declined to its lowest level since 1996, $3,800 a year less than its peak in 1999. By 2012, for the first time people had a lower income than thirteen years before.

For minorities, the poverty data was bleaker: 26.6 percent of Hispanic households and 27.4 percent of black households lived below the poverty line in 2010, compared with 13 percent for white households. Nearly a third of families with a single mother were below the poverty line, while 22 percent of children subsisted in poverty. Twenty-two percent of Americans were now poor, about the same share as a half-century ago. Per projections based on the current rate, the recession would have added almost 10 million people to ranks of the poor by the middle of the decade. Also, the number of uninsured people rose by nearly 1 million to 49.9 million.

Where do we turn; where to shift our attitudes, ideologies, and treasury? Assuredly, matters may be worse over the coming months as 2012 unfolds, but as a nation we have already created a wasteland where a huge number of citizens, both very young and old, face a decaying future of opportunity. The government, private sector, and public must aspire to generosity and reinvent the greatness that made the United States a beacon of possibility. Failure to respond to the fallout from the Great Recession may remain our legacy. Failure to generate both jobs and heighten aspirations may doom the American dream to a lost generation. We owe everything to our future; there is no recourse, but to advance or submit.

* * *

It seemed to be a calm and typical summer. In mid-2008, the American economy was in a strong position as its gross domestic product grew by an annualized 3.3 percent, in part reflecting a strong trade performance. U.S. wealth had reached $14 trillion annually. Despite rising unemployment, soaring fuel prices, and constricting credit, consumer spending managed to grow at a 1.7 percent annual rate. President George W. Bush introduced a fiscal stimulus package that included $110 billion in tax rebates, of which $92 billion had been disbursed by early July. Then, the second half of the year began to look weaker. Real consumer spending tumbled at a 0.4 percent monthly rate. Thus began what today is referred to as the Great Recession.

By the end of 2008, the S&P 500 had declined 38 percent, jobs lost came to 1.9 million, and the U.S. government owned stock in 206 banks. The $700 billion bank bailout plan—the Troubled Asset Relief Program (TARP)—was passed by Congress on October 3, 2008, yet failed to fulfill the needs of the nation. And 2009 looked worse. Moving quickly, once he was inaugurated in January, President Barack Obama succeeded in getting a complex, expensive, and lengthy economic stimulus package passed by Congress in February, followed by the new Treasury secretary's plans for ways to effectively use the unspent $350 billion of TARP funds. The next day, the Dow Jones Industrial Average plummeted nearly 5 percent in response to what was considered to be the administration's lack of clarity; specifics were missing.

As the rescue tab rose, taxpayers were not being "adequately informed or protected." These gambles are the reason the government should have attached more strings to its help, including a say in how the money was used. To finance the bailouts, the U.S. Treasury was borrowing money and the Federal Reserve Bank was printing it. That bodes ill for a heavily indebted nation, presaging higher interest rates and higher prices—perhaps sharply higher. By mid-February 2009, the president had signed into law the American Recovery and Reinvestment Act, followed by a housing plan to help nearly 10 million homeowners avoid foreclosure, with promises of more funds to come as needed.

Comparisons were inevitable with the collapse after 1929. In the year following the economic peak in 2008, industrial production declined by as much as it did in the first year of the Great Depression. Equity prices and worldwide trade collapsed even more. Although global industrial output fell by 13 percent forging a major recession, it dropped by nearly 40 percent in the 1930s. In Europe and the United States unemployment had been stuck at one point at roughly 10 percent, while the Great Depression estimates were over 25 percent.

By summer 2009, there were more than five unemployed American workers for every job opening. The ranks of the poor continued to swell, welfare rolls were rising, and those under thirty years of age had sustained nearly half the job losses since November 2007. A month before the meltdown began there were about 7 million Americans counted as unemployed; today there are about 15 million. By the end of the year, there were six times as many Americans seeking work as there were job openings, and the average duration of unemployment—the time the average job-seeker spends looking for work—was more than six months, the highest level since the 1930s. As promised by the government, new regulators and complicated federal regulations were appearing, all purporting to stop the leakage and misuse of the public trust. On Wall Street, 2010 would likely be known as the year of the regulator, with the most significant overhaul in seventy-five years.

This recession had touched Americans across incomes and races. It had slashed family earnings, increased poverty, created increased anxieties and emotional depression, and left more people without health insurance. Median household income fell 3.6 percent to just over $50,000, the steepest year-over-year fall in forty years. The poverty rate, at 13.2 percent, was the highest since 1997. And, about 700,000 more people didn't have health insurance in 2008 than twelve months prior.

One year following the collapse of Lehman Brothers on September 15, 2008, few of the numerous government proposals to reshape the banking and financial industries were in place. Today, most of the institutions that received government funds are doing well. In mid-September 2009, the chairman of the Federal Reserve declared that it appeared that the recession had come to an end and that the economy was turning upward, while at the same time, housing foreclosures and unemployment continued to climb. The jobless rate then hit 10.2 percent in October, the highest since 1982; more than one out of every six workers—17.5 percent—were unemployed or underemployed. Officially, the Great Recession began in December 2007; unofficially, it ended in the early fall 2009. However, for the 15 million unemployed and for those experiencing the meltdown, the year 2010 was part of their nightmare.

Further forestalling the recovery was the debt crisis, first in Greece, then spreading into Italy, Portugal, Spain, and other European Union nations. In April 2010, an attempt to secure funding from the richer European Union nations may have led to a further deterioration of the euro against the U.S. dollar and failed to curtail the mismanaged economies of many of the countries on the continent.

By the mid-term elections of 2010, the last U.S. government labor report announced that September's figures were assuredly disappointing to President Obama and his administration. The economy had lost another 95,000 jobs, as a modest gain in private sector jobs was swamped by large losses in the government sector. Far worse was that most of the net private sector positions did not appear to be particularly good ones—bars and restaurants added the most positions of any sector, followed by temporary hiring services. State and city governments cut jobs, including 58,000 teachers and other education employees who were not recalled for the 2010 school year.

While corporations held $1.6 trillion in cash, they were not hiring. The monthly September figures showed an unemployment rate of 9.6 percent, and without the stimulus plan of 2009 it would have been another 2 percentage points higher. In addition, 3.5 million citizens had either stopped searching for work or had not entered the labor force during the meltdown. President Obama was under great pressure to seek a new, detailed job-creating program.

On December 6, 2010, the president, in his determination to extend unemployment benefits for another thirteen months, retreated from his 2008 campaign promise of not extending the tax cuts of President G. W. Bush for those couples earning $250,000 or more. He compromised and decided to extend the tax cuts for another two years, accepting trade-offs from the Republicans. On December 17 the president signed the new tax cuts regulations.

The Great Recession that began at the end of 2007 has led to the worst unemployment in nearly thirty years. Nearly 42 percent in November 2010 of the 14.8 million jobless workers have been sidelined for six months or more. There is a profound scarcity of jobs. Federal benefits by year's end 2010 averaged $290 a week, about half of what the typical family spent on basics and hardly enough to dissuade someone from working. As unemployment has deepened, benefits have become less generous.

As the lame-duck Congress was to end in December 2010, President Obama chose to accept the Republicans' charge of extending the Bush era's tax cuts for another two years, receiving in part of this exchange, to fund extended unemployment benefits for another thirteen months. With a 9.8 percent unemployment rate, many liberal Democrats were outraged with the administration. Indeed, the sluggish pace of job creation hasn't been strong enough to absorb the growth of the labor force.

Following the collapse of the financial system in 2008 the world attempted to rescue it. Nations went deeply into debt to keep banks afloat and prevent a major recession. Now, stock markets around the world are at least 75 percent higher than they were then. Financial stocks have also risen.

On August 4, 2011, the Dow Jones Industrial Average had its worst retreat in two years, falling 11 percent in two weeks and almost 11 percent since July 22. Stocks were down 4.6 percent. While the Great Recession I was primarily caused by a sudden withdrawal of credit from the economy and formally concluded in 2009 when credit conditions recovered, the double-dip recession, often referred to as the Great Recession II, began when the traditional government policies to fight economic weakness were apparently unavailable. Housing prices had not recovered; millions of people owed more in mortgage debt than their homes were worth. Low interest rates helped push up corporate profits, but new hires had not followed. Washington appeared to be committed to lowering spending. And, to most of the experts' surprise and dismay, the following day Standard & Poor's pulled the U.S. government from its list of risk-free borrowers, reducing its rating to AA+ from AAA. The U.S. Treasury Department would accuse the rating agency of a $2 trillion calculating error.

On the heels of the "Arab Spring" there were the "Occupy Wall Street" protesters, who raised the debate on economic inequity and fairness, the one to ninety-nine ratio. The failure in November 2011 of the U.S. Debt-Reduction Super Committee to secure ways to cut the $1.2 trillion deficit further eroded public confidence in the nation's future. The mid-December European Union summit meeting to save the euro neither solved the long-term problem nor restored faith in the ability to create job growth throughout the eurozone. Fear of the return of autocratic rule in the European Union was spreading. For many experts, Europe's depression (not quite equal to that of the Great Depression) was slowly dragging the United States down.

Most economists forecast a modest 2 percent growth rate in 2012, all being shaped by four factors:

1. Global weakness, which threatens to undermine U.S. exports and could snowball if the European crisis deepens or another problem erupts
2. The foreclosure problem, which will keep the housing market flat on its back
3. A lackluster job market, which means U.S. businesses will keep adding jobs, but at a rate too slow to put much of a dent in unemployment
4. Government belt tightening, which will keep subtracting from growth

Standard & Poor's closed out 2011 nearly dead even with the end of 2010, while the Dow Jones Industrial average gained 5.5 percent for the year. Nevertheless, 2012 will be a year of austerity and continuing sacrifice. As the new year 2012 dawned with an 8.5 percent unemployment rate, one in three Americans—100 million people—were either poor or close to it. U.S. Census Bureau data indicated that 49.1 million citizens were below the poverty line—in general, $23,343 for a family of four. "Near poor" included another 51 million with incomes less than 50 percent above the poverty line.

At the end of January 2012 the government released figures to show that four years after the Great Recession began, real gross domestic product per person was down $1,112, while 5.8 million fewer Americans were working than when the recession commenced. Following two years of false starts, the February 3 report was more optimistic, indicating that the U.S. economy had added 243,000 jobs. The unemployment rate was down to 8.3 percent, the fifth consecutive monthly fall. Should the economy add 200,000 or more jobs each month, the unemployment rate will continue to drop.

The Great Depression of the 1930s, with about one-third of the workforce without jobs, was accompanied by two back-to-back recessions; it seems to be reappearing seventy-five years later. Some will argue that in the 1930s the focus was on people, family security, and the risks to economic well-being. At that time the government was "us," sharing circumstances, frights, and obligations. For some, by 2012 the focus on "the people" had faded, while the politicians in Washington had become an alien presence standing between the population and the realization of individual ambitions.

GOALS

Global understanding is a major part of the new world economic order. This volume attempts to spell out the activities and events of the past two years and to be a guide to help navigate the reader through this economic downturn. With current, accurate, and sufficiently detailed explanations of the economic seesaw of 2008 into 2012, this book should help readers to better understand the reasoning, motives, hidden agendas, and power plays of those who are responsible for this debacle and, most important, what the government has done to try to overcome it. At the same time, this historical and factual encyclopedia, based on daily reports from the media and from specialists in the field, will provide readers with the necessary resources for planning future moves for themselves and their families, friends, and colleagues.

To the user of this volume, it is my hope that this volume will prove to be a rewarding learning experience. I look forward to receiving your comments and suggestions that may assist me in the continuous upgrading of this book.

ACKNOWLEDGMENTS

No work of this nature can be the exclusive product of one person's effort. Even when written by one individual, such a work requires the tapping of many sources, which is especially true of this book. By the very nature of the subjects and fields included, I have had to rely on the able and extensive efforts of others, especially writers, practitioners, and specialists. I have not deliberately quoted from any copyrighted source. Any apparent similarity to existing, unreleased explanations in these cases is purely accidental and the result of the limitations of language. Various organizations have aided me directly by providing informative sources. Some government agencies and nonprofit associations have provided a considerable amount of usable information. In addition, being, according to the *New York Times*, "the leading business and technical lexicographer in the nation" has allowed me to borrow entries from my eight business dictionaries.

During the preparation of this new edition, starting with fall 2007 and covering until early 2012, numerous reliable sources have been tapped. The *Wall Street Journal*, the *International Herald Tribune*, and the *New York Times* have been particularly useful tools. To a lesser extent, the *Economist,* the *Financial Times* of London, and the federally funded *Financial Crisis Inquiry Commission Report* were also critical resources. In addition, most of the country introduction write-ups are drawn extensively from recent information provided by the Organisation for Economic Co-operation and Development (OECD). I could not have realized my goals without their professional wisdom and input.

On a personal level, I thank the many professionals and specialists whom I used as a sounding board to clarify my ideas and approach; they offered valuable suggestions and insight and encouraged me to move ahead. A special thanks to Gregory Henderson, my former MBA student who is currently vice president with a major New York City finance company. During the writing of the first edition of this book, covering 2007 to 2010, he devoted an enormous amount of hours and talent to reviewing my listings and correcting errors, thereby validating many of the entries. To my present editor, Bennett Graff, and publisher, Scarecrow Press, I add my appreciation for their willingness and encouragement to proceed with this second edition.

Then, there are those who have been closest to me. Nothing has been more fulfilling than sharing an adult lifetime with my wife, Ellen, who for more than fifty-one years has contributed immensely to my limited talents by providing her gifts of charm, responsibility, orientation to family, and intellect, and as a partner sharing adventure. Lauren and Bob, Liz, and Jon are the next generation, and they appear already in place as contributors to their communities and chosen areas of work. Of course, four grandchildren—Bess, Ella, Celia, and Rita—make this all come full circle, with the delights of just watching and being fascinated by the ever-changing rainbow in their lives.

NOTE TO READERS

A Concise Encyclopedia of the Great Recession, 2007–2012, has been prepared with the hope that the reader's understanding of the entries will help in the sharing of information and ideas. Hopefully, the confusion about the events that have occurred during this difficult time will be reduced, and this record will serve as a consistent, accurate, and informative resource. Most important, it should help people gain clarity about the significant economic issues of the past several years. Entries can take on different meanings in different contexts and situations, and a goal of this encyclopedic dictionary is to be inclusive and to present all the key elements for each entry. I have organized this work to provide these elements easily and rapidly.

DATES

Some entries provide dates that are essential to understanding the sequence of events. At the first appearance, a date is given by month, day, and year; the year may not be repeated when placed alongside different months and days within the same year. It should be assumed that the year remains constant until the next year appears. For example, January 8, 2008, is given, followed by February 5, March 14, and so on, all in 2008. When the next full date is given, for example, January 12, 2009, that triggers a new year for the subsequent months and days. In addition, most entries are clustered in one lengthy paragraph when they occur in a given year. In addition, nearly all entries within a specific year are encased in a single paragraph.

ALPHABETIZATION

Entries are presented alphabetically. The listings are alphabetized up to the first comma and then by words following the comma, thus establishing clusters of related terms. Entries with numerals are listed according to the spelling of the number.

ENTRIES

The current most common entry is usually given as the principal one, with others cross-referenced to it. Some terms have been included for historical significance only; some entries are given as background to enhance the user's understanding of the recent meltdown events; others are included to assure the smoothness of transition from the past one hundred years of political and economic institutions, regulations, and rules.

CROSS-REFERENCES

"See" and "See also" references are suggested to provide the reader with additional, often related and significant information. Utilizing these listings will provide a deeper and expanded sense of the entry. The use of "Cf." suggests entries to be compared with the original one. "Synonymous with" or "synonym" following a description does not imply that the entry is exactly equivalent to the principal title under which it appears. Usually, the entry only approximates the primary sense of the original term.

FEEDBACK

Major entries have been reviewed by bank/finance/legal specialists and educators. However, I am solely responsible for including the entries and descriptions. I welcome suggestions and critical comments bringing errors to my attention at ejrosenber@aol.com.

A

AAA RATING. A credit-rating agency's rating considered for the best-quality borrowers, reliable and stable—many of the sovereign governments.
See also STANDARD & POOR'S.

AA+ RATING. A credit-rating agency's rating considered for quality borrowers with a bit higher risk than AAA. Includes AA+ high quality, with very low credit risk, but with greater susceptibility to long-term risks.
See also STANDARD & POOR'S.

A RATING. A credit-rating agency's rating considered for quality borrowers whose financial stability could be affected by certain economic situations.
See also STANDARD & POOR's.

ABA. *See* AMERICAN BANKERS ASSOCIATION.

ABACUS 2007-ACI. *See* GOLDMAN SACHS.

ABBOTT LABORATORIES. The company reported a 40 percent fall in third-quarter 2010 earnings, with a near 12 percent increase in revenue. The company announced in 2011 that it would eliminate 1,900 positions, or 2 percent of its workforce.

In April 2011, Abbott reported a fall in earnings, though with a 17 percent increase in revenue. Its last quarter profit climbed 12 percent to $1.6 billion. Net sales rose 4 percent to $10.4 billion.

ABC. The television division of the Walt Disney Company announced on January 29, 2009, that it would eliminate about 400 jobs from its workforce of 6,500 to 7,000 because of the weakening economy. First-quarter profit dropped 46 percent. Ongoing promotion helped increase its hotel occupancy to 89 percent, up slightly from the previous year in their Florida resort. Its theme division shed about 1,900 jobs through a combination of layoffs and buyouts and restructured many of its behind-the-scenes operations. Profit declined in the second quarter 2009 by 26 percent. Net income fell to $954 million from $1.28 billion the year earlier. Fourth-quarter 2009 profit at Walt Disney rose 18 percent, with an $895 million profit. ABC profit climbed 26 percent on a 14 percent revenue gain.

Disney's quarterly revenue and profit surged, with net income for its fiscal third-quarter ending July 3, 2010, rising 40 percent to $1.3 billion from the year before, as revenue increased 16 percent to $10 billion. The Disney Company reported unexpected fourth-quarter 2010 earnings on November 11. For the quarter, Disney reported a profit of $835 million, with net income climbing 20 percent to $3.96 billion. Revenue increased 5 percent to $38.1 billion.

Management reported net income for the three months ending April 2, 2011, of $942 million, with revenue increasing 5.8 percent to nearly $9.1 billion. Net income for the first three months ending July 2 climbed to $1.5 billion, an increase of 11 percent from the year before. Walt Disney reported that its profit jumped 30 percent to $1.09 billion, with revenue climbing 11 percent to $3.13 billion in its fourth quarter 2011.

ABCP. *See* ASSET-BACKED COMMERCIAL PAPER.

ABERCROMBIE & FITCH CO. Reported a 68 percent drop in its fiscal fourth-quarter earnings of 2008. The firm expected deep losses into 2009. Abercrombie lowered prices as much as 90 percent over the Christmas 2008 buying season.

After showing a larger-than-expected fiscal first-quarter 2009 loss in May the firm had a 24 percent decline in revenue for the quarter ending May 2, while sales at stores open for more than a year fell a sharper 30 percent. Abercrombie & Fitch posted a quarterly loss of $26.7 million on August 14, 2009. Sales fell 23 percent to $648.5 million; revenue decreased 15 percent to $765.4 million. Its fiscal fourth-quarter 2009 earnings fell 31 percent. The company posted a profit of $47.5 million, compared with $68 million the year before, with revenue falling 4.6 percent to $936 million.

By January 2010, Abercrombie reported the largest sales surprise with same-store sales up 8 percent. The company decided to close sixty of its 1,098 stores in 2010 and another fifty in 2011, as they reported a 5 percent increase in quarterly sales. However, they noted that average prices fell 15 percent as other retailers increased their discounts.

By early 2011, Abercrombie & Fitch saw a 15 percent increase in same-store sales. The retailer's net rose 95 percent by 2011, as it posted higher international sales. The retailer had a fiscal first-quarter profit of $25.1 million, with total sales of $836.7 million, a rise of 22 percent. For the third quarter the apparel retailer posted a 1.7 percent climb in profit to $50.9 million. Sales had surged 21 percent to $1.08 billion.

See also RETAILING.

ABORTION RATE. Following a decade of decline, the U.S. abortion rate rose 1 percent to 19.6 abortions per 1,000 women of child-bearing age in

2008. The recession probably played a role, leading some people to consider the costs of raising a child.

See also BIRTHS.

ABS. *See* ASSET-BACKED SECURITY.

ABU DHABI. The $10 billion bailout for Dubai from oil-wealthy Abu Dhabi announced in December 2009 is in reality only half the amount promised. On January 18, 2010, a 20 percent reduction would occur, for a $20 billion cut.

See also BARCLAYS; DAIMLER; DUBAI; UNITED ARAB EMIRATES.

AB VOLVO. *See* FORD; GEELY; VOLVO.

ABX.HE. A series of derivatives indices constructed from the prices of twenty credit default swaps that each reference individual subprime mortgage-backed securities.

ACCOR. The global hotel company announced on July 16, 2009, that its second-quarter sales fell 9 percent.

On August 24, 2011, the company reported a first-half net profit of $59.2 million, with revenue increasing 4.4 percent.

See also MARRIOTT.

ACCOUNTABILITY. The quality or state of being accountable; an obligation or willingness to accept responsibility or to account for one's actions. Becoming more important since the Great Recession took hold.

See also EMERGENCY ECONOMIC STABILIZATION ACT OF 2008; FINANCIAL STABILITY OVERSIGHT BOARD; REGULATION; TRANSPARENCY; WALL STREET REFORM ACT (2010).

ACCOUNTANTS. Accountants have been accused of failing to protect the public interest before, during, and following the Great Recession. Questions remain—why didn't they know that the major banks were hiding assets off their balance sheets and stretching regulations, if not outright breaking them?

See also ERNST & YOUNG.

ACCOUNTING RULES. *See* FINANCIAL CRISIS ADVISORY GROUP.

ACQUISITIONS. *See* MERGERS AND ACQUISITIONS.

ADB. *See* ASIAN DEVELOPMENT BANK.

ADIDAS. Reported a 93 percent fall in second-quarter 2009 net profit. Adidas's total quarterly sales fell 2.5 percent.

In April 2011, the German company reported a 25 percent increase in its first-quarter net profit.

See also RETAILING.

ADJUSTABLE-RATE MORTGAGE (ARM). A mortgage whose interest rate changes periodically over time.

ADMINISTRATION. In the United Kingdom, a term synonymous with bankruptcy protection.

ADVANCED MICRO DEVICES (AMD). Plans to cut 10 percent of its workforce, or about 1,400 positions, in 2012. The chip maker recorded about $105 million in restructuring charges. The firm had a fourth-quarter 2011 loss of $177 million. Revenue rose 2.6 percent to $1.69 billion.

ADVERSE FEEDBACK LOOP. The combination of job losses and falling corporate profits that creates new loan defaults, which hurt banks beyond the original mortgage problems that began the 2008–2009 economic collapse.

ADVERTISING. Worldwide, in 2009 spending for advertising slipped 0.2 percent to $490.5 billion, led by a 6.2 percent drop in the United States, the first decline since 2001. Advertising spending in the United States fell 2 percent in the third quarter 2008 as the recession prompted cutbacks, with the steepest toll on national spot radio spending, which dropped 18 percent from 2007. Most forecasts for 2009 predicted general advertising to fall by 5 percent or more, and 9 percent specifically on television. The fate of the car industry is critical, as it spends around $20 billion a year on advertising. Car ads contribute up to 25 percent of advertising revenues for local television channels. Assuredly, advertising agencies will suffer. U.S. advertising spending on media such as TV, print, and online display ads dropped 14 percent to $30.18 billion in the first quarter 2009 from a year earlier. The top ten advertisers for the first quarter 2009, by ad spending in millions, were:

1. Procter & Gamble—$674.1
2. Verizon Communications—$577.1
3. AT&T—$459.4
4. General Motors—$424.2
5. Johnson & Johnson—$397.2
6. News Corporation—$341.2
7. Sprint Nextel—$317.7
8. Walt Disney—$303.7
9. Time Warner—$263.4
10. General Electric—$261.4

In 2011, it was projected that advertising around the world would grow by 4.5 percent, doubling the rate of 2010. Online advertising should grow by 16

percent in 2011, boosting its share of all advertising to over 15 percent. Television advertising should climb by 5.5 percent. Newspapers and magazines will see their advertising slipping further, by 1.5 percent.
See also INTERNET ADVERTISING; LUXURY GOODS; RETAILING.

AER LINGUS. In November 2009, the airline reported that revenue for the three months ending September 30 fell 9.7 percent from the year before, slowing from a 12 percent year-to-year decline in the first half.
See also AIRLINES.

AETNA. In October 2011, management of this large insurance firm reported that revenue rose 8 percent.

AFGHANISTAN. The nation's GDP growth in 2011 was 7.9 percent, with a GDP of $17 billion, an inflation rate of 4.5 percent, and a GDP per head of $570.
See also WARS IN AFGHANISTAN AND IRAQ.

AFRICA. At first minimally affected by the 2008 meltdown, South Africa, the region's largest economy closely linked to the outside world, was the first to feel the impact of the global meltdown. By November 1, 2008, its currency—the rand—lost about 30 percent of its value against the U.S. dollar; its stock market also fell significantly. Nevertheless, South Africa was in good shape with capital controls, financial-sector regulations, and sound banking practices. Most of sub-Saharan Africa was minimally affected, except for Nigeria and Lagos, where their stock markets declined abruptly. Plunging commodity prices and lower overseas demand will also impact this region, as will the drop in oil prices. In Zambia, there had been a 25 percent drop in their currency against the dollar as copper prices tumbled. From 2000 to 2008 Africa's annual output grew by 4.9 percent. Foreign direct investment increased from $10 billion to $88 billion, more than India and close to China.

The International Monetary Fund said on October 25, 2010, that growth for Africa, with forty-seven nations, should reach 5 percent in 2010, with a rise to 5.5 percent in 2011. The IMF expected Africa's economy to expand by 6 percent in 2011 and nearly 6 percent in 2012. A decade earlier Africa was labeled as "the hopeless continent." By the end of 2011, labor productivity grew by an average of 2.7 percent. Trade between the continent and the rest of the world increased by 200 percent since the year 2000. Inflation has fallen by 22 percent in the past ten years to 8 percent. Foreign debts fell by a quarter, budget deficits by two-thirds.
See also AUTOMOBILE INDUSTRY; SOUTH AFRICA; "THIRD WORLD."

AFRICAN AMERICANS. Historically, the automobile industry employed blacks when many industries would not. For many, jobs at car factories were the route to a better life for several generations, but those gains have been threatened since 2008.

African Americans were the most likely to get higher-priced subprime loans, leading to higher foreclosure rates, and have replaced Hispanics as the group with the lowest homeownership rates. The unemployment rate for African Americans is nearly twice that of whites. And nearly half of young black men without a high school diploma have no job. Black workers are also unemployed for about five weeks longer, on average, than the rest of the population. Forty-five percent of unemployed blacks have been out of work for twenty-seven weeks or longer, compared with just 36 percent of unemployed whites.

In October 2009, the unemployment rate for African American men reached 17.1 percent. In the summer 2010, the black unemployment rate was nearly twice as high as the white rate, as in 1975. Today, people at the nine-tieth percentile of the black income spectrum are making about as much as those at the seventy-fifth percentile of the white spectrum.

By 2011, the percentage of the U.S. African American population living in the southern portion of the states hit its highest level in more than fifty years, with the young and educated leaving northern and midwestern cities. In August, the black teen jobless rate jumped to 46.5 percent from 39.2 percent. In November, black unemployment climbed to 15.5 percent from 15.1 percent.

See also BLACKS; CHILDREN IN POVERTY; LIVING STANDARDS; MEN UNEMPLOYMENT; MIGRATION; UNEMPLOYMENT; WOMEN UNEMPLOYMENT.

Cf. HISPANICS.

AGGREGATE DEMAND. *See* KEYNES, JOHN MAYNARD.

AGGREGATOR BANKS. Institutions where the private sector plays a role in pricing bad assets. Of major importance since 2008 meltdown.

Synonymous with "BAD BANKS."

AGING. As more citizens during the Great Recession turn sixty-five in 2012, many are receiving financial help from their children. Eighteen percent have borrowed from their families.

AGRICULTURE. While the country remained in a sluggish performance into summer 2010, the nation's agriculture sector had a surge in exports, indicating that U.S. farmers would ship $107.5 billion in products in the fiscal year ending September 2010. That is the second highest amount, just below $115.3 billion in 2008. At year's end 2010, the prices farmers received for their crops, livestock, and other products were up 18.5 percent from the year before, surpassing the record high set in July 2008. Cotton, soybeans, and turkeys were among the gainers, while tomatoes, lettuce, and rice were among the decliners.

See also CORN; FARMING.

AIG. *See* AMERICAN INTERNATIONAL GROUP.

AIG FINANCIAL PRODUCTS. *See* AMERICAN INTERNATIONAL GROUP.

AIR BAGS. *See* AUTOLIV.

AIRBUS. January 15, 2009, signaled the start of a "very soft year" as the global downturn cut demand for aircraft, and Airbus in turn cut its forecasts. The European aircraft maker held the top spot in global airliner production for the sixth year in a row in 2008, with a 7 percent rise in deliveries to a record 483 planes, compared with Boeing, its U.S. rival. By April, Airbus trimmed its jumbo output as carriers deferred orders primarily based on the economic meltdown. Originally, Airbus planned to deliver more than thirty super-jumbos in 2010 carrying a catalog price of $327 million each. Airbus, which expected to sell about 300 planes in 2009, projected that sales would stabilize in 2010 and would rise by as much as 4.6 percent. The decline in 2009 traffic was 2 to 4 percent. On November 16, 2009, a third-quarter net loss at $129.9 million was posted. Revenue also fell 1.8 percent.

Then, on July 30, 2010, the European Aeronautic Defense and Space Company, the owner of Airbus, reported that its first-half net profit halved to $241.3 million; also for the first half of the year, revenue was 1 percent higher than the year before.

On November 10, 2011, the European Aeronautic Defense and Space Company announced that it expected 2011 revenue to increase by more than 4 percent with profit increasing to about 1.45 euros. Its third-quarter earning surged to 312 million euros, with revenue in its Airbus division falling by 10 percent.

See also AIRLINES.

Cf. BOEING.

AIR CARGO. *See* DHL; FEDERAL EXPRESS; UPS.

AIR FARES. *See* AIRLINES.

AIR FRANCE-KLM. Warned on March 26, 2009, that it would have an operating loss of about $272 million for its fiscal year ending March 31 because of shrinking passenger traffic and cargo activity and the costs of fuel. It expected revenues to decline 6 percent for 2009. The airline had a net loss for its fiscal fourth quarter of $684.5 million, with revenue declining 12 percent.

On July 30, Air France-KLM posted its fiscal first quarter with a net loss of $599 million, compared with a net profit of more than $200 million a year earlier. Its first-quarter 2009 revenue declined 21 percent to 5.17 billion euros. Air France-KLM had a net loss for its fiscal second quarter 2009 of $218.6 million. Revenue dropped 19 percent.

The carrier reported on May 19, 2011, that it had an approximately $1 billion profit despite a $1.42 billion increase in its fuel costs. Revenue climbed 13 percent to about $35 billion.

See also AIRLINES.

AIRLINES. The upheaval of airlines in the world continued throughout the economic crisis of 2008–2009 as passenger volumes continued to decline even though the price of fuel dropped. Lufthansa airlines made a bid for Austrian airlines; Iberia had a drop of 11 percent air travel in October; and British Airways' traffic fell 5.9 percent in November. Passenger travel worldwide declined 4.6 percent from a year earlier for a third straight month in 2008. Freight traffic dropped almost 14 percent. Further hurting the industry, on December 10 the government of China urged its state-owned airlines to cancel or defer new aircraft purchases at a time of global economic turmoil, hurting American and European aircraft makers. State-owned airlines had total losses of $612 billion in the first ten months of 2008.

Losses for the world's airlines, announced on March 24, with its deepest crisis in sixty years, were projected to total nearly $5 billion for 2009, as passenger and freight traffic continued to fall. The loss forecast made in December 2008 was $2.5 billion. Projections for 2009 were losses for global airlines of $9 billion because of low demand and poor yields in a global economic slump and the spread of H1N1 flu virus—double the $4.7 billion loss estimated in March 2009.

In 2008, the loss was $10.4 billion. By summer 2009, it was clear that profits for airlines were down. In the first four months of the year, premium traffic dropped by 15 percent, while traffic within Europe dropped by 37 percent. The industry lost $9 billion in 2009. The five largest hub-and-spoke carriers reported second-quarter 2009 losses, including AMR Corporation's American Airlines, Delta Air Lines, UAL Corporation's United Airlines, Continental Airlines, and US Airways Group. Passenger air traffic, measured in revenue passengers per kilometer, fell 2.9 percent from a year earlier in July, an improvement from the 7.2 percent fall in June 2009 and the 6.8 percent decline for the first eight months of the year. Cargo volumes, measured in freight ton per kilometer, fell 11.3 percent in July, better than the 16.5 percent fall in June 2009.

In September 2009, the global airline industry was facing $11 billion in losses for the year, $2 billion more than originally projected. Its trade association expected airlines to lose $3.8 billion worldwide in 2010, marking a third straight annual loss. The industry had lost $16.8 billion in 2008. The association representing airlines reported on September 17 that the world's airlines lost a combined $11 billion in 2009, on top of a $16.8 billion loss in 2008. Estimates were that the world's airlines would lose about $11 billion in 2009 as the meltdown sharply reduced air traffic. By December 2009, business-class sales were up. The industry appeared to be headed toward a recovery as fuller planes, fewer discounted fares, lower fuel prices, and revenue from a variety of formerly free services started to pay off.

Although it was expected that air travel would expand in 2010, airlines still had significant losses, perhaps $5.6 billion. The global airline industry expected a possible $4.6 billion loss in 2010. That would be an improvement on its estimated $11 billion loss for 2009. In May 2010, international air-passenger traffic soared 12 percent. Overall, airlines were expected to post a $2.5 billion profit in 2010, a turnaround from the $9.9 billion loss in 2009.

By mid-July 2010, it was clear that eight of the largest nine carriers had turned the corner as the economy improved to post its first meaningful profit since 2007's third quarter. This was a significant change from two years before when U.S. airlines were pounded by soaring fuel prices followed by the recession.

The pre–Great Recession airfare costs were nearly back to their price by September 2010, with as much as a 30 percent rise in international flights. Domestic airfare costs were also rising rapidly, along with other in-flight charges. The average price that passengers paid to fly each mile in July, excluding taxes, was the second-highest of the last decade. It was predicted on September 21 that global airlines would show a combined profit of $8.9 billion in 2010, more than triple the June forecast of $2.5 billion. Demand for air travel increased 11 percent in the year. Profits were up for the first time in years. Airline passenger traffic climbed 8.2 percent and freight increased 21 percent in 2010. On average, the profit margin was 2.7 percent.

By February/March 2011, airlines were spending about one-third of their revenue on fuel. It was expected that carriers' combined 2011 net profit of $8.6 billion would be down from an earlier forecast of $9.1 billion on revenues of $594 billion. The recession had resulted in large cutbacks in flights across the nation, minimally affecting large airports but significantly impacting mid-size and smaller airports. The smallest airports lost 10 to 15 percent of their scheduled flights from June 2006 to June 2011. Medium-size airports lost 18 percent of their scheduled flights, while at the largest airports passenger traffic fell by only 2.3 percent. By mid-September it was projected that global airline industry earnings would fall 29 percent to $4.9 billion in 2012. Earnings forecast for 2011 were $6.9 billion from the $4 billion profit projected in June.

See also AER LINGUS; AIRBUS; AIR FRANCE-KLM; AIRTRAN; ALL NIPPON AIRWAYS; AMERICAN AIRLINES; AMERICAN IN-TERNATIONAL GROUP; AUSTRIAN AIRLINES; BOEING; BRITISH AIRWAYS; CATHAY PACIFIC AIRWAYS; CONTINENTAL; DELTA; FINNAIR; IBERIA; JAPAN AIRLINES; JETBLUE; LUFTHANSA; MESA AIR GROUP; QUANTAS; SCANDINAVIAN AIRLINES; SOUTHWEST AIRLINES; TRAVEL AND TOURISM (2011); UNITED AIRLINES; UNITED CONTINENTAL HOLDINGS; US AIRWAYS.

AIR TRAFFIC. *See* AIRLINES.

AIRTRAN. A Florida-based airline, it posted a profit of $78.4 million, with revenues falling in the second quarter 2009 by 13 percent to $603.7 million.

By March 2010, its traffic gained 9.6 percent from a year before on a 5.5 percent increase in capacity. The world's airlines were expected to turn an industry-wide profit of $2.5 billion in 2010, compared to an earlier forecast of a global loss of $2.8 billion.

See also AIRLINE INDUSTRY.

ALCATEL-LUCENT. The French-American telecommunications equip-ment maker announced on December 11, 2008, that it would eliminate 1,000 management positions, or about 7 percent of its managers, in an austerity plan that aimed to save 750 million euros. The job cuts, about 1.3 percent of the global workforce of 77,000, suggested more hard times ahead.

A fourth-quarter 2008 report indicated a net loss of $5.07 billion. Their first-quarter 2009 loss was $536 million. On July 30, 2009, the company posted its first quarterly profit since its creation in 2006. Alcatel-Lucent had earnings of $19.6 million. It reported on October 30 that its third-quarter loss more than quadrupled from a year earlier as demand dropped for older-generation wireless network gear. Its loss climbed to $270 million. Sales in the third quarter fell 9.8 percent from a year earlier.

The firm posted a wider first-quarter 2010 loss. The Paris-based company had reported a quarterly profit only twice since its creation in 2006. Its loss widened to $660.3 million in the three months ending in March. Revenue dropped 9.8 percent.

ALCOA. Cut 13 percent of its workforce in early 2009, and 1,700 contrac-tors were eliminated. Alcoa, the third-largest aluminum company in the world and the largest U.S. aluminum producer, lost $1.19 billion during the fourth quarter 2008, as prices and demand for the metal plunged in the troubled global market. Alcoa announced in mid-March 2009 that it would slash its dividend 82 percent. In addition to reducing operational expenses by $2.4 billion, it would embark on a new round of cost-cutting. These measures were in addition to the earlier cuts in 2009 that included 15,000 layoffs, asset sales, and plant closures. In the first quarter 2009, Alcoa revealed that it was significantly hit by falling aluminum prices and a 41 percent decline in sales; a loss of $497 million resulted. The price of its metal fell 26 percent, since January 1.

Alcoa, on July 8, became the first blue-chip company to report its second-quarter 2009 earnings, with a $454 million loss. Revenue fell 42 percent to $4.24 billion in the quarter, compared with $7.25 billion one year earlier. Meanwhile, the price of aluminum fell 49 percent from the second quarter 2008 to $1,485 a metric ton.

On October 7, 2009, Alcoa posted a profit of $77 million in the third quarter. This was a 71 percent decline from a year before, but indicated a hopeful turnaround. By month's end, Alcoa reported its first profitable quarter in a year. Alcoa's fourth-quarter 2009 earnings showed a $277 million loss, a minor drop following the firm's $1.2 billion loss in 2008.

The company reported on April 12, 2010, that it had a narrower loss than expected. Sales increased 18 percent to $4.89 billion. Management reported on July 12 that the firm swung to a profit in the second quarter. Earnings were $136 million; revenue increased 22 percent to $5.19 billion from $4.24 billion one year before. The company reported on October 7, 2010, that its third-quarter sales had increased 15 percent to $5.3 billion.

For the fourth quarter 2010, Alcoa reported a profit of $258 million, compared with the year before loss of $277 million. Sales grew 4 percent to $5.65 billion. The company returned to profit in the first quarter, earning $308 million in the quarter, compared with a $201 million loss the year before. Revenue rose 22 percent to $5.96 billion.

On July 11, 2011, management reported that income soared 7.9 percent, with profit totaling $322 million. Sales climbed 27 percent to $6.59 billion. On October 11, management reported that its third-quarter earnings were short of expectations. Net income nearly tripled to $172 million, with revenue climbing 21 percent to $6.42 billion.

On January 5, 2012, management announced that it would slash global smelting capacity by 12 percent as a result of higher costs and lower prices. Prices had dropped more than 27 percent from their peak in 2011, significantly related to slower housing construction in China, which consumes about half the world's aluminum. Fourth-quarter 2011 losses posted a loss of $191 million, compared with a profit of $258 million the year before. Shares rose 2.9 percent to $9.43.

ALDRICH-VREELAND ACT. A forerunner of the Federal Reserve Act. Congress in 1908 passed legislation as a temporary relief measure until new banking rules could be formulated.

ALGERIA. In 2011, the economy was projected to expand by 4 percent, aided by improving hydrocarbon exports. The nation's GDP growth was 4 percent, GDP of $202 billion, an inflation rate of 4.2 percent, and a GDP per head of $5,560.

ALLIANZ. Europe's largest insurer by premiums and market capitalization, reported in November 2010 an 8 percent fall in net profit of $1.74 billion for the third quarter. Total revenue rose 11 percent.

ALLIED IRISH BANKS. *See* IRELAND.

ALL NIPPON AIRWAYS. Reported a fiscal first-quarter 2009 net loss of $308.6 million in the three months ending June 30. Revenue dropped 22 percent.
   See also AIRLINES.

ALLSTATE. The nation's largest publicly traded home and auto insurer reported that its fourth-quarter 2010 profit fell 43 percent to $296 million.

ALLY FINANCIAL. Formerly GMAC.
   See also FEDERAL HOUSING FINANCE AGENCY; GMAC.

ALTERNATIVE ENERGY. *See* EMERGENCY ECONOMIC STABILIZATION ACT OF 2008.

ALTERNATIVE MINIMUM TAX. *See* TAX CUTS.

ALUMINUM. *See* ALCOA; PROPERTY (2011); RIO TINTO.

AMAZON.COM INC. Shares on October 23, 2009, surged 27 percent to $118.49, an all-time closing high following strong third-quarter results. Its fourth-quarter 2009 net income rose 71 percent. The firm's profit for the quarter rose to $384 million, with revenue climbing to $9.52 billion from $6.70 billion.
   Amazon.com posted a sharp increase in first-quarter 2010 profit. Sales grew 72 percent. Its first quarter profit climbed 69 percent to $299 million; revenue rose to $7.13 billion from $4.89 billion. For its second quarter, Amazon's earnings climbed 45 percent on a 41 percent increase in sales. The quarter's profit grew to $207 million, with revenue rising to $6.57 billion from $4.65 billion. On October 21, 2010, Amazon.com posted a 16 percent profit gain, with sales rising 14 percent in the fourth quarter from the year before to $51 billion. The firm's third-quarter profit was driven by a 39 percent increase in total sales to $7.56 billion.
   The world's largest online retailer reported that its second-quarter 2011 revenue surged 51 percent to $9.9 billion. Profit, however, fell 8 percent to $191 million as operating costs climbed 54 percent. The firm's fourth-quarter

revenue climbed 35 percent to $177 million, down from $416 million the year before. At the same time, profit plunged 57 percent. For 2011, Amazon.com earned $631 million in profit on $48.1 billion in sales, compared with $1.2 billion in profit and $34.2 billion the year before. A total of 56,200 workers were on the payroll, up 67 percent from 2010.

On January 31, 2012, management announced that its fourth-quarter 2011 revenue rose 35 percent, while profits fell 57 percent. Operating costs climbed 38 percent. For the first quarter 2012 Amazon.com predicted revenue of $12 billion to $13.4 billion.

Cf. BARNES & NOBLE; BORDERS.

AMD. *See* ADVANCED MICRO DEVICES.

AMERICAN AIRLINES (AMR). Reported fourth-quarter 2008 losses, capping a miserable year that saw soaring fuel prices drop sharply, only to be replaced by a recession-induced drop in travel. Demand was off 2.5 percent from 2007, and international bookings were down about 8 percent. American Airlines would cut its mainline capacity by 6.5 percent in 2009, after trimming it by 8 percent in 2008. AMR lost $2.07 billion in 2008. On April 15, it was announced that the airline lost $437.5 million in the first quarter, cutting the company's revenue by 15 percent. Prices of the average fare fell by 4.5 percent from a year earlier.

Then, on July 15, American Airlines reported a $390 million second-quarter loss as collapsing travel demand continued to erase gains from lower fuel costs. Its second-quarter revenue fell 21 percent to $4.89 billion from a year before. Average fares dropped 15 percent. On September 1, AMR announced that it was cutting 921 flight-attendant positions effective October 1. Two hundred twenty-eight employees would be furloughed, and 244 others placed on leave for two months. Another 449 would take voluntary options such as leave. AMR reported that its traffic fell 8.1 percent in August from a year before. The airline's capacity fell 9.4 percent. AMR reported a loss of $359 million for the third quarter 2009, with revenue falling 20 percent from a year earlier. By December 2009, AMR announced that it was prepared to invest $1.1 billion in Japan Airlines.

In March 2010, traffic grew by 2.5 percent on 0.7 percent fewer seats. Its second quarter was among the worst in the industry to $10.7 million from $390 million the year earlier. The airline on October 20 presented its first profitable quarter in two years. The company posted a profit of $143 million, reversing the loss of $359 million the year before. AMR achieved a unit-revenue gain of 11 percent, with traffic increasing 3.7 percent. AMR reported a fourth-quarter loss of $97 million.

Management reported a first-quarter 2011 loss of $436 million and showed a revenue rise of 9.2 percent to $5.53 billion. On October 3, the airline's shares plunged 33 percent on fears that the third-largest airline by traffic may seek bankruptcy protection. In October it was reported that the airline had a third-quarter loss, becoming financially the weakest of the big U.S. carriers. The airline incurred nearly $5 billion in losses since 2008, and it was expected to post its fourth-consecutive annual loss in 2011. Then, on November 29, the parent airline filed for bankruptcy protection, hoping to reduce costs and emerge more competitive after losing more than $10 billion since 2001. AMR management stated that its annual labor costs, including pensions, were about $800 million more than competitors'. AMR shares collapsed 84 percent.

In February 2012, AMR indicated that it would seek to eliminate 13,000 positions and terminate pensions in the hopes of $2 billion in annual cost savings. It plans to lower labor costs by $1.25 billion a year, or 20 percent, including reducing its workforce of 88,000 by nearly 15 percent.

See also AIRLINES; JAPAN AIRLINES.

AMERICAN ASIATIC UNDERWRITERS. *See* AMERICAN INTERNATIONAL GROUP.

AMERICAN BANKERS ASSOCIATION (ABA). The national organization of banking formed in 1875 to "promote the general welfare and usefulness of banks and financial institutions." Critiques are that the ABA failed the public by not staying on top of the evolving banking crisis.

AMERICAN DREAM. *See* HOUSING PLAN; MODIFYING MORTGAGES.

AMERICAN EAGLE OUTFITTERS. Fiscal second-quarter 2011 earnings more than doubled, with a profit of $19.7 million. Sales climbed 3.7 percent to $675.7 million. The retailer's fiscal third-quarter earnings surged 59 percent by December 2011, with a profit of $52.4 million. Sales climbed 11 percent to $832 million.

AMERICAN EXPRESS (AMEX). In February 2009, the credit card company offered select customers a $300 AmEx prepaid gift card if they paid off their balances and closed their accounts. As the economic crisis widened and unemployment rose, there was growing concern that credit card defaults would soar. AmEx customers reduced spending by 16 percent in the first quarter 2009, sending the company's quarterly net income down 56 percent. The firm's three-month net income was $437 million, down from $991 million a year earlier. With customers reducing their spending by 16 percent in the second quarter, the company's quarterly net income fell 48 percent. Its net income was $337 million, down from $653 million a year earlier. AmEx's fourth-quarter 2009 profit tripled and overall cardmember spending climbed 8 percent. AmEx posted a profit of $716 million, up from $240 million a year before. Revenue fell 0.3 percent to $6.49 billion.

AmEx reported a first-quarter 2010 net income of $885 million, up from $437 million the year before. Management declared that its fourth quarter 2010 showed a net income soaring 48 percent. Net income in the quarter was $1.06 billion, up from $716 million the year before. Revenue climbed 13 percent to $7.32 billion.

The company announced on January 19, 2011, that it would cut about 550 jobs. In April, AmEx reported a first-quarter net income of $1.18 billion, up from $885 million the year before, and a revenue picture of $7.03 billion. The firm's second-quarter earnings rose 31 percent, posting a net income of $1.33 billion. Revenue, net of interest, rose 12 percent to $7.62 billion. Reported in October, AmEx profit climbed 13 percent to $1.2 billion, with revenue increasing 9 percent to $7.6 billion.

See also CREDIT CARDS.

AMERICAN INTERNATIONAL GROUP (AIG). Founded in Shanghai in 1919 and called American Asiatic Underwriters, the world's largest insurance company on May 9, 2008, announced a record $7.8 billion first-quarter loss. AIG provides insurance protection to more than 100,000 entities, including small businesses, municipalities, 401(k) plans, and *Fortune* 500 firms, which together employ over 100 million workers. AIG had over 375 million policyholders in the United States, with a face value of $19 trillion, and remained a major source of retirement insurance. On August 7, AIG announced a $5.4 billion second-quarter loss as the housing market continued to pose problems.

The U.S. government created an $85 billion emergency credit line in September to keep AIG from folding and added $38 billion more in early October when it became obvious that the initial amount was insufficient. As part of the revised plan, the Federal Reserve indicated that it would reduce that credit line to $60 billion. The government then announced on November 10 an overhaul of its rescue of the insurance giant, indicating that it would purchase $40 billion of the firm's stock, after indications that the initial bailout was placing too much strain on AIG.

When the reorganization was finalized, taxpayers would have invested and lent a total of $150 billion to AIG, the most the government had ever invested in a single private enterprise. But Federal Reserve officials said the $40 billion investment would permit them to reduce their exposure of $112 billion from $152 billion and improve the condition of the collateral for its loan. The government invested an additional $22.5 billion in AIG to help the firm buy residential mortgage-backed securities that it also insured. Treasury Department officials stated that the $40 billion AIG investment was separate from the $250 billion the Treasury had earmarked for buying stakes in banks. AIG reported a loss of $24.47 billion for the third quarter, compared with a profit of $3.09 billion a year earlier. Together with the U.S. government, AIG on December 3 agreed to clear itself of its obligations on about $53.5 billion in toxic mortgage debt. By December 31, AIG was prepared to ask the Federal Reserve to relax its rules on its $60 billion-plus disposal program to permit bidders to use a greater proportion of shares to pay for its assets. The government's $153 billion bailout of AIG had effectively made it a majority owner of the insurance group.

By mid-February 2009, the staggering infusion had not been able to stem losses at the company, as it tried to raise as much as $60 billion in fresh capital to stay afloat. At the beginning of March, the government overhauled its $150 billion bailout of AIG, hoping to support the ailing insurers. The arrangement, the government's fourth, represented a near reversal of the one first given in mid-September. Going from the government serving as a demanding lender, thereby forcing AIG to pay a steep interest rate on an anticipated short-term loan, the government eliminated interest charges and acted as a majority shareholder. The focus was on splitting the firm, with businesses made into separate stock offerings. AIG would combine its giant property-casualty insurance activities into a new unit, with a different name and separate management, and sell nearly 20 percent of it to investors. Another $30 billion in new cash from the Troubled Asset Relief Program would cut the firm's $60 billion credit line with the Federal Reserve to between $20 billion and $25 billion.

Since the Federal Reserve first bailed out AIG in September 2008, government aid to the insurer had almost doubled, as follows:

September 16—Government seized AIG, exchanging an $85 billion loan for a 79.9 percent equity stake.

October 8—Federal Reserve increased its loan by $38 billion, for a total of $123 billion.

November 9—The government scrapped the original loan in favor of a new deal that included lending and an equity share, for a total of $150 billion.

March 1—The government made $30 billion of TARP money available and cut the loans by up to $25 billion.

By March, the government was resigned to a long stewardship after failing to sell the insurer into smaller units, with the government owning nearly 78 percent of the firm. The AIG bailout was now up to $173.3 billion in taxpayer assistance. On March 2, AIG reported a $61.7 billion fourth-quarter loss that brought their losses for 2008 to $99.3 billion. Its assets also dropped, from over $1 trillion as of September 30 to $860 billion at year end 2008. In the fourth quarter 2008, the firm took $13 billion in charges on distressed investments, particularly related to commercial mortgages. Another $7 billion came from interest and other costs associated with a federal loan central to the bailout. On March 23, fifteen of the top twenty recipients of $165 million in bonuses to employees of the AIG Financial Products division (the division blamed for most of AIG's losses and woes) agreed to give back their bonuses—amounting in excess of $30 million in cash. A major portion of these monies would be returned, according to the New York attorney general, Andrew Cuomo. AIG reported the largest quarterly loss in history, around $62 billion. The quarterly losses suffered by Merrill Lynch and Citigroup, $15.4 billion and $8.3 billion, respectively, pale in comparison with AIG. The federal government would provide a third plan of assistance, on top of the $150 billion in loans, investments, and equity injections, to keep it afloat. Once again, in March the government provided AIG with its fourth round of assistance. On March 17, the government sought to recoup from AIG the $165 million in bonuses paid to employees in the wake of a national furor over the payments.

AIG reported a roughly $5 billion first-quarter 2009 loss. The first-quarter deficit was small in comparison to the $62 billion loss AIG reported for 2008's fourth quarter. AIG closed a deal with the Treasury Department on April 20 in which the government would make new funds available to AIG. Subtracted from the new monies was an amount to offset the bonus payments AIG made in March to employees of its financial products unit. The arrangement was originally set at $30 billion, and now $165 million was subtracted, leaving a total of $29.835 billion. In addition, the Treasury would invest in the company as long as AIG didn't file for Chapter 11 bankruptcy protection and the Treasury would hold more than 50 percent of the voting power. Then, on August 7, AIG reported a quarterly profit, its first since late 2007.

AIG's International Lease Finance Corporation, the largest airplane-finance firm in the world, was on the brink of collapse by mid-September 2009, unable to pay its coming debts. Over the coming three years, the company had about $18 billion of debt coming due, and $30 billion overall. AIG reported its second consecutive quarterly profit on November 6, 2009, but it was about 15 percent lower than a year earlier. The company earned $455 million in the quarter, with $363 million allotted to the federal government, which owned about 80 percent of AIG.

On March 23, 2010, the U.S. pay czar cut total executive compensation at AIG by 15 percent. His half-million-dollar restriction on cash salaries covered 82 percent of the 119 top executives, AIG being one of the five under his jurisdiction. Not surprisingly, AIG reported a first-quarter 2010 profit of

$1.45 billion, with a net income of $1.45 billion in the first quarter, in contrast to a net loss of $4.35 billion the year before. Then, at the beginning of October, the government announced that it would sell off its stake in AIG in order to terminate the controversial bailout as soon as feasible, which would involve selling at least $50 billion of shares to private investors. More than $120 billion in taxpayer support provided to AIG remained outstanding in mid-year 2010, of which $49 billion came from TARP.

AIG's management posted a $2.4 billion net loss for the third quarter 2010, with pre-tax income up 6.4 percent to $2.1 billion. On December 8, AIG entered into an agreement with the Treasury Department, which hoped to sell at least $15 billion of its shares in the insurer in the first of a series of stock offerings beginning in the first quarter of 2011. The shares sales were projected to bring in $60 billion over two years. The government had already provided $120 billion in aid to AIG. For the fourth quarter 2010, AIG posted a net income of $11.2 billion. At the end of the year, AIG had 63,000 workers, down from 96,000 the year before. For the entire year, AIG noted net gains of $7.8 billion, versus a $10.9 billion net loss in 2009. Its 2008 loss was $99 billion.

AIG, in early August 2011, had a profit of $1.84 billion in the second quarter, with operating income of $1.28 billion, as contrasted with $793 million the year before. On August 7, AIG announced that it would sue Bank of America over hundreds of mortgage-backed securities in order to recover more than $10 billion in losses on $28 billion of investments. AIG argued that the Bank of America misrepresented the quality of the mortgages placed in securities and sold to investors.

See also FEDERAL RESERVE; FINANCIAL CRISIS INQUIRY REPORT; GEITHNER, TIMOTHY; GREENBERG, MAURICE RAYMOND "HANK"; LEHMAN BROTHERS; "TOO BIG TO FAIL"; TROUBLED ASSET RELIEF PROGRAM; U.S. TREASURY.

AMERICAN INTERNATIONAL UNDERWRITERS (AIU). *See* AMERICAN INTERNATIONAL GROUP.

AMERICAN JOBS ACT (PROPOSED). On September 8, 2011, before a joint session of Congress, President Obama proposed a $447 billion economic plan, highlights of which were as follows:

Tax Cuts and Credits
$253 billion: Provides tax credits to encourage hiring of long-term unemployed veterans (cost is less than $500 million); $175 billion for workers, cuts payroll taxes in half in 2012, to 3.1 percent of wages; $65 billion for businesses, cuts payroll taxes in half, to 3.1 percent on the

first $5 million of payroll; eliminates payroll taxes for new hires and wage increases up to $50 million; and $5 billion to extend deductions for business equipment and machinery into 2012.

Employment Projects
$89 billion: $49 billion to extend unemployment benefits and make un-employment insurance reforms; $35 billion to retain and hire teachers, police, and firefighters; $5 billion to create a fund for subsidized employment, training programs, and jobs for youth.

Infrastructure Projects
$105 billion: $50 billion to modernize transportation, including roads, railways, airports, and waterways; $30 billion to modernize at least 35,000 public schools investing in science laboratories, Internet-ready classrooms, and renovations; $15 billion to rehabilitate vacant properties; $10 billion to create a National Infrastructure Bank.

TOTAL: $447 billion.

Estimated, if passed, would add 2 percentage points to real GDP growth and 1.9 million new jobs—almost 1.3 million in 2012 and nearly another 800,000 by 2013. By 2012, it would add 1.3 percentage points to the economy's growth rate and another 0.2 percentage points by 2013. It was projected that the jobs package of tax cuts and spending initiative would create 100,000 to 150,000 jobs a month over the year ahead.

AMERICAN JOBS AND CLOSING TAX LOOPHOLES ACT. Proposed U.S. legislation that would add $134 billion to the federal deficit. A mini-stimulus plan, on June 24, 2010, Democratic leaders withdrew the proposal after failing for the third time to get the sufficient sixty votes in the Senate to proceed. The administration had wanted $266 billion of new stimulus funds over a five-year period. This act called for $79 billion but failed to receive support.

AMERICAN PROTESTS. *See* "OCCUPY WALL STREET."

AMERICAN RECOVERY AND REINVESTMENT ACT (OF 2009). Originally suggested by president-elect Obama on January 3, 2009, this proposal would be combined with one-time measures that were more typical of federal stimulus packages to jump-start a weak economy, like spending for roads and other job-creating projects. President Obama's proposed $825 billion act would be the largest stimulus measure ever. He urged $275 billion in tax cuts and credits to jump-start the economy and $550 billion in spending for clean energy, road construction, social welfare programs, and emergency assistance to states. Then, on February 17, following two differing bills from the House of Representatives and the Senate, reconciliation negotiations were successful and the bill received the president's endorsement. The House of Representatives and the Senate on February 11 struck a deal on a $787.2 billion economic stimulus bill in just twenty-four hours of negotiations. Final congressional action occurred on February 13; the bill arrived on President Obama's desk for his signature on February 16. Conservatives and many other well-informed citizens believed that this piece of legislation would mark the largest single-year increase in domestic federal spending since World War II; it would send the budget deficit to heights not seen since the Great Depression; it would create a new and higher spending baseline for years to come. In the end, the concern was that the United States was about to test the outer limits of our national balance sheet.

The 407-page act included $507 billion in spending programs and $282 billion in tax relief, including a scaled-back version of the president's middle-class tax cut proposal, which gave credits of up to $400 for individuals and $800 for families within certain income limits. It provided a one-time payment of $250 to recipients of Social Security and government disability support. Selected programs include the following:

Spending

a. $30 billion—Modernization of the electric grid, advanced battery manufacturing, energy efficiency grants.
b. $19 billion—Payments to hospitals and physicians who computerize medical-records systems.
c. $8.5 billion—National Institutes of Health biomedical research into diseases, such as Alzheimer's, Parkinson's, cancer, and heart diseases.
d. $5 billion—Home weatherization grants to low- and middle-income families.
e. $6.3 billion—Energy efficiency upgrades to federally supported and public housing, including new insulation, windows, and frames.
f. $29 billion—Road and bridge infrastructure construction and modernization.
g. $8.4 billion—Public transit improvements and infrastructure investments.
h. $8 billion—High-speed rail investments.
i. $18 billion—Grants and loans for water infrastructure, flood prevention, and environmental cleanup.

Tax Cuts

j. $6.6 billion—Tax credit for first-time homeowners buying between April 2008 and June 2009 was raised from $7,500 to $8,000 and would not have to be repaid.

k. $116.2 billion—Workers earning less than $75,000 would get a payroll tax credit of up to $400; married couples filing jointly for less than $150,000 would get up to $800.

l. $69.8 billion—Middle-income taxpayers got an exemption from the alternative minimum tax of $46,700 for an individual and $70,950 for a married couple.

m. $5.1 billion—Businesses can more quickly deduct the cost of investment in plant and equipment from taxable income.

Aid

n. $40.6 billion—Aid to local school districts to balance educational budgets, prevent cutbacks, and modernize schools.

o. $87 billion—A temporary increase in federal funding for Medicaid to states.

p. $2 billion—Funds for communities to buy and rehabilitate foreclosed and vacant properties.

q. $8 billion—Aid to states for public safety and critical services.

r. $14 billion—Education tax credit, a partially refundable $2,500 credit or tuition and book expenses.

s. $17.2 billion—Increase in student aid, including raising maximum Pell Grant to $5,350 in 2009 and $5,550 in 2010.

t. $200 million—Extra grants for colleges' work-study programs.

u. $27 billion—Jobless benefits extended to a total of twenty weeks on top of regular unemployment compensation, and thirty-three weeks in twenty-nine states with high unemployment.

Critically, the act gave states more than $150 billion over a period of two and a half years to help them balance their budget. Nevertheless, huge state deficits remained.

Six months after its passage, the Recovery Act's single largest distribution of the entire $787 billion—more than one-third of it—was for tax cuts, with 95 percent of working citizens seeing their taxes lowered. The second largest part—just under one-third—was for direct relief to state governments and individuals. The final third was for roads and construction projects. By mid-July 2009, more than 30,000 projects had been approved. Seventy percent of the funds were to be spent by September 2010.

On September 10, 2009, the White House estimated that 1 million more people would have been out of work in August without programs funded by the stimulus plan. Recalling that the $787 billion stimulus package was expected to increase the nation's GDP by enough to create 3.6 million jobs, most economic experts concluded by mid-September 2009 that government transfers and rebates failed to increase consumption. Initially there were one-time payments of $250 to eligible individuals and temporary reductions in income-tax withholding for a refundable tax credit of up to $400 for individuals and $800 for families with incomes below certain thresholds. The government pointed to the sharp reduction in the decline in real GDP from the first to the second quarter 2009 as evidence that the stimulus program was succeeding. The growth improvement that followed in the second quarter was largely due to factors other than the stimulus program. By the end of October 2009, the government's $787 billion stimulus program had created or saved 640,239 jobs. More than half—325,000—were in education, and only about 80,000 were in construction. One year after the stimulus package was signed into law on February 17, 2009, federal agencies had spent about 66 percent of the allocated funds. About half of the original monies had been paid out.

The Congressional Budget Office in late August 2010 declared that the American Recovery and Reinvestment Act had lowered the unemployment rate by up to 1.8 percent and raised the level of gross domestic product by up to 4.5 percent.

See also COBRA; CONGRESSIONAL BUDGET OFFICE; EDUCATION; EXECUTIVE PAY; FINANCIAL CRISIS INQUIRY REPORT; FIRST-TIME HOMEBUYERS' CREDIT; GOLDMAN SACHS; HOME AFFORDABLE REFINANCE PROGRAM; KEYNES, JOHN MAYNARD; MAKING WORK PAY; MASS TRANSIT; NATIONAL DEBT; PART-TIME WORKERS; PAYROLL TAX CUTS; "READY TO GO" PROJECTS; STIMULUS PLAN (EUROZONE); U.S. COMMERCE DEPARTMENT; U.S. ENERGY DEPARTMENT; U.S. TREASURY DEPARTMENT.

Cf. CITIGROUP; ECONOMIC STIMULUS PLAN (BILL FROM HOUSE OF REPRESENTATIVES); ECONOMIC STIMULUS PLAN (BILL FROM THE SENATE); ECONOMIC STIMULUS PLAN (FINAL BILL); EMERGENCY ECONOMIC STABILIZATION ACT (OF 2008); FRAUD; MERRILL LYNCH.

Synonymous with RECOVERY ACT.

AMERICA ONLINE. *See* AOL.

AMEX. *See* AMERICAN EXPRESS.

AMR. *See* AMERICAN AIRLINES.

ANDORRA. *See* TAX HAVENS.

ANGELIDES, PHIL. *See* FINANCIAL CRISIS INQUIRY COMMISSION.

ANGLO IRISH BANK. *See* IRELAND.

ANGOLA. With an oil-and-diamond-fueled economy in 2011, expansion is projected to be about 7 percent. The nation's GDP growth of 7 percent will have a GDP of $108 billion, an inflation rate of 13.4 percent, and a GDP per head of $5,500.

ANHEUSER-BUSCH. Posted a second-quarter 2010 profit of 7.3 percent to $1.15 billion on a revenue of $9.17 billion, down from $9.5 billion.
   Net profit rose to $964 million in May 2011.
   Cf. CARLSBERG.

ANN TAYLOR STORES. Ann Taylor posted a net loss of $375.6 million, or $6.66 a share, for the period ending January 31, compared with a previous year's loss of $6.7 million, or 11 cents a share. The company reported a sharp sales decline in its fiscal third quarter 2009 but went into profit on low inventory levels and fewer markdowns. Sales at stores open at least one year fell 26 percent, with a profit of $2.1 million. Net sales fell 12 percent to $462.4 million.
   The firm announced on February 2, 2010, that its fiscal fourth-quarter 2009 sales approached $470 million, compared with its previous sales projection in the third quarter of $462.4 million.
   The company returned to profit in its fiscal second quarter 2010 of $18.6 million, with revenue climbing 2.8 percent to $483.5 million. Management expected sales for the year to approach $1.95 billion.

ANTI-FORECLOSURE PLAN. *See* FORECLOSURES; MODIFYING MORTGAGES.

AOL (AMERICA ONLINE). On January 28, 2009, announced that it was discharging around 700 workers, or 10 percent of its workforce, as a sharp decline in ad spending continued to pressure its transition from an Internet service provider to an advertising business. On November 19, 2009, AOL announced further plans to cut about a third of its staff. The company would ask up to 2,500 people to take buyout packages, leaving the firm with about 4,400 workers.
   Management reported on August 4, 2010, a loss of more than $1 billion for the second quarter. Its net income was $90.7 million, though revenue fell 26 percent to $584.1 million from $791.5 million the year before. For the fourth quarter, AOL had earnings of $66.2 million, with advertising revenue dropping 29 percent to $331.6 million. In total, revenue fell 26 percent to $596 million.
   On March 10, 2011, AOL's management laid off about 20 percent of its workforce, or 200 of its employees. In 2010, AOL cut about a third of its

total workforce, or about 2,300 workers. By May, profit had plummeted 86 percent. On August 9, the company reported that it lost a quarter of its market value. AOL stated that its second-quarter loss of $11.8 million was also followed by a revenue loss of 8.4 percent to $542.2 million.

AOL lost $11.8 million in the second quarter 2011, contrasted with the $1.06 billion loss of the previous year. Revenue was $542 million, compared with $584 million the earlier year. Its third-quarter loss was $2.6 million, with revenue falling 5.8 percent to $531.7 million.

On February 1, 2012, management reported a 66 percent fall in fourth-quarter 2011 profit. Advertisement revenue increased 10 percent to $364 million and a profit of $22.8 million.

See also ADVERTISING; TIME WARNER.

A&P. Weighed down by a crushing debt and competition from low-price rivals, the Great Atlantic and Pacific Tea Company filed for Chapter 11 bankruptcy on December 12, 2010. Its total debts stood at more than $3.2 billion, with assets of about $2.5 billion. It posted a $153.7 million loss for the quarter ending September 11.

APARTMENT. By July 2009, the vacancy rate for U.S. apartments hit a twenty-two-year high in the second quarter. Rents fell sharpest in markets where white-collar workers lost their jobs. Of the seventy-nine markets that were tracked, forty-five showed an increase in vacancies. In October 2009, the apartment vacancy rate hit its highest since 1986. The vacancy rate reached 7.8 percent, a twenty-three-year high. As a result, monthly rents continued to fall. Nearing 10 percent unemployment, more would-be renters were moving in with friends and families. The collapse of the rental market in 2009 has benefited renters. In many cities, landlords are offering tenants up to six months of free rent, flat-screen TVs, and new appliances. At the same time, they are slashing monthly rates and easing application standards. Rents fell a record of 3.5 percent in 2009, with 2010 projections for another 2 percent decline. Nationwide, apartment vacancy is 7.8 percent, up from 4.8 percent at the end of 2007.

Apartment rents rose during the first quarter 2010, ending five straight quarters of declines. Nationally, apartment vacancies remained flat at 8 percent—the highest level since tallying began in 1980. The apartment market improved in the third quarter 2010, with vacancies falling to its sharpest declines on record. The vacancy rate was 7.2 percent at the end of the quarter, down from the second quarter's 7.8 percent and 7.9 percent at the end of the third quarter one year before. The fourth-quarter vacancies fell below 7 percent for the first time in two years.

By 2011, apartment building values soared, with prices of some properties approaching values last seen in mid-2007. Some values have climbed

16 percent after falling 27 percent between 2006 and 2009. In March 2011, the apartment rental market witnessed vacancy rates falling to 6.6 percent from 8 percent the previous year. At the same time, rates increased 2.3 percent. Occupied apartments climbed by about 58,000 in the fourth quarter, the largest increase for that period in a decade. By April, vacancies fell to their lowest rate in over two years, from 6.6 percent to 6.2 percent. The average effective rent was $997 in the second quarter 2011. Vacancies dropped in seventy-two of the eighty-two markets with a vacancy rate of 6 percent, the lowest since 2008 and compared with 7.8 percent one year before. At the end of the third-quarter, 5.6 percent of the nation's apartments were vacant, down from 5.9 percent in the second quarter and the lowest level since 2006. Apartment values are now on the rise and rents up with them. The apartment vacancy rate in the fourth quarter 2011 fell to its lowest level since late 2011 following more people continuing to favor renting homes instead of buying them. In the quarter the vacancy rate fell to 5.2 percent from 6.6 percent the year before.

See also HOUSING; UNEMPLOYMENT.

A.P. MOLLER-MAERSK. *See* MOLLER-MAERSK; SHIPPING.

APPLE. Resisting the recession, Apple posted a 15 percent jump in second-quarter 2009 profit. Apple sold 5.2 million iPhones in the quarter, more than seven times what it sold a year earlier. Throughout the meltdown Apple Inc. continued to prosper. The company posted a 47 percent quarterly profit as consumers continued to buy their iPhones and Macintosh computers. Apple sold 7.4 million iPhones in its quarter ending September 26, up 7 percent from the year before and 41 percent more than the previous quarter. The company also sold 3.1 million Macintosh computers in the quarter, up 17 percent from the year before.

On January 25, 2010, Apple reported that it earned $3.38 billion in its most recent quarter, up nearly 50 percent from the year before. Revenue for the first quarter of Apple's fiscal year rose to $15.68 billion, from $11.88 billion in the first quarter of 2008. Only three years since introducing its iPhone, on April 20, 2010, the company reported a 131 percent surge of its iPhone sales. Posting its highest every quarter outside of the holidays, profits rose 90 percent, with a 49 percent increase in sales. Apple reported on July 20, 2010, that its profit climbed 78 percent for the quarter, with 3.47 million computers sold in the quarter and 8.4 million iPhones also sold. Its net income rose to $3.25 billion. Apple, on October 18, posted a 70 percent surge in quarterly earnings. Its profit was $4.31 billion in the quarter, with revenues up 67 percent from the year before. Sales at Apple's U.S. stores soared 83 percent to $2.8 billion in the fourth quarter of 2010.

Apple reported on April 20, 2011, a near double profit for the quarter of $5.99 billion, up 95 percent from the year before; revenue climbed 83 percent to $24.67 billion. On July 19, Apple surprised the investing community as it announced its quarterly revenues at $28.6 billion. Its gross margin was 41.7 percent. The technology firm sold 20.3 million iPhone units in the quarter, along with 9.2 million iPods and 3.9 million Mac units. In addition, Apple is moving quickly into China's market, with China already accounting for $8.8 billion in revenues, mostly for the iPhone. In addition, Apple's cash war chest continues to expand, with $76 billion in cash and short-term and long-term investments.

On August 9, Apple overtook Exxon Mobil Corporation to become the world's most valuable company when Apple reached a market capitalization of $343 billion, above Exxon's market value. Since the iPod was introduced in 2001, Apple shares have risen nearly 4,000 percent. Then, rather suddenly, Steve Jobs, Apple's CEO, announced that he was unable to continue as chief executive and handed the reins to his chief operating officer. Shares of the prospering firm slid 5.13 percent in after-hours trading. Jobs died soon after.

On January 24, 2012, Apple reported that it had posted one of the most profitable quarters for a U.S. firm, pulling in $13.1 billion on sales of $46.3 billion. Sales climbed 73 percent, up from $26.7 billion. Profits more than doubled to $13.87 per share.

Cf. YAHOO!.

APPLIANCES. Appliance manufacturers were counting on a similar "cash for clunkers" type of rebate program in fall 2009. These rebates were expected to be for purchases of high-efficiency household appliances. Earlier in 2009, Congress had authorized $300 million for the program as part of the economic stimulus bill. Rebates were expected to range between $50 and $200 per appliance.

By year's end, the appliance rebate program was only available in Delaware and wouldn't be available in many states until spring 2010. Delaware issued mail-in rebates in December 2009 for $25 to $200, allowing anyone to participate, and did not require that old appliances be turned in. The government allocated funds to states based on population.

By mid-October 2011, appliance sales had tumbled. North American appliance sales in 2011 were projected to be 25 percent below the 2005 peak. Western European sales were expected to be down 15 percent from 2006.

Cf. CASH FOR CLUNKERS; ELECTROLUX; WHIRLPOOL.

APPRAISALS. On May 1, 2009, under the Home Valuation Code of Conduct, a major change took effect to lower the conflicts of interest in home appraisals while safeguarding the independence of the people who do them.

Brokers and real estate agents can no longer order appraisals. Lenders now control the entire process.

ARAB SPRING. *See* MIDDLE EAST.

ARCANDOR. A German tourism and retailing giant that filed for insolvency on June 9, 2009.

ARCELORMITTAL. The world's largest steel maker said on November 5, 2008, that it would cut output by about one-third amid deteriorating demand from automakers and the construction industry. Its net debt at that time was $33 billion, and market capitalization was $35 billion.

Nevertheless, the company had sufficient liquidity to cover maturing debts for 2009. In South Africa alone, ArcelorMittal cut 1,000 contractor jobs and lowered 2009 capital spending by more than half as a plunge in steel prices pushed the firm to slow expansion. The steel giant had a $1.06 billion first-quarter loss. Sales declined 49 percent to $15.12 billion from $29.81 billion and its plants were slowed down to operate at about 50 percent capacity by the end of April 2009. The firm swung to a $792 million loss in the second quarter 2009. The company reported in fall 2009 a loss of $53 million, from a $3.82 billion profit in 2008. By year's end the company planned to eliminate about 10,000 jobs, or about 3.5 percent of its 287,000 employees.

For its second quarter 2010, the company had a net profit of $1.7 billion from the previous year's net loss of $792 million. Sales climbed 43 percent to $21.7 billion, up 43 percent from the previous year. Management called for a 10 percent price rise. On October 26, 2010, the firm reported that its third-quarter profit rose 48 percent to $1.35 billion. Sales jumped 30 percent to $21.04 billion, with profit falling 21 percent from the second quarter, while sales fell 2.8 percent.

On May 11, 2011, management reported a 67 percent jump in first-quarter profit, posting a net profit of $1.07 billion, up from $640 million the year before. Sales climbed 27 percent to $22.18 billion. The firm's operating profits surged to $64 a ton from $27 the year before.

ARCHER DANIELS MIDLAND. On August 2, 2011, announced that its fiscal fourth-quarter earnings fell 15 percent, with revenue climbing 46 percent to $22.87 billion from $15.7 billion the year before. Revenue rose to $80.67 billion.

On January 11, 2012, the firm announced that it would cut 1,000 jobs, or 3 percent of its workforce.

ARGENTINA. Many experts consider Argentina to be Latin America's most vulnerable country. Since 2008, Argentines were pulling money out of the country's banking system at an alarming pace, creating the potential for a crippling default on international debt that brought the country's seven-year expansion to a halt. The stock exchange tumbled to a five-year low in the fourth quarter of 2008. Its pension grab was seen as an admission that Argentina might not meet 2009's debt payments, approximately $20 billion.

By mid-December 2009, the government reported that it would set aside a portion of the central bank's foreign-currency reserves into a fund dedicated to debt service. Argentina moved to earmark $6.57 billion, of its total $47.54 billion in reserves, for debt service.

In mid-June 2010, Argentina closed the second round of its debt restructuring effort with a 66 percent acceptance rate, bringing its total share of defaulted bonds that have been exchanged to 92 percent. At the end of summer 2010, most experts forecast growth of up to 8 percent for the year, with tax revenues climbing to $50 billion.

For 2011, it was projected that Argentina's growth would slow as global demand falls, sliding to 4 percent from 6.8 percent the year before. The nation's GDP growth was 4.0 percent, a GDP of $375 billion, an inflation rate of 13.7 percent, and a GDP per head of $9,160. The nation's economy grew by over 6 percent a year for seven of the last eight years, unemployment was under 8 percent from over 20 percent in 2002, and the poverty level has dropped by almost half in the past decade. In the second-quarter, the economy surged 9.1 percent. Argentina depends greatly on Brazil's economy and is threatened by its neighbor's economic slowdown. For example, 80 percent of Argentina's auto exports go to Brazil.

See also LATIN AMERICA; WORLD TRADE.

Cf. BRAZIL.

ARION. *See* ICELAND.

ARM. *See* ADJUSTABLE-RATE MORTGAGE.

ARMENIA. A land-locked country of 3 million people in the Caucasus that has been dependent on the monies received from citizens living abroad. With the meltdown, many are returning to their birthplace, and remittances that once contributed significantly to support relatives are quickly disappearing.

It was also drawing $540 million from the International Monetary Fund and $550 million from the World Bank. Exports accounted for only 10 percent of the nation's GDP.

ARMS SALES. The Great Recession significantly affected the purchase of weapons in 2009, bringing it to the lowest level since 2005. Worldwide arms sales in that year were $57.5 billion, a fall of 8.5 percent from 2008. U.S. arms sales alone, which control 39 percent of all weapons sales globally, was in 2009 worth $22.6 billion, down from $38.1 billion in 2008.

ARS. *See* AUCTION RATE SECURITIES.

ARTS, THE. Art organizations are pulling back as they are having increasing difficulty attracting support. About 10,000 arts organizations, or 10 percent of the U.S. total, are at risk of closing. Arts groups get about 40 percent of their income, more than other nonprofits, from private donations, which are down considerably.

See also METROPOLITAN OPERA.

ASIA. Approximately $2 trillion of market value was lost in Asia in 2008.

By mid-May 2010, fear of Greece's debt would slow the recovery down throughout the United States, Europe, and assuredly around Asia. This downturn did not materialize, especially in Asia.

Following the March 2011 earthquake in Japan, including a tsunami and nuclear fallout, the overall GDP of Asia is expected to grow by 7.5 percent to 8.0 percent. It is expected that trade between Japan and other Asian nations will fall in the short term. Japan is the largest source of foreign direct investment for many nations in Asia.

See also AUTOMOBILE INDUSTRY; CHINA; FORMOSA; GREECE; INFLATION; JAPAN; KOREA; MALAYSIA; SINGAPORE; THAILAND; "THIRD WORLD"; VIETNAM.

ASIAN DEVELOPMENT BANK (ADB). At their annual meeting on May 3, 2009, finance officials agreed to set up an emergency $120 billion liquidity fund that thirteen Asian nations could tap to help overcome the global financial meltdown. In addition, the Chiang Mai Initiative was created to become a network of bilateral currency-swap arrangements among the nations. Small Asian economies would be able to borrow larger amounts in proportion to their contributions than the more developed economies.

See also GLOBAL ECONOMIC OUTPUT.

ASSET-BACKED COMMERCIAL PAPER (ABCP). Short-term debt secured by assets.

See also FINANCIAL CRISIS INQUIRY REPORT.

ASSET-BACKED SECURITIES (SECURITY) (ABS). Debt instrument secured by assets such as mortgages, credit card loans, or automobile loans.

See also FEDERAL RESERVE; FINANCIAL REGULATION PLAN (2009); STRUCTURED INVESTMENT VEHICLE.

ASSET GUARANTEE PROGRAM. A 2008 government effort providing a U.S. government guarantee for assets held by firms that "face a high risk of losing market confidence due in large part to a portfolio of distressed or illiquid assets." This new insurance program of the U.S. Treasury was announced on January 2, 2009, for bad loans and other troubled assets that it could use to further help financial institutions.

See also U.S. TREASURY.

ASSET-MANAGEMENT FIRMS. Companies that specialize in taking over all or part of a firm's servicing activities and then running them more efficiently. BlackRock merged with Barclays Global Investors in mid-June 2009, making it the world's largest asset manager.
See also BLACKROCK; EMERGENCY ECONOMIC STABILIZATION ACT OF 2008.

ASSET PROTECTION SCHEME. Developed by the British Treasury, a plan in which a bank's riskiest assets will be covered for up to 90 percent of future losses. The Royal Bank of Scotland was the first to participate, putting $430 billion of assets in the scheme.
See also BARCLAYS; UNITED KINGDOM.

ASTRAZENACA. On February 2, 2012, the U.K. drug maker announced that it would eliminate an additional 7,300 workers. In five years nearly 30,000 employees will have lost their jobs. Its fourth-quarter 2011 net profit was $1.49 billion, down from $1.62 billion the year before. Revenue in the quarter was $8.66 billion.

AT-RISK HOMEOWNERS. *See* HOUSING PLAN.

AT&T. The telecommunication's company's fourth-quarter 2009 sales to businesses fell 5.5 percent from the year before.

At the end of July 2010, AT&T reported a 26 percent increase in its second-quarter earnings, adding nearly a half million new subscribers. Its profit was up $4.02 billion, from $3.2 billion the year before.

Management reported a 39 percent jump of first-quarter profit in April 2011, with earnings of $3.41 billion and revenue increasing 2.3 percent to $31.25 billion. Its subscriber base was 97.5 million, 12 percent higher than the year before.
See also UNEMPLOYMENT.

AUCTION HOUSES. *See* CHRISTIE'S INTERNATIONAL; SOTHEBY'S.

AUCTION RATE SECURITIES (ARS). Long-term bonds whose interest rate may be reset at regular short-term intervals by an auction process.

AUDI. In mid-March 2009, this car company announced that it expected a sharp decline in profits and its first such drop in sales in fourteen years. Sales declined around 11 percent to 63,400 cars. Its first-quarter operating profit declined 29 percent amid waning demand for luxury cars.

March 2010 global sales of Audi soared 22 percent from the year before, with 110,400 cars sold. Nevertheless, profit fell 40 percent in 2009 to $1.77 billion and revenue sank 13 percent. A total of 949,700 of its cars were sold in 2009. Audi's management reported in early August 2010 that its first-half net profit nearly doubled to $1.28 billion, up 46 percent from the year before. Revenue climbed 21 percent and sales in the first half of 2010 rose 19 percent to 554,950 cars. Management reported that its 2010 operating profit rose to 3.34 billion euros from 1.6 billion euros in 2009, while revenue climbed to 35.4 euros.

See also AUTOMOBILE INDUSTRY.

AUDITOR. U.S. government auditors urged the Treasury Department in December 2008 to act quickly to develop internal controls to ensure that its $700 billion financial rescue package was operating effectively and ethically. This was to fulfill the obligations of the Economic Stabilization Act passed on October 3.

See also ACCOUNTANTS; ERNST & YOUNG.

"AUSTERITY." Selected as the word of the year for 2011.

See also KRUGMAN, PAUL.

AUSTRALIA. Having been less affected by the crisis than most other countries of the Organisation for Economic Co-operation and Development, Australia is likely to experience a relatively more robust recovery. Large public transfer and tax incentives stimulated private consumption and capital expenditure by firms. In addition, strong imports by China and other dynamic Asian economies buoyed exports of mining products. Growth is projected to pick up to 2.5 percent in 2010 and 3.5 percent in 2011, with unemployment peaking at around 6.25 percent in 2010 and inflation moderating. Current economic trends and the reduction in negative macroeconomic risks argue in favor of a gradual tightening of monetary policy. Furthermore, the planned reduction of the federal budgetary stimulus seems to be an appropriate response to the needs of the economy. To maximize the positive impacts of their investment program, the authorities should submit proposed projects more systematically to a rigorous and transparent cost-benefit analysis.

GDP growth weakened from 2.5 percent in 2008 to about 1.75 percent in 2009 before picking up, as forecast, to 2.75 percent in 2010. This would still imply that, despite the depressed international environment, the impact of the financial crisis and the fall in terms of trade should be relatively contained. Unemployment was likely to increase, however, and inflation would dip below 3 percent in 2010. The expected reduction of inflation due to the current slowdown, along with the need to preserve the stability of the financial system, suggests for looser monetary conditions. Budget measures made possible by the significant fiscal leeway built in the previous years will also support activity, although their effectiveness might be limited if confidence is not restored. It is important for the ongoing reform of industrial relations to preserve labor-market flexibility. Australia's central bank cut the policy interest rate by a percentage point, to 4.25 percent, on December 2, 2008.

The government announced at the outset of 2009 that it began a spending program of $11.8 billion to stimulate the economy. The program came after Australia's economy expanded at its weakest rate in eight years in the third quarter of 2008. The prime minister announced in early February that it would wipe $73.37 billion from government revenues in the next four years. Analysts predicted a deficit equaling up to 4 percent of Australia's trillion-dollar-a-year economy.

The government also reported a stimulus package worth $27 billion to keep the economy growing. Growth predictions in 2009 were for a drop from 2.7 percent to 1 percent, and just 0.75 in the following year. That same day, the central bank cut interest rates by a percentage point to a cash rate of 3.25 percent, the lowest in forty-five years. In mid-March, the government said it planned to crack down on excessive executive pay packages and curb so-called golden parachute termination payments, prompting an angry response from business groups. Shareholder approval will be required for any termination payments that exceed average annual base salary, which excludes additional compensation such as shares or stock options. On April 7, the Reserve Bank of Australia cut interest rates another one-quarter of a percentage point to a forty-nine-year low.

Australia's economy grew in the first quarter 2009, defying a global slowdown to become one of the few developed nations to have sidestepped a technical recession. The nation's GDP rose 0.4 percent in the first quarter from the fourth quarter of 2008, and rose 0.4 percent from a year earlier. In the second quarter the nation's economy grew significantly, reducing any threat of recession. GDP grew at the fastest pace, 0.6 percent, among the globe's thirty-three advanced economies. The economy expanded 0.6 percent from the first quarter. On October 6, 2009, Australia became the first G-20 nation to raise interest rates since the beginning of the Great Recession, setting a stage for further central bank increases. The Reserve Bank of Australia raised its main interest rate target one-quarter of a percentage point to 3.25 percent. The nation's Reserve Bank increased its benchmark interest rate by twenty-five basis points to 4.5 percent in May 2010. GDP climbed by 2.7 percent in the year to the end of the first quarter. Then, at the beginning of November, the bank raised its short-term rate by a quarter of a point to 4.75 percent.

The nation's unemployment rate rose surprisingly in October 2010 to the highest level in six months. The number of people without work rose to a seasonally adjusted 5.4 percent from 5.1 percent in October. The nation's economy expanded by 2.7 percent in the final 2010 quarter.

It was projected that Australia's terms of trade would climb by 17 percent in 2011 to their highest level on record. The nation's GDP growth was 2.6 percent, a GDP of $1,190 billion, an inflation of 2.5 percent, and a GDP per head of $52,830. In the three months opening the year, Australia's economy shrank 1.2 percent, its largest contraction in twenty years. GDP rose by only 1 percent, compared with 2.7 percent in the last quarter of 2010. The nation's trade surplus in goods and services widened to $2.5 billion in May. By mid-August, Australia's real-estate market indicated a significant fall in home prices and fears of overbuilding was on the horizon. In 2011, home and apartment prices were down about 4.0 percent.

See also G-20.

AUSTRIA. In 2010, Austria was expected to recover from its worst recession in decades thanks to the improved external environment and supportive policies. If these conditions continued to prevail, growth should have accelerated to its potential in 2011. Nevertheless, unemployment was set to increase until the end of 2010, and inflation, while inching up, would remain subdued. The deterioration in the fiscal positions called for committing soon to a credible medium-term consolidation strategy that would be implemented once the recovery was in train. Administrative reforms should be continued to facilitate consolidation efforts. Growth may prove strong in the short term given the brisk improvement in the global economy. The risk of a financial crisis in central and eastern Europe had diminished, but rising nonperforming loan ratios would put the Austrian banking sector under pressure, entailing a downside risk to fiscal projections.

Former Communist countries of Europe contributed 42 percent of the Austrian financial sector's profit in 2007. In 2008, Austrian banks were owed $290 billion by borrowers from Russia to Albania. This exposure was much higher than that of Italy or Germany and was equal to Austria's gross domestic product. On December 14, 2009, the government nationalized the local unit of a German bank, Hypo Group Alpe Adria, following huge losses. That bank had assets of about $58 billion. This was the second bank to be nationalized in Austria since the beginning of the Great Recession.

In 2011, Austria would face a difficult budget. The fiscal boost of 2009–2010 would give way to austerity in 2011 and weak growth. The nation's GDP growth of 0.9 percent and GDP of $376 billion had a 1.8 percent inflation and a GDP per head of $44,520.

See also AIRLINES; TAX HAVENS.

AUSTRIAN AIRLINES. Lufthansa completed its takeover of the Austrian carrier on September 3, 2009. Austrian Airlines was 42 percent government owned before the takeover.

See also AIRLINES.

AUTO CZAR. *See* RATTNER, STEVEN.

AUTO DEALERS. During the January–March 2009 quarter, 271 auto dealers in the United States went out of business. At the end of the quarter there were 19,738 auto dealers in the United States, down from 20,009 at the end of 2008. Another 1,200 dealers were expected to permanently close their doors before the end of the year.

On another front, in April 2010 auto dealers, numbering 17,000, sought an exemption from the financial-regulation bill.
See also AUTOMOBILE INDUSTRY.

AUTOLIV. The world's largest maker of air bags for cars said in March 2009 that it would cut 3,000 jobs in the first two months of the year, eliminating 2,600 permanent positions. In June 2008, it further reduced its total workforce by 20 percent, or 9,000 positions.

AUTOMAKERS. *See* AUTOMOBILE INDUSTRY.

AUTOMATIC STABILIZERS. Known in Europe and barely used in the United States, where spending on unemployment benefits automatically rises more the longer a downturn lasts.

AUTOMOBILE BAILOUT. The government reported on June 1, 2011, that taxpayers would lose about $14 billion of the $80 billion on automobile bailouts.

AUTOMOBILE CZAR. *See* RATTNER, STEVEN.

AUTOMOBILE INDUSTRY. The years 2008–2009 were the worst years for selling cars and trucks since 1992. The U.S. motor vehicles and parts manufacturing industries employed 703,900 people in 2008. The sector had shed 116,500 jobs since November. The Big Three carmakers employed about 201,000 workers. Indirectly the industry employed between 2.5 million and 3 million workers who were usually employed by suppliers or in services such as warehousing and ports. As a whole, the industry accounted for 13 percent of U.S. manufacturing jobs. General Motors, Chrysler, Ford, and Toyota announced on April 2, 2008, that they had a double-digit drop in U.S. vehicle sales in March. Lenders were making fewer auto loans. After rescuing the banks in October, governments on both sides of the Atlantic turned their attention to the ailing automobile industry. President George W. Bush sought help to spur a merger between General Motors and Chrysler.

In the first nine months of the year, GM earned nearly $2 billion in Latin America, Asia, the Middle East, and Africa, even as its North American operations recorded a $5.7 billion loss. Similarly, Ford earned more than $1 billion in Latin America, while it lost $4 billion in North America. Ford earned $1.4 billion in Europe in the first half of 2008, and nearly $1 billion in 2007. GM lost $18.8 billion in the first six months of 2008. A merger with Chrysler would give GM access to approximately $11.7 billion in cash that was on Chrysler's books as of June. New car sales fell across Europe in October, with sales down 40 percent in Spain, the worst hit among four countries publishing data. With 55,000 workers spread across twenty plants, GM's European workforce was now down 40 percent from a decade ago. But with market share shrinking to about 9.5 percent currently from roughly 12 percent, GM remained under pressure to cut overhead.

If the "Big Three" automobile firms were to collapse, 3 million people would potentially lose their jobs, counting autoworkers, suppliers, and the employees of a variety of businesses dependent on the companies. The cost to local, state, and federal governments could be as much as $156 billion over three years in lost taxes and higher outlays for such things as unemployment and health care assistance. The car and parts industries employed 732,800 workers directly in September and the three U.S. automobile carmakers, Ford, GM, and Chrysler, employed 239,341 workers at the end of 2007. Some 2 million present and former workers depend on carmakers for health care, a costly part of the automobile industries dilemma.

In Europe, car sales fell almost 15 percent in October, the sixth straight monthly decline. For example, Renault, the French carmaker, cut its output to reduce inventories by the end of 2008 to the same level as the end of 2007. For October 2008, its sales were down 14.1 percent from a year earlier. New car sales in the United States fell below 800,000 in November for the first time in decades. Sales of new luxury cars in the United States were 39 percent lower in November than a year before. For example, Mercedes-Benz saw American sales decline by 43 percent and Porsche by more than half. The same held true in Asia and Europe. This in great part is a result of the credit crunch and the lack of available financing. In addition, the U.S. automakers owed more than $100 billion to their bankers and bondholders, and experts wondered how much of that would be repaid.

The proposed rescue bill of December 10 would have extended $14 billion in emergency loans to General Motors and Chrysler, the two most imperiled automakers, and subjected them to far-reaching government oversight at the direction of a so-called car czar. The czar (never appointed) would have been required by March 31, 2009, to certify that the automakers and their stakeholders—including creditors, labor unions, and dealers—had agreed to carry out a long-term viability plan and that they would have provided a hard economic definition of what it meant to be a viable firm. The proposed plan would give the government stock warrants in the automakers, allowing taxpayers to profit should share prices rise. It would also have prevented shareholder dividends, executive bonuses, and golden parachute severance packages. It would have required the car czar to call in the emergency loans for repayment should the auto firms fail to carry out an aggressive reorganization plan or meet other requirements found in the law. The following day, December 11, prospects of the $14 billion rescue plan seemed to vaporize as Republican leaders spoke out forcefully against the bill. The Bush administration shifted position on December 12 and said it would dip into the money set aside for the $700 billion financial bailout to keep General Motors and Chrysler from going bankrupt. The Treasury Department promptly indicated that it would provide short-term relief to the automakers. By mid-December, there was increasing concern for the overseas operations of U.S. carmakers Ford and GM, which were profitable in the first half of the year. Ford earned $1.4 billion in Europe in the first half of the year, while GM earned nearly $300 million in the first half of 2008. Their collapse could also imperil the survival of automobile manufacturers in both Asia and Europe that are dependent on U.S. components. In addition, European car sales fell 26 percent in November, the biggest drop since 1999. Registrations declined to 932,537 from 1.26 million a year earlier.

With one month left in office, President George W. Bush announced on December 19 that he would extend up to $17.4 billion in emergency loans to prevent the collapse of General Motors and Chrysler. He then shifted onto the Obama administration, commencing on January 20, 2009, how to apply these funds and what sacrifices it would mean to the firms and workers. Ford Motor Company was excluded, as they were still able to fulfill their financial obligations and did not seek or require government assistance. The loans were considered to be critical, as the companies were already on the brink of insolvency and with taxpayers monies would now remain afloat until March 31, 2009. At that time, a decision would be made to determine if the conditions of the loans were met, allowing them to receive additional monies, or whether they would have to repay the loans and face bankruptcy. The events of rescue were as follows:

September 2008—Auto executives began lobbying for U.S. loans.

November 18 and 19—CEOs of Big Three were grilled before Congress about their need for rescue.

November 20—Lawmakers turned down automakers' pleas and told CEOs to return in December.

December 2—Automakers returned to Congress, this time with turnaround plans in hand.

December 11—In a huge blow to the industry, Senate relief effort collapsed amid partisan disputes.

December 19—White House agreed to $17.4 billion in bailout loans.

February 17—GM and Chrysler requested another $14 billion in bailout funds.

March 30—White House agreed to provide additional aid to GM and Chrysler on conditions of change, including fulfilling auto task force recommendations.

April 30—Chrysler Corporation declared bankruptcy.

June 1—General Motors declared bankruptcy.

June 10—Chrysler signed papers formally establishing relationship with Fiat.

The monies would come from the U.S. Treasury's $700 billion financial stabilization fund; Congress had released the second $350 billion for that program. The rescue of GM and Chrysler cost taxpayers more than $62 billion. January 2009 automobile sales were down, with an industry-wide 656,976 cars and light trucks sold, down 37 percent from January 2008. It was the lowest total since December 1981, and the first time U.S. sales were lower than in China, where about 790,000 cars were sold in January. On February 17, both Chrysler and General Motors requested $21.6 billion more to move them toward recovery, in addition to the $7.6 billion they had previously requested but not received. Deep cuts were promised.

Despite the offering of deep car discounts, vehicle sales in the United States still fell to their lowest level in twenty-eight years. Reported on March 3, industry sales declined 4.9 percent from January and plummeted 41 percent from February of 2008. It was equally sour for European car sales, shrinking 18 percent in February. Only Germany prospered, as sales rose 22 percent following the government's offering of $3,230 to people who trade in their old cars for new ones. There was a bit of optimism. Despite major sales declines in March, the leaders of automakers saw signs of the industry's downturn bottoming out. All the big carmakers suffered sales declines of 36 percent or more compared to March 2008. U.S. sales industry-wide totaled 857,735 cars and trucks, down 37 percent from a year before. But that's up from 688,909 vehicles sold in February and was the highest total since September 2008. February's sales were down 41 percent from a year earlier. On April 30, the Chrysler Corporation filed for bankruptcy after months of negotiations with regulators, unions, and creditors. Meanwhile, car sales continued to plummet. April results indicated:

General Motors—down 33.2 percent, retaining 21.0 percent of global sales.

Ford—down 31.5 percent, retaining 16.3 percent of global sales.

Chrysler—down 48.1 percent, retaining 9.4 percent of global sales.

Toyota—down 41.9 percent, retaining 15.4 percent of global sales.
Honda—down 25.3 percent, retaining 12.3 percent of global sales.
Nissan—down 37.8 percent, retaining 5.8 percent of global sales.
Hyundai—down 13.6 percent, retaining 4.1 percent of global sales.
KIA—down 14.8 percent, retaining 3.1 percent of global sales.
Volkswagen—down 14.8 percent, retaining 2.9 percent of global sales.
BMW—down 38.4 percent, retaining 2.4 percent of global sales.

U.S. car sales fell 34 percent in May to 925,824 vehicles but began to show some signs of improving. By July, the three biggest carmakers in the United States envisioned a bottom to the long decline in auto sales as the industry reported its smallest monthly sales drop in 2009. New vehicle sales in June declined 28 percent from a year earlier to 860,000 cars and light trucks, making it the smallest fall in any month of the year. U.S. carmakers sold 1,261,977 cars and pickup trucks industry-wide in August 2009, up about 1 percent from the year before, and up from July's 997,824. It was the highest total sales since May 2008 and the first time automobile executives saw a year-over-year increase since October 2007.

U.S. auto sales dropped 23 percent in September 2009 following the termination of the U.S. government's "cash for clunkers" incentive program. Car manufacturers sold 745,997 vehicles in September, compared with 964,783 in the same month one year earlier. GM's sales fell 45 percent in September, Chrysler's car sales dropped 42 percent, Honda's sales declined 20 percent, and Toyota's sales dropped 13 percent. October 2009 auto sales were 838,052 new cars and light trucks, just 104 fewer than in the year before, with an increase of 12 percent from September. By mid-November 2009, the global automobile industry noted that it had sufficient capacity to produce 85.9 million cars and trucks each year, about 30 million more than it made in 2009. The manufacturers were only utilizing about 65 percent of their available production capacity. Global auto sales were projected to grow by 25 million vehicles over the next six years; however, the industry-wide capacity utilization would only reach 85 percent by 2015.

U.S. auto sales continued to improve, selling an estimated 750,000 cars and trucks in November 2009 compared with 746,789 in the same month in 2008. The industry ended 2009 with its worst U.S. sales year since 1982. Even with sales climbing 15.1 percent in December compared with a year before, sales fell 21.2 percent to 10.4 million vehicles, compared with 2008.

By March 2010, U.S. auto sales surged 24 percent to more than one million cars (up from 857,735 in 2009) and light trucks. And in July auto sales climbed 5.1 percent from a year before to 1,049,101 cars and light trucks. After a promising spring 2010, automobile makers reported on September

1, that their sales dropped an average 21 percent during the month compared to the year before. Also, there was a 5 percent month-to-month decrease in sales from July and the expectation that the market would remain stagnant for months ahead.

Automobile makers reported on November 3, 2010, a 12 percent increase in new vehicles sales for the previous month and an increase in the annual selling rate to its highest level in more than one year. A sales total of more than 900,000 would be the strongest month for automakers in three years. New car sales failed to reach that level in 2008 and 2009. In October 2007, just prior to the official beginning of the Great Recession, automakers sold 1.23 million cars and trucks. November sales totaled 873,323 cars and light trucks, up almost 17 percent from the year before. The seasonally adjusted annualized sales pace was 12.26 million vehicles. Sales of new cars rose 11 percent to around 11.4 million in 2010. More than 859,000 new cars were sold in 2010.

For 2011, it was projected, following the 2010 rapid recovery of the industry, that global car registrations would climb by 6.9 percent, a bit slower than the previous year. Growth of car sales in China and India would spur the recovery rapidly where there would be 46 cars per 1,000 people in China and only 14 in India. The global average is 137. Car sales should rise in 2011 by 8.5 percent, and in western Europe sales would grow only by 1 percent. December U.S. sales rose 11 percent.

By January 2011, U.S. carmakers reported a 27 percent increase in U.S. new vehicle sales. Both GM and Chrysler Group reported that their car and truck sales climbed 23 percent in January, compared with the same month in 2010. In January 2011, new vehicle sales rose an annualized selling pace of 12.6 million employees. In February 2011, car sales were 490,994 and light truck sales were 502,393, for a total of 993,387, compared to February 2010 of 398,818 car sales and 381,447 light truck, for a total of 780,265; the grand total change was plus 27.3 percent, with annual sales of $13.4 million. Sales climbed 37 percent for pickups and 34 percent for SUVs, and demand for smaller vehicles rose 24 percent. GM had a 46 percent increase, with Toyota's sales climbing 42 percent, and Ford up 10 percent. Sales jumped in July 2011 by 5.2 percent.

By March 2011, U.S. auto sales rose 17 percent. Chrysler showed an increase of 31 percent from the year before, and GM's increase was 10 percent. By June, U.S. auto sales climbed another 7.1 percent. August sales were upbeat, rising industry-wide 7.5 percent from the year before, attributed to GM, Ford, and Chrysler. In September, U.S. auto sales jumped nearly 10 percent from the year before. GM, Chrysler, and Nissan Motor Company noted U.S. sales up at least 20 percent, while Ford Motors sales climbed 8.9 percent. For September, luxury car sales posted significant gains: Audi was up 17 percent with 120,200 cars, BMW up 9.3 percent with 128,446 cars, and Mercedes-Benz up 2.0 percent with 120,082 cars. U.S. sales climbed 7.5 percent in October.

By December 2011, it was predicted that employment in the automobile sector would return to prerecession levels by 2015, adding about 167,000 jobs. The job growth would represent a 28 percent surge over existing levels but only account for about a third of the jobs lost throughout the past ten years. About 590,000 people are employed in the automobile industry, 13 percent more than in July 2009. That figure is projected to grow to 756,000 in 2015.

On January 5, 2012, auto sales for December 2011 were up, with Chrysler posting a 37 percent climb, Ford with a 10 percent gain, and GM with a 4.6 percent climb. For the entire year Chrysler's sales rose 26 percent, Ford's 11 percent, and GM 13 percent. In total, automakers sold 913,287 cars and light trucks by the end of the month.

See also ADVERTISING; AMERICAN RECOVERY AND REINVESTMENT ACT (OF 2009); AUDI; AUTO DEALERS; AUTOLIV; AUTOMOBILE BAILOUT; AUTONATION; AUTO PARTS; AUTO TASK FORCE; AUTO TRANSPLANTS; AVIS; BMW; CANADA; CAR CZAR; CASH FOR CLUNKERS; CHINA; CHRYSLER; CONTROLLED BANKRUPTCY; DRIVING; ENTERPRISE; EXPORTS (U.S.); FIAT; FORD; FRANCE; FUEL TAX; GENERAL MOTORS; GOLDEN PARACHUTE; GOODYEAR TIRE AND RUBBER COMPANY; HERTZ; HONDA; HUMMER; HYUNDAI MOTOR COMPANY; JAGUAR; JAPAN; LAND ROVER; MAZDA MOTORS; MITSUBISHI MOTORS; NISSAN; PEUGEOT-CITROEN; RATTNER, STEVEN; RENAULT; SAAB; SPAIN; SUBARU; SWEDEN; TATA MOTORS; TOYOTA; TRADE DEFICIT (U.S.); TROUBLED ASSET RELIEF PROGRAM; TRUCKING INDUSTRY; TURKEY; UNFAIR TRADE SUBSIDIES; U.S. TREASURY; VEBA; VOLKSWAGEN.

AUTOMOBILE SAFETY. *See* CAR SAFETY.

AUTO PARTS. By 2009, following the lead from the U.S. automobile industry, auto parts makers sought a bailout, asking the U.S. Treasury for $25.5 billion. Four hundred parts makers applied for Chapter 11 bankruptcy protection in 2008. By mid-February, President Obama's auto task force met with senior procurement executives from GM, Chrysler, and Ford. Suppliers had raised concerns over their finances and submitted plans to the Treasury Department on February 13, arguing that 1 million jobs were at risk. In mid-March the Treasury Department announced a $5 billion program to aid struggling auto parts suppliers drawing money from the bailout fund, the Troubled Asset Relief Program (TARP). It offered financing to help suppliers to bridge the gap between delivering parts to carmakers and receiving payment.

The Treasury Department announced on April 8 a program to assist ailing auto parts makers, providing $3.5 billion in aid to be funneled to suppliers through GM and Chrysler. GM would oversee $2 billion and Chrysler $1.5 billion (Ford continued to claim that it could make supplier payments from its own funds). Auto parts firms announced in June 2009 that they would seek up to $10 billion in loan guarantees from the federal government. On June 16, the Obama administration rejected the request, concluding that the government shouldn't further interfere in the industry's contraction.

By summer 2010, most U.S.-based automobile parts suppliers had turned profitable, with their stocks climbing and hiring on the upswing.

See also AUTOMOBILE INDUSTRY; DELPHI; OBAMA, BARACK.

AUTO SUPPLIERS. *See* AUTO PARTS; DELPHI.

AUTO TASK FORCE. Before providing additional funding to General Motors and Chrysler, at the end of March 2009 the task force concluded that the firms' survival depended on greater concessions from the workers' union because the cost of funding retiree benefits had become unmanageable, especially given the economic meltdown. They called on President Obama to urge hourly workers and retirees to be ready to accept more sacrifices if they hoped to keep their employers afloat.

See also AUTOMOBILE INDUSTRY; AUTO PARTS; RATTNER, STEVEN.

AVIS. Congress was asked in January 2009 to allow Avis and other car renters to use funds from the Troubled Asset Relief Program to finance new auto purchases. As part of the car rental business, firms purchased as many as 1.8 million new vehicles each year, making them the auto industry's largest customer.

Cf. ENTERPRISE; HERTZ.

AVON PRODUCTS. Reported on May 5, 2009, a 37 percent drop in first-quarter profit as beauty industry sales continued to sag. Profits fell to $117.3 million, down from $184.7 million. Avon reported a fourth-quarter 2009 profit jump of 16 percent. The firm reported a profit of $269.4 million, with net sales climbing 13 percent to $3.15 billion.

B

BA. *See* BRITISH AIRWAYS.

BABY-BOOMERS. In 2011, the first of the baby-boomers, born between 1946 and 1964, reached age sixty-five, moving them into retirement. The nation's official pension age had risen to sixty-six, but people on average retire at sixty-four and are expected to live another sixteen years. By year's end, baby-boomers between ages fifty-five to sixty-four had an average duration of unemployment of 56.6 weeks. That number had nearly doubled in five years.

See also RETIREMENT; UNEMPLOYMENT.

BACK-TO-SCHOOL SALES. *See* RETAILING.

"BAD BANKS." Banks with troubled assets that were held by the government and then sold over time when market and economic conditions improved. In the meantime, the government uses taxpayer money to provide enough capital to allow banks to resume normal lending. Bad banks could have troubled assets exceeding $5 trillion if defined as assets that could show a loss rate close to or above 10 percent, an amount that is just over 40 percent of the $12.3 trillion in total assets of U.S. commercial banks.

Experts predicted that over five years, from 2009 to 2014, as many as one thousand banks could close, which is six times more than the Treasury Department placed on the regulatory problem list in 2009.

By March 2010, the government considered creating multiple investment funds to purchase bad loans and other distressed assets that were at the center of the financial crisis. Obama's intention was for the government to partner with the private sector to purchase $500 billion to $1 trillion of distressed assets as part of its revamping of the $700 billion bank bailout plan. The administration was considering a private-public financing partnership to deal with troubled assets.

Sweden nationalized its bad banks in the early 1990s and a rapid recovery followed that led to taxpayers making money in the long run.

See also EUROPEAN UNION; "GOOD BANKS"; IRELAND; "NEW BANKS"; "TOO BIG TO FAIL"; TOXIC MORTGAGE ASSETS.

Synonymous with AGGREGATOR BANKS.

BAILOUT. The dictionary publisher Merriam-Webster chose "bailout" as its word of the year for 2008.

See also EUROPE (BAILOUT); GOVERNMENT BAILOUT; GREECE; IRELAND; PAULSON, HENRY; PORTUGAL; SPAIN; TOXIC MORT-GAGE ASSETS.

BAILOUT FUND (PLAN) OF 2008 (U.S.). *See* BANK BAILOUT (PLAN) OF 2008; BANK RESCUE (PLAN) OF 2009 (U.S.); EMERGENCY ECO-NOMIC STABILIZATION ACT OF 2008; TROUBLED ASSET RELIEF PROGRAM.

BAILOUT HOUSING PLAN. *See* HOUSING BAILOUT; MORTGAGE BAILOUT.

BAILOUT RESCUE (PLAN) OF 2009 (U.S.). *See* BANK RESCUE (PLAN) OF 2009 (U.S.); TROUBLED ASSET RELIEF PROGRAM.
See also EUROPE (BAILOUT).

BAILOUT RESCUE PLAN (U.K.). *See* UNITED KINGDOM.

BAIR, SHEILA C. Chairwoman of the Federal Deposit Insurance Corpo-ration since June 2006. "They should have let Bear Stearns fail." She sup-ported "market discipline" where shareholders and debt holders would take losses ahead of depositors and taxpayers over bailouts, which she disliked. She also felt that "avoiding foreclosure would protect neighboring proper-ties and hasten the recovery." Her five-year term at FDIC ended on July 8, 2011.

See also FEDERAL DEPOSIT INSURANCE CORPORATION; HOME AFFORDABLE MODIFICATION PLAN.

BALANCED BUDGET ACT (1997). Aimed to achieve $127 billion in net savings by 2002, primarily by slowing the rise in Medicare spending. Raised billion of dollars by increasing excise taxes on tobacco products.
Cf. BUDGET ENFORCEMENT ACT (1990); DEBT DEAL.

BALL BEARINGS. *See* SKF.

BALTICS. The three Baltic countries were experiencing a spiraling eco-nomic downturn in 2009. Latvia, in December 2008, received a $10 billion bailout from the IMF and was facing a 13 percent decline in its GDP. Estonia and Lithuania expected a decline of a tenth. All three Baltic states were facing double-digit economic declines in GDP throughout 2009, all following the collapse of credit bubbles created by reckless lending and spending.
See also ESTONIA; LATVIA.

BALTIMORE SUN. Maryland's largest newspaper discharged sixty-one people at the end of April 28, 2009. It represented about 27 percent of the newsroom staff.
See also NEWSPAPERS.

BANCA ROTTA. *See* BANKRUPT.

BANCO SANTANDER. Spain's bank lender reported in October 2011 a 10 percent rise in third-quarter profit to 180 billion euros.

BANGKOK. *See* THAILAND.

BANGLADESH. Since 2004 and ending in 2007, the economy of Bangladesh grew at more than 6 percent each year, with a falling poverty rate. With the recent global downturn, the country concluded that it was hard to feed its people. According to the World Bank, nearly 56 million out of a total 147 million people found it difficult to feed themselves.

BANK. *See* BANKS.

BANK AID (EU). *See* EUROPEAN UNION.

BANK BAILOUT FUND. *See* HOUSE (U.S.) FINANCIAL OVERHAUL PLAN.
Synonymous with TROUBLED ASSET RELIEF PROGRAM.

BANK BAILOUT (PLAN) OF 2008 (U.S.). The bailout plan, officially the "Troubled Asset Relief Program," was announced on Monday, October 27, 2008, when the U.S. government started doling out $125 billion to nine major banks to get credit flowing again. These deals were intended to bolster the banks' balance sheets so they would be able to commence more normal lending. This action marked the first deployment of resources from the government's $700 billion financial rescue package passed by Congress on October 3.

Treasury Secretary Paulson used $250 billion of the $700 billion to make direct purchases of bank stock, partly nationalizing the U.S. banking system, as a way to get money into the financial system more quickly. The plan aimed to clear banks' balance sheets of bad assets. Then on November 12, Treasury Secretary Paulson announced a major shift in the thrust of the $700 billion financial rescue program. He stated that the funds would not be used to purchase up troubled mortgage-related securities, as the rescue effort was originally conceived, but would instead be used in a broader campaign to help financial markets and, in turn, make loans, including car and student loans, more accessible for creditworthy borrowers.

Of the initial $350 billion out of the $700 billion that Congress authorized, all but $60 billion had been committed by early November 2008.

By month's end, more than $1 trillion was allocated globally in giant bank rescues from governments in the United States, Europe, and Asia. The Treasury Department concluded that there were some banks that were "too big to fail" out of fear that their collapse would severely damage the world's economy.

See also AUDITORS; BANK RESCUE (PLAN) OF 2009 (U.S.); BASEL II ACCORD; CITIGROUP; CREDIT UNIONS; EMERGENCY ECONOMIC STABILIZATION ACT OF 2008; FAILED BANKS; FEDERAL DEPOSIT INSURANCE CORPORATION; FORECLOSURES; GINNIE MAE; LEHMAN BROTHERS; NATIONAL DEBT; PUBLIC-PRIVATE INVESTMENT PROGRAM; TERM AUCTION FACILITY; "TOO BIG TO FAIL"; TROUBLED ASSET RELIEF PROGRAM.

Synonymous with TROUBLED ASSET RELIEF PROGRAM.

BANK BAILOUT (REPAYMENT). The U.S. government, and therefore the U.S. taxpayer, has profited from its investment to save the nation's banks.

See also BANK COMPENSATION; TROUBLED ASSET RELIEF PROGRAM.

BANK BONUSES. *See* BANK COMPENSATION; TROUBLED ASSET RELIEF PROGRAM; WALL STREET REFORM ACT (2010).

BANK BUYOUTS. At the end of August 2009, the five-member board of the Federal Deposit Insurance Corporation voted for new rules that required buyout firms to hold on to failed banks they purchase for at least three years. Investors would also be required to maintain larger amounts of high-quality capital at their acquired banks.

See also BANK STOCKS; FEDERAL DEPOSIT INSURANCE CORPORATION; MARKET CAPITALIZATION; SECURITIES LENDING; "TOO BIG TO FAIL."

BANK CAPITAL. Proposal not requiring legislative approval that would increase the amount of capital banks must have as a percentage of their assets. By mid-September 2009, the Obama administration had proposed new principles for capital requirements, but it does not plan to announce rules for some time.

See also STRESS TESTS.

BANK COMPENSATION. Once the thirty-eight top financial companies reported their fourth-quarter profits in January 2010, they began to pay their workers a total of about $145 billion for 2009 as compensation. Nearly 18 percent more was paid than in 2008 and slightly more than the record year of 2007. Overall, pay is on pace to be equivalent to about 32 percent of revenue, a decline from 40 percent in 2008.

BANK CREDIT CARDS. *See* CREDIT CARDS.

BANK DEPOSIT INSURANCE ACT OF 1934. Federal legislation to protect depositors, extended to June 1935 for bank deposit insurance, originally established by the Banking Act of 1933. This act eventually led to the creation of a permanent deposit insurance program in 1935.

BANKER BONUSES (EU). The European Parliament agreed in mid-June 2010 to provide the most stringent rules on bankers' bonuses, capping large cash awards across the European Union in 2010. The new law limited upfront cash to 30 percent of a banker's total bonus and to 20 percent in the case of very large bonuses. Between 40 percent and 60 percent of bonuses were to be deferred for at least three years.

BANK FAILURES. There were a total of 25 bank failures in 2008. By February 2009, of the nation's 8,300 banks, 83 had failed, and by the end of August 252 banks were on the agency's watch list, meaning that they were at risk of failing. In September alone, regulators took over 11 banks in nine states that were saddled with soured commercial real estate loans. By mid-October, as the one hundredth bank failed for the year, the rate further indicated a growing divide between the small and the large bank as the economy improved. The Federal Deposit Insurance Corporation feared that hundreds of small lending institutions would fail over the coming years, pulling down the economy and adding to the strain on the FDIC. By the end of October, U.S. bank failures reached 105, the highest number since 1992. On August 20, 2010, regulators shut down three banks, raising the number of bank failures to 113. Regulators, after seizing two small banks in Georgia and one in Arizona, brought the total bank failures in November 2010 to 146 for the year.

The FDIC revealed that it was conducting about fifty criminal investigations of former executives, directors, and workers at U.S. banks that had failed since the start of the financial crisis. More than 300 banks and savings institutions had failed since the start of 2008, with a few leading to criminal charges. The September 2008 collapse of Washington Mutual was the biggest ever. On December 10, regulators seized two banks in Michigan and Pennsylvania, marking 151 failures in 2010. By mid-December, regulators had closed eleven more banks in 2010 than the previous year. A total of 319 banks have been closed since 2007. By the end of the year 2010, 98 banks had received bank bailout funds of $4.2 billion under the Troubled Asset Relief Program. When created, TARP provided monies to healthy banks, but some slipped into failure, resulting in more than $27 billion in lost TARP funds.

More banks failed in 2010 than any year since the savings-and-loan crisis ended in 1992 with 157 banks holding $92.1 billion in assets. Since 2008, 322 banks have failed, with combined assets of $633.7 billion and a total cost to the FDIC of $79.5 billion.

By February 23, 2011, the FDIC reported that nearly 12 percent of U.S. banks remained at risk of failing. A total of 884 of the nation's 7,657 banks were on the list at the end of December 2010. Bank profit for all of 2010 was $87.5 billion, compared with a loss of $10.6 billion in 2009. Twenty-one percent were profitable. In mid-March, the FDIC announced that it had paid out nearly $9 billion to cover losses on loans and other assets at 165 failed institutions that had been sold to stronger firms during the financial meltdown.

See also BANK PROFITS; BANK STOCKS; CAPITALISM; COLONIAL BANCGROUP; FAILED BANKS; FEDERAL DEPOSIT INSURANCE CORPORATION; MARKET CAPITALIZATION; SECURITIES LENDING; STRESS TESTS (U.S.); "TOO BIG TO FAIL."

BANK FOR BAILOUTS. A novel idea where the eurozone bailout fund is put into a special bank. Would permit much more lending to calm markets but provide little help for insolvent countries.

See also EUROZONE.

BANK HOLDING COMPANY. Any company that owns or controls one or more banks. As defined in the Bank Holding Company Act of 1956, a company that controls two or more banks. Such companies must register with the Board of Governors of the Federal Reserve System and are commonly referred to as registered bank holding companies.

See also BANK HOLDING COMPANY ACT OF 1956; BANK HOLDING COMPANY ACT AMENDMENTS OF 1966; BANK HOLDING COMPANY ACT AMENDMENTS OF 1970.

BANK HOLDING COMPANY ACT OF 1956. Applied to any corporation controlling 25 percent or more of the voting shares of at least two banks or otherwise controlling the election of a majority of the directors of two or more banks. The law formulated standards for the formation of bank holding companies. These firms were strictly limited to the business of banking managing banks, and providing services to affiliated banks.

See also BANK HOLDING COMPANY; BANK HOLDING COMPANY ACT AMENDMENTS OF 1966; BANK HOLDING COMPANY ACT AMENDMENTS OF 1970.

BANK HOLDING COMPANY ACT AMENDMENTS OF 1966. Established uniform standards for bank agencies and the court in evaluating the legality of bank holding company acquisitions.

See also BANK HOLDING COMPANY; BANK HOLDING COMPANY ACT OF 1956; BANK HOLDING COMPANY AMENDMENTS OF 1970.

BANK HOLDING COMPANY ACT AMENDMENTS OF 1970. Ended the exemption from the Bank Holding Company Act that one-bank holding companies had enjoyed since 1956. This amendment clearly regulated the ownership of bank shares and limited bank holding company entries into activities related only to the business of banking.

See also BANK HOLDING COMPANY; BANK HOLDING ACT OF 1956; BANK HOLDING COMPANY ACT OF 1966.

BANKING. Primarily the business of receiving funds on deposits and making loans. Three decades ago, banks supplied three out of every four dollars' worth of credit worldwide. In 2009, that share had dropped to about one in three dollars.

U.S. Thrifts reported that they had their fifth consecutive quarterly profit in the third quarter 2010. The Office of Thrift Supervision noted that the country's 741 thrifts reported a $1.77 billion profit for the July–September quarter, up from $149 billion in the second quarter. In addition, the number of problem thrifts running the highest risk of failure was fifty-three at the end of the quarter, up from forty-three the year before.

See also CANADA; CAPITALISM; CAPITAL ONE FINANCIAL CORPORATION; CHASE; CHECKING; CITIGROUP; FEDERAL HOUSING FINANCY AGENCY; HSBC; INVESTMENT BANKING; OFFICE OF THRIFT SUPERVISION; U.S. BANCORP.

BANKING ACT OF 1933. Created the Federal Deposit Insurance Corporation to insure deposits of member banks. Other sections, known as the Glass-Steagall Act, prevented national banks from most investment banking. As the first major piece of banking legislation during the Roosevelt administration, it led to significant changes in banking laws.

See also PECORA COMMISSION.

BANKING REGULATIONS. *See* BANKING ACT OF 1933; BANK HOLDING COMPANY ACT OF 1956; BASEL II ACCORD; FEDERAL HOME LOAN BANK ACT OF 1932; FEDERAL RESERVE ACT OF 1913; FINANCIAL INSTITUTIONS REFORM, RECOVERY, AND ENFORCEMENT ACT OF 1994; GRAMM-LEACH-BLILEY ACT OF 1999; NATIONAL BANK ACT OF 1863; RIEGLE-NEAL INTERSTATE BANKING AND BRANCHING EFFICIENCY ACT OF 1994; SAVINGS AND LOAN HOLDING COMPANY ACT OF 1967; WALL STREET REFORM ACT (2010).

BANKING SUPERVISION. *See* BASEL COMMITTEE ON BANKING SUPERVISION.

BANK LENDING. *See* LENDING.

BANK LOSSES. *See* BASEL II ACCORD; EUROPEAN CENTRAL BANK.

BANK MERGERS AND ACQUISITIONS. December 2010 was the busiest month for bank mergers and acquisitions in more than two years, with a total $6.25 billion in deals.

BANK NATIONALIZATION. *See* NATIONALIZATION.

BANK OF AMERICA (BOFA). On January 12, 2008, Bank of America agreed to purchase the nation's largest mortgage lender, Countrywide Financial, for $4 billion in stock, protecting a casualty of the mortgage-default crisis from possible collapse. When the acquisition occurred in July, it was valued at only $2.5 billion. In late 2008, management announced plans to cut 30,000 to 35,000 positions over the next three years as it completed its acquisition of Merrill Lynch. That was more than 11 percent of the combined firms' global workforce of 308,000. The $19.36 billion purchase of Merrill Lynch & Company enabled Bank of America to announce that it was the largest U.S. bank by assets, with $2.7 trillion on its balance sheet.

Key dates in Bank of America's acquisition of Merrill Lynch were:

September 15, 2008—announced deal to buy Merrill Lynch for $50 billion in stock.

November 30—Merrill Lynch had accumulated $13.34 billion in pretax quarterly losses.

December 5—shareholders for both firms approved the deal. Nothing was said about Merrill Lynch's problems.

January 1, 2009—The Merrill Lynch Bank of America deal closed on New Year's Day.

January 16—Bank of America announced the new bailout and a fourth-quarter net loss of $1.79 billion. Merrill Lynch reports a net loss of $15.31 billion for the fourth quarter.

The government extended a new multibillion-dollar lifeline on January 16, 2009, providing Bank of America with an additional $20 billion in support from the government's $700 billion financial rescue fund. Bank of America agreed to pay the government an 8 percent dividend on the $20 billion capital injection and restrict executive pay and benefits. The same month, an additional $20 billion was received by Bank of America from the government to help the bank, based in Charlotte, North Carolina, absorb the losses at its just-acquired unit, Merrill Lynch. Bank of America had received a total of $45 billion in capital injections from the Troubled Asset Relief Program, including $10 billion originally given to Merrill Lynch prior to its merger with Bank of America.

Bank of America reported on April 20 a $4.2 billion first-quarter 2009 profit. Shares of the bank fell 24 percent to $8.02 on concerns that major banks could face more credit losses or write-downs or a need to secure further capital. On April 29, during the huge criticism of the takeover procedures of Merrill Lynch, shareholders voted to strip Kenneth Lewis of his duties as chairman of the nation's largest bank, as measured in assets. He remained as president and chief executive officer following a vote of 50.34 percent by the shareholders.

Bank of America reported a $3.2 billion profit for the second quarter 2009. Its chief executive announced at the end of July his intention to shrink the company's 6,100 branch network by about 10 percent. A federal judge on September 14, 2009, threw out the Securities and Exchange Commission's proposed settlement with Bank of America over its disclosure of controversial bonuses paid to Merrill Lynch workers. On September 21, Bank of America announced it would soon reduce its dependence on federal assistance and repay its $45 billion loan; it would also hopefully convince U.S. regulators that the bank was sound enough by repaying billions in federal aid. Kenneth D. Lewis, chief executive of Bank of America, finally resigned on September 30, 2009, effective at the end of the year, following criticism of his taking over of Merrill Lynch.

On October 16, 2009, Bank of America during the Merrill Lynch takeover reported a $1 billion net loss, revealing continued exposure to bad loans and a weak U.S. consumer. The third-quarter results were down from a net profit of $1.18 billion a year before. Bank of America announced on December 2 that it had reached an agreement to repay $45 billion in federal bailout funds and thus escape pay restrictions and other curbs imposed by the U.S. government. Bank of America became the first of several companies to return their taxpayer-funded TARP monies. The bank planned to raise about $18.8 billion in new equity through the sale of securities, a move required by federal regulators to ensure that the bank has adequate capital reserves and would not find it necessary to come back to the government for further aid.

In early February 2010, Bank of America approved more than $4 billion in 2009 pay for its investment bankers and traders, with an average payout of $300,000 to $500,000. Its first-quarter 2010 profit was $3.2 billion, following two consecutive quarters of losses. Its total revenue was $32 billion, contrasted with losses of $194 million in the last quarter of 2009 and $1 billion the quarter before. On July 16, 2010, Bank of America upset the market with a statement that their second-quarter 2010 earnings were weak and that their overhaul would cost them as much as $4.3 billion a year in lost revenue, plus a one-time charge of $7 billion to $10 billion.

On October 8, 2010, altering its initial response to government pressure to reexamine their documentation with a stop to the entire foreclosure procedures in twenty-eight states, Bank of America imposed a nationwide moratorium on foreclosures and the sale of foreclosed homes throughout the country. Then suddenly, Bank of America announced that it would restart its home seizures that were frozen by documentation concerns, opening more than 100,000 foreclosure actions. The bank declared that it had found no significant problems in its procedures for seizing homes. It began preparing new affidavits for pending foreclosures in twenty-three states where a judge's approval was required, presenting the paperwork on October 25. This action puts the bank and other involved banks on a collision course with state attorneys general. Following Bank of America's announcement, their stock climbed 3 percent.

In the fall 2010, Brian Moynihan, chief executive officer for one year of the nation's largest bank, was in the thick of decision-making as more than 1.3 million of its customers were behind on their home loans and all U.S. state attorneys general were investigating the industry's foreclosure practices, with Bank of America, a leading symbol of all that went wrong. A major concern is how to react should his and other banks be forced to buy back a portion of the hundreds of millions in mortgages gone bad, worth an estimated $2.1 trillion from 2004 to 2008. Bank of America had a fourth-quarter loss of $1.2 billion, with revenue falling 11 percent to $22.7 billion.

At the outset of 2011, Bank of America began to pay Fannie Mae and Freddie Mac almost $3 billion to cover bad mortgages the government bought from the bank's Countrywide Financial mortgage unit. On March 8, 2011, the management rejected the idea of lowering home loans to write off tens of billions of dollars' worth of mortgage debt.

On June 29, Bank of America's management announced an $8.5 billion settlement with investors and that the bank would also absorb an addition $5.5 billion to buy back other defective mortgages. Lawsuits and foreclosure problems will absorb another $6.6 billion. On August 8, following the downgrading of the U.S., Bank of America's stock fell 20 percent and the cost of insuring its bonds against default jumped 50 percent. Other banks' stock would also fall.

Bank of America announced in mid-August that it would cut 3,500 jobs in the quarter, amounting to 3.5 percent of its workforce. The bank's shares fell 47 percent since the beginning of 2011, and 6 percent on the day of the announcement of cuts. The chief executive's goal was to lower expenses of the bank by $1.5 billion each quarter. On August 25, Warren Buffett purchased $5 billion of Bank of America stock. The bank announced on September 8 that under its $5 billion cost-pruning plan, 30,000 positions (at $5 billion) would be cut by the end of 2013. Then on September 21, Moody's cut its credit rating on the bank's long-term senior debt to BAA1, three levels above junk.

On December 21, 2011, Bank of America agreed to pay $335 million to settle the U.S. Department of Justice's allegations that its Countrywide Financial unit discriminated against black and Hispanic borrowers between 2004 and 2008 in the largest residential fair-lending settlement in history. It involved more than 210,000 minority borrowers who were charged higher fees or who could have qualified for a prime mortgage, one offered to borrowers with the best credit history, but instead were steered into more costly subprime loans.

Bank of America reported on January 19, 2012, that it swung to its first annual profit of $2 billion in the fourth quarter 2011.

See also AMERICAN INTERNATIONAL GROUP; BERNANKE, BEN; BUFFETT, WARREN E.; COUNTRYWIDE FINANCIAL; FEDERAL HOUSING FINANCE AGENCY; MERRILL LYNCH; MOODY'S; STRESS TESTS (U.S.); "TOO BIG TO FAIL"; TROUBLED ASSET RELIEF PROGRAM; UNEMPLOYMENT.

BANK OF CHINA. On March 24, 2009, Bank of China announced a 59 percent drop in fourth-quarter net profit as its overseas investments were hit by the global financial crisis. The bank's fourth-quarter net fell to $646.8 million (4.42 billion yuan) from 10.77 billion yuan a year earlier.

At the end of March 2011, Bank of China, the fourth-largest lender by assets, reported that its net profit rose 29 percent in 2010. The bank had a net profit of $15.9 billion for the twelve months ending December 31, 2010.

See also CHINA.

BANK OF ENGLAND. November 6, 2008, the central bank slashed the base rate by an astonishing 1.5 percentage points, bringing it down from 4.5 percent to 3 percent, the lowest since early 1955.

It cut its policy rate to a record low of 1 percent on February 5, 2009. Then again, on March 5, the Bank of England cut key interest rates by a further half a percentage point, pushing the rate to their lowest levels ever. The benchmark rate, at the lowest in the bank's 315-year old history, became 0.5 percent.

In August 2009, the Bank of England received permission from the government to inject an additional $85 billion into the economy. The Bank of England on August 11 cut its economic growth forecast with a new annual growth to peak at 3 percent, less than the 3.6 percent it had predicted earlier. On September 10, the Bank of England decided to leave its benchmark interest rate at a record low 0.5 percent amid signs that the nation's economy was recovering more slowly than those in other parts of Europe. The central bank also left its $290 billion program of buying bonds intact.

See also UNEMPLOYMENT; UNITED KINGDOM.

BANK OF IRELAND. *See* IRELAND.

BANK OF NEW YORK MELLON (BNY MELLON). Posted a steeper-than-expected 51 percent decline in first quarter 2009 and net profit.

Its second-quarter 2010 earnings nearly quadrupled to $658 million. Earnings were up 16.8 percent for the fourth quarter.

In March 2011, the bank reported that its quarterly dividend surged 44 percent and that it planned to repurchase as much as $1.3 billion of its stock. The financial institution had a market capitalization of about $35.09 billion.

America's largest custody bank saw volume fall, with profits dropping 26 percent to $505 million. Revenue fell 5.6 percent to $3.54 billion.

BANK OF WYOMING. Federal Deposit Insurance Corporation regulators shut down the Bank of Wyoming on July 10, making it the fifty-third failure of a federally insured bank in 2009.

BANK PAYBACK. *See* TROUBLED ASSET RELIEF PROGRAM.

BANK PROBES. *See* BANK FAILURES.

BANK PROFITS. Bank profits surged over the summer 2011 to their highest level since mid-2007, with a net profit of $35 billion, up nearly 50 percent from the year before. Nevertheless, revenue was flat.

See also BANK FAILURES.

BANK REGULATION. *See* FEDERAL RESERVE.

BANK RESCUE (PLAN) OF 2009 (U.S.). Treasury Secretary Timothy Geithner's announcement on February 10, 2009, led to a near 400-point drop (almost 5 percent) in the Dow Jones Industrial Average. The lack of clarity was given as the reason by many disappointed Wall Street traders.

The government's bank rescue plan, using $350 billion of the Troubled Asset Relief Program, described the Obama administration's roadmap to "financial stability and recovery," which included a fresh round of capital injections into banks, an expansion of a Federal Reserve lending program, and a public-private effort to relieve banks of toxic assets. These steps were aimed at getting $1 to $2 trillion in financing into the economy to kick-start both consumer and business lending. The idea was to entice private capital to buy bad loans and derivatives in an effort to set the "market price."

The government would be committed to spending $50 billion to stem home foreclosures and to creating a Public-Private Investment Fund to remove bad assets off banks' books. The goals were to encourage lending through a variety of efforts:

a. To stabilize banks with a fresh round of capital injections. It would provide a financial cushion for banks and encourage them to lend. Large banks would have to undergo "stress tests" to measure their capacity to absorb future losses. Investments can be converted into common equity if needed. Banks faced restrictions on dividends, stock repurchases, acquisitions, and executive compensation.

b. To stabilize banks by purchasing toxic assets. It would create a public-private investment fund to purchase bad loans that were causing bank losses and eroding confidence in the financial system. The fund was designed to attract capital for large-scale asset purchases and to allow the private sector to determine the price of current troubled and previously illiquid assets.

c. To unfreeze consumer lending by offering financing for loans. It would expand a Federal Reserve program designed to jump-start markets that provided funding for debt such as student loans and car loans. Investors would purchase newly packaged securitized loans with AAA ratings using attractive financing from the Federal Reserve.

d. To help homeowners by modifying home loans. Attempts would be made to halt the spiral of foreclosures and falling home prices, one of the root causes of the crisis. One option was committing funds for programs to reduce monthly payments and setting guidelines for loan modification.

President Obama's first budget, presented on February 26, 2009, included a $250 billion placeholder for government losses associated with further financial rescue efforts. Those losses would come from the possible deployment of an additional $750 billion, a sum that would double the size of the current bailout and was based on estimates that the government would get back two-thirds of its investment. The International Monetary Fund reported in April that U.S. banks had $510 billion in write-downs by the end of 2008 and faced another $550 billion in 2009 and 2010.

One year following the collapse of Lehman Brothers on September 15, 2008, banks were returning to their normal way of conducting business.

2008

September 15—Lehman Brothers declared that it would file for bankruptcy.

September 16—U.S. officials agreed to bail out American International Group.

September 22—The Federal Reserve approved emergency bank holding company applications for Goldman Sachs and Morgan Stanley.

September 25—Washington Mutual failed; largest bank failure in U.S. history.

September 29—Federal Deposit Insurance Corporation agreed to help Citigroup acquire Wachovia; House defeats initial bank bailout proposal.

October 3—President Bush signed into law $750 billion financial market bailout package.

October 13—U.S. officials told top bankers that government wanted to buy stakes in their firms.

November 23—U.S. officials agreed to purchase more stock in Citigroup and insured large chunks of assets.

2009

January 16—U.S. agreed to bolster Bank of America with more bailout funds and guaranteed assets.

March 22—Treasury Secretary Geithner detailed plans for a public-private investment structure to rid banks of bad assets.

May 7—Bank regulators released results of bank stress tests.

June 17—President Obama proposed overhaul of financial market rules.

July 15—U.S. rejected deal to save CIT Group.

August 25—Obama nominated Ben Bernanke to another four-year term as Federal Reserve chairman.

See also BANK BAILOUT (PLAN) OF 2008 (U.S.); FORECLOSURES; GEITHNER, TIMOTHY; PUBLIC-PRIVATE INVESTMENT FUND; STRESS TESTS (U.S.) ; "TOO BIG TO FAIL"; WALL STREET REFORM ACT (2010); ZOMBIE BANKS.

Synonymous with FINANCIAL STABILITY PLAN; TARP 2.0.

BANKRUPT. A person, corporation, or other legal entity that, being unable to meet its financial obligations, has been declared by a decree of the court to be insolvent, and whose property becomes liable to administration under the Bankruptcy Reform Act of 1978. Originally came from Italy, deriving from *banca rotta*, or "broken bench." When a medieval money lender could not pay his debts, his bench was broken in half.

See also BANKRUPTCY.

BANKRUPTCY. The conditions under which the financial position of an individual, corporation, or other legal entity are such as to cause actual or legal insolvency. Two types are (a) involuntary bankruptcy—one or more creditors of an insolvent debtor file a petition having the debtor declared bankrupt; and (b) voluntary bankruptcy—the debtor files a petition claiming inability to meet debts and willingness to be declared a bankrupt. A court adjudges and declares a debtor bankrupt.

See also BANKRUPT; BANKRUPTCY FILINGS; CHRYSLER; CONTROLLED BANKRUPTCY; CRAMDOWN; GENERAL MOTORS.

BANKRUPTCY COURT. *See* BANKRUPTCY FILINGS; MODIFYING MORTGAGES.

BANKRUPTCY FILINGS. In the United States, filings rose 40 percent in October 2008 as home values sank and individual credit grew, with more than 880,000 bankruptcy petitions filed from January 1 through November 1, 2008, equal to the total for all of 2007. However, the credit crisis of 2008–2009 had forced more firms that would have filed for bankruptcy protection to close down and liquidate rather than restructure because they could not obtain enough financing to operate while they reorganized. Filings jumped nearly 33 percent in 2008 and were expected to climb through 2009. Consumer filings reached 1,064,927 in 2008, up from 801,840 in 2007.

For many people, declaring personal bankruptcy could be the step needed to solvency. More than a million people filed for personal bankruptcy in one year, a staggering 30 percent increase from earlier years. In some cases, individual credit could emerge in better shape once debts were dealt with via bankruptcy. Chapter 7 or Chapter 13 is often used for personal bankruptcy filings.

An average of 5,945 bankruptcy petitions were filed each day in March 2009, up 9 percent from February and up 38 percent from one year earlier. A total of 130,793 people filed for bankruptcy in March. Experts believed it would rise to at least 1.4 million by the end of 2009, compared to 1.1 million at the end of 2008. Consumer bankruptcies rose 27.9 percent in October 2009 from the year before. Filings rose to 135,913 in October, an 8.9 percent jump from September's 124,790. Businesses filing for bankruptcy protection in October numbered 7,771, compared to 7,271 in September, a 7 percent rise in commercial filings.

The year 2009 became the seventh-worst year on record, with more than 1.4 million bankruptcy petitions submitted, up 32 percent from 2008. The number of personal bankruptcies rose by nearly a third in 2009, primarily due to foreclosures and job losses. Personal bankruptcy filings hit 1.41 million in 2009, up 32 percent from 2008.

In January 2010, consumer bankruptcies jumped 15 percent from the year before. There were 102,254 consumer bankruptcies in January, representing a 10 percent fall from December 2009, but filings at the end of last year were abnormally high. Three months in July 2010 bankruptcy filings pointed to the financial struggles of many people. Personal bankruptcies were 137,698 in July, a 9 percent increase from the month before. While there were 1.4 million bankruptcy protection filings in 2009, by mid-year 2010 there were more than 900,000.

Personal bankruptcy filings continued to climb in October on a pace to reach their highest level in five years. A total of 132,173 consumer bankruptcies were filed in October, up 1.4 percent from the month before. Nearly 1.3 million bankruptcies were filed between January and October, with expectations that they would reach 1.6 million by the end of the year, making it the largest number since Congress overhauled the bankruptcy system in 2005. More than 1.6 million Americans filed for bankruptcy-court protection in 2010. While most debtors earned less than $30,000 and were without a college degree, more than a fifth of them had a college degree, a 4.1 percentage point increase.

In January 2011, the number of personal bankruptcy filings fell to the lowest level in two years. Down 22 percent, 92,669 consumer bankruptcy filings occurred. Consumer bankruptcies reached their highest level in five years in 2010. In the first half of 2011, fewer people filed for bankruptcy than in the same period a year before. Through June, 709,303 personal-bankruptcy petitions were filed, down 7.9 percent from the first six months of 2010. In 2010, there were more than 1.5 million such filings, the highest count since Congress overhauled the system in 2005. Personal bankruptcy filings in April 2011 fell nearly 6.5 percent.

See also GENERAL GROWTH PROPERTIES; GENERAL MOTORS; LEHMAN BROTHERS.

BANKRUPTCY PROTECTION. A mechanism where each sovereign nation attempts to assure the public that funds in a bankrupt company will be secure and that regulations are in place to sustain the institution and/or that the government will, via its laws guarantee procedures, so that overtime the bankrupt organization can pull out of bankruptcy and become viable again.

Synonymous with ADMINISTRATION, used in the United Kingdom.

BANKS. By mid-summer 2011, bank profits continued to fall, now facing a leaner future. Jobs were being cut. At the same time, banks were seeking ways to generate revenue that could translate to higher costs for consumers. Lending, the prime driver of profits, had been depressed for years. Trading profits had also been falling thanks to a slowdown in stock purchase volume. Revenue fell 4.4 percent to $188 billion, which was equivalent to the industry's level in 2005.

BANK STOCKS. On October 14 and 15, 2010, bank stocks of large institutions were struck as the mortgage-foreclosure processing debacle spread, leaving millions of delinquent borrowers confused and at risk. Bank stocks lost as much as 5 percent of their value each of these two days, as the cost of protecting against the default of bank bonds surged along with higher banking operating and legal costs. By October 20, recovery would begin as the banks claimed that the panic was uncalled for and that all was under control. In 2010, bank stocks regained strength for the first time in four years. From 2007 to 2009, investors lost 66 percent on bank stocks. In 2010, bank stocks outperformed the broader market, returning 20 percent compared with 15 percent for the S&P 500 as a whole.

On August 8, 2011, following Standard & Poor's downgrading of the U.S. credit rating, bank stocks plunged 11 percent in their biggest one-day fall since April 2009. All six of the largest U.S. banks traded on August 10 for less than book value or net worth. By September, financial stocks in the United States and Europe were down as much as in 2011 as they were in 2008. For example, percent changes in stock prices were as follows between September 2008 and 2011:

European Banks

HSBC (Britain)—51 percent
Banco Santander (Spain)—48 percent
UBS Switzerland—55 percent
BNP Paribas France—52 percent
Standard Chartered (Britain)—59 percent
BBVA Spain—51 percent
Deutsche Bank Germany—57 percent
Barclays Britain—59 percent
Nordau Sweden—27 percent
ING Netherlands—70 percent
Credit Suisse (Switzerland)—60 percent
Unaccredited (Italy)—75 percent
Society General (France)—72 percent
Lloyds (Britain)—78 percent
Intense Sangallo (Italy)—74 percent

U.S. Banks

JP Morgan—42 percent
Wells Fargo—22 percent
Citigroup—85 percent
Bank of America—79 percent
Goldman Sachs—34 percent
U.S. Bancorp—35 percent
Bank of New York Mellon—50 percent
PNC—36 percent
Morgan Stanley—59 percent

Capital One—9 percent
State Street—55 percent
BB&T—39 percent
SunTrust—61 percent
M&T Bank—10 percent
Fifth Third—36 percent

See also BANK OF AMERICA; MORTGAGE FORECLOSURES; SE-
CURITIES LENDING; SECURITIZATION.

BANK TAX. On January 14, 2010, the president proposed a $90 billion
bank tax by saying, "We want our money back, and we're going to get it."
The ten-year assessment on bank liabilities, referred to as the Financial
Crisis Responsibility Fee, would fall most heavily on the nation's top six
banking institutions. Under the plan, a 0.15 percent tax would be levied
on liabilities and would apply to a range of firms that received taxpayer
assistance. The tax would be levied on total assets, minus a type of capital
considered high quality, such as common stock, and disclosed and retained
earnings.

Synonymous with FINANCIAL CRISIS RESPONSIBILITY FEE.

BANK TURALEM. *See* KAZAKHSTAN.

BARCLAYS. The British bank raised nearly 10 billion U.S. dollars by selling shares to Abu Dhabi and Qatar to meet Britain's new capital requirements
for banks seeking to avoid the government's help.

The United Kingdom's second-largest bank, founded more than 300 years
ago, told the country's government not to forward them assistance. Instead of
participating in a program in which the government injected $60 billion into
other British banks, Barclay's raised capital without state aid.

Barclays' shareholders showed their displeasure with the British bank's
fund-raising even as they approved the plan. The issue revolved around
the attractive investment terms that were granted to investors from several
Middle East countries. Part of the funds carried a long-term interest rate of
14 percent.

On January 14, 2009, the bank announced that it was in the process of cutting an additional 2,100 jobs in its consumer and commercial banking business and at its credit card unit, bringing the total job cuts to 4,600, including
400 information technology positions in Britain. To deal with its credibility
gap, Barclays announced on January 26 that it would write down an additional $11 billion for 2008 but wouldn't seek a bailout.

In early April, Barclay's chose not to participate in the British government's Asset Protection Scheme, in which a bank's riskiest assets were

surrounded and then protected against future losses. In mid-June 2009, Barclays accepted Blackrock's offer to purchase Barclays Global Investors for $13.5 billion. On August 6, 2010, Barclays reported a 29 percent climb in net profit for the first half of the year. Barclays announced on November 10, 2010, that its profit fell 76 percent in the third quarter from the year before. It had a pretax profit of $528 million. Fourth-quarter profit surged 36 percent to $5.77 billion. However, profit declined to $5.7 billion from $15.1 billion one year earlier.

Barclays announced on August 2, 2011, that its profit fell 38 percent, with net income dropping to $2.4 billion in the first half of 2011.

See also BLACKROCK; FEDERAL HOUSING FINANCE AGENCY; LEHMAN BROTHERS; SECURITIES AND EXCHANGE COMMISSION; UNITED KINGDOM.

BARCLAYS GLOBAL INVESTORS. *See* BLACKROCK.

BARNES & NOBLE. The world's largest chain of bookstores laid off 100 people in its New York headquarters on January 14, 2009. Its Christmas 2008 sales were down 5.2 percent from a year earlier. Online sales were down 11 percent. At that time there were no plans to close any of the 799 stores.

Its net income plummeted 29 percent for its fiscal fourth quarter as a result of weak store traffic, poor holiday spending, and charges. It had a net income of $81.2 million, down from $115 million in the quarter one year earlier. Fourth-quarter losses at Barnes & Noble were announced on May 21. Online sales fell 7 percent to $93 million in the quarter ending May 2. Revenue fell 4.4 percent to $1.11 billion, while sales at stores open at least a year fell 5.7 percent. Barnes & Noble's sales fell five consecutive quarters. Revenue dropped 5.3 percent by August 2009, with earnings falling 20 percent to $12.3 million from $15.4 million a year before. Its loss widened to $24 million for its second quarter, compared to a loss of $18.4 million a year before. Revenue climbed 4.3 percent to $1.2 billion. Holiday sales in December 2009 for the nine-week holiday period to the end of the year were $1.1 billion, down 5 percent from the same period one year before.

For its fiscal third quarter, profit fell 1 percent from the year before. Revenue increased 33 percent to $2.17 billion. Barnes & Noble's store sales fell 4.7 percent to $1.4 billion. Following seventeen years of growth, Barnes & Noble slipped in 2008 and afterward. Revenue declined 3 percent to $5.12 billion for the fiscal year ending January 31, 2009, while earnings fell about 45 percent to $76 million. Its stock is less than half its peak from four years earlier.

The bookseller expected the gross margin to fall between 26 percent and 26.3 percent in 2010. In August 2010, Barnes & Noble announced that the corporation was for sale. The company posted a net loss of $62.5 million for the first quarter ending July 31, 2010. Its revenue fell 0.9 percent. Barnes & Noble's fiscal second-quarter 2010 loss narrowed to $12.6 million, with gross profit falling 23.6 percent from 29.5 percent. Its online operation climbed 59 percent. In November, Barnes & Noble commenced negotiations with Borders for a possible merger.

In mid-February 2011, management announced that its revenue had fallen 25 percent and it canceled its quarterly dividend to free up $60 million. By summer's end, Barnes & Noble remained the only large U.S. bookstore chain. A fiscal first-quarter loss narrowed less than expected, with sales falling 3 percent. However, online sales increased 37 percent. Indicating a lack of expansion in the book store business, Barnes & Noble reported lower sales in its fiscal second quarter of 0.6 percent to $1.89 billion from $1.90 billion the year before. Its stock fell 16 percent once it was reported that the company had a loss of $6.6 million for the quarter.

On January 5, 2012, management warned that it would lose twice as much money in the year and that it was considering splitting off its growing digital-book business. The company's stock fell 17 percent that day.

Cf. AMAZON.COM; BORDERS GROUP.

BAROFSKY, NEIL. Special Inspector for the Troubled Asset Relief Program since December 2008, he announced his resignation and left the job on March 30, 2011. His interim replacement was Christy Romero, Robert Brodsky's one-time deputy.

He frequently testified before Congress and completed nine quarterly reports and thirteen audits. He also criticized the rescue of the American International Group. His office over the years had won criminal convictions of eighteen people and helped to keep $555 million in taxpayer funds. As for TARP, he ended his service with, "It has increased the potential need for future government bailouts by encouraging the too-big-to-fail financial institutions to become even bigger and more interconnected than before, therefore increasing their ultimate danger to the financial system."

See also HOME AFFORDABLE MODIFICATION PROGRAM; TROUBLED ASSET RELIEF PROGRAM.

BASEL COMMITTEE ON BANKING SUPERVISION. Sets capital standards for banks across the globe. On December 17, 2009, it published a report for more stringent rules for bankers, in particular calling for a change in the manner banks' capital is measured.

The Group of Twenty (G-20), following the financial meltdown, asked the Basel Committee, made up of regulators from twenty-seven nations, including the United States, to come up with new rules to moderate the banks' wanton risk-taking and strengthen their balance sheets. Such rules, if approved, would tighten capital requirements for the globe's largest banks, requiring them to set aside a larger cushion of cash and other easy-to-sell securities and set stricter limits on their leverage and liquidity.

See also BASEL III ACCORD; COMMON EQUITY.

BASEL I ACCORD. Its strength lay in being reasonably simple to negotiate and administer. Then, banks soon started to favor profitable businesses, which under Basel I's crude definitions escaped the appropriate capital charges. There was a need for Basel II during the meltdown of 2008.

Synonymous with BASEL STANDARDS.

Cf. BASEL II ACCORD; BASEL III ACCORD.

BASEL II ACCORD. A set of rules on banks' capital adequacy created in 1988, implemented in Europe in 2008, and expected to become a force in the United States in 2009, its objective is to align the amount of capital that banks set aside to absorb unexpected losses with the amount of risk that they are taking. Under Basel II, banks will be rewarded if they take fewer risks with lower capital requirements. It failed its first big test in part because global diplomatic initiatives were difficult to implement. A shortcoming of such models is that their risk projections come with a caveat that they are assumed to be accurate during normal market conditions. This often is not true.

See also BANK BAILOUT; BASEL I ACCORD; BASEL III ACCORD.

BASEL III ACCORD. In mid-May 2010, new capital and liquidity rules were being debated. Basel III would govern the capital and liquidity buffers that banks carry. Basel III is likely to demand excluding low-quality instruments such as preference shares from capital. On September 12, 2010, twenty-seven nations negotiated new banking regulations that limit the risk at the world's largest financial companies. The regulators were determined to create a more resilient banking system to prevent future financial crises. Some banks argued that overly restrictive rules would make it costlier for people to borrow money, potentially harming economic growth, while regulators countered that new rules would make the banking system safer.

Now each member nation of Basel III needs to adapt the rules to their individual banking systems. To avoid crimping credit, regulators agreed that the rules will likely take at least eight years to be fully implemented, with some technical changes not being fully in place until 2023.

The far-reaching steps would require global banks to maintain basic levels of capital equal to at least 7 percent of their assets, considerably more than present standards of roughly 4 percent for large U.S. banks. If the regulations are supported, it would transform banking, forcing banks to take fewer risks, make less profit, and face more government scrutiny.

Banks would not be able to move risky investments or trading off their balance sheets to shield assets from capital requirements. The reforms have the potential to somewhat lower profits at large banks because the higher capital requirements could discourage riskier and lucrative activities. On December 16, the Basel Committee on Banking Supervision released its study. Their conclusion was that had the newly created regulations been in place in 2009, the ninety-four largest lenders in the world would have needed $762 billion of extra capital.

See also BASEL I ACCORD; BASEL II ACCORD; BASEL COMMITTEE ON BANKING SUPERVISION; COMMON EQUITY; G-20; TIER 2 CAPITAL.

BASEL STANDARDS. *Synonymous with* BASEL I ACCORD.

BASF. A Germany-based global chemical company. It announced in November 2008 that it was temporarily shutting down around eighty plants and reducing production at one hundred factories around the world.

BASF's first-quarter 2009 net profit fell 68 percent, with sales falling 23 percent. BASF's second-quarter 2010 profit tripled to 1.18 billion euros. On October 28, 2010, the company reported a higher third-quarter net profit of $1.72 billion. Sales rose 23 percent. Third-quarter earnings fell to $1.69 billion euros.

See also GERMANY.

BASIC-MATERIAL COMPANIES. *See* ARCELORMITTAL; CEMEX; LAFARGE; RIO TINTO; TATA STEEL; XSTRATA.

BAYERISCHE MOTOREN WERKE. *See* BMW.

BBC (BRITISH BROADCASTING CORPORATION). With the United Kingdom's government reducing expenditures, BBC agreed in mid-October 2010 to a deal that secure its income for the next six years but required the news organization to absorb many of its costs. The government announced that it would freeze the annual TV license fee that funds the BBC, fixed at $228.50 for each color TV household in the United Kingdom. It would permit the broadcaster to collect roughly $3.5 billion each year.

See also UNITED KINGDOM.

BEAR MARKET. A 20 percent drop from its recent peak.

BEAR STEARNS. On March 16, 2008, the Federal Reserve came forward and rescued Bear Stearns, the country's fifth-largest investment bank, by guaranteeing a large portion of its assets against losses in order to get JP Morgan to agree to acquire the bank. By lending money to banks for longer against worse collateral, the Federal Reserve hoped to stem panic and buy time.

It was to be the first indication of how financial services were spreading, mostly without being regulated or checked on. There were conflicts of interest and fraud in the sale of subprime mortgages, which significantly contributed to Bear Stearns's collapse becoming the first bank crisis of securitization in 2008. Bear Stearns was particularly active in the credit default swaps market.

Eventually, JP Morgan Chase saved Bear Stearns and purchased the investment house. As recently as January 2007, Bear Stearns was worth $20 billion. However, due to risky business practices and massive exposure to subprime mortgages, its customers and investors lost confidence in the company and the value of Bear Stearns stock plummeted.

Cf. BAIR, SHEILA; FINANCIAL CRISIS INQUIRY REPORT; JP MORGAN; LEHMAN BROTHERS.

BED BATH & BEYOND. On September 21, 2011, management posted a 26 percent surge in its fiscal second-quarter earnings, with revenue climbing 8.3 percent. For the quarter ending August 27, the firm reported a profit of $229.4 million.

BEER BREWERS. *See* CARLSBERG; SABMILLER.

BEGGAR THY NEIGHBOR. *See* BUY AMERICAN; PROTECTIONISM.

BEIGE BOOK. A survey from the twelve regional Federal Reserve banks. In its mid-summer 2010 regional report evidence was presented that the nation's economy struggled under the weight of a depressed real estate market, high unemployment, and consumers with low confidence. Only the retailing and transportation segments showed growth. On September 8, 2010, the Federal Reserve's survey concluded that the U.S. economy showed "widespread signs" of slowing. Broken down by the twelve district banks, the declaration indicated:

- Minneapolis: The economy grew moderately, with an increase in consumer spending, tourism, services, energy, manufacturing, mining, residential construction, and agriculture.
- San Francisco: Economic activity improved modestly. Upward pressures on prices and wages were quite limited. Sales of retail items and services were mixed but grew on balance.
- Chicago: Manufacturing production growth slowed and private construction decreased, while consumer spending increased and business spending continued at a steady pace.
- Cleveland: Manufacturers reported that new orders and production levels were stable or marginally lower. An uptick was seen in residential and nonresidential construction.
- Boston: The economy was positive on average but varied within sectors. Reports are upbeat among contacts in software, information technology, and manufacturing firms. Retail was mixed.

- New York: The economy continued to weaken, input prices have continued to rise moderately, while consumer prices appear to be steady to down slightly. Real estate remained soft.
- Philadelphia: Business conditions were mixed. Manufacturers reported slight decreases in shipments and new orders. Retailers and auto dealers saw an increase in sales.
- Richmond: Manufacturing activity increased modestly, and there was an improvement in tourism. Service-providing firms reported mixed activity, while retailers had flat to weakening sales.
- Atlanta: The economy remained sluggish. Retail traffic and sales decreased and retailers' outlook was less positive than in previous months. Tourism was mixed.
- St. Louis: Economic activity in the manufacturing and service sectors increased. Retail sales were mixed, while auto sales increased. Residential real estate markets remained firm.
- Kansas City: The economy posted increases, with consumer spending up slightly and high-tech and transportation firms reporting moderate growth. Manufacturing was flat, and factory orders declined.
- Dallas: The economy expanded modestly. The energy sector, agriculture, transportation services, and staffing firms reported solid growth. The manufacturing sector was mixed. Retail sales increased.

On October 19, 2011, the Beige Book reported that all of its twelve bank regions had stronger economic activity than earlier reports, with most showing a modest or slight improvement.

See also FEDERAL RESERVE.

BEIJING. *See* CHINA.

BEIJING AUTOMOTIVE INDUSTRY HOLDING COMPANY. *See* SAAB.

BELARUS. The International Monetary Fund loaned Belarus $2.5 billion in early 2009 to help the country cope with the global economic crisis. Belarus received access to about $800 million of the financing. Belarus's central bank sharply devalued the country's ruble, allowing the currency to plunge 20 percent. This action was a condition of the loan from the IMF.

In June 2011, the government appealed to the IMF for a loan of up to $8 billion.

See also INTERNATIONAL MONETARY FUND.

BELGIUM. The economy embarked on a slow recovery during the second half of 2009, supported by fiscal and monetary easing and an acceleration in world trade. Consumer confidence and business sentiment have improved, albeit from some of the lowest levels on record. Growth will not suffice to prevent further increases in unemployment until mid-2011, which is likely to push up the already high level of structural unemployment. As the economy recovers, attention must return to securing fiscal sustainability. Consolidation measures should concentrate on achieving medium-term expenditure restraint at all levels of government and on controlling aging-related costs. About two-thirds of the deficit reduction in 2010 and 2011 is to be achieved by the federal government and the social security system, and the remainder by communities and regions, although the implementation details have yet to be finalized. This should be complemented by implementing labor market reforms to increase the flexibility of wage formation and enhance job search incentives.

Activity was projected to contract slightly and, thereafter, growth would remain below potential well into 2010, before rebounding on the back of easier monetary conditions, renewed growth in real incomes, and a recovery in world trade. As a result, unemployment would increase over the projection period. Headline inflation should decline with the fall in energy and food prices, although core inflation would show more persistence. The automatic stabilizers should be allowed to work fully during the downswing, but securing fiscal sustainability over the longer term would at some point require long-term structural measures to achieve expenditure restraint at all levels of government.

Belgium had a debt level in mid-November 2010 of about 100 percent of GDP. By the end of November 2010, Belgium's borrowing costs rose, as high levels of public debt makes investors edgy. By year's end, the nation's public debt was 100.2 percent of GDP, the third-highest level in the eurozone, after Greece and Italy.

Shoring up the economy in 2011 would require a stable government that was not distracted by constitutional issues. Even as the economic policy got the required focus, growth would dip to 1 percent in 2011 as the authorities struggled to reduce the fiscal deficit. The nation's GDP growth was 1.0 percent and a GDP of $444 billion, with an inflation of 2.5 percent and a GDP per head of $41,760. On November 25, 2011, Standard & Poor's cut Belgium's rating by one notch, citing a slowing economy and "protracted political uncertainty." The nation's long-term sovereign credit rating was reduced to AA from AA+, leaving it two steps below the coveted AAA rating. On December 6 a new cabinet was sworn in, terminating a world record of 541 days without a federal government.

See also BNP PARIBAS; FORTIS BANQUE; TAX HAVENS.

BENCHMARK INTEREST RATE. *See* FEDERAL RESERVE.

BENEFITS. *See* RETIREMENT BENEFITS; UNEMPLOYMENT; WAGES.

BENETTON GROUP. In August 2009, Benetton posted a drop in first-half net profit, with revenue falling 11 percent.

BERKSHIRE HATHAWAY. In May 2009, Berkshire reported a loss of $1.53 billion in the three months ending March 31, its first unprofitable period since 2001. The company then returned to profitability in the second quarter 2009, with a net income of $3.3 billion.

Third-quarter 2009 profit tripled as the improving economy and stock market increased the value of its derivatives contracts. The investment company generated $3.2 billion in net income, up from $1.1 billion the year before. Berkshire shed 8 percent of its workforce. It had 21,000 fewer employees than it had at the end of 2008; along with its subsidiaries, it has about 225,000 workers. For 2009, Berkshire Hathaway reported one of its strongest growth periods in its forty-five-year history as its book value gained 19.8 percent in 2009 from the previous year. In dollar terms, its book value increased to $21.8 billion from 2008, when its book value per share slid 9.6 percent, the biggest decline since 1965.

The firm's management reported that second-quarter 2010 net income fell 40 percent to $1.97 billion from $3.30 billion the year earlier. There was a 73 percent increase in operating profit, however. In early November, management reported that third-quarter profit fell 7.7 percent to $2.99 billion, with operating earnings at $2.79 billion. A 36 percent increase in operating profit was shown, with a profit nearly doubled to $645 million. Its second-quarter profit surged 74 percent to $3.42 billion, and its operating earnings fell 12 percent to $2.7 billion.

Berkshire Hathaway report that its third-quarter 2011 profit fell 24 percent to $2.28 billion. Operating profits were $3.81 billion.

See also BUFFETT, WARREN E.

BERLUSCONI, SILVIO. Prime Minister of Italy for seventeen years; resigned in November 2011.

See also ITALY.

BERNANKE, BEN. Sworn in on February 1, 2006, as chairman and a member of the Board of Governors of the Federal Reserve System. Before his appointment as chairman, Dr. Bernanke was chairman of the President's Council of Economic Advisers from June 2005 to January 2006. He had been a chaired professor of economics and public affairs at Princeton University since 1985.

Bernanke was born in 1953 in Augusta, Georgia, and grew up in Dillon, South Carolina. He received his BA in economics in 1975 from Harvard University and a PhD in economics in 1979 from the Massachusetts Institute of Technology.

Dr. Bernanke is one of the few government officials that had an active role through both the Bush and Obama administrations. His comments before congressional committees were powerful and had an enormous impact on government policy.

Addressing the Federal Reserve's annual symposium in Jackson Hole, Wyoming, on August 17, 2007, he said: "It is not the responsibility of the Federal Reserve—nor would it be appropriate—to protect lenders and investors from the consequences of their financial decisions. But developments in financial markets have broad economic effects felt by many outside the markets, and the Federal Reserve must take those effects into account when determining policy."

On March 5, 2008, Bernanke called on lenders to aid homeowners by reducing their principal to lessen the likelihood of foreclosure.

As U.S. Federal Reserve chairman, he authorized putting $800 billion into the financial system during the September–October 2008 meltdown.

On April 29, he announced that the Federal Reserve would hold official interest rates low and would continue to purchase government bonds and other debt, in an effort to pump credit into banks and companies. Also, he indicated plans to substantially increase the Federal Reserve's holdings of mortgage-backed securities and Treasury securities in the months to follow.

Bernanke announced at the same time that the Federal Reserve had purchased $74 billion of Treasury securities. On June 25, Bernanke faced open hostility from lawmakers barraging him during a congressional hearing over his handling of the financial crisis and the Federal Reserve's role in reshaping the banking system. In particular, they focused on the aid package given to the Bank of America to complete its acquisition of Merrill Lynch in January 2009. It was clearly the harshest treatment of a Federal Reserve chairman in a decade.

During his July 22 presentation before the Senate Banking Committee stating that President Obama's call for a consumer protection agency for risky financial products was not needed, he argued that consumer oversight was part of the Federal Reserve's mission to oversee the safety and soundness of banks. On August 25, President Obama, seeking continuity in U.S. economic policy, nominated Ben Bernanke for another four-year term as chairman of the Federal Reserve. As chairman, he will have to make decisions regarding how and when to withdraw federal support without undermining the recovery. Moving too slowly could lead to a period of inflation, as happened in the 1970s.

One year after the collapse of Lehman Brothers on September 15, 2008, Ben Bernanke stated that the recession was "very likely over. . . . At this point we are in a recovery." This confidence was in part based on the government's report that retail sales climbed 2.7 percent in August 2009 after falling 0.2 percent in July.

Bernanke warned the nation on November 28, 2009, that he opposed the revamping of the government's proposed financial legislation changes. He criticized a provision that he said "would strip the Fed of all its bank regulatory powers" and stated that he wants "to protect monetary policy from short-term political influence." *Time* magazine announced on December 15, 2009, that Ben Bernanke was the 2009 Person of the Year. On December 17, the Senate Banking Committee backed Bernanke for a second term as chairman of the Federal Reserve by a vote of 16–7.

On January 28, 2010, Bernanke won the backing of the U.S. Senate for a second four-year term as the Federal Reserve's chairman. By the end of July 2010, referring to the nation's recession he characterized the economy as "unusually uncertain." He chose not to announce any new measures but said that the Federal Reserve was "prepared to take further policy action" if needed.

At the Federal Reserve's annual meeting in Jackson Hole, Wyoming, on August 27, 2010, Bernanke indicated that the Federal Reserve was prepared to take additional steps if the economy continued to weaken, including significant purchases of government debt. He argued that the Federal Reserve was determined to prevent the economy from slipping into a cycle of falling wages and prices. Options include purchasing more government debt and long-term securities. It could ride it out and keep short-term rates extremely low for a longer period. It could also lower the interest rate it pays on the funds banks hold at the Federal Reserve, and it can raise it medium-term target for inflation that would discourage banks from holding onto their cash.

On October 15, 2010, Bernanke declared that he would consider using "non-conventional" tools to spur growth. He called for buying up Treasury bonds to push down long-term interest rates in order to weaken the value of the dollar and thus increase exports and reduce imports. At the same time, his intention was to minimize the chances of deflation. Bernanke, in early December, called the inflation fears "way overstated" and said he had 100 percent confidence that he could act quickly enough to keep prices in check. As for the recession, he also said that "it doesn't seem likely" the economy would fall into recession again but suggested that could happen if the unemployment rate remained high "for a protracted period of time."

On July 13, 2011, he said, "We don't know where the economy is going to go," and declared that the Federal Reserve was ready to act again if necessary. While at the annual meeting of the Federal Reserve in Jackson Hole, Wyoming, Bernanke spoke but offered no new stimulus programs. On October 4, the chairman warned that the U.S. economic recovery was "close to faltering" and that Congress and the White House had a "shared responsibility" with the central bank to respond. Bernanke argued, "Monetary policy can be a powerful tool, but it is not a panacea for the problems currently faced by the U.S. economy. Fostering healthy growth and job creation is a shared responsibility of all economic policy makers. Fiscal policy-other policies-pertaining to labor markets, housing, trade, taxation, and regulation-have important roles."

On February 2, 2012, speaking before the House Budget Committee, Bernanke said that he would "not actively seek to raise inflation or to move away from our (2 percent) target." He warned that "interest rates can soar quickly if investors lose confidence in the ability of a government to manage its fiscal policy." Republicans criticized him for working to lower unemployment and revive the housing market instead of maintaining a single-minded focus on inflation, to which Bernanke said that he would "not actively seek" to raise inflation, but if inflation and unemployment both rose about its targets, it could choose to lower inflation more slowly in order to reduce unemployment more quickly.

For many followers of the global and national economic trends, Ben Bernanke is right on target and history will show that he saved the day for America, leading to the start of a great bull market of the century.

See also CONSUMER FINANCIAL PROTECTION AGENCY; DEFLATION; DEPRESSION 2.0; EMERGENCY ECONOMIC STABILIZATION ACT OF 2008; FEDERAL RESERVE; WALL STREET REFORM ACT (2010).

BERTELSMANN. Europe's largest media firm, which reported on March 23, 2010, its first net loss in decades. In 2009, sales fell 5.4 percent and earnings before interest and taxes also declined.

BEST BUY. Sales declined in same-store sales during the December 2008 peak holiday period. The company posted its fiscal fourth-quarter profit as declining 23 percent compared to 2007. Earnings dropped 4.9 percent, with net earnings of $570 million.

The company said that its fiscal first-quarter earnings fell 15 percent, with sales falling 4.9 percent. The government reported that sales at electronics and appliance stores had decreased 10.4 percent in August 2009, but that was a significant improvement from July when sales dropped 14.1 percent. Best Buy raised its annual revenue forecast to between $48 billion and $49 billion from September 2009 until February 2010 and forecast revenue of $46.5 billion to $48.5 billion, with sales falling as much as 5 percent. Revenue increased 12 percent to $11.02 billion. On December 14, 2009, Best Buy reported that revenues grew and earnings quadrupled for its third quarter ending in November.

However, its fourth-quarter profits were lower than expected because purchasers sought less expensive electronics, offering smaller corporate profits.

The company showed a 4.6 percent increase in revenue, with sales rising 1.7 percent following a 5.3 percent fall in 2008. Best Buy's fiscal fourth-quarter 2009 earnings rose 37 percent. In the three months ending August 28, 2010, revenue fell 0.1 percent. Second quarter net income rose to $254 million, compared to $158 million one year earlier. Revenue climbed 3 percent to $11.34 billion from $11.02 billion one year before. Third-quarter 2010 net income for Best Buy fell. With shares down nearly 15 percent; revenue dropped 5 percent in the United States; net income in the quarter fell 4 percent to $217 million.

On March 24, 2011, management reported that its fourth-quarter income plummeted 16 percent, with net income falling to $651 million from $779 million the year before. Revenue fell 2 percent to $16.26 billion. For the quarter ending May 28, Best Buy had a profit of $136 million, with revenue climbing 1.4 percent to $10.94 billion. On September 13, management of the world's largest electronics chain reported a 30 percent fall in quarterly profit, with sales falling for the fifth consecutive quarter. Best Buy's heavy Black Friday promotions were achieved at the expense of profits, which dropped 29 percent.

See also RETAILING.

"BETS AGAINST CLIENTS." *See* GOLDMAN SACHS.

BGI. Barclays Global Investors.
See also BLACKROCK.

BILATERAL TRADING. *See* DERIVATIVES.

BILLABLE HOUR. *See* LAW FIRMS.

BILLIONAIRES. *See* WEALTH.

BIPARTISAN POLICY CENTER DEBT REDUCTION TASK FORCE. A November 2010 report, headed by Dr. Alice Rivaling and former Senator Peter Domenici, formed a panel of experts dealing with the overhaul of the U.S. tax code. The center was created in 2007. The report called for an overhaul of tax and spending program, including:

a. Changing the formula for social security taxes so that they are levied against 90 percent of all wages, compared with the current system, which caps the tax at a certain income level.
b. Major cuts in discretionary spending. Singled out a government policy that permits military retirees to collect full benefits after twenty years.
c. Cuts to farm subsidies and either eliminating or limiting certain politically popular tax breaks, such as mortgage-interest tax deduction.

The deficit reduction would total $5.9 trillion, with spending cuts of $2.7 trillion to include a freeze on discretionary spending (defense and nondefense), a tax on sweetened drinks, increase in Medicare part B premiums, smaller payments to drug firms and other health care savings, higher incomes subject to payroll tax, and smaller cost-of-living increases; $0.4 trillion of new revenue and offset to include a 6.5 percent national Deficit Reduction Sales Tax, one-year holiday from Social Security payroll taxes, income taxed at rates of either 15 percent or 27 percent, and corporate tax rate drops to 27 percent from 35 percent; $1.9 trillion of other tax changes to include replacing deductions for mortgage interest and charitable giving with 15 percent tax credits, reduce or eliminate most other tax credits, replace earned income tax credit for low-income families, and eliminate standard deduction; and $0.9 trillion of interest savings.

See also NATIONAL COMMISSION ON FISCAL RESPONSIBLITY AND REFORM.

BIRTHS. The U.S. birthrate fell to its lowest level in 100 years as many people decided that the costs of having children during the Great Recession was too great. The birthrate fell for the second year in a row to 2.6 percent in 2009, even with an increasing population. The birthrate fell 13.5 births for every 1,000 people in 2009; down from 14.3 in 2007.

Probably due to the weak economy, for a third year in a row U.S. births fell after an all-time high of more than 4.3 million in 2007. In 2010, births fell 3 percent to slightly more than 4 million. During the recession, rates dropped to 64.7 births per 1,000 women ages 15 to 44 from 69.6 births per thousand women, about 7 percent. (During the 1936 period, in the depths of the Great Depression, birthrates fell 26 percent.) Hispanics saw the largest drop, with birthrates down 5.9 percent from 2008 to 2009. Rates fell by 2.4 percent among black women and by 1.6 percent among white women.

See also ABORTIONS; GREECE; ICELAND.

BLACKROCK. BlackRock purchased Barclays Global Investors (BGI) for $13.5 billion. BGI, which is based in San Francisco, combined with Black-Rock creates the globe's biggest money manager, with nearly $2.8 trillion in assets.

BlackRock's second-quarter 2009 net profit fell 20 percent from a year earlier, despite the money-management giant's cost controls and stronger stock and bond markets. The nation's largest publicly traded asset manager by market capitalization posted earnings of $218 million, down from $274 million the year before. Revenue fell 26 percent to $1.03 billion.

The company reported a 74 percent increase in its third-quarter 2010 earnings, with its operating margin to widen to 40 percent from 33.8 percent. A profit of $551 million was up from $317 million the year before, with revenue climbing 84 percent to $2.09 billion. The firm's fourth-quarter net profit more than doubled from the year before, receiving $23.9 billion from clients.

In April 2011, BlackRock's profit climbed 34 percent to $568 million. In mid-July, the world's largest asset manager reported that earnings rose 25 percent to $578 million, with revenue increasing 16 percent to $2.35 billion. Blackrock's third-quarter profit climbed 8 percent, with a profit of $595 million.

BLACKS. See AFRICAN AMERICANS; BIRTHS; CHILDREN IN POVERTY.

BLACKSTONE GROUP. Its fourth-quarter 2010 loss narrowed with this private equity firm loss for the quarter at $11 million, from the previous year's loss of $143.3 million. Revenue climbed 49 percent to $1.08 billion.

Blackstone had a first-quarter profit with assets climbing to $150 billion and a profit of $42.7 million.

See also CHINA.

BLACK THURSDAY. See IRELAND.

BLAIR, DENNIS C. See GLOBAL UNEMPLOYMENT.

BLAIR, TONY. See FRANCE; UNITED KINGDOM.

BLANKFEIN, LLOYD. Born in the Bronx, New York City, educated at Harvard University, and became the chief executive officer at Goldman Sachs in 2006 after twenty-four years at the firm.

In November 2009, during an interview Blankfein said that Goldman Sachs was doing "God's work." The reputation of the chief executive and his 140-year-old firm was on the line and indeed might have been at the point on the edge that convinced questioning members of Congress to support new federal regulations for the investment/banking industry.

Indicating a year of financial industry retrenchment, Blankfein's stock bonus fell for the first time since the financial crisis began. He received from his firm restricted shares worth $7 million for 2011, down 44 percent from the previous year and his lowest payout since he received no bonus for 2008, when he accepted government funds.

See also GOLDMAN SACHS.

BLOCKBUSTER. For more than twenty-five years a video rental giant, it filed for bankruptcy protection September 22, 2010.

In mid-January 2011, Blockbuster asked its creditors to put up more money to help it exit bankruptcy protection. In addition, the chain was considering closing more of its stores, perhaps as many as 1,000 of its 5,000 remaining. On February 21, management decided to sell itself for $290 million to a consortium of its shareholders to convert its Chapter 11 bankruptcy into Chapter 7 liquidation. The agreement called for the closing of more than 600 stores by month's end. In mid-March 2011, a judge cleared the way for Blockbuster to sell itself to a group of hedge funds, thus staving off an imminent liquidation of its assets. On April 5, bidding began, with offers reaching more than $300 million. Ultimately, Blockbuster closed all of its stores.

BLS. *See* BUREAU OF LABOR STATISTICS.

BLUE CHIP. A corporation maintaining a good dividend return and having sound management and good growth potential.
See also DOW JONES INDUSTRIAL AVERAGE; STOCK MARKET.

BLUE/RED BONDS. A novel idea dealing with the eurozone nations; jointly backing a portion of each nation's debt. Would lower volume of troublesome debt, but not likely to help market access in a liquidity crisis.
See also EUROZONE.

BMW (BAYERISCHE MOTOREN WERKE). November 2008 sales were down 25 percent. BMW swung to a rare loss in the fourth quarter 2008, and its full-year net profit plunged 90 percent. It had sustained a net loss of $1.24 billion for the quarter. Revenue fell 18 percent as auto sales for the year dropped 30 percent.

In January 2009, BMW announced that a total of 26,000 workers would move to shorter shifts on some days in February and March, with four plants affected. BMW employed about 75,000 people in Germany. In February, BMW announced that it would eliminate 850 positions from its national responsibility. The world's best-selling premium automaker by sales reported a loss of $204 million, compared to a previous year net profit. BMW had a first-quarter 2009 net loss.

BMW posted a 76 percent fall in second-quarter net profit as demand for luxury cars sagged. Profit declined to $171.5 million, while revenue fell 11 percent. In August 2009, BMW indicated that sales for the month had fallen by 11 percent. Sales fell 18 percent in the year's first nine months. In October 2009, BMW reported that monthly sales increased year-on-year for the first time in 2009. BMW's third-quarter profit slumped 74 percent from a year earlier. Quarterly sales fell 7.2 percent to 324,100 vehicles. With a sales rise in November, the automaker expected full-year sales to fall 10–15 percent lower than in 2008.

BMW's management reported on April 12, 2010, that global sales rose in the first quarter. Sales rose to 141,701 cars, up 12 percent from the previous year. A few days later, on May 5, BMW reported that it had jumped to a profit in the first quarter 2010 with a net profit of $420 million. Revenue rose 8.1

percent to $420 million. In July 2010, BMW's management predicted that sales for the year would climb by about 10 percent to more than 1.4 million cars. In 2009, 1.29 million cars were sold, down 10 percent from the previous year. Its second quarter showed a net profit of $1.1 billion, with revenue increasing 18 percent.

By mid-March 2011, BMW said it would boost its dividend fourfold. It had a 19 percent climb in revenue, reflecting an 85 percent climb in Chinese auto sales. First-quarter 2011 profit more than tripled, posting a $1.78 billion profit, with car sales climbing 21 percent. On July 12, 2011, management reported that BMW predicted sales increases of more than 10 percent in the year to more than 1.6 million cars. The car marker posted a 20 percent sales rise to 833,366 cars. By year's end 2011, BMW had sold 221,073 cars and sports-utility vehicles in the United States, a rise of 12.3 percent.

See also AUTOMOBILE INDUSTRY.

BNP PARIBAS. Its shares fell to a six-year low on December 23, 2008, resulting from its failure to purchase part of Fortis. BNP shares closed down 71 cents, or 2.3 percent. BNP Paribas, one of the largest French banks, had a fourth-quarter 2008 net loss of about €1.4 billion, but managed a net profit for the year of about €3 billion, helped by its retail banking, asset management, and services unit.

BNP Paribas, by market capitalization France's largest bank, reported in early August 2010 a net profit of $2.78 billion; up 31 percent in the second quarter. It fourth-quarter net profit climbed 14 percent, with its net rising $2.1 billion and revenue increasing 2.6 percent.

See also FORTIS BANQUE.

BNY MELLON. *See* BANK OF NEW YORK MELLON.

BOEHNER, JOHN. The U.S. House Speaker who agreed on December 22, 2011, to a two-month extension of a payroll tax break.

See also PAYROLL TAX CUTS.

BOEING. This rival of Airbus delivered 375 planes in 2008, making it the second-largest producer of airplanes. The company reported an unexpected fourth-quarter loss and forecast 2009 earnings well below Wall Street estimates. It expected delivery of 480 to 485 commercial planes in 2009. The plane maker expected to cut a total of l0,000 jobs in 2009, about 6 percent of its workforce.

The number included 4,500 layoffs announced in January 2009 by Boeing's commercial plane unit. Boeing announced in April that it would scale back production of some of its jetliners, along with job cuts. Orders for their commercial planes had declined. It reduced its monthly production of its twin-aisle 777 to five airplanes from seven beginning in June 2010 and planned to cut a total of 10,000 positions after reporting a loss for the fourth quarter 2008. Boeing cut its full-year earnings forecast as it reported in April a 50 percent drop in first-quarter profit. Earnings for the year were lowered to $4.70 from $5 a share.

Boeing is by far the largest beneficiary of the U.S. Export-Import Bank financing, with $11.2 billion in the value of loans and guarantees. Boeing's fourth-quarter 2009 profit was $1.27 billion, compared to a loss of $86 million the year before. Revenue increased to $17.94 billion. Management projected that by 2011 its cash flow would reach about $5 billion. For the first quarter 2010, Boeing posted a profit of $519 million, down 15 percent from $610 million a year before. Revenue fell 7.8 percent to $15.22 billion. The airline swung to a third-quarter 2010 profit of $837 million, compared with a yearly 2009 loss of $1.56 billion.

On January 20, 2011, management announced that it would cut about 1,100 jobs through the end of 2012. The firm reported a profit of $1.16 billion for the fourth quarter, compared with $1.27 billion the year before. At the end of July, Boeing reported that its earnings had increased 20 percent to $941 million, with revenue climbing 6 percent to $16.5 billion from $15.6 billion. The firm's third-quarter profit surged 31 percent. Net income was $1.1 billion, with revenue climbing 4 percent to $17.73 billion.

See also AIRLINES; EXPORT-IMPORT BANK; TRADE DEFICIT (U.S.). *Cf.* AIRBUS.

BOFA. *See* BANK OF AMERICA; COUNTRYWIDE FINANCIAL.

BOLIVAR. *See* VENEZUELA.

BOLIVIA. For 2011, its economy was projected to expand by 3.8 percent, down slightly from 2010. The nation's GDP growth was 3.8 percent, GDP at $21 billion, an inflation rate of 6.0 percent, and a GDP per head of $2,080.

BOLLYWOOD. *See* INDIA.

BOND BUYBACKS. Popularized in Europe, bond buybacks permit an indebted nation to borrow money from Europe's bailout fund and use it to buy up their own bonds at depressed prices from investors or the central bank. It also permits nations to lower their total debt burdens by paying less than the face value of their bonds.

BOND BUYING. The Federal Reserve declared in mid-March 2009 that it would purchase as much as $300 billion of long-term U.S. Treasury securities in the coming months and hundreds of billions of dollars more in mortgage-backed securities. The Federal Reserve pumped as much as an extra $1.15 trillion into the economy via bond purchases.

By mid-summer 2010, should ten-year interest rates, which were 2.8 percent, climb to 4 percent as they did in spring 2009, bondholders would suffer a capital loss more than three times the current yield.

See also FEDERAL RESERVE; MORTGAGE-BACKED SECURITIES; MUNICIPAL BONDS.

BONDS. *See* STOCK MARKET; YIELD CURVE.

BONUSES. In 2008, payouts were $20.3 billion, below the record-high bonuses of $34.3 billion in 2006. Bonuses on Wall Street increased 17 percent in 2009.

On February 7, 2011, the Federal Deposit Insurance Corporation approved a draft rule that aimed to tie the final payments of bonuses to the outcomes of the employees' trades and other decisions over time. At the end of the year, Wall Street cash bonuses had fallen by about 8 percent. Financial institutions paid out $20.8 billion in cash bonuses, down from $22.5 billion in 2009 and down by one-third from the $34.3 billion paid in 2006—the highest ever. By mid-March, CEO bonuses at fifty major corporations had surged 30.5 percent, the largest gain in at least three years. It was projected that Wall Street year-end 2011 bonuses would be on average 20 percent to 30 percent lower than the previous year. Bonuses for Wall Street employees were expected to fall 35 percent to 40 percent on average from the year before.

Bonuses for 2011, as reported in January 2012, were the lowest since 2008, with many major financial and corporate bonuses cut by at least half from 2010.

See also AMERICAN INTERNATIONAL GROUP; BANKERS BONUSES; BANK OF AMERICA; BLANKFEIN, LLOYD; BONUS TAX BILL; EXECUTIVE PAY; GOLDMAN SACHS; LAW FIRMS; RETENTION BONUS; WALL STREET REFORM ACT (2010); WINDFALL TAX.

BONUS TAX BILL. The U.S. House of Representatives passed legislation on March 19, 2009, that would significantly curb Wall Street bonuses in 2009. The measure was approved on a 328–93 vote and imposed a 90 percent surtax on bonuses granted to employees who earn more than $250,000 at firms that have received at least $5 billion from the government's financial rescue program. If approved by the Senate and signed into law by President Obama, it would be retroactive to December 31, 2008. On March 22, President Obama expressed doubt about the constitutionality of the Bonus Tax Bill.

BORDERS GROUP. The country's second-largest bookstore chain reported in May 2009 a 12 percent decline in revenue. Sales declined to $650.2 million from $735.8 million a year earlier. Sales at their superstores fell by 14 percent. The Borders Group posted a wider loss for its fiscal second quarter 2009, with a loss of $45.6 million compared to a loss of $9.2 million one year earlier. Revenue fell 18 percent to $624.7.

For its fiscal third quarter 2009, the company reported a loss of $37.7 million compared to a loss of $175.4 million one year before. Revenue declined 13 percent to $602.5 million. The company announced a sharp decline in revenue and same-store sales for the eleven-week holiday period, ending January 2010. Revenue fell 15 percent to $649.2 million, with sales of $846.8 million, a 14 percent decline. Borders reported a drop of 14 percent in sales and laid off 884 workers, more than 3 percent of its workforce, in 2009. Management then reported on September 1, 2010, a loss for the fifth time in six quarter as revenue fell and profit margins declined. The net loss widened to $46.7 million.

Borders reported that it would close 200 of its mall stores in January 2010, discharging approximately 1,500 employees from its workforce of 25,000, many of whom work part time. On December 10, the company reported a very poor quarter with lower sales and falling margins, as it proceeded in talks with Barnes & Noble for a possible merger. The loss was $74.4 million, with revenue falling 18 percent to $475.6 million. By year's end 2010, Borders management announced that it was delaying payment to some publishers, a growing indication of the bookstore's continuing troubles. The delay was to enable the company to refinance its debt during this time of turbulence in the bookstore and publishing business. Borders estimated that it had 8.1 percent of new printed book retail sales for 2010, compared with 17.3 percent for Barnes & Noble and 22.5 percent for Amazon.com.

Burdened by too much debt, Borders Group filed for Chapter 11 protection on February 16, 2011, and announced that it would close about 30 percent of its stores (200 of its 642 stores). The bookseller employed 17,500 people and had about $287 million in total rental expenses in 2010. Closing of stores left 4.9 million square feet of space available, creating huge retailer rental space to remain unused. Borders identified its assets of $1.28 billion and its liabilities of $1.29 billion. By May, Borders would close an additional 28 stores, leaving the chain with 405 stores. By the end of March, Borders sought from the bankruptcy court approval to hand out as much as $8.3 billion in executive bonuses.

By July 15, Borders' future was uncertain, as a deadline approached to either find a buyer or face liquidation. On July 19, management announced that it would liquidate after failing to receive any offers to save it. The following day, the bookstore of 399 stores started to close and the company expected to go out of business by September.

Cf. AMAZON.COM; BARNES & NOBLE.

BORN, BROOKSLEY. Chairperson of the Commodity Futures Trading Commission, the federal agency that oversees the future and commodity op tions market. She lobbied Congress at the CFTC to give the agency oversight of off-exchange markets for derivatives in addition to its role with respect to exchange-trade derivates, but her warnings were opposed by regulators and most members of Congress.

Born was especially concerned about swaps, financial instruments traded over the counter between banks, insurance firms, and other funds or companies and have no transparency except to the two counterparties and regulators, if any. CFTC regulation was strongly opposed by the Federal Reserve, the secretary of the Treasury, and other key players noting that capital markets could be trusted to regulate themselves. As the Great Recession took hold, there was considerable support for what Born had proposed.

In March 2009, she said: "The market grew so enormously, with so little oversight and regulation, that it made the financial crisis much deeper and more pervasive than it otherwise would have been." She also lamented the influence of Wall Street lobbyists on the process and the refusal of regulators to discuss even small reforms. In 2009, Born was awarded the John F. Kennedy Profiles in Courage Award in recognition of the "political course she demonstrated in sounding early warnings about conditions that contributed to the current global financial crisis."

See also Commodity Futures Trading Commission.

BORNEO. *See* MALAYSIA.

BORROWING. *See* INTEREST RATES.

BOSTON GLOBE. *See* NEWSPAPERS; *NEW YORK TIMES*.

BOUND RATES. *See* WORLD TRADE ORGANIZATION.

BOUNTIES. *See* SECURITIES AND EXCHANGE COMMISSION.

BOWLES, ERSKINE. *See* NATIONAL COMMISSION ON FISCAL RESPONSIBILITY AND REFORM.

BP. *See* BRITISH PETROLEUM.

BRANDEIS UNIVERSITY. On January 26, 2009, the trustees of Brandeis University voted unanimously to close the Rose Art Museum in order to sell its collection to help shore up the university's finances. Following outcries from the public, students, and alumni, the board canceled this decision in February.

See also ENDOWMENTS.

BRAZIL. GDP grew in the second quarter, following a decline in the previous two. Activity rebounded robustly on the back of resilient private consumption and an ongoing recovery in industrial production, which had contracted sharply in the previous months. Capacity utilization was approaching precrisis levels in a number of manufacturing sectors. Investment had yet to recover. Domestic demand was set to grow vigorously in the last quarter of 2009 and into 2010, supported by a still accommodative policy mix. The monetary easing cycle came to an end in September, following a cumulative 500-basis-point cut in the policy interest rate over the previous twelve months. Fiscal outcomes continued to weaken due to cyclical factors, a ratcheting-up of recurrent expenditure, especially the central government payroll, and the discretionary measures that have been put in place in response to the global crisis. The end-of-year fiscal target was therefore unlikely to be met. A judiciously planned withdrawal of policy stimulus would be advisable from early 2010, if the recovery is well in hand as expected.

The expansion that gathered pace during 2007 was sustained in the first half of 2008, although activity appears to be slackening due to a worsening of financial conditions. Domestic demand had been the main driver of growth. The trade surplus was shrinking, essentially due to buoyant demand for imports, and the current account shifted into deficit. Dynamism in the labor market continued to deliver robust job creation. Inflation picked up considerably through mid-year. Further monetary tightening was expected in the near term, despite a falling-out gap in 2009, to quell the inflationary pressures arising from sharp exchange rate depreciation. The primary budget surplus target was expected to be met, although the 2009 draft budget law calls for further increases in expenditure. Reversing the trend of increased public spending is among Brazil's main macroeconomic policy challenges.

Brazil's currency fell as the nation's trade surplus narrowed to a six-year low in 2008, propelled by a deepening economic slowdown that curbed demand for their exports. The currency declined 0.1 percent to 2.3176 per dollar from 2.3145 at the start of 2009. The government reported its first monthly trade deficit since 2001 as the global economic crisis cut exports. Exports fell 26 percent in January 2009 from a year earlier to $9.8 billion, while imports dropped 17 percent to $10.3 billion.

Brazil lowered interest rates below 10 percent, to 9.25 percent, on June 10, following two decades of double-digit levels. Its central bank lowered its 10.25 percent overnight-lending rate by more than half a percentage point, its fourth cut so far in 2009. On September 11, Brazil reported that it had returned to growth after a short-lived recession with a 1.9 percent growth in its GDP in its second quarter 2009. Industrial production increased by 2.2 percent in October, but it was still 3.2 percent lower than a year before.

Brazil's third-quarter GDP expanded 1.3 percent but fell short of estimates for growth of 1.9 percent. According to its fourth-quarter inflation report submitted on December 22, 2009, Brazil's growth could swell to 5.8 percent in 2010 from near zero in 2009, with the possibilities of a climb in the inflation rate to 4.6 percent.

By April 2010, there was a growing concern that the nation's economy was overheating. The economy grew at least 10 percent in the first quarter 2010; car sales climbed 18 percent in the same period. Expectations were that Brazil's economy would expand by 5.5 percent in 2010. Industrial production surged by 17.4 percent until the end of April.

The nation's GDP grew by 9 percent in the first quarter of the year compared to one year earlier. It was the fastest pace of growth in fourteen years. By June 2010, industrial production fell by a seasonally adjusted 1 percent but was 11.1 percent higher than a year before. By the second quarter 2010, Brazil's economy continued to boom, with its GDP expanding 8.8 percent from a year before. Of the world's major economies, only China exceeds Brazil's remarkable record. In addition, Brazil's government began requiring its banks to cover 60 percent of their bets against the dollar with deposits at the central bank that do not attract interest.

For 2011, it was projected that GDP would continue to climb, as would foreign direct investment into Brazil, and growth would remain stable at 4.5 percent. The nation's GDP growth was 4.5 percent, GDP at $2,052 billion, an inflation rate of 4.4 percent, and a GDP per head at $10,530. On February 2, the central bank raised the benchmark lending rate by a half percentage point to 11.75 percent per year. This high interest rate tightened monetary policy for the second time in three months and attracted a flood of overseas investment. The nation's trade surplus climbed to $1.2 billion in February from $0.4 billion in January 2011. Import growth of 18.4 percent in the year until February was outpaced by a 23.5 percent expansion in exports.

On March 3, it became evident that Brazil's economy surged by 7.5 percent, a rate unmatched since 1986, making it the world's seventh-largest economy. In mid-April, Brazil's GDP expanded 4.2 percent. Yet, there were signs of difficulty ahead—inflation was 6.5 percent and rising in April and the minimum wage would rise by 7.5 percent in real terms in 2012 at a great fiscal cost since pension payments were tied to the minimum wage. Nevertheless, Brazil noted that it had its second-greatest trade surplus in nearly two years. There were record exports (up 265 percent from the year before) and higher commodity prices, creating the surplus of $3.5 billion.

On August 29, the government declared that it would set aside $6.3 billion of tax resources to curtail spending. On August 31, the government slashed its overnight-lending rate, which questions their intent to control inflation in addition to the independence of its central bank. The bank lowered its overnight rate by half a percentage point to 12 percent, among the highest in the world. Consumer prices soared by 7.2 percent, the first time inflation had breached the 7 percent mark since 2005.

By September, Brazil became the world's most overvalued currency. The real has weakened 6 percent against the U.S. dollar, but it still was up 36 percent since January 1, 2009. Soaring currency hurt manufacturing and helped drive rising real estate prices and consumer loans. In response, the government tripled taxes on foreign bond purchases, making currency bets more expensive. The central bank bought dollars, while an interest-rate cut in August deterred speculative capital.

On October 19, 2011, the central bank cut the nation's benchmark rate for the second time in two months, doubling down on its bet that a slowing economy was more troubling than high inflation. The overnight rate was lowered by 0.5 percentage point to 11.50 percent. At the end of November, the central bank dropped half a point from its base interest rate.

In 2012, Brazil's interest rates could fall below 10 percent, following a high of 12.5 percent in 2011. On February 3, Brazil's currency climbed against the U.S. dollar, gaining about 8 percent. The government's intervention did not stop the real's gain.

See also ARGENTINA; LATIN AMERICA; WORLD TRADE.

BRETTON WOODS. In 1944, one year before the end of World War II, the focus of Bretton Woods was on creating a new system. It sought to avoid a repeat of the Great Depression of the 1930s by creating the World Bank to rebuild Europe after the war and the International Monetary Fund to oversee an economic system based on fixed exchange rates. The meeting took place at a time when trade and financial cooperation had virtually ceased. The 700 representatives gathered at the luxury Mount Washington Hotel in New Hampshire. The meeting lasted three weeks and was preceded by more than two years of technical preparation.

Since the 2008–2009 meltdown, many specialists and governments are urging a reexamination of the Bretton Woods concepts and outcome. By 2012, nothing appears to be on the agenda for revisiting the Bretton Woods system.

See also BRETTON WOODS II; HYUNDAI MOTOR COMPANY; LATIN AMERICA.

BRETTON WOODS II. Following the meltdown in the fall of 2008, there was a push to replace the original Bretton Woods concepts of the World Bank and the International Monetary Fund with a new, updated version. By 2012, there has been little talk of change.

Cf. BRETTON WOODS.

BRIC. Brazil, Russia, India, and China. *See* BRICS.

BRICS. Brazil, Russia, India, China, and South Africa. These five nations combined account for about 40 percent of the globe's population and 18 percent of its GDP. On April 14, 2011, a summit was held in Sonya, Hainan Province, China, with recommendations to change the structure of the international monetary system and the possibilities for a common currency.

BRIDGES. *See* AMERICAN RECOVERY AND REINVESTMENT ACT (OF 2009).

BRITAIN. *See* UNITED KINGDOM.

BRITISH AIRWAYS (BA). In early April 2009, management announced that ongoing layoffs would mean a bigger-than-expected operating loss for the fiscal year just ending. Operating losses amounted to $220.5 million. On May 22, British Airways announced that it had a significant full-year loss. BA had a loss of $594.6 million for the twelve months ending March 31. Passenger and cargo volumes slumped and fuel costs climbed $45 percent. To cut costs during the meltdown, in mid-June BA asked its staff to voluntarily work for no pay or take an unpaid leave for up to one month to help the company "fight for its survival."

BA reported in July 2009 that it would further reduce summer and winter capacity and lay off another 3,700 jobs in its fiscal year through March. BA would cut capacity by 3.5 percent in the April–October period and would cut its winter schedule by 5 percent. BA reported its first pretax loss for the fiscal first quarter since its shares were posted twenty-two years ago. Ending June 30, 2009, its quarterly loss was $247.2 million. BA had lost $465 million in the six months prior to September 2009.

BA announced on November 6, 2009, that it would reduce an additional 1,200 jobs, raising the reductions to nearly 5,000. The cuts represented about 13 percent of its total staff of 39,000. Its net loss climbed to a record $345 million for the six months prior to September 30. Revenue during this period fell nearly 14 percent. On November 12, BA and Iberia Lineas Aereas de Espana agreed to merge, creating a carrier with annual revenues of about $20 billion. The new firm would be called International Airlines, with both carriers retaining separate brands.

At the end of July 2010, BA announced that its fiscal first-quarter net loss widened to $190.5 million. Then in early November 2010, BA announced its first profit in two years. Pretax income for the six months ending in

September came in at $240 million. Their cargo business performed well, with revenue increasing 39 percent.

See also AIRLINES; IBERIA.

BRITISH PETROLEUM (BP). Adjusting to $50 a barrel of crude oil, BP's earnings dropped 64 percent by the end of April 2009. On July 28, BP posted a 53 percent fall in profit for the second quarter. Profit was $4.39 billion for the three months ending on June 30, from $9.36 billion a year before. In October 2009, BP reported a decline in third-quarter results. The giant oil company expected to slash costs by $4 billion in 2009, twice its original forecast.

Major problems would then affect BP, including the April 2010 explosion of its gulf rig off the coast of Louisiana. In time it would become the world's worst oil spill, finally capped in August 2010.

On July 26, 2011, BP's management reported a profit in the second quarter of $5.6 billion, which was 21 percent lower than the $7.1 billion generated in the first quarter. Third-quarter profit was $5.3 billion, down 3.6 percent. Revenue climbed 35 percent to $95.4 billion.

See also OIL COMPANIES.

BRITISH POUND. *See* POUND.

BRITISH UNIVERSITIES. *See* UNITED KINGDOM.

BROADBAND ACCESS. The economic stimulus package of 2009 gave $183 million in stimulus grants to expand broadband Internet service to rural areas in seventeen states. It was approved in late December 2009.

See also AMERICAN RECOVERY AND REINVESTMENT ACT (OF 2009).

BROKER-DEALER. A firm, often the subsidiary of an investment bank, that buys and sells securities for itself and others.

BROKERS. *See* STOCK BROKERS.

BROWN, GORDON. Holding his first meeting in Washington, D.C., with President Obama on March 3, 2009, the prime minister of the United Kingdom called for a "global New Deal" to set common principles for regulation of banks, declaring that the fiscal crisis could help to overcome past resistance to increased oversight across borders. Prime Minister Brown urged and then hosted the April 2 economic summit in London.

See also BUSINESS 20; FINANCIAL PROTECTIONISM; G-20; GOLDMAN SACHS; UNITED KINGDOM.

BRUSSELS SUMMITS. *See* MERKEL, ANGELA; SARKOZY, NICOLAS.

BRYSON, JOHN. Became U.S. commerce secretary in November 2011.

BTA (BANK TURALEM). *See* KAZAKHSTAN.

BUDGET (CITY). *See* CITY BUDGETS.

BUDGET (U.S.) (FISCAL YEAR 2010). President Obama's proposed U.S. budget of $3.6 trillion for the fiscal year beginning October 1, 2009, marked the most significant change in nearly thirty years on the subjects of national health care, moving energy away from oil and gas, and boosting the federal role in education. Federal outlays were to soar in fiscal 2009 to $4 trillion, or 27.7 percent of GDP, from $3 trillion, or 21 percent of GDP, in 2008 and 20 percent in 2007. This was higher as a share of the economy than any year since 1945. It was more spending by far than during the recessions of 1974–1975 or 1981–1982.

A 134-page booklet described the priorities of the Obama administration, with income tax rates sharply increasing. Rates would rise for single people earning $200,000 and for couples earning 250,000 beginning in 2011. Limits would be set on personal exemptions and itemized deductions, as well as higher capital-gains rates.

The president also called for an additional $75.5 billion for the wars in Iraq and Afghanistan for the remainder of 2009 and an additional $130 billion for 2010. It set aside contingency funds of $250 billion in the event that more funds would be required to bail out teetering banks and other firms. The president's plan indexed Pell Grants to inflation plus 1 percent, making it akin to Medicare and Social Security.

It envisioned raising $646 billion between 2012 and 2019 by capping carbon levels and auctioning off permits for the emission of greenhouse gases. The government established a $630 billion reserve fund for the creation of a national health care plan to provide universal access to health insurance.

The deficit, which by 2009 was $1.75 trillion, or 12.3 percent of the GDP, was the highest it had been since 1942, when World War II began. With a return to economic well-being, the president looked forward to 2013 when stability will have returned.

The top tax rate for couples would rise to 39.6 percent from 35 percent to fund expanded benefits. Top earners would see mortgage deductions fall $70 for every $1,000 in deductions.

Programs of the proposed 2010 fiscal budget were as follows:

a. Defense—includes war spending; shake-up in weapons-buying process: $663.7 billion, a 1.4 percent change from 2009.
b. Health and Human Services—$630 billion fund to finance health care overhaul; crackdown on fraud in Medicare and Medicaid: $78.7 billion.

    c. Transportation—$5 billion to improve high-speed rail corridors; $800 million for satellite-based air-traffic control: $72.5 billion, change of 2.8 percent.

    d. Veterans affairs—boost spending by $25 billion; expand centers for prosthetics, mental health, and other medical needs: $52.5 billion, 10.3 percent change.

    e. State and other international programs—expands foreign service positions; doubles spending on foreign aid: $51.7 billion, 40.9 percent change.

    f. Housing and urban development—crackdown on mortgage fraud; $1 billion in funds for an affordable-housing trust fund: $47.5 billion, 18.5 percent change.

    g. Education—removes private lenders from student-loan market: $46.7 billion, 12.8 percent change.

    h. Homeland security—deporting illegal immigrants who commit crimes; boosting airline-passenger screening: $42.7 billion, 1.2 percent change.

    i. Energy—seeks cap on U.S. carbon emissions; companies would bid for right to pollute: $26.3 billion, minus 0.4 percent change.

    j. Agriculture—cut subsidies to wealthiest farmers; reduced funding for overseas promotion of U.S. brand-name products: $26 billion, 8.8 percent change.

    k. Justice—$8 billion for the Federal Bureau of Investigation to combat financial fraud; funds for local governments to hire 50,000 police officers: $23.9 billion, minus 6.3 percent change.

    l. Commerce—boosts funding for research into climate change; $4 billion for 2010 census: $13.8 billion, 48.4 percent change.

    m. Labor—"Green jobs" training; action to curb improper benefits mistakenly paid; targets employer tax evasion: $13.3 billion, 4.7 percent change.

    n. Treasury—$250 billion placeholder for losses tied to more rescue efforts; funds for IRS enforcement: $13.3 billion, 4.7 percent change.

    o. Interior—excise tax on oil and gas output in the Gulf of Mexico; new fees on companies that drill on federal lands: $12 billion, 6.2 percent change.

    p. Other—Securities and Exchange Commission would receive 13 percent funding boost; Environmental Protection Agency's budget would jump nearly 35 percent, the largest in its history; new fund to finance infrastructure: $78.2 billion, 15 percent change.

Congress passed a $3.5 trillion budget for 2010 on April 29, by a vote of 233–193, without any Republicans voting for it and seventeen Democrats voting against it. The Senate vote was 53–43, with four Democratic defections. The budget outline included $530 billion in basic spending for domestic programs.

See also DEFICIT (BUDGET, U.S.); WARS IN AFGHANISTAN AND IRAQ.

BUDGET CONTROL ACT (2011). *Synonymous with* DEBT DEAL.

BUDGET DEFICIT. The budget deficit for the fiscal year topped the $1 trillion mark in July 2011. The United States spent $129.38 billion more than it collected in July, raising the shortfall for the first ten months of fiscal 2011 to $1.1 trillion. The federal government ran an estimated $1.3 trillion budget deficit in fiscal 2011, the same as the previous year. This was equivalent to 8.6 percent of GDP, down from 8.9 percent in fiscal 2010 but still the third-highest percentage since 1945.

See also DEFICIT (BUDGET, U.S.); FEDERAL RESERVE; WARS IN AFGHANISTAN AND IRAQ.

BUDGET ENFORCEMENT ACT (1990). A $482 billion reduction package that broke President George H. W. Bush's pledge: "Read my lips, no new taxes." Included cuts in agriculture subsidies and higher taxes on gasoline, cigarettes, alcohol, and luxury items.

Cf. BALANCED BUDGET ACT (1997); DEBT DEAL.

BUDGET (FISCAL 2011) PROPOSED. President Obama presented his budget for 2011 on February 1, 2010. It called for nearly $1 trillion in tax increases on families with income above $250,000 over the next decade, largely by allowing tax cuts from George W. Bush's administration to expire. For 2011, the budget was projected to be $3.8 trillion and projected a deficit of $16 trillion.

Then, on February 19, 2011, the House of Representatives, controlled by the Republicans, voted to slash more than $60 billion from the budget and impose large spending reductions over the remaining months of the year. Cuts would have been made in domestic programs, foreign aid, and some military projects. The Senate, controlled by the Democrats, failed to support this bill. It soon was pulled.

BUDGET (FISCAL 2012) PROPOSED. On February 14, 2011, the president proposed his 2012 budget that purported to lower the federal deficit over time, leaving spending at historically high levels because of mushrooming health and retirement programs. As proposed, spending as a percent of GDP would be 23.6 percent in 2012, down from 25.3 percent in 2011. If fully accepted by Congress, the federal deficit would drop from 10.9 percent of GDP in 2011 to 3 percent in 2017.

In 2012, the plan would place the deficit at $1.1 trillion, down from $1.6 in 2011. It would lower the government's accumulated red ink over the coming ten years by a similar $1.1 trillion.

By department, the proposed 2012 breakdown of funds were as follows:

Department 2012 Requested Change from 2010

Department	2012 Requested	Change from 2010
Education	$77.4 billion	+ 21 percent
Energy	$29.5 billion	+ 18 percent
Veterans Affairs	$58.8 billion	+ 11 percent
State/International Programs	$61.4 billion	+ 8 percent
Treasury	$14.0 billion	+ 4 percent
Interior	$12.1 billion	no change
Defense	$670.6 billion	– 3 percent
Health/Human Services	$82.2 billion	– 3 percent
Housing/Urban Development	$41.7 billion	– 3 percent
Homeland Security	$43.5 billion	– 4 percent
Labor	$12.8 billion	– 5 percent
Transportation	$13.4 billion	– 9 percent
Agriculture	$22.0 billion	– 14 percent
Justice	$20.9 billion	– 25 percent
Commerce	$8.8 billion	– 334 percent

BUFFETT RULE. *See* BUFFETT, WARREN E.

BUFFETT, WARREN E. A renowned investor and one of the world's wealthiest people, Buffett's Berkshire Hathaway recorded a loss of $5.1 billion in 2008. The firm reported a 62 percent drop in net income for the year and posted negative results for only the second time since he took control in 1965.

Buffett said on March 9, 2009, that the U.S. economy was facing an economic Pearl Harbor and it had fallen off a cliff. Moody's, on April 8, lowered the long-term issuer rating of Berkshire to Aa2 from its top rating, citing the weakening economy and "severe decline in equity markets." Berkshire had seen its shares decline by 33 percent over the past year. Berkshire Hathaway had a loss of $1.5 billion in the first quarter 2009, compared with a profit of $940 million a year earlier.

Buffett proposed a "Public-Private Partnership Fund" to act as a quasi-private investment fund backed by the government with the sole purpose of buying up whole loans and residential mortgage-backed securities.

On August 15, 2011, following the August 1–5 volatile ups and downs of the stock market, he argued that "billionaires like me should pay more taxes."

He humbly noted that in 2010 he paid $6,938,744 in federal taxes, only 17.4 percent of his taxable income. This contrasted with the tax burdens ranging from 33 percent to 41 percent for most, an average of 36 percent. He wants the federal government to "stop coddling the super-rich." "For those making more than $1 million, there were 236,883 such households in 2009, I would raise rates immediately on taxable income in excess of $1 million, including, of course, dividends and capital gains. And for those who make $10 million or more, there were 8,274 in 2009, I would suggest an additional increase in rate."

The Buffett Rule was named after Warren Buffett's urging the government to raise the tax rates paid by the wealthiest Americans. The average tax rate for the top 400 earners in the United States fell to as low as 16.62 percent in 2007 from a peak of 29.9 percent in 1995. Republicans argued that the Buffett Rule was "class warfare." He remarked: "My friends and I have been coddled long enough by a billionaire-friendly Congress."

On August 25, Warren Buffett purchased $5 billion worth of stock in Bank of America.

See also BANK OF AMERICA; BERKSHIRE HATHAWAY.

BUILD AMERICA BONDS. Introduced in April 2009 as part of the government's economic stimulus plan to create jobs building roads, schools and hospitals. Intended to create jobs in struggling cities that often charged municipalities higher costs than for traditional bond deals. The United States paid 35 percent of the interest, although fees had declined and were nearly comparable today to tax-exempt fees.

BUILDING PERMITS. *See* HOME CONSTRUCTION.

BULGARI. Sales dropped to $410.7 billion in the fourth quarter 2008, a 10 percent declined from a year earlier.

In March 2011, LVMH paid $6 billion for the Italian jeweler, including its debt.

See also JEWELRY; LUXURY GOODS; LVMH; RETAILING.

BULGARIA. Cut its forecast for economic growth in 2009 by nearly two percentage points, with the global financial crisis expected to hurt investments and exports. The current account deficit was 24 percent in 2008. By mid-September 2009, the government of Bulgaria reduced its budget deficit to $76.5 million. There was an 81 percent reduction in Bulgaria's budget.

When Bulgaria joined the European Union in 2007, it posted the smallest budget deficit of the twenty-seven EU nations. Bulgaria's growth forecast for 2010 increased to 0.2 percent from minus 2 percent.

Economic growth in 2011 improved as employment began to rally. The nation's currency is pegged to the Euro and will probably apply for membership of the EU's exchange rate mechanism in preparation for full adoption. The nation's GDP growth was 2.6 percent, with a GDP of $46 billion, an inflation rate of 2.4 percent, and a GDP per head of $6,270.

BURBERRY. The British luxury-goods firm said on January 20, 2009, that it would cut 540 jobs in Britain and Spain as part of a plan to save about $49 million. Burberry reported on July 15 a further drop in sales growth for its fiscal first quarter as the economic meltdown continued to hold back demand.

On October 13, 2010, Burberry reported an 11 percent climb in second-quarter sales of $603.6 million. Management raised its earnings forecast for the entire year by 5 percent. Burberry posted in November a 46 percent surge in profit for its fiscal first half. Sales grew 6 percent, with net profit of $133.3 billion; revenue climbed 18 percent.

On January 18, 2011, the 155-year-old label announced a 27 percent increase in revenue to $770 million for the last quarter of 2010 and huge surges in Asia, up 68 percent for same quarter one year earlier. Its net profit, announced on May 26, more than doubled to $339.2 million. On October 12, management reported first-half year sales up 30 percent to $1.29 billion.

BUREAU OF CONSUMER PROTECTION. *See* WALL STREET REFORM ACT (2010).

BUREAU OF LABOR STATISTICS (BLS). A research agency of the U.S. Department of Labor, it compiles statistics on hours of work, average hourly earnings, employment and unemployment, consumer prices, and many other variables.

"BURGER-KING KIDS." Walk-in hires who worked on mortgage foreclosure documents in 2010, most with minimal experience or knowledge. These people were often employed, some outside of the lending firms, with little training and were found to dispose of some paperwork by throwing the documents into the garbage. Some were under so much pressure to dispose of their paperwork that they barely had time to see what there were signing. *See also* ROBO-SIGNERS.

BUSH, GEORGE W. President of the United States from 2001 to 2009. Between January 2001 and 2008, the U.S. economy under his watch added about 3 million nonfarm jobs, including 1.34 million in the private sector.

Bush outlined a sweeping plan on April 1, 2008, to streamline the U.S. financial regulatory system, with proposals that consolidated bank regulation, created a new type of insurance charter, improved the oversight of mortgage lending, and allowed the Federal Reserve to peek into more corners of finance. On July 31, President Bush signed a housing-rescue bill into law, completing Congress's ambitious legislative effort to head off foreclosures and stabilize jittery financial markets.

See also AUTOMOBILE INDUSTRY; BUDGET (FISCAL 2011) PROPOSED; OBAMA, BARACK; TAX BREAKS; TAX CUTS; TROUBLED ASSET RELIEF PROGRAM; UNFAIR TRADE SUBSIDIES.

BUSINESS BANKRUPTCY FILINGS. *See* BANKRUPTCY FILINGS.

BUSINESS CYCLE DATING COMMITTEE. *See* NATIONAL BUREAU OF ECONOMIC RESEARCH.

BUSINESS STARTS. *See* NEW COMPANIES.

BUSINESS 20. Proposed by Gordon Brown, prime minister of the United Kingdom in January 2009, a group of multinational firms to work with leaders of G-20 nations to tackle the financial crisis.

See also BROWN, GORDON; G-20.

BUY AMERICAN. Legislation originally adopted in 1933 that set up the basic principles of buying national. Amended in 1954, the scope of the act was expanded to allow procuring entities to set aside procurement for small businesses and firms in labor-surplus areas and to reject foreign bids either for national interest reasons or national security reasons.

A protectionist concept in the 2009 economic stimulus package that created conflicts and reactions from other nations, this program was spreading protests against foreign workers, fueled a backlash on trade, and invited retaliation by other nations.

See also BUY LOCAL; PROTECTIONISM; SMOOT-HAWLEY ACT.

BUYBACKS. *See* STOCK BUYBACKS.

BUY LOCAL. An argument made by some Americans since 2008–2009 to purchase goods and services from within the boundaries of the country, state, and/or community. Buy Local is a policy purporting to protect local industries and stores against imports.

See also BUY AMERICAN.

BUYOUT FIRMS. These private equity groups tapped the public markets for cash during the borrowing booms and were having increasing difficulty since summer 2008, with lower reported values.

The American Recovery and Reinvestment Act (of 2009) permitted firms to defer income taxes when they repurchase their own debt at a discount. This allows companies restructuring debt to defer possible taxes for as long as five years and then pay the taxes over the following five years.

See also AMERICAN RECOVERY AND REINVESTMENT ACT (OF 2009); BANK BUYOUTS; DEBT-BUYBACK.

BUYOUTS. *See* BANK BUYOUTS.

C

CADILLAC. *See* GENERAL MOTORS.

CALIFORNIA. *See* FURLOUGHS.

CAMERON, DAVID. Prime Minister of the United Kingdom. On December 9, 2011, he rejected the proposed new European Treaty, the only leader of twenty-seven European Union governments to do so. "I said if I couldn't get adequate safeguards for Britain in a new European treaty, I wouldn't agree to it," creating for some "two Europes," for putting Britain "on the sidelines." Praised by others for his "bulldog spirit," he refused to participate in an urgent 200 pound/billion euro funding boost for the International Monetary Fund to deal with the ongoing crisis. The following day, a major newspaper poll supported Cameron's decision, even though it would lower the United Kingdom's influence in the European Union.

See also EUROPEAN UNION.

CAMEROON. Growth was projected in 2011 to be 3.9 percent. GDP will be about $21 billion, with an inflation rate of 4.3 percent and a GDP per head of $1,040.

CAMPBELL SOUP. The largest soup company in the world. Management reported on September 3, 2010, that its fourth-quarter 2010 profit climbed 64 percent, although its sales fell by 5 percent. For the quarter, income was $113 million, with revenue falling 1 percent to $1.52 billion.

On November 10, management reported that its fiscal 2011 forecast was weak, with per-share earnings falling 5–7 percent on sales growth of 2–3 percent. Campbell's Soup earned $279 million, with revenue falling 1 percent to $2.17 billion from $2.2 billion.

Reporting lower 2010 quarterly earnings, management projected a deadline for the full year. Profit for its fiscal second quarter 2010 ending January 30 fell 7.7 percent to $239 million; revenue fell 1.2 percent to $2.13 billion. It earned $239 million in the quarter, down from $259 million. Sales fell to $2.13 billion from $2.15 billion.

In May 2011, management reported an 11 percent increase in third-quarter earnings of $187 million. Revenue climbed 0.6 percent to $1.81 billion, with overall sales down 7 percent for the quarter. In November, management announced that its fiscal first-quarter sales fell 0.5 percent to $2.15 billion, with earning declining 5 percent. The soup company reported a profit of $265 million, down from $279 million the year before.

CANADA. The contraction that began in the last quarter of 2008 seems to have ended in the second half of 2009. External demand and domestic investment appeared to be rebounding, but they also posed the greatest risks to the recovery's sustainability. Unemployment was projected to keep rising until the end of 2009 and underlying disinflation to continue for several more quarters under the weight of persistent slack. The Bank of Canada should hold the policy rate at its current near-zero level until the end of June 2010, as it has committed, and probably beyond. Given the time required to roll out fiscal stimulus and the nascent recovery, additional expansionary measures, including extending the window of eligibility for extraordinary unemployment benefits, should be resisted. Instead, governments should be preparing detailed and credible medium-term fiscal consolidation plans to be announced soon and implemented when the recovery is firmly under way.

In December 2008, the Bank of Canada cut its benchmark interest rate three-quarters of a percentage point to 1.5 percent, a fifty-year low. The lack of a mortgage and banking crisis in Canada did shield the country from the economic downturn to a certain extent. However, a drop in exports, like car and auto parts to the United States, as well as a collapse in energy and commodity prices, brought an end to the nation's privileged isolation. Canadian output fell in the last three months of 2008 at the sharpest rate since 1991 as the nation entered its first recession in almost twenty years. GDP contracted at a 0.8 percent quarterly rate as exports, capital investment, and personal spending all fell.

Also in December, moving to preempt a possible shift of auto production back to the United States, the governments of Canada and the Ontario province offered the auto industry Can$4 billion in emergency loans. The Canadian auto industry exported about 90 percent of its production employed about 400,000 people.

The Bank of Canada revised its economic forecast downward for the first quarter of 2009, saying it expected growth to shrink 4.8 percent. In January 2009, employers cut 129,000 jobs, more than in any single month during earlier downturns. Canada's jobless rate climbed from 6.6 percent to 7.2 percent. Canada remains uncomfortably dependent on the United States as a market, with 76 percent of its exports coming into its southern neighbor.

The Bank of Canada announced on April 21 that it cut its interest rates by a quarter of a percentage point to a historic low of 0.25 percent and that it would maintain its benchmark overnight-lending rate for fourteen months.

The April stress-test program in the United States of its largest nineteen banks could be turned onto the Canadian banking system. Canada's five largest banks would have passed the U.S. government stress test brilliantly. They were profitable in the fourth quarter 2008, are adequately capitalized, and have had no difficulty securing additional private capital. On average, only 7 percent of their mortgage portfolios consisted of subprime loans (versus 20 percent in the United States). No major Canadian bank has required direct government infusions of capital.

Canada's economy improved with 27,000 new jobs in August 2009, climbing to 16.8 million. However, unemployment rose slightly to 8.7 percent and Canada's economy shrank unexpectedly in August. Its GDP contracted 0.1 percent to U.S. $1.11 trillion. By December 2009, Canada's GDP grew by 0.1 percent, the first quarter of economic growth since the third quarter of 2008. Projections for 2010 were for a 3.7 percent growth in its economy.

While the United States suffered its Great Recession, Canada's economy suffered only a mild recession and by 2010 was making a fast economic recovery. Strict financial regulation with a strong commodity boom had made Canada a model of economic strength.

The emphasis for 2011 would be on closing the fiscal gap, although Canada's public finances were the most comfortable among the G-7 nations, given that the deficit in 2009–2010 was the first following five years of surpluses. Less fiscal stimulus and a slowdown in the United States would reduce economic growth to 2.1 percent, down from 3.2 percent in 2010. The nation's GDP growth was 2.1 percent, a GDP of $1,616 billion, an inflation rate of 1.8 percent and a GDP per head of $47, 070.

Canada cut its corporate tax rates from 18 percent to 16.5 percent, compared to the U.S. federal rate of 35 percent, on January 1, 2011, making the nation one of the world's most cost-effective areas to do business. This rate is less than half of the United States' 35 percent. In the last three months of 2010, Canada's GDP grew at a 3.3 percent annualized rate, up from 1.8 percent for the earlier three months.

By February 2011, employment climbed by 15,100, with the unemployment rate remaining at 7.8 percent. In February, the nation's economy contracted to its sharpest pace since May 2009. GDP fell 0.2 percent to US$1.32 trillion, with the manufacturing sector falling 1.6 percent, the sharpest decline since March 2009. Inflation rose to 3.7 percent in the year until May, the highest rate since March 2003. The nation's economy shrank in the second quarter, the first contraction in two years. GDP fell 0.1 percent from the first quarter, for an annualized contraction of 0.4 percent.

The unemployment rate in Canada climbed to 7.3 percent with a loss of 5,500 jobs in August, representing the second straight month of poor employment data. The rise in the jobless rate was the first in seven months. By September, the economy added 60,900 new positions and unemployment fell to 7.1 percent, its lowest level since December 2008.

See also AUTOMOBILE INDUSTRY; MAGNA.

CANON. In January 2009, management reported a 91 percent tumble in its fourth-quarter 2008 net profit, caused primarily by plummeting overseas demand. The Tokyo-based maker of digital cameras and precision electronics, which generates about 80 percent of its total revenue outside of Japan, projected a poor 2009.

Canon's first-quarter 2009 net profit fell 83 percent, with revenues dropping 32 percent. Management reported weaker third-quarter 2009 results as profits fell 56 percent to $398.3 million and revenue slipped 22 percent.

Canon's first-quarter 2010 earnings more than tripled, with net profit climbing to $604.2 million. The firm's operating profit rose, while revenue was up 10 percent. For the entire year, Canon expected an 82 percent increase in net profit. Its second quarter 2010 indicated a surge in profit to $778.4 million, doubling from the year before, with revenue increasing.

See also JAPAN.

CAPITAL. Assets minus liabilities; what a firm owns minus what it owes. Regulators often require financial firms to hold minimum levels of capital.

CAPITAL ASSISTANCE PROGRAM. *See* STRESS TESTS (U.S.).

CAPITAL FLOWS. *See* BRAZIL; CHILE; CHINA; COLOMBIA; INDIA; INDONESIA; RUSSIA; SOUTH AFRICA; SOUTH KOREA; TURKEY.

CAPITAL GAINS. *See* TAX CUTS.

CAPITALISM. Accused by some governments and individuals as a primary contributor to the 2008 meltdown, it is usually defined as an economic system based on freedom of ownership, production, exchange, acquisition, work, and movement and open competition.

The 2008 meltdown to 2012 has, not for the first time but acutely because of its gravity, introduced the huge question of capitalism's survival and value. The capitalist economy, while dynamic and productive, is presently unstable. At its core is a banking system that allows large-scale borrowing and lending. Without this procedure, the majority of businesses cannot deal effectively with incurring costs and receiving revenues, and most consumers cannot achieve their level of consumption. When the banking system collapses, and credit consequently seizes up, economic activity falls.

Capitalism has created its own rules in and outside the boundaries of government. Business people want to maximize profits within a framework created by the government. Once it is determined what people want to purchase, firms generate profits, which induces competitors to enter the market until excess profit is eliminated and resources are allocated more efficiently.

It appears that greater regulation, not less, is needed within the banking industry, especially to pull the nation out of its present recession. The failure that drove the nation into its present predicament can be blamed on both the banks and on the U.S. government regulators. The government, as it is argued, failed to develop contingency plans to deal with future concerns that most experts believed were on the horizon. Others, including professional economists, are to be included in their judgment calls as to the future of our traditional capitalist system.

CAPITAL ONE FINANCIAL CORPORATION. Wrote off an additional $1 billion for bad loans and posted a worse-than-expected loss in the fourth quarter 2008 due to a rising default rate. The bank expected losses to worsen in 2009 based on estimates that the unemployment rate would hit 8.7 percent and home prices would drop another 10 percent. Capital One Financial posted a loss of $275.5 million in July compared with a profit of $452.9 million.

Capital One shifted to a first-quarter 2010 profit of $636 million from a $172 million loss a year before.

CAPITAL PURCHASE PROGRAM (CPP). A part of the Troubled Asset Relief Program providing financial assistance to 700-plus U.S. financial institutions through the purchase of senior preferred shares in the corporations on standardized terms.

See also TROUBLED ASSSET RELIEF PROGRAM.

CAPITAL REQUIREMENTS DIRECTIVE. A requirement for financial institutions to retain at least the equivalent of 5 percent of the capital value of an asset that they securitize. Introduced as part of the 2008 bailout fund.

See also BANK BAILOUT (PLAN) OF 2008 (U.S.); TROUBLED ASSET RELIEF PROGRAM.

CAPITAL RESERVES. *See* FEDERAL HOUSING ADMINISTRATION.

CAR ALLOWANCE REBATE SYSTEM (CARS). *See* CASH FOR CLUNKERS.

CAR CZAR. Would help press the automakers as well as their various constituents, employees and unions, creditors, and suppliers to make concessions to reorganize the businesses to become profitable.

On February 15, 2009, the president announced that he would drop the idea of appointing a single, powerful "car czar" to oversee the revamping and restructuring of GM and Chrysler. Instead, he would maintain the task in the hands of his senior economic advisers.

The president created a panel—the Presidential Task Force on Autos—drawing officials from several federal agencies and being led by his senior economic advisers. A few days later, GM and Chrysler placed on file with the Treasury Department their plans for a complete restructuring of their companies.

See also AUTOMOBILE INDUSTRY; AUTO TASK FORCE; PRESIDENTIAL TASK FORCE ON AUTOS; RATTNER, STEVEN.

CARD ACT. *See* CREDIT CARDS; WALL STREET REFORM ACT (2010).

Synonymous with CREDIT CARD ACCOUNTABILITY RESPONSIBILITY AND DISCLOSURE ACT OF 2009.

CARGO SHIPPING. *See* SHIPPING.

CAR-INDUSTRY SUPPLIERs. *See* AUTO PARTS.

CAR LEASING. *See* GENERAL MOTORS.

CARLSBERG. The beer producing company, Carlsberg of Denmark based in Copenhagen, said on January 15, 2009, that it would cut 270 jobs in the face of an uncertain market.

On August 17, 2010, management posted a 36 percent rise in second-quarter profit of $454.2 million, with revenue climbing 2 percent.

The world's fourth-largest brewer announced on August 17, 2011, that it expected net profit to increase 5 percent to 10 percent for the year. Second-quarter profit fell to nearly $400 million, with sales climbing 4.3 percent.

Cf. ANHEUSER-BUSCH.

CARLYLE CAPITAL. Mortgage-securities hedge fund that on March 11, 2008, sought a moratorium on more forced sales of assets after about $5 billion of their $21 billion in holdings had been liquidated.

CARMAKERS. *See* AUTOMOBILE INDUSTRY.

CARNEGIE BANK (OF SWEDEN). *See* SWEDEN.

CARNIVAL CRUISES. A major cruise-ship operator, it reported its earnings in mid-June 2009, which fell 33 percent. For its fiscal second quarter ending May 31, Carnival reported a profit of $264 million, down from $390 million a year earlier. Revenue fell 12 percent to $2.95 billion. At the end of July, Carnival posted its second consecutive quarterly loss.

On March 23, 2010, Carnival estimated that its net revenue yield, how much it earns from each passenger, would climb 2 to 3 percent in 2010. Its last quarter 2009 net income fell 33 percent to $175 million from $260 million the year before.

Carnival's earnings rose 22 percent during the summer 2010 season, with 5 percent more passengers than the year before. It showed a profit for the quarter of $1.3 billion, with revenue increasing 6.9 percent to $4.4 billion. Carnival's fiscal fourth-quarter earnings climbed 29 percent, with a profit at the end of November 2010 of $248 million.

Management reported that its fiscal 2011 second-quarter earnings fell 18 percent, with a profit of $206 million. Revenue climbed 11 percent to $3.62 billion, with operating margin falling 7.7 percent from 10.7 percent. A major cause was $150 million in higher fuel prices. Fiscal third-quarter earnings climbed 2.6 percent on higher revenue and lower-than-expected costs. For the quarter ending August 31, management posted a profit of $1.34 billion, with revenue climbing 12 percent to $5.06 billion.

Cf. ROYAL CARIBBEAN CRUISES.

CAR PARTS MAKERS. *See* AUTO PARTS.

CARREFOUR. A French firm, the world's second-largest retailer announced on December 18, 2008, that its net income fell 7.4 percent. The group, with more than 15,000 stores in thirty countries, blamed a downturn in consumer spending across its markets and the cost of promotions to maintain market share in the face of competition from discounters.

Carrefour met its fourth-quarter sales forecast and announced on January 14, 2010, that sales increased in the last three months of the year by 1 percent to $37.61 billion.

On July 13, 2011, the retail giant predicted a 23 percent fall in first-half year earnings, with a profit of $1.06 billion. Second-quarter sales rose 1.6 percent. In November, it lost market share in France, its home market, accounting for 42 percent of sales. Its chares dropped by 45 percent in one year.

See also RETAILING.

CARRIER AIR CONDITIONERS. *See* UNITED TECHNOLOGIES.

CARRY TRADE. Any investment that appears suspiciously profitable. A foreign-exchange trading of borrowing cheaply in a funding currency to exploit high interest rates in a target currency.

CARS. Official name for Car Allowance Rebate System.
See also AUTOMOBILE INDUSTRY; CASH FOR CLUNKERS.

CAR SAFETY. In 2009, vehicle traffic deaths in the United States fell to the lowest level since 1950, in part a function of the Great Recession. A total of 33,808 people were killed in 2009, down 9.7 percent from 37,423 in 2008.

CASH BUILDUP. By September 2010, U.S. corporations' cash pile had reached its highest level in half a century, at $1.93 trillion in cash and other liquid assets, accounting for 74 percent of firms' total assets—the largest share since 1959. This holding back on spending is indicative of corporations' hesitation about investing in expansion while the economic recovery remains slow and high unemployment continues to limit consumers' ability to spend.

By the end of the 2010, cash and other liquid assets made up 7 percent of the total assets of nonfarm, nonfinancial corporations, the highest level since late 1963.

CASH BUYING. *See* HOME SALES.

CASH FOR CLUNKERS. A 2009 government proposal to give money to consumers who trade in their old car for a new one. Used extensively in Europe to encourage car sales. July 24 was the first day of the federal government program to purchase more fuel-efficient cars.

Officially, the Car Allowance Rebate System (CARS) provided up to $4,500 for a traded-in vehicle. It was aimed at lifting sales for the automobile industry and taking gas-guzzlers off the road. To qualify, buyers had to turn in a car or light truck that gets no more than eighteen miles per gallon and purchase or lease one that gets at least twenty-two miles per gallon. The vehicle also had to be less than twenty-five years old.

The program was federally funded by $1 billion and was to terminate on November 1, 2009. The program was so popular that by August 19, 435,000 vouchers worth either $3,500 or $4,500 had been distributed to consumers. The government then added another $2 billion to the $1 billion and announced that the program would be terminated at 8:00 PM on Monday, August 24.

On August 27, 2009, the government reported that buyers bought 690,000 new vehicles under the program. U.S. automakers accounted for 38.6 percent, while Japan's largest carmakers sold 41 percent. While the program was terminated at the end of August 2009, European automakers in September were urging their governments to continue the Cash for Clunkers program out of fear that car sales would plunge if programs ended abruptly.

Cf. APPLIANCES; KERUGER, ALAN; TOYOTA.

CASH HOLDINGS. *See* CASH BUILDUP.

CATERPILLAR. The maker of heavy equipment announced in January 2009 that it would cut 20,000 jobs after it forecast that this would be one of its worst years in decades and would slash its payroll by 16 percent. In March, Caterpillar announced that it would lay off nearly 2,500 U.S. workers and close a plant in Georgia. The cuts were in addition to the 22,100 layoffs that were announced in January. Buyouts were offered to about 25,000 U.S.-based employees. On April 21, Caterpillar moved into a first-quarter 2009 loss and cut its full-year sales and profit forecasts, underestimating the severity of the global economic slump. Caterpillar reported a first-quarter net loss of $112 million, compared with a previous-year profit of $922 million.

On July 21, Caterpillar reported a 66 percent drop in second-quarter profit. The company's second-quarter profits were $371 million, down from $1.106 billion a year before. By mid-July, Caterpillar's layoffs approached 15 percent of its total workforce. Caterpillar management announced on October 26 that it would recall 550 laid-off workers by the end of 2010 but would permanently trim about 2,500 idle workers. The company had already dismissed more than 30,000 permanent and temporary workers.

Caterpillar's fourth-quarter 2009 earnings fell by 65 percent. Sales were at $7.89 billion, a 39 percent fall from the year before, with a quarterly profit of $232 million. For the entire 2009, the firm's earnings fell 75 percent to $895 million. Revenue plunged 37 percent and the company trimmed its workforce by more than 20,000 people.

Caterpillar reported in April 2010 that its quarterly profit was strong. The company noted that its first-quarter 2010 profit was $233 million, compared with a year-earlier loss of $112 million. The firm had already dismissed nearly 30,000 full-time and contract workers throughout the world. The firm's retail sales of equipment rose in the three-month period ending May 2010 by 11 percent, the first year-over-year sales growth since September 2008. Management announced on July 22, 2010, that the company doubled its profit in the second quarter and raised its forecast for the year, with profits surging 91 percent for the quarter to $707 million. Revenue climbed 31 percent to $10.41 billion. Its fourth-quarter earnings more than quadrupled, while revenue surged 62 percent.

Caterpillar's sales climbed 49 percent in the three months ending January 31, 2011. Profits in the second quarter surged 44 percent. In mid-August, Caterpillar announced that its global retail sales rose 35 percent in the three months ending July. It was the fifteenth straight three-month period of sales growth. Its third-quarter earnings surged 44 percent, with projected profit increases between 10 and 20 percent projected for 2012. Caterpillar's income in the quarter was $1.14 billion, with sales up 31 percent. On November 19, management reported that its global retail sales rose 31 percent.

Caterpillar expects earnings in 2012 to climb by about 25 percent, with sales in the range of $68 billion to $72 billion. For the fourth quarter 2011, Caterpillar's profit was $1.55 billion, with sales and revenue increasing 35 percent to $17.24 billion.

CATHAY PACIFIC AIRWAYS. Announced in April 2009 that it would reduce passenger and cargo capacity, delay new aircraft deliveries, and ask staff to accept unpaid leaves following a dramatic drop in first-quarter

revenue. Passenger capacity would fall by 8 percent and the airline asked its 17,000 workers to take unpaid leaves of one to four months.
See also AIRLINES.

CATTLE PRICES. *See* HIDE PRICES.

CBO. *See* CONGRESSIONAL BUDGET OFFICE.

CDO COLLATERALIZED DEBT OBLIGATION. *See* CDO SQUARED; FINANCIAL CRISIS INQUIRY REPORT; SYNTHETIC CDO.

CDO SQUARED. CDO that holds other CDOs.
See also FINANCIAL CRISIS INQUIRY REPORT.

CDS. *See* CREDIT DEFAULT SWAP.

CDX. *See* CREDIT DEFAULT SWAP.

CEA. *See* COUNCIL OF ECONOMIC ADVISERS.

CELL PHONES. *See* MOTOROLA; NOKIA CORPORATION; VODA-FONE.

CEMEX. Mexico's Cemex had in November 2008 a net debt of $16 billion, with $8 billion of that debt maturing by the middle of 2010, but only $560 million in cash. In mid-December, shares of Cemex, the largest cement maker in the Americas, rose sharply after it reached an agreement with lenders that cleared the way for the company to refinance $6 billion in debt coming due in 2009. Shares had plunged 24 percent in two days on concern that it might fall short in efforts to refinance its debt.

CENSUS (U.S.). *See* U.S. CENSUS; U.S. DEPARTMENT OF COMMERCE.

CENTER ON BUDGET AND POLICY PRIORITIES. *See* CHILDREN IN POVERTY; STATES (U.S.).

CENTRAL ASIA. Kazakhstan's annual average GDP growth since 2000 was 10 percent; in 2008, it dropped to 5 percent. Predictions were for a national insolvency, even with its $48.4 billion in foreign reserves. The government injected 15 percent of its GDP into the economy, including a $5 billion bailout for local banks.
See also KAZAKHSTAN.

CENTRAL BANK. The national bank of a sovereign nation. A bank holding institution that maintains the bank reserves of a nation and is the prime reservoir of credit. It has impacts on monetary policy, regulates not just banking but a whole range of financial services and markets, encourages economic innovation and legal infrastructure, and possesses proper links with other global financial centers. Central banks played a major role in the 2008 meltdown and in nations' futures.

On November 30, 2011, the major central banks of the world announced that they would provide inexpensive, emergency U.S dollar loans to banks in Europe to cushion the effects of the euro crisis. Six central banks announced participation: the Federal Reserve (U.S.), the Bank of Canada, the Bank of England, the Bank of Japan, the European Central Bank, and the Swiss National Bank.

See also BANK OF CANADA; BANK OF ENGLAND; BANK OF JAPAN; EUROPEAN CENTRAL BANK; FEDERAL RESERVE; SWISS NATIONAL BANK; "TOO BIG TO FAIL."

CENTRAL BANKERS. Meeting at the end of August 2009 in Jackson Hole, Wyoming, central bankers from around the globe expressed growing confidence that the worst of the financial crisis was over and that a global economic recovery was moving forward.

CENTRAL BANK (U.S.). *See* FEDERAL RESERVE.

CENTRAL EUROPE. *See* EASTERN EUROPE.

CEO COUNCIL. The *Wall Street Journal*'s CEO Council held its annual meeting in mid-November 2010 and then again in 2011 of nearly 100 chief executive officers from the largest U.S. companies (representing more than $3 trillion in market capitalization) to present their agendas for the future of the country.

See also CONFIDENCE BUILDING; ENERGY INNOVATION; GLOBAL FINANCE; SUSTAINABLE JOBS.

CERBERUS. Cerberus Capital Management bought Chrysler from the German automaker Daimler in August 2007. Chrysler then cut 33,000 jobs and reduced its production capacity by 1.2 million units a year.

By the end of March 2009, Cerberus was expected to lose its entire stake in Chrysler under the latest bailout offer to the automaker. By summer's end 2009, investors in Cerberus had withdrawn more than $5.5 billion, or nearly 71 percent of the hedge fund's assets, in response to the significant investment losses and their own personal requirement for cash.

See also AUTOMOBILE INDUSTRY; CHRYSLER; DAIMLER; FIAT; GMAC.

CFPA. *See* CONSUMER FINANCE PROTECTION AGENCY.

CFTC. *See* COMMODITY FUTURES TRADING COMMISSION.

CHAIN RESTAURANTS. *See* FRIENDLY'S ICE CREAM CORPORATION.

CHALLENGED WORKERS. *See* DISABLED WORKERS.

CHAMMAH, WALID A. Co-president of Morgan Stanley.

CHAMPAGNE. Indicating the sharp decline in consumer spending in the recession, champagne producers agreed in the summer 2009 to pick 32 percent fewer grapes for the year. Champagne sales throughout the world were expected to fall as low as 260 million bottles in 2009, compared to 339 million bottles in 2007. In 2008, as the meltdown hit hardest, sales fell to 322 million bottles, the first decline since 2000.

CHAPTER 7. *See* BANKRUPTCY FILINGS.

CHAPTER 11. *See* BANKRUPTCY FILINGS; LEHMAN BROTHERS.

CHAPTER 13. *See* BANKRUPTCY FILINGS.

CHARITABLE GIVING. *See* CHARITY.

CHARITY. Charity donations in the United States fell by 3.2 percent to $304 billion in 2009. Most of the fall was accounted for by a 24 percent decline in charitable bequests.

With an improvement in the 2010 economy, givers increased their charitable giving by 3.8 percent to $290.89 billion, up from $280 billion in 2009. More than two-thirds of donations in 2010 were to religious institutions.

See also FOUNDATIONS.

CHARLES SCHWAB. A discount brokerage firm; its stock declined 8.2 percent after it announced that its earnings were crimped by a slowdown in the retail business, expected to continue in both 2009 and 2010.

Charles Schwab's third-quarter 2009 profit fell 34 percent, with its net income declining to $200 million. The largest discount broker by market capitalization projected fourth-quarter 2009 profit below estimates. Schwab expected fourth-quarter earnings would be 2 to 4 cents a share lower than the third quarter's 17 cents.

On April 15, 2010, the firm reported its first-quarter results with net income of $119 million on net revenue of $978 million, a significant drop. In mid-July 2010, the firm posted flat second-quarter profit, with earnings at $205 million. Management reported that its year-over-year increase of 36 percent ($248 million) in trading revenue occurred during its third quarter 2011. Revenue increased in the third quarter by 11 percent to $1.18 billion.

CHARTER SCHOOLS. In order to tap the $5 billion in federal stimulus funds, charter schools are expanding. Typically, they are nonunionized, publicly funded alternative schools.

See also EDUCATION.

CHAVEZ, HUGO. President of Venezuela. *See also* VENEZUELA.

"CHEAP MONEY." *See* FEDERAL RESERVE.

CHECKING. By summer 2010, many large banks were preparing new fees on basic banking services as they attempted to replace lost revenue resulting from regulatory rules. Free checking is expected to end for many depositors.

CHEVROLET. *See* GENERAL MOTORS.

CHEVRON. On July 31, 2009, Chevron announced that its profit fell 71 percent in the second quarter. Net income amounted to $1.75 billion, compared with $5.98 billion one year earlier. Revenue fell 51 percent to $4.2 billion from $81 billion.

Chevron's fourth-quarter 2009 profit fell 37 percent, and still it posted a profit of $3.07 billion. Revenue increased 7.7 percent to $48.68 billion.

In May 2010, Chevron quarterly profit more than doubled, beating forecasts as the rise in profit rose to $4.55 billion. Chevron's second-quarter 2010 profit more than tripled, with earnings of $5.41 billion. Revenue climbed 29 percent to $51.05 billion.

Chevron announced on October 29, 2010, that its third-quarter earnings fell 1.6 percent from the previous year. The second-largest U.S. oil company by market value reported a quarterly profit of $3.77 billion.

On May 1, 2011, Chevron reported its earnings for the first quarter as climbing 36 percent. On July 29, management reported that the oil giant had a 43 percent surge in quarterly profit to $7.7 billion from $5.4 billion the year prior. Revenue climbed 30 percent to $69 billion. Its third-quarter earnings more than doubled, with a profit of $7.83 billion. Revenue surged 30 percent to $64.43 billion. Chevron's fourth-quarter profit fell, with output down 5.2 percent.

CHIANG MAI INITIATIVE. *See* ASIAN DEVELOPMENT BANK.

CHICO'S FAS. The women's apparel retailer said in January 2009 that it would cut about 180 jobs, or about 11 percent of its headquarters staff, and planned to close as many as twenty-five stores. The company aimed to reduce expenses by approximately $15 million in 2009.

CHILD CARE. By 2010, with 6.7 million people unemployed for six months or longer, many states were rolling back child care. The 2009 stimulus package added $2 billion for subsidized child care programs for 2009 and 2010 on top of the expected $5 billion a year. In 2010, the number of families eligible for help climbed. The Obama administration proposed another $1.6 billion increase for 2011.

By the end of 2011, child care assistance was falling. Federal stimulus money had dried up, state budgets were reduced, and more of the poor were unemployed. In thirty-seven states, families were worse off in 2011 as waiting lists grew, co-payments climbed, eligibility was tightened, and reimbursement had stagnated. Parents who need help the most, not having the funds, struggled to seek other arrangements so that they could hold on to their jobs. *See also* WELFARE.

CHILDREN IN POVERTY. "The State of America's Children 2011," a report released in July 2011 by the Children's Defense Fund, found the following:

a. The number of children living in poverty had increased by 4 million since 2000, and the number of children who fell into poverty between 2008 and 2009 was the largest single-year increase ever recorded.
b. The number of homeless children in public schools increased 41 percent between the 2006–2007 and 2008–2009 school years.
c. In 2009, an average of 15.6 million children received food stamps monthly, a 65 percent increase over ten years.
d. A majority of children in all racial groups and 79 percent or more of black and Hispanic children in public schools cannot read or do math at grade level in the fourth, eighth, or twelfth grades.
e. The annual cost of center-based child care for a four-year-old is more than the annual in-state tuition at a public four-year college in thirty-three states and the District of Columbia.

The nonpartisan Center on Budget and Policy Priorities noted, "Of the forty-seven states with newly enacted budgets, 38 or more states are making deep, identifiable cuts in K–12 education, higher education, health care, or other key areas in their budgets for fiscal year 2012. Even as states face rising numbers of children enrolled in public schools, students enrolled in universities, and seniors eligible for services, the vast majority of states (thirty-seven of forty-four states for which data are available) plan to spend less on services in 2012 than they spent in 2008—in some cases, much less. These cuts will slow the nation's economic recovery and undermine efforts to create jobs over the next year."

By summer 2011, a fifth of children in the United States were living in poverty, and more were living in homes affected by foreclosure and unemployment. In addition, some states were cutting programs that helped the poor, making situations even more difficult. In September, new reports indicated that one in three young families with children were living in poverty the year before. At 37 percent, it was the highest level on record, surpassing the previous peak of 36 percent in 1993. In 2000, the rate was about 25 percent. By mid-2011, it was found that millions of children were receiving free or low-cost meals for the first time, rising to 21 million from 18 million in 2006–2007, a 17 percent increase.

See also CHILD CARE; POVERTY.

CHILDREN'S DEFENSE FUND. *See* CHILDREN IN POVERTY.

CHILE. As a small open economy with a strong dependence on mining and agricultural exports, Chile has been hit hard by the collapse in world trade and commodity prices. Output has fallen sharply and annual average growth is projected to be negative in 2009. However, a good part of the earlier fall in copper prices through the end of 2008 has been reversed since and activity bottomed out toward mid-year with support from a substantial macroeconomic stimulus. Growth is set to accelerate gradually through 2010 to reach rates above potential in 2011. The central bank has reduced interest rates decisively by 775 basis points since the beginning of the year and enacted some unconventional measures when policy rates fell to 0.5 percent in July. The finance ministry was quick to implement a well-targeted fiscal stimulus. These measures should be gradually withdrawn if Chile embarks on the projected return to robust economic growth.

After several years of robust expansion, activity was projected to moderate and inflation to recede. The slowing world economy, tighter financial conditions, and lower investments in mining and energy will all slow growth. Inflation will decline gradually as second-round wage increases from high commodity prices wear off and expectations are re-anchored to the central bank's target. Past current account surpluses have disappeared as copper prices have retreated from high levels. To ensure an orderly decline in inflation, policies remained prudent. Depending on world macroeconomic and financial developments, a gradual loosening of the monetary policy stance may be warranted unless the recent depreciation of the peso revives inflationary pressures. The fiscal rule provided an appropriate mild countercyclical cushion to activity.

Chile's growth rate during the first ten years of the decade was about half the level of the decade before. The economy was projected to grow in 2011 by 5.7 percent. The nation's GDP growth was 5.7 percent, GDP at $207 billion, an inflation rate of 2.7 percent, and a GDP per head at $12,000.

In January 2011, Chile's government announced that it would purchase $12 billion of foreign reserves. Over time, capital inflows and commodity prices sent the peso soaring. The central bank had announced a $12 billion program to purchase dollars.

See also WORLD TRADE.

CHIMERICA. Term coined by Niall Ferguson, the financial historian and Moritz Choleric, describing the significant trade and financial relationship between China and the United States. Together they projected an often testy tug of war, with China challenging the United States as the wealthiest country on earth. "For without the availability to the American consumer of both cheap Chinese labor and cheap Chinese capital, the bubble of the years 2002–2007 would not have been so egregious." It is believed that China's leadership has a plan to wind up Chimerical and reduce their dependence on dollar-reserve accumulation and subsidized exports.

CHINA. Vigorous growth has resumed in China, thanks to a very large monetary and fiscal stimulus. Momentum picked up in the second quarter and annual GDP growth is projected to exceed 8 percent in 2009 and 10 percent in 2010, before easing slightly in 2011 as the impact of the fiscal stimulus ends. The strong increase in domestic demand stemming from the stimulus has drawn in imports, while exports have been weak and may not recover to a pre-crisis rates. As a result, the current account surplus is set to fall sharply to 5.5 percent of GDP by 2010 before rising somewhat in 2011, as domestic demand growth eases. Inflationary pressures are likely to remain subdued. The fiscal stimulus has not endangered public finance sustainability. Indeed, starting from a sizable surplus and negative net government debt on the eve of the crisis, the government can afford to keep spending at higher levels. The composition of public spending, however, ought to be changed to favor outlays on social services, notably education, health, and pensions. By contrast, credit growth will need to be reined in to avoid a renewed build-up in poor-quality loans.

Thirty years after the official beginning of economic reform in China, 200 million fewer people lived in poverty, and the country had a 6 percent share of global GDP compared with 1.8 percent in 1978. Importantly, to feed its people there had been a nearly 70 percent increase in grain production in the thirty years since reform took hold.

In 2000, China's reserves were less than $200 billion; today, China has a $2 trillion arsenal of reserves, a current-account surplus, little connection to foreign banks, and a budget surplus that offers lots of room to increase spending.

In the past decade, China invested more than $1 trillion, mostly earnings from manufacturing exports, in U.S. government bonds and government-backed mortgage debt. That helped lower U.S. interest rates and fuel the consumption binge and housing bubble.

Low-cost Chinese goods helped to keep a lid on U.S. inflation, while the flood of Chinese investment helped the U.S. government finance mortgage and a public debt of nearly $11 trillion.

China's $3.3 trillion economy accounted for about a quarter of the world's economic growth in 2007. Its GDP growth rate slowed to 9 percent in the third quarter in 2008, year on year the lowest in five years, creating worries.

Most experts believe that China needs a minimum 7 percent growth each year to contain social unrest. China, in 2008, held $652 billion in Treasury debt, up from $459 billion a year ago. China owns $1 out of every $10 of America's public debt.

The slowdown in exports contributed to the closing of at least 67,000 factories across China in the first half of 2008. Middle-class homeowners were having their first housing downturn in 2009 after years of boom, with earlier buyers wanting their money back.

On November 9, China announced a huge economic stimulus package aimed at bolstering its weakening economy. Beijing said it would spend an estimated $586 billion by 2010 on a wide array of national infrastructure and social welfare projects. China's central bank cut interest rates by more than a full percentage point, the largest Chinese rate reduction since the Asian financial crisis of a decade ago, amid signs of existing slowdowns.

Exports, which make up 40 percent of GDP, slipped toward the end of November, sliding 2.2 percent and marking the first fall in seven years. In October, by contrast, exports had surged 19.2 percent. The sudden shift provided clear evidence that the global financial crisis had arrived. Exports to all of China's trading partners suffered, with those to the United States down 6.1 percent. Additionally, the stock market was in the doldrums and property values in many cities were off by 30 to 40 percent. Power generation, a reliable tool for measurement in China, fell by 7 percent. Growth in industrial production slowed to 5.4 percent in November from 8.2 percent in October.

Since ascending to membership in the World Trade Organization in 2001, China's exports had quadrupled, helping transform it into the world's fourth-largest economy after the United States, Japan, and Germany. Converting the export figures into China's own currency, a better measure of the effect on China's economy, exports plunged 9.6 percent. As reported by the government on December 10, imports also plunged sharply in November, falling 17.9 percent, which widened the trade surplus to $40 billion from $35.2 billion in October.

The International Monetary Fund cut its 2009 forecast for Chinese economic growth to around 5 percent in its revision as the global economy continued to fall. The central bank cut interest rates for the fifth time in four months, effective the end of December, in a new effort to revive economic growth as the government worried about spreading job losses and worker protests. The one-year lending rate fell by 0.27 percentage point to 2.24 percent. The reduction came just four weeks after China's biggest rate cut in eleven years.

The gap between average urban and rural incomes expanded to about $1,600 in 2008, with the ratio between the richer city residents to those in the countryside rising to 3.36 to 1. China's urban incomes had increased much more quickly, with average annual income jumping 74 percent since 2003, while rural incomes rose only 31 percent. The official urban unemployment rate for the end of 2008 was 4.2 percent, up from 4 percent in 2007, the first time the official rate had risen after five consecutive years of decline. Some studies showed as large as a 9.4 percent urban unemployment rate. About 670,000 businesses shut down and 6.7 million jobs evaporated in 2008.

The government said that its economy expanded 6.8 percent in the fourth quarter of 2008 from a year earlier, confirming a dramatic slowdown that cut growth rates. This downturn marked the first time since 2002 that China's economy had expanded by less than 10 percent annually. The current growth rate put China in danger of falling below the government's longstanding annual target of 8 percent.

The government announced in January 2009 that it would dole out $1.3 billion to 74 million people as a one-time living subsidy. On January 14, China revised upward its gross domestic product growth for 2007 to 13 percent from 11.9 percent, which meant that it had passed Germany to become the third-largest economy in the world. The Chinese premier, Wen Jerboa, on January 28 blamed the U.S.-led financial system for the world's deepening economic slump. China had $2 trillion in foreign exchange reserves and continued to buy U.S. government debt, surpassing Japan in September 2008 as the biggest foreign holder of the Treasury.

The year 2009 saw China surpassing the United States in auto sales; 790,000 vehicles were bought by Chinese consumers in January compared with 656,976 vehicles sold in the United States. On February 9, the government announced plans to create jobs, lower distribution costs, and improve the quality and availability of products sold in rural areas. The government planned to establish 150,000 stores in the countryside in 2009 to offer rural residents easy access to safe consumer goods. These stores were expected to create 775,000 new jobs by 2010.

China's exports plummeted in January, falling 17.5 percent from a year earlier. The decline was far worse than the 2.8 percent fall recorded in December 2008. The U.S. trade deficit with China narrowed sharply in December 2008 to $19.9 billion from $23.1 billion in November but left China reeling amid lower demand for its goods. Chinese bank lending more than doubled in January as the government pushed banks to free up credit to hard-hit sectors of the economy. Foreign direct investment in China plunged 33 percent in that month compared to a year before. The government reported on February 16 that the fourth consecutive monthly decline was indicative of the dire situation in China.

The nation's manufacturing sector declined in February 2009 for the seventh straight month. A sharp drop in its trade surplus signaled a shift in the nation's financial balance with the rest of the world and lowered the speed with which it piled up foreign-currency assets such as U.S. Treasury bonds. Once a year, China's parliament convenes. On March 4, 2009, Premier Wen Jerboa promised to bolster the economy and reaffirmed an economic growth forecast of 8 percent for the year.

China moved to minimize the sale of state-owned stakes in financial firms at below-market prices. New rules were to take place on May 1, 2009, requiring that state-owned shares of listed financial firms be sold through stock exchanges and further stated that sale prices in block trades should be no lower than the average weighted stock price on the trading day closest to the date of transaction.

Meanwhile, on March 18 the World Bank lowered its forecast for economic growth in China to 6.5 percent in 2009. This figure was down from the bank's earlier forecast of 7.5 percent and was well below the 8 percent projected by Chinese officials. China called for the establishment of a new currency on March 23 to replace the U.S. dollar as the world's standard, proposing a major overhaul of global finance, which reflected developing nations' growing displeasure with the U.S. role in world economics.

More than 40 percent of China's GDP was traced to factory construction and other kinds of fixed-asset investments. Over the past decade entrepreneurs created 5 million businesses of at least eight employees each. They spawned about 75 million jobs for China's university graduates, workers discarded from state firms, and streams of people from the countryside. The output of China's private firms and their investment spending made up half of 2008's $4.42 trillion GDP.

To the dismay of the government, it was announced on April 15 that the country had its worst quarterly economic growth in nearly two decades. China's GDP in the first quarter 2009 rose 6.1 percent from the same period one year earlier. That was lower than the 6.8 percent from the fourth quarter 2008 and a dramatic slowdown from the past growth hitting 13 percent for the year 2007. Although economic growth slowed to 6.1 percent in the first quarter 2009, retail sales, after adjusting for price changes, rose 15.9 percent for the same time frame. While that was slower than the 17.7 percent rise in spending in the fourth quarter 2008, it indicated that growth in consumption was encouraging compared to other major economies.

China's exports fell 22.6 percent from a year earlier to $91.94 billion in April, deeper than March's 17.1 percent decline. Beijing's stimulus spending was expected to aid China's economy to grow 7.5 percent in 2009 and 9 percent in 2010. The World Bank raised its forecast in mid-June for China's economic growth in 2009 to 7.2 percent (in March it was predicted to be as low as 6.5 percent).

China's government had turned its economy around far faster than expected. On July 15, it was announced that growth had accelerated to 7.9 percent in the second quarter 2009. On September 11, 2009, the government issued data showing that industrial expansion accelerated in August, with output rising 12.3 percent from a year before. By mid-September, China's economy roared back following its stimulus plan. The central bank said that the nation's economy surged at an annualized rate of 14.9 percent at the second quarter, compared to the U.S. economy, which shrank at an annualized rate of 1 percent in the same period.

Government data released on October 22 showed that China's GDP grew by 8.9 percent in the third quarter from a year before. Industrial output accelerated further to 13.9 percent in September. China allowed the yuan to rise by 21 percent against the dollar in the three years prior to July 2008, but since then it has more or less kept the rate fixed. China's industrial output grew 16.1 percent in October, the fastest in over one year. The increase accounts for two-thirds of China's economic output. By November 2009, China had transformed itself from a global font of low-price items fueled by cheap labor, creating significant disparities of wealth.

Today, there are billionaires—the fastest growing in the world—and a lot of poverty in China. Per capita income is small, roughly $3,200, which is less than 10 percent of the United States, with many farmers earning as little as $1 a day. China provides multibillion-dollar loans to other developing countries and retains large holdings in Wall Street giants, such as Morgan Stanley and the Blackstone Group. China is poised to eclipse the United States by selling nearly 15 million cars in one year. No nation has ever acquired larger foreign exchange reserves ($2.2 trillion). The country leads the world in initial public stock offerings. China's imports increased 26.7 percent from the year before, to $94.56 billion, countering the October fall of 6.4 percent. It was the first increase in thirteen months.

By the end of 2009, China was rapidly moving out of deflation after nearly a year of falling consumer prices. The return of inflation highlighted the recovering economy, with prices rising for a range of items. For example, gasoline prices were up 50 percent since the beginning of the year.

China purported to have an industrial-production growth in 2010 of about 11 percent to help fulfill its economic-growth target of 8 percent. December automobile sales in China almost doubled, increasing 92 percent from a year before to 1.41 million cars. Consequently, China's auto sales for the year 2009 surpassed U.S. sales for the first time.

China's reserves of foreign currency, by far the world's largest, rose to $2.4 trillion at the end of 2009, an increase of $126.56 billion since September. Foreign direct investments to China more than doubled from a year before to $12.14 billion in December.

China's exports turned upward in December 2009, resuming growth following thirteen months of decline. For the year, exports fell 16 percent to $1.202 trillion and imports slid 11.2 percent to $1.006 trillion. It was China's first annual export fall since 1983, when exports fell a mere 0.4 percent. In December, exports surged to $130.7 billion, with imports growing to $112.3 billion. Consumer prices rose 1.9 percent in December, up sharply from 0.6 percent in November following nine months of decline, thereby raising inflationary concerns. In December, China sold a record amount of its U.S. Treasury holdings, ceding its place as the world's biggest foreign holder of U.S. debt to Japan. On January 7, 2010, the central bank of China edged up the interest rate on its three-month treasury bill by 0.04 point to 1.3684 from the 1.3280 percent yield that had prevailed since August 2009. By tightening credit, it indicated that the Chinese consumer was slowing down its consumption.

The government reported on January 21, 2010, that its economy expanded 8.7 percent in 2009, surpassing the 8 percent expected target. Growth in fourth quarter 2009 was up 10.7 percent from a year before, with consumer prices in December rising 1.9 percent. Profit at China's major industrial enterprises more than doubled in the year's first two months (2010). There was a 119.7 percent rise in industrial profits in January/February. Industrial firm profits averaged 5.7 percent. China's first quarter profit 2010 rose 11.9 percent from a year before.

With the fall of the euro against the U.S. dollar, the euro by mid-May 2010 had declined against the renminbi (China's currency), whose value was pegged to that of the dollar, reaching its lowest level since late 2002. This had made Chinese exports to the EU less competitive and gave European firms an advantage in the Chinese market. This shift in Europe has complicated China's plan to let the renminbi rise against the U.S. dollar. Equally important, the euro's difficulties had also inflicted tens of billions of U.S. dollars in losses on the value of China's $2.4 trillion in foreign exchange reserves. On August 10, 2010, the government reported that the nation's largest trade surplus in a year and half had an unexpected surge in Chinese exports and the slowing down of imports emerged. The nation's surplus jumped to $28.7 billion in July, the highest since January of the previous year. Exports climbed 38.1 percent. The same month, China's trade surplus narrowed to $20.03 billion from $28.7 billion in July on surging imports. Exports climbed 34.4 percent in August from the year before to $139.3 billion. The economy jumped 13.9 percent from a year before, accelerating from 13.4 percent growth in July. In addition, inflation jumped to 3.5 percent in August from 3.3 percent, the highest in nearly two years.

With little fanfare, China surpassed Japan in 2010 as the world's second-largest economy. Second-quarter GDP figures from Japan fell short of the $1,339 trillion that China reported for the three months ending in June.

More than ten years ago, China was the world's seventh-largest economy. It surpassed Germany to become number three in 2007. For September, China posted a $16.9 billion trade surplus, capping the largest quarterly excess since the meltdown in 2008. Exports climbed 25.1 percent compared to a year earlier, and imports rose 24.1 percent to $128.1 billion. In August, the excess was $20 billion. In October, China's premier, reacting to increased pressure from the United States and other nations to revalue its currency, the renminbi, declared that such a rapid shift would be a "disaster for the world" and would cause social unrest throughout China.

The nation's foreign exchange reserves jumped to $2.648 trillion at the end of September 2010 in a record surge. These reserves, already the largest in the world, climbed by $194 billion in the third quarter. China's monthly trade surplus reached $16.9 billion in September, with exports up 25 percent and imports rising 24 percent. Suddenly, on October 19, the central bank shocked investors by raising its interest rates, leading to a worldwide sell-off of stocks, commodities, and emerging markets' currencies as investors lowered their expectation for the nation's growth, which has often been seen as the critical economy to pull the world out of the Great Recession. Key rates were to be increased by a quarter percentage point, the first such change since the bank lowered rates in December 2008.

The government announced on October 20 that GDP rose 9.6 percent from a year before in the third quarter, slowing from 10.3 percent growth in the second quarter. A property battle was a persistent threat to the nation's growth. On November 2, China's central bank indicated that it would raise interest rates, remaining concerned about inflationary risks. On November 17, the government pledged to use measures to tame rising prices of goods and energy and to cushion the poor with higher welfare payment, all in the hope of alleviating the possibility of social unrest in the country. In addition, China's exports rose from a year earlier by 34.9 percent, while imports also expanded, increasing 37.7 percent from the year before. The result was that trade surplus narrowed slightly to $22.89 billion in November. On December 10, China raised banks' reserve requirements for the third time in a month in order to cool its economy. The government reported on December 11 that the nation's consumer price index, their best measure of inflation, rose 5.1 percent for the previous moth, the largest jump in twenty-eight months. Food costs soared and construction climbed significantly. The government planned to restrain growth and fight inflation.

China believes it could become the world's biggest manufacturer around 2011, ending the 110-year supremacy of the United States. Expansion is causing havoc in the banking system and in regional finances tied to a volatile property sector. The nation's GDP growth was 8.4 percent, a GDP of $6,460 billion, an inflation rate of 3.5 percent, and a GDP per head of $4,800. Europe is China's largest market, purchasing roughly $282 billion of the nation's goods in the first eleven months of 2010, or nearly a fifth of China's total exports.

China announced that its trade surplus narrowed sharply, shrinking to $13.08 billion in December from $22.9 billion in November. Her exports in December grew 17.9 percent from the year before, down from 34.9 percent in November and below the median forecast for a 24.0 percent rise. Imports climbed 25. 6 percent down from November's 37.7 percent. The government's trade surplus totaled $183.1 billion in 2010, down from $196 billion in 2009.

On January 22, 2011, it was reported that China's biggest bank signed an agreement to acquire retail bank branches in the United States. On February 8, in order to minimize the impact of spreading inflation, the central bank raised its interest rates by one-quarter of a percentage point to 3 percent for the third time in four months. Its one-year lending rate was raised to 6.06 percent. On February 14, it was announced that China, with its $5.88 trillion GDP, had passed Japan, with its $5.47 trillion GDP, to become the second-largest economy in the world, only surpassed by the United States, with a GDP of $14.66 trillion. In addition, consumer prices climbed 4.9 percent, apparently losing the inflation battle. On February 18, the central bank indicated that it would raise the bank reserve requirement ratio by 0.5 percentage point. Also, in attempting to counter currency criticism, China allowed its currency to move higher, reaching 6.5732 renmindi against the U.S. dollar.

China reported a surprise trade deficit for February 2011, its first in eleven months, as export growth slowed and imports remained strong. China imported $7.3 billion more than it exported, compared with a trade surplus of $6.45 billion in January. Her exports climbed 2.4 percent, while imports rose 19.4 percent. At the same time, China targeted total spending of almost $200 billion in 2011, with $198 billion for construction of subsidized housing. When the consumer price index rose 4.9 percent in February, the government decoded to log a 4.9 percent increase in prices. Food prices rose 11 percent in the month. The producer price index, a measure of inflation at the wholesale level, rose 7.2 percent in February, the biggest increase since October 2008. Then, on April 5, China raised interest rates for the fourth time in six months, attempting to rein in inflation and a growing real estate bubble and slow its overheating economy. A one-year benchmark deposit rate increased one-quarter of 1 percent to 3.25.

Surprisingly, China reported its first quarterly trade deficit of $1.02 billion from January to March, when surging prices for commodities pushed up its import bill. The government reported a small trade surplus of $140 million in March, up from a deficit of $7.3 billion the month prior.

Inflation continued to be of great concern to the government. On April 15, with an expanding economy of 9.7 percent, its consumer price index rose 5.4 percent from the year before, the sharpest increase in thirty-two months. In March, food costs jumped 11.7 percent. Gasoline increased from $3.82 a gallon to about $4.50.

Another indication of China's concerns about its debt, in late June the government reported that local government debts totaled about $1.65 trillion, or 27 percent of the nation's GDP in 2010. In total, public debt was more than 80 percent of its GDP. And in May, the annual inflation rate jumped to 5.5 percent, the highest in thirty-four months. The central bank raised commercial banks' required reserve ratios by half a percentage point.

The central bank announced in July 2011 its fifth-interest rate increase in eight months to fend off growing inflation. The National Bureau of Statistics reported on July 9 that the consumer price index in June surged by 6.4 percent from the year before, a climb from May's 5.5 percent rate and closing in on the high of three years prior. For the second quarter 2011, GDP surged 9.5 percent, noting that the nation had high consumer inflation of 6.5 percent in July, its highest level in more than three years. The consumer price index topped 6.4 percent as prices continued to surge in the country. On September 8, the government reported that its consumer prices increased 6.2 percent, while price growth slowed to 6.5 percent. Foreign capital flows helped drive inflation, which could potentially create social unrest. The central bank purchased dollars and sidelined them in massive stockpiles of reserves. The government tightened bank reserve requirements. China had its first monthly outflow of foreign currency since 2007 in October 2011, indicating that investors were withdrawing their money on fears over the global economy and lowered expectation that the yuan would appreciate.

Toward the end of 2011, China's exports showed troubling signs. Annual growth in monthly exports was now crawling from 34 percent in 2010 to 16 percent. Growth in the nation's imports from the rest of Asia slowed from 90 percent year on year in early 2010 to about 20 percent in October 2011. At the end of November, in order to stimulate the economy, the government and banks cut their bank reserve requirements for the first time in nearly three years, as trade and real estate sectors were sagging. The People's Bank of China reported on November 30, 2011, that it would reduce the reserve requirement ratio for banks by 0.5 percentage point, freeing up more money for lending.

In November, China's inflation and industrial activity slowed down, with consumer price inflation going from 6 percent at the beginning of 2011 to 4.2 percent. Industrial output expanded just 12.3 percent. By year's end, China had shifted some of its policies to avoid a crash landing of its economy. It had succeeded in applying the brakes to its runaway real estate market, as declining global demand had softened its export growth—all indicating that its economy was expanding at a more moderate pace, with a continuing anxiety that the slowdown would be abrupt.

China's trade surplus in 2011 was its smallest since 2005, falling to $155.14 billion, down 14.5 percent from 2010. At the same time, China's GDP growth slowed to 8.9 percent in the last quarter of the year. The previous time China's economy slowed like this was in the last quarter of 2008 when the globe felt the worst of the Great Recession. In addition, property prices in seventy major cities fell in December, marking the third straight fall after developers cut prices to boost sales. Prices fell on average about 0.22 percent.

See also AIRLINE; AUTOMOBILE INDUSTRY; BANK OF CHINA; CHIMERICA; DOW JONES INDUSTRIAL AVERAGE; EXPORTS (U.S.); GENERAL MOTORS; INDUSTRIAL & COMMERCIAL BANK OF CHINA; INTERNATIONAL MONETARY FUND; ITALY; JAPAN; LENOVO; PROPERTY (2011); RENMINBI; STEEL; TRADE DEFICIT (U.S.); U.S.–CHINA TRADE; YUAN.

Cf. INDIA.

CHINA CERAMICS AND POTTERY. *See* WATERFORD WEDGWOOD

CHIP SALES. In November 2008, global semiconductor sales fell almost 10 percent from a year earlier to $20.8 billion. November sales were 7.2 percent lower than the $22.4 billion in October 2008.

By January 2009, chip sales plunged by almost a third from a year earlier to $15.3 billion.

CHRISTIE'S INTERNATIONAL. Sold $1.8 billion of fine and decorative arts in the first half of 2009, falling nearly 49 percent from one year earlier. In the United States, sales fell by half to $462.9 million.

Cf. SOTHEBY'S.

CHRISTMAS SALES. *See* RETAILING.

CHRYSLER. On December 11, 2008, during congressional debates, it appeared that Chrysler's demise was all but inevitable regardless of whether it received government aid. The automaker warned that it could soon run out of money without a $7 billion loan and would be forced to sell off its parts or merge with a foreign automaker. By the end of the month, President Bush came forward and announced a rescue plan. Chrysler was owned by Cerberus Capital Management in 2008–2009, but the federal government changed this relationship. Chrysler received $4 billion in emergency loans at the end of 2008 and planned to submit a restructuring plan by March 2009 showing how the carmaker would shrink in response to the sharp decline in auto sales. The company needed $7 billion every forty-five days in order to pay parts suppliers.

The Treasury Department announced on January 14, 2009, that a $1.5 billion, five-year loan would be given to Chrysler Financial, enabling the firm to offer 0 percent financing on select 2008 and 2009 vehicles. That same month, Chrysler's U.S. sales fell 55 percent compared with a year earlier to 62,157 vehicles. On February 17, the automaker requested another $5 billion from the government to survive through 2009 (Chrysler had already received $4 billion in loans). On the same day, Chrysler announced that it was cutting another 3,000 jobs and discontinuing three of its models. Without this funding, management would likely be forced to declare bankruptcy. President Obama made a speech on March 30 declaring that Chrysler could file for bankruptcy, giving it until April 30 to complete a deal. It was clear on April 1 that Cerberus would lose its entire stake in the Chrysler auto division, but would continue to control its finance arm. The Treasury was pressing the Italian automaker Fiat to take 20 percent ownership initially of Chrysler. The Treasury, on April 2, made opening offers of $1 billion to lenders at a meeting in Washington, D.C. On April 20, the banks made their first offer to the Treasury, proposing $4.5 billion in new debt, a 40 percent equity stake, a $1 billion investment from Fiat, and $1 billion in preferred equity and a board seat. In rapid succession:

On April 22, the Treasury proposed the bank group take $1.5 billion in new debt and 5 percent equity.

On April 26, the United Auto Workers (UAW) and the Treasury agreed to a labor contract deal and it is announced. UAW-Chrysler members begin voting the next day.

On April 28, lead banks agreed to back a $2 billion cash offer. Other lenders do not.

On April 29, the government made a last offer of $2.25 billion. Lenders were informed on a 4:30 PM call that they had ninety minutes to vote on the offer. It failed. A new UAW deal was ratified by Chrysler workers.

As the April 30 Treasury deadline approached for Chrysler to seal an agreement with Fiat of Italy, a group of large banks and other lenders rebuffed a Treasury Department request that they slash 85 percent of Chrysler's secured debt, proposing instead to eliminate about 35 percent in exchange for a minority stake in the restructured car market and a seat on its board.

Under the government plan, a restructured Chrysler would be owned by Fiat, the lenders, the UAW, and the Treasury. Under the agreement, the Treasury or Chrysler, if it returned to profitability, would pay in cash half of the $10.6 billion that the company owed a retiree health care fund. The remainder would be paid in an undetermined amount of Chrysler equity.

Chapter 11 bankruptcy protection was nearing even as a deal was struck with Chrysler's lenders or an alliance forged with Fiat. Even with an agreement with its lenders, bankruptcy protection would permit Fiat to pick and choose which operations it wanted, and the U.S. government would provide bankruptcy financing while the reorganization played out.

The UAW union was on board with the plan and would end up owning a significant stake in the restructured automaker. The union would eventually own 55 percent of a restructured Chrysler, as announced on April 27, with Fiat owning another 35 percent. Chrysler's secured lenders together would end up owning 10 percent of the firm once it was reorganized.

Chrysler would also issue a $4.59 billion note to the health care trust fund of the union for retired workers. Chrysler would pay $300 million in cash into the trust fund in 2010 and 2011, with increasing amounts up to $823 million in the years 2019 and 2023. Daimler would surrender its remaining 19.9 percent stake in Chrysler and pay as much as $600 million into the carmaker's pension fund. Fiat, on the other hand, would produce at least one small car in a Chrysler plant in the United States and permit Chrysler to use a 3.0-liter diesel engine and a 1.4-liter gasoline engine in its cars. Fiat's investment was estimated to be worth $8 billion and would create 4,000 union jobs for Chrysler.

By the end of April, key lenders agreed to Chrysler's debt swap, allowing movement toward reorganization. Lenders accepted $2 billion in cash in exchange for the $6.9 billion in secured debt they held. Meanwhile, adding to the plight of the carmaker, sales fell 48 percent in April, which was considerably worse than the industry average of 34 percent compared to a year before. On April 30, Chrysler filed for bankruptcy protection. The eighty-four-year-old firm would have new owners. The UAW union's retirees would own 55 percent, Fiat up to 35 percent, the U.S. government 8 percent, and the Canadian government 2 percent.

A bankruptcy judge said on May 3 that the automaker could use $4.5 billion in government loans for bankruptcy financing while attempting to win court approval for a sale of its assets to Fiat. Also, after losing nearly $17 billion in 2008, Chrysler projected a return to profitability by 2012. Chrysler planned to close 789 dealerships, almost one-quarter of its retail stores. A group of pension funds on June 6 opposed to the sale of Chrysler to Fiat asked the U.S. Supreme Court to put the deal on hold while they continued their attempt to block it. Then, on June 9, the Court cleared the way for Chrysler to exit bankruptcy court, lifting a stay on its proposed sales to a group, including Fiat.

On June 10, with a wire transfer from the federal government, Chrysler both received $6.6 billion in exit financing and cemented its alliance with Fiat, thus ending its forty-two days of bankruptcy. Chrysler announced on

June 17 that it would restart production in June 2009 at seven of its twelve assembly plants.

Chrysler Financial, in mid-July, reimbursed the U.S. government with $1.5 billion, becoming the first auto-sector company to pay off the loans provided by the Treasury Department. Even during the cash-for-clunkers program in August 2009, Chrysler sales dropped by 15 percent. Sales had fallen significantly over the past two years. In November 2009, cars and light trucks were down from 11.4 percent for the same month a year before. Five years ago, it had 14 percent of the market. A year after emerging from bankruptcy, Chrysler on August 9 announced a net loss of $172 million for the second quarter. Its revenue climbed to $10.5 billion, up 8.2 percent from the first quarter. On November 8, management posted a third-quarter net loss of $84 million, with expectations to break even in 2011. The loss was almost half of the $172 million that the automaker lost in the second quarter. Chrysler made $239 million in operating profit in the quarter, compared to $183 million in the second quarter. Chrysler car sales in November were 74,152, a 17 percent increase over last year.

On January 31, 2011, Chrysler announced that it lost $199 million in the fourth quarter 2010. The firm lost $652 million on revenue of $41.9 billion for the entire 2010 but was able to sustain an operating profit of $763 million. Chrysler ended 2010 with $7.3 billion in cash, down from $8.3 billion at the end of the third quarter. By September, the automaker announced that sales up at least 20 percent from the year before, with 127,334 vehicles sold. In October 2011, Chrysler reported its second quarterly profit of $212 million for its third quarter. Revenue jumped 19 percent to $13.1 billion. In October, Chrysler sales surged 27 percent to 114,512 cars.

The carmaker projected to earn $3 billion in 2012, with sales reaching two million cars and truck in 2011, rising 20 percent to 2.4 million in 2012. Profit for 2012 was expected to increase to $1.5 billion with revenue climbing 18 percent over 2011 to $65 billion. On February 1, 2012 management reported a fourth-quarter 2011 and full-year profit for the first time since leaving bankruptcy in 2009.

See also AUTOMOBILE INDUSTRY; AUTO TASK FORCE; CERBERUS; DAIMLER; FIAT; GENERAL MOTORS; GMAC; JOB BANKS; MARCHIONNE, SERGIO; U.S. TREASURY; VEBA.

CHRYSLER FINANCIAL. *See* CHRYSLER; FIAT.

CHURCHES. Throughout the country, churches during the Great Recession were having increasing difficulty paying their mortgages. Some were closing, others are merging. Since 2008, nearly 200 religious institutions have been foreclosed by banks, up from eight during the previous two years and virtually none in the decades before.

CIRCUIT BREAKERS. *See* "FLASH CRASH."

CIRCUIT CITY STORES. Filed for bankruptcy court protection on November 11, 2008, amid a worsening financial state and store closings.

On Friday, January 16, 2009, Circuit City became the first major post-holiday casualty of the retail slump and announced that it would close all of its 567 stores and begin selling off its assets. More than 30,000 employees would lose their jobs and no value would remain in the firm for shareholders. Circuit City officially closed its stores on Sunday, March 8. The company initially filed for restructuring and then later switched to liquidation.

CISCO SYSTEMS. A giant networking-equipment company, it reported a 24 percent drop in profit and a 17 percent drop in revenue for its fiscal quarter ending April 25, 2009. Revenue for the quarter fell to $8.16 billion from $9.79 from a year earlier. Profit was $1.35 billion, down from $1.77 billion a year earlier. Over the past three quarters, Cisco eliminated nearly $1.5 billion in costs and planned to cut up to 2,000 positions in 2009.

Cisco Systems laid off several hundred workers on July 16, 2009, as its sales continued to decline. Between 600 and 700 workers were laid off out of its total 66,558 employees. By August 2009, Cisco posted a 46 percent fall in quarterly profit. Cisco reported a 19 percent profit decline and a 13 percent revenue fall for its fiscal first quarter 2009. Profit fell to $41.8 billion and revenue declined to $9 billion from $10.3 billion the year before.

The firm posted on May 12, 2010, a profit surge of 63 percent in its fiscal third quarter on revenue that climbed 27 percent. On August 11, management reported that the company earnings were $1.9 billion in its fourth quarter ending July 31, 2010. Revenue increased 27 percent to $10.8 billion. It was the fifth straight quarter of sales gains. The company's management posted on November 10 an 8 percent rise in profit on 19 percent revenue growth. Fiscal second-quarter 2010 income fell to $1.5 billion from $1.9 billion the year before. An 18 percent fall in profit was also announced, with revenue rising to $10.4 billion from $9.8 billion the prior year.

Cisco's profit in its third fiscal quarter fell nearly 18 percent, as reported on May 11, 2011, while its revenue climbed about 5 percent. It had a profit for the period ending April 30 of $1.8 billion, with revenue climbing to $10.9 billion. In July 2011, management announced plans to terminate 6,500 workers, or 9 percent of its staff. In August, the firm reported that its net income in the fourth quarter fell 36.3 percent to $1.2 billion, with revenue climbing 3.3 percent to $11.2 billion. Its quarterly profit declined 8 percent, as revenue climbed 5 percent. Net income was $1.8 billion, and revenue climbed to $11.3 billion from $10.8 billion.

CITADEL BROADCASTING. The nation's third-largest radio broadcaster filed for bankruptcy on December 20, 2009. Owning 224 stations, the bankruptcy reflected the troubles plaguing radio shows and significant declines in advertising revenue during the meltdown period.

CIT GROUP (CIT). A lender to almost a million mostly small and midsize businesses across the United States, CIT was narrowly saved from bankruptcy on July 19, 2009. The 101-year-old company had $68 billion of liabilities as of March 31, 2009. CIT is registered as a bank holding company—the twenty-sixth-largest bank holding company in the country. It received $2.33 billion from the federal TARP in December 2008, after winning approval to become a bank holding firm.

On July 15, the U.S. government rebuffed pleas to rescue the struggling company a second time. It would be the largest American bank to fail since Lehman Brothers collapsed in 2008. CIT avoided imminent bankruptcy protection when on July 19 its bondholders rescued the company through a $3 billion emergency loan. It gave CIT time to restructure its business model and reduce its voluminous debt load, even if only temporarily. Another $1.7 billion in debt payments was due by the end of 2009, and CIT had to pay off an additional $8 billion in 2010.

CIT was charged high interest rates (10.5 percentage points above the London interbank-offered rate) but avoided the pressure to pay down $1 billion in debt that came due in August. It also preserved the U.S. Treasury's $2.33 billion investment made as part of TARP. By the end of September 2009, CIT had readied a plan to hand over control of the company to its bondholders. By doing this, CIT would eliminate 30 to 40 percent of its more than $30 billion in outstanding debt. The plan offered bondholders new debt secured by CIT assets and nearly all of the equity in a restructured firm. Then, on October 30, CIT decided it would declare an abbreviated bankruptcy filing to relieve its debilitating debt burden. With its $71 billion in assets, its bankruptcy filing would be the fifth-largest in U.S. history. The U.S. Treasury, which in 2008 injected $2.33 billion of funds from TARP to help stabilize the company, became a major loser from the bankruptcy. The result was that CIT's lending capacity would fall to less than 20 percent of what it was two year before. CIT lent about $60 billion to retailers and small firms, providing capital for operations, purchases, and other expenses.

CIT filed for bankruptcy protection on November 1, 2009, creating problems for nearly 1 million small and midsize firms. CIT gained support from about 90 percent of voting debt holders for a prepackaged reorganization plan that would permit the lender to speed through Chapter 11 and emerge with a new business model by the end of the year. At that time, CIT's assets were about $71 billion and nearly $65 billion in liabilities. On December 8, 2009,

CIT listed liability of nearly $65 billion in its bankruptcy filing. A restructuring plan took effect on December 10 giving creditors new debt aid. CIT's major history is:

1908—founded in St. Louis by Henry Ittleson.
1916—works with Studebaker to provide financing to car buyers.
1924—first listed on the New York Stock Exchange.
1930s—signs contract with Sears Roebuck for purchases of refrigerators.
1941—during World War II, acquires two manufacturing companies and sends 2,000 employees to war.
1958—purchases Bank of North America.
1965—merges two banks to create the National Bank of North America.
1980 acquired by RCA, which sells CIT's four manufacturing businesses.
1986—transfers its consumer loan portfolio to Manufacturers Hanover Trust.
1997—holds its initial public offering, posts earnings of $300 million.

It was announced by management on April 27, 2010, that the commercial lender returned to profit following its emergence from bankruptcy protection in 2009 and said that it would pay down $1.5 billion in high-cost debt.

CIT Group's first-quarter earnings 2011 dropped 55 percent, with a profit of $65 .6 million.

Cf. LEHMAN BROTHERS.

CITIBANK. *See* CITIGROUP.

CITIES. By the summer 2010, U.S. cities were in their worst fiscal shape in twenty-five years, with a continuing slide anticipated. Numerous municipalities were in their fourth straight year of declining revenues, with lower property tax collections. Cities on average projected a 1.8 percent decrease in property tax collections, resulting in significant layoffs in the public sector.

See also CITY BUDGETS; STATES (U.S.).

CITIGROUP. On January 16, 2008, this financial services company wrote down certain assets by $18.1 billion as it showed fourth-quarter 2007 losses of about $10 billion that were linked to the subprime-mortgage crisis. Then, on April 19, Citigroup posted a $5.1 billion quarterly loss.

Citigroup announced on November 17, 2008, that it would cut 50,000 jobs, from investment bankers to the back office. Investment bankers would bear the brunt of the losses because senior managers were asked to reduce expenses significantly. In addition, the bank would trim expenses by 16 to 19 percent to about $50 billion in 2009. Citigroup reported four consecutive quarterly losses, including a $2.8 billion in the third quarter 2008. Its share price continued to fall in November. On November 21, it dropped 20 percent, after falling 26 percent the day before and 23 percent the previous day. For the week, Citigroup plummeted 60 percent.

Citigroup, once the largest and mightiest U.S. financial institution, was brought to its knees by more than $65 billion in losses, write-downs for troubled assets, and charges to account for expected future losses. More than half of that amount stemmed from mortgage-related securities. Its stock had fallen to its lowest price in more than a decade, closing on November 21 at $3.77. At that price the company was worth just $20.5 billion, down from $244 billion two years before. Waves of layoffs accompanied that slide, with about 75,000 jobs lost or soon to disappear from a workforce that numbered about 375,000 in 2007. On Monday, November 24, Citigroup agreed to halt dividend payments for the next three years and to put restrictions on executive compensation under terms of the U.S. government rescue of the struggling bank. These concessions were made in return for the U.S. government's direct investment of about $20 billion in the bank and an agreement to back about $306 billion in loans and securities, largely residential and commercial real estate loans and certain other assets that remained on the bank's balance sheet. Citigroup would shoulder losses on the first $29 billion of that portfolio.

Any remaining losses would be split unequally between Citigroup and the government, with the bank absorbing 10 percent and the government absorbing 90 percent. The Treasury Department would use its bailout fund to assume up to $5 billion of losses. If necessary, the Federal Deposit Insurance Corporation would bear the next $10 billion of losses. Beyond that, the Federal Reserve would guarantee any additional losses.

In exchange, Citigroup issued $7 billion of preferred stock to government regulators. In addition, the government bought $20 billion of preferred stock in Citigroup. The preferred shares would pay an 8 percent dividend and only slightly erode the value of shares held by investors. Citigroup lost 77 percent of its stock value in 2008. On December 31, Citigroup's chief executive and chairman announced that senior staff would forgo their 2008 bonuses. Citigroup posted an $8.29 billion loss, twice as much as analysts estimated.

Events since the government got involved with Citigroup were as follows:

October 14, 2008—Treasury Department announced plans to inject $125 billion into eight banks, including $25 billion into Citigroup.

November 23—The United States pumped another $20 billion into Citigroup, but demanded that the company revamp its strategy and shrink.

January 13, 2009—Under federal pressure, Citigroup announced a deal to spin off Smith Barney into a joint venture with Morgan Stanley.

January 16—Citigroup reported an $8.3 billion fourth-quarter loss.

January 21—The company named a new chief executive, Vikrim Pandit, handing him responsibility for pushing out more directors and recruiting fresh blood.

January 27—After being publicly scolded by President Obama, Citigroup reneged on its plans to buy a luxury corporate jet.

February 11—Citigroup's chief executive testified before a congressional committee, saying he would get paid $1 a year until Citigroup returns to profitability.

February 21—Negotiations intensified about expanding the government's stake in Citigroup to as much as 40 percent.

February 27—Treasury Department announced that it would increase its ownership in Citigroup to 36 percent from 8 percent.

July 16—Citigroup said it earned a $4.3 billion profit.

Taxpayers had already put more than $50 billion in capital into the bank while guaranteeing $301 billion of its bad assets. Still, Citigroup remained unable to stop its slide.

Citigroup announced on March 3 a new plan to aid unemployed homeowners. Citigroup would temporarily lower mortgage payments to an average of $500 per month for some borrowers who had recently lost their positions and were at least sixty days behind on their mortgage payments. Borrowers would then be permitted to make the lower payments for three months and the bank would waive interest and penalties during this time period. Citigroup held in excess of 1.4 million mortgages. To qualify, borrowers had to have loans of no more than $417,500 and they had to live in their home and possess a mortgage serviced by CitiMortgage. In mid-April, Citigroup reported a $1.6 billion first-quarter 2009 profit by the way it accounted for the decline in the value of its own debt. By the end of April, Citigroup, soon to be one-third owned by the U.S. government, asked permission to pay special bonuses to key workers. Pay restrictions imposed on banks receiving bailout funds were resulting in the threat of important employees finding work elsewhere and receiving significantly higher incomes. Citigroup referred to these bonuses as "retention awards." The U.S. government had a 33.6 percent stake in Citigroup.

Following results of the stress test, Citigroup needed to raise as much as $10 billion in new capital. Citigroup made a $101 million profit in the third quarter 2009 on revenue of about $20.4 billion. On December 14, 2009, Citigroup announced that it would repay $20 billion that had been given to them under the Troubled Asset Relief Program. Hours later, Wells Fargo, the last of the big banks, announced that it would repay its loans to the government. The U.S. Treasury would earn a profit of nearly $14 billion on its Citigroup investment.

The nation's third largest bank by assets reported 2010 quarterly earnings in April of $4.4 billion, its best showing since the Great Recession began. Profits more than doubled the $1.5 billion from the first quarter of 2009. Revenues climbed 3 percent to $8.1 billion. In mid-July 2010, Citigroup reported a second-quarter profit of $2.7 billion, indicating a 37 percent drop from a year earlier. On July 29, management agreed to pay $75 million to settle federal claims that it failed to disclose vast holdings of subprime mortgage investments that were failing during the meltdown and badly crippled the bank. It was also the first time that the Securities and Exchange Commission had brought charges against high-ranking bank executives over their involvement with subprime mortgage bonds.

Citigroup reported third-quarter 2010 net income, posting a profit of $2.2 billion. However, earnings fell 20 percent from the second quarter. The results far exceeded income of $101 million in the third quarter 2009. One result is that Citigroup's stock rose 5.6 percent the following day. By December 2010, the U.S. Treasury set plans to sell the last of its Citigroup common shares in a $10 billion offering that would cap the government's largest bank bailout of the financial-market meltdown. When completed, the taxpayers made a profit of $12 billion on their $45 billion cash investment in the bank.

By mid-January 2011, the bank reported quarterly profits of $1.3 billion, up from a $7.6 billion loss in the fourth quarter of 2009. Then, on March 21, just two years after approaching collapse, when its stock price was measured in cents, not dollars, the bank reported that it would reinstate a dividend and engineer a reverse split to lift its stock out of the single digits. Management noted that the bank's earnings surged 24 percent to $3.3 billion from $2.7 billion the year before. In the second quarter, revenue fell 1 percent.

In mid-July 2011, management reported a second-quarter 24 percent profit increase of $3.3 billion, up from $2.7 billion the year before. Then, on September 21, Moody's downgraded its credit rating on Citigroup, cutting its ratings on short-term debt to Prime 2 from Prime 1, while affirming its A3 long-term rating. Then, in December, Citigroup management announced that it would eliminate about 4,500 positions over the coming few quarters, or about 1.6 percent of its workforce. It was reducing employment by a combined 20,332 jobs, or 2.5 percent.

See also BANK BAILOUT (PLAN) OF 2008 (U.S.); FEDERAL HOUSING FINANCE AGENCY; FINANCIAL CRISIS INQUIRY REPORT; MOODY'S; PRINCE, CHARLES O.; RUBIN, ROBERT E.; STRESS TESTS (U.S.) ; "TOO BIG TO FAIL."

Cf. AMERICAN INTERNATIONAL GROUP; MERRILL LYNCH; WELLS FARGO.

CITIMORTGAGE. *See* CITIGROUP.

CITY BUDGETS. By the end of summer 2009, the recession hit city budgets hard, with overall city revenues down for the year for the first time in seven years. In 379 cities studied, it was found that revenues declined by 0.4 percent as expenses climbed 2.5 percent. It was the worst outlook in twenty-four years.

Cf. CITIES; STATES (U.S.)

CITY UNEMPLOYMENT. *See* UNEMPLOYMENT.

CIVETS. The countries of Colombia, Indonesia, Vietnam, Egypt, Turkey, and South Africa projected to be the next generation of tiger economies. They have large, young populations with an average age of twenty-seven. This suggests that these nations will benefit from fast-rising domestic consumption.

CIVILIAN CONSERVATION CORPS. *See* ROOSEVELT, FRANKLIN DELANO.

CLARIANT. In January 2009, the chemical giant posted a 5 percent drop in full-year sales, cut a further 1,000 jobs, and canceled its dividend in the face of the global economic slump.

CLARITY. *See* TRANSPARENCY.

CLASSICAL ECONOMICS. *See* KEYNES, JOHN MAYNARD.

CLASS SIZE. *See* EDUCATION.

"CLASS WARFARE." *See* BUFFETT, WARREN E.

CLAWBACKS. Payments that are given back due to unfulfilled promises or other circumstances. President Obama, on February 4, 2009, placed limits on severance packages for dismissed employees whose firms received government funds, allowing for clawbacks of such payments.

Many alleged that the current financial collapse was caused by employees in the mortgage and financial products industries pursuing short-term gains without regard for long-term losses and/or consequences. Prior to the financial crisis of 2008–2009, clawback provisions were rare or nonexistent, so an employee's only incentive was to work to make the current year's bonus as large as possible.

See also EXECUTIVE PAY; G-20; GOLDEN PARACHUTES; NAME AND SHAME; UNEMPLOYMENT.

CLINTON, HILLARY. President Obama's first secretary of state, starting in January 2009.

CLUB MED (MEDITERRANEE) (MEDITERRANEAN). The largest European resort company, it lowered planned spending for 2009 by almost half to €50 million and set a goal of lowering costs by €31 million following a travel slump that cut into bookings.

CLUNKERS. *See* CASH FOR CLUNKERS.

COACH. This upscale company operated 324 full-priced stores and 106 factory outlets in North America and another158 locations in Japan. Profits fell 14 percent in the fourth quarter 2008. Coach posted net income of $216.9 million, down from $252.3 million. Management fired 150 employees (10 percent of its workforce). Profit ending the quarter of June 27 fell to $145.8 million. Sales declined less than 1 percent.

The company reported a 3.4 percent fall in its fiscal first-quarter 2009 earnings, as sales rose slightly by 1.2 percent to $761.4 million. For the quarter ending September 26, earnings were $140.8 million. For the fiscal quarter ending December 2009, Coach reported a profit of $241 million compared with $216.9 million the year before, with revenue rising 11 percent to $1.07 billion.

Coach's fiscal third-quarter 2010 earnings rose 37 percent of $157.6 million, compared to $157.6 a year before. Earnings climbed 28 percent and revenue rose 12 percent to $830.7. The firm's fourth-quarter 2010 profit climbed 34 percent to $195.5 million. The retailer reported fiscal first-quarter profit jumped 34 percent, with earnings of $188.9 million; revenue climbed 20 percent to $911.7 million. Its inventories jumped percent to $367 million at the end of its fiscal second quarter.

Coach's fiscal first-quarter earnings rose 14 percent, announced on October 25, 2011. Profit was $215 million, with revenue climbing 15 percent to $1.05 billion.

COAL USAGE. *See* ENERGY EFFICIENCY.

COBRA. A law—the Consolidated Omnibus Budget Reconciliation Act—under which severed employees can remain on their employer's group health plan for a limited time. On December 21, 2009, President Obama signed a measure to extend the federal subsidy for continued health-insurance coverage for involuntarily terminated workers under employer group programs. The stimulus package provided a federal subsidy for 65 percent of the COBRA premium for nine months for workers who qualify. The subsidy applied to workers who lost their jobs between September 1, 2008, and December 31, 2009. Workers who may have preexisting conditions must maintain coverage to protect insurability. An estimated 14 million people were eligible for the subsidy.

See also AMERICAN RECOVERY AND REINVESTMENT ACT (OF 2009).

COCA-COLA. Management reported on April 20, 2010, its first-quarter profit of $1.61 billion, up from $1.35 billion the year before, climbing 20 percent. Revenue increased 5 percent to $7.53 billion. The firm's second-quarter 2010 global profit climbed 16 percent, with a profit of $2.37 billion. Revenue increased 5 percent to $8.67 billion.

By mid-April 2011, Coca-Cola's profit had grown 18 percent. On July 19, management reported that its earnings in the latest quarter climbed 18 percent to $2.8 billion. Revenue jumped 47 percent to $12.74 billion. Its third-quarter earnings climbed 8.1 percent. A $2.2 billion profit was reported, with revenue increasing 45 percent to $12.25 billion.

COLGATE-PALMOLIVE COMPANY. At the end of October 2009, Colgate reported profit of $590 million, up 18 percent from $500 million a year earlier. Revenue was flat at $3.99 billion.

Colgate posted a profit of $624 million for 2010, down 1 percent from the year before, with sales falling 2.5 percent to $3.98 billion. Its fourth-quarter global sales reported a profit of $5.77 billion, up from $1.54 billion the previous year. Revenue increased 40 percent to $10.5 billion.

Cf. KELLOGG; PROCTER & GAMBLE.

COLLATERALIZED DEBT OBLIGATION (CDO). Type of security often composed of the riskier portions of mortgage-back securities.

See also FINANCIAL CRISIS INQUIRY REPORT.

COLLECTIVE BARGAINING. *See* UNIONS.

COLLECTIVE BOND. *Synonymous with* EURO-BOND.

COLLEGE ENDOWMENTS. *See* ENDOWMENTS.

COLLEGE GRADUATES. The unemployment rate for workers twenty-five years and older with a bachelor's degree or higher was 4.6 percent in the summer 2010, compared with 10.3 percent for those possessing only a high school diploma. That is a 5.7 percent point gap, contrasted with a spread of only 2.6 percent at the very beginning of the meltdown.

See also UNEMPLOYMENT.

COLOMBIA. Colombia's peso fell the most in one week (January 2009) on concern of a deepening global recession. The currency declined as much as 1.4 percent. The central bank cut its key rate on March 21 to 7 percent from 8 percent.

Growth in 2011 was projected to fall to 4.4 percent in line with weakening global demand. The nation's GDP growth was 4.4 percent, GDP was at $301 billion, with an inflation rate of 3.8 percent, and a GDP per head of $6,320.

The rising peso squeezed noncommodity industries. The central bank then purchased dollars and held interest rates pat firm.

See also LATIN AMERICA.

COLONIAL BANCGROUP. A Southern-based large lender. On August 14, 2009, it was seized by federal regulators, making it the largest bank failure of the total of seventy-seven banks in 2009.

Cf. INDYMAC BANCORP.

COLUMBIA UNIVERSITY. The university's endowment investments lost 16.1 percent in the year ending June 30, 2009, with a value of about $5.7 billion. On June 30, 2008, the endowment fund was valued at $7.1 billion.

On September 15, 2010, the university indicated that its endowment performed well, posting a 17.3 percent return on its investment, more than four percentage points higher than other private universities.

Cf. HARVARD UNIVERSITY; PRINCETON UNIVERSITY; STANFORD UNIVERSITY; YALE UNIVERSITY.

COMBINED LOAN-TO-VALUE. *See* LOAN-TO-VALUE RATIO.

COMCAST CORPORATION. The largest U.S. cable operator by subscribers (3.3 million customers) posted an 8.2 percent fall in third-quarter 2010 earnings. Profits were $867 million, and revenue climbed 7.3 percent to $9.49 billion.

On February 16, 2011, the company reported that its revenue climbed 7 percent in the fourth quarter 2010. It had $9.72 billion in revenue for the quarter, up 7.2 percent from the year before, and $2.01 billion in operating income, up 10.8 percent. Earnings rose to $1.02 billion from $955 billion a year earlier. For the second quarter, Comcast's revenue rose 51 percent to $14.3 billion, with net income climbing to $1.02 billion. Its third-quarter profit climbed 4.7 percent to $908 million, with revenue up 51 percent to $14.34 billion. During the quarter, it lost a net 165,000 video subscribers.

COMMERCE DEPARTMENT. *See* U.S. COMMERCE DEPARTMENT.

COMMERCIAL BORROWERS. *See* COMMERCIAL REAL ESTATE.

COMMERCIAL PAPER (CP). Short-term unsecured corporate debt.

See also CONSUMER CREDIT; FINANCIAL CRISIS INQUIRY REPORT.

COMMERCIAL PAPER FUNDING FACILITY. Emergency program created by the Federal Reserve in 2008 to purchase three-month unsecured and asset-backed commercial paper from eligible firms.

See also FEDERAL RESERVE.

COMMERCIAL REAL ESTATE. One thousand large, commercial properties in the United States, representing $25.7 billion, were already bank-owned or the landlord was in default by the end of 2008. Possibly another $80.9 billion, more than 3,700 properties, faced a similar situation in 2009. Retail vacancy rates were expected to climb to 11 percent in 2009. Rents declined between 4 and 6 percent as property owners contended with more tenant bankruptcies, store closures, and fewer retailer expansions.

Commercial real estate debt could be more dangerous to a financial system than debt classes such as credit card and student loans, as $6.5 trillion was invested in such holdings and financed by about $3.1 trillion in debt.

More than 6 percent of commercial-mortgage borrowers fell behind in their payment throughout 2009. This portended trouble ahead as nearly $40 billion of commercial-mortgage-backed bonds came due in 2010. The percentage of loans thirty days or more delinquent rose to 6.07 percent in December 2009 from 5.65 percent a month before.

By October 2010, the commercial real estate market was showing signs that office rents had begun to stabilize. Commercial real estate, with $1.4 trillion of debt coming due by the end of 2014, remained in an undetermined situation. Rents, on average at $22.05 per square foot per year, were 12 percent lower than the 2008 high of $25.07. Office buildings in seventy-nine metropolitan areas lost 1.9 million square feet of occupied space in the third quarter 2010, pushing the national office vacancy rate to 17.5 percent, the highest level since 1993.

The national office-vacancy rate was 17.3 percent in the fourth quarter 2011, slightly down from 17.4 percent three months before. Rents were up 0.4 percent in the quarter.

See also COMMERCIAL REAL ESTATE LOANS; GENERAL GROWTH PROPERTIES; PROPERTY (2011).

COMMERCIAL REAL ESTATE DEBT. *See* COMMERCIAL REAL ESTATE.

COMMERCIAL REAL ESTATE LOANS. By March 2009, commercial real estate loans were delinquent at an accelerating pace, possibly threatening additional losses to banks of tens of billions of dollars. The delinquency rate on about $700 billion in securitized loans from office buildings, hotels, stores, and other investment properties had more than doubled since September 2008 to 1.8 percent in March 2009. It had been estimated that as much as $250 billion in commercial real estate losses could occur during the meltdown period, with as many as 700 banks failing as a result of their involvement with commercial real estate.

See also COMMERCIAL REAL ESTATE.

COMMERZBANK. By the end of 2011, Commerzbank, the second-largest German bank, was pressured by regulators to increases its capital buffer. The bank was reported to be on the verge of asking for another government bailout of $6.9 billion by the middle of 2012.

See also GERMANY; UNEMPLOYMENT.

COMMODITIES. Commodities were strong at the beginning of 2008 and then dropped in 2009.

See also COPPER; CROP PRICES; DOW JONES-AIG COMMODITY INDEX; GOLD; NATURAL GAS; OIL; SILVER.

COMMODITIES REGULATIONS. *See* COMMODITY EXCHANGE ACT OF 1936; COMMODITY FUTURES MODERNIZATION ACT OF 2000; COMMODITY FUTURES TRADING COMMISSION ACT OF 1974; FUTURES TRADING PRACTICES ACT OF 1992.

COMMODITY EXCHANGE ACT OF 1936. Broadened the types of agricultural commodities that can trade through futures contracts on an organized exchange.

COMMODITY FUTURES MODERNIZATION ACT OF 2000. Allowed trading of over-the-counter financial derivatives between certain sophisticated counterparties, such as regulated financial institutions and pension funds, to be exempted from being executed on an exchange.

COMMODITY FUTURES TRADING COMMISSION (CFTC) ACT OF 1974. Transferred authority over futures markets from the secretary of agriculture to the new Commodity Futures Trading Commission; gave the CFTC jurisdiction over nonagricultural futures and options on those contracts.

President Obama's 2011 budget proposed increasing the Commodity Future Trading Commission's budget by $93 million to $261 million, up 55 percent from 2011.

See also BORN, BROOKSLEY; DERIVATIVES LEGISLATION; FINANCAL REGULATION PLAN (2009); WALL STREET REFORM ACT (2010).

COMMON EQUITY. Banks holdings of capital; considered the most effective type of capital because it is used to directly absorb losses. New regulations now require large banks to have a common equity of at least 7 percent of the assets, higher than the approximately 2 percent on the international banking scene or 4 percent with larger U.S. banks. Banks, under the Basel III Accord, that fail to maintain these standards will face restrictions.

See also BASEL III ACCORD.

COMMUNITY BANKS. *Synonymous with* SMALL BANKS.

COMMUNITY REINVESTMENT ACT (CRA). 1977 federal law encouraging depository institutions to provide loans and services in the local communities in which they take deposits.

See also FINANCIAL CRISIS INQUIRY REPORT.

COMPENSATION. Major banks and securities firms planned to pay their workers about $140 billion in 2009, a record high. Employees at the top twenty-three investment banks, hedge funds, asset managers, and stock and commodities exchanges expected to earn more than they did during the peak year of 2007. Total compensation and benefits at publicly traded companies were expected to increase 20 percent from 2008's $117 billion and to top 2007's $130 billion payout. That translates into $143,400 on average, up almost $2,000 from 2007 levels.

See also BONUSES; PAY CZAR.

COMPENSATION CZAR. *See* PAY CZAR.

COMPTROLLER OF THE CURRENCY. A federal office created in 1863 to oversee the chartering and regulation of national banks.

See also NATIONAL BANK SUPERVISOR; WALL STREET REFORM ACT (2010).

COMPUTER SALES. Following a difficult period, computer sales and home-office equipment rose in the summer 2009, up 7.3 percent from a year before.

See also APPLE; DELL; GOOGLE; INTEL; INTERNATIONAL BUSINESS MACHINES CORPORATION; YAHOO!.

CONAGRA FOODS. ConAgra's fiscal first-quarter 2010 earnings declined 12 percent, with revenue falling 2.4 percent to $2.82 billion. Net income dropped 16 percent at the company in its second fiscal quarter 2010. On December 21, the firm's revenue rose 2 percent to $3.16 billion.

On September 20, 2011, management reported that its quarterly profit, with net income, fell 41 percent to $85.3 million. On December 19, ConAgra posted double-digit percentage declines in its fiscal second-quarter earnings. Profit fell to $171.8 million from $200.9 million, while revenue increased 8.1 percent to $3.4 billion

CONFERENCE BOARD. An organization supported by business executives that conducts research. By the end of November 2008, the Conference Board, with a financial-industry research study, concluded that its confidence index was 44.9 in November, up from a revised 38.8 the month before. The October reading was the lowest since the index was established in 1967.

By March 2009, the index was flat, with slight indications of a positive turn. In early April, the Conference Board found that confidence among chief executives improved in the first quarter 2009. Its index rose to 30 from 24 in the fourth quarter of 2008, though well below the 50 mark reflecting a positive position. In a sign of economic recovery, the Conference Board said its index of leading economic indicators rose 1 percent in April, after seven straight monthly declines. It was the largest gain in nearly four years.

On September 21, 2009, the Conference Board index rose 0.6 percent, indicating the public's expectation that there are signs of recovery ahead. In late December 2009, the Conference Board's consumer-confidence index rose to 52.9 from 50.6 in November. That was up from the 25.3 showing in February, which was the lowest level in its forty-two-year history. The index remained below pre-meltdown levels.

The Conference Board announced on January 4, 2010, that working Americans were becoming increasingly unhappy with their jobs, in part blamed on the Great Recession. Only 45 percent of people were satisfied with their work, the lowest level in twenty-two years. In early 2010, the Conference Board indicated that the U.S. economy shrank by around 2.5 percent in 2009, with hours worked falling at twice that rate, allowing productivity (GDP per hour) to climb by 2.5 percent. The board also indicated that the average drop in GDP in the fifteen nations of the European Union before its expansion in 2004 was larger, at 4.2 percent. Hours worked fell less sharply than in the United States and, as a result, EU productivity fell by 1.1 percent. The board's consumer-confidence index rose to 57.9 in April 2010 from 52.3 a month earlier, reaching its highest point since the financial crisis was at its lowest in September 2008. Chief corporate executives' level of confidence deteriorated in the third-quarter 2010. Their level of confidence hit 50 (a score of 50 means there was an equal number of negative and positive responses), down from 62 in the second quarter, becoming the lowest score since the first quarter of 2009, when it was 30.

On February 22, 2011, the Conference Board reported that its index rose to 70.4 in February, up from a revised 64.8 in January, reaching its highest level since February 2008. Its consumer-confidence index plummeted to 44.5 percent in August from 59.2 in July. In mid-September, the Conference Board put the odds of a double-dip recession at 45 percent. "The consumer has never really thought that we got out of the recession." By the end of September, consumers remained in the doldrums, with the board's announcement that their confidence index registered 45.4 for the month, near its lowest levels since early 2009. The board reported in October that the confidence level with the economy dropped to a 2.5 level low, slipping to 26.3 from 33.3 on their index. By December 1, the Conference Board said that its index of consumer confidence has surged to its highest point since July. Then, in December, the Conference Board's index climbed to 64.5, its highest level since April.

January 2012's consumer confidence index suddenly fell more than three points to 61.1.

See also CONSUMER CONFIDENCE; RECESSION.

CONFIDENCE. *See* CONFERENCE BOARD; CONSUMER CONFIDENCE; CONTAGION; RETAILING.

CONFIDENCE BUILDING. The *Wall Street Journal*'s 2010 CEO Council summary of recommendations for building U.S. confidence:

1. A New Stakeholder Approach—Companies should talk less about benefits to shareholders and short-term profits and instead focus on customer needs, investment in workers, and sustainability (from ecology to education). We talk too much about benefits we provide to shareholders. We should be talking about benefits provided to our employees, customers, and to the public. This will boost public confidence in business.
2. Long-Term Recommendations—Business needs to advocate for long-term solutions such as education reform, more research and development, and changing the U.S. visa policy to keep foreign students working in the U.S. after they graduate from schools here. The discussion is too focused on the short term.
3. Face Reality—The United States needs to engage in the global marketplace rather than complain. This effort needs to be led by the Obama administration and business. The public needs to understand that there are benefits to be had from engaging globally, and business needs to do a better job of explaining what we're doing well in the international market.
4. Presidential Leadership—The president must advocate for a competitive business environment to create healthy companies, jobs, and rising standards of living. He must be an advocate for business in general.
5. Invest in America Now—Winning public confidence is all about job creation. Business and government should stimulate long-term investment in the United States and make U.S. companies more competitive globally. It should include a cut of 10 percentage points in corporate tax rate; 100 percent depreciation on capital equipment through 2012; permanent research and development tax credit; and a cut in taxes on repatriated earnings, provided earnings are reinvested.

See also CEO COUNCIL.

CONGRESSIONAL BUDGET OFFICE (CBO). On February 24, 2010, the Congressional Budget Office, a nonpartisan government unit, reported that the economic stimulus law added between 1 million and 2.1 million workers to employment rolls by the end of 2009. The office also reported that the $862 billion stimulus added 1.5 to 3.5 percentage points to economic growth in 2009.

In late August, the Congressional Budget Office declared that the president's economic stimulus plan had increased the number of employed Americans by between 1.4 million to 3.3 million during the second quarter 2010, and that the American Recovery and Reinvestment Act had lowered the unemployment rate by up to 1.8 percent and raised the level of GDP by up to 4.5 percent. On November 30, 2010, the Congressional Budget Office announced that the cost to taxpayers of the $700 billion financial rescue, the Troubled Asset Relief Program (TARP), had fallen to $25 billion and that the government would recoup most of the funds spent.

The Congressional Budget Office believed that U.S. debt would rise from 62 percent of GDP in 2010 to 109 percent by 2025 and 185 percent by 2035. The CBO was charged with finding ways to reduce the deficit by at least $1.2 trillion over the coming decade. The committee projected that deficits would total $3.5 trillion over ten years, significantly lower than the $7 trillion it estimated in January.

At the end of August 2011, the CBO presented its budget forecast expecting the budget deficit to reach 8.5 percent of GDP in 2011, before reducing to 6.2 percent in 2012, 3.2 percent in 2013, and then to average 1.2 percent of GDP from 2014 to 2021. On September 13, the director of the CBO, Douglas W. Elmendorf, testified before the deficit reduction plan that the government's growing debt would "lead to lower output and incomes" and could "increase the possibility of a sudden fiscal crisis."

At the end of January 2012, the CBO reported that tax increases and spending cuts scheduled to take effect in January 2013 would slow the economy and raise unemployment. In its semi-annual statement, the CBO projected a $1.2 trillion federal deficit for fiscal year 2012.

See also DEFICIT (BUDGET, U.S.).

CONOCOPHILLIPS. The third-largest U.S. oil company, it announced in January 2009 that it would cut its workforce 4 percent, slashing capital spending by 18 percent. ConocoPhillips reported on April 23 that its first-quarter profit fell 80 percent from the year before. ConocoPhillips lost money in the second quarter 2009, with profit down 76 percent. The company earned $1.3 billion in the quarter, down from $5.4 billion a year earlier. On October 28, 2009, the company reported a 71 percent decline in third-quarter earnings because of lower commodity prices and a weak environment for refining operations. A profit of $1.5 billion was announced, up from $5.19 billion from the year before. Revenue fell 42 percent to $41.31 billion.

The firm announced on July 30, 2010, that its second-quarter earnings tripled. Reversing a year-earlier loss, management reported a profit of $1.22 billion by year's end 2009, compared to a loss in 2008 of $31.76 billion. Revenue of $43.6 billion was down from $44.9 billion. ConocoPhillips reported profit of $3.06 billion, with revenue climbing to $45.5 billion.

Profits rose 44 percent in April 2011. On October 26, management reported that its third-quarter earnings fell 14 percent, with net income of $2.6 billion. Revenue increased 28 percent to $63.63 billion.

The firm reported on January 25, 2012, that its fourth-quarter earnings surged 66 percent, with a profit of $3.39 billion. Revenue climbed 17 percent to $62.39 billion.

See also COMMODITIES; OIL; OIL COMPANIES.

CONSOLIDATED OMNIBUS BUDGET RECONCILIATION ACT. *See* COBRA.

CONSOLIDATED SUPERVISED ENTITIES (CSE) PROGRAM. A Securities and Exchange Commission program created in 2004 and terminated in 2008 that provided voluntary supervision for the five largest investment bank conglomerates.

CONSTRUCTION. By December 2009, construction industry jobs had fallen by 1.6 million since the recession began. In October, unemployment climbed to 19.1 percent, up from 10.7 percent the year before. The transportation and material-moving sector had a rise in unemployment to 11.6 percent from 7.9 percent over the same time frame. Construction jobs fell by 53,000 in December 2009.

It was predicted that a slow recovery would begin in 2011, climbing to $445.5 billion, an increase of 8 percent from the year before. By December 2010, although remaining in a slump, construction spending climbed 0.7 percent to a seasonally adjusted annual rate of $802.3 billion. Overall, construction spending was 34 percent below its March 2006 high. Construction spending fell 0.7 percent in January 2011 to an annual rate of $ 791.8 billion.

CONSTRUCTION SPENDING. *See* CONSTRUCTION; CONSUMER SPENDING.

CONSUMER AND BUSINESS LENDING INITIATIVE. A 2009 federal administration plan designed to finance lending to consumers and higher spending. Purports to help increases in spending and reduce trillion-dollar deficits.

CONSUMER BANKRUPTCIES. *See* BANKRUPTCY FILING.

CONSUMER CONFIDENCE. The U.S. government reported at the end of October 2008 that consumers sharply cut their spending during the summer months, causing the longest American shopping spree on record to come to an end. The U.S. economy contracted at an annual rate of 0.3 percent in the third quarter of 2008.

The housing bust, the resulting credit crunch, and the deteriorating job market had pushed most Americans to cut back. Personal consumption fell at an annual rate of 3.1 percent in the third quarter of 2008, its biggest drop since the spring of 1980. Disposable personal income dropped at an 8.7 percent rate in the third quarter, the biggest decline since the quarterly data was first recorded in 1947.

At the same time, the U.S. Conference Board found that consumer confidence had plunged to the lowest point on record in October 2008, as Americans complained about fewer jobs, lower net worth, and smaller incomes. Citizens also believed that the economy would worsen before it improved, a sign of deep pessimism that reflected a year of painful declines in stocks, jobs, and home values. The survey's confidence index with 5,000 households fell to 38 in October from 61.4 in September. In October, consumer prices tumbled by a record amount, carried lower by skidding energy and transportation prices, while new home construction continued to fall.

Consumer spending was expected to decrease in 2009, the first time since 1980 and perhaps by the largest amount since 1942. By the end of 2008, gloom over the state of the economy had led to a huge disappointment around the world. Five out of six people surveyed in France expressed pessimism. The average was seven in ten in many other European nations, with the most optimistic European country, Germany, having only 37 percent expressing pessimism. The negative response compared to two years earlier was about 25 percent, except for Spain, which was even more optimistic. In December 2006, only 15 percent of Spaniards were pessimistic; now the number was 59 percent.

A year earlier, the Conference Board index was at 90.6. In February 2009, the confidence of the U.S. consumer tumbled to its lowest level in more than forty-one years, with home prices continuing to decline, accompanied by bank-loan delinquencies and a worsening consumer market. In August, consumer confidence climbed more than expected, rising to an index of 54.1 from a July level of 47.4. Consumer confidence increased by December 2009, with the Conference Board's index climbing from 50.6 to 52.9.

September 2010 consumer confidence reached its lowest level since February, falling to 48.5 points from 53.2.

See also CONFERENCE BOARD; CONSUMER PRICES; CONSUMER SPENDING; FEAR GAUGE; FEDERAL RESERVE; FRANCE; RECESSION; RETIREMENT.

CONSUMER CREDIT. In August 2009, consumer credit by commercial banks stood at $834 billion, about $45 billion less than at the end of 2008.

Banks' outstanding commercial and industrial loans fell to $1.411 trillion in September 2009, $170 billion lower than a year before. Commercial paper issued by nonfinancial businesses fell 40 percent from the year before. Consumer lending shrank at an annual rate of 1.7 percent in October, its ninth consecutive fall. The $3.5 billion decline caps a 4 percent drop in consumer lending from its July 2008 peak. By December, lending to consumers continued to shrink as the credit squeeze dragged on.

Consumer lending sagged in February 2010 by cutting back on borrowing as they pare back debt. Consumer borrowing fell at a 5.6 percent annual rate to $2.45 trillion. Overall consumer credit outstanding increased by $3.4 billion from September 2010 to $2.399 trillion.

See also CREDIT CARDS; WALL STREET REFORM ACT (2010).

CONSUMER FINANCIAL PROTECTION AGENCY (BUREAU) (CFPA). Proposed by President Obama as a new regulatory agency to assist consumers to make informed decisions about financial products, save for retirement, and receive improved investment guidance. Under this plan, firms will be given the option of offering products, such as credit cards without hidden fees or penalty interest rates, without having to maneuver regulatory hurdles.

The agency, if approved by Congress, would have the authority to write regulations and require upgraded disclosure with enforcement capability. Ben Bernanke, chairman of the Federal Reserve, argued before the Senate Banking Committee that this proposed agency was not needed and that the Federal Reserve had a sound handle on consumer protection. By mid-September 2009, the Obama administration had submitted draft legislation, and the House Financial Services Committee had drafted a bill under the chairmanship of Barney Frank.

Its powers were watered down from the original Obama proposal and would examine only the nation's largest banks, but it would be able to write regulations that applied to any firm offering financial products.

By mid-January 2010, scrapping Senate Banking Committee Chairman Dodd was considered the idea of the CFPA, the initiative at the heart of the president's proposal to revise financial-sector regulations. CFPA would have ten members, who, act on a two-thirds vote and an initial working budget of about $500 million per year.

By mid-July 2011, the new bureau began supervising the nation's largest banks. The agency's stated goal was to make certain that banks weren't engaging in discriminatory lending practices and that their products and services wouldn't put consumers at risk. Examiners began their first round of on-site examinations after July 21. On July 17, President Obama announced that he would nominate Richard Cordray to head the agency, and not the more controversial Elizabeth Warren. Mr. Cordray, in testimony, said he would streamline regulations. Regulation can be overturned by a two-thirds vote of the ten-member Financial Stability Oversight Council, which included the directors of most federal banking and financial regulation agencies.

See also BERNANKE, BEN; CORDRAY, RICHARD; FEDERAL RESERVE; FINANCIAL REGULATION PLAN (2009); FEDERAL RESERVE; HOUSE (U.S.) FINANCIAL OVERHAUL PLAN; WALL STREET REFORM ACT (2010); WARREN, ELIZABETH.

CONSUMER GOODS (2011). It was projected for 2011 that retail sales in the United States would grow by 2.4 percent, while Europe would cut spending by 1.8 percent and Japan would reach the 1.1 percent rate. However, in China consumer spending was expected to expand by 22 percent. Online sales would grow at annual rates of 10 to 11 percent.

See also PROCTER & GAMBLE; RETAILING; UNILEVER.

CONSUMER LENDING. *See* CONSUMER CREDIT.

CONSUMER LOANS. *See* HOME EQUITY LOANS.

CONSUMER-PRICE INDEX. *See* CONSUMER PRICES.

CONSUMER PRICE INFLATION (EUROZONE). Fell from 3.2 percent to 2.1 percent in November 2008.

CONSUMER PRICES. In the United States, consumer prices dropped by 1.7 percent in November 2008, the largest one-month decline on record. Prices were only 1.1 percent higher than one year before.

The consumer price index, the broadest measure of product and service costs across the country, fell 0.4 percent in March 2009 compared to the year earlier, the first time since August 1955 that prices declined over the year. Consumer prices posted their largest annual decline in fifty-nine years. The consumer-price index rose 0.1 percent in May from April. Consumer prices held steady in July 2009, with prices 2.1 percent lower than in July 2008. Consumer prices rose in August 2009. The consumer price index rose 0.4 percent from July. Consumer prices declined 1.5 percent, the largest decline in any twelve-month period since February 2004. Consumer prices rose modestly in September by 0.2 percent. By December 2009, the index of consumer prices rose a mere 0.1 percent from November. Nevertheless, industrial capacity shrank, suggesting the possibility of creeping inflation. In addition, industrial production rose 0.6 percent in December and manufacturing declined 0.1 percent.

Consumer prices rose in August 2010. The consumer-price index rose 0.3 percent from July.

In October 2011, consumer prices fell 0.1 percent, thus easing inflation fears. Should these price declines continue, they would free up more disposable income for shopping.

See also CONSUMER CONFIDENCE; DEFLATION; EUROZONE; WAGES.

CONSUMER PROTECTION. *See* HOUSE (U.S.) FINANCIAL OVER-HAUL PLAN.

CONSUMER SPENDING. Rose just 0.1 percent in February 2008, before inflation, continuing months of lethargic activity. Consumer spending, which accounted for more than two-thirds of U.S. economic activity, fell 1 percent in December 2008 for the fifth month in a row. Residential spending slumped by about 27 percent for all of 2008, and total construction spending dropped 5.1 percent to $1.08 trillion, the biggest annual drop since records began in 1993.

For a second consecutive month in February 2009 consumer spending climbed. It rose at a seasonally adjusted annual rate of 0.2 percent. Consumers cut their spending in March as incomes dropped, leading to a 0.2 percent fall from February. The drop in consumer spending, the first since December 2008, showed that a recovery was short-lived. On August 4, 2009, the government indicated that consumer spending rose 0.4 percent in June. But, adjusted for inflation, it fell 0.1 percent. Personal income also declined 13 percent in June, the largest single-month drop in four years. By the end of September 2009, consumer spending was showing growth. Personal income climbed 0.2 percent in August compared with July, and spending increased 1.3 percent. Personal savings as a percentage of disposable income was 3 percent compared with 4 percent in July. However, GDP growth forecast rose to 3.1 percent from 2.7 percent. Consumer spending climbed modestly, 0.5 percent for the sixth time in seven months. Adjusted for inflation, spending increased 0.2 percent in November 2009.

November 2010 figures indicated that consumer spending rose at a 2.8 percent annualized rate in the third quarter, up from the 2.6 percent previously estimated. For October, it rose 0.5 percent. Retail sales jumped 0.8 percent from the month before, reaching its highest level since 2007. Sales were up 7.8 percent from a year before for the three-month period through November. Consumer spending jumped 0.4 percent in November from October, lifting spirits. There were indications of job market improvement, a pickup in business orders for new equipment, and improved consumer sentiment. In December, borrowing by consumers climbed 3 percent.

Consumer spending climbed 0.7 percent in February 2011, the largest increase since October 2010 and the eighth straight month of gains. Following an adjustment for inflation, consumption climbed 0.3 percent. Consumer spending fell 0.2 percent in June, the largest fall since September 2009. Consumer spending posted strong gains in July, rising 0.8 percent. In November, consumer spending inched upward.

See also CONSUMER CONFIDENCE; CREDIT CARDS; FOOD SPEND-ING; RETAILING.

CONSUMPTION. *See* CONSUMER CONFIDENCE.

CONTAGION.
1. Where a loss of market confidence in one economy transmits to others.
2. Where investors look across from a troubled economy and see similar problems elsewhere.
3. In investor portfolios, where falling prices in one asset class cause investors to sell other assets.
4. Where a blow to one economy hits investor faith across a swath of others.

Synonymous with DEBT INFECTION.
See also BELGIUM; CONSUMER CONFIDENCE; FOOD SPENDING; PORTUGAL; SPAIN.

CONTAINER SHIPPING. *See* SHIPPING.

CONTINENTAL. The German tire maker reported on April 29, 2009, that it had a net loss of $350.9 million compared with a year-earlier net profit. In the first quarter 2009, revenue fell 35 percent.

CONTINENTAL AIRLINES. The airline's revenue decreased 8.3 percent to $3.18 billion. The firm reported earnings of $85 million compared with a year earlier loss of $269 million.

Its passenger unit revenue rose in March 2010 by between 14.5 percent and 15.5 percent from a year before. Reversing its earlier losses, on July 22, 2010, Continental announced that it earned $233 million in its second quarter, the airline's highest second-quarter profit in eleven years. Revenue climbed 19 percent to $3.7 billion. Then, it announced a merger with United Airlines.
See also AIRLINES; UNITED CONTINENTAL HOLDINGS.

CONTINGENT CAPITAL. *See* WALL STREET REFORM ACT (2010).

CONTRACTION. By the end of 2011, it was clear that the eurozone economy had contracted. Retail sales in Germany fell in December. Eurozone GDP dropped 1 percent to 1.5 percent in the fourth quarter.

CONTROLLED BANKRUPTCY. By March 2009, the government reintroduced controlled bankruptcy for General Motors, which attempted to persuade some creditors to agree to a plan that would divide the company into two pieces.
See also CHRYSLER; GENERAL MOTORS.

CONVERTIBLE-ARBITRAGE FUNDS. Funds that attempt to exploit price anomalies among corporate bonds. These funds lost 46 percent of their value in 2008.

CONVERTIBLE WRAPAROUND MORTGAGE. *See* FLEXIBLE MORTGAGE; FLEXIBLE-PAYMENT MORTGAGE; RENEGOTIABLE-RATE MORTGAGE; VARIABLE-RATE MORTGAGE.

COPPER. On May 17, 2010, copper prices plunged 6.4 percent, the largest one-day fall since the Great Recession began. The metal fell below the $3-a-pound level for the first time since February 10, 2010. By January 2011, with a 33 percent climb for 2010, the price of the futures contract rose 1.9 percent to $4.495 a pound. In February, fueled in part by the conflicts in the Middle East and North Africa, copper hit an all-time high of $4.62 a pound, and then in March fell 11 percent. Copper, by mid-June, plummeted to 4 percent. On September 19, copper prices fell 3.8 percent to $3.7715 a pound, the lowest level since November 2010. Then, on September 22, copper futures dropped by more than 7 percent to their lowest levels in a year at $3.48 a pound.

Prices reached a record $4.62330 per pound in mid-February 2011, a 68 percent gain in eight months. By year's end, it fell nearly 26 percent, ending 23 percent down at $3.41315 per pound.

See also PROPERTY (2011).

CORDRAY, RICHARD. On July 17, 2011, President Obama announced that he would nominate former Ohio Attorney General Richard Cordray to head the Consumer Financial Protection Bureau without Senate approval. He is a specialist in lawsuits against mortgage lenders accused of poor foreclosure practices. During the Christmas recess of Congress in December/January 2011–2012 the appointment was made.

See also CONSUMER FINANCIAL PROTECTION BUREAU.

CORN. The largest crop in the United States hardly changed in 2011, up 3 percent at $6.465 per bushel, 18 percent below the all-time high of $7.87 per bushel in June.

For the month of January 2012, corn prices rose nearly 10 percent.

CORNING. Shifted many employees to four-day work weeks and began eliminating 1,400 temporary and contract workers. Corning's first-quarter 2009 profits allowed the firm to rehire some of its laid-off staff. Corning reported on July 27 that its second-quarter earnings fell 81 percent to $611 million. Sales dropped 18 percent to $1.4 billion from $1.69 billion. The company's management reported that third-quarter 2009 profit declined 16 percent. Earnings were $643 million, down from $768 million a year earlier.

Revenue fell 4.9 percent to $1.48 billion. Corning's fourth-quarter 2009 profit nearly tripled, with strong sales. Earnings were $740 million and revenue increased 41 percent to $1.53 billion.

Corning's first-quarter 2010 earnings soared, with sales rising 57 percent from one year before. Earnings climbed to $816 million and sales to $1.55 billion.

At the end of November 2011, Corning slashed its fourth-quarter profit, with earnings falling 30 percent. Its New York City store closed at the end of December.

CORPORATE CREDIT UNIONS. *See* CREDIT UNIONS.

CORPORATE PROFITS. *See* PROFITS.

CORUS BANKSHARES. On September 11, 2009, the Federal Deposit Insurance Corporation closed this Chicago-based bank (the ninety-first bank failure in 2009), whose loan portfolio tripled to $4.5 billion in the four years from 2001 to 2005.

COSTCO WHOLESALE. Earnings at this retailer known for selling household goods in bulk dropped 29 percent for its fiscal third quarter 2008. For the period ending May 10, 2009, Costco posted net income of $209.6 million. Sales at stores open at least a year fell 7 percent. The company reported on December 10 that it had flat fiscal first-quarter earnings with a profit of $266 million compared to $263 million one year before. Total revenue increased 7.9 percent to $17.3 billion from $16.4 billion, with sales increasing 5.5 percent to $16.92 billion. By year's end 2009, the company posted a 5 percent jump in sales compared to a year earlier.

Costco Wholesale posted a gain of 11 percent in early 2010. The firm's fiscal third-quarter 2010 earnings rose by nearly half. Sales rose 10 percent with revenue increasing 12.3 percent to $17.78 billion. On December 8, Costco reported that its sales climbed 11 percent to $18.82 billion from $16.92 billion, with total revenue at $189.24 billion.

For January 2011, Costco had a 9 percent gain in same-store sales. For the quarter ending on May 8, the firm reported a profit of $324 million, with revenue climbing 16 percent to $20.62 billion. By year's end, Costco reported a 6 percent increase in sales. Costco's fiscal first-quarter earnings climbed 2.6 percent, with a profit of $320 million. Revenue jumped 12 percent.

COST-CUTTING. By mid-November 2009, many companies were reporting strong earnings. However, a large portion of their profits came from cost-cutting, not from hoped-for revenue growth.

COSTS OF WAR. *See* WARS IN AFGHANISTAN AND IRAQ.

COTTON. In March 2010, cotton farmers were content to contract for about 80 cents per pound. By harvest time, prices had doubled. In December 2010, cotton futures hit a nominal record of $1.59 a pound. The last time prices were so high was during the U.S. Civil War and its aftermath.

In mid-August 2011, cotton futures surged, up 4.1 percent to $10.052 a pound.

COUNCIL OF ECONOMIC ADVISERS (CEA). A group of economists charged with advising the U.S. president on a variety of matters, including the preparation of the budget message to Congress and the American people.

At the end of August 2011, the president nominated Princeton University's Alan Krueger to be chairman of the White House Council of Economic Advisers. Professor Krueger, fifty years old, would succeed Austan Goolsbee.

COUNCIL ON JOBS AND COMPETITIVENESS. As advisers to the president, its mission is to streamline regulations and encourage start-up firms to create more jobs. On October 11, 2011, they backed efforts to spend more on U.S. infrastructure projects. Created in January and mostly comprising corporate executives, the council recommended to eliminate taxes on income from investments of $25 million or less in privately held firms as long as the investment is held for at least five years. It also recommended cuts to corporate incomes taxes for the first three years of a firm's existence to encourage it to expand. Among the ideas from the council were as follows:

- Accelerated investment infrastructure and energy projects.
- Programs to support entrepreneurship and held young, fast-growing firms.
- National initiative to boost foreign investment in the United States.
- Simplified regulatory reviews and streamlined project approvals.
- Training and skills-development programs created with the private sector.

COUNTERCYCLICAL POLICIES. Lower interest rates and undiminished public spending often created by fiscal austerity and tight money.

COUNTERFEITING. *See* EUROPEAN CENTRAL BANK.

COUNTERPARTY. A party to a contract.

COUNTERPARTY RISK. *See* CREDIT DEFAULT SWAPS.

COUNTRYWIDE FINANCIAL. Mortgage lender that posted an $893 million loss in April 2008 as a federal probe found that sales executives at the company deliberately overlooked inflated income figures for borrowers.

In August 2010, the Securities and Exchange Commission claimed that the management of Countrywide Financial hid from investors growing risks and problems in their loan portfolio. Loan problems ultimately led to the 2008 sales of Countrywide to Bank of America. Angelo R. Mozilo, born in the

Bronx, New York City, founder of Countrywide, was a pioneer of subprime and adjustable-rate mortgages that were at the heart of the housing boom. He agreed on October 15, 2010, to charges of wrongdoing in the housing crisis and said he would pay $67.5 million in penalties to settle civil fraud and insider-trading charges; $22.5 million would be for civil penalties and $45 million in disengagements that were returned to Countrywide shareholders.

On December 21, 2011, Bank of America, owners of Countrywide Financial, settled with the U.S. Justice Department on discrimination charges by paying $335 million, making it the largest residential fair-lending settlement in history. For example, in 2007, the bank charged Hispanic applicants in Los Angeles an average of $545 more in fees for a $200,000 loans than they charged non-Hispanic white applicants with similar credit histories, and independent brokers processing applications for the bank charged Hispanics $1,195 more.

See also BANK OF AMERICA.

COVERED BONDS. Typically preferred by investors because they offered a claim on mortgages or public-sector loans held on a bank's balance sheet if the issuer became insolvent, offering more protection than lower-ranked unsecured debt.

COX, CHARLES CHRISTOPHER. Chairman of the Securities and Exchange Commission. Became partner at Bingham McCutchen.

See also SECURITIES AND EXCHANGE COMMISSION.

CP. *See* COMMERCIAL PAPER.

CPP. *See* CAPITAL PURCHASE PROGRAM.

CRA. *See* COMMUNITY REINVESTMENT ACT; CREDIT-RATING AGENCY.

CRABTREE & EVELYN. The purveyors of specialty soaps, fragrances, and lotions filed for Chapter 11 bankruptcy protection on July 1, 2009. It operated 126 stores in thirty-four states and employed 950 people. The retailer lost $13.3 million on revenue of about $100 million in the current fiscal year.

CRAMDOWN. A measure by which should the mortgage industry fail to modify mortgage loans, bankruptcy judges could cut payments more sharply by cramming down mortgage loan balances on primary residences for people filing for bankruptcy protection. The cramdown would have allowed bankruptcy judges to rewrite contracts to reduce the amount that people owe on their mortgages.

President Obama's hope for a mortgage cramdown passage in Congress failed.

See also BANKRUPTCY PROTECTION; MODIFYING MORTGAGES; OBAMA, BARACK.

CREDIT. *See* EXPORTS; G-20; INTEREST RATES; MICROLENDING.

CREDIT AGRICOLE. In mid-September 2011, Moody's Investors Service lowered the French bank's credit rating to AA2. On November 10, France's third largest bank reported a 65 percent fall in third-quarter net profit to $349 million, with revenue climbing 6.2 percent. The fall in the lender's second quarter net profit was closely tied to Greece's debt write-down.

On December 14, 2011, Credit Agricole announced plans to significantly downsize its investment bank to lower its reliance on volatile market funding. France's third-largest bank, employing 160,000 people around the globe, with 54 million clients, and $2.25 trillion in assets, expects to cut 2,350 positions. It also planned to leave twenty-one of the fifty-three countries in which it operates.

See also MOODY'S.

CREDIT CARD ACCOUNTABILITY RESPONSIBILITY AND DISCLOSURE ACT. *See* CREDIT CARDS.

CREDIT CARD ACT OF 2009. *See* CREDIT CARDS.

CREDIT CARD LEGISLATION. *See* CREDIT CARDS.

CREDIT CARDS. Toward the end of April 2009, the Obama administration turned its attention to high credit card rates in order to put limits on the industry. Banks had come under considerable pressure over raising their credit card rates during the meltdown.

Congress was determined to minimize the rising costs of credit cards, from higher interest rates on past balances to fees for paying by phone or online. The president threw his support behind legislation moving through Congress that would restrict the ability of banks to impose higher fees and interest rates on consumers. Credit card delinquencies increased in the first quarter 2009 from a year earlier. The delinquency rate rose to 1.32 percent for consumers who were three months or more behind payments on their cards, up 11 percent from 1.19 percent a year earlier.

Banks almost always tighten credit standards in an economic slowdown. By the summer 2009, many banks were tightening things up before many of the restrictions of Congress were to go into effect. Banks had until February 2010 to comply with the government's key provisions. Their responses to legislative and economic changes include:

a. Tightening standards for credit card applicants, rejecting more people, and offering smaller credit lines.

   b. Raising interest rates and fees and switching customers with fixed rates to variable ones.

   c. Enhancing rewards programs for a few customers but adding more fees.

On August 20, 2009, banks, as stated in the Credit Card Accountability Responsibility and Disclosure Act of 2009 (also known as the Card Act), are required to mail bills at least twenty-one days before their due dates and provide at least forty-five days' notice before making a significant change to their rates or fees. The new rules bar banks from increasing fees and rates without warning when a consumer misses a payment or exceeds a credit limit. Consumers will also be permitted to avoid future interest rate increases and pay off any outstanding balance over time under the original rate terms. The bulk of the legislation's key provisions took effect in February 2010, including limits on interest rate increases on existing balances. Then, in July 2010, new disclosure rules were introduced.

The banks want to find ways to make up for losses under the Card Act. As much as $390 million a year in fee revenue is now gone. Already, ordinary bank charges have climbed since the act was passed, such as:

- Foreign transaction fees—up 50 percent
- Balance transfers—up 33 percent
- Cash-advance fees—up 33 percent
- Annual fees—up 18 percent
- Penalty interest rates—up 3.4 percent

In addition, delinquency rate, a measure of future losses, slowed down for most credit card users in December 2009. The number of credit card holders shrank by 32 million, or 11 percent, in 2009.

U.S. credit card issuers faced a $12 billion revenue shortfall in 2010 from price limitations imposed by the new rules found in the Card Act, effective February 22, 2010. Over five years, the overall loss to the industry could exceed $50 billion. For the 381 million U.S. credit card accounts, borrowing rates by mid-summer 2010 continued to climb. New regulations that went into effect on August 22, 2010, limit banks' ability to charge penalty fees. These regulations follow other rule changes restricting issuers' ability to adjust rates on the fly. The result is that bank issuers have raised card rates to their highest in nine years. For example, in the second quarter 2010, the average interest rate on existing cards approached 14.7 percent, up from 13.1 percent the year before, the highest level since 2001.

Consumer credit, almost entirely credit card debt, fell $4.4 billion to $827.8 billion in July 2010 from the previous month. That was down 15 percent from an August 2008 peak of $973.6 billion. On October 19, 2010, the Federal Reserve announced its intention to amend some credit card regulations and reduce some practices issuers have employed to circumvent new credit-card laws. The proposed rules would restrict offers designed to get around regulations governing interest rate increases. They would also minimize "fee harvester" cards that use high up-front charges to skirt fee limits. The Federal Reserve proposed on December 16 that new restrictions would be urged to cap the amount of money that debit card issuers could charge merchants for so-called swipe fees.

By 2011, new card credit regulations would cost as much as $25 billion a year in lost revenue. The result might be that issuers of credit cards would lower rewards and charge higher annual fees. In addition, holders sharply reduced their use of credit cards in January 2011, slipping $4.2 billion from December to $795.5 billion, the lowest level since 2004. In addition, by the end of September, some beleaguered banks began to charge customers $3 to $5 monthly fees to use their debit cards. The industry argued that it needed the fees to recoup revenue it lost because of new government regulations taking effect on October 1. Without these new fees, the banks claim that they would lose about $6.6 billion in revenue each year.

See also AMERICAN EXPRESS; FEDERAL RESERVE; REGULATION; TALF; WALL STREET REFORM ACT (2010).

CREDIT DEFAULT SWAP (CDS). Insurance-like contracts that Wall Street created in the early 1990s allowing bondholders to protect themselves against losses if a company or a debt issuer defaults.

A way for market participants to bet on the likelihood that a firm or other debt issuer will default on its obligation. There is a viable and legitimate use for CDSs, especially when they permit bondholders and firms to limit their risks to actual economic exposure. Recently, they became a haven for speculators who were doing nothing more than betting on whether a debt issuer would survive.

Buyers of CDSs pay premiums to firms issuing the contract. If a debt default occurs, the party providing the credit protection has to make the buyer whole on the amount of insurance bought. It is similar to payments that insurers pay to homeowners if their houses burn down.

CDSs provide insurance against an organization defaulting on its debt by providing a real-time gauge of credit risk. They permit the investor to purchase insurance against a firm defaulting on its debt payments.

CDSs, made many firms and investors feel comfortable owning corporate debt because they could eliminate the risk of the issuer failing, which helped lower the cost of capital.

The value of outstanding CDSs exploded from nearly zero a decade ago to $62 trillion at the end of 2007 and fell back to $55 trillion in 2008. The collapse of Lehman Brothers in September 2008 indicated that the main systematic risk posed by CDSs came not from widespread losses on underlying debts but from the demise of a major dealer.

By January 2010, prices for CDS contracts soared as investors snapped them up on worries about the growing debt of nations including Greece, Portugal, Spain, and Latvia.

See also BEAR STEARNS; DERIVATES LEGISLATION; EMPTY CREDITOR; FINANCIAL CRISIS INQUIRY REPORT; HEDGE; SYNTHETIC CDO.

CREDIT ENHANCEMENT. Insurance or other protection that can be bought for a loan or pool of loans to offset losses in the event of default.

CREDIT EXPANSION. *See* FINANCIAL CRISIS INQUIRY REPORT.

CREDIT INFORMATION BUSINESS. *See* CREDIT-RATING AGENCIES.

CREDIT LOSS. Loss from delayed payments or defaults on loans.

CREDIT RATING. *See* FINANCIAL CRISIS INQUIRY REPORT; FITCH RATINGS; MOODY'S; MUNICIPAL BONDS; RATERS; STANDARD & POOR'S.

CREDIT-RATING AGENCIES. A firm issuing credit ratings for the debt of public and private corporations and governments. It is a designated statistical rating organization by the Securities and Exchange Commission.

In April 2010, a U.S. Senate investigation committee revealed how these agencies became beholden to the largest issuers of mortgage-backed bonds. Ratings, to be useful and fair, must be transparent. Agencies should be obliged to publish their methodologies and include the inputs so investors can check. All rating should be based on published information. On August 6, Standard and Poor's downgraded the United States from a AAA rating to AA+.

See also FINANCIAL CRISIS INQUIRY REPORT; FITCH RATINGS; MOODY'S; RATING AGENCIES; STANDARD & POOR'S.

CREDIT RATING AGENCY REFORM ACT OF 2006. Empowered by the Securities and Exchange Commission to register nationally recognized statistical rating organizations and impose disclosure and record-keeping requirements.

CREDIT REPORT. *See* CREDIT SCORE.

CREDIT RISK. Risk to a lender that a borrower will fail to repay the loan.

CREDIT SCORE. Prior to 2011, credit applicants who were turned down were permitted to get a free copy of their credit report but not their actual credit score. Generally, only those applying for mortgage loans were given free copies of their scores. As of January 1, 2011, lenders now have a choice: they can send the credit score used to any consumer who is approved for a loan, or they can send a letter explaining how credit reports were used in the decision if the applicant doesn't receive the best terms available. Effective July 21, 2011, under the Dodd-Frank Act, if a credit score negatively affects a consumer's financial transaction or hiring decision, the credit score used must be disclosed.

CREDIT SQUEEZE. By November 2011, nervous investors were increasingly exiting from the debt of European governments and banks, increasing the risk of a credit squeeze that might lead to a downward spiral. Financial institutions were dumping some of their vast holdings and European government debt and avoiding new bond issues. Many will not renew short-term loans to European banks, which are needed to finance day-to-day operations. Such risks would lead to rising costs of borrowing, larger spending cuts, and slower economic growth. All is based on the concern that nations will not be able to fully repay their bond borrowings.

CREDIT SUISSE. One of Europe's strongest banks, in December 2008 it announced a cut of about 5,300 jobs, or 11 percent of its workforce. Its top executives would not receive any bonuses for 2008. For the third quarter 2008, the bank posted a loss of 1.26 Swiss francs, worth about $1 billion.

On July 23, 2009, Credit Suisse's second-quarter profit rose 29 percent.

Credit Suisse announced on October 21 that its third-quarter 2010 profit shrank 74 percent to $632.6 million.

On July 28, 2011, management announced its plans to cut about 2,000 positions (about 4 percent of its workforce) as their net income fell to $958 million in the three months ending June 30.

See also FEDERAL HOUSING FINANCE AGENCY; UNEMPLOYMENT.

CREDIT UNIONS. Federal regulators announced on January 28, 2009, that they would guarantee $80 billion in uninsured deposits at credit unions. Regulators also injected $1 billion of new capital into the largest of the wholesale credit unions.

A federal plan introduced in February 2009 to rescue troubled wholesale credit unions had a provision requiring credit unions to pay an extra $4.7 billion into a government insurance fund.

Federal authorities took control of the two largest wholesale credit unions on March 20 after learning that their losses on mortgage-related securities were larger than originally believed. These institutions do not have impact on the general public in that they provide critical financing, check clearing, and other tasks for the retail institutions. They are referred to as "corporate credit unions" that are owned by their retail credit union members.

On September 23, 2010, U.S. regulators announced a rescue of the nation's wholesale credit unions with a federal guarantee valued at $30 billion or more. As part of the credit union sector, these institutions had been battered by losses on subprime mortgages. The National Credit Union Administration, which supervises about 7,500 credit unions, released $30 billion to $35 billion in government-backed guaranteed bonds backed by the shaky mortgage-related assets. Five of the nation's twenty-seven wholesale credit unions have closed since March 2009.

At the end of March 2011, federal regulators and the National Credit Union Administration (NCUA) blamed Wall Street's largest firms for the collapse of five credit union firms and began to secure tens of billions of dollars in losses on securities directly related to their collapse. They are seeking over $50 billion of mortgage-backed securities sold to the five institutions, called wholesale credit unions, also known as corporate credit unions.

CREDIT-WORTHY BORROWERS. *See* SUBPRIME.

CREMATION. By the end of 2011, 41 percent of all deaths in the United States resulted in cremation. Of the numerous reasons, a major one was the high cost of a traditional funeral as opposed to the lower expense of a cremation.

CRIME. Violent crime fell in 2009, challenging the widely held belief that recessions drive up crime rates. The incident of violent crimes such as murder, rape, and aggravated assault was down 5.5 percent from 2008 and 6.9 percent in big cities.

On December 19, 2011, the government showed that crime across the country was down, hitting a 4.5-year low. Unexpected during the recession, with high unemployment violent crime fell 6.4 percent in the first half of 2011.

See also HACKING.

CROATIA. Its government, rejected in December 2008, planned to run a balanced budget in 2009. In 2008, Croatia's economy expanded at the slowest pace in eight years. GDP climbed at an annual rate of 1.6 percent compared with 3.4 percent earlier.

After its economy decline in 2010, its growth would expand by 2 percent in 2011. Wages were expected to also rise as unemployment fell. The nation's GDP growth was 2.0 percent, a GDP of $57 billion, and an inflation rate of 2.4 percent, with a GDP per head of $12,670.

CROP PRICES. Prices of corn and soybeans jumped 4 percent in January 2011, with wheat gaining 1 percent. Prices of corn futures rose 94 percent, soybeans 51 percent, and wheat 80 percent.
See also COMMODITIES; CORN.

CROSS-BORDER INVESTMENT FLOWS. Investments between nations collapsed in 2009, with the value of mergers and acquisitions likely to be 56 percent lower than in 2008. Foreign direct investment fell to $600 billion in 2009 from $1.02 trillion.

CRUDE OIL. *See* OIL.

CRUISE LINE. In 2009, projections showed a 2.3 percent drop in travelers to 13.5 million people.
See also CARNIVAL CRUISES.

CSE. CONSOLIDATED SUPERVISED ENTITY.
See also CONSOLIDATED SUPERVISED ENTITIES PROGRAM.

CUBA. Economic reforms will continue into 2011, with more goods taken off the regulated price list and ties on private firms loosened somewhat. The nation's GDP growth was 3.7 percent, with a GDP of $61 billion, an inflation rate of 5.4 percent, and a GDP per head of $5,400.
See also VENEZUELA.

CUOMO, ANDREW. The New York State attorney general.
See also AMERICAN INTERNATIONAL GROUP.

CURRENCY-SWAP ARRANGEMENTS. *See* ASIAN DEVELOPMENT BANK.

CURRENCY WAR. Originally described in September 2010 where nations were blaming each other for distorting global demand with currency intervention and capital controls.

CURRENT RECESSION. *See* CHINA; RECESSION.

CYBER MONDAY. *See* RETAILING.

CYPRUS. The central bank warned on July 20, 2011, that the island nation was in a state of emergency and may need financial support. The budget deficit stood at 5.1 percent of GDP. Moody's cut Cyprus's long-term government bond rating two levels to BAA from A2. The government is hoping to lower a budget deficit that hit 5.3 percent of GDP in 2010.

CZECH REPUBLIC. Falling investment and recession in major export markets contributed to a sharp downturn at the beginning of this year. Real

GDP turned slightly positive in the second quarter, largely due to a pick-up in exports and continued, albeit weak, consumption growth. A gradual recovery is projected for 2010 and 2011, driven by stronger investment and export demand, though weak consumption will act as a drag on growth. Inflation has been negative during part of 2009 but is expected to rise gradually to about 2 percent in 2011. The government responded to the downturn with two stimulus packages, and cyclical factors will further increase the general government deficit. However, there is little room for further discretionary fiscal easing, and parliament has already approved a fiscal consolidation plan to reduce the government deficit. Sustaining the consolidation effort over the longer term will require addressing large unresolved spending issues, particularly in health care, welfare, and pensions, as part of the necessary exit strategy.

By mid-January 2009, unemployment rose to 6.8 percent compared with 6 percent a year before. After growing about 4 percent in 2008, its economy contracted by 2 percent in 2009, a sharp decline from a growth peak around 7 percent in 2006. Until the meltdown of 2008, nearly 40 percent of new jobs in the Czech Republic were filled by foreigners. By the end of 2008, more than 360,000 foreigners were working there. By the end of April, the economy having soured, the Czech government announced in February that it would provide one-way plane tickets to its citizens who wanted to return home.

A tight budget in 2011 and a weaker demand abroad will pull the economy back, holding growth to 2 percent for the year. The nation's GDP growth is 2.0 percent, with a GDP of $184 billion, an inflation rate of 2.1 percent, and a GDP per head at $18,050. GDP growth in the Czech Republic fell to 2.4 percent in the second quarter 2011.

See also EASTERN EUROPE; MIGRATION; SPAIN.

D

DAIMLER. The German maker of luxury cars announced in December 2008 that it would cut working hours at Mercedes-Benz plants in Stuttgart and Berlin as the recession in Europe and the United States continued to hurt car sales. On February 17, 2009, Daimler reported a net loss of €1.53 billion, or $1.93 billion, for the fourth quarter 2008, as the economic slowdown intensified. This net loss compared with a profit of €1.7 billion in the quarter a year earlier indicated the depths of the fallout. In a deal worth $2.65 billion announced in mid-March, Daimler ceded a 9.1 percent stake in the company to an Abu Dhabi investment firm.

Daimler planned to cut labor costs in Germany by $2.66 billion in 2009, with measures including salary reductions. It was announced on April 1 that its vehicle sales had dropped 40 percent in February. Daimler said on April 8 that it expected a significant decline for the first quarter 2009, resulting in company-wide cost-cutting and efficiency programs in response to the downturn in auto markets worldwide. Labor savings would be $2.68 billion in Germany, with other reductions possible. On April 27, Daimler agreed to give up its remaining 19.9 percent stake in Chrysler and pay as much as $600 million into the automaker's pension fund. This stake would be turned over to Chrysler's parent, Cerberus Capital Management (Daimler sold an 80.1 percent stake in Chrysler to Cerberus in August 2007).

The following day, Daimler posted a worse-than-expected net loss of €1.29 billion for the first quarter as revenue fell 22 percent. In the first three months of the year sales were down 34 percent from the previous year. The number two master luxury carmaker indicated that sales had dropped 12 percent in August. Daimler's third-quarter 2009 earnings before interest and tax were about $700 million.

In June 2010 there was a 20 percent increase in Mercedes-Benz sales. Then, on July 16, 2010, Daimler's management reported a profit with revenue of $32.46 billion. Daimler announced on October 29, 2010, that its profit climbed to $2.222 billion, with earnings before interest and tax rising to 2.42 billion euros; revenue increased by 30 percent.

On February 16, 2011, the company posted fourth-quarter profit of $1.54 billion from a year before loss. Net profit rose in the first quarter $1.75

billion, with revenue increasing 17 percent. In October, 24,449 cars were sold for a 28 percent gain.

See also AUTOMOBILE INDUSTRY; CERBERUS; CHRYSLER; GERMANY.

DARK POOLS. Trading venues that match buyers and sellers anonymously. By hiding identities, in addition to the quantity of shares bought or sold, dark pools help institutional investors avoid price movements as the wider market reacts to their trades. Stock quotes aren't displayed until after the trade is completed.

Synonymous with TRADING DESKS.

DAVOS. *See* WORLD ECONOMIC FORUM.

DEAD, THE. *See* CREMATION; SOCIAL SECURITY.

DEATH TAXES. One of the results of the Great Recession has been a huge fall in federal and states tax revenues. Defined as States of Confiscation, the combined federal and state death tax rates, including inheritance and estate taxes, in 2011 were as follows:

New Jersey	54.1 percent	New York	45.4
Maryland	50.9	North Carolina	45.4
Indiana	48.0	Oregon	45.4
Washington	47.4	Rhode Island	45.4
Nebraska	46.7	Vermont	45.4
Delaware	45.4	Iowa	44.8
Hawaii	5.4	Pennsylvania	44.8
Illinois	45.4	Connecticut	42.8
Kentucky	45.4	Tennessee	41.2
Maine	45.4	Ohio	39.6
Massachusetts	45.4	All other states	35.0
Minnesota	45.4		

DE BEERS. On February 11, 2011, posted a rise in profit and sales for 2010, with a net profit of $894 million, compared with $327 million the year before. Earnings climbed to $1.43 billion from $654 million in 2009. Total sales were $5.88 billion, a 53 percent increase from the year earlier.

DEBIT CARD FEES. The Federal Reserve in July 2011 cut banks slack on debit card fees, allowing them to charge double to 12 cents per transaction permitted.

DEBIT CARDS. *See* CREDIT CARDS.

DEBT. Money, services, or materials owed to another person as the result of a previous agreement.

The International Monetary Fund urges wealthy nations to cut spending substantially and boost their taxes to keep debt levels from expanding further. The IMF estimates that the United States, western Europe, and Japan are likely to increase 37 percentage points on average to 110 percent of GDP in 2015, from 73 percent in 2006. Higher debt can undermine economic growth.

In 2011, it was expected that debt would strain governments, banks, and companies. Debt owed by the globe's governments reached a huge $43 trillion, of which Japan alone accounted for a quarter (with the United States not far behind). Debt can be lowered in several ways: it can be paid off with the help of higher savings; its burden can be lowered through higher inflation or faster growth; or it can be defaulted on.

See also DEBT SPIRAL; HOUSEHOLD DEBT; INTERNATIONAL MONETARY FUND; ROLLOVER RISK.

DEBT-BUYBACK. *See* BUYOUT FIRMS.

DEBT CEILING. The limit that the U.S. government can borrow. The debt cap's legal limit is presently $12.1 trillion. On December 24, 2009, the government approved a short-term increase in federal borrowing authority of $290 billion, fearful of it exceeding the legal limit and not having the ability to pay its debts. Then suddenly on December 29, the president delayed submitting his request to Congress for a $1.2 trillion increase in the debt ceiling.

On January 18, 2012, the House voted to reject President Obama's request to raise the federal debt limit by $1.2 trillion, a symbolic act to let lawmakers oppose the increase while letting it take effect.

See also DEBT DEAL; OBAMA, BARACK.

DEBT DEAL (BUDGET CONTROL ACT OF 2011). On July 31, 2011, the president and congressional leaders reached a "deal" to raise the government's debt ceiling while reducing spending by about $2.4 trillion, thus avoiding a government default. It would raise the debt ceiling in two stages and provide initially for $917 billion in spending cuts over ten years. A special committee, the Joint Select Committee on Deficit Reduction, with a three-month schedule was charged with securing another $1.5 trillion in deficit reduction via a tax overhaul and changes to safety net programs. A November 2011 deadline had been set for the committee and, should they fail to find at least $1.2 trillion in savings or should Congress not adopt its proposals, a preset array of spending cuts would kick in, including Medicare payments to health-care providers and cuts in military spending. The government would raise its borrowing limit to $14.29 trillion in three phases. The first round of spending cuts would fall $25 billion, or 2.1 percent. Another $47 billion of discretionary-spending cuts in fiscal year 2013 would amount to another 3.9 percent reduction.

Divided into forthcoming dates, the debt deal, officially the Budget Control Act (2011), shows:

1. Immediately: $400 billion increase in the debt ceiling to stave off default.
2. Additional increase: Additional $500 billion increase in the debt ceiling to carry through February 2012. Congress can vote to halt this, but it would largely be symbolic because the president can veto.
3. If Congress approves or overrides the increase, the bill retains a strategy first proposed by Senate Republicans that permits conservatives in the House to vote against a debt ceiling rise without actually defeating it by giving the president authority to raise it subject to approval by Congress. The president can veto the override.
4. October 1, 2011: Spending caps begin. Caps on spending will lower the deficit by $917 billion over ten years. Only $21 billion will be saved in the first year, 2012. Wars in Afghanistan and Iraq will not be subject to spending caps. Defense cuts in 2012 and 2013 are mild. Over a decade, about $350 billion of savings will come from national security programs, including intelligence and veterans programs. Pell grants would be exempted. The president won authority to increase financing for grants to poor college students by a total of $17 billion in 2012 and 2013.
5. November 23, 2011: A twelve-member Special Joint House-Senate Super Committee is charged, no later than this date, to come up with a $1.2 trillion to $1.5 trillion in further cuts or revenue. It can consider tax measures that increase revenue, as well as cuts in entitlements and defense.
6. December 23, 2011: No later than this date, Congress votes (up or down) on the joint committee's plan with no amendments and no delays.
7. If enacted or if not enacted, Democrats and Republicans can strive to make this option unpalatable to force serious changes by the joint committee. Defense cuts could be half the total, a prospect tailored to make many conservatives angry. By January 15, 2012, there were across-the-board spending cuts where half the funds would come from national security. Medicare subject to limited cuts. Social security and Medicaid are excluded.

8. December 31, 2011: Prior to this date—A balanced budget amendment where Congress is required to hold a vote on sending a balanced budget amendment to the states, which requires a two-thirds majority. The balanced budget vote is a largely symbolic action, potentially useful in reelection races for conservative Republicans but unlikely to get enough Democratic votes to pass.
9. If passed or if not passed: The president can request a second debt ceiling increase of up to $1.2 trillion to $1.5 trillion.
10. Congress is then required to vote on whether to approve the President's request. Should Congress approve the increase, or should Congress override the increase, the President can veto the override.
11. The second debt ceiling increase is final.

A super committee failed to draw any conclusions by the end of 2011.

Cf. BALANCED BUDGET ACT (1997); BUDGET ENFORCEMENT ACT (1990); DOUBLE-DIP RECESSION; SEQUESTER; STANDARD AND POOR'S; SUPER COMMITTEE.

Synonymous with BUDGET CONTROL ACT (2011).

DEBT, FEDERAL (U.S.). *See* DEBT DEAL; DEFICIT (BUDGET, U.S.); NATIONAL COMMISSION ON FISCAL RESONSIBILITY AND REFORM; OBAMA, BARACK.

DEBT HOLDER. *See* CHINA; JAPAN.

DEBT INFECTION. *Synonymous with* CONTAGION.

DEBT LIMIT. *See* DEBT CEILING.

DEBT MASKING. *See* MASKING.

DEBT MONETIZATION. The process by which the national debt is used to increase currency in circulation. Essentially, this is carried out by the purchase of government bonds, thus releasing Federal Reserve notes into circulation. These purchases may be affected through member banks.

DEBT PAYBACK. Companies worldwide had $4 trillion in debt due to be repaired or renewed before the end of 2010. That sum, roughly equivalent to Japan's annual economic output, could be the next phase of the global financial crisis.

Synonymous with REFINANCE.

DEBT RATIO. The ratio of U.S. federal public debt to GDP. When the Democrats took control of Congress in 2007, the debt ratio was 36.2 percent, and within a year it rose to 40.2 percent. It is expected to reach 63.3 percent in 2010, 68.6 percent in 2011, and more than 70 percent in the last years of the decade.

DEBT REDUCTION. *Synonymous with* DELEVERAGE.

DEBT RULE. *See* SHORT-TERM BORROWING.

DEBT SPIRAL. A vicious circle of sinking confidence, rising borrowing costs, and, finally, rising debt burdens. When investors lose confidence in a nation, its bond prices fall, its bond yields rise, and its government must pay higher interest rates to borrow. The result is a greater debt problem, leading to a repeat of this vicious cycle.

DEBT-TO-INCOME RATIO. One measure of a borrower's ability to repay a loan, usually calculated by dividing the borrower's monthly debt payments by gross monthly income.

DEBT TRAP. *See* PORTUGAL.

DECEMBER 2007. The government's official date set by the National Bureau for Economic Research (NBER) for the beginning of the recession in the United States. By April 2010, the bureau had not declared the recession over.
See also NATIONAL BUREAU FOR ECONOMIC RESEARCH; RECESSION.

DECLINING GROWTH. With a $14.4 trillion U.S. economy, the output of goods and services had been declining by nearly $50 billion a month since September 2008.

DEED. A formal, written agreement of transfer by which title to an estate or other real property is transmitted from one person to another.

DEED-FOR-LEASE PROGRAM. *See* FANNIE MAE.

DEED IN LIEU OF FORECLOSURE. A mortgagor's way of presenting title to the mortgagee to prevent foreclosure of property.
See also FORECLOSURE.

DEERE & CO. The world's largest manufacturer of agricultural equipment posted a 27 percent fall in its fiscal third-quarter 2009 profit. Net sales fell 24 percent.

In May 2010, Deere reported its full-year profit after a 16 percent rise in fiscal second-quarter earnings. For its quarter ending in April, profits were $547.5 million, up from $472.3 million the year before, and revenue increased 5.7 percent to $7.13 billion. In November, management reported that the firm had swung to a fiscal fourth-quarter profit, from a year-earlier loss. The company expected profits of about $2.1 billion in 2011. Profit reported was $457.2 million, with revenue climbing 35 percent to $7.2 billion as equipment sales climbed 39 percent from the year before.

On February 16, 2011, Deere reported that its quarterly net income more than doubled. Earnings were $513.7 million, up from $243.2 million the year before. Revenue climbed 27 percent to $6.12 billion from $4.83 billion. Quarterly earnings were expected to climb 15 percent in 2011. The firm reported a profit of $712 million, with revenue climbing 22 percent to $8.37 billion. On November 23, management reported that its fourth-quarter profit climbed by 46 percent to $670 million. Revenue surged 20 percent to $8.6 billion. Sales were up 20 percent in the quarter.

DEFAULT. *See* DEBT DEAL.

DEFERRAL. *See* PROMOTE AMERICA'S COMPETITIVE EDGE (PACE).

DEFICIT (BUDGET, U.S.). Between 2004 and 2007, the budget deficit narrowed from $413 billion to $162 billion thanks to rapid growth in tax revenue. Before the 2008 meltdown, the Congressional Budget Office projected the 2009 deficit at $438 billion; now expected to be at least $750 billion. At 5 percent of GDP, that would be the highest level since 1986.

In February 2009, several weeks after passage of the American Recovery and Investment Act, President Obama set a goal to cut the annual deficit at least in half by the end of his first term. The reduction would come in large part through Iraq troop withdrawals and higher taxes on the rich.

For 2009, the deficit was about $1.2 trillion, which could reach more than $1.5 trillion. Starting in fiscal year 2010, the ten-year program would result in an annual deficit declining to $33 billion in 2013. Measured against the size of the economy, the projected $533 billion shortfall for 2013 would mean a reduction from a deficit equal to more than 10 percent of the GDP—larger than any deficit since World War II—to 3 percent.

To implement slashing the deficit, President Obama would tax the investment income of hedge funds and private equity partners at ordinary income tax rates. The Congressional Budget Office presented on March 20 its forecast that the president's spending program would produce significantly deeper long-run deficits. Summarizing, the deficits would average nearly $1 trillion a year over the coming decade. The cumulative deficit from 2010 to 2019 would total about $9.3 trillion, $2.3 trillion more than President Obama's original forecast. The Treasury Department reported on April 10 that the deficit had reached nearly $1 trillion—$956.80 billion—for the first half of the 2009 fiscal year. In the first six months of fiscal year 2008, the government ran a deficit of $312.75 billion. For the entire fiscal year 2008, it ran a deficit of $454.80 billion.

Spending on government bailouts combined to widen the deficit in the fiscal year that began on October 1, 2008. Gross spending through the Troubled Asset Relief Program was $2.89 billion for March 2009. Another $46 billion went to mortgage firms. For the first six months of the fiscal year, government receipts were down about 13.6 percent to $990 billion compared with the first half of fiscal 2008. Government expenditures grew by some 33.5 percent compared with a year earlier to $1.95 trillion.

The U.S. federal budget deficit broke through the $1 trillion mark in June. By August 2009, with falling tax receipts, soaring spending, and a sluggish recovery, the country's deficit was predicted to rise higher over the next decade. The White House Office of Management and Budget forecast a $9 trillion debt over the coming ten years, $2 trillion more than it had previously projected. On October 7, 2009, the Congressional Budget Office and the Treasury estimated that the federal deficit for fiscal 2009 would be $1.4 trillion, or about 10 percent of the U.S. GDP. In 2009, the U.S. debt rose from 41 percent of the nation's output of goods and services, the GDP, to 53 percent. Without changes in taxes or spending, it will climb to 85 percent of GDP by 2018, 100 percent by 2022, and 200 percent by 2038.

On January 25, 2010, the president said that he would ask for a three-year freeze (that would account for one-sixth of the federal budget) in spending on many domestic programs and for increases no greater than inflation to reduce the budget deficit. The freeze would cover the agencies and programs for which Congress allocates specific budgets each year. The estimated $250 billion in savings over ten years would be less than 3 percent of the roughly $9 trillion in additional deficits the government was expected to accumulate over that time.

On February 1, the president proposed a $3.8 trillion budget for fiscal 2011, projecting that the deficit would shoot up to a record $1.6 trillion in 2010, with a fall of about $700 billion, or 4 percent of GDP, by 2013. On July 23, the government raised its forecast for the 2011 fiscal budget deficit to $1.4 trillion or 9.2 percent of the economy, up from $1.267 forecast in February. Over the coming decade, the government projects $8.5 trillion of more debt. Under these new projections, federal debt held by the public would reach 77.4 percent of GDP by 2020, with $114 billion of debt.

According to experts, the projected deficit for 2015 is 4 to 5 percent of GDP. A sustainable level is more like 3 percent or lower. The nation therefore requires deficit reduction of 1 to 2 percent of GDP, or about $200 billion to $400 billion, a year by 2015.

The government spent about $1.3 trillion more than it collected during the first eleven months of fiscal 2010, or about $100 billion less than the shortfall for the same period in fiscal 2009. "This year's deficit is expected to be the second-largest shortfall in the past sixty-five years. On October 15, 2010, the Treasury reported a near $1.3 trillion deficit for the year, down from 2009 but still the second largest in more than sixty years.

The deficit, up more than $1.29 trillion in 2010, was projected to be $1.5 trillion in 2011 and caused by a weak economy, higher spending, and fresh tax cuts. By 2017, the level of U.S. debt subject to the debt ceiling will hit $20.9 trillion. On April 13, President Obama called for reducing the deficit by $4 trillion over the next twelve years, including cuts in spending, pulling back on Medicare and Medicaid, and controlling tax loopholes.

By the end of June 2011, reducing the U.S. deficit turned into a political issue more than one of economics and the plight of the poor, the most vulnerable Americans. In 2008, the number of poor citizens climbed by 1.7 million to nearly 47.5 million. In 2009, the rise was leveled thanks to the stimulus packages. By 2011 and projected into 2012, the problems would expand, dealing with Medicaid, unemployment benefits, food aid, temporary assistance for needy families, etc.

For the first eleven months of the fiscal year, the budget deficit ($1.234 trillion) continued to run lower than in the same period one year earlier. The U.S. government spent $134.15 billion more than it collected the month before. The government predicted that the country would run a deficit of $1.28 trillion in fiscal 2011, which would be a bit less than the 2010 deficit of $1.294 trillion. On September 19, the president offered a new plan to reduce the federal deficit by more than $3 trillion over ten years, where about half would come from tax increases.

See also BUDGET (FISCAL 2011) PROPOSED; CONGRESSIONAL BUDGET OFFICE; DEBT; DEBT DEAL; DEFICIT (BUDGET, U.S.); DEFICIT-REDUCTION COMMITTEE; EXPORTS (U.S.); FEDERAL DEFICIT; FEDERAL RESERVE; FOOD AID; IMPORTS; MEDICAID; MISERY INDEX; NATIONAL COMMISSION ON FISCAL RESPONSIBILITY AND REFORM; SOCIAL SECURITY; TEMPORARY ASSISTANCE FOR NEEDY FAMILIES; TROUBLED ASSET RELIEF PROGRAM; UNEMPLOYMENT BENEFITS; WALL STREET REFORM ACT (2010).

DEFICIT COMMISSION. *Synonymous with* NATIONAL COMMISSION ON FISCAL RESPONSIBILITY AND REFORM.

DEFICIT PLAN. *See* DEFICIT (BUDGET, U.S.)

DEFICIT-REDUCTION COMMITTEE. Aimed to reduce the deficit by $433 billion over five years through $192 billion in spending cuts and tax increases of $241 billion. The panel was to recommend ways to lower federal deficits by at least $1.2 trillion over ten years or else the government would make across-the-board cuts in many federal programs to achieve those savings.

On November 21, 2011, the deficit-reduction super committee failed to reach its mandated goal of writing a bipartisan bill to reduce deficits over the next ten years by at least $1.2 trillion. Therefore, $1.2 trillion in automatic spending cuts were on track to begin in 2013, with roughly half coming from the Pentagon. The absence of an agreement threatened to send that country back into recession by raising taxes on almost everyone while lowering government spending on nearly everything. Failure meant cuts in 2013. Applications were expected in November, unless changed by Congress, would be as follows:

Defense: war funding—$9.9 billion reduction; other nonwar funding—$36.7 billion; funding carried over from previous years—$8.1 billion; military personnel—no reduction.

Nondefense: regular spending set by Congress—$38.5 billion reduction; mandatory spending, mostly farm support—$5.2 billion; Medicare payments to providers and plans—$10.8 billion; veterans health and Pell grants—no reduction.

Cf. BALANCED BUDGET ACT (1997); BUDGET ENFORCEMENT ACT (1990); DEBT DEAL; SEQUESTER.

Synonymous with JOINT SELECT COMMITTEE ON DEFICIT REDUCTION.

DEFICIT-REDUCTION PLANS. *See* DEBT DEAL; DEFICIT-REDUCTION COMMITTEE; NATIONAL COMMISSION ON FISCAL RESPONSIBILITY AND REFORM; TAX CUTS.

DEFLATION. Symptoms occur when goods pile up without buyers and prices steadily fall, suffocating new investment and worsening joblessness. Deflation occurs when falling prices become embedded in the mindset of households and businesses, causing them to delay spending, investing, and hiring because they believe goods, services, and labor will cost less in the future. Deflation accompanied the Great Depression of the 1930s. The decline in the general price level results in an increase in the purchase power of money.

Consumers and businesses worldwide lose their ability to purchase, and prices for many goods fall. Production is slowed, and layoffs are accelerated, taking more paychecks out of the economy, further weakening demand for products and services. Dropping profits reduce opportunities for profit, making firms reluctant to invest even when they can borrow money for free. From 1929 to 1933 prices fell by 27 percent.

As prices of consumer goods continued to fall in 2009, projected to be 1 percent, it brought the total drop from summer 2008 to the end of 2009 to about 4 percent. Twenty-two percent of U.S. consumers expected deflation during 2009, the highest proportion to anticipate declining prices in the past half a century.

Consumer prices in the United States advanced at their slowest pace in fifty years in 2008, raising concerns about deflation as the weakening economy suppressed demand for cars, clothing, electronics, and a host of goods and services. The consumer price index fell by a seasonally adjusted 0.7 percent in December 2008, its third consecutive monthly decline, after sliding 1.7 percent in November.

In July 2009, the annual contraction in eurozone consumer prices increased the risk of deflation. The rate fell 0.6 percent from a year earlier.

See also CONGRESSSIONAL BUDGET OFFICE; EUROZONE; FRUGALITY; JAPAN; SPAIN; SWITZERLAND.

Cf. INFLATION; REFLATION; STAGFLATION.

Synonymous with FALLING PRICES.

DELEVERAGE. A company's attempt to decrease its financial leverage, a leading issue in the Great Recession meltdown. The best way for a firm to deleverage is to immediately pay off an existing debt on its balance sheet; otherwise, there is the significant risk of defaulting.

See also DEBT; EURO.

Synonymous with DEBT REDUCTION.

DELEVERAGING. *See* DELEVERAGE.

DELINQUENCY RATES. On February 23, 2009, the Federal Reserve announced that delinquency rates on consumer and business loans at large banks were higher in the fourth quarter 2008, led by increases in residential-mortgage delinquencies, which neared 7 percent of outstanding mortgages.

See also COMMERCIAL REAL ESTATE LOANS.

DELINQUENT TAXPAYERS. *See* TAXPAYERS.

DELL. On May 28, 2009, the computer maker announced that it had a 63 percent drop in quarterly profit amid a 23 percent decline in revenue. This marked the third consecutive quarter of shrinking sales and profit at the company. Dell reported a 20 percent decline in laptop revenue and a 34 percent drop in desktop PCs for the quarter. The division that sells to large firms posted a 31 percent revenue slide. In August 2009, Dell reported that its revenue from consumers had climbed 2 percent in the second quarter, while revenue from large businesses fell 3 percent over the same time period.

Management reported in May 2010 that its profit for the quarter ending April 30 rose 52 percent from a year before to $441 million, with revenue climbing 21 percent to $14.87 billion. Still, the firm's gross profit margin fell to 16.9 percent from a year earlier at 17.6 percent. On August 19, 2010, management indicated that profit climbed 15 percent to $545 million in its fiscal second quarter. Revenue rose 22 percent to $15.53 billion. Dell then reported one of its strongest quarters in November 2010. Revenue was $15.4 billion. Fourth-quarter profit almost tripled; its shares surged 5 percent. Earnings climbed to $927 million, with revenue increasing 5 percent to $15.7 billion from the previous year.

Dell's profit nearly tripled for the quarter ending April 29, 2011, to $945 million. Revenue climbed 1 percent to $15.02 billion. The firm's second quarter 2011 profit surged 63 percent, with revenue climbing 0.8 percent to $15.66 billion. On November 15, management reported quarterly sales with revenue declining to $15.37 billion, with net income climbing to $893 million.

Cf. HEWLETT-PACKARD COMPANY; INTEL.

DELPHI. The Pension Benefit Guaranty Corporation (PBGC) agreed on July 22, 2009, to take on $6.2 billion in pension liabilities from the bankrupt auto supplier Delphi Corporation. The $6.2 billion rescue is PBGC's second-largest ranked by dollar. On July 30, Delphi won court approval to sell its assets to its lenders and General Motors, allowing the auto parts supplier to end its four-year stay in bankruptcy.

DELTA AIR LINES. Delta Air Lines reported in January 2009 a wider fourth-quarter loss. The world's largest carrier by traffic expected a 4 percent decline in passenger revenue in 2009. It was reducing its capacity by 6 to 8 percent to match the weaker demand.

Delta stated on April 6 that its international passenger traffic declined 15.1 percent in March. Business fell 13.9 percent in March, measured in revenue passenger miles. Delta posted a loss of $257 million for the second quarter 2009, compared with a loss of $1.04 billion a year before. Seat capacity was expected to decline 9 percent in 2009. In mid-September 2009, the airline projected an operating margin of 3 to 4 percent, while its passenger capacity would drop 5 to 6 percent from a year before. Delta's fourth-quarter 2009 loss was $25 million.

For the first quarter 2010, Delta announced on April 20 that it had narrowed its loss to $256 million. Delta's revenue rose 2 percent in the first-quarter to $6.85 billion from the year before. The airline reported on July 19 its best quarterly profit in a decade of $467 million, compared with a previous year loss of $257 million; revenue climbed 17 percent to $8.17 billion.

In October, the airline predicted that it would post its first fourth-quarter profit in ten years. Delta's revenue jumped 18 percent to $8.95 billion, with earnings of $363 million, compared with $161 million the year earlier. Delta expected to produce an operating margin of 6 to 8 percent for the fourth quarter. Third-quarter 2011 earnings were $549 million. Delta posted record fourth-quarter net of $425 million, with revenue climbing 8 percent to $8.4

billion. As US Airways examines possibilities and benefits of acquiring Delta, Delta in turn is looking at the possibly acquisition of US Airways.
See also AIRLINES.

DENMARK. The Danish economy was hit hard, if belatedly, by the global economic crisis but is projected to recover gradually as world trade regains momentum and as support is provided by the large automatic stabilizers, substantial fiscal easing, and low interest rates. Private consumption fell very steeply in late 2008 and early 2009 but less so subsequently, as it is being supported by tax cuts, withdrawals from the special pension scheme, and less depressed equity prices. Sentiment is up in manufacturing, and industrial production seems to have stabilized at a low level, while the number of new bankruptcies is coming down. Despite some withdrawal of the fiscal stimulus imparted in response to the crisis, the budget deficit is expected to remain large in 2011. Additional consolidation measures will be needed in due course to bring the fiscal position back on track with the long-term targets, and these measures should be spelled out sooner rather than later.

After years of strong expansion, the construction boom was now over and falling house prices have put an end to debt-financed consumption growth. As the impact of global financial turmoil materialized, forecasts remained weak during 2009, leading businesses to cut back investment. Denmark entered the slowdown with severe capacity pressures and wages rising much faster than warranted by productivity growth. There was thus little need for fiscal demand stimulus, especially since monetary conditions were set to ease along with those of the eurozone. Aggressive fiscal stimulus to keep unemployment at recent record-low levels would magnify the loss of competitiveness and, ultimately, challenge the stability of the fixed exchange rate regime. This would make it difficult to lower interest rates in line with cuts in the eurozone.

The nation's economy was expected to shrink 0.5 percent in 2009. Unemployment was 1.6 percent. Denmark announced on December 8, 2008, a bank support plan aimed at allaying the worst global credit crunch since the Great Depression. On February 23, Denmark seized control of Fiona Bank, a bank of 90,000 customers, by injecting about 1 billion Danish kroner, or about $172 million, in a deal that took away shareholder control and split the bank into two parts until a sale could be found.

It was projected that Denmark's economy would continue to recover in 2011, expanding by 1.6 percent. The nation's GDP growth was 1.6 percent, with a GDP of $292 billion, an inflation rate of 1.8 percent, and a GDP per head of $52,320.
See also FLEXICURITY; ICELAND.

DEPOSIT INSURANCE. *See* FEDERAL DEPOSIT INSURANCE CORPORATION.

DEPOSITORY AGREEMENT. *See* MORTGAGE CERTIFICATE.

DEPOSITORY INSTITUTION. A financial institution, such as a commercial bank, thrift, or credit union, that accepts deposits, including deposits by the Federal Deposit Insurance Corporation.

DEPOSITORY INSTITUTIONS DEREGULATION AND MONETARY CONTROL ACT. Legislation passed in the spring of 1980, this act committed the government to deregulating the banking system. It provided for the elimination of interest rate controls for banks and savings institutions within six years, and it authorized them to offer interest-bearing accounts beginning in 1981 anywhere in the country.

The act also wiped out all state usury laws on home mortgages above $25,000. It also modernized the mortgage instrument by repealing dollar limits, thus permitting second mortgages.

DEPRESSION (OF THE 1930S). *See* DOUBLE-DIP RECESSION; GREAT DEPRESSION.

DEPRESSION 2.0. Federal Reserve Chairman Bernanke's description for the Great Recession.

DERIVATIVE(S). A financial contract that specifies the terms of a future transaction (or set of transactions in some underlying assets). Its origin is from "derived"—the underlying asset price. A derivative is a powerful and mostly unregulated investment that became a primary source of controversy before and following the 2007 meltdown. It is a security whose price is dependent on or derived from one or more underlying assets. Derivatives enable people and companies to insure themselves against risk, allowing them to lower that risk. The derivative itself is merely a contract between two or more parties. Its value is determined by the fluctuations in the underlying asset. The most common underlying assets include stocks, bonds, commodities, currencies, interest rates, and market indexes. Most derivatives are characterized by high leverage.

This multitrillion-dollar market is presently traded as buyers and sellers go through one of a small group of big banks to trade these contracts. The banks mostly work among themselves to find a customer to complete the transaction, a system known as bilateral trading. Unlike the stock market, customers cannot see pricing or other trading information. Buyers and sellers are left uncertain if they have overpaid or have gotten a good deal. With the banks trading directly with each other, it heightens the risk that the failure of one bank could bring down the others. They system also tends to hide risks that big players such as hedge funds might be taking.

European regulators proposed new measures in July 2009, fueling concern that trading of these exotic contracts could be pushed onto exchanges, crimping the profits of banks that currently handle such transactions. The measures of the European Commission include expanding collection of trading information and broadening efforts to standardize the market. For the year, banks reported $22.6 billion in derivatives revenue.

Under the Dodd-Frank financial overhaul of 2010, many derivates will be in the future traded via clearinghouses. If regulators are successful in placing this new system, the clearinghouses will stand between the banks that trade derivates. Participants will post money with the clearinghouses, ensuring they can meet their obligations. Key committees at the clearinghouses are to be dominated by people from the banks that control the market. Other institutions will have been blocked from entering the market, and trading information is still not freely available.

See also BEAR STEARNS; BORN, BROOKSLEY; COMMODITY FUTURES MODERNIZATION ACT OF 2000; CREDIT DEFAULT SWAP; DERIVATIVES LEGISLATION; FINANCIAL REGULATION PLAN (2009); GOLDMAN SACHS; HOUSE (U.S.) FINANCIAL OVERHAUL PLAN; LEHMAN BROTHERS; LONG-TERM CAPITAL MANAGEMENT; SUMMERS, LAWRENCE; SWAP CONTRACT; WALL STREET REFORM ACT (2010).

Synonymous with DERIVATIVE CONTRACT.

DERIVATIVE CONTRACT. *Synonymous with* DERIVATIVE.

DERIVATIVE DEPOSIT. A deposit that is created when a person borrows money from a bank. A customer is lent a sum, not in money but by credit to his or her account, against which he or she may draw checks as required.

DERIVATIVE MARKET. The manipulation of options and futures stemming partly from the huge leverage they afford.

Synonymous with SHADOW MARKET.

DERIVATIVES LEGISLATION. Proposals in Congress that would have these products, which have not been regulated, fall under the jurisdiction of the Securities and Exchange Commission and the Commodities Future Trading Commission. Credit default swaps would also be regulated. By mid-September 2009, the House of Representatives was considering several bills.

See also WALL STREET REFORM ACT (2010).

DESTOCKING. The recession-induced paring back of inventories. By mid-2010, destocking appeared to end as firms began increasing inventory to keep pace with rising demand.

DEUTSCHE BANK. A German bank that has kept itself from resorting to public bailouts but now has the German government as an indirect shareholder. The state owns 30 percent of Deutsche Post, which on January 14, 2009, agreed to take an 8 percent stake in Deutsche Bank.

Deutsche Bank reported in late October 2009 that its third-quarter profit would be about €1.4 billion. The bank reported a net profit in the fourth quarter 2009 of 1.32 billion euros, compared to a net loss the year before of 4.79 billion euros.

For the first quarter 2010, the bank's net income rose by half compared with the year before. Deutsche Bank, on December 21, agreed to pay $553 million and admit to criminal wrongdoing. The bank therefore avoided prosecution for helping 2,100 customers evade taxes through 2,300 financial transactions occurring between 1996 and 2002, with attempts to assist wealthy Americans to lose more than $29 billion in fraudulent tax losses. The bank had a fourth-quarter 54 percent net profit of 601 million euros, with a record revenue of $10.2 billion.

The bank's profit and revenue soared nearly 5 percent after it reported its best first quarter since the meltdown began in 2007. Profit climbed 17 percent to $3.11 billion, with net revenue climbing 17 percent. On October 4, the bank, the largest in Germany, said it would not meet its profit goals for the year. It planned to cut costs and raise capital. It would not meet its 2011 profit goal of $13.3 billion and it would take a loss of 250 million euros on its Greek debt and eliminate 500 investment banking jobs, mostly outside of Germany. Third-quarter net income was $1.08 billion.

On February 2, 2012, it was reported that the bank's profit fell 69 percent in the fourth quarter 2011, earning $244.8 million. Deutsche Bank's net income for the year was 4.3 billion euros.

See also FEDERAL HOUSING FINANCE AGENCY; GERMANY.

DEUTSCHE POST. *See* DEUTSCHE BANK; DHL.

DEVELOPING ECONOMIES. *See* WORLD BANK, THE.

DEVELOPMENTALLY CHALLENGED POPULATION. *See* UNEMPLOYMENT.

DEXIA SA. A Belgian-French Bank that is one of the European Union's twenty largest in assets. On October 4, bank executives and government personnel came forward with a drastic plan to break up the bank. The bank gave governments across the United States easy access to cheap financing by agreeing to "backstop," or purchase unsold bonds, in the $2.9 trillion municipal-debt market. By June 2011, management stated that they had taken back about $400 million in main debt because of troubled remarketing. Its shares fell about 20 percent. As of June 30, the bank had total assets, including derivatives of $689.5 billion, and a leverage ratio of 74.5. Then, on October 7, Standard & Poor's lowered its credit rating on Dexia to A-/A2 from A/A1.

On October 9, France, Belgium, and Luxembourg agreed on a plan for the restructuring of Dexia to permit the breakup of the bank and the government ownership of its Belgian subsidiary. The board approved the sale of the Belgian arm, calling for the Belgian government to pay $5.4 billion for the Belgian unit. The federal government therefore will own all of Dexia Bank Belgium at first, but later shares of the banks will probably be sold to the Belgian regional governments.

DHL. Owned by Deutsche Post of Germany, the package delivery company cut 9,500 jobs at its U.S. unit on November 10, 2008, and effectively conceded the American domestic market to its rivals, FedEx and United Parcel Service.

DIAMOND, ROBERT E. President of Barclays PLC and chief executive officer of Barclays Capital.

DIAMOND SALES. *See* TIFFANY.

DIET. The Great Recession has led to a decrease in fruit and vegetable consumption. With a 1 percent increase in unemployment, a 2 percent to 4 percent fall in fruit and vegetable consumption, and an 8 percent drop in salad consumption resulted. After the beginning of the economic meltdown in December 2007, the national unemployment rate doubled from 5 percent to 10 percent in two years. Fruit and vegetable consumption fell by 10 percent to 20 percent among the unemployed.

DIMON, JAMIE. Chairman and chief executive officer of JP Morgan Chase.

DINING OUT. *See* EATING OUT.

DISABLED WORKERS. Disabled workers during the Great Recession were more likely than the overall workforce to be older and working part time or jobless. In 2009, the average unemployment rate for disabled workers was 14.5 percent, far above the 9 percent rate for those without disabilities. There are 27 million Americans sixteen years and older with a disability. The unemployment rate for those people with disabilities climbed to 16.4 percent in July 2010.

Those with disabilities were three times as likely as those without to be sixty-five years or older. Nearly one-third of workers with disabilities worked only part time compared to a fifth of those without disabilities. Disabled workers with college degrees had a jobless rate of 8.3 percent compared to 4.5 percent of those without disabilities.

In 2001, 5 million workers collected a federal disability benefit. Ten years later, it had increased to 8.2 million, costing taxpayers $115 billion a year, or about $1,500 per household.

DISCLOSURE REQUIREMENTS. *See* REGULATORS; SECURITIES AND EXCHANGE COMMISSION.

DISCOUNT WINDOW. *See* FEDERAL RESERVE.

DISCOVER FINANCIAL SERVICES. On September 20, 2010 Discover reported a fiscal third-quarter profit of $260.6 million, with revenue falling 7 percent from the year before to $1.7 billion.

DISNEY. *See* ABC.

DISPLAY ADVERTISING. *See NEW YORK TIMES.*

DISPOSABLE INCOME. *See* SAVINGS RATE.

DISTRESSED ASSETS. *See* "BAD BANKS."

DISTRESSED SALES. In the housing industry, a situation when sellers face foreclosure or are forced to sell their home for less than the value of the mortgage.
See also HOUSING.

DIVIDENDS. For the first time in fifty years, U.S. firms announced more negative dividend actions (reductions or eliminations) than positive ones (increases and resumptions) in 2009. In the peak quarter for bad news, the first quarter of 2009, almost two-thirds of the changes were negative. But by the end of the year, positive actions were beginning to predominate.
See also TAX CUTS.

DIVORCE. *See* MARRIAGE.

DODD, CHRISTOPHER J. The head of the U.S. Senate Banking Committee, Senator Dodd of Connecticut wanted in the fall 2009 to merge four agencies and diminish the role of the Federal Reserve as a system-wide overseer, a plan significantly different from President Obama's position.

On February 3, 2010, Senator Dodd argued that he backed the concept to curb risky activity but felt that its late emergence as presented by the Volcker Rule imperiled his own bill. The Wall Street Reform Act was his achieving legacy in the Senate before retiring.
See also CONSUMER FINANCIAL PROTECTION AGENCY; VOLCKER, PAUL; WALL STREET REFORM ACT (2010).

DODD-FRANK FINANCIAL REFORM. *See* WALL STREET REFORM ACT (2010).

DODD-FRANK REGULATORY LAW. *See* WALL STREET REFORM ACT (2010).

DODD-FRANK WALL STREET REFORM AND CONSUMER PRO-TECTION ACT. *See* WALL STREET REFORM ACT (2010).

DOLE FOODS. On March 15, 2011, management reported a brisk fourth-quarter loss, with an 11 percent sales increase for its foods. Dole posted in the quarter ending January 1, 2011, a loss of $37 million, compared to a profit in the previous year of $16 million.

DOLLAR GENERAL. Throughout the meltdown, Dollar General discovered the value to the consumer of their low-ticketing policy. By February 2010, the firm reported that it would add 5,000 jobs as its opened 600 stores in 2010. In total, Dollar General operates 8,800 stores with about 78,000 workers.

The retailer's fiscal third-quarter 2010 profit was $128.1 million, climbing 69 percent. Sales climbed 10 percent to $3.22 billion.

On January 3, 2011, management announced plans to open 625 new stores after its revenue climbed 10 percent to $3.22 billion. On June 1, management reported that its fiscal first-quarter profit rose 15 percent to $157 million. Sales climbed 11 percent to $3.45 billion. The retailer's fiscal second-quarter 2011 earnings climbed 3.4 percent, with a profit of $146 million. Sales climbed 11 percent to $3.58 billion. In December, management said that its fiscal third-quarter earnings surged 34 percent, with a profit of $171.2 million. Sales climbed 12 percent to $3.6 billion.

See also DOLLAR STORES; RETAILING.

DOLLAR INDEX. *See* U.S. DOLLAR INDEX.

DOLLAR STORES. Throughout the recession, these $1 items stores have witnessed an increase in sales as more people could only afford inexpensive items in small quantities as sold in dollar stores. From June 2009 to June 2010, dollar stores increased the number of customer visits by 2.6 percent compared to the year before.

See also DOLLAR GENERAL; RETAILING.

DOLLAR (U.S.). On February 29, 2008, the dollar hit a record low against the euro, deepening a six-year slide in which it was off more than 40 percent against the currency amid a softening U.S. labor market, weak housing, and slowing growth. As the economic crisis unfolded during the third quarter into the fourth of 2008, the dollar strengthened against the euro, the British pound, and the Swiss franc. The dollar remained the world's reserve currency. By December 15, the dollar had commenced a downward trajectory as the world digested the implications of a difficult recession in the United States. The euro soared past $1.44 in its sharpest daily movement ever. The euro gained

15 percent against the dollar after it hit a low for the year of $1.2453 on November 20. The dollar's December performance was good, as the currency emerged from a seven-year downtrend in 2008. The dollar had fallen against the yen but ended 2008 higher against the sterling (pound) and the euro. For the year 2008, the dollar strengthened 4.5 percent against the euro, 36 percent against the British pound, and 22 percent against the Canadian dollar. It also jumped 30 percent or more against the Brazilian real, the South Korean won, and the Turkish lira, and strengthened 24 percent against the Russian ruble.

The year 2009 began with a three-week high against the yen. China proposed on March 23 a replacement of the U.S. dollar as the world's standard. On October 8, 2009, the U.S. dollar fell to a fourteen-month low against other world currencies. The dollar was down 11.9 percent against a basket of currencies since President Obama's administration took office in January.

The dollar fell on October 7, 2010, to new lows against nations vying to keep their currencies weak and exports competitive. Since the end of August, the dollar had fallen 7 percent against a basket of currencies.

The U.S. dollar dropped on April 29, 2011, to its lowest point since the summer of 2008.

See also CHINA; EURO; POUND.

DOMENICI, PETER. *See* BIPARTISAN POLICY CENTER DEBT REDUCTION TASK FORCE.

DOMESTIC MIGRATION. *See* MOBILITY.

DOUBLE-DECKER FUNDS. Originally developed in the Japanese financial markets, funds that bundle high-return assets with high-yield currencies. The first layer is to invest in assets like stocks or bonds, often with large coupons or dividends. Those returns are then turbocharged with foreign-exchange derivatives, which make an equal-sized currency bet. Yields then become attractive.

DOUBLE-DIP RECESSION. Usually commences with a recession where unemployment rises to a high level and then drops at a disappointingly slow rate. Prior to employment returning to normal, there is a second recession. As long as the economic recovery isn't complete, that is a double recession, even if there are years between the declines. Historically, there has only been one U.S. double-dip recession. It began with the 1929–1933 recession, followed by the 1937–1938 recession. Between those declines, the unemployment rate never dropped below 12.2 percent.

By August 2011, following huge falls in global markets, many experts were increasingly talking of a double-dip recession, some declaring that it was already present. It had been three decades since the country suffered a recession that followed on the heels of the previous one. By late summer, many experts believed a double-dip recession had crossed the 50/50 line of possibility, with job growth slowed in the past four months to a pace that is typically associated with the start of a recession. Job growth was slower than population growth, which ultimately causes unemployment to rise, another major indicator of a relapsed economy. In nations of the eurozone by the mid-end of 2011, many experts believed that the seventeen countries were already in a double-dip recession.

See also BANK STOCKS; CONFERENCE BOARD; RECESSION.

Synonymous with GREAT RECESSION II.

DOW. *See* DOW JONES INDUSTRIAL AVERAGE.

DOW CHEMICAL. On December 8, 2008, it was announced that 5,000 jobs would be cut due to the economic slowdown. It would close twenty facilities and cut 11 percent of its global workforce in light of the global economic slump. On December 10, Dow forecast fourth-quarter earnings of 30 cents a share.

Then, on February 3, 2009, it reported a loss before exceptional items of 62 cents a share. Dow cut operating capacity in the face of slumping demand but couldn't cut fast enough; utilization slumped to 44 percent in December. On July 30, the company reported a quarterly loss of $435 million. Dow Chemical met a fourth-quarter estimate with a profit as revenue climbed 15 percent. The firm posted a profit of $172 million, following a previous year loss of $1.55 billion. Revenue increased to $12.47 billion from $10.85 billion a year before.

In August 2010, Dow Chemical reported that its second-quarter results remained weak and that revenue rose 20 percent to $13.62 billion, with a profit of $651 million. Dow Chemical's third-quarter 2010 profit fell 25 percent to $595 million.

Reported in October 2011 earnings of $900 million. Net sales increased 17 percent to $15.1 billion.

See also GENERAL MOTORS; PUBLIC-PRIVATE INVESTMENT PROGRAM; STOCK MARKET.

DOW JONES-AIG COMMODITY INDEX. A broad benchmark, it finished 2008 with a 37 percent loss, the worst year since the index began in 1998.

DOW JONES INDUSTRIAL AVERAGE (DJIA) (DOW). The averages of closing prices of thirty representative industrial stocks, fifteen public utility stocks, twenty transportation stocks, and an average of the sixty-five computers at the end of a trading day on the New York Stock Exchange.

On January 3, 2008, the Dow fell 220.86 points, or 1.7 percent, in the first trading session of the year. Twelve months later, on January 2, 2009, it rose 258.3 points, or 2.94 percent, to 9,034.69. It ended at 8,000.86, down 148.15, 8.84 percent for the month, making January 2009 the worst January in its 113-year history. On February 20, the Dow lost nearly half its value, or 47 percent, since its record close sixteen months earlier.

The Dow Jones Industrial Average tumbled on March 2 below 7,000 for the first time in twelve years as investors appeared to be giving up hope and girding for a prolonged recession. The Dow fell 4.2 percent to 6,763.29, its lowest close since April 1997, thus losing almost one-quarter of its value in 2009 and more than half since its high in October 2007. On March 23, in reaction to the Treasury secretary's announcement of the Public-Private Investment Program, the Dow soared 6.8 percent, or 497.48 points, to 7,775.86 in its biggest gain since October 2008. It finished the first quarter 2009 at 7,608.92, down 13 percent. The string of quarterly declines was the longest stretch since the six quarters that ended in June 1970, and the worst first quarter in percentage terms since 1939.

By the end of April, the Dow was up 24 percent from its March low. Then, on May 6, 2010, the DJIA, over a period of about one hour, plunged nearly 1,000 points and then made a partial recovery. The following day, the DJIA, following the commitment of nearly $1 trillion to bailout Europe, soared to the largest point gain since March 23, 2009. The DJIA on May 20 fell 376 points, a plunge of more than 1,000 points in a matter of weeks. Partially, this was a reaction to the plunge on fears of a spreading European crisis, with a close at 3.6 percent. On May 28, 2010, the DJIA fell 122.36 points, or 1.2 percent, its worst May fall since 1940. Stocks fell 7.92 percent. On October 19, the DJIA had its worst day since mid-August, falling below 11,000. This behavior was attributed to China's sudden decision to raise rates. The DJIA then, on November 4, climbed 219.71 points, or 2 percent, to 11,434.84, its highest close since September 8, 2002, just before the Lehman bankruptcy filing began the most intense phase of the Great Recession. The index was now up 75 percent from its March 2009 low, with a need to climb 24 percent to return to its all-time high set in October 2007. The DJIA jumped to a two-year high on December 14, 2010, climbing 47.98, or 0.4 percent, ending the day at 11,476.5, the highest since September 8, 2008.

On January 1, 2011, the DJIA closed above 12,000 for the first time since June 2008. The Dow rose 148.23 points, or 1.25 percent. By the end of January, the Dow was up 4 percent, having surged 20 percent since the end of August. For the entire month of January, the DJIA had its strongest monthly gain in fourteen years. The Dow's 2.7 percent gain for the month was the strongest since 1997 and the first positive January in four years.

Following the resignation of Egypt's president, Hosni Mubarak, the DJIA on February 11, 2011, reached a 2.5-year high, climbing 0.4 percent to 12,273.36, its highest close since June 13, 2008. On July 19, the DJIA posted its biggest percentage and point advance in 2011, rebounding 202.26 points, or 1.6 percent, to 12,587.42. The day following the president's signing of the debt ceiling, the DJIA fell below 12,000, plunging 265.87 points, or 2.2 percent, to 11,866.62. Then, on August 4, the DJIA posted its worst point fall since the financial crisis in December 2008, dropping 512.76 points, or 4.31 percent, to 11,383.68. The decline was the ninth worst by points for the Dow.

Standard & Poor's downgrade of the U.S. credit rating devastated the DJIA on August 9; the selloff was the sharpest one-day fall since the financial meltdown began in 2008. The DJIA closed that day down 634.76 points, or 5.5 percent, at 10,809.85, its lowest close since October 2010. This was the sixth-largest point decline ever. Marking the first time in the 115-year old history, the DJIA moved by more than 400 points for four consecutive days. It surged 423.37 points, or 3.9 percent, on August 11 to 11,143.31.

Worldwide total stock value ranges from about $30 trillion to about $55 trillion. During the week of August 1–5, losses in total stock value worldwide was estimated at between $2.5 trillion and more than $4 trillion. The DJIA tumbled on September 2, with the worst start to September since 1974. The DJIA fell 253.31 points, or 2.20 percent, to 11,240.26. On September 9, the DJIA plunged 303.68 points, or 2.69 percent, to 10,992.13 based primarily on new fears on Europe. Two critical members of the European Central Bank resigned in protest over the bank's strategy to resolve Europe's debt problems. On September 22, the DJIA fell 391.01 points, or 3.5 percent, to 10,733.83. The Dow had fallen 16 percent from its April high, approaching the 20 percent fall that would signal a bear market. For the week ending on September 24, the DJIA lost 6.4 percent of its value, the worst week since October 2008. The DJIA ended the third quarter down 12 percent, its worst percentage fall since the first quarter of 2009. The selloff was illustrative of a dismal quarter marked by anxiety about the European sovereign-debt crisis, the U.S. economy approaching a possible double-dip recession, and the fall of gold prices. In late November 2011, with growing uncertainty in European financial markets, the DJIA had its worst Thanksgiving week since 1942, losing 7.6 percent of its value over the previous two weeks.

On November 30, 2011, following the announcement by central bankers that a program was in place to contain the European debt crisis, the DJIA rose more than 4 percent, or 490.05 points. It was the largest rise since March 23, 2009. The day following the European Union's summit on December 9, the reaction was negative, with Germany's main stock index falling 3.4 percent, France's down 2.6 percent, and Italy's plunging 3.8 percent. The DJIA lost

162.87 points, or 1.34 percent, to 12,021.39. By year's end, the DJIA reached a five-month high by adding 124.35 points, or 1 percent, to 12,294.00. The Dow was back to where it was in July 2010, just as the European debt crisis and the congressional deficit-reduction confrontations were coming to a head. Then, on December 29, the DJIA rose 135.63 points, or 1.12 percent, to 12,287.04, taking back nearly all the previous session's 140-point decline.

On January 2, 2012, with a burst of the U.S. credit rating downgrade and the EU debt crisis, investors had endured a volatile 2011. The DJIA began the new year by rising nearly 6 percent. On the last trading day in 2011, the DJIA fell 69.48 to 12,217.56, leaving it up 5.53 percent for the year. Following a brief turnaround on August 9, the following day the DJIA fell 519.83 points, or 4.62 percent, to 10,719.94. It was the fourth triple-digit move in five days and brought its declines since its April peak to more than 16 percent. At that time, the DJIA was less than 500 points away from officially being in a bear market, defined as a decline of 20 percent. Blue chips were the stars in 2011 as the DJIA ended a 12 percent rally for the fourth quarter. By month's end the DJIA rose 3.4 percent, the best performance to open a year since 1997. On February 3, the DJIA broke through to its highest close since May 2008, gaining 156.82 points, or 1.23 percent, to 12,862.23.

See also EUROPE (BAILOUT); EUROPEAN CENTRAL BANK; FEDERAL RESERVE; "FLASH CRASH."

Cf. STANDARD & POOR'S.

DOWNTOWN. By fall 2010, office space rental had slipped in suburban areas when firms sought lower rentals, less crime, and shorter commuting time for workers. Now, city downtowns were filling up again as the office space in the surrounding suburbs continues to empty. Suburbs have been harder hit by the recession

DP WORLD. *See* DUBAI.

DRAGHI, MARIO. Became the European Central Bank's president in October 2011. On December 2, he offered a road map for policy makers, asking eurozone governments to evolve a "new fiscal compact." In his first month, he presided over an interest rate cut, signaled a greater willingness to deploy the bank's resources to fight the debt crisis in the European Union, and turned up the pressure on governments to remake the eurozone.

In early 2012, he would face the choice between escalating the Ebb's bond purchases or letting the borrowing costs approach ruinous levels. Crisis-hit nations on the eurozone periphery must repay about $115 billion of bonds that are due in the first three months of 2012.

See also EUROPEAN CENTRAL BANK.

DRESSING UP BOOKS. *See* MASKING.

D.R. HORTON. One of the two largest home builders in the United States, it reported on August 4, 2009, its ninth consecutive quarterly loss, where revenue fell 36 percent to $914.1 million and orders fell 7.5 percent to 5,089.

The home builder posted a profit for the quarter ending March 31, 2010, with a 55 percent increase in new orders compared to the year before. It had a profit of $11.4 million for its fiscal second quarter, with home sales gross margin rising to 18 percent from 13.3 percent. On August 3, the home builder reported a 60 percent surge in quarterly closings.

Cf. PULTE.

DRIVING. U.S. citizens drove more miles in 2010 than in any year since 2007. Three trillion miles were driven in 2010, the third highest total on record and an increase of 0.7 percent from 2009.

See also AUTOMOBILE INDUSTRY.

DUBAI. By November 2008, the world financial crisis hit Dubai, slamming the door nearly shut on its galloping development. Projects were delayed as tourism was declining and the government explored ways to collect taxes.

Life in the United Arab Emirates changed rapidly. Before 2008, a typical government position paid $3,600 a month; marriage prospects were supported with a free piece of land and about $200,000 to build a house, plus access to a ten- to twenty-year interest-free loan. Dubai's debt was $50 billion more than the GDP of the entire Emirates in 2006. On November 24, the United Arab Emirates began to bail out rattled lenders, consolidate the financial sector, and cap a building spree as it moved to cut spending in the face of the credit crisis. Dubai's sovereign debt stood at $10 billion, while the debts of state-affiliated companies amounted to $70 billion. By December, Dubai held $90 billion in government assets and $260 billion in assets. While Dubai started 2008 on a high, it ended the year with the Emirates' economic model unraveling. Its problems could mean a drastic change in economic power within the United Arab Emirates.

The United Arab Emirates announced on February 22, 2009, that it would spend $10 billion to bail out the once-high-flying emirate of Dubai. A debt crisis in Dubai in November 2009 brought a stock market tumble throughout Europe and Asia, creating the largest one-day fall in values since April. On November 25 the sprawling conglomerate—the state-owned Dubai World—sought a six-month standstill on interest payments tied to roughly $60 billion in debts. Dubai gorged on debt and borrowed too much to finance a building boom that went bust in the global meltdown. Dubai's debt debacle had created a new fear that government default by heavily indebted nations was spreading around the globe. Dubai's stock market fell 6.4 percent as its debt concerns continued to spin downward by 27 percent since November 25, 2009.

Throughout 2009, Abu Dhabi committed $25 billion to Dubai in subordinated loans yielding a mere 4 percent. By mid-May 2010, Dubai World reached an agreement to pay off its creditors and reduce its $23.5 billion in debt, which hopefully would revive global confidence in the Dubai government. On August 17, 2010, Dubai World posted a 10 percent rise in first-half net profit of $206 million, up from $188 million in 2009. On Friday, September 10, the state-run investment arm Dubai World reported that 99 percent of its creditors had agreed to the terms for restructuring $24.9 billion in debt.

See also ABU DHABI; MIDDLE EAST.

DUBAI WORLD. *See* ABU DHABI; DUBAI.

DUNCAN, ARNE. Secretary of the Department of Education in the first term of the Obama administration.

See also EDUCATION.

DUPONT. The chemical company posted a fourth-quarter 2008 net loss on a $500 million restructuring charge and cut its 2009 earning guidance amid slowing global chemical demand.

Sales fell 17 percent in its first quarter 2009, and DuPont reported on April 21 that profits fell 59 percent in their product sales volume. First-quarter net income fell to $488 million from $1.2 billion a year before. DuPont expected to cut an additional 2,000 jobs in a restructuring plan announced in April. DuPont's second-quarter profit plunged 61 percent as the meltdown continued for its products. The company reported earnings of $417 million, down from the $10.08 billion a year earlier. The company's third-quarter 2009 earnings rose 11 percent from a year before to $409 million. Sales declined 18 percent to $5.96 billion. DuPont jumped to a fourth-quarter 2009 profit of $441 million, with revenue climbing 12 percent to $6.81 billion.

The firm's first-quarter 2010 profit more than doubled to $1.13 billion from $488 million the year before. Net sales grew 23 percent to $8.48 billion. Its revenue rose 6 percent in the first quarter, with earnings up 10 percent. DuPont's second-quarter profit nearly tripled to $1.16 billion.

On January 24, 2012, DuPont reported a fourth-quarter profit of $373 million, with net sales up 14 percent.

See also UNEMPLOYMENT.

DURABLE GOODS. Durable goods orders rose 3.4 percent in February 2009 following a 7.3 percent decline in January. Orders for durable goods fell 0.8 percent in March.

In July 2009, new orders for durable goods increased 4.9 percent from their level in June, suggesting that companies' inventory levels had reached the point where they needed to increase orders to keep pace with demand. Durable goods were up 2.9 percent in November, with orders up 0.2 percent to a seasonally adjusted $166.87 billion.

Business items for long-lasting manufactured items fell for a second consecutive month in October 2011, with an overall drop of 0.7 percent on top of the September decline of 1.5 percent.

DUTCH. *See* NETHERLANDS, THE.

E

EARMARKS. President Obama signed a $410 billion spending bill on March 11, 2009, that included thousands of pet projects inserted by lawmakers, even as he unveiled regulations to restrict such activity.

The 2010 federal spending bills disclosed $10.2 billion for pet projects earmarks—a decline of nearly a third since 2008. The 9,297 earmarks in spending legislation for 2010 would be down from 11,282 reported for the fiscal year ending September 30. The 2009 earmarks were worth $14.3 billion.

EARNED INCOME TAX CREDIT. The 2009 economic stimulus plan sought to expand the Earned Income Tax Credit temporarily in order to raise the pay of the working poor.

See also TAX CUTS.

EARNINGS. *See* COST-CUTTING.

EASTERN EUROPE. By the end of November 2008, the European Bank for Reconstruction and Development cut its growth forecast for the region by half. The future appeared to include several years of low or no growth. The average growth among countries of Eastern Europe dropped to 3.2 percent in 2008 from 5.4 percent in 2007. Since peaking in the summer 2008, Poland's currency slumped 48 percent against the euro, Hungary's had fallen 30 percent, and the Czech Republic's was off 21 percent.

On February 26, 2009, the World Bank, European Bank for Reconstruction and Development (EBRD), and the European Investment Bank announced the offer of $31 billion for struggling banks in Eastern Europe to help head off a precipitous slide in the economies of these nations. In response to a call for assistance, on March 1 European Union leaders rejected a call for a sweeping bailout, further straining the bonds holding together the twenty-seven EU nations. A special EU fund of up to $241 billion to protect the weakest members was requested. Governments of the EU had by March already spent $380 billion in bank recapitalizations and put up $3.17 trillion to guarantee banks' loans and try to get credit moving again. By mid-month, the recession hit consumers with higher food prices. In Hungary, monthly food inflation had jumped 2.7 percent in January, as well as in many other Eastern European nations.

In both Slovakia and Latvia, GDP dropped 11.2 percent in the first quarter. Hungary's economy would contract by 2.3 percent. The International Monetary Fund forecast a 4.9 percent average decline in GDP, while the EBRD projected a 5.2 percent drop. By June, the biggest concern was the Baltic three, which saw the sharpest falls in GDP. Estonia's first-quarter figures indicated a decline of 15.6 percent, Latvia's drop was 18 percent, and in Lithuania, 12.6 percent. The economies of eight nations in Eastern Europe were predicted to grow by 1.7 percent in 2012, half of what it had earlier expected. The eurozone slowdown was expected to hurt 2012 GDP for Eastern European nations.

See also CZECH REPUBLIC; EUROPEAN BANK FOR RECON-STRUCTION AND DEVELOPMENT; EUROPEAN UNION; HUNGARY; INTERNATIONAL MONETARY FUND; POLAND; ROMANIA; RUS-SIA; SLOVENIA.

EASTMAN KODAK. The 130-year-old company planned 3,500 to 4,500 more layoffs in 2009, or 14 to 18 percent of its workforce, and disclosed on February 4 that it anticipated a loss from continuing operations of $400 million to $600 million. Sales in 2008 fell 24 percent to $2.43 billion, with film down 27 percent and digital products such as cameras, printers, and picture frames down 30 percent.

The company's first-quarter net loss widened to about triple the previous year's level. Kodak's cash shrank 40 percent to $1.3 billion. On July 30, Eastman Kodak posted a second-quarter 2009 loss of $189 million; its gross profit margin fell to 18.5 percent, and revenue declined by 29 percent. The company announced on October 29 that it had lost $111 million in the third quarter as sales fell 26 percent. Sales dropped to $1.78 billion from $2.41 billion. Reversing a fourth-quarter 2009 loss, the company's profit was $443 million, with revenue climbing 6 percent to $2.58 billion.

Kodak swung to a profit in the first quarter 2010 of $119 million, compared to a loss the year before of $353 million. The company narrowed its third-quarter 2010 loss to $43 million, with net sales climbing 25 percent to $670 million. Fourth-quarter profit was down 95 percent.

Management reported on July 26, 2011, that it had its fifth consecutive quarter of losses. Its stock was selling at $1.77, a fall of 10 percent. Kodak hadn't closed below $2 since the 1950s. Kodak's stock price has slipped nearly 70 percent since the beginning of 2011.

In early January 2012, the firm's stock was trading at 50 cents a share, and bankruptcy was imminent. On January 19, running low on cash, the firm put itself into bankruptcy court.

EATING OUT. Americans ate out an average of 3.3 times a week before the meltdown of 2007. In 2010, that figure fell to 3.1. In 2007, 53 percent of all meals were prepared outside the home; today, it is 47 percent. As of September 2010, there were 579,102 restaurants in the country, down 1 percent from 584,653 the year before.

See also CHAIN RESTAURANTS; FRIENDLY'S ICE CREAM CORPORATION.

EATON CORPORATION. A diversified manufacturer in Cleveland, Ohio, it announced on January 20, 2009, that it planned to cut 5,200 jobs, or about 6 percent of its workforce. This figure was in addition to the 3,400 layoffs announced in the second half of 2008, bringing the total to 10 percent. Eaton posted a 39 percent decline in third-quarter 2009 profit, declining to $193 million from $315 million a year before. The firm's net sales in the quarter dropped 26 percent to $3.03 billion.

Its second-quarter 2010 earnings soared with a profit of $226 million. Eaton's third-quarter 2010 earnings jumped 39 percent. Management reported a profit of $268 million, and revenue increased 18 percent to $3.57 billion. Gross margin increased to 30.6 percent from 28.1 percent.

EBAY. First-quarter profit in 2009 dropped 22 percent amid consumer reluctance to spend in the meltdown economy. eBay's revenue fell 8 percent from a year before to $2.02 billion.

For its first quarter 2010, eBay reported higher revenue and profit, with income rising to $397.6 million from $357.1 million the year before. Revenue climbed to $2.2 billion from $2.02 billion the year earlier. Its second-quarter profit then rose 26 percent following a 6 percent growth in revenue. eBay's third-quarter earnings climbed 23 percent, with a 0.5 percent increase in revenue. Revenue increased 22 percent to $838 million. The firm posted a 5 percent revenue increase for its fourth quarter, with profit falling 59 percent—new revenue at nearly $2.5 billion with profit totaling $559.2 million.

In October 2011, eBay had its largest quarterly revenue surge in five years. It posted a 14 percent climb in net income to $491 million and a 32 percent increase in revenue to $3 billion.

eBay reported on January 18, 2012, that it had its largest revenue increase in six years, as sales in the fourth quarter 2011 climbed 35 percent from the year before. Income rose 79 percent to $3.2 billion.

EBRD. *See* EUROPEAN BANK FOR RECONSTRUCTION AND DEVELOPMENT.

EC. *See* EUROPEAN COMMISSION.

ECB. *See* EUROPEAN CENTRAL BANK.

ECONOMIC STIMULUS PLAN • 185

ECONOMIC CYCLE RESEARCH INSTITUTE. A private forecasting firm in New York City founded by Geoffrey H. Moore, a one-time Rutgers University and Columbia University economist who died in 2000. Forecasts and projects the economy utilizing huge amount of economic data. The institution had a perfect fifteen-year record in calling recessions. Management predicts that the GDP rate is likely to go negative by the first quart of 2012, if not earlier, and that a second recession would commence.
See also NATIONAL BUREAU OF ECONOMIC RESEARCH.

ECONOMIC NATIONALISM. The urge to keep jobs and capital at home. This urges banks to support businesses and jobs within their boundaries, not abroad.
See also NATIONALIZATION; PROTECTIONISM.

ECONOMIC PEARL HARBOR. *See* BUFFETT, WARREN E.

ECONOMIC OUTPUT. *See* GLOBAL ECONOMIC OUTPUT.

ECONOMIC RECOVERY. By April 2010, there were hopeful signs of an economic recovery, with strong performances in a cross-section of economic sectors indicating a robust turnaround:

- Retail sales: + 9.1 percent in March
- New homes sales: + 26.9 percent in March
- Durable goods: +2.8 percent in March
- Exports: +14.8 percent in January–February

See also RECOVERY.

ECONOMIC RECOVERY ADVISORY BOARD (ERAB). Intended to help craft the Obama administration's response to the financial crisis.
See also VOLCKER, PAUL.

ECONOMIC STIMULUS PLAN (BILL FROM HOUSE OF REPRE-SENTATIVES). The House passed an $819 billion tax-and-spending bill on Wednesday, January 28, 2009, to reshape policies on energy, education, health care, and social programs. Major goals included:

- Doubling generating capacity for renewable energy over three years.
- Undertaking a program to weatherize 75 percent of federal buildings and 2 million homes.
- Computerizing every American's health record within five years.
- Launching a school-modernization program sufficient enough to upgrade 10,000 schools.

• Enacting a large investment increase in roads, bridges, and major transit systems.

The Senate measure, to come to a vote in early February, was valued at nearly $900 billion. Not a single Republican voted for the House bill. The act, signed by the president, would be called the American Recovery and Reinvestment Act (of 2009).

See also AMERICAN RECOVERY AND REINVESTMENT ACT (OF 2009); EARNED INCOME TAX CREDIT; MAKING WORK PAY; STIMULUS PLAN (EUROPE).

Cf. ECONOMIC STIMULUS PLAN (BILL FROM SENATE).

ECONOMIC STIMULUS PLAN (BILL FROM SENATE). On February 6, 2009, the U.S. Senate completed what became an $827 billion stimulus bill, only slightly more than the $820 billion cost of the measure adopted by the House.

The plan, as with the House plan, was intended to blunt the recession with a combination of tax cuts and government spending on public works and other programs to create more than 3 million jobs. The Senate bill cut $40 billion of aid to help states and localities and created $30 billion in tax incentives to encourage people to buy homes and cars within 2009.

Another significant difference between the House and Senate bill was the Senate's inclusion of nearly $70 billion to protect thousands of middle-class Americans from paying the alternative minimum tax in 2009, sparing them from a system originally intended to prevent the wealthy from claiming too many tax deductions. The Senate version also eliminated $19.5 billion in construction aid for schools and colleges and sliced proposed new aid for the Head Start program.

On Tuesday, February 10, the Senate passed the $838 billion stimulus bill, beginning the process. The act signed by the president would be called the American Recovery and Reinvestment Act (of 2009).

See also AMERICAN RECOVERY AND REINVESTMENT ACT (OF 2009).

Cf. ECONOMIC STIMULUS PLAN (BILL FROM HOUSE OF REPRESENTATIVES).

ECONOMIC STIMULUS PLAN (FINAL BILL). Final bill following negotiations between members of the U.S. House of Representatives and the U.S. Senate. Signed into law by President Obama on February 17, 2009, as the American Recovery and Reinvestment Act (of 2009).

See also AMERICAN RECOVERY AND REINVESTMENT ACT (OF 2009).

Cf. ECONOMIC STIMULUS PLAN (BILL FROM HOUSE OF REPRE-
SENTATIVES); ECONOMIC STIMULUS PLAN (BILL FROM SENATE);
EUROPEAN UNION.

ECUADOR. Borrowed $2.58 billion in 2009 from regional lenders after
defaulting on its international debt for the second time in a decade.

Ecuador made a $30.9 million interest payment on its global 2015 bonds
despite vowing to stop paying some other debts. The nation's GDP growth,
projected to 2011, was 2.5 percent, with a GDP of $61 billion, an inflation
rate of 3.4 percent, and a GDP per head of $4,250.

See also LATIN AMERICA.

EDDIE BAUER HOLDINGS. A specialty retailer, it announced in January
2009 that it was eliminating 193 jobs, or about 15 percent of its nonretail
staff.

The company filed for Chapter 11 bankruptcy protection on June 17. With
371 stores in North America, it is seeking to sell the company. On July 17,
Eddie Bauer Holdings was successfully auctioned for a purchase price of
$286 million. Initially, it would keep the majority of the retailer's stores open.

EDUCATION. The American Recovery and Reinvestment Act (of 2009)
provided $100 billion in emergency aid for public schools and colleges. With
the stimulus program, the budget of the department doubled. The bill, signed
by President Obama on February 18, 2009, doubled federal spending on dis-
advantaged and disabled children, Head Start, and school renovation.

Most of the funds, $54 billion, would be used to prevent public sector lay-
offs, mostly in schools. Another $5 billion was for setting high standards and
narrowing achievement gaps between poor and affluent students. Nationwide,
in fiscal 2009, which began July 1, 2008, for most states, state funding for
higher education fell $2.8 billion to $77.9 billion, though the drop was largely
offset by $2.3 billion in stimulus funds.

On January 19, 2010, the president asked Congress for an extra $1.35 bil-
lion to expand his signature education objectives purporting to assist states
into revamping their school systems during their tight budget. This was all
part of the Race to the Top program. About forty states applied for funding
on the first deadline date.

President Obama's proposed 2011 budget would boost education spending
9 percent. As many states slashed education spending, fiscal woes pushed up
class sizes, a reversal of the trend of previous years. In California, about 75
percent of the state's public elementary schools increased their class sizes. By
April 2010, with revenue cuts, school districts around the country were warning hundreds of thousands of teachers that their jobs might be eliminated in
June. The 2010–2011 school year could well be the most austere in the past
half century. At risk were 100,000 to 300,000 public school jobs.

See also AMERICAN JOBS ACT (PROPOSED); AMERICAN RECOV-ERY AND REINVESTMENT ACT (OF 2009); CHARTER SCHOOLS; CHILDREN IN POVERTY; COLLEGE GRADUATES; HARVARD UNIVERSITY; HIGH SCHOOL GRADUATES; LIBRARIES; PREP SCHOOLS; PRIVATE SCHOOLS; PUBLIC SCHOOLS; RACE TO THE TOP PROGRAM; TAX CUTS; YALE UNIVERSITY.

EDUCATION DEPARTMENT. *See* U.S. DEPARTMENT OF EDUCA-TION.

EDUCATION JOBS. *See* AMERICAN JOBS ACT (PROPOSED); UNEM-PLOYMENT.

EGYPT. The country ranks 137 in the world in per-capita income, with a population in the top twenty. While growth for the past few years has been respectable, averaging 4 percent to 5 percent save for 2009, that has been considered a poor showing. Egypt's government promised a 5 percent GDP growth during 2010, 6 percent in 2011, and the following year 7 percent, as it was prior to the Great Recession. Inflation had slowed somewhat from a peak of 13.3 percent in November 2009, with a budget deficit consuming about 8 percent of GDP. Foreign direct investment declined to about $8.1 billion from a high of $13.2 billion in 2008. On December 25, 2010, Egypt's president announced that he would deliver an 8 percent economic growth over the coming five years.

Growth in 2011 was projected to be 5.5 percent, with a combined GDP of $253 billion and a GDP per head of $2,940. Then came the January/February 2011 crisis—part of the Arab Spring, where banks and stock exchange was closed for a week. The central bank claimed its official reserves were $36 billion, with another $20 billion held with commercial banks. Prior to the crisis in January and February 2011, foreigners held just 7 percent of Egypt's total public debt, equivalent to over $11 billion. The Egyptian pound suffered a sharp selloff on February 7, dropping to its lowest level in six years against the U.S. dollar. Tourism brought in $12 billion in 2010, accounting for about 5 percent of the nation's GDP.

In 2012, life in Egypt remains austere, volatile, and unpredictable.
See also MIDDLE EAST.

EHLP. *See* EMERGENCY HOMEOWNERS' LOAN PROGRAM.

EISENHOWER, DWIGHT DAVID. *See* FEDERAL AID HIGHWAY ACT; OBAMA, BARACK.

EL CENTRO, CALIFORNIA. *See* UNEMPLOYMENT.

ELDERLY, THE. The number of unemployed workers seventy-five and older increased to more than 73,000 in January 2009, up 46 percent from the prior January. Among workers sixty-five and older, the jobless rate stood at 5.7 percent. Although below the national average, it was well above what it was in previous recessions, including the recession of 1981, when it reached 4.3 percent.

The percentage of people sixty-five and older who are in the workforce rose to 16.8 percent at year-end, from 11.9 percent a decade earlier. Among those who are seventy-five and older, the increase was even greater, to 7.3 percent from 4.7 percent.

See also UNEMPLOYMENT.

ELECTRIC CARS. *See* AUTOMOBILE INDUSTRY; CHINA.

ELECTRIC GRID. *See* AMERICAN RECOVERY AND REINVEST-MENT ACT (OF 2009).

ELECTRICITY. The recession sent demand and rates for electricity lower. By August 2009, it was clear that electricity demand had fallen 4.4 percent in the first half of the year. Electricity sales remained sluggish in the third quarter 2009. Overall electricity sales declined 3.3 percent in the year.

ELECTROLUX. The largest European appliance maker, based in Sweden, it announced on December 15, 2008, that it would fall short of its yearly earnings forecast and cut more than 3,000 jobs globally as a result of an abrupt slowdown in demand. On October 26, 2009, it posted a 93 percent rise in third-quarter net profit amid cost cuts, higher prices, and lower raw-material costs, a net profit of $239.9 million.

On April 27, 2010, Electrolux posted a first-quarter net profit of $127.27 million after a net loss the previous year. Management reported on July 19 that its quarter profit was $140 million, although revenue fell to 27.3 billion kroner. In late October 2010, management announced a 15 percent fall in third-quarter earnings, with profits falling $204.9 million. Sales declined 5 percent.

By mid-October 2011, it was clear that appliance sales were dramatically lower than the year before. Profits had fallen 40 percent in the third quarter, and sales fell 2.6 percent.

See also APPLIANCES; SWEDEN; WHIRLPOOL.

ELECTRONIC HEALTH RECORDS. Under the $787 billion stimulus package approved in February 2009, more than $20 billion was set aside for health information technology. Doctors using electronic records would be eligible for more than $40,000 each in incentive payments over several years beginning in 2011. Hospitals would also qualify for millions of dollars in incentive payments. Doctors and hospitals not going electronic by 2015 would be subject to penalties. It was projected that the jobs package of tax cuts and spending initiative would create 100,000 to 150,000 jobs a month over the year ahead.

Synonymous with ELECTRONIC MEDICAL RECORDS.

ELECTRONIC MEDICAL RECORDS. *Synonymous with* ELECTRONIC HEALTH RECORDS.

ELI LILLY. Profits fell 27 percent to $858.2 million in its fourth quarter 2011. Revenue fell 2 percent to $6.05 billion.

ELMENDORF, DOUGLAS W. The director of the Congressional Budget Office.

See CONGRESSIONAL BUDGET OFFICE; DEFICIT-REDUCTION COMMITTEE.

EMERGENCY ECONOMIC STABILIZATION ACT OF 2008. Signed into law by President George W. Bush on October 3, 2008, the legislation that created TARP, the Troubled Asset Relief Program. It was a $700 billion bailout package to minimize the impact of a financial meltdown. Initially rejected by the House of Representatives, the Senate version approved the funds with a higher limit for insured bank deposits and tax breaks for businesses and alternative energy. The Treasury secretary, Henry Paulson Jr., was given access of up to $700 billion to purchase and later resell troubled securities clogging the financial system. Needed support was also given by the Federal Reserve chairman, Ben Bernanke.

The bailout plan attempted to place a dollar value on mortgage-related assets that no one appeared to want in order to move them off the books of ailing banks and unlock the frozen credit markets. The U.S. Treasury would not manage the mortgage assets alone. Instead, they outsourced nearly all the work to professionals who oversaw huge portfolios of bonds and other securities for management fees.

The asset-management firms received a portion of the $250 billion that Congress allowed the Treasury to spend in the first phase of the bailout. Some of the funds were used to help restructure many subprime mortgages in the hopes of enabling troubling homeowners to avoid foreclosure. The 2008 federal deficit was $455 billion, or about 3.3 percent of gross domestic product.

The government said it would temporarily guarantee $1.5 trillion worth of new senior debt issued by banks, as well as insuring $500 billion in deposits in noninterest-bearing accounts. The potential cost of the bailout package might be $2.25 trillion, triple the size of the original bailout rescue plan. According to Neil M. Barofsky, the special inspector general for the Troubled Asset Relief Program, until March 30, 2011, "Treasury's plan for TARP shifted from the purchase of mortgages to the infusion of hundreds of billions of dollars into the nation's largest financial institutions, a shift that came with the express promise that it would restore lending."

See also AUDITORS; BAROFSKY, NEIL; BERNANKE, BEN; BRETTON WOODS II; CAPITAL REQUIREMENTS DIRECTIVE; FINANCIAL STABILITY OVERSIGHT BOARD; GREENSPAN, ALAN; RESOLUTION TRUST CORPORATION; REVULSION STAGE; SUBPRIME; TROUBLED ASSET RELIEF PROGRAM.

Cf. AMERICAN RECOVERY AND REINVESTMENT ACT (OF 2009).

EMERGENCY HOMEOWNERS' LOAN PROGRAM (EHLP). Created under the Dodd-Frank financial overhaul to aid 30,000 homeowners by providing zero-interest loans of as much as $50,000, which could be forgiven after five years if they remained current on their mortgage payments.

EMERGING CURRENCIES. *See* CHINA; EMERGING MARKETS.

EMERGING MARKETS. At first, these economies (including Poland, Hungary, Ukraine) seemed healthy, even thriving, but they were swept up in global financial panic by the end of October 2008. Of the four biggest emerging markets, Brazil, Russia, India, and China, India has the largest current-account deficit, which widened to 3.6 percent of GDP in the second quarter of 2008.

Before the Great Recession, the world economy was dominated by the rich nations (where 17 million people lost their jobs) mostly found in Western countries. That share by 2010 had fallen to just over half and was expected to decline to 40 percent in another ten years. Clearly, the bulk of global output would be produced in the emerging world. Between 2002 and 2008, more than 85 percent of developing economies grew faster than the United States.

See also BRAZIL; CHINA; INDIA; RUSSIA; WORLD BANK.

EMERSON ELECTRIC. A maker of industrial-automation equipment, power systems, and heating and cooling gear, it reported on May 5, 2009, a 32 percent drop in fiscal second-quarter earnings. Revenue fell 16 percent to $5.09 billion. Sales for 2010 were estimated to decline by 10 percent.

EMIGRATION. *See* IRELAND; MIGRATION.

EMPLOYEE FREE CHOICE ACT. Supported by union leaders in March 2009, the bill would make it easier for unions to recruit workers because it would permit them to join unions merely by signing cards rather than through secret-ballot elections where firms can campaign against the union.

EMPLOYMENT. Employment in residential construction and carmaking was, by 2010, down by almost a third, in retailing and banking by 8 percent. In March 2010, 162,000 new jobs were added to the U.S. payroll, the largest increase in three years. On May 7, 2010, the Labor Department reported that employers had added 290,000 jobs in April, the largest increase in four years. However, the unemployment rate went up to 9.9 percent from 9.7 percent in March. By November, private-sector employers added just 50,000 jobs, offsetting the 11,000-job drop in government employment driven by local budget reductions.

On May 6, 2011, the government indicated that the United States created 244,000 jobs in April and the private sector another 268,000 positions, the largest jump since 2006. By year's end there were increasing signs that new hires were emerging. The United States added jobs for thirteen straight months, and new jobless claims had been falling since the spring. Unemployment fell to 8.6 percent, and most economists projected fourth-quarter economic growth to be at a robust annual rate of 3.5 percent or so. The year would end with the addition of 200,000 new jobs, a good improvement, but weak and inadequate.

See also INSOURCING; PRIVATE-SECTOR PAYROLLS; TEMPORARY HIRINGS; UNEMPLOYMENT.

EMPTY CREDITOR. A hypothesis that purchasers of credit insurance can profit by permitting, or even encouraging, firms to file for bankruptcy. Used by credit default swaps where traders insure themselves against a firm's default. Empty creditors are investors who hedge with credit default swaps and benefit if firms fail because the payout on the swap would make them whole on the value of their debt.

See also CREDIT DEFAULT SWAPS.

ENDOWMENTS. The value of university endowments fell about 23 percent on average in the four months ending in November 2008. Many universities were predicting layoffs following the stock market decline, the worst since the 1970s.

By the end of June 2009, when the fiscal year ended for endowments, the five largest single-school endowments acknowledged a decline of 25 to 30 percent. Specifically, by the end of June, the two largest higher education endowments lost 30 percent in their value. Combined, Yale and Harvard lost a staggering $17.8 billion. In 2009, university endowments declined an average of 18.7 percent, the worst since the 1930s. The wealthiest universities lost more than 26 percent of their endowment values. For the ten wealthiest universities, the losses were as follows:

Change	2008	2009
Harvard—29.8 percent	$36.6 billion	$25.7 billion
Yale—28.6 percent	$22.9 billion	$16.3 billion

Stanford—26.7 percent	$17.2 billion	$12.6 billion
Princeton—22.8 percent	$16.3 billion	$12.6 billion
Texas—24.8 percent	$16.2 billion	$12.2 billion
Michigan—20.7 percent	$7.6 billion	$6.0 billion
Columbia—19.8 percent	$7.3 billion	$5.9 billion
Northwestern—24.8 percent	$7.2 billion	$5.4 billion
Pennsylvania—16.8 percent	$6.2 billion	$5.2 billion
Chicago—23.2 percent	$6.6 billion	$5.1 billion

See also BRANDEIS UNIVERSITY; COLUMBIA UNIVERSITY; HARVARD UNIVERSITY; STANFORD UNIVERSITY; YALE UNIVERSITY.

ENERGY. *See* ELECTRICITY.

ENERGY DEPARTMENT. *See* U.S. ENERGY DEPARTMENT.

ENERGY EFFICIENCY. The American Recovery and Reinvestment Act, signed by President Obama on February 17, 2009, called for $80 billion to be used to promote energy efficiency, renewable energy sources, higher-mileage cars, and coal technology that is cleaner. $2 billion was made available for research into advanced car batteries and $3.4 billion to develop coal-fired power plants that could capture and store greenhouse gases. Of the $25 billion provided for energy efficiency, more than half was aimed at helping low-income households weatherize 1 million homes and helping governments at all levels retrofit public buildings.

Tax incentives of $20 billion were offered for wind, solar, hydroelectric, and other renewable power sources.

See also AMERICAN RECOVERY AND REINVESTMENT ACT (OF 2009).

ENERGY INNOVATION. The *Wall Street Journal*'s November 2010 CEO Council recommended the following:

1. Develop Domestic Energy—Promote development of all domestic resources with appropriate environmental safeguards and a regulatory system that is timely and predictable and avoids a back-door, de factor moratorium.
2. Support Research and Development—Ensure long-term commitment by the federal government to basic research and development for new energy sources and carbon mitigation, and provide stable incentives for research and development in the private sector and universities. Energy storage is crucial, yet technological breakthroughs are necessary before deploying batteries and fuel cells at scale. Focus on research and development to bring down costs rather than mandates and subsidies for immediate deployment.

3. Consistent Federal Regulation—A comprehensive energy policy that provides consistency and predictability for investment. Clearer policy on auto fuel efficiency and carbon constraints avoiding a patchwork of state rules. Consider the country's massive natural gas resources and create a path for nuclear and renewable. Be honest about the continued primacy of fossil fuels and costs.
4. Competitiveness—Restore U.S. companies' leadership in developing and exporting energy technology around the world. Remove tax policies and other burdens that impede U.S. firms' global competitiveness.
5. Energy Efficiency—Put the United States at the forefront of energy-efficiency technology, both to curb waste at home and to create markets abroad. Policies should include building codes, appliance standards, and incentives to deploy new energy-efficient technologies.

See also CEO COUNCIL.

ENFORCEMENT. *See* REGULATION.

ENTERPRISE. A car-rental firm, it laid off 2,000 employees, about 3 percent of its workforce, in November 2008 to trim about $200 million from its overall cost structure. Enterprise sought funds from the Troubled Asset Relief Program.
Cf. AVIS; HERTZ.

ENTITLEMENTS. A guarantee of access to benefits because of rights or by agreement through law. Often refers to a person's belief that one is deserving of some particular reward or benefit.

The United States is a nation of entitlements where nearly half of the population resides in a household in which someone received government benefits, more than at any time in history. In 2005, 39 percent of the population did not pay any federal income taxes; that figure has climbed to 45 percent during the meltdown.

ENVIRONMENT. *See* GREEN ENVIRONMENT.

ENVIRONMENTAL CLEANUP. *See* AMERICAN RECOVERY AND REINVESTMENT ACT (OF 2009).

EQUITY BUYOUT. The purchase of a company without using any borrowed money the "leveraged" portion of a leveraged buyout.
See also LEVERAGED BUYOUT FIRMS.

EQUITY FIRMS. *See* FORECLOSURE; FORECLOSURE MILLS.

ERICSSON. The world's largest telecommunications network company by sales, it posted a 31 percent drop in fourth-quarter 2008 net profits. It had already cut 4,000 workers in 2008 and projected another 5,000 people would be released, or about 6.4 percent of its workforce.

Ericsson reported a first-quarter 2009 profit drop of 35 percent, falling to $212.9 million, and a 56 percent drop to $111.3 million in the second quarter. *See also* SONY.

ERNST & YOUNG. A major U.S. accounting/consulting firm. New York prosecutors filed on December 21, 2010, in New York State civil fraud charges against Ernst & Young for its alleged involvement in the collapse of Lehman Brothers, accusing the firm of standing by while the investment bank misled investors about its financial health by shifting debt off the books.

The outside auditor certified the bank's financial statements from 2001 until it filed for bankruptcy in September 2008. The lawsuits brought the return of more than $150 million in fees that Ernst & Young collected, plus investor damages. Federal agent brought charges against Ernst & Young, Lehman Brothers' auditor, on fraud charges for failing to properly follow up on a whistleblower's claim that Lehman was misstating the value and size of its assets.

See also LEHMAN BROTHERS.

ESCADA. An international women's luxury fashion company. On August 13, 2009, Escada filed for bankruptcy protection.

ESPRIT HOLDINGS. Manufacturer of apparel, accessories, and house wares. In February 2009, it reported a 13 percent decline in first-half net profit, its first earnings decline since 1998. The company noted that the global economic downturn had squeezed its operating profit margin.

ESTATE AND GIFT TAX. *See* TAX CUTS.

ESTEE LAUDER. Beauty brand and perfume maker, it reported in February 2009 sharply lower sales and a 30 percent drop in profit for its fiscal second quarter ending December 31. Reported on May 3 a fiscal third-quarter 70 percent decline in profits. Posted sales of $1.7 billion were down 9.8 percent from a year earlier. Profit was $27.2 million, down from $90.1 million the year before.

The firm's fiscal third-quarter 2010 profit more than doubled, with a profit of $57.5 million. Skin care sales climbed 16 percent, while fragrance sales role 19 percent. Then, in August, management reported a profit of $23.9 million, with sales increasing 9 percent to $1.84 billion. At the end of October 2010, management reported fiscal first-quarter earnings of 36 percent. Its profit was $191.1 million, with revenue climbing 14 percent to $2.09 billion, or 15 percent.

In May 2011, the firm reported that its fiscal third-quarter earnings more than doubled. On August 15, management reported that earnings rose 72 percent. For the quarter ending June 30, the firm had a profit of $41.1 million, with revenue increasing 12 percent to $2.06 billion.

ESTONIA. Real GDP is projected to fall by 14.4 percent his year, broadly stabilize in 2010, and recover in 2011, when growth of 3.9 percent is expected. This projection depends largely on developments in major export markets, the speed with which resources are reallocated toward expanding export activities, and the country's ability to attract renewed foreign direct investment inflows to the export sector as the recovery takes hold. Maintaining the currency board with a view to adopting the euro as soon as possible remains the primary objective of economic policy. The need to meet the 3 percent of GDP Maastricht criterion implies that fiscal policy will remain very tight. External assessments of the credibility of Estonia's economic policies—and, in particular, of its prospects for euro accession—will also become critical for foreign direct investment flows and credit conditions.

GDP fell by 3.5 percent in the third quarter of 2008. There were concerns that without an improved social safety net, the public would suffer greatly, as unemployment could hit 20 percent during the meltdown.

By the end of October 2009, Estonia set its 2010 budget with a deficit of 2.95 percent. Its gross debt in 2009 was only 7.2 percent of GDP and the government deficit was 1.7 percent.

By 2011, the long march back for Estonia's economy was slow. The nation's GDP growth was 3.2 percent, with a GDP of $18 billion, an inflation rate of 2.6 percent, and a GDP per head of $13,500. By mid-summer, unemployment had fallen significantly from 18.8 percent to 13.8 percent, there had been soaring growth with exports, and the country had a budget surplus. GDP rate of growth in the first quarter 2011 was 8.5 percent, the highest in the European Union. Its debt was the lowest in the European Union at 6.6 percent of GDP.

See also BALTICS; LATVIA.

ETF. *See* EXCHANGE-TRADED FUND.

ETHIOPIA. The economy was projected to grow by 10 percent in 2011, with a GDP of $26 billion, an inflation rate of 11 percent, and a GDP per head of $342.

EU. *See* EUROPEAN UNION.

EURO. The sharp contraction in eurozone activity appears to have ended sooner than anticipated, with further improvements in financial conditions, fiscal stimulus measures, and stabilization of export demand. However, headwinds from financial sector deleveraging and rising unemployment suggest that the recovery will be gradual. Bank lending standards are tight, credit growth to households and firms is weak, and property prices are declining in many countries. Despite the improved outlook, core inflation should continue to moderate until the end of 2010 due to substantial economic slack. Low core inflation, tight credit conditions, and a persistent negative output gap make it appropriate for the current expansionary monetary policy stance to be maintained until late 2010. Thereafter, emergency credit support measures should be withdrawn and policy rates gradually increased. Medium-term growth prospects would be enhanced by clear and credible plans for future fiscal consolidation and further structural measures to deepen the single market, enhance competitive pressures, and strengthen financial operations

The euro is the single currency of most European Union nations designed to replace the currencies of individual nations. There are seven euro-denominated notes and eight coins. Starting January 2002, the euro became the official legal tender of these countries (the eurozone). As it was originally conceived, the euro required countries to share a currency and at the same time retain responsibility for their own fiscal policies, including the consequences of default.

On February 13, 2009, figures showed that the eurozone GDP shrank at an annualized rate of around 5 percent in the fourth quarter of 2008. GDP was projected by the International Monetary Fund to decline by 2 percent in 2009, and then barely recover in 2010. By year's end 2009, the euro was considered to be overvalued by between 7 and 8 percent relative to other major currencies.

The euro plummeted to a twelve-month low against the U.S. dollar on April 27, 2010, as concerns that a sovereign debt crisis would spread across the euro-zone prompted investors to run from the common currency. The euro fell to a low of $1.3166, down more than 1.5 percent against the dollar. By mid-May, the euro had depreciated about 15 percent against the U.S. dollar since December. Many specialists believed that the euro could reach parity against the dollar by the middle of 2011. If so, it would be the lowest since 2002. A gradual recovery of the euro followed in the summer 2010. Then, on August 4, the euro tumbled, closing at $1.4093, a 1.6 percent fall against the U.S. dollar.

During the week of December 5, 2011, European leaders met to save the euro. The "new euro" as described was negotiated on four main lines. It combined new promises of fiscal discipline to be embedded in amendments to European treaties; a leveraging of the current bailout fund, the European Financial Stability Facility, to perhaps two or even three times its current balance; a tranche of money from the IMF to augment the bailout fund; and participation of the European Central Bank to keep purchasing bonds aggressively in nations nearing default. The euro had hit a 2011 high of $1,484 in early May. Days after the eurozone debt crisis summit on December 9, the euro tumbled to its lowest level against the dollar in almost one year. The currency fell 2.6 percent to 1.3037, a level last seen in January. The euro was down 12 percent from its May high.

The euro on January 5, 2012, fell to its lowest level against the U.S. dollar since September 2010, hitting $1.2790. It was down almost 10 percent since October 2011.

See also CHINA; DELEVERAGE; DOLLAR (U.S.); EUROPEAN CENTRAL BANK; EUROPEAN FINANCIAL STABILITY FACILITY; EUROZONE; EXCHANGE RATES; ICELAND; MERKEL, ANGELA.

EURO-AREA. *Synonymous with* EUROZONE.

EUROBONDS. Where members of the eurozone sell joint bonds to investors, guaranteeing them collectively. The funds raised would be split up among euro members to cover each nation's borrowing needs, which would have to be collectively approved in advance. Joint borrowing would create a highly liquid bond market of more than $11 trillion. The primary objection to eurobonds is that they would remove financial market pressure on national governments to curb deficit spending. Decided for the time being (August 17, 2011), these collective bonds would not be recommended. If the countries of the eurozone were to collectively issue eurozone bonds, instead of each nation individually issuing debt, their combined borrowing would create a large liquid market that could offer a real alternative to the U.S. Treasury market.

The pros and cons of issuing eurobonds are as follows:

Benefits—combine the financial muscle of the eurozone and ease the debt crisis; reduce borrowing costs for most members of the euro zone; make nations less likely to fall prey to market mood swings; and offer competition to the U.S. Treasury market and the dollar as the main reserve currency.

Drawbacks—delay incentives for action by weak economies; bloat overall debt and damage credit standing of strong economies; deepen European Union divisions because of the bonds' unpopularity; and long implementation time at a time when quick action is required.

See also MERKEL, ANGELA.
Synonymous with COLLECTIVE BOND.

EURODOLLARS. Dollar balances held by private people or firms in European banks. They provide a stock of international currency not appearing in governmental returns. Traffic is not confined to dollars. It is also a fund of international short-term capital that usually flows to those nations offering the highest interest rates. The system came into being in 1957.

See also LIBOR.

EUROFIRST. *See* FTSE.

EUROPEAN AERONAUTIC DEFENSE AND SPACE. *See* AIRBUS.

EUROPEAN BANK. *Synonymous with* EUROPEAN BANK FOR RECONSTRUCTION AND DEVELOPMENT.

EUROPEAN BANK FOR RECONSTRUCTION AND DEVELOPMENT (EBRD). Commenced operations in April 1991 to help former Soviet-bloc nations make the transition to market economies.

The bank forecast in November 2008 that Eastern Europe's economic growth would fall by half in 2009 to 3 percent as a result of declining consumption and rising unemployment.

In February 2009, the bank warned that the economic crisis "is threatening to throw nearly two decades of economic reform into reverse." In its 2009 annual report, the EBRD reported that the combined GDP of the twenty-nine nations in which it invests would shrink 6.3 percent for the year, with the region hit harder than other emerging markets.

See also EASTERN EUROPE.

Synonymous with EUROPEAN BANK; EUROPEAN DEVELOPMENT BANK.

EUROPEAN BANKING AUTHORITY. In March 2011, the European Union's regulators proceeded to measure, via stress tests, eighty-eight of Europe's largest banks. Instead of a European Union across-the-board set of standards, regulators will use each country's definition of an important capital ratio, such as Tier 1. The problem remains that regulators in different countries have different means of calculating the Tier 1 ratio, thus preventing a pan-European standard.

See also STRESS TESTS (EUROPEAN UNION); TIER 1.

EUROPEAN CAR SALES. *See* AUTOMOBILE INDUSTRY.

EUROPEAN CENTRAL BANK (ECB). Inaugurated in Frankfurt, Germany, on June 1, 1998, and became operational on January 1, 1999, it set interest rates along with the participating member national central bank chiefs in the eurozone.

On November 6, 2008, the European Central Bank reduced its main borrowing gauge by a half a percentage point to 3.25 percent. In Britain, the Bank of England cut its benchmark interest rate by 1.5 percentage points. The new rate, at 3 percent, was the lowest the country had seen since 1954.

In mid-January 2009, the ECB slashed its main interest rate by half a percentage point to 2 percent as it sought to protect the 330 million people in the countries that use the euro against a deepening recession. The ECB said that the number of counterfeit euro bank notes it removed from circulation rose 19 percent in 2008 to 666,000. The twenty-euro bill was most popular among forgers, accounting for 43 percent of notes taken from circulation. The ECB developed guidelines to prevent bailout plans from one country being significantly more generous than plans from another. On March 5, the ECB cut its main interest rate by a half point to 1.5 percent, the lowest since the creation of the euro and the bank itself ten years earlier. The president of ECB said in mid-month that Europe didn't need to boost spending more to combat the global financial crisis, giving the bank's support in Europe's battle with the United States over how to overcome the economic recession. On April 2, the ECB cut its key rate by a quarter percentage point to 1.25 percent.

The ECB forecast further financial-sector weakness restraining countries from expanding their economies before mid-2010. By the end of June, the ECB pumped $622 billion into its lenders to revive the sagging eurozone economy. The bank on July 2 left its main interest rate steady for the second consecutive month. On October 8, 2009, the ECB left its key interest rate unchanged at 1 percent, indicating concerns for growth in the future. The ECB took steps on December 3 to absorb some of the hundreds of billions of euros it gave to banks. Now the ECB is planning to pull back some of its stimulus aid as inflation remained just under 2 percent, considered to be low. By year's end 2009, the ECB reported that banks in the eurozone faced higher losses than earlier thought. Updated losses for all loans and securities were $796.57 billion for 2007 to 2010. On December 30, 2009, the ECB reported that lending to the private sector was down 0.7 percent from November 2008, the third straight month of decline, reflecting a lower demand for credit.

On May 8–9, 2010, the ECB announced steps to head off the debt crisis in Europe. It would:

- *Buy debt*—It will purchase European government and corporate debt on the open market to support bond prices.
- *Expand lending*—It will expand the cash it provides to European banks by granting loans with 1 percent interest rates for up to six months. There is no limit on the amounts banks can borrow, as long as they provide collateral.
- *Provide dollars*—In conjunction with the U.S. Federal Reserve Board, it will provide unlimited short-term loans to banks in dollars in return for collateral in order to prop up the euro.

At the end of July 2010, the European Central Bank announced a new set of discounts that it would apply from January 1, 2011, when accepting low-quality assets as collaterals from bank, hoping to lower the risk of the ECB. Discounts will not apply to government bonds. On October 9, 2010, the ECB took steps to address the credit risk it takes on its balance sheets, thus increasing the discretionary powers of the national central banks in the euro-area. The measures made it harder for banks with weak balance sheets to borrow from the ECB.

On March 3, 2011, the European Union's banking regulator announced that he would commence a new health check of banks. These "stress" tests would measure the banks' ability to withstand economic shocks and downturns. On June 24, 2011, European leaders appointed Mario Draghi, an economics professor and former World Bank official, as the new president of the European Central Bank. He became head of the ECB on November 1. On July 7, the ECB raised interest rates for the second time since April to control inflation. On August 8, the ECB announced that it would purchase government bonds of Italy and Spain on a large scale to stem Europe's unfolding debt crisis. The cost of a bailout for Italy would be about $1.4 trillion, and for Spain an additional $700 billion. This purchase would put an additional strain on the central bank's $2.86 trillion balance sheet. On September 15, the ECB announced that it would coordinate leading global central banks (U.S. Federal Reserve, Bank of England, Bank of Japan, and Swiss National Bank) to ensure that eurozone banks would have unlimited dollar funding through the end of 2011. The ECB increased aid to struggling financial institutions on October 6, leavings its benchmark rate unchanged at 1.5 percent.

On November 3, the new president of the ECB cut the eurozone's benchmark interest rate to 1.25 percent from 1.5 percent. Then, on December 8, the day before the EU summit to deal with the eurozone crisis, the ECB decided to lower interest rates back to record lows to avert a recession and to assist cash-strapped banks. The bank also refused to permit EU national central banks from channeling funds to governments via third parties, such as the International Monetary Fund or Europe's bailout funds. One result was that the Dow Jones Industrial Average fell nearly 200 points, or 1.63 percent, to 11,997.70.

A total of 523 banks in the eurozone had demanded three-year loans to help them survive the financial crisis. Hundreds of lenders took out $640 billion in low-interest loans from the ECB on December 22. The three-year average of the ECB benchmark rate was 1 percent. It was the largest package of such loans that the central bank had every made. The loans are for three years; previously, the longest loans were for 371 days.

As the year 2011 closed, the ECB warned of the difficult year before them as the sovereign debt crisis collided with slower economic growth and difficulties of bank financing. Their half-year report said that financial tensions among the region's governments and commercial banks had taken on "systemic crisis proportions not witnessed since the collapse of Lehman Brothers three years ago."

See also CREDIT SQUEEZE; DOW JONES INDUSTRIAL AVERAGE; DRAGHI, MARIO; EUROPE (BAILOUT); EUROZONE; EUROZONE LENDING; FINANCIAL PROTECTIONISM; SWITZERLAND.

EUROPEAN CLEAN URBAN TRANSPORTATION INITIATIVE. *See* EUROPEAN COMMISSION.

EUROPEAN COMMISSION (EC). The European Commission is the driving force of European Union policy and the starting point for every European Union action, presenting proposals and drafts for legislation. It is obliged to act on behalf of its members. The EC has lawmaking powers and is the guardian of its treaties. It monitors applications for new members and institutes infringement proceedings in the event of any violation of its laws.

The EC announced at the end of November 2008 a stimulus package worth 130 billion euros aimed at bolstering the bloc's economy. On November 24, the EC outlined a €200 billion (US$254 billion) wish list of measures for Europe to spend its way out of recession and gave national capitals permission to temporarily break budget deficit ceilings if required. This amounted to 1.5 percent of the EU's GDP, calling for the twenty-seven member governments to provide €170 billion of the total. The remaining €30 billion would come from the EU budget and the European Investment Bank.

The bank also announced that it would provide the automobile industry of Europe with €4 billion in low-interest loans in both 2009 and 2010 as part of the European Clean Urban Transportation Initiative. The European Commission would spend €5 billion over two years for the same ends.

The EC agreed in mid-December to loosen rules on state subsidies to allow governments to double the amount of money, to $720,000, that they could pump into cash-strapped firms without first checking with regulators.

On May 9–10, 2010, the EC announced steps to head off the debt crisis in Europe by providing the following:

- *Loans to governments*—If needed; already financed.
- *Buy government debt*—If necessary, a special purpose vehicle (SPV) would be created to raise money from investors and buy government debt in the EU. Members of the eurozone have pledged to guarantee the SPV's investments up to 440 billion euros.

On September 13, 2010, the EC significantly raised its growth forecast, predicting a growth rate for the year of 1.7 percent in the sixteen-nation eurozone, and 1.8 percent for the twenty-seven-member EU.

See also AUTOMOBILE INDUSTRY; DERIVATIVE(S); STIMULUS PLAN (OF EUROPE); and individual countries.

EUROPEAN COURT OF JUSTICE. At the January 30, 2012, eurozone summit, the Court of Justice was empowered to impose fine on euro nations running excessive deficits, capping the fines at 0.1 percent of GDP. It will require that nations keep their budget deficits to an average of 0.5 percent of GDP over the economic cycle and lower their total government debt toward 60 percent of GDP over time.

EUROPEAN DEVELOPMENT BANK. *Synonymous with* EUROPEAN BANK FOR RECONSTRUCTION AND DEVELOPMENT.

EUROPEAN FINANCIAL STABILITY FACILITY. The current eurozone bailout fund. Eurozone leaders agreed to expand its capacity to more than a half billion dollars and permit it more flexibility, but the changes await ratification.

By the end of October 2011, eurozone leaders agreed to provide guarantees for about $1.4 trillion of bonds. Ceases operation of new bailouts in 2013.

See also EURO; EUROPEAN STABILITY MECHANISM; EUROZONE; IRELAND.

EUROPEAN FINANCIAL STABILIZATON MECHANISM. A 60 billion pound fund that is guaranteed by the European Union, using the budget contributions of all twenty-seven European Union member states as collateral. Like the European Financial Stability Facility, it raised funds from the financial markets by issuing bonds. There has been no discussion, to date, of expanding it.

EUROPEAN INVESTMENT BANK. Authorized by the Treaty of Rome in 1957, the bank provides loans and guarantees in all economic sectors of the European Union, especially to promote the development of less-developed regions, modernize or convert undertakings or create new jobs, and assist projects of common interest to several member states.

On March 12, 2009, the European Investment Bank approved €3 billion in loans to the European automotive industry.

See also EUROPEAN COMMISSION; KOENIGSEGG; UNITED KINGDOM.

EUROPEAN PARLIAMENT. Although the Parliament cannot enact laws, it has a co-decision procedure that empowers it to veto legislation in certain policy areas. It can question the European Commission, amend or reject the European Union budget, and dismiss the entire commission through a vote of censure.

A law was passed on January 13, 2009, to help mutual funds expand abroad. The bill lets funds regulated by the European Union attract investors anywhere in the region with a harmonized, two-page offering document. It has made it easier for mutual funds to merge and allows asset managers to manage funds more easily across the European Union. Management firms can easily notify regulators when they want to offer new products across the European Union. It was estimated that fund managers could save €6 billion to €8 billion each year.

EUROPEAN REGULATORS. On January 1, 2011, three new European regulators commenced for the first time to exert centralized control over large European financial markets. The new bodies succeeded three committees that previously tried to coordinate the supervision of European banks, insurers, pension funds, and securities. The new rules brought credit derivatives and credit-rating agencies into the regulatory net.

See also EUROPEAN BANKING AUTHORITY.

EUROPEAN STABILITY MECHANISM. A 500 billion pound fund envisaged as the permanent rescue vehicle for the eurozone, replacing the European Financial Stability Facility in mid-2013.

See also EUROPEAN FINANCIAL STABILITY FACILITY.

EUROPEAN SYSTEMIC RISK COUNCIL (PROPOSED). *See* EURO-PEAN UNION.

EUROPEAN TOURISM. *See* TOURISM.

EUROPEAN UNION (EU). The twenty-seven nations of western and central Europe. The European Union was created by means of the Treaty of Maastricht, signed on February 7, 1992. The European Union is governed by five institutions.

On December 2, 2008, finance ministers called for EU member states to inject an average of 1.3 percent of their own GDP into the economy. At the end of the month, the EU approved bank rescue measures for many of the continent's major economic powers, clearing the way for cash injections and loan guarantees expected to help lenders through the financial crisis.

The EU announced in mid-January 2009 that the economy in the sixteen nations that use the euro would shrink by 1.9 percent in 2009, with the entire EU contracting 1.8 percent, and that 3.5 million jobs would disappear in 2009. At the same time, the EU predicted a moderate recovery in 2010, when the EU could grow 0.5 percent.

Finance ministers of the EU agreed on February 10 to guidelines for handling bad assets on banks' balance sheets. Principles for governments helping resuscitate banks hurt by nonperforming loans and other impaired assets were spelled out. Remedies included the formation of a so-called bad bank or series of bad banks to hold troubled assets. The guidelines call for a "correct and consistent approach of valuation" for these assets selected. The goal was to restore bank lending while preserving a level playing field across the EU.

On February 27, unemployment rose in the EU to 8.2 percent, up from 8 percent in December. Inflation slowed to 1.1 percent from 1.6 percent in December 2008 as businesses cut costs across the board. By March, the EU feared that the jobless rate would increase to 10 percent, but its governments continued to argue that there was no immediate need for further fiscal stimulus measures. While the unemployment rate in the twenty-seven nations had dipped below 7 percent in 2008, it rose to 7.6 percent in January 2009. Spain had the highest at 14.8 percent in January, while the Netherlands had the lowest at 2.8 percent.

The EU reversed course on assistance to eastern Europe's troubled nations by doubling a fund to €50 billion. On March 21, the twenty-seven countries put aside funds by offering $102.55 billion for the International Monetary Fund to rescue economies. The International Monetary Fund estimated in April that nations of the EU would have to write down $1.19 trillion in loans and securities. The EU announced on May 3 that the ongoing recession would last at least six months longer than originally expected and predicted a 4 percent contraction for the EU economy in 2009, more than double its earlier forecast.

EU economies contracted sharply in the first quarter. The economy in every major European nation fell. For the EU as a whole, including the sixteen countries that use the euro, GDP shrank by 2.5 percent in the first quarter, or at a 10 percent annual rate. Meeting on June 18, EU leaders agreed to broad principles for forming new supranational financial supervisors, stopping short of giving those regulators the power to force national governments to bail out firms. The Brussels two-day summit meeting concluded its session by endorsing the creation of a European Systemic Risk Council to track the financial system for stability. A second group would set standards for governments to supervise banks, insurers, and other financial firms.

The EU bounced back with strength in the second quarter 2009, a significant improvement from the first quarter, with rebounds primarily in France and Germany. Their economies both grew following four negative quarters. On October 1, 2009, the EU declared that their largest twenty-two banks would survive a potential $485 billion in credit losses in 2009.

In an act of unity, on May 9, 2010, finance ministers from the EU agreed on a deal to provide $560 billion in bilateral loans and $76 billion under an existing lending program managed by the European Commission. The IMF gave up to an additional $280 billion to weak nations to calm markets throughout the globe. Totaling $640 billion, it would rival the U.S. 2008 economic stimulus plan, all in an attempt to reduce the crises starting in Greece, then Spain, Portugal, and Ireland. On September 2, the EU reached a preliminary accord to create four new European regulators to strengthen supervision of the region's financial services industry.

In October, representatives of the nations achieved agreement to tighten rules governing the bloc's public finances. This fiscal-sanction regime purported to stall the sort of runaway accumulation of government debt that fueled Europe's meltdown. The EU voted on October 20 to increase the bloc's spending by about 6 percent, double the increase that national governments said they could afford. The result would be a budget of about $180 billion in 2011, mostly for the common agriculture policy needs and the poorest regions of the EU. On November 24, 2010, the EU floated a proposal to double the size of Europe's $588 billion bailout fund for eurozone nations, but the concept was dismissed by the German government. Meeting in Brussels, leaders of the EU decided on December 16 to do "whatever is required" to defend their embattled euro. They agreed to establish a permanent support fund for the currency after 2013, in part to increase investor confidence.

On February 14, 2011, EU officials signaled that the bloc's new bailout fund would be capable of lending $677 billion, nearly twice the current pool of money. In July, inflation fell unexpectedly and consumer prices climbed 2.5 percent. At a critical summit on December 8 and 9, 2011, European leaders, except for the United Kingdom, agreed on a new fiscal treaty to adopt tighter spending controls. The chancellor of Germany was the apparent victor by persuading every current member of the union, except Britain, to endorse a new agreement calling for tighter regional oversight of government spending. If supported, it would permit the European Court of Justice to strike down a member's laws if they violated fiscal discipline. Participants in the Brussels session agreed to raise up to $270 billion that could be used by the IMF to aid indebted European nations, and they moved up the date that a European rescue fund would come into operation.

The financial and euro problems of 2011 had key dates for making critical decisions. They were:

February 4—As rumors of contagion grew, EU leaders argued that plans made in September would be reality by June.
March 11—With combined IMF-EU-ECB participation in Ireland and Greece, eurozone countries agreed to coordinate economic policies more

closely and urged faster work on bailout to reinforce markets' impressions that they are merely talking and talking.

July 21—A rift between all twenty-seven EU nations and the seventeen euro members appeared when the latter agreed to steps to ease the Greek debt crisis, including a bailout for some 109 billion euros.

October 27—Leaders agreed to a second bailout for debt-stricken Greece, an ambitious privatization plan with increases to the common currency's bailout funds.

December 9—By agreeing to an intergovernmental treaty shift at the level of twenty-six countries (the United Kingdom chose not to participate), a shift between the United Kingdom and the continental nations would arise.

The December 9 summit in Brussels was expected to salvage the euro for the seventeen participating nations for the immediate future, with acceptance of greater oversight and control of national budgets. Ultimately, however, four major concerns needed to be resolved before "victory" could be declared: how much money would be required to protect the debt-ridden nations from speculative attack; whether banks in the EU would falter because of the crisis; the probable isolation of the United Kingdom; and whether the found solution can improve the European Union's continuing economic dilemma. Ultimately, Germany's remedy for the sovereign debt crisis won out with promises of greater discipline, central oversight, and sanctions on nations that exceed the regulations on debt limits. These limits were set twenty years ago with the Maastricht Treaty at the time of the creation of the euro, identifying limits not to exceed 3 percent of the GDP and cumulative debt no more than 60 percent of GDP.

See also CAMERON, DAVID; DOW JONES INDUSTRIAL AVERAGE; EUROPE (BAILOUT); EUROPEAN PARLIAMENT; EUROPEAN UNION YOUTH; EUROZONE; ICELAND; INTERNATIONAL MONETARY FUND; IRELAND; MERKEL, ANGELA; STRESS TESTS (EUROPEAN UNION).

EUROPEAN UNION YOUTH. Unemployment among job seekers in the age range 15–24 is over one in five, or 20.3 percent. Youth unemployment was lowest in the Netherlands (7.1 percent), Austria (8.2 percent), and Germany (9.1 percent). It was highest in Spain at 45.7 percent and Greece at 38.5 percent.

See also UNEMPLOYMENT.

EUROPE (BAILOUT). A near trillion-dollar package, secured on May 8–9, 2010, intended to head off Greece's default and stop the crisis from dragging other weak economies of Europe into greater crisis. The reaction of the markets was impressive on their first day of trading after the bailout. The Dow Jones Industrial Average rose 3.9 percent and the Paris CAC-40 index rose nearly 10 percent. It afforded the European Central Bank to begin buying European debt immediately. In sum, the bailout tried to solve debt crisis with more debt.

See also DOW JONES INDUSTRIAL AVERAGE.

EUROZONE. In 2003, twelve European Union nations adopted a cooperative single-currency effort, now extended to most of the twenty-seven countries of the EU. In 2008, sixteen of the European Union countries were part of the eurozone.

The eurozone slipped into a recession during the third quarter of 2008. The figures pointed to the region's first recession since the inception of the euro in 1999. There was a sharp increase in imports into the eurozone compared with a surplus in 2007. Statistics of the EU indicated that the external trade deficit of the countries using the euro totaled $7.1 billion.

For the fourth quarter 2010, the EU's economy grew more slowly than expected. At 0.3 percent growth for the sixteen countries, it was below what analysts were prepared for. Following concerns of increased inflation, with the economic crisis in fall 2008, eurozone inflation declined in November. Evidence of a slowdown showed that consumer price inflation in the eurozone fell by 1.1 percentage points to 2.1 percent. It was expected that the inflation rates would fall below 1 percent in 2009 and might even turn negative.

The economies of nations sharing the euro had their worst performance in three decades. GDP shrank an annualized 5.9 percent in the fourth quarter. The eurozone's manufacturing sector had its worst month in more than ten years in February, the ninth consecutive month of contraction. In the final three months of 2008, the number of people at work in the then fifteen countries that used the euro plummeted by 453,000, an acceleration from the 80,000 jobs lost in the third quarter. This represented a drop in employment of 0.3 percent in the fourth quarter, compared with a fall of 0.1 percent in the prior period.

In February 2009, eurozone industrial producer prices posted their biggest year-on-year decline since 1999, while retail sales had their largest drop since 2000, when records were first kept. The International Monetary Fund reported in April that its bank reported just $154 billion in write-downs by the end of 2008, and in 2009 it still faced $750 billion in projected write-downs.

The inflation rate across the eurozone dropped to zero in May, the lowest in thirteen years of records, underlining the increasing risk of deflation—a damaging decline in wages and prices that could dampen recovery prospects worldwide. Prices were declining in six of the nations that shared the euro. The eurozone reported a trade surplus in May. Nonseasonally adjusted figures indicated that the surplus narrowed to $2.7 billion in May.

Consumer prices in the eurozone fell for the first time ever in June, while an index of producer prices fell by 6.6 percent in June from a year before, the sharpest fall since records began in 1982. Unemployment in the eurozone nations rose in July 2009 to the highest level in more than ten years. The jobless rate rose to 9.5 percent, the highest reading since May 1999. Nearly 22 million people in the EU were out of work. The European Commission estimated that the nations of the eurozone would see their economies stop contracting in the third quarter 2009. The eurozone had its fourth straight monthly increase in industrial output in August 2009. Industrial output in the sixteen countries increased 0.9 percent that month from July. Output growth was greatest in Germany, up 1.5 percent from July, France grew 1.5 percent, and Italy's factory output rose 7 percent.

The eurozone's trade balance swung to a deficit in August 2009 from a surplus in July after exports declined to their lowest level in four and a half years. The nations of the eurozone reported a combined trade deficit of $5.97 billion. Unemployment rose to 9.6 percent in August and 9.7 percent in September 2009. In the third quarter 2009, the eurozone economy returned to modest growth, marking the end of five months of recession. Economic activity expanded at an annualized rate of 1.5 percent in the period from July to September. Eurozone producer prices rose 0.2 percent in October from September. Producer prices fell 6.7 percent from October 2008. Bank lending fell in October 2009 at the fastest rate on record. Credit to the private sector was down 0.8 percent from a year before. By November, the pace of economic recovery gained momentum, with economic activity increasing 0.55 percent in November from 0.33 percent in October. Industrial producer prices rose by 0.2 percent but were still 6.7 percent lower than a year before.

In April 2010, a crisis appeared to be spreading throughout the euro-area. Greece's credit situation continued to deteriorate and appeared to be spreading to Portugal and perhaps beyond. The euro was threatened, and it was questionable whether the EU could or would protect its common currency. The euro tumbled to its lowest point in a year against the dollar, affecting world markets. In addition, the inflation rate was 1.5 percent in April 2010, up from 1.4 percent in March and considerably higher than the 0.6 percent of April 2009. The jobless rate as a whole climbed in April 2010 by a tenth of a percentage point to 10.1 percent. Eurozone finance ministers approved on June 7 a $520 billion rescue package. The bloc's currency rescue plan was the largest piece of a 750 billion euro package that included participation from the International Monetary Fund (matching funds of 250 billion euros) and the European Commission (60 billion euros). The remaining 440 billion euros would be raised and used as follows:

a. The market—capital markets will be the source for any bailout money. The rescue vehicle will borrow directly from markets, which should be more comfortable lending to it than directly to a troubled nation.

   b. The rescue vehicle—The special purpose vehicle is guaranteed by eurozone nations. Each participates in proportion to its share in the European Central Bank.

   c. The country in need of aid—It can use the funding to refinance its debt or pay bills. It will have to repay the rescue vehicle at a variable rate that currently is around 5 percent.

The eurozone economy grew by 1 percent in the second quarter 2010. Then, on September 23, bad news indicated that the eurozone's economy had reached a seven-month low. Consumer confidence across the sixteen nations using the euro was stable for October. The eurozone's economy slowed in the third quarter 2010 by 1.5 percent. That was less than half the second quarter's 3.9 percent growth rate. GDP in the sixteen-country region expanded by 0.4 percent compared with the previous three months; after increasing 1 percent in the second quarter, growth appeared to have slowed down. In November 2010, it was reported that eurozone consumer prices rose at their fastest rate in two years. The consumer prices climbed by 0.4 percent from September and were up 1.9 percent from October 2009. Unemployment in the eurozone climbed in October 2010 to its highest level in more than twelve years with a seasonally adjusted rate of 10.1 percent. The year before it was 9.6 percent. The lowest unemployment was in the Netherlands, at 4.4 percent, with 20.7 percent as the highest, in Spain.

By the outset of 2011, inflation in the eurozone climbed past the EU central bank's target for the first time in more than two years. Inflation throughout the EU was 2.2 percent, 0.2 percent above the EU's goal. Inflation in the eurozone raced at its fastest pace since late 2008. Industrial orders rose 1.4 percent from September and were up 14.8 percent from October 2009. In one year since January 2010, consumer prices in the seventeen nations rose 2.4 percent, well above the 2.0 percent EU target. In mid-March 2011, leaders agreed to expand the eurozone's current bailout capacity to 500 billion euros ($710 billion) from an earlier 300 billion euros. They also pledged to create a new 500 billion euro permanent bailout fund in 2013. In April, unemployment was still at 9.9 percent. The eurozone's trade balance fell into deficit in April after their collective exports dropped more sharply than imports from March. The seventeen nations' combined trade deficit was $5.8 billion following a March surplus, with exports falling more than 11 percent. The eurozone by mid-year 2011 showed that nearly one in ten people in the eurozone area remained unemployed. Inflation slowed slightly to 2.7 percent in May. Retail sales fell by 1.1 percent in May.

Following the sharp changes in stock market prices between August 1 and 5, 2011, the president of France and chancellor of Germany met on August

16 to set proposals in place to deal with the eurozone's growing financial crisis. Across the eurozone, GDP rose only 0.2 percent in the second quarter from 0.2 percent in the first quarter, in France GDP growth was flat, and in Germany, GDP expanded a mere 0.1 percent. To evolve fiscal bonding in the seventeen nation eurozone, they proposed to elect a eurozone president, recommended to be the twenty-seven-nation European Council President Herman Van Rompuy; enshrine fiscal discipline in the constitutions of the seventeen eurozone countries; introduce a tax on financial transactions with the eurozone; align French and German corporate tax rates; and prepare French and German future annual budgets on the basis of shared macro-economic analysis. A "golden rule" was called for where each nation in the eurozone would enshrine this practice into their national constitutions to work toward balanced budgets and debt reduction. By mid-September, the euro-zone's business activity shrank for the first time in more than two years. On October 4, eurozone officials had to live with the possible break up of Dexia SA, a Belgian-French bank and Moody's downgrading of Italy's debt rating by three notches to A2.

By the end of October 2011, economic activity in the currency bloc shrank for the first time since the 2009 recession. Predictions for the zone's GDP were expected to slow from the meager 0.2 percent. Inflation remained stuck at a three-year high, and unemployment climbed by 188,000, pushing the job-less rate up 0.1 percentage points to 10.2 percent. Unemployment was now at its highest level, 16.2 million, since records were kept in January 1998. By December, the possible default on its debts appeared to be secondary in importance to whether the eurozone would survive in its current form. The European Central Bank was considering a dramatic extension of its longest loans to commercial banks to fight off a potential collapse of the bloc's bank-ing system. At the same time, leaders of the three largest economies in the EU pledged to work toward a closer political and economic integration. The four largest eurozone economies indicated a slowdown in November. By year's end, the eurozone economy had slowed markedly from a 3.1 percent annual growth pace in its first quarter to just 0.8 percent.

The Organisation for Economic Co-operation and Development expected the eurozone to have a mild recession lasting until April 2012. Eurozone governments had to repay nearly $1.5 trillion of long- and short-term debt in 2012, with about $695 billion of Italian, French, and German debt maturing in the first half of the year.

On December 16, it was announced that only nine nations of the eurozone would have to approve the new fiscal treaty. Then on December 19, eurozone finance ministers confirmed plans to contribute $195.6 billion in additional bilateral loans to the IMF as part of a move to boost its resources for crisis response. The year 2012 would require further action. The eurozone's annual inflation fell to 2.8 percent in December from 3 percent the previous month. For the year 2011, eurozone unemployment was 10.4 percent.

On January 6, 2012, a new report indicated that business and consumer confidence in the eurozone had worsened, with strong possibilities that the area was in a recession well into the year. Its economic sentiment indicator fell for a tenth straight month to its lowest point in more than one year. At their January 30 summit in Brussels, leaders of the EU nations agreed to move closer to fiscal union and signed off on the details of a permanent bailout fund for the eurozone. They noted "tentative signs" of economic stabilization in Europe, but financial market tensions continued to weigh on the economy.

See also BANK FOR BAILOUTS; BLUE/RED BONDS; CONSUMER-PRICE INFLATION; CREDIT SQUEEZE; DEFLATION; DEXIA SA; EURO; EUROBONDS; EUROPEAN CENTRAL BANK; EUROPEAN COMMISSION; EUROPEAN COURT OF JUSTICE; EUROPEAN UNION; EUROZONE LENDING; FINLAND; ICELAND; IRELAND; MERKEL, ANGELA; MOODY'S; PORTUGAL; RETAIL SALES; SARKOZY, NICOLAS; STANDARD & POOR'S; UNITED KINGDOM.

Synonymous with EURO-AREA.

EUROZONE BONDS. *See* CREDIT SQUEEZE; EURO-BONDS.

EUROZONE DEBT CRISIS. *See* EUROPEAN UNION.

EUROZONE LENDING. In 2008, eurozone loans stagnated as the economy slumped and lenders tightened credit standards. Lending had expanded at the slowest rate in seventeen years. The annual growth of lending to the private sector slowed to 7.1 percent in November from a rate of 7.8 percent in October. The annual growth rate of loans to households fell to a low of 2.5 percent in November from 3.3 percent in October.

Employment failed to grow across the eurozone nations in the third-quarter 2010, with divergence between the larger economic nations and the struggling ones becoming more obvious. Third-quarter employment growth was zero after a 0.1 percent jump in the second quarter from the first. In October, the unemployment rate reached a high, standing at 10.3 percent. The average youth unemployment rate for those under twenty-five was 21.4 percent.

In addition, inflation surged by the end of September 2011, with consumer prices climbing at their fastest rate, 3 percent, in nearly three years—the most rapid climb in prices since October 2008.

See also AMERICAN RECOVERY AND REINVESTMENT ACT (OF 2009); EUROPEAN CENTRAL BANK; EUROZONE; LENDING.

EUROZONE RESCUE PACKAGE. *See* EUROPEAN UNION; EUROZONE.

EUROZONE SUMMIT (DECEMBER 2011). *See* EUROPEAN UNION.

EVER GREENING. *See* ZOMBIES.

EXCHANGE RATES. Most major currencies had weakened against the dollar since the end of 2008. By April 22, 2009, the biggest loser had been the Swiss franc, which fell by 8.4 percent in 2009. The euro, the Korean won, and the Swedish krona also weakened by more than 6 percent against the U.S. dollar, and the yen had fallen by 7.6 percent. The British pound had risen by 1.1 percent against the dollar, but only after collapsing against the dollar in 2008.

EXCHANGE-TRADED FUND (ETF). An investment that uses futures to hedge against broad market declines instead of shorting individual stocks. Fees for exchange-traded funds are small compared to management charges by many hedge funds. ETFs did not exist more than a decade ago; today, there are nearly 1,000 U.S. listings. Originally, ETFs dealt with passive investments in specific securities.

Cf. HEDGE FUNDS.

EXECUTIVE COMPENSATION LEGISLATION. Proposal to give shareholders the right to vote on compensation and required that independent directors sit on compensation committees. If enacted, it would allow regulators to prohibit inappropriate or risky compensation practices for banks and other financial institutions.

By mid-September 2009, this legislation had passed the House of Representatives but had yet to be considered by the Senate.

See also EXECUTIVE PAY; HOUSE (U.S.) FINANCIAL OVERHAUL PLAN.

EXECUTIVE PAY. Many have criticized the six- and seven-figure paychecks that Wall Street's top brass collected in pre-2008 years while driving their companies—and the entire financial system—into the ground.

President Obama, on February 4, 2009, laid out a plan for executive compensation with a cap of $500,000 for top executives at firms that accepted "extraordinary assistance" from the government, except for restricted stock. The pay would be disclosed to shareholders for a nonbinding vote. Bonuses would be clawed back if they provided misleading information. No golden parachutes would be permitted upon severance, and the board would decide policies on luxuries such as airplanes and entertainment. The rules were not retroactive to firms that had already been bailed out.

A provision of the $787 billion economic stimulus plan imposed restrictions on executive bonuses at financial institutions. The restrictions prevented top executives from receiving bonuses that exceeded one-third of their annual pay. Any bonus would have to be in the form of long-term incentives, like restricted stocks, which would not be cashed out until the TARP money was paid back in full.

On March 22, the president called for increased oversight of executive pay at all Wall Street institutions as part of a sweeping plan to overhaul financial regulations. The president was seeking a broader new role for the Federal Reserve to oversee large firms, including major hedge funds, proposing that numerous derivatives and other exotic financial instruments that contributed to the crisis be traded on exchanges or through clearinghouses so they are more transparent and can be more rigorously regulated. It also called for federal standards for mortgage lenders beyond what the Federal Reserve adopted in 2008, as well as greater enforcement of mortgage regulations.

See also AUSTRALIA; BONUSES; CLAWBACKS; COMPENSATION; EXECUTIVE COMPENSATION LEGISLATION; FEDERAL RESERVE; FINANCIAL REGULATION PLAN (2009); GOLDEN PARACHUTES; HOUSE (U.S.) FINANCIAL OVERHAUL PLAN; MORGAN STANLEY; NAME AND SHAME.

EX-IM BANK. See EXPORT-IMPORT BANK.

EXPAND REGULATORY POWERS LEGISLATION. Proposal that would give the Federal Deposit Insurance Corporation the power to seize and liquidate any troubled financial institution; it would require hedge funds to register with the Securities and Exchange Commission and to open their books. The legislation gives the Federal Reserve the power to regulate and oversee any large financial institution whose failure would threaten the economy.

By mid-September 2009, there had been no action in either the House or Senate committees. There has been much disagreement over whether the Federal Reserve should be a systematic regulator.

EXPORT-IMPORT BANK (EX-IM BANK). Created in 1934 to help fight the Great Depression.

See also BOEING.

EXPORTS (U.S.). The spiraling financial crisis severely affected the U.S. export market. The trade deficit widened in October 2008 for the first time in three months as exports dropped 2.2 percent, with large declines in sales of American-made products like automobiles and consumer goods. China, one of the larger sources of export demand, had cut back sharply. October exports totaled $151.7 billion. Sales of U.S.–made cars and car parts fell $236 million, consumer goods exports dropped $156 million, and industrial supply sales fell $1.4 billion. Exports by the end of 2008 and into 2009 declined in almost every country as the world endured a recession. The decline began in the summer of 2008 after Lehman Brothers failed. Credit became harder to obtain for importers and confidence waned among would-be buyers of many products. Overall, the total reported exports from forty-three countries peaked in July 2008 at $1.03 trillion. By November, it was down 26 percent to $766 billion.

In February 2009, U.S. exports rose by 1.6 percent to $126.8 billion, the first gain since July 2008. Farming exports, once a major source of income for U.S. farmers, declined during the meltdown. Developing nations were slowing their food imports, the price of dairy products was slumping, and the strengthening U.S. dollar made imports more costly. Farm commodities fell 40 to 50 percent from six months before. Farm exports, which account for about 20 percent of the value of farm production, dropped to $96 billion in 2009 from $117 billion in 2008.

By the end of the first quarter, exports from the United States declined 30 percent from the previous three months. The dollar value of exports, which surged in July 2009, rose another 0.2 percent in August. That put exports at their highest gain since December 2008 but still 21 percent below the same time one year earlier. Between 2008 and 2009, U.S. exports fell by $272 billion, while imports dropped by $589 billion. As a result, the trade deficit narrowed sharply to $379 billion from $696 billion. As a share of GDP, it was the lowest since 1998.

Not since before the financial meltdown began had there been so great a surge in U.S. exports. In October 2010, along with a 0.5 percent fall in imports, the U.S. trade deficit fell to a nine-month low of $38.7 billion. Exports during the month hit their highest level since August 2008. Export prices increased 6.5 percent in 2010, the largest calendar-year jump on record. Prices for exports rose 3.4 percent in 2009. By January 2011, U.S. exports climbed to a record level. The deficit increased 15 percent to $46.3 billion. Exports surged 2.7 percent during the month to a record of $167.7 billion. During this period, exports rose 21 percent compared with an average of 11 percent in other recoveries. The problem was that the export sector wasn't significant enough to drive the whole $14 trillion economy.

See also AUTOMOBILE INDUSTRY; DEFICIT (BUDGET, U.S.); NATIONAL EXPORT INITIATIVE; TRADE DEFICIT (U.S.).

Cf. IMPORTS.

EXTENDERS. See TAX CUTS.

EXURBIA. By 2011, people who had moved to exurbia to find homes less costly than in suburbia were finding the cost of gas prices pushing more of them into foreclosure on their houses.

See also FORECLOSURE.

EXXON (EXXONMOBIL). The energy company, the world's largest publicly traded oil firm, reported on July 30 that its second-quarter 2009 profit tumbled 66 percent. Its net income fell to $3.95 billion from $11.68 billion one year before.

Exxon's second-quarter 2010 earnings climbed 91 percent. Management reported a profit of $7.56 billion with revenue climbing 24 percent to $92.48 billion. Its fourth-quarter earnings surged 53 percent, with its profit climbing to $9.25 billion, from $6.05 the year earlier.

In January 2011, Exxon management reported a 53 percent increase in its fourth-quarter 2010 profit, the strongest quarterly profit in more than two years. The quarterly profit was $9.25 billion, contrasted with $6.05 billion the year earlier. Total revenue in the quarter was $105.2 billion, an increase from $89.8 billion twelve months before. For 2010, ExxonMobil made $30.46 billion, compared with $19.28 billion for 2009. Revenue climbed to $383 billion from $310 billion the previous year. ExxonMobil reported that its first-quarter 2011 earnings surged 69 percent, with earnings climbing to $10.65 billion from $6.3 billion. On July 29, ExxonMobil reported earnings of $10.7 billion for the quarter, climbing from $7.56 billion the year before. Management reported on October 27 that its profit surged 41 percent, with net income of $10.33 billion and revenue up 32 percent to $125.33 billion.

Its fourth-quarter profit, announced on January 31, 2012, climbed 1.6 percent. Its profit was $9.4 billion, with revenue increasing 16 percent to $121.61 billion.

See also APPLE.

F

"FABULOUS FAB." *See* GOLDMAN SACHS; TOURRE, FABRICE.

FACEBOOK. The pioneering social network set a historic initial public offering when on February 1, 2012, it filed for an initial public offering that could be valued at between $75 billion and $100 billion, one of the largest U.S. stockmarket debuts of all time. The firm hopes to raise as much as $10 billion when it begins to sell shares in the spring of 2012. In 2011, Facebook showed a $1 billon profit with growing revenue of 88 percent from the year before at $3.71 billion. Founded by twenty-seven year-old Mark Zuckerberg, who owns about 28 percent of the company and holds 57 percent of its voting share power.
　　See also INITIAL PUBLIC OFFERING.
　　Cf. GOOGLE; MICROSOFT; YAHOO!.

FACTORY ORDERS. Factory orders declined 0.8 percent in August 2009 from a month before, following four months of increases. Orders rose 0.6 percent in October, the sixth gain in seven months. Durable goods orders rose 0.6 percent and nondurable goods 1.6 percent.
　　Factory output surged 0.9 percent in March 2010. U.S. industries operated at 73.2 percent of capacity that month, up 3.7 percentage points from the year before.
　　See also DURABLE GOODS.

FACTORY OUTPUT. *See* FACTORY ORDERS.

FAILED BANKS. By August 1, 2009, regulators, usually the Federal Deposit Insurance Corporation, had closed 68 failed banks nationwide in 2009, compared with 25 in 2008 and 3 in 2007. It would reach 100 by mid-October 2009. By mid-November, the FDIC had taken over 150 failed banks.
　　Of the failed banks since February 2007, 75 of them were created after 1999. The result was that in the past two years, the banking industry had lost about 188,000 jobs, or 8.5 percent, since 2007. Failures alone have cost 11,210 positions, or 32 percent of workers, at failed banks. By the end of September 2010, 279 banks had collapsed since September 25, 2008. By mid-November, the number had grown to 149 banks. By year's end, 98 banks

that had aided by TARP monies slipped into failure. In total, 92 banks failed in 2011, far below the previous two year's totals: 140 banks failed in 2009 and 157 failed in 2010.

Going into 2012, 844 banks remain on regulator's list.

See also BANK FAILURES; COLONIAL BANCGROUP; MARKET CAPITALIZATION; TROUBLED ASSET RELIEF PROGRAM; WALL STREET REFORM ACT (2010).

FALLEN ANGELS. Blue chip companies at risk of losing investment-grade ratings. A cut to junk status invariably adds to financing risks. Before the meltdown, banks were healthy enough and provided alternative funding, and high-yield investors were keen to purchase bonds from large firms as the bank debt was refinanced.

Today, a downgrade to junk may be just the start of a firm's problems. If financing is unavailable, and raising equity proves troublesome, management can be forced into disposals or spending cuts that further harm credit quality. This could lead to fallen angels continuing their fall.

FALLING PRICES. *Synonymous with* DEFLATION.

FAMILIES. *See* CHILDREN IN POVERTY; POVERTY.

FAMILY DOLLAR STORES. Posted a 23 percent climb in fiscal fourth-quarter profit on September 29, 2010, with sales growth of 5 percent to 7 percent. Its profit rose to $74 million from $60.1 million the year before.

First-quarter 2011 earnings climbed 9.9 percent, with sales up 6.9 percent. On January 6, the company announced that its December sales grew by 4 percent. In March 2011, management reported that sales climbed during the quarter ending February 26 to $2.26 billion from $2.09 billion the year earlier. Management stated that in September its fiscal fourth-quarter profit rose 8 percent, with its more than 7,000 stores. It had a net profit of $79.8 million, up 8 percent from $74 million the year before. Per-share earnings climbed nearly 18 percent, with sales rising 9.1 percent to $2.13 billion.

See also RETAILING.

FANNIE AND FREDDIE. Fannie Mae and Freddie Mac, the bailed-out mortgage giants, cost the taxpayers upward of $125 billion during the Great Recession, with more to come. Their combined importance is astounding in that nine of every ten new mortgages are sold to or guaranteed by the two institutions. Their troubles began when they faced competition of securitizing loans and providing liquidity to the mortgage market, resulting in their losing profits and stock prices. Eventually, their debts reached a shocking level of 100 times their capital. Since late 2008, they both have been wards of the state.

By May 2010, both Fannie and Freddie consumed a combined $145 billion in taxpayer cash, with an unlimited funnel to the U.S. Treasury. In June 2010, the federal regulator of Fannie Mae and Freddie Mac ordered the two mortgage finance giants to delist their common and preferred stock from the New York Stock Exchange, resulting from their shares falling below the $1 share-price required threshold.

On February 11, 2011, the president outlined his plans to begin shrinking the government's broad support of the nation's crippled mortgage market and would include phasing out Fannie Mae and Freddie Mac. The administration wanted maximum loan limits to fall to $625,000 from $729,750 and to increase minimum down payments to 10 percent on loans. In addition, the role of the government would be limited to the Federal Housing Administration and other smaller housing units. Other options remained on the table and whatever is passed might take years to implement.

See also FANNIE MAE; FREDDIE MAC.

FANNIE MAE (FEDERAL NATIONAL MORTGAGE ASSOCIATION) (FNMA). An independent, government-sponsored enterprise (GSE) agency originally chartered in 1938 and reconstituted in 1954. Its major function is to purchase mortgages from banks, trust companies, mortgage companies, savings and loan associations, and insurance companies to help these institutions with their distribution of funds for home mortgages. Nicknamed Fannie Mae, the mortgage finance company is now under government control. On March 20, 2008, federal regulators eased Fannie Mae's capital requirements, a move that allowed the agency to buy an additional billion dollars of mortgage securities.

The U.S. mortgage financial company announced on November 10 a $29 billion loss for the third quarter and that it was losing money so fast that it would have to tap the federal government for cash to avoid shutting down. Along with Freddie Mac, Fannie Mae owns or guarantees about half of all mortgages in the United States. Credit expenses soared to $9.2 billion in the quarter as mortgage credit conditions deteriorated and as home prices declined. On November 11, both Freddie Mac and Fannie Mae announced that they planned a broad new effort to reduce the loan burdens of homeowners facing foreclosure. The program was offered to people who are at least ninety days behind on their payments. The goal was to modify the mortgage—most likely by reducing the interest rate—so that the monthly loan payment would be no higher than 38 percent of the borrower's monthly income. The plan would help as many as 300,000 families that were delinquent in their mortgage payments. Borrowers would have to provide evidence that they had suffered a hardship, such as losing a job. They would have to be occupying the home, and they would have to go through a ninety-day trial period before the loan modification became final.

On February 26, 2009, Fannie Mae reported a $25.2 billion loss for the fourth quarter 2008, with homeowner defaults continuing to increase even as the government redirected the company to focus its attention on preventing foreclosures and propping up the housing market. For the entire 2008, Fannie had a loss of $58.7 billion, compared with a year-earlier loss of $2.1 billion. The loss for 2008 exceeded net income for the preceding seventeen years. The "Deed for Lease" program permits borrowers who don't qualify for loan modifications to transfer their property to Fannie Mae for a lease. Fannie May acquired 57,000 properties through foreclosures during the first half of 2009. The government announced on December 24 significant new financial support for Fannie Mae, no matter how poorly it performs in the coming two years. The U.S. government already owns 79.9 percent of Fannie Mae and permitted its chief executive to receive up to $6 million in compensation for two years. The pay package includes a $900,000 salary, $3.1 million in deferred payments in 2010 that are not dependent on performance, and an additional $2 million to meeting certain goals.

On May 10, 2010, Fannie Mae reported its eleventh consecutive quarterly loss of $11.5 billion and requested another $8.4 billion in government assistance. Fannie Mae posted a narrower third-quarter 2010 net loss of $1.3 billion, becoming the thirteenth consecutive quarterly loss. A 13 percent increase in revenue, to $5.1 billion, was also given, along with an increase in credit losses, rising 13 percent to $5.6 billion. Fannie announced on November 27 that it had lifted a moratorium on foreclosure sales after a review of the affected properties it had acquired.

On February 11, 2011, President Obama announced his intention to phase out Fannie Mae, thus curbing the government's role in housing finance. Then, in early May 2011, Fannie Mae reported a net loss of $6.5 billion for its first quarter. It would request an additional infusion of $6.2 billion from the U.S. government. Fannie Mae posted a loss of $2.9 billion for the second quarter 2011, up from a year-before loss of $1.2 billion. The mortgage finance firm reported losses in fifteen of the last sixteen quarters. Fannie Mae has to date received $104 billion in government aid and raised its loss reserves to $75 billion. On August 8, Standard & Poor's downgraded Fannie Mae's stock from AAA to AA+. On October 3, the government revealed that Fannie Mae had learned as early as 2003 of extensive foreclosure abuses among law firms hired to remove troubled borrowers from their homes. The firm did little to adjust the law firms' practices. By mid-2011, Fannie Mae started to scrutinize this conduct.

See also FANNIE AND FREDDIE; FEDERAL HOUSING FINANCE AGENCY; FEDERAL RESERVE; FINANCIAL CRISIS INQUIRY REPORT; FORECLOSURE; FREDDIE MAC; GINNIE MAE; HOUSING

PLAN; MODIFYING MORTGAGES; MORTGAGE-BACKED SECU-RITY; SECURITIES AND EXCHANGE COMMISSION; STANDARD & POOR'S; UNDERWATER; U.S. TREASURY.

FARM EXPORTS. *See* EXPORTS (U.S.).

FARMING. The Agriculture Department forecast on August 27, 2009, that U.S. farm profits would fall 38 percent for the year. Net farm income was expected to drop to $54 billion, down $33.2 billion from a year earlier.

Rising demand in the agriculture sector led by the end of November 2010 to a 31 percent jump in profit ability to $81.6 billion from $62.2 billion in 2009.

See also AGRICULTURE; CORN; FARM REAL ESTATE; UNEM-PLOYMENT.

FARM REAL ESTATE. Values of farm real estate fell for the first time in more than twenty years, according to the U.S. Department of Agriculture. The value of all land and buildings on U.S. farms averaged $2,100 an acre on January 1, 2009, down 3.2 percent from a year before. The decline was the first since 1987. Farmland values across the upper Midwest jumped 10 percent since the end of 2009, with the highest of 12.2 percent in Kansas. Affected by the increase in prices, there is growing concern that a collapse may occur during this frenzy period of growth.

By 2011, farmland values rose at their fastest rate since the 2008 boom, jumping around 14.8 percent in some areas. In a few districts, farmland prices rose 23.4 percent and prices on nonirrigated farmland rose 21.2 percent.

FASB. *See* FINANCIAL ACCOUNTING STANDARDS BOARD.

FCIC. *See* FINANCIAL CRISIS INQUIRY COMMISSION.

FDI. *See* FOREIGN DIRECT INVESTMENT.

FDIC. *See* FEDERAL DEPOSIT INSURANCE CORPORATION.

FEAR GAUGE. Prices investors are willing to pay to buy and sell stocks or options.
See also CONSUMER CONFIDENCE.

"FEAR INDEX." *See* VIX.

FED. Short for Federal Reserve (System).
See also FEDERAL RESERVE.

FEDERAL ADVISORY COUNCIL. A committee of the Federal Reserve System that advises the Board of Governors on major developments and activities.

FEDERAL AID HIGHWAY ACT (OF 1956). Signed by President Dwight David Eisenhower, ultimately resulting in the construction of 42,795 miles of roads, dramatically improving highway travel. In 1991, the government concluded that the total cost of the act was $128.9 billion. Eisenhower's interstate highway system, at $400 billion in today's dollars, cost four times as much and took three times as long as planned.

In September 2008, the nonpartisan Congressional Budget Office estimated it would take two years to spend just 60 percent of $37 billion in infrastructure funds in a stimulus bill. President Obama was considering spending taxpayers' monies to rebuild U.S. infrastructures, including roads and highways.

FEDERAL CREDIT UNION. A cooperative association organized under the Federal Credit Union Act for the purpose of accepting savings from people, making loans to them at low interest rates, and rendering other financial services to members.

FEDERAL DEBT. By the end of 2007, the federal debt was 64.4 percent of the economy. By the summer 2011, it was about 100 percent of GDP, an amount not seen since the end of World War II.

See also AMERICAN RECOVERY AND REINVESTMENT ACT (OF 2009); DEBT (U.S.).

FEDERAL DEFICIT. A public or federal debt; the difference that exists between revenue and government expenditures. The deficit hit a record $311 billion for the first half of fiscal 2008 as corporate tax revenue fell.

See also DEFICIT (BUDGET, U.S.); EMERGENCY ECONOMIC STABILIZATION ACT OF 2008; FEDERAL RESERVE; SOCIAL SECURITY.

FEDERAL DEPOSIT INSURANCE CORPORATION (FDIC). A government corporation that insures the deposits of all banks that are entitled to the benefits of insurance under the Federal Reserve Act. The Federal Deposit Insurance Corporation was created through the Banking Act of 1933 and was affected by amendments of 1935. All national banks and all state banks that are members of the Federal Reserve System are required by law to be members of the FDIC. Mutual savings banks are also encouraged to join.

In January 2009, the FDIC began asking banks getting capital injections from the $700 billion financial rescue program to report how they were using the funds to support consumer lending and foreclosure relief.

The FDIC, which insures deposits on accounts worth up to $250,000, estimated that it would lose $65 billion through 2013 as a result of bank failures. Its board imposed on February 27 a one-time $15 billion increase in insurance premiums on the nation's 8,300 banks. Banks were required to pay $27 billion to replenish the insurance funds in 2009, nine times more than in 2008.

A three-page bill, proposed in March 2009, to give greater clout to the FDIC would temporarily allow the FDIC to borrow $500 billion to replenish the fund it employed to guarantee bank deposits. The Federal Reserve and Treasury Department must support this presidential request, which would permanently raise the level that the FDIC could borrow from the Treasury, now $30 billion, to $100 billion, and the FDIC could use these funds without prior approval from the Federal Reserve and the Treasury.

Banks have benefited from the purchase of FDIC-backed bonds (in billions), as follows:

Bank of America	$44.0
JP Morgan Chase	$45.0
General Electric	$37.7
Citigroup	$27.6
Morgan Stanley	$23.8
Goldman Sachs	$21.1
Wells Fargo	$9.5
American Express	$5.6
State Street	$3.9
PNC Financial Services	$3.9

On August 27, 2009, the FDIC reported that it had 416 U.S. banks on its problem list, equivalent to 5 percent of the nation's banks, up from 305 at the end of March and 117 at the end of June 2008. These problem banks had a combined $299.8 billion of assets at the end of June, compared with $78.3 billion a year before. By this time in 2008, the FDIC had closed 25 banks, compared to 95 in 2009. Then, in early October, the FDIC seized three small lenders in Michigan, Minnesota, and Colorado, bringing the number of banks that had failed in 2009 to 98. The FDIC insurance fund guards $6.2 trillion in U.S. deposits. These funds dropped $10.4 billion at the quarter's end, the lowest since mid-1993.

By the end of September 2009, the FDIC was considering asking healthy banks to lend them billions of dollars to rescue its insurance fund, which was quickly running out of money because of a wave of bank failures. Under the law, the FDIC does not require permission from the U.S. Treasury to tap into a credit line of up to $100 billion. Borrowing from the banks is allowed under a 1991 law adopted during the savings and loan crisis. The lending institutions would receive bonds from the government at an interest rate that would be set by the Treasury Department and ultimately be paid by the rest of the industry. The bonds would be listed as an asset on the books of the banks. On September 29, the government announced that the FDIC funds that protect consumer bank deposits had fallen into the red and would remain there into

2012. The FDIC asked the banking industry to prepay $45 billion in fees by the end of the year to give the government more breathing room to handle future failures. By mid-November 2009, the FDIC had taken over 150 failed banks. In this process, the FDIC had seized more than 5,000 homes, subdivisions, buildings, parcels, and other foreclosed assets.

The FDIC planned to add more than 1,600 employees in 2010, with a budget boost of 35 percent to handle bank failures. The agency would spend $2.5 billion to fund its bank failure operations out of its total budget of $4 billion. The FDIC presented its plans, as required by the Wall Street Reform Act, to replace private credit ratings in their review of bank capital levels. Among its options under discussion is a greater use of credit spreads, having supervisors develop their own risk metrics, and a reliance on existing internal models.

The FDIC outlined on October 12 how it would respond to the Wall Street Reform Act to be a receiver for bringing about the "orderly liquidation" of huge financial firms as an alternative to bankruptcy court. The authority is intended to avoid a recurrence of bank failures. The proposals will require the creditors of a large financial firm to suffer losses if the firm fell apart. It would bar further payments to shareholders and holders of long-term senior debt and subordinated debt.

On February 7, 2011, the FDIC announced that large financial institutions would pick up a great portion of the cost to protect deposits when banks fail. The new fee took placed in April 2011, resulting in about 110 large banks covering about 80 percent of the premiums paid into the government's deposit insurance fund each year, up from 70 percent. In 2011, the FDIC was expected to generate $14 billion in premiums. As part of her legacy, Sheila Bair, who stepped down as chairman of the FDIC in mid-July 2011, at her last meeting finalized a rule allowing the government to recover compensation from executives responsible for a financial firm's collapse.

On January 17, 2012, the FDIC announced a stress-test proposal for the twenty-three qualifying banks it overseas.

See also ASSETS; BANK FAILURES; SYSTEMATIC RISK EXCEPTION; TROUBLED ASSET RELIEF PROGRAM; WALL STREET REFORM ACT (2010).

FEDERAL DISCOUNT RATE. The interest rate charged on federal funds. The interest is charged on a discount basis and is a key factor in determining the prime rate charged for commercial loans.

FEDERAL EXPRESS (FEDEX). Coping with slumping volumes, the package delivery company slashed pay for 35,000 employees in December 2008.

In early February 2009, FedEx cut another 900 positions, representing about 2.5 percent of the roughly 35,000 employees working in the freight division of the Memphis, Tennessee, company. In mid-March, FedEx reported a 75 percent drop in quarterly profit. By June, FedEx posted a loss of $876 million in the quarter. On September 17, FedEx reported a 53 percent fall in quarterly profit. The company reported a profit of $181 million for the first quarter ending on August 31. Then on November 10, 2009, the company forecast that it would ship more than 13 million packages on the busiest day of the year, December 14, an increase of 8 percent from the year before. The company reported on December 9 that its second-quarter 2009 earnings would easily surpass its previous forecast. FedEx shipped 14.1 million packages on December 13, with sales falling 9.9 percent to $8.6 billion. Profit fell to $345 million.

By June 2010, shipments from Asia climbed 1 percent and its U.S. ground delivery volume rose 7 percent in the quarter ending in May. Management projected growth for the fiscal year at 3.1 percent. On September 16, 2010, FedEx announced that its fiscal first-quarter profit 2010 more than doubled, with a profit of $380 million, up from $181 million the year before. Revenue for the quarter increased 18 percent, as contrasted to the 20 percent decline the year before. The company announced that it earned $380 million and that it would cut 1,700 jobs in its U.S. operations, representing about 5 percent of its workforce. Toward year's end, management reported that its revenue rose 12 percent to $9.63 billion, up from $8.60 billion the year before.

On June 22, 2011, FedEx management announced a 33 percent surge in profit for its fourth quarter. In mid-September, management reported that earnings climbed 22 percent to $464 million in the firm's fiscal first quarter ending August 31, up from $380 million a year before. Revenue climbed 11 percent to $10.5 billion. On December 15, management reported a 76 percent increase in quarterly profit of $497 million. Revenue climbed 10 percent to $10.59 billion from $9.63 billion the year earlier.

Cf. UNITED PARCEL SERVICE.

FEDERAL FINANCING BANK (FFB). Established in 1973 to assist in financing U.S. government agencies, the Federal Financing Bank is authorized to acquire any obligation that is issued, sold, or guaranteed by any federal agency, except those of the Farm Credit System, the Federal Home Loans Banks, the Federal Home Loan Mortgage Corporation, and the Federal National Mortgage Association.

FEDERAL FUNDS. Funds available at a Federal Reserve Bank, including excess reserves of member banks and checks drawn in payment for purchases by the Federal Reserve Bank of government securities.

FEDERAL FUNDS MARKET. The market in which excess bank reserves are borrowed and lent by federal banks.

FEDERAL FUNDS PAYMENT/TRANSFER. Payment made by check or wire transfer against a bank's account with a Federal Reserve Bank.

FEDERAL FUNDS PURCHASED. Short-term borrowing of reserves from another bank.

FEDERAL FUNDS RATE. The interest rate charged on loans by banks that have excess reserve funds (above the level required by the Federal Reserve) to those banks with deficient reserves. The Federal Reserve funds rate is closely watched as an early warning indication of major changes in the national economy.

FEDERAL FUNDS TRANSACTIONS. The reporting bank's lending (federal funds sold) or borrowing (federal funds purchased) of immediately available funds for one business day or under a continuing contract, regardless of the nature of the contract or of the collateral, if any. Due bills and borrowings from the Discount and Credit Department of a Federal Reserve Bank are excluded from federal funds.

FEDERAL GOVERNMENT SECURITIES. All obligations of the U.S. government.

FEDERAL HOME BANK (FEDERAL HOME LOAN BANK). One of twelve regional banks established in 1932 to encourage local thrift and home financing during the Depression. The banks are owned jointly by various savings and loan associations. The Federal Home Loan Bank Board serves as a management body.

On July 2, 2009, the Federal Home Loan Banks' net income dropped 51 percent to $345 million in the first quarter 2009 from $697 million a year earlier. The drop reflected $516 million of write-downs on mortgage securities held by some of the twelve regional banks. By the end of October, the Federal Home Loan Banks continued to struggle with soured investments in mortgage securities, with a combined third-quarter 2009 loss of $165 million. The loss showed write-downs totaling $1.04 billion in the value of private-label mortgage-backed securities.

FEDERAL HOME LOAN BANKS. See FEDERAL HOME BANK.

FEDERAL HOME LOAN BANK ACT OF 1932. A system that provided a stable source of funds for residential mortgages during the Great Depression. Members could obtain advances on home mortgage collateral and borrow from home loan banks under certain conditions.

FEDERAL HOME LOAN MORTGAGE CORPORATION. See FREDDIE MAC.

FEDERAL HOUSING ADMINISTRATION (FIIA). Government agency that insures mortgage loans. By September 2009, the Federal Housing Administration's reserves were being pushed below the level required by Congress. At the end of June, 7.8 percent of FHA-backed loans were ninety days late or more or in foreclosure, up from 5.4 percent a year earlier. By the end of September, the FHA indicated that its reserves were shrinking rapidly. The agency might require a federal bailout. About 20 percent of FHA loans insured in 2008, and as many as 24 percent of those from 2007, faced serious problems, including foreclosures. The FHA's capital reserves fell far below the minimum of 2 percent. On November 12, 2009, the FHA noted that its reserves had been depleted much faster than the agency had anticipated. The capital reserve fund fell to $3.6 billion as of September 30, down 72 percent from the year before, leaving reserves at just 0.53 percent of the $685 billion in total loans insured by the FHA.

On November 12, 2010, the president tapped Joseph A. Smith Jr. to head the regulatory agency that oversees mortgage giants Fannie Mae and Freddie Mac. Then, it was announced that the FHA could run out of funds, suggesting that it would require a government bailout for the first time in its seventy-seven-year history.

See also SMITH, JOSEPH A.; STEVENS, DAVID.

FEDERAL HOUSING ENTERPRISE OVERSIGHT. *See* OFFICE OF FEDERAL HOUSING ENTERPRISE OVERSIGHT.

FEDERAL HOUSING FINANCE AGENCY (FHFA). Independent federal regulator of government-sponsored enterprises created by the Housing and Economic Recovery Act of 2008 as successor to the Office of Federal Housing Enterprise Oversight and the Federal Housing Finance Board.

On September 2, 2011, the FHFA filed lawsuits against seventeen financial institutions, including some of the nation's largest banks, alleging a pattern of fraud in their packaging and selling of roughly $200 billion worth of mortgage-linked securities. The suits amounted to one of the most significant legal actions to emerge from the fallout of the financial crisis of 2008. The FHFA claimed that these institutions knowingly peddled shoddy deals without informing investors. When the housing market crashed and those deals went sour, the damage rippled through economies around the world, plunging nations into recession.

The named banks—Ally Bank, Bank of America, Barclays, Citigroup, Credit Suisse, Deutsche Bank, First Horizon, General Electric, Goldman Sachs, HSBC, JP Morgan Chase, Morgan Stanley, Nurture, Royal Bank of Scotland, and Society General—are also concerned about the adequacy of their capital reserves and could face large losses. The FHFA alleged that many of the banks repeatedly made false claims to the mortgage giants Fannie Mae and Freddie Mac about the very nature of the loans banks were selling. The government claims that banks sold shoddy loans even after a third-party analysis company informed them that billions of dollars' worth of mortgages failed to meet the specifications that the banks made in legal filings and in statements to Fannie and Freddie.

See also FANNIE MAE; FEDERAL HOUSING ADMINISTRATION; FREDDIE MAC; HOME PRICES; MORTGAGES.

FEDERAL INSURANCE RESERVE. A general loss reserve required to be established by a federal association under the rules and regulations of the Federal Savings and Loan Insurance Corporation.

FEDERAL INTERMEDIATE CREDIT BANKS (FICB). Regional banks created by Congress to provide intermediate credit for ranchers and farmers by rediscounting the agricultural paper of financial institutions.

FEDERAL LOAN AGENCY. See RECONSTRUCTION FINANCE CORPORATION.

FEDERAL NATIONAL MORTGAGE ASSOCIATION. See FANNIE MAE.

FEDERAL OPEN MARKET COMMITTEE (FOMC). The Federal Reserve's most important policy-making group, with responsibility for creating policy for the system's purchase and sale of government and other securities in the open market.

In September 2009, the Federal Open Market Committee held interest rates at a record low. It also extended its $1.25 trillion program of buying mortgage-backed securities into the first quarter of 2010.

See also FEDERAL RESERVE.

FEDERAL PAY FREEZE. On November 30, 2010, President Obama proposed a two-year salary freeze for all federal workers, except for those in the military. This would have impact on two million people in 2011 and 2012 and save about $5 billion.

FEDERAL REGULATORY POWERS. See HOUSE (U.S.) FINANCIAL OVERHAUL PLAN; WALL STREET REFORM ACT (2010).

FEDERAL RESERVE. The central banking system of the United States as established by the Federal Reserve Act of 1913. The system regulates money supply, determines the legal reserve of member banks, oversees the mint, effects transfers of funds, promotes and facilitates the clearance and collection of checks, examines member banks, and discharges other functions. The Federal Reserve System, or the Fed, consists of twelve Federal Reserve Banks, their twenty-four branches, and the national and state banks that are members of the system. All national banks are stockholding members of the Federal Reserve Bank of their district. Membership for state banks or trust companies is optional.

On August 20, 2007, the Commerzbank of Germany borrowed $350 million at the Fed's discount window. Two days later, Citigroup, JP Morgan Chase, Bank of America, and Wachovia each received $500 million. As collateral for all of these loans, the banks put up a total of $213 billion in asset-securities, commercial loans, and residential mortgages. This bank run set off the financial crisis of 2008.

The Fed cut its main interest rate target by three-quarters of a percentage point to 3.5 percent on January 23, 2008. With global markets in free-fall amid recession fears, this reduction temporarily shored up confidence. Nine days later, on January 31, the Fed lowered interest rates by half a percentage point to 3 percent, seeking to nip an oncoming recession. The 2.25 points in rate cuts since September 2007 approximated the initial pace in early 2001 as the most rapid in two decades. On October 29, 2008, the Fed cut its benchmark interest rate by 50 basis points to 1 percent, its lowest level since June 2004. Together with the U.S. Treasury, the Fed announced $800 billion in new lending programs on November 25, essentially stepping in as a substitute for the crippled American banking system to provide financing for homebuyers, consumers, and businesses. They created a $200 billion lending program that bought up loans to consumers and small businesses. The Fed then announced that it would try to push down home mortgage rates by purchasing $600 billion in debt ties to home loans guaranteed by Fannie Mae, Freddie Mac, and other government-controlled financing firms.

The U.S. central bank on December 16 lowered interest rates by as much as 75 basis points to just 0.25 percent. That meant that since the financial crisis escalated in September 2007, the Fed had cut rates from 5.25 percent to the current 1 percent in an effort to pump money into both the banking system and the recessionary economy. Between September and mid-December, the U.S. government had printed more than $1 trillion in new money, yet it failed to slowdown the economy's sinking. "Cheap money" would be introduced. The Fed's lending to financial institutions peaked at $1.6 trillion in December but was subsequently expanded its holdings by buying Treasury and mortgage-related debt securities.

The Fed would turn to "quantitative easing," which involves injecting money into the economy rather than aiming at an interest rate. This strategy was a rather new approach at the Fed, with risks of increased inflation or perhaps even another speculative bubble.

On June 24, 2009, the Fed, believing that the economy was showing signs of a slight improvement, kept interest rates near zero. President Obama reappointed Ben Bernanke on August 25 to a second four-year term as Federal Reserve chairman. On September 24, the Federal Reserve said that it would shorten the maturity on loans it makes to banks under the Term Auction Facility, a program created in December 2007 to provide banks with sufficient cash as the credit crunch worsened. In its place, the Fed would shift the program toward its shorter-term loans of twenty-eight days. The House of Representatives' Financial Services Committee, in a vote of 43–26 approved a measure on November 19, 2009, strongly opposed by the Fed, that would instruct the Government Accountability Office to expand its audits of the Fed to include decisions about interest rates and lending to individual banks. The Fed argued that the provision threatened its ability to make monetary policy without political interference. Some called for Treasury Secretary Geithner to resign. On December 11, the House of Representatives, in a wave of anti–Wall Street feeling, passed (with a vote of 223–202) sweeping legislation aiming to limit the operations of big banks and the powers of the Federal Reserve. Under the stewardship of Congressman Barney Frank, chairman of the House Financial Services Committee, it would bring the biggest change to financial regulations since the 1930s. The bill would strip nearly all of the Fed's powers to write consumer-protection laws and permit an arm of Congress to audit the Fed's monetary policy decisions. It would also create a new Consumer Financial Protection Agency under the House Financial Overhaul Plan.

On August 10, 2010, the Fed moved to keep interest rates low in order to encourage economic growth. To fight the slowing economy, the Fed planned to use the proceeds from its huge mortgage bond portfolio to purchase long-term government debt. For the consumer, it meant that mortgage rates would remain at record lows for an extended time period. One week later, the Fed unveiled rules aimed at protecting consumers from abusive lending practices blamed for luring millions of people into unaffordable home loans. These rules took effect April 1, 2011.

The Fed initiated 189 enforcement actions against banks or their workers for the first eight months of 2010, up from 104 in the same period one year earlier and only 21 in 2008. On November 3, 2010, the Federal Reserve announced that it would purchase $600 billion in treasuries over the next eight months in a second round of "quantitative easing." That decision to add more liquidity into the economy to bring down long-term interest rates and spur growth prompted modest rises in stock markets around the globe. The

Fed would purchase long-term bonds with newly created money. Specialists opposed to the Fed's move call it a "Hail Mary" pass. In the same month, the Fed downgraded their outlook for the U.S. economy, projecting that it wouldn't return to its former vitality for five years or more and that the jobless rate could exceed 8 percent for two more years. Their forecasts for unemployment were as follows:

2010	9.5–9.7 percent
2011	8.9–9.1 percent
2012	7.7–8.2 percent
2013	6.9–7.4 percent

In January 2011, the Fed held $2.40 trillion in assets, up $84 billion from the year before and almost triple what it held prior to the Great Recession. On February 16, the Fed upgraded its forecasts for how much the economy would grow in 2011, which included the output of goods and services by 3.4 percent to 3.9 percent. If correct, it would be the fastest annual growth since 2004, when the economy expanded by 3.6 percent.

On March 18, 2011, the Fed approved the large financial banks to raise their dividends and buy back stock. When the U.S. Supreme Court denied the move to bar details of a Federal Reserve bailout on March 21, the Fed announced that it would publish details about its emergency lending to banks during the 2008 financial crisis. The Fed's data about its main emergency aid program, the "discount window," shattered a policy of confidentiality dating to its founding in 1913. Then, on March 22, it was reported that profit at the Federal Reserve Bank surged to a record $82 billion in 2010. The twelve regional banks held $2.4 trillion in government debt, mortgage-backed securities, and other investments. Then, on August 9, the Federal Reserve announced that it planned to keep interest rates near zero for at least the next two years. One of the results was that the Dow Jones Industrial Average shot up 4 percent, the biggest daily gain since March 2009.

On September 7, the Federal Reserve announced that its twelve-bank region grew over the summer, primarily because consumers purchased more goods. Most of the gains were a result of stronger automobile sales. Then, on September 21, the Fed attempted to dramatically recast its $2.65 trillion securities portfolio to lower long-term interest rates. The Fed would shift its holdings so that it would have more long-term U.S. Treasury bonds and more mortgage debt than earlier planned. It expected that the lower rates would boost investment and spending and give a shot to the housing market. Referred to as "operation twist," the Fed would boost its share of long-term treasuries it owns by $400 billion by June 2012.

On November 30, the Federal Reserve and other large global central banks announced that they would attempt to calm the public's fears by providing a joint action to offer inexpensive, emergency U.S. dollar loans to banks in Europe. The Federal Reserve has a number of tools it can use to help overcome the financial crisis, including:

a. *The Discount Window*—one way the Fed provides banks with short-term loans if they run short of cash. The Fed in December 2011 charged 0.75 percent on overnight loans to banks, a rate it can alter. During the 2008 financial crisis, these loans hit $111 billion. They totaled just $113 million in the week ending November 30, 2011.

b. *Term Auction Facility*—during the crisis, some banks were reluctant to take funds from the discount window for fear of being seen as weak, so the Fed began to auction funds en masse in December 2007, ending in March 2010.

c. *Commercial Paper Funding Facility*—in October 2008, the Fed created this entity to assist firms having trouble obtaining short-term loans. Closed in February 2010.

d. *Asset-Backed Commercial Paper Money Market Mutual Fund Liquidity Facility*—this operation helped money-market funds holding asset-backed commercial paper. A run on the $2.5 trillion money-market industry in 2008 amplified the crisis.

e. *Term Asset Backed Securities Loan Facility*—this entity was engineered to stabilize the market for consumer loan-backed securities for a year starting in March 2009. It was back-stopped by the now-ended Troubled Asset Relief Program but could be used again.

f. *Primary Dealer Credit Facility*—in March 2008, the Fed began providing overnight emergency cash in exchange for collateral to primary dealers, a group of about twenty banks and broker-dealers. The program is the first time the Fed lent to nondepository institutions since the Great Depression; closed in February 2010.

By year's end 2011, the Fed closed its books, maintaining that its ongoing efforts to increase growth was adequate and that there was evidence that the U.S. economy was moving forward. Meanwhile, the Federal Reserve announced provisional profits for the year of $77 billion. The result: the Fed had outperformed the rest of America's financial industry put together for four consecutive years.

In January 2012, the Federal Reserve began detailing its plans for short-term interest rates. In its latest attempt to increase transparency, the short-term interest rate projections will be added to the already existing quarterly forecasts. The Fed expected to keep short-term interest rates near zero for almost three more years.

See also AMERICAN INTERNATIONAL GROUP; BAILOUT RESCUE PLAN (OF 2009) (U.S.); BEAR STEARNS; BEIGE BOOK; BERNANKE, BEN; BOND BUYING; BORN, BROOKSLEY; BUSH, GEORGE W.; CENTRAL BANKS; CENTRAL BANKERS; COMMERCIAL PAPER FUNDING FACILITY; CREDIT CARDS; DEBIT CARD FEES; DOW JONES INDUSTRIAL AVERAGE; EMERGENCY ECONOMIC STABILIZATION ACT OF 2008; EXECUTIVE PAY; EXPAND REGULATORY POWERS LEGISLATION; FEDERAL OPEN MARKET COMMITTEE; FINANCIAL CRISIS INQUIRY REPORT; FINANCIAL REGULATION PLAN (2009); GEITHNER, TIMOTHY; GERMANY; GMAC; GOLDMAN SACHS; GREENSPAN, ALAN; HOME MORTGAGES; HOME OWNERSHIP AND EQUITY PROTECTION ACT; HOUSE (U.S.) FINANCIAL OVERHAUL PLAN; INDUSTRIAL PRODUCTION; MONEY-MARKET MUTUAL FUND; MORGAN STANLEY; MORTGAGE LEGISLATION; MORTGAGE RATES; NEW MONEY; PAY; PRIMARY DEALER CREDIT FACILITY; QUANTITATIVE EASING; ROOSEVELT, FRANKLIN DELANO; SECTION 13 (3); STRESS TESTS (U.S.); "TOO BIG TO FAIL"; TOXIC ASSETS; U.S. TREASURY; WALL STREET REFORM ACT (2010).

FEDERAL RESERVE ACT. Legislation signed by President Wilson on December 23, 1913, establishing the Federal Reserve System to manage the nation's money supply. It is the nation's central bank, which sets monetary policy.

See also FEDERAL RESERVE BANK; FEDERAL RESERVE DISTRICT BANKS; SECTION 13 (3).

FEDERAL RESERVE BANK. One of twelve banks created by and operating under the Federal Reserve System. Each Federal Reserve Bank has nine directors.

FEDERAL RESERVE BOARD. The seven-member governing body of the Federal Reserve System; the governors are appointed by the president of the United States, subject to Senate confirmation, for fourteen-year terms. Created in 1913 to regulate all national banks and state-chartered banks that are members of the Federal Reserve System, the board possesses jurisdiction over bank holding companies and also sets national money and credit policy.

FEDERAL RESERVE CURRENCY. Paper money issued by the Federal Reserve Banks that circulates as a legal medium of exchange and is legal tender.

FEDERAL RESERVE DISTRICT BANKS. There are twelve of these central banks, or "banker's banks." They are:

1st District—Boston
2nd District—New York
3rd District—Philadelphia
4th District—Cleveland
5th District—Richmond
6th District—Atlanta
7th District—Chicago
8th District—St. Louis
9th District—Minneapolis
10th District—Kansas City
11th District—Dallas
12th District—San Francisco

FEDERAL RESERVE OVERSIGHT. To tighten their rules for dealing with multinational banks, the U.S. Congress adopted in 1991 a Federal Reserve proposal for policing foreign banks operating in the United States. The law provides that all foreign banks operating in the United States be subject to firm, consolidated supervision in their home country. The legislation gave the Fed new powers to gather financial and ownership information regarding such banks and clarified the Fed's power over these banks in the United States if they superseded state authority.

See also REGULATORS; WALL STREET REFORM ACT (2010).

FEDERAL RESERVE REQUIREMENTS. The amount of money that member banks of the Federal Reserve system must hold in cash or on deposit with a Federal Reserve Bank in order to back up their outstanding loans. The requirement is expressed as a percentage of outstanding loan volume.

FEDERAL RESERVE SYSTEM. *See* FEDERAL RESERVE.

FEDERALS. Items drawn on banks in a large city in which a Federal Reserve Bank is located, although the banks do not belong to the city's clearinghouse association.

FEDERAL SAVINGS AND LOAN ASSOCIATION. One of the associations established by the Home Owners' Loan Act of 1933 and amended in the Home Owners' Loan Act of 1934, which brought existing and newly formed mutual savings banks and building and loan associations under a federal charter.

FEDERAL TAXES. *See* DEATH TAXES.

FEDEX. *See* FEDERAL EXPRESS.

"FEE HARVESTER." *See* CREDIT CARDS.

FEINBERG, KENNETH. *See* PAY; PAY CZAR.

FERGUSON, NIALL. *See* CHIMERICA.

FERRAGAMO. The Italian fashion house saw double-digit growth in sales for the opening weeks in January 2011. Revenue increased more than 25 percent.

FERRE. The Gianfranco Ferré label was placed in bankruptcy administration, a victim of the recession that is impacting luxury-goods firms worldwide. The Italian government placed the firm under the supervision of three government-appointed administrators, who will attempt to keep the group operating. The company racked up more than $375 million in net debt to finance expansion.
See also ITALY; LUXURY GOODS.

FFB. *See* FEDERAL FINANCING BANK.

FHA. *See* FEDERAL HOUSING AGENCY.

FHFA. *See* FEDERAL HOUSING FINANCE AGENCY.

FHLMC. *See* FREDDIE MAC.

FIAT. On December 16, 2008, the Italian automaker announced temporary plant closures resulting from a decline in key markets.
Chrysler, in January 2009, seeking to bolster its case for long-term survival after its $4 billion government bailout, was trading a 35 percent stake in Italy's Fiat for access to small-car technology and a global sales network. Fiat would use this partnership to expand its U.S. foothold, now limited to its luxury brands. Fiat had the option to increase its stake to as much as 55 percent. Fiat would provide technology and engineering for Chrysler to make small cars that would meet coming stricter U.S. federal fuel-economy standards, saving Chrysler $3 billion or more to develop. Fiat would let Chrysler build small cars using its "platforms"—the automobile industry term for the mechanical underpinnings of a vehicle, including engines—so that Chrysler could broaden its lineup beyond large pickups, SUVs, and minivans. The alliance had raised questions about whether the U.S. taxpayers were indirectly providing aid to a foreign automaker.
On March 21, Fiat management said that it wouldn't assume any of Chrysler's debt in a potential deal for a 35 percent stake in the company. By month's end, the U.S. Treasury Department pressed Fiat to take an initial 20 percent

ownership of Chrysler. At the end of April, following the United Auto Workers union with Chrysler, Fiat would eventually own 35 percent of Chrysler. Chrysler requires the Fiat merger as well as the cost concession from its debt holders to receive more U.S. aid to avoid bankruptcy. Fiat now agreed to produce at least one small car in a Chrysler plant in the United States and permit Chrysler to use a 3.0 liter diesel engine and a 1.4 liter gasoline engine in its vehicles. Fiat's investment could be worth $8 billion and hopefully will create 4,000 new jobs. Fiat reported lower third-quarter 2009 earnings on a fall of 16 percent in revenue. Incentive programs raised sales volume by 4.3 percent from a year before. Fiat's third-quarter profit fell $37.5 million. On June 10, Fiat completed its alliance agreement with Chrysler, largely ending Chrysler's forty-two days of bankruptcy. Management reported on October 21 that it expected to be profitable in the year, achieving an annual net profit of about $558 million.

With the beginning of 2011, Fiat spun off its truck and tractor division into a separate firm, with its cars and vans retaining the name of Fiat. Then, on April 12, Fiat reported that it increased its stake in Chrysler to 30 percent from 25 percent. At the beginning of June, Fiat's management agreed to purchase the remaining U.S. Treasury's 6 percent stake in Chrysler. Fiat would pay the Treasury $500 million and the Treasury would hold onto 80 percent of the $75 million purchase right, sharing the remaining 20 percent with the Canadian government. The result is that Fiat would own 52 percent of Chrysler while formally cutting the U.S. government's final ties to the automaker.

See also AUTOMOBILE INDUSTRY; CERBERUS; CHRYSLER; ITALY.

FICB. *See* FEDERAL INTERMEDIATE CREDIT BANKS.

FICO SCORE. A measure of a borrower's creditworthiness based on the borrower's credit data.

FILENE'S BASEMENT. The retailer filed for Chapter 11 bankruptcy on May 3, 2009, and then was purchased by Syms Corporation, which filed for Chapter 11 bankruptcy protection on November 2, 2011, and liquidated.

FINANCIAL ACCOUNTING STANDARDS BOARD (FASB). Voted at the end of March 2009 to change one of its rules and allow banks more leeway to determine for themselves what the mortgage securities they own are worth.

See also MARK-TO-MARKET RULES; SEIDMAN, LESLIE.

FINANCIAL CONS. *See* SCAMS.

FINANCIAL CRIMES ENFORCEMENT NETWORK (FINCEN). Treasury office that collects and analyzes information about financial transactions to combat money laundering, terror financing, and other financial crimes.

FINANCIAL CRISIS ADVISORY GROUP. This group seeks ways to make the regulatory system less pro-cyclical by allowing banks to postpone recognition of profits in good times so that losses would not be as large as in bad times. In July 2009, the group issued a report dealing with accounting rules and warned against changing rules in ways that would make it easier for banks to manage earnings.

See also FINANCIAL CRISIS INQUIRY COMMISSION (REPORT); MARKET CAPITALIZATION.

FINANCIAL CRISIS INQUIRY COMMISSION (REPORT) (FCIC). Created by both the House of Representatives and the Senate in May 2009. An outgrowth of the Fraud Enforcement and Recovery Act of 2009, the commission was given broad authority to examine the domestic and global causes of the current U.S. financial and economic crisis.

Under the act, the commission would have roughly eighteen months to investigate the circumstances that led to the financial crisis and issue a report to Congress with its findings and recommendations. The commission was given broad investigative authority, including subpoena power and the ability to refer any evidence of criminal activity to the U.S. attorney general and state attorneys general. It was to report its findings no later than December 15, 2010.

The commission had ten members, who had to be private citizens and were not employed by any government entity. Its chair was Phil Angelides, a former California treasurer. Six members of the commission were appointed by the Democratic leadership of Congress and four members by the Republican leadership. The commission has been charged to examine topics such as fraud and abuse in the financial sector; capital requirements and regulations on leverage and liquidity; lending practices and securitization; the availability and terms of credit; the quality of diligence undertaken by financial institutions; derivatives and unregulated financial products and practices; and compensation structures. Formal public hearings started in December 2009. More than 700 witnesses were interviewed over a nineteen-day period. In mid-November 2010, the panel voted to delay its final report until the end of January 2011.

The document was released on January 27, 2011. The commission believed that the financial crisis was "avoidable" and was brought on by actions of government officials and private-sector players. The report singled out the federal banking regulators for particularly sharp criticism, including "the Federal Reserve's pivotal failure to stem the flow of toxic mortgages" over the past ten years. Six commissioners voted to adopt the report; four commissioners dissented from the report. A total of eighty pages in the report were devoted to notes identifying sources and references. More than one million pages of documents, including materials never before made public, were examined.

The conclusions of the Financial Crisis Inquiry Commission were that the financial crisis was avoidable; the government was ill prepared for the crisis, and its inconsistent response added to the uncertainty and panic in the financial markets; there was a systematic breakdown in accountability and ethics; collapsing mortgage-lending standards and the mortgage securitization pipeline lit and spread the flame of contagion and crisis; over-the-counter derivatives contributed significantly to this crisis; and the failure of credit rating agencies were essential cogs in the wheel of financial destruction.

The January 2011 commission and report, sponsored by the U.S. government, identified specific areas of failure and gave the following conclusions:

a. *Credit Expansion*—there was untrammeled growth in risky mortgages. Unsustainable, toxic loans polluted the financial system and fueled the housing bubble. Subprime lending was supported in significant ways by major financial institutions. Some firms, such as Citigroup, Lehman Brothers, and Morgan Stanley, acquired subprime lenders. In addition, major financial institutions facilitated the growth in subprime mortgage lending companies with lines of credit, securitization, purchase guarantees, and other mechanisms. Regulators failed to rein in risky home mortgage lending. In particular, the Federal Reserve failed to meet its statutory obligation to establish and maintain prudent mortgage lending standards and to protect against predatory lending.

b. *Mortgage Machine*—the monetary policy of the Federal Reserve, along with capital flows from abroad, created conditions in which a housing bubble could develop. However, these conditions need not have led to a crisis. The Federal Reserve and other regulators did not take actions necessary to constrain the credit bubble. In addition, the Federal Reserve's policies and pronouncements encouraged rather than inhibited the growth of mortgage debt and the housing bubble. Lending standards collapsed, and there was a significant failure of accountability and responsibility throughout each level of the lending system. This included borrowers, mortgage brokers, appraisers, originators, securitizes, credit rating agencies, and investors, and ranged from corporate boardrooms to individuals. Loans were often premised on ever-rising home prices and were made regardless of ability to pay. The nonprime mortgage securitization process created a pipeline through which risky mortgages were conveyed and sold through the financial system. This pipeline was essential to the origination of the burgeoning numbers of high-risk mortgages. The originate-to-distribute model undermined responsibility and accountability for the long-term viability of mortgages and mortgage-related securities and contributed to the poor quality of mortgage loans. Federal and state rules required or encouraged financial firms and some institutional investors to make investments based on the ratings of credit rating agencies, leading to undue reliance on those ratings. However, the rating agencies were not adequately regulated by the Securities and Exchange Commission or any other regulator to ensure the quality and accuracy of their ratings. Moody's, the commission's case study in this area, relied on flawed and outdated models to issue erroneous ratings on mortgage-related securities, failed to perform meaningful due diligence on the assets underlying the securities, and continued to rely on those models even after it became obvious that the models were wrong. Not only did the federal banking supervisors fail to rein in risky mortgage-lending practices, but the Office of the Comptroller of the Currency and the Office of Thrift Supervision preempted the applicability of state laws and regulatory efforts to national banks and thrifts, thus preventing adequate protection for borrowers and weakening constraints on this segment of the mortgage market.

c. *CDO Machine*—declining demand for riskier portions (or tranches) of mortgage-related securities led to the creation of an enormous volume of collateralized debt obligations (CDOs). These CDOs—composed of the riskier tranches—fueled demand for nonprime mortgage securitization and contributed to the housing bubble. Certain products also played an important role in doing so, including CDOs squared, credit default swaps, synthetic CDOs, and asset-backed commercial paper programs that invested in mortgage-backed securities and CDOs. Many of these risky assets ended up on the balance sheets of systemically important institutions and contributed to their failure or near failure in the financial crisis. Credit default swaps, sold to provide protection against default to purchasers of the rated tranches of CDOs, facilitated the sale of those tranches by convincing investors of their low risk, but greatly increased the exposure of the sellers of the credit default swap protection to the housing bubble's collapse. Synthetic CDOs, which consisted in whole or in part of credit default swaps, enabled securitization to continue and expand even as the mortgage market dried up and provided speculators with a means of betting on the housing market. By layering on correlated risk, they spread and amplified exposure to losses when the housing market collapsed. The high ratings erroneously given CDOs by credit rating agencies encouraged investors and financial institutions to purchase them and enabled the continuing securitization of nonprime mortgages. There was a clear failure of corporate governance at Moody's, which did not ensure the quality of its ratings on ten of thousands of mortgage-backed securities and CDOs.

The SEC's poor oversight of the five largest investment banks failed to restrict their risk activities and did not require them to hold adequate capital and liquidity for their activities, contributing to the failure or need for government bailouts of all five of the supervised investment banks during the financial crisis.

d. *All In*—firms securitizing mortgages failed to perform adequate due diligence on the mortgages they purchased and at times knowingly waived compliance with underwriting standards. Potential investors were not fully informed or were misled about the poor quality of the mortgages contained in some mortgage-related securities. These problems appear to have been significant. The SEC failed to adequately enforce its disclosure requirements governing mortgage securities, exempted some sales of such securities from its review, and preempted states from applying state laws to them, thereby failing in its core mission to protect investors. The Federal Reserve failed to recognize the cataclysmic danger posed by the housing bubble to the financial system and refused to take timely action to constrain its growth, believing that it could contain the damage from the bubble's collapse. Lax mortgage regulation and collapsing mortgage-lending standards and practices created conditions that were ripe for mortgage fraud.

e. *The Madness*—that credit rating agencies abysmally failed in their central mission to provide quality ratings on securities for the benefit of investors. They did not heed many warnings signs indicating significant problems in the housing and mortgage sector. Moody's, the commission's case study in this area, continued issuing ratings on mortgage-related securities using its outdated analytical models rather than making the necessary adjustments. The business model under which firms issuing securities paid for their ratings seriously undermined the quality and integrity of those ratings; the rating agencies placed market share and profit considerations above the quality and integrity of their ratings. Despite the leveling off and subsequent decline of the housing market beginning in 2006, securitization of collateralized debt obligations (CDOs), CDOs squared, and synthetic CDOs continued unabated, greatly expanding the exposure to losses when the housing market collapsed and exacerbating the import of the collapse on the financial system and the economy. During this period, speculators fueled the market for synthetic CDOs to be on the future of the housing market. CDO managers of these synthetic products had potential conflicts in trying the serve the interests of customers who were betting mortgage borrowers would continue to make their payments and of customers who were betting the housing market would collapse. There were also potential conflicts for underwriters of mortgage-related securities to the extent they shorted the products for their own accounts outside of their roles as market makers.

f. *The Bust*—the collapse of the housing bubble began the chain of events that led to the financial crisis. High leverage, inadequate capital, and short-term funding made many financial institutions extraordinarily vulnerable to the downturn in the market in 2007. The investment banks had leverage ratios by one measure of up to 40 to 1. This means that for every $40 of assets, they held only $1 of capital. Fannie Mae and Freddie Mac had even greater leverage with a combined 75-to-1 ratio. Leverage or capital inadequacy at many institutions was even greater than reported when one takes into account "window dressing," off-balance-sheet exposures such as those of Citigroup, and derivates positions such as those of AIG. The government-sponsored enterprises (GSEs) contributed to, but were not a primary cause of, the financial crisis. Their $5 trillion mortgage exposure and market position were significant, and they were without question dramatic failures. They participated in the expansion of risky mortgage lending and declining mortgage standards, adding significant demand for less-than-prime loans. However, they followed, rather than led, the Wall Street firms. The delinquency rates on the loans that they purchased or guaranteed were significant lower than those purchased and securitized by other financial institutions. The Community Reinvestment Act (CRA)—which requires regulated banks and thrifts to lend, invest, and provide services consistent with safety and soundness to the areas where they take deposits—was not a significant factor in subprime lending. However, community lending commitments not required by the CRA were clearly used by lending institutions for public relations purposes.

g. *Early 2007—Spreading Subprime Worries*—entities such as Bear Stearn's hedge funds and AIG Financial Products that had significant subprime exposure were affected by the collapse of the housing bubble first, creating financial pressures on their parent companies. The commercial paper and repo markets—two key components of the shadow banking lending markets—quickly reflected the impact of the housing bubble collapse because of the decline in collateral asset values and concern about financial firms' subprime exposure.

h. *Summer 2007—Disruptions in Funding*—the shadow banking system was permitted to grow to rival the commercial banking system with inadequate supervision and regulation. That system was very fragile due to high-leverage, short-term funding, risky assets, inadequate liquidity, and the lack of federal backstop. When the mortgage market collapsed and financial firms began to abandon the commercial paper and repo lending markets, some institutions depending on them for funding their operations failed or, later in the crisis, had to be rescued. These markets and other interconnections created contagion, as the crisis spread even to markets and firms that had little or no direct exposure to the mortgage market. In addition, regulation and supervision of traditional banking had been weakened significantly, allowing commercial banks and thrifts to operate with few constraints and to engage in a wider range of financial activities, including activities in the shadow banking system. The financial sector, which grew enormously in the years leading up to the financial crisis, wielded great political power to weaken institutional supervision and market regulation of both the shadow banking system and the traditional banking system. This deregulation made the financial system especially vulnerable to the financial crisis and exacerbated its effects.

i. *Late 2007 to Early 2008—Billions in Subprime Losses*—some large investment banks, bank holding companies, and insurance companies, including Merrill Lynch, Citigroup, and AIG, experienced massive losses related to the subprime mortgage market because of significant failures of corporate governance, including risk management. Executive and employee compensation systems at these institutions disproportionally rewarded short-term risk taking. The regulators—the SEC for the large investment banks and the banking supervisors for the bank holding companies and AIG—failed to adequately supervise their safety and soundness, allowing them to take inordinate risk in activities such as nonprime mortgage securitization and over-the-counter (OTC) derivatives dealing and to hold inadequate capital and liquidity.

j. *March 2008—The Fall of Bear Stearns*—the failure of Bear Stearns and its resulting government-assisted rescue were caused by its exposure to risky mortgage assets, its reliance on short-term funding, and its high leverage. These were a result of weak corporate governance and risk management. Its executive and employee compensation system was based largely on return on equity, creating incentives to use excessive leverage and to focus on short-term gain such as annual growth goals. Bear experienced runs by repo lenders, hedge fund customers, and derivatives counterparties and was rescued by a government-assisted purchase by JP Morgan because the government considered it too interconnected to fail. Bear's failure was in part a result of inadequate supervision by the SEC, which did not restrict its risky activities and allowed undue leverage and insufficient liquidity.

k. *March to August 2008—Systemic Risk Concerns*—banking supervisors failed to adequately and proactively identify and police the weakness of the banks and thrifts or their poor corporate governance and risk management, often maintaining satisfactory ratings on institutions until just before the collapse. This failure was caused by many factors, including beliefs that regulation was unduly burdensome, financial institutions were capable of self-regulation, and regulators should not interfere with activities reported as profitable. Large commercial banks and thrifts, such as Wachovia and Indy Mac, that had significant exposure to risky mortgage assets were subject to runs by creditors and depositors. The Federal Reserve realized far too late the systemic danger inherent in the interconnections of the unregulated OTC derivatives market and did not have the information needed to act.

l. *September 2008—Takeover of Fannie Mae and Freddie Mac*—the business model of Fannie Mae and Freddie Mac (the GSEs), as private-sector, publicly traded, profit-making companies with implicit government backing and a public mission, was fundamentally flawed. The risky practices of Fannie Mae, the commission's case study in this area, particularly from 2005 on, led to its fall—practices undertaken to meet Wall Street's expectations for growth, regain market share, and ensure generous compensation for its employees. Affordable housing goals imposed by the Department of Housing and Urban Development (HUD) did not contribute marginally to these practices. The GSEs justified their activities, in part, on the broad and sustained public policy support for homeownership. Risky lending and securitization resulted in significant losses at Fannie Mae, which, combined with its excessive leverage permitted by law, led to the company's failure. Corporate governance, including risk management, failed at the GSEs in part because of shrewd compensation methodologies. The Office of Federal Housing Enterprise Oversight (OFHEO) lacked the authority and capacity to adequately regulate the GSEs. The GSEs exercised considerable political power and were successfully able to resist legislation and regulatory actions that would have strengthened oversight of them and restricted their risk-taking activities. In early 2008, the decision by the federal government and the GSEs to increase the GSEs' mortgage activities and risk to support the collapsing mortgage market was made despite the unsound financial conditions of the institutions. While these actions provided support to the mortgage market, they led to increased losses at the GSEs, which were ultimately borne by taxpayers, and reflected the conflicted nature of the GSEs dual mandate. GSE mortgage securities essentially maintained their value throughout the crisis and did not contribute to the significant financial firm losses that were central to the financial crisis.

September 2008—Bankruptcy of Lehman—the financial crisis reached cataclysmic proportions with the collapse of Lehman Brothers. Lehman's collapse demonstrated weaknesses that also contributed to the failures or near failures of the other four large investment banks: inadequate regulatory oversight, risky trading activities (including securitization and OTC derivatives dealing), enormous leverage, and reliance on short-term funding. While investment banks tended to be initially more vulnerable, commercial banks suffered from many of the same weaknesses, including their involvement in the shadow banking system, and ultimately many suffered major losses, requiring government rescue. Lehman, like other large OCT derivatives dealers, experienced runs on its derivatives operations that played a role in its failure. Its massive derivatives positions greatly complicated its bankruptcy, and the impact of its bankruptcy through interconnections with derivatives counterparties and other financial institutions contributed significantly to the severity and depth of the financial crisis. Lehman's failure resulted in part from significant problems in its corporate governance, including risk management, exacerbated by compensation to its executives and traders that was based predominantly on short-term profits. Federal government officials decided not to rescue Lehman for a variety of reasons, including the lack of a private firm willing and able to acquire it, uncertainty about Lehman's potential losses, concerns about moral hazard and political reaction, and erroneous assumptions that Lehman's failure would have a manageable impact on the financial system because market participants had anticipated it. After the fact, they justified their decision by stating that the Federal Reserve did not have legal authority to rescue Lehman. The inconsistency of federal government decisions in not rescuing Lehman after having rescued Bear Stearns and the GSEs, and immediately before rescuing AIG, added to uncertainty and panic in the financial markets.

m. *September 2008—Bailout of AIG*—AIG failed and was rescued by the government primarily because its enormous sales of credit default swaps were made without putting up initial collateral, setting aside capital reserves, or hedging its exposure—a profound failure in corporate governance, particularly its risk-management practices. AIG's failure was possible because of the sweeping deregulation of OTC derivatives, including credit default swaps, which effectively eliminated federal and state regulation of these products, including capital and margin requirements that would have lessened the likelihood of AIG's failure. The OTC derivatives market's lack of transparency and effective price discovery exacerbated the collateral disputes of AIG and Goldman Sachs and similar disputes between other derivatives counterparties. AIG engaged in regulatory arbitrage by setting up a major business in this unregulated product, locating much of the business in London, and selecting a weak federal regulator, the Office of Thrift Supervision (OTS). The OTS failed to effectively exercise its authority over AIG and its affiliates; it lacked the capability to supervise an institution of the size and complexity of AIG, did not recognize the risks inherent in AIG's sales of credit default swaps, and did not understand its responsibility to oversee the entire company, including AIG Financial Products. Furthermore, because of the deregulation of OTC derivates, state insurance supervisors were barred from regulating AIG's sale of credit default swaps even though they were similar in effect to insurance contracts. If they had been regulated as insurance contracts, AIG would have been required to maintain adequate capital reserves, would not have been able to enter into contracts requiring the posting of collateral, and would not have been able to provide default protection to speculators; thus, AIG would have been prevented from acting in such a risky manner. AIG was so interconnected with many large commercial banks, investment banks, and other financial institutions through counterparty credit relationships on credit default swaps and other activities such as securities lending that its potential failure created systematic risk. The government concluded AIG was too big to fail and committee more than $180 billion to its rescue. Without the bailout, AIG's default and collapse could have brought down its counterparties, causing cascading losses and collapses throughout the financial system.

n. *Crisis and Panic*—as massive losses spread throughout the financial system in the fall of 2008, many institutions failed or would have failed without government bailouts. As panic gripped the market, credit markets seized up, trading ground to a halt, and the stock market plunged. Lack of transparency contributed greatly to the crisis; the exposures of financial institutions to risky mortgage assets and other potential losses were unknown to market participants, and indeed many firms did not know their own exposures. The scale and nature of the OTC derivatives market created significant systemic risk throughout the financial system and helped fuel the panic in the fall of 2008; millions of contracts in this opaque and deregulated market created interconnections among a vast web of financial institutions through counterparty credit risk, thus exposing the system to a contagion of spreading losses and defaults. Enormous positions concentrated in the hands of systemically significant institutions that were major OTC derivatives dealers added to uncertainty in the market. The "bank runs" on these institutions included runs on their derivatives operations through collateral demands, and refusals to act as counterparties. A series of actions, inactions, and misjudgments left the country with stark and painful alternatives— either risk the total collapse of our financial system or spend trillions of taxpayer dollars to stabilize the system and prevent catastrophic damage to the economy. In the process, the government rescued a number of financial institutions deemed "too big to fail"—so large and interconnected with other financial institutions or so important in one or more financial market that their failure would have caused losses and failures to spread to other institutions. The government also provided substantial financial assistance to nonfinancial corporations. As a result of the rescues and consolidation of financial institutions through failures and mergers during the crisis, the U.S. financial sector is now more concentrated than ever in the hands of a few very large, systemically significant institutions. This concentration places greater responsibility on regulators for effective oversight of these institutions.

o. *Foreclosure Crisis*—the unchecked increase in the complexity of mortgages and securitization has made it more difficult to solve problems in the mortgage market. This complexity has created powerful competing interests, including those of the holders of first and second mortgages and of mortgage servicers; reduced transparency for policy makers, regulators, financial institutions, and homeowners; and impeded mortgage modifications. The resulting disputes and inaction have caused pain largely borne by individual homeowners and created further uncertainty about the health of the housing market and financial institutions.

See also FINANCIAL CRISIS ADVISORY GROUP; PRINCE, CHARLES O.; RECESSION OF 2007–2012; RUBIN, ROBERT E.
Cf. PECORA COMMISSION.

FINANCIAL CRISIS RESPONSIBILITY FEE. Originally meant to help pay back the $700 billion Troubled Asset Relief Program and draw in possibilities of risk-taking.
Synonymous with BANK TAX.

FINANCIAL INSTITUTIONS REFORM, RECOVERY, AND ENFORCEMENT ACT OF 1989. Created the Office of Thrift Supervision to regulate federal and most state-chartered thrifts and their holding companies.

FINANCIAL ISOLATIONISM. *See* FINANCIAL PROTECTIONISM.

FINANCIAL OVERHALL BILL. *See* WALL STREET REFORM ACT.

FINANCIAL OVERHAUL PLAN. *See* GOLDMAN SACHS; HOUSE (U.S.) FINANCIAL OVERHAUL PLAN.

FINANCIAL PROTECTIONISM. A tactic introduced by Gordon Brown, the British prime minister, in January 2009 for the setting of guidelines to prevent countries (primarily of the European Union) from carrying out rescue plans that favor their banks over others. This form of protectionism involves banks retreating behind national borders by lending more at home and less abroad. One result is the loss of credit from foreign banks.
See also PROTECTIONISM.

FINANCIAL REFORM ACT (2010). *See* WALL STREET REFORM ACT.

FINANCIAL REGULATION. *See* EXECUTIVE PAY; FINANCIAL REGULATION PLAN (2009); REGULATION; WALL STREET REFORM ACT (2010).

FINANCIAL REGULATION PLAN (2009). Proposed by the Obama administration on June 17, 2009, and requiring congressional approval, this sweeping and historic program would overhaul U.S. finance rules, including:

a. Creating a Financial Services Oversight Council to guide regulators' activities.
b. Financial firms big enough to be a risk to the financial system would be heavily regulated by the Federal Reserve.
c. Allowing the Federal Reserve to collect reports from U.S. financial firms that met "certain minimum size thresholds."
d. Treasury would reexamine capital standards for banks and holding firms.
e. Regulators would issue guidelines on executive pay.
f. Creating national bank supervisors and terminating Office of Thrift Supervision.
g. Hedge funds, private-equity funds, and venture-capital funds would register with the Securities and Exchange Commission.
h. Urging the SEC to stem runs on money market mutual funds.
i. Beefing up oversight of insurance by creating an office in the Treasury to coordinate information and policy.
j. Over-the-counter derivatives, asset-backed securities would be in a regulatory framework.

k. Giving the Federal Reserve more power over infrastructure that governs these markets, such as pay and settlement systems.
l. Harmonizing powers and authority of SEC and Commodity Futures Trading Commission to avoid conflicting rules.
m. Requiring certain loan originators to retain some economic interest in securitized products.
n. Urging SEC to strengthen credit-rating-firm regulation.
o. Creating Consumer Financial Protection Agency, with authority over consumer-oriented products.
p. Requiring nonbinding shareholder votes on executive pay packages.
q. Requiring certain employers to offer an "automatic IRA plan" for retirement.
r. Creating a mechanism that allows the government to take over and unwind large failing financial institutions.
s. The Federal Deposit Insurance Corporation would act as conservator or receiver, except with broker dealers or securities firms, then SEC takes over.
t. Amending the Fed's lending powers to get Treasury secretary's approval.

See also CONSUMER FINANCIAL PROTECTION AGENCY; TIER 1 FINANCIAL HOLDING COMPANIES; TRANSPARENCY; WALL STREET REFORM ACT (2010).

FINANCIAL REGULATORS. *See* REGULATORS; TIER 1 FINANCIAL HOLDING COMPANIES; WALL STREET REFORM ACT (2010).

FINANCIAL SERVICES (2011). It was projected that profit growth at large banks in the United States and Europe could have a rapid return to its premeltdown state. Earnings would come in large part from lower loss provisions, accounting items, and trading income. Lending could assuredly remain subdued.

New bank loans globally would climb by 4.4 percent, making up for a 3.1 percent fall in 2010. Facing stricter regulations and capital requirements, restrictive regulatory reforms, and more than $3 trillion in debt maturing in 2011 and 2012, banks would not part with capital easily. Future efforts to repair capital ratios and limit exposure to wholesale funding markets could see banks compete fiercely for retail deposits. This should lead to safer but less profitable banks.

FINANCIAL SERVICES COMMITTEE (HOUSE OF REPRESENTATIVES). *See* FEDERAL RESERVE.

FINANCIAL SERVICES OVERSIGHT COUNCIL. *See* FINANCIAL-REGULATION PLAN (2009).

FINANCIAL STABILITY (AND RECOVERY) PLAN. Under the administration of President Obama, the replacement name for the Troubled Asset Relief Program, a bank bailout plan in 2008 from the administration of President George W. Bush. Designed to attack U.S. credit crisis on all fronts.
See also "TOO BIG TO FAIL"; TROUBLED ASSET RELIEF PROGRAM.
Synonymous with BAILOUT RESCUE PLAN (OF 2009) (U.S.); TARP 2.0.

FINANCIAL STABILITY FORUM (FSF). See REGULATORS.

FINANCIALSTABILITY.GOV. The U.S. Treasury's website dedicated to "transparency, oversight, and accountability."

FINANCIAL STABILITY OVERSIGHT BOARD (COUNCIL). Regulators from the Federal Reserve and the Treasury Department. This unit was established by the Emergency Economic Stabilization Act of 2008 to help oversee the Troubled Asset Relief Program granted to the Secretary of the Treasury and to help restore liquidity and stability to the U.S. financial system. The board is committed to transparency and accountability in all of its programs and policies, including those established under the Emergency Economic Stabilization Act. Met for the first time in September 2010 to "establish an integrated road map for the first stages of reform," not including the plans for the consumer agency. It is composed of a group of regulators headed by the U.S. Treasury secretary.

These regulators define "shadow banking" as "credit intermediation involving entities and activities outside the regular banking system." It offers financial institutions a source of funding and liquidation on a day-to-day basis. At worst, it permits the buildup of leverage and systemic risk, as revealed by the 2008 financial crisis.

See also TROUBLED ASSET RELIEF PROGRAM; WALL STREET REFORM ACT (2010).

FINANCIAL TIMES. The British newspaper publisher announced on February 23, 2009, that it would reduce staffing costs by offering employees the option of working a shortened week in the summer and extending their annual leave.

FINCEN. See FINANCIAL CRIMES ENFORCEMENT NETWORK.

FINLAND. Output continued to decline in Finland over the first half of 2008, as the collapse in exports deepened. However, a recovery should get under way by the end of 2009 with a bounce in exports from the current very low levels and substantial restocking. Harmonized inflation has remained above the euro-area average due to large negotiated wage increases. The unemployment rate has climbed sharply and is expected to continue to rise, magnified by significant labor market rigidities. The government's initial response to the downturn, including assistance to banks and businesses and a modest fiscal stimulus, provided material support to activity. Further significant fiscal loosening is planned, but it may be counterproductive if its comes just as the recovery gets under way. While some consolidation measures have been announced, a coherent plan for a substantial fiscal consolidation should be articulated as soon as possible and put in place once the recovery is on a firm footing. The forthcoming wage negotiations should align outcomes more closely to productivity within firms.

By 2010, Finland's public debt was moderate as the nation recovered from the Great Recession. The government was expected to maintain the policy of economic growth, with exports doing quite well. The nation's GDP growth was 1.6 percent, with a GDP of $229 billion, an inflation rate of 1.5 percent, and a GDP per head of $42,720.

The influence of Finland goes beyond its small GDP. In August 2011, Finland threatened to upend an agreement that eurozone countries made in July 2011 to expand the European Union bailout fund. Finland would contribute less than 2 percent of the guarantees provided by the eurozone fund. Growth was 2.9 percent in the second quarter 2011, down from a revised figure of 4.8 percent in the first three months of the year.

See also FINNAIR; NOKIA.

FINNAIR. In August 2009, the airline posted its fourth consecutive quarterly net loss, with revenue falling 22 percent.

FIONIA BANK. *See* DENMARK.

FIRST HORIZON. *See* FEDERAL HOUSING FINANCE AGENCY.

FIRST LOOK. *See* FANNIE MAE.

FIRST LOSS. *See* TRANCHE.

FISCAL COMPACT. *See* EUROPEAN UNION.

FISCAL RESPONSIBILITY AND REFORM COMMSSION. *See* NATIONAL COMMISSION ON FISCAL RESPONSIBILITY AND REFORM.

FISCAL RESPONSIBILITY SUMMIT. *See* DEFICIT (BUDGET, U.S.); NATIONAL COMMISSION ON FISCAL RESPONSIBILITY AND REFORM.

FISCAL TREATY. *See* EUROPEAN UNION.

FISHER, IRVING. A long-forgotten economist of the Depression era, he was called by John Maynard Keynes the "great-grandparent" of his own theories. Throughout the Great Depression, he was considered America's foremost economist. In October 1929, he predicted that stocks would reach a "permanently high plateau." His great contribution was an ability to convince decision makers that monetary forces were instrumental in the direction of a real economy. His debt-deflation theory argued that it was critical to defend a nation against deflation and to also concern itself with inside debt and abandoning the gold standard.

In 1911, he wrote *The Purchasing Power of Money* describing with models and flowcharts the quantity theory of money, which holds that the supply of money times its velocity is equal to output multiplied by the price level. He explained how interest rates could deviate from nominal ones. He held that the dollar's value should be maintained relative not to gold but to a basket of commodities. To the end, he remained convinced that the Depression of the 1930s would be short lived. In addition, he urged President Hoover to veto the Smoot-Hawley Act but failed to get the attention of the administration.

See also KEYNES, JOHN MAYNARD; SMOOT-HAWLEY TARIFF ACT.

FITCH RATINGS. One of the major credit rating agencies in the United States.

Cf. ITALY; MOODY'S; PORTUGAL; SPAIN; STANDARD & POOR'S.

"FLASH CRASH." The Securities and Exchange Commission proposed in May 2010 that trading would pause in certain stock if and when the price moved 10 percent or more in a five-minute time frame. The May 6 "flash crash" caused some stocks to fall to as low as one penny. If approved, these circuit breakers would begin in mid-June 2010 and have a six-month pilot period. The Dow Jones Industrial Average on May 6 suffered its biggest, fastest decline ever, and hundreds of stocks momentarily lost nearly all of their value. So many things went wrong so quickly that months later regulators hadn't pieced together exactly what had happened. Stock price data from the New York Stock Exchange's electronic trading arm were so slow that at least three other exchanges simply cut it off from trading. A flash crash could happen again, warn many experts. The challenge for regulators and exchange operators is whether they can find ways to protect investors in a market even more defined by high-speed trading.

On February 18, 2011, a joint panel of regulators on the flash crash recommended rules and incentives for traders to continually post quotes close to market prices and considered imposing market-wide fees on order cancellations. The panel's report argued that delays in the transmission of quote and price information could have fueled traders' selling: "If traders are uncertain, some high-frequency and algorithmic traders simply withdraw until they feel more certain while others sell to get out of the market altogether."

See also DOW JONES INDUSTRIAL AVERAGE; FLASH ORDERS (TRADING).

FLASH ORDERS (TRADING). Permits traders to peek at other investors' orders before they are sent to the wider marketplace. This method gives some traders an edge over everyone else, and the Securities and Exchange Commission is determined to stamp it out. On September 17, 2009, the SEC proposed banning these so-called flash orders, which utilize power computers to look at investors' orders. By July 2009, flash orders represented 2.8 percent of the roughly 9 billion shares of stocks traded in the United States. This was known as high-frequency trading. Critics claim that flash orders favor sophisticated, fast-moving traders at the expense of slower market participants. Utilizing lightning-quick technology, these high-frequency traders often issue and then cancel orders almost simultaneously and find out how others trade, creating a two-tiered market.

See also "FLASH CRASH"; HIGH-FREQUENCY TRADING.

FLEMING, GREGORY J. President and chief operating officer of Merrill Lynch; became president of investment management of Morgan Stanley.

FLEXIBLE MORTGAGE. *See* CONVERTIBLE WRAPAROUND MORTGAGE; FLEXIBLE-PAYMENT MORTGAGE; RENEGOTIABLE-RATE MORTGAGE; VARIABLE-RATE MORTGAGE.

FLEXIBLE-PAYMENT MORTGAGE. An interest-only type of loan for the first five years. Two major restrictions apply: each monthly payment must cover at least the interest due, and after five years, payments must be fully amortizing. A rarely used mortgage because it offers the homebuyer only a slight reduction in monthly payments during the early years.

See also CONVERTIBLE WRAPAROUND MORTGAGE; RENEGO-TIABLE-RATE MORTGAGE; VARIABLE-RATE MORTGAGE.

FLEXICURITY. First used in Denmark, the concept that Europeans will tolerate flexible labor markets, i.e., increased layoffs, as long as they have the security of generous social assistance if things go bad.

FLIPPING HOMES. *See* HOME FLIPPING.

FLOOD PREVENTION. *See* AMERICAN RECOVERY AND REIN-VESTMENT ACT (OF 2009).

FNMA. *See* FANNIE MAE.

FOMC. *See* FEDERAL OPEN MARKET COMMITTEE.

FOOD AID. The government reported on November 16, 2009, that the number of families struggling to purchase enough food in 2008 climbed 31 percent over the previous year. Seventeen million households indicated some form of food insecurity in 2008, an increase from 13 million families in 2007.

In 2008, 6.7 million households had very low food security, up 43 percent from 47 million households in 2007.

By summer 2011, in an effort to reduce the U.S. deficit, food aid programs were threatened. Some 44.6 million Americans use food stamps, at a cost to taxpayers of $71.5 billion.

See also FOOD STAMPS; UNEMPLOYMENT.

FOOD BANKS. Indicating how hard times are in the United States, by December 2008, food banks were trying to feed more people with less food. Signing people up for benefits became more crucial than ever, as more working-class people were finding it difficult to make ends meet and were coming to food banks for assistance. Demand at food banks increased by 30 percent in 2008.

See also UNEMPLOYMENT.

FOOD PANTRIES. *See* FOOD BANKS.

FOOD PRICES. In February 2011, world food prices climbed 2.2 percent from the previous month, the eighth monthly rise in a row, to the highest level in real and nominal terms since monitoring prices began in 1990. Wholesale food prices surged 3.9 percent the same month in the United States, the largest increase in more than thirty-six years. In August, food costs propelled wholesale prices. The cost of food surged 4.6 percent in November from the year before.

FOOD SECURITY. *See* FOOD AID.

FOOD SPENDING. In 2008's fourth quarter, consumer spending on food fell at an inflation-adjusted rate of 3.7 percent from the third quarter, the greatest fall in sixty-two years.

By 2009, the money spent by consumers in food markets and for eating out was lower than the previous year. Generic brands increasingly replaced standard ones as more and more people ate at home. The packaged-food industry was assumed to be recession proof, considering people must eat no matter what.

FOOD STAMPS. Food stamps at one time had a stigma projecting an image of welfare and poverty. Since 2008, the number of people who receive food stamps has increased nearly a third, resulting in a program that feeds more than 36 million citizens. One in eight Americans and one in four children are dependent on food stamps, expanding at a pace of approximately 20,000 people a day. There are 239 counties in the country where at least a quarter of the population receives food stamps.

Nearly 12 percent of Americans receive stamps, 28 percent are African American, 15 percent Latino, and 8 percent white. Benefits average about $130 a month for each person in the household. By November 2010, the number of people relying on food stamps surged 14.2 percent from the year before. About 43.6 million people received food stamps for the month, up 0.9 percent from October. Mississippi had the highest use with more than a fifth of all residents utilizing food stamps.

See also FOOD AID; UNEMPLOYMENT; WELFARE.

FORD. Ford Motor's U.S. sales plummeted as much as 30 percent in October 2008. Ford, Lincoln, and Mercury car sales were off 27 percent, while light truck sales for the three brands were down more than 30 percent. When President George W. Bush announced a program to bail out the automobile industry in late December, only General Motors and Chrysler were to be recipients of government monies. Ford claimed that it was not in need of funds to continue operations, thereby relieving them, at least for the time being, from further government controls. Ford sold 138,458 light vehicles in December, down from 204,787 in the same month in 2007. It was a 32 percent drop in December.

Ford reported on January 2, 2009, that their car and truck sales fell almost 19 percent in 2008. Ford's U.S. market share slipped to about 14 percent for 2008, down from 14.7 percent in 2007. Executives forecast overall 2009 sales to come in at $12.5 million in car sales, while light vehicle sales could hit $12.2 million. The year 2008 ended up the worst year for selling cars and trucks since 1992. For example, Ford had projected total industry sales of about $13.5 million, a full $3 million less than in 2007. Not since 1974 had the market collapsed that much in a single year. On January 29, after closing the books on a $14.6 billion loss in 2008, the worst annual result in its 105-year history, Ford Motor Company said that it was drawing the last $10.1 billion from its lines of credit to add to its cash hoard so that it could survive the increasingly bleak vehicle market. Ford's January sales dropped 40 percent to 93,041.

In mid-March, hourly workers at Ford ratified sweeping cost-cutting changes in their labor contract. Restrictions were made on overtime and unemployment pay, and cutbacks made in work rules and cost-of-living wage increases. Up to half of Ford's cash obligation to its retiree healthcare fund was replaced with company stock. On April 6, the automaker said its investors agreed to exchange $9.9 billion in debt for cash and stock, a 28 percent reduction in its overall debt. By the end of April, the Ford Motor Company said it likely wouldn't require a government bailout, reporting a smaller-than-expected loss for the first quarter 2009. Nevertheless, Ford was not out of the woods. On April 24, it announced having lost $1.4 billion, sales fell 43 percent, and it spent $3.7 billion of its cash during the first quarter 2009. It still had $21 billion in the bank and continued not to request federal bailout funds.

Ford Motor Company returned to profitability in the second quarter 2009 with signs of stabilizing. It reported a profit of $2.3 billion. It was projected that Ford would break even or perhaps make money in 2011. After four quarterly losses, Ford had its first quarterly profit. On August 13, 2009, Ford announced plans to build 495,000 cars and trucks in the third quarter of the year, up 18 percent from a year before. It estimated that its first production goal for the fourth quarter would be 570,000 vehicles, up 33 percent from the 2008 quarter. Ford posted a 17 percent gain in sales in August, during the cash-for-clunker program, while other U.S. automakers saw sales falling. And, by October, Ford had weathered the industry's downturn far better than its U.S. competitors, thanks to its ability to minimize its year-over-year sales declines and taking advantage of its competitors' weaknesses and securing market share. Ford secured more than five percentage points of U.S. retail market shares in the third quarter 2009 compared with the same period one year earlier, while GM and Chrysler lost ground. At the beginning of November, the company reported a third-quarter 2009 profit of nearly $1 billion.

In June 2010, Ford management reported that its April sales finished at an annual rate of 11.2 million cars, for a 13 percent increase in sales. On July 21, the company stated better-than-expected earnings of $2.6 billion for the second quarter 2010, up 15 percent from the year before. Revenue climbed 17 percent to $31.3 billion, giving Ford a profit of $4.6 billion for the first half of the year. Ford went from losing the most money in its history over the 2008–2009 period to earning $26 million each day.

In mid-October 2010, the Ford Motor company reported a huge 70 percent jump in its third-quarter profit. By this time in the year, the firm had earned $6.3 billion, more than any full year since 1999. On October 26, the company said that its third-quarter revenue totaled $29 billion. Ford car sales in November were 146,956 for an increase of 20 percent over last year. In the third quarter 2010, Ford's operating profit was $2.3 billion, twice as much as the year prior and the fifth quarterly surplus in a row, on revenue of $29 billion, with anticipated profit for the year of $10.5 billion. Ford also cut $12.8 billion of its debt of $33 billion. This impressive showing must be tempered by the fact that nearly all of Ford's growth came from China, India, and Brazil.

On January 10, 2011, Ford announced plans to hire 7,000 workers in the year, with at least 2,500 more new manufacturing positions. The firm had about 41,000 hourly workers and 20,000 salaried employed in the United States. On January 28, Ford reported a large decline from the $1.7 billion made in the third quarter. Nevertheless, for the year income totaled $6.6 billion, up from $2.7 billion in 2009. Revenue was $120.9 billion, $17 billion more than in 2009. The carmaker made just $1,130 in operating profit on each of the 593,000 cars and trucks produced in North America. In the third quarter of 2010, it made $2,707 a vehicle. In early February, Ford announced that it would boost car production by 13 percent in the first quarter. On June 15, management reported that its second-quarter pretax profit fell short of expectations, with a profit of $2.8 billion. By September, sales of 175,199 vehicles were sold, up 8.9 percent from the year before.

On October 26, management reported a 2 percent fall in earnings to $1.65 billion, as revenue climbed 14 percent to $33.1 billion. Pretax operating profit was $581 million. Ford earned $6.6 billion through the first nine months of the year. Ford sales climbed 6.2 percent to 167,502 vehicles in October. On December 8, management declared that it would pay a quarterly dividend for the first time in more than five years after canceling its dividend in September 2006. Earning $6.6 billion in 2011 through October, on March 1, 2012, it would pay a five-cents-a-share dividend to owners as of January 31, 2012.

On January 27, 2012, Ford management reported a record fourth-quarter profit of $12.4 billion resulting from an accounting change. Net income was $13.6 billion, and revenue climbed 6.4 percent to $34.6 billion.

See also AUTOMOBILE INDUSTRY; GEELY; JOB BANKS; VOLVO.

Cf. GENERAL MOTORS; GENERAL MOTORS–FORD PROPOSED MERGER; TOYOTA; VOLKSWAGEN.

FORECLOSURE(S). A legal process whereby a mortgagor of a property is deprived of his or her interest therein, usually by means of a court-administered sale of the property. In November 2008, the U.S. Treasury developed a $40 billion program to help delinquent homeowners avoid foreclosure. It was intended to help as many as 3 million beleaguered homeowners by reducing their monthly payments. More than 10 million homeowners were desperate for help.

Experts believed that nearly 5 million families could lose their homes between 2009 and 2011. With this, JP Morgan Chase, Morgan Stanley, and Bank of America said they would halt foreclosures through March 6, 2009. It was predicted that as many as 4 million homeowners faced foreclosure proceedings in 2009. On Wednesday, February 18, the administration outlined a proposal to spend at least $50 billion to prevent foreclosures. Then, on April 14, it was noted that the nation's largest mortgage companies were stepping up foreclosures on delinquent homeowners. Major banks and lending institutions had increased foreclosure activities since March following a temporary halt to foreclosures in February. The result was a further depression of home prices and increased pressure on bank earnings as troubled loans were written off. The government, in hoping to expand its $50 billion plan to lower home foreclosures, announced on April 28 a new program to help troubled homeowners modify second mortgages. The Treasury Department would offer cash incentives and subsidies to lenders who agreed to modify the primary or first mortgages of homeowners who had fallen delinquent or were in danger of doing so.

By July, four months into the administration's antiforeclosure effort, the president estimated that "over 50,000" at-risk loans had been modified so that homeowners could afford their payments and keep their homes. By the end of August, the government predicted that the existing program would modify 20,000 bad loans each week. Unfortunately, this effort would not be sufficient. Of the nearly 4.5 million foreclosures, distress sales could follow, thereby prolonging the recession. On August 4, 2009, the Treasury Department indicated that more than 400,000 borrowers had been offered government assistance. Over 235,000 borrowers, or roughly 9 percent of those eligible for the program, who were at least sixty days past due began trial mortgage modifications, the first step to getting a loan reworked. By summer's end 2009, one out of eight U.S. households with mortgages were in foreclosure or behind on its mortgage payment during the second quarter.

During this period, 6 million loans were either past due or in foreclosure in the second quarter 2009, the highest level ever recorded. Worse, loan defaults were not the only cause of foreclosures, even for homeowners otherwise current on their payments. As cities and counties struggled for income, they sold their delinquent tax bills to private firms. These firms, which often charge double-digit interest rates and large fees, get to keep what they collect. They also get the right to foreclose on the homes, taking priority over mortgage lenders. Home prices continued to fall in November 2009. It was expected that another 2.4 million homes would be lost in 2010, while home prices continued to drop another 10 percent or more.

By 2010, the previously immune rich were feeling the impact of the Great Recession. Houses with loans of $5 million or more saw a sharp increase in foreclosures. In February alone, 352 homes nationwide in this range were scheduled for foreclosure activity, making it the largest monthly increase. In 2009, there were only 1,312 notices. In early October 2010, some of the nation's largest lenders acknowledged that their foreclosure procedures could have been improperly handled, including GMAC Mortgage, JP Morgan Chase, and Bank of America. In some cases, bank officials signed papers that failed to verify crucial information like amounts owed by borrowers. Notarization of documents were also under question. In addition, a single official's name is signed radically different, suggesting forgeries.

Robo-signers, uncovered in October, were used by some major large banks to sign documents (more than 10,000 each month) without proper review and notarizing. Many such banks under inquiry ceased their practice of closing on foreclosures, at least for a brief period. The effect may be to prolong the foreclosure process, which in mid-2010 could deepen the housing crisis entering its fourth year. On October 7, the president announced that he would make his first significant veto, blocking the foreclosure bill over banks' paperwork. The veto would make it more difficult for banks to complete paperwork and speed the foreclosure process, giving homeowners more time to rework loans. Then, on Friday, October 8, Bank of America imposed a nationwide moratorium on all of its foreclosures in fifty states, just as the government pressed for a solution to the documentation problem. Earlier in the week, other large banks disclosed that they would temporarily cease foreclosure procedures in twenty-three U.S. states, hoping to find a "tailored" response to the foreclosure problem that wouldn't cause serious greater issues for the fragile housing market.

Attempting to slow down foreclosures, in October 2010, President Obama said he would veto the "Notary Bill" concerned that it would facilitate foreclosure fraud. The bill would have mandated that the notarizations of mortgages and other financial documents done in a particular state, including those done electronically, be recognized in other states. Latest numbers indicated that 4.2 million loans were in or near foreclosure. An estimated 3.5 million homes could be lost by the end of 2012, on top of the 6.2 million already surrendered. During that month, major banks were involved in the unfolding mortgage-foreclosure crisis. On October 14, the crisis entered the financial markets, forcing down bank stocks and weighing on mortgage bonds. Bank stock fell more than 5 percent along with bank bonds and the cost of buying protection against a possible debt default by banks.

To many experts, a foreclosure moratorium was a bad idea, as it would delay a needed resolution to move the housing market forward. In addition, it would create more losses for investors, homeowners, and taxpayers, and have little impact on keeping delinquent borrowers in their homes. By October 20, some of the major banks chose to move ahead with foreclosures of homes, declaring that the crisis was overblown and procedures were followed. Then, suddenly, both the Bank of America and GMAC Mortgage, on October 18, announced that they would restart home seizures that were frozen by documentation concerns. This was a strategy for counterattacking a financial and political threat over allegations that certain employees signed hundreds of documents a day without properly reviewing their contents when foreclosing on homes.

By year's end 2010, the foreclosure crisis had claimed more than 5 million U.S. homes, about 10 percent of all homes with a mortgage. It commenced in lower-income neighborhoods and then spread to the wealthier. One in six homeowners were "underwater," owing more on their houses than they were worth.

By March 2011, the Justice Department investigated allegations that a mortgage subsidiary of a major bank had foreclosed on almost two dozen military families from 2006 to 2008 in violation of the Service Members Civil Relief Act. This law bars lenders from foreclosing on active-duty service members without a court hearing. Banks initiated fewer foreclosures in April than in any month since late 2008. New foreclosures were 187,400, a 31 percent fall from the previous month and a 15 percent drop from one year earlier.

See also BANK OF AMERICA; BERNANKE, BEN; "BURGER-KING KIDS"; CHURCHES; DEED IN LIEU OF FORECLOSURE; EMERGENCY ECONOMIC STABILIZATION ACT OF 2008; FANNIE MAE; FEDERAL DEPOSIT INSURANCE CORPORATION; EXURBIA; FORECLOSURE GATE; FORECLOSURE LEGISLATION; FORECLOSURE MILLS; FORECLOSURE PREVENTION PLAN; GMAC MORTGAGE; HOME ASSISTANCE MODIFICATION PROGRAM; HOMEOWNERSHIP; HOME PRICES; HOME REPOSSESSION; HOUSE (U.S.) FINANCIAL OVERHAUL PLAN; HOUSING BAILOUT PLAN; JP MORGAN CHASE; MAKING HOME AFFORDABLE PROGRAM; MERS; MODIFYING MORTGAGES; MORTGAGE-FORECLOSURE CRISIS; MORTGAGE LOAN; MORTGAGE MODIFICATION; MORTGAGE SCAMS; REO (REAL ESTATE OWNED); ROBO-SIGNERS; SHORTCUT FORECLOSURE; STRATEGIC DEFAULT; TROUBLED ASSET RELIEF PROGRAM; UNDERWATER; WELLS FARGO.

FORECLOSURE FRAUD. *See* FORECLOSURE; FORECLOSURE GATE.

FORECLOSURE GATE. With a combination of sloppy (possibly fraudulent) paperwork, a securitization process of poorly reviewed repossessions leading to premature foreclosures. The name given a scandal on sales of mortgaged-foreclosed homes.

FORECLOSURE LEGISLATION. Proposed legislation that would permit bankruptcy judges to lower the payments on home loans to prevent debtors from losing them. By mid-September 2009, the proposal was blocked in Congress after vehement opposition from the banking industry.

FORECLOSURE MILLS. Usually, law firms specializing in the processing of thousands of foreclosures on behalf of lenders. There is a connection between Wall Street private equity companies and these law firms. Often, a private equity firm, in a transaction worth tens of millions of dollars, purchases a wide range of services used by the law firm. Then, a subsidiary of that private equity firm or an entity it controls makes money by providing those services back to that law firm or other businesses for a fee.

See also "BURGER-KING KIDS"; FORECLOSURE; FORECLOSURE GATE; MERS.

FORECLOSURE-PREVENTION PLAN. Announced in mid-March 2009, designed to give several million troubled borrowers another chance to lower their mortgage payments. The government warned that it was also an opportunity for firms to fleece unsuspecting borrowers by charging fees for what they promised would be quick results in negotiating with banks to get easier loan terms. In numerous situations, the firms took the homeowner's money and never delivered the services promised. Some of these companies delivered on their promises but charged fees, often more than $1,000, for services that borrowers can obtain for free.

In July, Congress increased to $360 million the funds it had allocated for foreclosure-prevention counseling free of charge.

See also HOME AFFORDABLE MODIFICATION PROGRAM.

FOREIGN ACCOUNT TAX COMPLIANCE ACT. Under the jurisdiction of the Internal Revenue Service, a unit devoted to scrutinizing large firms and wealthy individuals. The act becomes operational in 2013, requiring U.S. citizens to declare offshore accounts or withholdings and pay a 35 percent tax on those accounts. Also requires the IRS to reviewer partnerships and wealthy individuals with at least $10 million in assets.

See also INTERNAL REVENUE SERVICE.

FOREIGN AID. Resulting from the Great Recession and a $1.5 trillion reduction in the federal deficit expected, the United States appears to be retreating from foreign aid, which today accounts for less than 2 percent of the federal budget. The budget was cut by $6 billion, or about 11 percent, in 2011, with a $2 billion reduction possible in 2012.

FOREIGN-BORN RESIDENTS. *See* IMMIGRATION.

FOREIGN CURRENCY LIQUIDITY SWAPS. A means for central banks to get foreign currencies to their local banks. Allows for any central bank to exchange currencies with one another.

See also SWAPS.

FOREIGN DIRECT INVESTMENT (FDI). Was up 49 percent in 2011 from 2009. Rose to $236 billion in 2010 from $159 billion in 2009, but far below the $310 billion in 2008.

See also INDIA; ORGANISATION FOR ECONOMIC CO-OPERATION AND DEVELOPMENT.

FOREIGN EXCHANGE RESERVES. *See* CHINA; DEBT.

FORINT. *See* HUNGARY.

FORMOSA. The central bank in early December 2008 cut its main benchmark interest rate by three-quarters of a point to 2.0 percent, the fifth such move in the last two months.

FOR-PROFIT COLLEGES. *See* STUDENT LOANS.

FORTIS BANQUE. A financial service bank, Fortis took on huge debt just after the peak of the credit boom in 2007. In the first nine months of 2008,

Fortis posted an $18.36 billion loss. It began to stall in September 2008 following the collapse of Lehman Brothers. Faced with imminent failure of the bank, the Dutch and Belgian governments initially agreed to a joint salvage operation; in the end, the Dutch went their own way, deciding on October 3 to nationalize the operation in the Netherlands. On October 5, BNP Paribas agreed to acquire Fortis's banking and insurance operations in Belgium and Luxembourg for €14 billion. Fortis's stock was down 95 percent in 2008. Then, on December 18, BNP Paribas suspended its takeover of the Belgian financial services firm following a court ruling that effectively froze the deal.

On April 29, 2009, Fortis shareholders voted to back a takeover by the French bank BNP Paribas, thus ending the run of Fortis as a ward of the Belgian state.

See also BNP PARIBAS.

FOUNDATIONS. Legislation was introduced on March 24, 2009, in the U.S. Senate that intended to encourage foundations to give away more of their funds. If passed, the measure would alter the way foundations are taxed on their investment income, replacing the existing two-tiered system with a single tax rate. Foundations had long argued that the present system effectively penalized them when they gave away more money than usual.

Under present law, private foundations must give their charitable gifts equal to at least 5 percent of the market value of their assets. The proposal urged a single tax rate of 1.32 percent.

401(K) PLANS. *See also* RETIREMENT BENEFITS.

FRANCE. After falling by 2.2 percent in 2009, real GDP was projected to grow slowly by 1.4 percent in 2010 and 1.7 percent in 2011, led by business investment and exports. This would not be enough to prevent the unemployment rate from rising until the beginning of 2011. A mix of appropriate discretionary measures and automatic stabilizers had cushioned the impact of the crisis. The investment tax cut embedded in the 2010 budget was also welcomed, but additional spending should now be resisted. Designing and clearly communicating a credible multiyear exit strategy was a priority. The needed consolidation represented an opportunity to rebalance public finances by cutting inefficient spending, increasing inheritance, property, and carbon taxes, and further reforming the pension system.

Business confidence fell to its lowest level in more than fifteen years in October 2008. On Thursday, November 20, 2008, President Sarkozy introduced a €20 billion ($25 billion) strategic investment fund. He also promised a stimulus package with the aim of investing massively in infrastructure, education, and research. Then on Friday, November 28, President Sarkozy said he would present a €19 billion program to help the struggling car industry and further invest in the nation's infrastructure. On December 5, President Sarkozy vowed to spend some €26 billion over two years in an effort to soften the blow of an economic crisis that had increased unemployment and risked pushing the economy into recession. His plan, worth about 1.3 percent of the French GDP, was designed to add as much as 0.8 percentage point to growth in 2009.

Among the planned investment projects was €4 billion in state spending on military, research, and infrastructure projects, while €1.8 billion was earmarked for the housing sector. Sarkozy's plan would widen the French deficit to 3.9 percent of GDP in 2009. The economy was projected to contract by 0.4 percent in 2009, falling into its first recession in more than fifteen years. French banks increased their lending to consumers and firms. The government pledged $13.3 billion to recapitalize six banks in exchange for promises to increase lending. President Sarkozy announced another stimulus package of €26 billion, or $37 billion, as business confidence fell to the lowest in fifteen years and the economic slump continued its downslide. It was projected in mid-December that France would loose 191,000 jobs in the first half of 2009, following a drop of 125,000 in the second half of 2008.

In mid-January 2009, the government considered helping U.S. automakers ride out the credit crunch by covering up to 50 percent of their financing needs. An auto summit was planned. After Germany, Europe's second-largest car market by volume is France. Registrations of new vehicles fell to 74,659 in January, down 7.9 percent from a year earlier and 2.8 percent from December. Renault sales plunged 21 percent in January; Peugeot-Citroen saw an 11 percent slump in registrations. In addition, the market share of French manufacturers fell to 50 percent from 54.1 percent a year earlier.

Unemployment in France had soared the previous month, pushing job losses in the fourth quarter to their highest level in more than two decades. The number of people seeking work rose by 45,000 in December, bringing the number of jobs lost in the fourth quarter to more than 156,000. Unemployment was expected to rise to 8 percent by mid-2009 from 7.3 percent in last year's third quarter.

Unemployment rose to 3.5 percent from the previous month to reach 2.38 million, up 19 percent for the year. On February 2, the prime minister detailed the government's plan for boosting the economy, including 1,000 investment projects and €200 million for payments to low-income families. France's GDP was projected to contract 1.8 percent. France announced on February 9 a sweeping $8.5 billion plan to supports its automobile industry. The two largest French carmakers, Peugeot-Citroen and Renault, would each get a five-year loan of €3 billion at an interest rate of 6 percent. Unemployment rose to 8.6 percent in February, above the European Union average. For the new school year, 13,500 public-sector teaching jobs had to be cut. The International Monetary Fund forecast that France's economy would shrink a little more than 1 percent over 2009 and 2010. Between 2002 and 2007, the economy averaged 1.9 percent growth. The French economy shrank for the fourth straight quarter, with GDP falling 1.2 percent from the fourth quarter of 2008.

On June 22, 2009, President Sarkozy addressed a joint session of the French Parliament at Versailles. He told lawmakers that he would sharply lower the state's "bad budget deficit" and introduce a government bond issue to finance industrial, education, and cultural projects. France's economy expanded at an annualized rate of 1.4 percent in the second quarter 2009. By September 2009, the nation's economic outlook appeared brighter. After four consecutive quarters of decline, GDP grew. However, the jobless total reached 2.5 million in July, a jump of 26 percent in the same month a year earlier.

On August 20, 2010, President Sarkozy downgraded the government's forecast for 2011, but he remained firm on reducing the nation's deficit to 6 percent of GDP in 2011. The government projected a growth of 2 percent for 2011, compared to an earlier optimistic forecast of 2.5 percent. Public-sector workers went on strike on September 7 to force the government to retreat on its plans to raise the retirement age to sixty-two from sixty.

While the nation ranks fifth in the world in exports of goods and fourth in services, the nation's performance is generally weak, with a trade balance deficit. The nation assuredly needs an economic overhaul. Beginning on October 17 and continuing for days, unions held huge demonstrations and strikes in opposition to the pension overhaul plan. High school students in large numbers were supportive, arguing that they would have to work more years, even though at present they hadn't found a career or job. In early November 2010, the French Parliament approved the final version of a controversial reform to the pension system that raises the minimum retirement age from sixty to sixty-two.

France's pace of recovery in 2011 was expected to be slow, as stimulus is withdrawn and demand falters among trading partners. The precarious state of the national accounts suggested a tight budget year. The nation's GDP growth was 1.1 percent, with a GDP of $2,490 billion, an inflation rate of 1.3 percent, and a GDP per head of $39,370.

On March 28, 2011, the government noted that the number of foreign direct investments into France surged 22 percent in 2010 from 2009 to 782 projects, thereby creating 31,000 jobs. It was the highest amount in fifteen years. France's deficit reached 7.1 percent in the year, and the president pledged to narrow it to 3 percent in 2013. Under the IMF's growth projections, the deficit would reach 3.8 percent in 2013 and 3 percent in 2014. On

August 10, the government promised to consider fresh tax rises, spending cuts, etc. At the same time, shares in the nation's second-largest publicly trade bank, Societe General, fell down 15 percent. By the middle of August, it was shown that France's economic growth in the second quarter dropped to zero, leading to concerns regarding the nation's prized AAA credit rating. GDP was flat in the quarter after expanding at nearly 4 percent in the first quarter. At the end of September, the government released its austerity budget attempting to lower its deficit to 4.5 percent of GDP in 2012, all through spending cuts and tax increases.

On November 7, 2011, the government outlined the country's second austerity package in less than three months. The prime minister's office introduced new measures that would save $16.5 billion through the end of 2012. Cutbacks included increasing in the lower-level value-added tax rate to 7 percent from 5.5 percent; curbs on rising health-care and benefits spending; temporary tax increases for high-revenue firms; acceleration of pension overhauls; and increased levies on dividends and interest payments. By mid-November, French borrowing costs began to signal danger, raising the burden of servicing its debt. This would be the single largest budget expenditure in 2012. France had the highest deficit level in 2010 at 7.1 percent of GDP. At the end of June 2011, France had $2.3 trillion of debt, and the government projected that public debt would peak at about 87 percent of GDP in 2012. Then, on December 9, Moody's Investors Service downgraded the three largest banks in France.

In addition, France's car market shrank sharply in December with 18 percent less sales than the year before. For the entire 2011, car registrations were down 2.1 percent. On December 29, the president outlined job plans to contain a sharp rise in unemployment by persuading firms and workers to agree to a new deal: pay cuts for job guarantees.

See also BNP PARIBAS; CONSUMER CONFIDENCE; EURO-PEAN COMMISSION; ING GROUP; MERKEL, ANGELA; PEUGEOT-CITROEN; SARKOZY, NICHOLAS; SOVEREIGN FUND; TRAVEL AND TOURISM (2011).

FRANCHISING INDUSTRY. The number of defaults by franchisees increased 52 percent in the fiscal year ending September 30, 2008, from fiscal 2007. Loan losses totaled $93.3 million, a 167 percent jump from $35 million just twelve months earlier.

FRANK, BARNEY (BARNETT). Congressman, chairman of the Committee on Financial Services, and co-author of the Dodd-Frank Bill (2010). Decided not to run for reelection in 2012.

See also FEDERAL RESERVE; HOUSE (U.S.) FINANCIAL OVER-HAUL PLAN; WALL STREET REFORM ACT (2010).

FRAUD. The watchdog and head of the Recovery Act Accountability and Transparency Board, nicknamed the Rat Board, over the $787 stimulus package believed that fraud consumed about 7 percent of all major contracts or over $55 billion.

See also GOLDMAN SACHS; INTERNAL REVENUE SERVICE; MORTGAGE FRAUD; UNEMPLOYMENT CLAIM FRAUD.

FRAUD ENFORCEMENT AND RECOVERY ACT OF 2009. *See* FINANCIAL CRISIS INQUIRY COMMISSION.

FREDDIE MAC (FEDERAL HOME LOAN MORTGAGE CORPORATION) (FHLMC). Established in 1970, responsible for aiding the secondary residential mortgages sponsored by the Veterans Administration and Federal Housing Administration in addition to nongovernment residential mortgages. The mortgage finance company, a government-sponsored enterprise (GSE), is now under government control.

On March 20, 2008, federal regulators eased Freddie Mac's capital requirements, a move that allowed the agency to purchase billions of dollars of mortgage securities. An $821 million loss was announced on August 7, with warnings of further losses. Its shares dropped 19 percent. Freddie Mac asked the U.S. Treasury on November 14, 2008, for $13.8 billion after a record quarterly loss caused its net worth to fall below zero. Freddie Mac, which had a net worth of negative $13.7 billion at the end of the third quarter 2008, received the money by November 29. The net loss widened to $25.3 billion after it wrote down tax assets and provided for bad mortgages and securities.

Freddie Mac's losses narrowed to $6.3 billion in the third quarter 2009. The government owned 79.9 percent of Freddie Mac, and on December 24, 2009, it offered significant new financial support to the housing giant no matter how poorly it performs in the next few years. In addition, it approved a compensation package for its chief executive officer to receive up to $6 million for the coming two years. The pay package includes $900,000 in salary, $3.1 million in deferred payments in 2010 that are not dependent on performance, and an additional $2 million tied to meeting certain objectives. On May 5, 2010, Freddie Mac asked the U.S. Treasury for an additional $10.6 billion after posting first-quarter losses. Then, in early November, Freddie Mac posted a $2.5 billion third-quarter loss, the smallest in more than a year, indicating that mortgage delinquencies were slowing.

On February 11, 2011, the president announced plans to eliminate Freddie Mac, thus curbing the government's role in housing finance. In May, Freddie Mac reported net income of $676 million for the first quarter, its best performance since the government took it over in 2008. On August 8, Standard & Poor's downgraded Freddie Mac's stock from AAA to AA+. In November, Freddie Mac secured another $6 billion from the U.S. government after the mortgage finance firm losses increased to $4.4 billion in the third quarter 2011. The loss, Freddie's worst quarterly showing in more than one year, compared to a $2.5 billion loss the year prior.

See also FANNIE AND FREDDIE; FANNIE MAE; FEDERAL HOUSING FINANCE AGENCY; FEDERAL RESERVE; FINANCIAL CRISIS INQUIRY REPORT; GINNIE MAE; HOUSING PLAN; MORTGAGE-BACKED SECURITY; SECURITIES AND EXCHANGE COMMISSION; U.S. TREASURY.

FREE CHECKING. *See* CHECKING.

FREE-FALL. *See* INTERNATIONAL MONETARY FUND.

FREIGHT HAULERS. The freight transportation industry remained in a sharp slump by the end of April 2009. U.S. air-cargo volumes dropped 21 percent in February 2009; railroad firms reported declines of 23 percent to 26 percent.

By July 2010, rail haulers noted a seasonally adjusted average of 289,320 carloads a week, up 3.2 percent from the month before. This increase suggested that firms are continuing to boost orders.

FRIENDLY'S ICE CREAM CORPORATION. As fewer people ate out during the recession, Friendly's filed for Chapter 11 bankruptcy protection on October 5, 2011, with about 10,000 workers and more than 400 restaurants. On that day, it closed sixty-three underperforming restaurants as part of an effort to trim costs; it will keep others open during the restructuring.

Chain restaurants have been struggling during the Great Recession. Many have declared bankruptcy resulting from consumer cutbacks on the number of meals out since the recession began. During the twelve-month period ending in August 2011, the average American ate at or got takeout from restaurants 195 times, down from 208 times in 2008. Sun Capital Partners, the private-equity firm that owns Friendly's, received court approval on December 29.

FRUGALITY. In 2009, consumers became increasingly cautious in their spending habits amid fears of a worsening economy over the coming twelve months. Deflation can result from a pattern of hesitation.

See also DEFLATION.

FSF (FINANCIAL STABILITY FORUM). *See* REGULATORS.

FTSE. Stocks in Europe had their worst annual fall in more than twenty years at the end of 2008, its worst performance since records began. FTSE Eurofirst lost 32.4 percent of its value in 2008, substantially larger than its previous biggest annual loss of 24.5 percent.

FUEL TAX. By 2009, there was a call for increasing the current 18.4 cents a gallon federal tax on gasoline and 24.4 cents a gallon tax on diesel. State fuel taxes vary from state to state.
See also AUTOMOBILE INDUSTRY.

FULD, RICHARD S. JR. Former chief executive officer of Lehman Brothers. Following its collapse, he became a Matrix adviser.

FUR INDUSTRY. In 2007, global fur retail sales were a record $15 billion. In this meltdown period, sales in 2008 and 2009 plummeted as much as 30 percent.

FURLOUGHS. On February 6, 2009, the first of the semimonthly work furloughs across California state agencies would trim $1.3 billion from that state's $143 billion budget, affecting 200,000 employees. For those forced on leave, it meant a 9 percent pay cut to aid the coffers of California. California's unemployment rate at that time was 9.3 percent, among the highest in the country.

By 2009, furloughs that were usually confined to factory workers were hitting the office scene as employers were digging deeper to cut costs. More and more firms were instituting these short-term furloughs as a humane alternative to permanent job cuts. School teachers were now included.

The arguments for and against unpaid furloughs are as follows:

a. Benefits—reduces labor costs quickly, helps keep highly skilled workers, and avoids rehiring and retraining.
b. Disadvantages—could drive away top performers, prolongs cost cutting, and drains long-term morale.

Furloughs as a cost-saving measure designed to minimize more layoffs were minimally used. Pay cuts became more pronounced.
See also PAY.
Synonymous with TEMPORARY LAYOFFS.

FURNISHINGS. *See* FURNITURE AND FURNISHINGS.

FURNITURE AND FURNISHINGS. By mid-August 2011, furniture and furnishings purchases remained 22 percent below the 2009 Great Recession.

FUTURES TRADING PRACTICES ACT (OF 1992). Authorized the Commodity Futures Trading Commission to exempt certain over-the-counter transactions from most of the Commodity Exchange Act. The CFTC would use its new authority to exempt some swap agreements, hybrid instruments, and energy contracts.

G

G-2 (GROUP OF TWO). Unofficially, by 2009, the two most powerful nations of the world—China and the United States.

G-5 (GROUP OF FIVE). Composed of the United States, Great Britain, France, Germany, and Japan.

G-7 (GROUP OF SEVEN). A group of industrialized nations, including the United States, Japan, Germany, France, and Great Britain, plus Canada and Italy.
See also G-8; G-20.

G-8 (GROUP OF EIGHT). Members of the G-7 plus Russia.
See also G-20.

G-20 (GROUP OF TWENTY). Leaders of the Group of Twenty met in Washington, D.C., on November 14–15, 2008, to revive their economies and overhaul financial regulations. The group planned its next meeting for the end of March 2009. These rich and emerging nations represent almost 90 percent of global GDP, comprising nineteen industrialized and emerging countries and the European Union.

Stimulus spending estimates for the G-20 countries as a percentage of their GDP in 2009 are as follows:

Saudi Arabia—3.3 percent
Spain—2.3 percent
Australia—2.1 percent
United States—2.0 percent
China—2.0 percent
South Africa—1.8 percent
Russia—1.7 percent
South Korea—1.5 percent
Mexico—1.5 percent
Germany—1.5 percent
Canada—1.5 percent
Japan—1.4 percent

United Kingdom—1.4 percent
Indonesia—1.3 percent
Argentina—1.3 percent
France—0.7 percent
India—0.5 percent
Brazil—0.4 percent
Italy—0.2 percent
Turkey— 0.0 percent

A global slump existed on the eve of the summit of the G-20. Gordon Brown, the architect and organizer of the summit, called for a "New Deal" to tackle the economic crisis. The day before the summit opened, President Obama conceded U.S. culpability in starting the global financial crisis, but he then called on those in attendance to do more to end it.

The one-day meeting was held on April 2, 2009, in London; new evidence was used as background for the meeting. The eurozone showed inflation at 0.6 percent through March, the lowest level since official records began in 1996. Together, the world economy shrank by 2.75 percent in 2009, according to the Organisation for Economic Co-operation and Development.

Leaders at this summit agreed to quadruple the financial capacity of the International Monetary Fund with a $1.1 trillion commitment in order to revive trade, which was expected to contract in 2009 for the first time in thirty years. It also promised to clamp down on tax havens and tighten financial regulations, making large hedge funds comply with domestic regulators and disclose how much they have borrowed, and making certain that there is effective oversight, even if the funds are operating across national borders.

The scorecard for the G-20 April 2 meeting, with a commitment of $1.1 trillion, was as follows:

Pledged Resources

- Increased resources for the IMF—$500 billion
- New special drawing rights allocation—$250 billion
- Increased lending by multilateral development banks—$100 billion
- Increased support for trade finance—$250 billion
- Additional lending to poorest countries, financed by IMF gold sales—$6 billion

Other Commitments

- Establish a Financial Stability Board, whose purpose would be to assess weaknesses in the global financial system and to oversee action to correct these weaknesses.

- Ensure that regulators have necessary access to financial information.
- Require that hedge funds are registered and regularly disclose their financial information, including leverage, to regulators.
- Develop means to control the use of illegal tax havens, in part by increasing disclosure requirements for taxpayers.
- Support greater transparency in the reporting of financial executives' compensation, and ensure that boards of directors play a greater role in the setting of executives' pay.

The $1.1 trillion pledge was deceiving. About $500 billion represented increased direct financing for the IMF. Less than half of that amount had been committed by Japan, the European Union, Canada, and Norway. China would provide $40 billion and the United States $100 billion (which must be authorized by Congress). A shortfall of $145 billion of the $500 billion was expected.

On September 24–25, 2009, the Group of Twenty met in Pittsburgh, Pennsylvania. Members agreed that the G-20 would henceforth be the permanent council for international economic cooperation, eclipsing the Group of 7 and Group of 8. Support was given to an agreement that would require members to subject their economic policies to a type of peer review. Another recommendation was that bonuses be reduced, or "clawed back," after being awarded if a bank's performance suffered. Throughout the meeting of the world's industrial nations, the police were out in force attempting to control protestors (estimated to be 3,000 to 4,000), some of whom were arrested. At the Pittsburgh meeting, China and Japan announced that they would rely less on exports and more on domestic consumption; the United States would work to cut its budget deficit; member nations would require higher levels of capital in banks and other financial institutions; and Europe would make tough structural reforms to prod business investment. In addition, it was agreed that there was to be a major shift in ownership of the International Monetary Fund.

On June 27, 2010, the wealthiest of the Group of Twenty nations agreed that they would halve their government deficits by the year 2013 and stabilize their debt by the year 2016. At the G-20 meeting in South Korea in November, the United States was unable to persuade other nations to take measures it believes are necessary to end currency wars and promote sustainable growth.

See also AUSTRALIA; BASEL COMMITTEE ON BANKING SUPERVISION; BASEL III ACCORD; BUSINESS 20; EUROZONE; G-7; G-NEXT; GLOBAL REBALANCING; HEDGE FUNDS; INTERNATIONAL MONETARY FUND; OBAMA, BARACK; ORGANISATION FOR ECONOMIC CO-OPERATION AND DEVELOPMENT; REGULATORS; SUMMIT OF NOVEMBER 4, 2008; TAX HAVENS; WORLD BANK.

G-77. Developing nations and others.

GAMBLING. Following the meltdown, state governments struggling to balance their budgets were seeking way to increase revenues. Gambling had become a growing source of income. The near $100 billion-a-year source of revenue was being considered by states across the country. However, with tourism down from past years, the risks of failure remained high.

GANNETT. The largest newspaper publisher in the nation, it reported in mid-April 2009 a 60 percent decline in first-quarter profits. Gannett publishes dozens of daily papers and earned $77.4 million in the first three months of the year compared to $192 million the year before. Gannet announced at the end of June 2009 that it would cut between 1,000 and 2,000 jobs out of its 41,500-person workforce as a result of dramatic drops in advertising income and lower circulation. Net income fell nearly 60 percent from a year before as publishing ad revenue declined more than 34 percent. By the end of the month, the newspaper publisher announced that 1,400 positions would be eliminated from its workforce of 41,500. On October 19, Gannett's management reported a 53 percent fall in third-quarter income. Publishing advertising fell 28 percent in the quarter from the year before, an improvement from the 32 percent ad-revenue decline in the second quarter.

Gannett reported on April 16, 2010, a 51 percent increase in first-quarter profit of $117.2 million, up from $77.4 million the year before. Nevertheless, revenue declined 4.1 percent to $1.32 billion. Gannett's second-quarter 2010 profit more than doubled to $195.5 million, with revenue falling 1.6 percent to $1.37 billion. On October 15, 2010, the company posted a 37 percent increase in its quarterly profit. Net income rose to $101.4 million, with a flat revenue of $1.31 billion. Fourth-quarter profit rose by 30 percent, with revenue increasing 4.7 percent.

On June 21, 2011, Gannett announced plans to lay off about 700 workers, representing approximately 2 percent of the firm's workforce. The slowness in the economy recovery was to blame. Its second-quarter earnings fell 22 percent, with ad revenue falling 7 percent and circulation revenue falling 2 percent. It had a quarterly profit of $151.5 million.

On January 30, 2012, management reported a 33 percent fall in fourth-quarter 2011 profit, with ad revenue falling 7.1 percent from the year before. Gannett reported a profit of $116.9 million.

See also NEWSPAPERS.

GAP. By the end of December 2008, the retailer suffered a 14 percent drop in same-store sales. Fiscal fourth-quarter 2008 net income fell 8.3 percent on a 13 percent sales drop. Gap's second-quarter 2009 profit fell slightly.

In November 2009, Gap announced that its quarterly profit climbed 25 percent following five straight years of declines. The company reported a profit of $307 million.

Gap posted first-quarter 2010 earnings. Sales for the quarter climbed 6 percent to $3.33 billion. Net income rose to $302 million. In early November, Gap management posted a 2 percent increase in same-store sales. In mid-November 2010, Gap posted a slight fall in profit by 1 percent to $303 million, with revenue climbing 2 percent to $3.65 billion.

By 2011, Gap posted a 3 percent decline. On November 17, Gap's management reported that its fiscal third-quarter earnings fell 36 percent, with net sales for the quarter falling 1.9 percent to $3.59 billion, and a profit of $193 million.

See also RETAILING.

GAS. *See* NATURAL GAS.

GASOLINE PRICES. By February 2011, gasoline rose to $3.14 a gallon, up from $2.61 a year before and the highest level since October 2008. Following months of increased prices, on August 7–8 consumers noticed a fall in their gas bill as the Standard & Poor's downgrading led to consumers spending less to fill up their cars and trucks.

By 2012, gasoline prices had again climbed high even though there was a drop in consumption. Foreign affairs and global conflicts contributed to this decline.

GATT. *See* GENERAL AGREEMENT ON TARIFFS AND TRADE.

GDI. *See* GROSS DOMESTIC INCOME (GDI) (U.S.).

GDP. *See* GROSS DOMESTIC PRODUCT (GDP) (U.S.).

GE (G.E.). *See* GENERAL ELECTRIC.

GE CAPITAL CORPORATION. *See* GENERAL ELECTRIC CAPITAL CORPORATION.

GEELY. The Chinese automaker reported on April 12, 2010, that its 2009 net profit rose 35 percent, with profits climbing $172.9 billion. Revenue more than tripled.

See also VOLVO.

GEITHNER, TIMOTHY F. President Obama's secretary of the Treasury. He graduated from Dartmouth College, majoring in government and Asian studies. He then completed his master's degree (1985) from Johns Hopkins School of Advanced International Studies and later joined the Treasury Department as an assistant financial attaché at the U.S. Tokyo Embassy. Following a stint at the International Monetary Fund, he was recruited in November 2000 as the president of the New York Federal Reserve, the second most prominent job in the country's central banking system.

On July 25, 2007, Geithner said, "Financial markets outside the United States are now deeper and more liquid than they used to be, making it easier for companies to raise capital domestically at reasonable cost."

A controversial aspect of his career was his role in failing to save Lehman Brothers while at the Federal Reserve in New York. It is believed that he was a key decision maker in September 2008 when the government let Lehman Brothers fail and then, two days later, bailed out the insurer American International Group for $85 billion. This was considered an abrupt reversal from the "no new bailout" position taken with Lehman and initially with AIG.

His much-anticipated speech on February 10, 2009, where he announced the administration's financial rescue plan was followed by a nearly 5 percent sell-off of stocks, the worst drop since President Obama assumed office. Then, on March 23, Geithner delivered the long-awaited details of his scheme to save the banking system, which dazzled Wall Street. He called for broad regulation of derivatives trading, nonbanks, and hedge funds.

The Troubled Asset Relief Program has been closely identified with the Treasury secretary. Some people are calling the TARP effort the Hotel Geithner. On November 19, 2009, the Treasury secretary announced his hope to end the bailout fund, TARP, as soon as possible and to use funds from the $700 billion program to reduce debt.

Following rumors that he would soon be leaving as secretary of the Treasury, he announced that he would stay on at least to complete the first term of the president. At the same time, on August 7 he argued that Standard & Poor's decision to downgrade the U.S. AAA credit rating to AA+ by saying that "S&P had shown really terrible judgment."

See also BANK RESCUE (PLAN) OF 2009 (U.S.); FEDERAL RESERVE; MAKING HOME AFFORDABLE PROGRAM; STANDARD & POOR'S; TROUBLED ASSET RELIEF PROGRAM; "TOO BIG TO FAIL"; WALL STREET REFORM ACT (2010).

GENDER. *See* WOMEN WORKFORCE.

GENERAL AGREEMENT ON TARIFFS AND TRADE (GATT). On January 1, 1948, a multilateral trade treaty was signed embodying reciprocal commercial rights and obligations as a means of expanding and liberalizing world trade. It established common regulations and obligations concerning international trading arrangements and the framework for the negotiation of agreements to liberalize world trade. It was accepted by more than eighty fully participating nations, with nearly thirty others signing under special arrangements. These nations at that time accounted for almost 80 percent of world trade.

With GATT, following the end of World War II, world trade expanded faster than global output did. Tariffs worldwide have been cut from an average of 40 percent in 1947 to less than 5 percent today, and consumers have reaped rich rewards in the form of lower prices and better merchandise. GATT, based in Geneva, Switzerland, has been remarkably successful and crucial to a strong world economy.

In 1995, GATT became the World Trade Organization (WTO).

See also PROTECTIONISM; WORLD TRADE ORGANIZATION.

GENERAL DYNAMICS. On March 5, 2009, the firm announced the cut of 1,200 jobs, sending its shares to a six-year low. The company's third-quarter 2009 earnings fell 9.8 percent. Overall profit for the period was $572 million. Revenue increased 8.1 percent to $7.72 billion.

GENERAL ELECTRIC (GE). Posted fourth-quarter 2008 earnings with shares dropping more than 50 percent. General Electric expected earnings growth of 0 to 5 percent in 2009 from its industrial and media divisions, down from 10 percent in 2008.

In February 2009, GE shrank its dividend by 68 percent, the first such cut since the Great Depression. GE lowered its dividend for the first time in seventy-one years to 10 cents a share per quarter from 31 cents. On March 6, in what was termed a "housekeeping exercise," GE's Capital Corporation unit offered to purchase back $1.46 billion of its bonds as a way to boost its financial flexibility and make it easier to participate in new government financing efforts. Then, on March 23, GE lost its coveted AAA credit rating, which it had first won in 1956. By one notch, GE's long-term debt was dropped to an AA+ rating by Moody's.

The company's profit fell sharply in the first quarter 2009 from a year earlier, down 36 percent to $2.74 billion. Its revenue for the quarter fell 9 percent to $38.4 billion. GE's second-quarter 2009 net income fell 49 percent. Profit at its financial division, GE Capital, declined 80 percent to $590 million. For its third-quarter 2009 profit there was a 42 percent decline, with a net income of $2.49 billion, down from $4.31 billion one year before. Revenue declined 20 percent to $37.8 billion from $47.2 billion. Earnings fell at GE Capital 87 percent to $263 million. The real estate group saw a $538 million loss from a $244 profit one year earlier.

GE projected revenue in 2010 to be roughly $155 billion, similar to 2009, with a profit margin of about 16 percent. The company reported net income of $1.9 billion in the first quarter 2010, even though revenue fell 5 percent to $36.6 billion and earnings were $2.3 billion, down 18 percent from a year before. Its profit fell 31 percent. In mid-July 2010, GE announced a profit increase for the first time since the meltdown began. The firm's second-quarter 2010 profit rose 16 percent to $3.11 billion; revenue fell 4.3 percent to $37.44

billion. On October 16, management reported that revenue fell 5 percent to $35.9 billion, with profit falling 18 percent to $2.1 billion. GE raised its quarterly 2010 dividend for a second time in the year. GE had a 51 percent increase ($4.52 billion) in fourth-quarter profit with expectations of revenue growth of up to 5 percent in 2011.

On March 24, 2011, it was reported that GE, after showing worldwide profits of $14.2 billion, in its tax returns claimed a tax benefit of $3.2 billion. Then, on April 21, management reported a 77 percent increase in its first-quarter profit of $1.8 billion, with revenue climbing 6.2 percent to $38.45 billion. For the second quarter, revenue rose 23 percent with sales outside the United States accounting for 59 percent. Net income rose 21 percent to $3.76 billion, up from $3.11 billion the year before. Revenue was $35.63 billion. Its third-quarter earnings increased 57 percent to $3.22 billion. The firm had an operating profit of $3.4 billion.

On January 20, 2012, GE reported an 18 percent fall in fourth-quarter 2011 earnings. Profit climbed 58 percent, and revenue surged 7.9 percent to $37.97 billion

See also FEDERAL HOUSING FINANCE AGENCY; MOODY'S.

GENERAL ELECTRIC CAPITAL CORPORATION (GE CAPITAL CORPORATION). See GENERAL ELECTRIC.

GENERAL GROWTH PROPERTIES. One of the nation's largest mall operators, it filed for bankruptcy on April 16, 2009, in one of the biggest such collapses in U.S. history. Founded more than fifty years ago, this giant in retailing had 200 malls in forty-four states. The company's shopping centers encompassed 200 million square feet of space and 24,000 tenants. It was unable to refinance the $3.3 billion in debt that had already matured or would be due in 2009.

By November 2009, General Growth Properties revealed to a bankruptcy court that it had reached a deal with lenders and servicers to restructure $8.9 billion of mortgages on seventy-seven malls in anticipation of getting out of bankruptcy protection by the end of December.

GENERAL MILLS. General Mills saw a lower profit for its fiscal third quarter 2008, hurt by high input costs, the strong dollar, and the impact of weak consumer spending on its foodservice business. Its shares dropped 11 percent, with a net income of $288.9 million, down 33 percent from a year earlier. Net sales rose 3.9 percent to $3.54 billion.

General Mills reported a 49 percent increase in fiscal second-quarter 2009 earnings. For the quarter ending November 29, 2009, the firm reported a profit of $565 million. Sales climbed 1.7 percent to $4.08 billion on top of 8 percent growth in the prior-year period.

General Mills' fiscal third-quarter earnings rose 15 percent, with profits increasing to $332.5 million from $288.9 million a year before. Its fiscal fourth-quarter 2010 earnings declined 41 percent, with a net income of $211.9 million. Sales dropped 2 percent to $3.56 billion. Management projected fiscal 2011 earnings to rise 7 percent to 8 percent. On September 22, management reported a 12 percent climb in net income, earning $472.1 million for the quarter, up from $420.6 million a year before. Revenue rose 1.5 percent to $3.53 billion.

On March 23, 2011, General Mills reported that its third-quarter (ending February 27) earnings rose 18 percent, with a profit of $392.1 million. Revenue increased 1.6 percent to $3.65 billion, with sales increasing 2 percent from the year before. Management reported at the end of June a 51 percent surge in fiscal fourth-quarter earnings, with a profit of $320.2 million. Revenue jumped 3 percent to $3.63 billion. The firm's fiscal first-quarter earning dropped 14 percent, with sales climbing 8.9 percent to $3.85 billion. General Mills' profit was $405.6 million, down from $472.1 million the year before. On December 19, the giant food packager posted double-digit percentage declines. Earnings dropped 28 percent. Profit declined to $444.8 million from $613.0 million the year before, while sales climbed 14 percent to $4.62 billion.

GENERAL MOTORS (GM). Founded in 1908 incorporating Buick Motor Company.

On February 13, 2008, GM announced that it ended 2007 $38.7 billion in the red, the largest annual loss ever by an automaker. In July, it indicated plans to sell assets, including its Hummer brand worth $2–4 billion.

GM sales in the United States plummeted 45 percent in October 2008. The company sold nearly 169,000 vehicles in October, down from about 307,000 a year earlier. Car sales dropped 34 percent, while light truck sales declined 51 percent. Rumors spread about a potential merger between GM and Chrysler. Its revenue in the third quarter fell 13 percent to $37.9 billion from $43.7 billion in November 2007, one year earlier. General Motors, the largest American automaker, had been losing more than $2 billion a month from its cash cushion.

GM shares tumbled on November 11 to 1946 prices; its stock was downgraded on worries that the company would soon run out of cash and shareholders would be wiped out by any federal bailout. In a bankruptcy, GM's labor contracts with its 479,000 retirees and their spouses would be at risk of termination. Shareholders had already lost much of the equity that would disappear in a bankruptcy case. Shares had fallen 90.5 percent throughout 2008. GM, with $111 billion in assets, would rank as one of the biggest bankruptcies ever. In December, GM secured $13.4 billion from the U.S. Treasury. GM was unable to meet conditions of the loan. GMAC converted itself into a bank holding company and took $6 billion bailout from the U.S. government. By late December, President Bush decided to provide funds to both General Motors and Chrysler in order to prevent them from running out of cash. The month's decline totaled 31 percent. GM sold 220,000 light vehicles in December compared with 319,837 a year earlier.

For the year 2008, GM had a $30.9 billion loss. Revenue fell 17 percent to $149 billion from the previous year, as sales plummeted 11 percent globally. GM consumed $5.2 billion in cash during the fourth quarter on an operating basis and $19 billion over the year, as the rate of sales decline outpaced the firm's ability to cut costs. GM lost $9.6 billion in the last three months of 2008, losing more than two-thirds of the money borrowed from the government.

January 2009 sales slid 49 percent to 128,198 vehicles. Then, on February 10, GM announced that it would cut 10,000 white-collar jobs worldwide in 2009, amounting to 14 percent of its salaried workers globally. GM began offering retirement incentives to 22,000 of its 62,000 union members. In February, GM presented another plan to Congress asking for up to $16.6 billion. Saab filed for bankruptcy protection and the German unit Opel sought state aid. On February 17, 2009, GM offered to drop half of its brands, cut 47,000 jobs out of its 244,000 worldwide workforce, and close five of its North American plants, leaving thirty-three. In exchange for restructuring and deep cuts, GM asked for another $16.6 billion of taxpayers' money (GM had already received $13.4 billion in loans). By March 31, a presidential task force ruled on whether the company had restructured sufficiently to be viable. Failure to receive these funds brought renewed questions of the automaker's survivability, with bankruptcy lying ahead. By mid-February, GM was subsisting on $13.4 billion in government bailout loans. The automaker claimed it had only about $14 billion in cash on hand, and that it was using it at the rate of $2 billion each month. It was asking the president's auto task force for as much as $16.6 billion more, including $4 billion to fund operations in March and April.

On March 12, GM announced that it had sufficient funds to keep operating through the end of March and would not seek the $2 billion government infusion that it had earlier requested. As part of its restructuring plans, 7,600 factory workers volunteered to leave GM under a buyout program. Before providing additional government funding for GM, on March 29, Rick Wagoner, GM's chief executive was ousted, assuredly indicating the Treasury Department's deep involvement in the affairs of the nation's largest and oldest car firm. By the end of March, GM had a 113-day supply of cars and a 123-day supply of trucks sitting unsold on dealer lots.

On April 27, GM outlined its new turnaround plan that would leave the U.S. government controlling the carmaker, creating a potential showdown with its bondholders. Under the program, GM was asking the Treasury Department for another $11.6 billion in loans on top of the $15.4 billion it had already received. The government would then have at least half ownership of GM as payment for half of the loans. At the same time, GM would use stock instead of cash to pay off half the $20.4 billion it owed a United Auto Workers fund to cover retiree health care, leaving the union owning 39 percent of GM.

GM projected a smaller, more-focused car company hoping for profits as early as 2010. By the end of April, management announced a restructuring plan that would nearly wipe out the company's unsecured debt holders and require 42 percent of its dealers to close their doors. GM had to convince its unsecured bondholders with $27 billion to accept GM stock instead—stock that might be wiped out in a bankruptcy filing. Unless holders of 90 percent of the debt agreed, the offer would be withdrawn. A May 26 deadline had to be met. GM also agreed to pay stock instead of $10.2 billion in cash to a trust fund to be managed by the UAW. At the same time, GM would cut 7,000 more union jobs than it had proposed in a February 17 revamping proposal, reducing these ranks to 40,000 from 61,000 by 2010.

It said it would shut down its Pontiac brand and stop making its Saturn vehicles by the end of 2009. Its U.S. dealer count would be reduced by 42 percent by the end of 2010, a reduction of 500 more dealers four years sooner than earlier stated. GM's first-quarter 2009 losses widened significantly to nearly $6 billion. Revenues shrank 47 percent to $22.43 billion from $42.38 billion a year before. The automaker consumed $10.2 billion in cash during the quarter, nearly double the amount it consumed in the fourth quarter 2008. On May 21, GM received $4 billion in U.S. aid, $1.4 billion more than it had originally requested. Magna on May 29 was chosen as the preferred bidder for GM Europe after Fiat pulled out.

GM, which hadn't made a profit since 2004, filed for bankruptcy protection on June 1, becoming the second-largest industrial bankruptcy in history (the largest bankruptcy was WorldCom's filing in 2002). The company announced that owners of 1,100 U.S. dealerships would be dropped from its retail network. For the past thirty years, it had been losing nearly one percentage point of market share each year. It sold 45 percent of new vehicles in the United States in 1980, 35 percent in 1990, 28 percent in 2000, and 19 percent by June 2009. GM planned to close seventeen factories and parts centers and lop off 20,000 more jobs by the end of 2011. GM and the UAW agreed to a new restructuring plan and left the U.S. government owning as much as 70 percent of the carmaker. Ten percent of the new GM would be owned by existing bondholders, while a UAW union health care fund would own 17.5 percent. The Canadian government would own the remaining 12.5

percent. GM ceased being part of the Dow Jones Industrial Average (after eighty-four years) one week later.

After finding purchasers for its Hummer and Saturn brands, GM negotiated an agreement to sell its Saab unit to Koenigsegg, a Swedish maker of high-performance cars. The arrangement was tied to a $600 million loan backed by the Swedish government. GM cut 4,000 U.S. white-collar jobs by October 1, 600 more than it earlier declared. This totaled more than 6,000 salaried jobs in total in 2009. Executive ranks were reduced by 34 percent.

On July 10, GM emerged from bankruptcy, and then announced plans to ask more than 400 of its 1,300 executives to resign or retire. The bankruptcy journey, which began on June 1, had in its forty days of bankruptcy protection reduced its debt by more than $40 billion, with the loss of factories, workers, brands, and scores of dealerships across the United States. The best of GM's assets, including the Chevrolet and Cadillac brands, were formally transferred to the "new" GM in court on July 10. GM posted on July 22 its sixth consecutive quarterly decline in global sales. These sales declined 15 percent worldwide to 1.93 million cars from the same period one year earlier. U.S. sales fell 32 percent in the same period. On August 1, 2009, GM returned to the auto-leasing market. Leasing represents about 20 percent of GM's new-car business. GM announced two days later that the expected layoffs of factory workers who volunteered through buyout and early retirement totaled about 6,000. The company was still about 48,000 hourly workers short, which is 7,500 employees more than its year-end goal of 40,500. Workers who resigned received cash payments of $20,000 to $115,000, with the largest amount going to those who gave up retirement benefits other than their pensions. Departing workers also received a voucher worth $25,000 toward a new-vehicle purchase.

Even during the Cash for Clunkers program in August 2009, GM sales dropped 20 percent. GM announced on September 2 that its sales growth in China, its fastest growing market, was expected to increase 40 percent in 2009. Sales from its Chinese passenger-vehicle joint venture more than doubled in August 2009 from a year before to 21,127. GM's sales doubled in China in the third quarter 2009 from the year before. The company's 478,000 vehicles sales in China help make GM a successful world player, with China accounting for at least 25 percent of GM's global sales in 2009, compared with 10 percent one year earlier.

In order to persuade people that its cars are as good as its competitors', GM launched in mid-September 2009 a campaign featuring a sixty-day money-back guarantee, running until November 30. Customers were able to return cars between thirty-one and sixty days after purchase and with less than 4,000 miles. On September 10, GM agreed to sell a 55 percent stake in its Opel unit to Magna, making Magna one of the world's largest car parts makers. However, on November 1, GM reversed its decision. In mid-November 2009, GM announced its plans to pay back a $6.7 billion loan to the U.S. government beginning toward the end of the year. The company hoped to repay its obligation by the middle of 2011 by returning $1 billion per quarter. It also expected to repay the Canadian government $200 million each quarter. On November 16, 2009, GM reported a $1.15 billion third-quarter loss. Its revenue fell 26 percent to $28 billion from the 2008 period. Since leaving bankruptcy protection, GM reported a net loss of $4.3 billion for the period between July 10 and December 31, 2009.

GM sales in China set a monthly record in March 2010, becoming the U.S. automaker's biggest market. A total of 230,048 cars were sold in China, a 68 percent gain from the year before, compared with 188,011 cars sold in the United States, a rise of 21 percent. To the surprise of many, China's largest automaker began negotiations to acquire about 1 percent of GM's worth of about $500 million.

In spring 2010, GM repaid $6.7 billion to the U.S. government, but this reflected a small portion of the $50 billion that the firm received from the U.S. government in 2009. The big payback won't come until GM goes public and the United States can begin to sell off its 60 percent stake in the firm.

Ten months after emerging from a government-orchestrated bankruptcy, GM reported on May 17, 2010, that it had its first quarterly profit in three years. GM made $863 million in the first three months of the year, compared with a $6 billion loss the year before. Revenue was up 40 percent to $31.5 billion and the automaker generated $1 billion in cash. In June 2010, GM said that its sales of cars and light trucks rose 12 percent from the year before. On August 12, GM reported net earnings of $1.3 billion for the three months prior to June 2010, its best profit since 2004. GM filed registration papers one week later for an initial public stock offering, preparing the foundation for the carmaker to begin cutting its relationship to the U.S. government, its majority owner. This 734-page document is the most detailed portrayal of the company postbankruptcy. Successful offering of the initial stock offering permitted the U.S. Treasury to begin selling the 61 percent stake it holds in GM after the 2009 $50 billion government bailout of the firm. GM management hoped to raise $10.6 billion by offering 365 million shares of common stock with an initial price range of between $26 and $29 and 60 million shares in preferred stock.

By the beginning of November 2010, the United States cut its ownership stake in GM from 50 percent to about 35 percent as the automaker relisted its stock by the end of the month. Its initial public offering was about $50 billion. GM received a tax break from the government that was worth as much as

$45 billion. The automaker did not have to pay this amount in taxes on future profits. The law permits firms to use losses in prior years and costs related to pensions and other expenses to shield profits from U.S. taxes for up to twenty years. On November 10, GM's management posted its third-quarter profit (a third straight quarter profit) of $2 billion, compared to its $1.2 billion loss from the year before. Revenue totaled $34.06 billion. The automaker earned $4.1 billion in the first nine months of 2010, compared to Ford's $6.4 billion.

GM was moving one week later to sell $18.1 billion in shares in an initial public offering, following an amazing two-year turnaround in which management successfully went from seeking a government bailout to posting its first steady profits in more than six years. A total of 478 million shares were sold at $33 each that day. An additional 71.7 million shares were to be sold by GM's bankers. $4.35 billion was also sold as preferred shares. Proceeds helped pay back the U.S. government for the $49.5 billion spent on its rescue; it had gone from losing billions each year to making $4.07 billion by mid-November 2010. The U.S. Treasury reduced its ownership stake in GM to about 26 percent from 61 percent through the stock sales. November car sales were 168,670, a 12 percent increase over the previous year.

On February 24, management reported that the company had earned $4.7 billion for 2010, the most in more than ten years. It was also the most profitable year since 2004. GM announced that 45,000 union workers would now receive profit-sharing checks averaging $4,300, the most ever. By mid-March, with the effects of Japan's multiple disasters, GM stopped work at two of its European factors, resulting from a shortage of Japanese-built electronic parts. GM also closed a plant in Spain and canceled shifts at a factory in Germany. On May 5, GM reported that its first-quarter profit tripled, with its profit rising to $3.2 billion. Revenue increased 15 percent to $36.2 billion from $31.5 billion. Sales in September were 207,145 vehicles, up 19.7 percent from the year before. GM sales of 186,895 in October saw a 1.7 percent rise.

On November 9, 2011, GM reported a 12 percent fall in third-quarter earning, producing 740,000 cars and trucks. Its overall quarterly profit was $1.73 billion, with revenue of $36.72 billion, up 7.8 percent from the year before. In 2011, GM earned $7.4 billion by November compared to $4.7 billion for all of 2010. On November 9, GM reported its seventh consecutive quarterly profit of 12 percent to $1.73 billion. Revenue climbed 8 percent to $36.72 billion.

See also AUTOMOBILE INDUSTRY; AUTO TASK FORCE; CHRYSLER; CONTROLLED BANKRUPTCY; DELPHI; GMAC; "GOVERNMENT MOTORS"; HUMMER; JAPAN; MAGNA; OPEL; PRESIDENTIAL TASK FORCE ON AUTOS; RATNER, STEVEN; SAAB; SUBSIDIES; U.S. TREASURY; WAGONER, RICK.

Cf. FORD; GENERAL MOTORS–FORD PROPOSED MERGER; TOY-OTA; VOLKSWAGEN.

GENERAL MOTORS–FORD PROPOSED MERGER. In the summer of 2008, almost one year before GM filed for bankruptcy, GM's secretly proposed a merger with Ford Motor Company. Savings would be great, the synergies significant, and a reduction in workers impressive. Ford rejected the idea and it never materialized.

GENERIC FOOD. *See* FOOD SPENDING.

GENWORTH FINANCIAL. Posted a fourth-quarter 2010 loss of $161 million, compared to the year-before profit of $40 million, due primarily to its U.S. mortgage-insurance business, which lost more than $1.3 billion since the start of 2008.

GEORGIAN BANK. *See* BANK FAILURES.

GERMANY. Following the sharp decline in the first quarter of the year, real GDP increased in the second quarter, helped by the temporary surge in private consumption growth in response to stimulus measures. The recovery continued in the third quarter on account of an improvement in world trade and stock-building. Going forward, the improvement in activity could be relatively slow, especially to mid-2010. Unemployment remains unusually low, not least due to the government-sponsored short-time working scheme that allows firms to reduce labor input without layoffs. While unemployment is projected to increase rapidly during 2010, the total employment loss will be mild compared with the depth of the recession. The budget balance is set to deteriorate sharply in 2009 and 2010 as revenues remain subdued and expenditures rise, not least due to higher unemployment. In addition, the fiscal stimulus package will worsen the budget deficit in 2010. Once economic activity is back on a sustainable growth path, the structural deficit will have to be reduced, also in view of future aging related expenditure. The implementation of income tax cuts in 2011 should be made conditional on the ability to meet the recently enacted fiscal rule.

On August 20, 2007, Cummerbund of Germany borrowed $350 million at the Federal Reserve's window. Thus began the bank run that set off the financial crisis of 2008. An index of business confidence fell to a five-year low at the end of October 2008, the lowest level since 2003. On November 5, 2008, Chancellor Merkel's cabinet approved a near $30 billion stimulus package in a bid to unlock more than twice that amount in investments and help Germany, the world's biggest exporter, to weather a sharp global slowdown. Officially, Germany, with the largest economy in Europe and the fourth-largest in the world, entered a recession on November 13. Germany's

GDP contracted 0.5 percent in the third quarter—more than the 0.2 percent decline that had been anticipated. That followed a fall in the second quarter of 0.4 percent. German unemployment fell to 7.1 percent in November as the number of people out of work hit a sixteen-year low. There were increasing signs that the economic crisis would soon hit the job market.

On December 4, the government announced a €500 voucher plan to be given to every adult on the condition that he or she purchases something. It would be an expensive program, costing about $51 billion. This complicated program required that Germans pay €200 to receive the €500 voucher. The central bank predicted in early December that its economy would shrink 0.8 percent in 2009. By contrast, a private research firm believed the German economy would shrink 2 percent in 2009. The government ended its economic summit on December 15 saying that their employers would sustain a "voluntary no-firing" policy as part of efforts to pull the country out of recession. Chancellor Merkel called the session to develop an approach to deal with the economic crisis. Evidence around the country indicated that many large firms had set policy to at least temporarily close factories, create shorter work weeks, and in some cases dismiss employees for the time period. Merkel's strategy appeared to run contradictory to most other European Union governments.

Pressure was put on the government to increase its stimulus package by a further €25 billion, or about 1 percent of GDP. On the last day of the year 2008, Germany received European Commission approval for two programs: a $21.2 billion loan effort for companies affected by the credit crunch and a measure permitting the government to provide aid of as much as €500,000 per firm.

Germany's chancellor agreed on January 5, 2009, to give Europe's biggest economy an extra stimulus of up to $70 billion in an effort to cushion it against a deepening recession. This added to an existing $31.35 billion package given earlier. On the day that China passed Germany as the third-largest economy in the world, it was announced that the German economy had contracted by as much as 2 percent in the final quarter of 2008. German GDP increased 1.3 percent for all of 2008, a modest growth rate that masked a steep decline late in the year and was significantly slower than the 2.5 percent rate for 2007.

Although the German government forecast in March that the GDP for 2009 would fall only 2.25 percent, the Commerzbank forecast projected a 6 to 7 percent drop. Germany, the largest European economy, led the way down with a 3.8 percent decline in the first quarter. Germany's GDP, the value of all its goods and services, fell by nearly 7 percent in the year ending June 2009, driven largely by foreigners purchasing fewer German goods. Germany's exports make up 47 percent of its GDP, but exports had been dropping 17 percent over the year. In mid-July, the government stated that its GDP shrank 2.2 percent in the fourth quarter of 2008 from the previous three months and then contracted a further 3.8 percent in the first quarter of 2009. Germany exported 23.5 percent less in the first six months of 2009 than it did in 2008.

Chancellor Angela Merkel and her party, the Christian Democrats, won reelection at the end of September 2009. The government projected that the economy would contract by 5 percent in 2009 and was expected to grow by 1.2 percent in 2010. Germany's industrial production rose 2.7 percent in September 2009, with a 5.9 percent increase in capital goods production. GDP was expected to grow in 2010 by only 1.4 percent, after falling 5 percent in 2009. Forty thousand firms were expected to enter insolvency in 2010, up 16.6 percent from 2009, surpassing 2003's record of 39,470.

The government announced on June 7, 2010, that $95.6 billion in budget cuts would be made over four years to rein in budget deficits. The austerity policy would commence in 2011 when the government aimed to save just under 0.5 percent of GDP, mainly by cutting spending but also with some extra taxes. Germany's exports climbed by 22.5 percent in the year up to September 2010, while imports grew by 18 percent. The country's trade surplus soared to $22 billion in the same month. The nation's economy in 2010 grew at the fastest pace, 3.6 percent, in a generation. German manufacturing orders dropped 3.4 percent in December, steered by a 4.2 percent fall in foreign orders, especially an 8.9 percent drop in demand and from outside the eurozone.

In 2011, Germany would enjoy faster GDP growth than the average in the richer parts of the currency zone. The country was less weighed down by household debt and had a smaller budget deficit than almost all its peers, and so had less of a need to increase taxes or curb public spending. In January, inflation accelerated to its highest rate, 1.9 percent, in over two years. It was the highest annual gain since October 2008, when prices rose 2.4 percent. The unemployment rate dropped to 7.3 percent in February. The number of people out of work fell by 52,000.

The government raised its official growth rate forecast on April 15 for 2011 from 2.3 percent to 2.5 percent. Yet, by August 2011, the service-sector economy had slowed to its lowest pace since February 2010. Including manufacturing, Germany's private sector expanded at its weakest rate in almost two years. By mid-August, an "obvious slowdown" was occurring in Germany, and its budget deficit was expected to shrink to just 1.5 percent of its GDP in 2011. In the first quarter, growth at an annualized rate was 5.5 percent, falling to 0.5 percent in the second quarter. For the second quarter, growth was 0.1 percent. GDP was up 2.7 percent on an annual basis in the second quarter. Germany's trade surplus was $16.3 billion in June, 17 percent lower than the year before.

Germany's industrial production continued to rise over the summer 2011. Total production increased 4 percent month to month. Manufacturing production climbed 4.5 percent. Basic goods increased 2.3 percent, and capital items jumped 7.5 percent. Construction was up 3.2 percent. Germany's inflation accelerated to its highest level since September 2008, with consumer prices climbing 2.6 percent for the month from the year before and up from 2.4 percent in August. For the year 2011, German exports would set a record, breaching $1.3 trillion for the first time.

The German Parliament voted on September 29 for the expansion of the bailout fund for heavily indebted European nations. Germany now promised to increase its share of the loan guarantees to 211 billion euros, or about $287 billion. On November 13, addressing members of her party, Chancellor Merkel noted that "not less Europe but more" was needed, saying that Europe had likely entered "the most difficult hours since World War II. . . . It is now the task of our generation to complete the economic and currency union in Europe and create, step by step, a political union." On November 21, the Bondsman significantly lowered its growth forecast for the nation's economy, expecting it to expand about 3 percent in 2011. (In June, the bank had predicted growth of 1.8 percent in 2012.) Growth was predicted to be 1 percent in 2012. On November 30, the government announced that its unemployment had hit a two-decade low of 6.9 percent, while the other eurozone nations had a record high of 10.3 percent.

By year's end, it was evident that change was occurring in Germany. The people had long had a reputation for being thrifty, saving an average of 11.3 percent of their income in 2010, one of the highest percentages in Europe. Industry has focused on export. GDP rose 0.5 percent in the third quarter 2011, and household spending increased by 0.8 percent from the second quarter. About 40 percent of Germany's exports go to eurozone nations, with unemployment down to 6.9 percent, a twenty-year low. The year 2012 is uncertain as most banks in Germany have cut the growth forecast for the year to 0.6 percent from 1.8 percent. Germany's economy contracted in the fourth quarter 2011. Its GDP fell at an annualized rate of about 1 percent.

See also ARCANDOR; AUTOMOBILE INDUSTRY; AUTO TRANSPLANTS; BASF; DAIMLER; DEUTSCHE BANK; JOB BANKS; MERKEL, ANGELA; METRO; TOYOTA; VOLKSWAGEN.

GILT EDGE. *See* MOODY'S.

GINNIE MAE (GOVERNMENT NATIONAL MORTGAGE ASSOCIATION). An agency formed in the Department of Housing and Urban Development. Its primary function is in the area of government-approved special housing programs, offering permanent financing for low-rent housing.

See also FANNIE MAE; FREDDIE MAC; GINNIE MAE PASS-THROUGH SECURITIES; GINNIE MAE TRUSTS; GINNIE MAE II; MORTGAGE-BACKED SECURITY.

GINNIE MAE II. Started in July 1983, similar to the original Ginnie Mae, with other advantages. Allows originators to join together to issue jumbo pools, which combine mortgages from different issuers into a single package, as well as continue to be sole issuers. Holders of Ginnie Mae II are paid on the twenty-fifth day of the month, in contrast to the fifteenth day of the month for the original Ginnie Mae; thereby, the ten-day delay lowers the yield on the securities by about five points.

GINNIE MAE PASS-THROUGH SECURITIES. Under this program, principal and interest payments collected on mortgages in specified pools are "passed through" to holders of certificates guaranteed by Ginnie Mae after deduction of servicing and guaranty fees. Actual maturity of these certificates is forty years, but the average life is approximately twelve years because of prepayments. The minimum denomination of certificates is $25,000 and issuance is in registered form only.

GINNIE MAE TRUSTS. Closed-end unit investment trusts made up of Ginnie Mae certificates. The cost is $1,000 per unit with a sales charge of around 4 percent. The monthly payments cover earned interest and amortization—the same as having direct participation in Ginnie Mae certificates, which are available only in larger denominations.

GLASS-STEAGALL ACT OF 1933. A federal legislative safeguard designed to prevent commercial banks from engaging in investment banking activities; it also authorized deposit insurance. No longer active. This legislation was an immediate outgrowth of the Pecora Commission investigation.

See also BANKING ACT OF 1933; GRAMM-LEACH-BLILEY ACT OF 1999; PECORA COMMISSION.

GLITNIR. See ICELAND.

GLOBAL COMPETITIVENESS. See GLOBAL ECONOMIC OUTPUT; WORLD TRADE (2011).

GLOBAL ECONOMIC OUTPUT. The Asian Development Bank warned on March 9, 2009, that the value of financial assets worldwide reached more than $50 trillion, the equivalent to a year's worth of global economic output, including $9.6 trillion of losses in developing areas of Asia alone. The bank took into account falling stock market valuations and losses in the value of bonds supported by mortgages and other assets. About a fifth of the losses in dollar terms arose from the depreciation of many currencies against the U.S. dollar.

By summer 2010, the U.S. economy's competitiveness fell two spots to rank fourth behind Switzerland, Sweden, and Singapore, with Germany advancing two steps to fifth; Japan was sixth.

GLOBAL FINANCE. The *Wall Street Journal*'s 2010 CEO Council recommendations were as follows:

1. *Reduce Debt, Fortify Dollar*—United States should reduce its budget deficit to stabilize its debt-to-GDP ratio and should sustain recent increases in private savings. Deficit reduction should include spending cuts, tax increases, and credible budget rules. Tax policy should encourage private savings. The United States should recognize the value of the dollar's reserve-currency role by avoiding policies that depress its value or undermine the creditworthiness of the United States.
2. *Foster Global Trade*—Rebuild the consensus around free trade by emphasizing the benefits to the developed world. Encourage the flow of intellectual capital through immigration across borders. Business should talk more about the jobs created from trade and the benefits to consumers and support retraining for those adversely affected and education for future prosperity.
3. *Enforce Global Financial Regulation*—Central banks and other regulators must be more forceful in defining and enforcing Basel III and other financial regulations consistently across countries. New financial regulations, including Dodd-Frank, must be implemented carefully, quickly, and transparently to provide the certainty that market participants need. Create rules that allowing failure of big institutions.
4. *Reshape Housing Finance*—Restructure housing finance in the United States to narrow the government's role to maintaining market stability and targeting groups such as first-time homebuyers. This means gradually reducing the role of government, including the government-sponsored enterprises in housing; reviving the private mortgage market; and reducing tax breaks for the mortgage-interest deduction.
5. *Encourage China's Domestic-Led Growth*—The United States and allies should encourage China and other emerging markets to adopt incentives for domestic-led growth, including incentives for consumption, developing services industries, beginning a social safety net, and allowing the yuan to rise.

See also CEO COUNCIL.

GLOBAL FINANCIAL ASSETS. The stock of all debt and equity around the world rose by 5 percent in 2010 to $212 trillion. Until August 2011, half of the growth came from rising stock markets, which accounted for a quarter of all financial assets. Global debt rose by 3 percent to $158 trillion.

GLOBAL MERCHANDISE TRADE. Shrank by 9 percent in 2009, the first decline since 1982.

GLOBAL MERGERS. Activity in 2008 fell 29 percent.
See also MERGERS AND ACQUISITIONS.

GLOBAL REBALANCING. A major point at the G-20 Seoul meeting in 2010. The concept was to change the world economy so that it relied less on American consumers and more on shoppers in evolving and richer nations. The goal was to build a firmer foundation for global growth and avoid financial instability.
See also G-20.

GLOBAL SECURITIES. In the fourth quarter 2011, sales of global securities fell 26 percent from the year before. For all of 2011, the volume of global debt sales fell just 5.7 percent to $5.76 trillion, but the volume of global stock sales slumped 30 percent to $628.3 billion.

GLOBAL SLUMP. *See* G-20.

GLOBAL TRADE. Tariff barriers may be the protectionists' primary wall to protect national industries, along with subsidies and currency levers.

Tariffs on goods fell from a worldwide average in 1986 of 26 percent to 8.8 percent in 2007.

The dollar value of exports in 2009 in nearly fifty countries was about one-third lower than in May 2008. The average value of exports, accounting for three-quarters of world trade, fell by 15.4 percent in November 2008 and dropped by 12.2 percent in January 2009. Global trade flows fell in August 2009 after climbing for the two previous months. Trade volumes fell 2 percent from July. The International Monetary Fund said that world trade fell 11.9 percent overall in the year, the biggest since the Great Depression. A modest 2.5 percent increase was projected by the IMF for 2010.

By summer 2010, it appeared that international trade was improving. Global GDP fell by 0.6 percent in 2009, and world export volume declined by 12.2 percent. However, by spring 2010, emerging-economy members were importing and exporting about 10 percent more than their premeltdown peaks. By June, trade was back to within 2 percent of its old peak, after falling 21 percent between April 2008 and May 2009.

By the middle of 2011, global trade was once again sliding downward.

See also PROTECTIONISM; SMOOT-HAWLEY ACT; TRADE; WORLD TRADE (2011); WORLD TRADE ORGANIZATION.

GLOBAL TRADE FLOWS. *See* GLOBAL TRADE.

GLOBAL UNEMPLOYMENT. In February 2009, Dennis C. Blair, director of U.S national intelligence, told Congress that instability caused by the global economic crisis had become the biggest security threat facing the United States, outpacing terrorism. Protectionism fears also abounded as countries throughout the world were seeking ways of cushioning their local economies and businesses.

See also PROTECTIONISM; UNEMPLOYMENT.

GLOBAL WEALTH. By early 2010, global wealth had been reduced by $50 trillion.

GM. *See* GENERAL MOTORS.

GMAC (FINANCIAL SERVICES). Provides financing for GM dealers and its customers as well as home mortgage loans through one of its divisions. The company was 51 percent owned by Cerberus Capital Management, the investment fund that also owned Chrysler. GM owned the remaining 49 percent of the firm. Investors holding about $10.5 billion in bonds agreed to revise terms of a debt swap, bringing the company closer to getting rescue funds from U.S. banking programs.

On December 24, 2008, the Federal Reserve approved the eighty-nine-year-old GMAC Financial Services' request to become a bank holding company. That designation made GMAC eligible to receive a portion of the $700 billion bailout fund and get emergency loans directly from the Federal Reserve. This decision bolstered General Motors' ability to survive. One week later, GMAC resumed financing to a wider range of car buyers, a day after the U.S. Treasury injected billions of dollars into the lender. Under the financing deal, the Treasury injected $5 billion into GMAC as part of a deal that let the lender convert itself into a bank holding company and enabled it to borrow money at low rates from the Federal Reserve.

The lender awaited approval from the Federal Deposit Insurance Corporation to issue FDIC-insured debt. On May 5, 2009, GMAC reported a loss for the first quarter 2009 of $675 million, widening from a loss of $589 billion a year before. The results were aided by a $631 million after-tax gain from retiring debt. Without this gain, GMAC's loss had totaled about $1.3 billion. On August 4, GMAC posted a wider second-quarter loss of $3.9 billion, compared to a loss of $280 million a year before. Revenue dropped during the quarter by 28 percent to $1.27 billion from $1.76 billion one year earlier. While other financial institutions were doing well, by October 2009 GMAC negotiated with the Treasury Department for its third helping of taxpayer funds. The government on December 30 said that it would provide GMAC Financial Services with an additional $3.8 billion in capital and assumed a majority stake in the firm. This would be in addition to the $12.5 billion already received since December 2008.

At the end of September 2010, GMAC reported that it had filed dubious foreclosure documents, violating legal rules to file as many foreclosures as rapidly as possible. Others would announce similar issues. On October 12, GMAC Mortgage announced that it was expanding its review of foreclosures across the country to all fifty states, hiring personnel to review their foreclosure process. This extended the review from an original twenty-three states. Then suddenly, on October 18, GMAC Mortgage reported that it was also pushing ahead with an unspecified number of foreclosures.

Now called Ally Financial.

See also CHRYSLER; FEDERAL RESERVE; FORECLOSURE; GENERAL MOTORS.

G-NEXT. An inclusion of new members such as China, India, and Brazil in the G-20.

See also G-20.

"GOD'S WORK." *See* BLANKFEIN, LLOYD.

GOLD. Gold climbed $22.10 to $857 a troy ounce on January 3, 2008, the highest ever. Gold closed at $857.20 at the end of the year, an advance of 5.8 percent. In another sign of flagging investor confidence, gold topped $1,000 an ounce on February 20. The previous high and record was on March 8, 2008, when gold hit $1,003.20. Then, on February 21, gold delivery rose $25.70, or 2.6 percent, to $1,001.80. It then dropped.

By mid-September 2009, gold traded at about $1,000 an ounce, the highest level since February. Gold had risen 9.7 percent since mid-July 2009. By December 2, gold surged to a record high of $1,200 a troy ounce, only to retreat by December 10 to $1,120.40 a troy ounce.

In September 2010, gold rose $8.10 an ounce to a record close of $1,257.30. Then, on September 16, gold set a record by rising 0.4 percent to $1,271.90 an ounce. On September 22, for its fifth record high in seven sessions, gold rose to $1,292.20 an ounce, after approaching the $1,300 mark in intraday trading, up 27 percent for the year. And then, on September 29, gold prices jumped to $1,306.60 a troy ounce for a 4.7 percent increase in the month. Since 2000, gold has climbed 353 percent, with the rally surging in late 2008 as the financial meltdown peaked.

Reacting to China's rate rise, on October 17, gold, which set a record high the week before, fell $36.10 per troy ounce, or 2.6 percent, to $1,335.10.

Gold futures dropped $15.10 in December but remained up 22 percent since January 2010. By year's end 2010, gold futures contracts rose 1.7 percent to $1,405.20 a troy ounce, just 0.7 percent off the December 6 record close.

By the beginning of 2011, gold inched up $1.50 to $1,422.60 a troy ounce. With turmoil in the Middle East, the price for March delivery of gold climbed $10.40 to $1,437.90, a record high. The price of gold rose $5.90 to $1,457.70 an ounce on April 6, but still below the high of $2,348.21 of 1980. Then, on April 21, 2011, gold reached above $1,500 an ounce. Gold was up for five consecutive weeks, gaining 5.8 percent since the beginning of the year. By mid-year 2011, gold had slid to its lowest level in more than six weeks. For July, gold delivery traded on the New York Mercantile Exchanged was down 1.2 percent from the previous week. On July 13, gold soared to a record $1,585.50, or 1.5 percent. Gold broke records on July 29, reaching $1,628.30 a troy ounce. The day following the president's signing of the Debt Deal, gold prices on August 3 hit a record high of $1,641.90 per ounce, up $22.90. On August 4, gold, which had peaked at $1,681.80 per troy ounce, fell and settled for the day at $1,656.20. And then, on August 8, gold closed at $1,700, settling at parity with sister metal platinum for the first time since the end of 2008. On August 18, gold jumped past $1,800 to $1,818.90 a troy ounce, creating a 12 percent jump for the month. Gold had increased almost 50 percent from a year earlier. Then, on August 24, gold sank 5.6 percent, losing $104.20 to $1,754.10 a troy ounce. On September 22, gold fell 3.7 percent to 1,739.20. For the week ending September 24, gold futures fell 5.8 percent, the largest one-day loss in five years and gold's worst week since 1983.

The first trading day after the December 2011 summit to deal with the sovereign-debt crisis, gold futures tumbled almost 3 percent. A delivery contract was lowered to $48.60, or 2.8 percent, to settle at $1,668.20 a troy ounce, the lowest settlement price since October 24. Then, on December 14, gold fell almost 5 percent to below $1,600, its lowest level since July.

With the close of 2011, worries about the debt crisis in Europe pulled gold prices down. Gold for December delivery fell $31.30, or 2 percent, to $1,562.90 a troy ounce, taking its year-to-date gain to 10 percent. Gold hit a five-month low. Gold futures posted their sixth consecutive loss as the metal climbed to record highs. Gold was up 8.4 percent for the year, but it fell 1.5 percent to $1539.90 a troy ounce on December 29 and was down more than 18 percent from a peak in mid-August.

By the beginning of 2012, gold ended up 10 percent for 2011 at $1,565.80. (The high was $1,888.70 a troy ounce on August 22, 2011.) For the month of January, gold rose 11 percent.

Cf. COPPER; PLATINUM; SILVER.

GOLDEN PARACHUTE. Employment contract for top management, usually long term, providing for continued compensation in the event that control of a company changes hands.

In February 2009, President Obama restricted severance packages for dismissed executives receiving government bailout funds.

See also AUTOMOBILE INDUSTRY; CLAWBACK; HOUSE (U.S.) FINANCIAL OVERHAUL PLAN.

"GOLDEN RULE." *See* EUROZONE.

GOLDMAN SACHS. Goldman Sachs transformed itself in September 2008 into a deposit-taking bank holding company with direct access to borrowing from the Federal Reserve. The firm was now legally bound to take fewer risks.

Goldman was founded by Marcus Goldman in 1869 as a small commercial paper deal operating in a one-room office on Pine Street. In 1906 Goldman became a major player in the nascent initial public offering business. Goldman in 1929 suffered big losses in the stock market collapse. By 1930, Sidney Weinberg took over Goldman and built its investment bank. In 1956, Goldman became the lead underwriter of Ford Motor Company. Then, in 1969, Gus Levy took over Goldman and built back up its stock-and-bonds-trading business. John Weinberg, in 1976, his son Sidney, and John Whitehead took over the firm and continued to expand its investment banking business. Then, in fall 1981, Goldman Sachs acquired J. Aaron & Company. The same year, Goldman acquired Jargon & Company, a commodities-trading shop.

Fifty years ago, Goldman Sachs had around $10 million of capital, which came from its partners. Today, the firm has upward of $74 billion of capital, derived mostly from the generosity of its shareholders and the creditors who have bought its public and private securities.

Goldman Sachs, the one-time envy of Wall Street, had not reported a loss since the U.S. stock market crash of 1929. But the panic of 2008 ended its profitable run. On December 16, 2008, Goldman announced a quarterly loss of $2.16 billion, or $4.97 a share, resulting from its investments plunging in value. Goldman shares were at $65.89 on December 15, down about 70 percent in 2008. At the end of the third quarter, 32,569 people were employed by Goldman, down by 8 percent. Revenue in Goldman's big trading and principal investment business was a negative $4.36 billion, in contrast to a positive $6.93 billion in the fourth quarter of 2007.

By February 2009, Goldman Sachs was determined to repay the $10 billion it got from the federal government as soon as possible in order to end the toughened scrutiny that came with the money. Returning these funds would put pressure on other financial institutions to do the same and would, in the long run, add to the prestige of Goldman. Goldman announced on April 13 its intentions to get out from under government control. It purported to raise $5 billion by selling new common shares to investors. It would be used to help repay the $10 billion government bailout money received in 2008. Goldman Sachs also paid a $1.1 billion interest charge to the government. By returning funds to the government, Goldman Sachs hoped that the restrictions on pay would be lifted, which would allow it to better compete with firms such as foreign banks that don't have these restrictions.

At the same time, Goldman Sachs announced profits of $1.66 billion in the quarter, or $3.39 a share, marking a strong comeback from a loss in late 2008. The day before, the investment bank sold $5 billion worth of shares in an effort to raise money to repay the U.S. government for its bailout funds. Then, on April 14, Goldman stocks fell $15.04, or 12 percent, to $115.11. Goldman announced on July 14 that its net income in the second quarter 2009 was $3.44 billion, or $4.93 a share, more than the company earned in all of 2008. Net revenue was up 46 percent to $13.76 billion. The firm set aside $11.36 billion for compensation and benefits during the year's first six months, enough to pay each employee $386,429 for the period. Goldman posted its richest quarterly profit in its 140-year history. Employees could, on average, earn roughly $770,000 in 2009. The firm earmarked $16.71 billion for employee compensation in 2009. On October 15, 2009, Goldman Sachs reported an impressive quarter, with a profit of $3.19 billion for the three months ending September 25, up from $845 million a year prior. Then, on November 17, the firm announced that it would launch a $500 million small-business assistance program along with Warren Buffett. This would be the firm's largest charitable gift in its history. There would be $250 million set aside for charities, $200 million for investor education, and $50 million for community-development grants. Goldman Sachs would fund firms employing at least four full-time workers and having revenues from $150,000 to $4 million in the most recent fiscal year. Firms had to be operating for at least two years and work "predominantly in underserved markets." To defuse public outrage over its year-end bonuses to its top thirty executives on December 10, 2009, the firm announced that these senior managers would not be receiving cash bonuses. Only stock would be offered, which cannot be sold for five years. This situation was only for 2009 and did not impact the more than 31,000 other employees, consultants, and temporary workers.

In mid-April 2010, the Securities and Exchange Commission decided to sue the Goldman Sachs Group. The five-member commission held a meeting and decided in a 3–2 vote in favor of going ahead with allegations. Goldman denied accusations that it "bet against" clients in the mortgage market at the height of the financial crisis by giving short shrift to criticism of its behavior and pay policies. Goldman was accused on April 16 of securities fraud in a civil lawsuit by the Securities and Exchange Commission, which claimed that the bank created and sold a mortgage investment that was secretly intended to fail and avoided telling its customers that mortgage investments they were purchasing consisted of pools of dubious loans. This SEC action was the first time that government regulators took action against a Wall Street deal that helped investors capitalize on the collapse of the housing market. In response, Goldman called the accusations "completely unfounded in law and fact," and stated that they would "vigorously contest them and defend the firm and its reputation." The same day Goldman Sachs stock fell by more than 12 percent.

Goldman Sachs profited with an initial fee of $15 million from the Paulson Fund. The SEC named vice president of Goldman Fabrice Tourre, who worked on the deal creating the misconception. The SEC charged Goldman with designing a financial product that had a high chance of failing in value and then lying about it to the customers who purchased it. Central to the SEC inquiry was an investment vehicle called Abacus 2007-AC1, created by Goldman in February 2007 for betting against the housing market. A prominent hedge fund manager John A. Paulson earned about $3.7 billion in 2007 by correctly wagering that the housing bubble would burst. Goldman had authorized Paulson to choose mortgage bonds that he believed were most likely to lose value. Shares of Goldman Sachs fell more than 10 percent in the first half-hour of trading and 15 percent for the day, reducing the value of Goldman Sachs stock by about $12.4 billion. Paulson chose the mortgage bonds he believed would perform poorly and purchased insurance on them from an Abacus vehicle. As the bonds performed poorly, Paulson received a payout.

Several months following the sale of the investments by Goldman, 83 percent of the bonds contained in the packaged securities were downgraded by rating agencies. On April 18, 2010, British Prime Minister Gordon Brown declared the "moral bankruptcy" of Goldman Sachs following the SEC's accusation that the world's most famous bank was the perpetuator of fraud. Brown demanded that the United Kingdom's authorities launch its own investigation.

Ultimately, a court would decide whether Goldman committed fraud. The SEC argued that the firm designed a derivative—a "synthetic collateralization debt obligation" that would have a significant chance of falling in value—at the request of a hedge fund client who wished to bet against it. The SEC charged that Goldman misled investors by not revealing the hedge fund's role in selecting the investments. Goldman argued that it was obligated to do so. On July 15, 2010, Goldman Sachs agreed to pay $550 million ($300 million in fines and $250 million in restitution to investors) to settle SEC claims that it misled investors in a subprime mortgage product as the housing market began to collapse. Goldman Sachs admitted no wrongdoing. That security, called Abacus 2007-AC1, enabled a prominent hedge fund manager to place a bet against mortgage bonds. Ninety-nine percent of the portfolio of mortgage bonds had been downgraded and investors lost more than $1 billion. Goldman Sachs shares rose 4.9 percent in after-hours trading. The chronology is as follows:

- February 2007—Goldman Sachs created the Abacus 2007-AC1 portfolio so that banks and some of its clients could bet against the housing market. The complex deal was composed of a kind of insurance credit default swaps that pays out if mortgage bonds hit trouble.
- 2004–2008—Goldman issued twenty-five Abacus deals, with a total value of $10.9 billion. The housing market collapsed.
- January 2009—99 percent of the portfolio of mortgage bonds had been downgraded. Investors lost more than $1 billion.
- April 16, 2010—The SEC filed a lawsuit contending that Goldman misled investors by telling them that an independent manager chose the mortgage bonds in Abacus. In fact, they had been chosen with significant input by the Paulson fund, which was beginning. Goldman Sach's second-quarter earnings plunged 82 percent. Goldman reported on August 5 that 25 to 35 percent of its revenue came from derivatives-based businesses. The firm generated $11.3 billion to $15.9 billion of its $45.17 billion net revenue for 2009.

In September, Goldman Sachs decided to terminate its principal-strategies unit, which conducted proprietary trading, in light of new financial regulations of 2010. This follows other banks closing their proprietary-trading business. On October 19, Goldman reported that its second consecutive quarterly profit declined, with net income of $1.9 billion, down 40 percent from the year before. Net revenue fell 28 percent to $8.9 billion from $12.37 billion. Goldman's profit fell 52 percent in the fourth quarter to $2.39 billion. Net revenue shrank 10 percent to $8.64 billion from $9.62 billion.

On January 10, 2011, Goldman Sachs agreed to release details on how and where the firm makes its money. A sixty-three-page report indicated that it would disclose how much revenue is generated from the firm's own trading and investing. In the second quarter 2011, Goldman's revenue from trading bonds, commodities, and currencies fell 53 percent to $1.6 billion from $3.37 billion the year before. Profit surged 78 percent to $1.09 billion. Goldman plans to cut about 1,000 jobs, or 3 percent of its workforce. By year's end 2011, Goldman was expected to earn its smallest annual profit since 1998. Its stock dropped 48 percent by December 19, compared with a fall of just 4.2 percent for the broader markets.

Goldman Sachs reported on January 18, 2012, a 58 percent fall in fourth-quarter 2011 profit with earnings of $1 billion in the quarter, down from

$2.39 billion. Goldman's full-year net income was $4.44 billion, a decline of 47 percent from $8.35 billion in 2010. Its net revenue in 2011 was down 9 percent for investment banking, down 4 percent for financial advisory, and down 14 percent in underwriting. For the fourth quarter, investment banking was down 43 percent year on year, financial advisory down 25 percent, and underwriting more than halved.

See also ABACUS 2007-AC1; AMERICAN INTERNATIONAL GROUP; BLANKFEIN, LLOYD; BUFFETT, WARREN E.; DERIVATIVES; FEDERAL HOUSING FINANCE AGENCY; FEDERAL RESERVE; FINANCIAL CRISIS INQUIRY REPORT; HIGH-FREQUENCY TRADING; INVESTMENT BANKING; PROPRIETARY TRADING; SECURITIES AND EXCHANGE COMMISSION; "TOO BIG TO FAIL"; TOURRE, FABRICE; TROUBLED ASSET RELIEF PROGRAM.

Cf. JP MORGAN CHASE; MORGAN STANLEY.

"GOOD BANKS." *See* "BAD BANKS"; "NEW BANKS."

GOODYEAR TIRE AND RUBBER COMPANY. America's largest tire manufacturer, it posted a fourth-quarter 2008 loss with plans, announced February 18, 2009, to cut another 5,000 jobs. The company broke a pattern of three quarterly losses, with earnings falling by as much as $125 million. For the third quarter 2009, earnings more than doubled to $72 million from $31 million a year before. Sales fell 15 percent to $4.39 billion.

A fourth-quarter 2010 loss of $177 million was reported compared with a profit of $107 million the year before. In mid-February 2011, the company predicted that its global tire sales would climb by as much as 5 percent. In July 2011, management reported a $40 million second-quarter profit, with revenue climbing 24 percent to a record $5.6 billion. Management reported that its third consecutive quarterly earnings totaled $168 million, with revenue climbing 22 percent to $6.06 billion. Operating profit jumped to $260 million from $77 million the year before.

See also AUTOMOBILE INDUSTRY.

GOODY'S FAMILY CLOTHING. Filed for Chapter 11 bankruptcy protection in January 2009.

GOOGLE. Google's growth remained slow in the second quarter 2009. The firm inched up 2.9 percent from a year earlier to $5.52 billion, down from a 6 percent growth in the first quarter and far below the 39 percent growth Google witnessed in the second quarter one year earlier. In the third quarter 2009, Google's revenue increased 7 percent from the year before to $5.94 billion. Net income rose 27 percent to $1.64 billion from a year before.

Google's first-quarter 2010 profit climbed 37 percent and revenue rose 23 percent. Eight hundred new employees were hired during this period, bringing their workforce to 20,621. For the quarter, earnings were $1.96 billion, up from $1.42 billion a year before. Revenue was $6.77 billion, compared with $5.51 billion the year earlier. Even as 90 percent of its profit comes from its search and competition continues to increase, in mid-July 2010 Google announced that its net income rose to $1.84 billion, with revenue climbing to $6.82 billion from $5.52 billion a year earlier.

On April 15, 2011, management reported an 18 percent profit jump and a 27 percent revenue increase. In mid-July, Google posted a 36 percent surge in quarterly profit of $2.51 billion and a 32 percent climb in revenue from $6.82 billion the year before to $9.03 billion for the second quarter. On October 13, Google reported that its sales grew, with a climb of 26 percent in its third-quarter profit. Revenue increased by 33 percent.

Following four straight quarter, of accelerating growth, on January 19, 2012, the firm reported fourth-quarter results of a 9 percent fall in share prices. Google posted a 7 percent profit and a 25 percent climb in revenue. Google posted a quarterly profit of $2.71 billion and had $44.6 billion in cash.

See also COMPUTERS.

Cf. FACEBOOK; MICROSOFT; YAHOO!.

GOOLSBEE, AUSTAN D. On September 10, 2010, the president appointed a longtime economic adviser Austan D. Goolsbee to replace Christina Romer as chairman of the Council of Economic Advisers. He had been the staff director of the president's Economic Recovery Advisory Board. He resigned his position at the end of summer 2011, returning to his professorship at the University of Chicago.

See also COUNCIL OF ECONOMIC ADVISERS.

GOVERNMENT BAILOUT. By mid-November 2010, U.S. bailouts were as follows in U.S. billions of dollars:

Money Committed	Projected	Final Cost to the United States
Banks	$250	$5 to 20 profit
Fannie Mae/Freddie Mac	$188	Up to $55 loss
Automakers	$82	$15 to $34 loss
AIG	$70	$50 loss to $17 profit
Housing	$46	$10 to $49 loss
Lending	$27	$2 loss to $0.2 profit

"GOVERNMENT MOTORS." Following the government's bailout of General Motors, some potential car buyers and unhappy investors used this term to describe their negative feelings toward the company and perhaps even the government.

GOVERNMENT NATIONAL MORTGAGE ASSOCIATION. *See* GIN-NIE MAE.

GOVERNMENT SPENDING. *See* ENTITLEMENTS; FISHER, IRVING; KEYNES, JOHN MAYNARD.

GOVERNMENT-SPONSORED ENTERPRISE (GSE). GSE debt is held by financial institutions around the world. Includes Fannie Mae and Freddie Mac.

See also FANNIE AND FREDDIE; FANNIE MAE; FREDDIE MAC.

GOVERNMENT TRANSFERS. *See* AMERICAN RECOVERY AND RE-INVESTMENT ACT OF 2009.

GRADUATED-PAYMENT ADJUSTABLE MORTGAGE. A mortgage with an adjustable rate; the borrower and lender share interest rate risk.

See also GRADUATED-PAYMENT ADJUSTABLE MORTGAGE LOAN.

GRADUATED-PAYMENT ADJUSTABLE MORTGAGE LOAN. A mortgage instrument that combines features of the graduated payment mortgage and the adjustable mortgage loan; authorized by the Federal Home Loan Bank Board in July 1981. Lenders are able to offer mortgage loans where the interest rate may vary to reflect changes in the market place and where the monthly payments for the first ten years may be set at a lower amount than required to fully amortize the loan.

GRADUATED-PAYMENT MORTGAGE. First insured by the Federal Housing Administration in 1977 where payments are much lower at first than for traditional level-payment mortgages. Prices then rise gradually and level off after a few years. The idea is to put homeownership within reach of young people who might otherwise be forced by spiraling housing prices and high interest rates to remain renters.

See also PLEDGED-ACCOUNT MORTGAGE.

GRAMM-LEACH-BLILEY ACT OF 1999. Repealed the Glass-Steagall Act's wall between banks and securities firms, allowing some institutions to engage in commercial banking, securities underwriting and dealing, and insurance underwriting.

See also GLASS-STEAGALL ACT.

GREAT ATLANTIC & PACIFIC TEA COMPANY (A&P). *See* A&P.

GREAT DEPRESSION (OF THE 1930S). In the 1930s, total government spending as a share of the economy was less than 20 percent and the unemployment rate averaged more than 17 percent. By 1933, the U.S. economy had shrunk by one-third in real terms since 1929. Industrial production had fallen by 40 percent. Job losses in 1930 shed 4.8 percent of the labor force. In 1931, it was 6.5 percent; in 1932, another 7.1 percent. Unemployment eventually soared to 25 percent, up from 3 percent in 1929.

Between 13 and 18 million Americans, nearly a third of the working population, were unemployed. One in six homes was foreclosed upon. Even the ill stopped visiting doctors as they could not afford medical care, and hungry physicians joined the growing breadlines. The president's early official act was to repeal Prohibition to reduce the nation's distress level. By 1935, 28 percent of the black population was on relief.

Due particularly to the entry of the United States into World War II, total government spending as a share of the economy rose to 52 percent and peaked at nearly 70 percent in 1944. Economists define "depression" differently. For example, some see it as a period of 10 percent unemployment plus two consecutive quarters of economic contraction. There are two major criteria—a decline in real GDP that exceeds 10 percent or a recession that lasts more than three years.

Unlike the depression of the 1930s, real gross domestic product rose in 2008 despite a bad fourth quarter. GDP declined 2 percent in 2009. The 1929 stock market crash didn't topple major banks or corporations; it merely wiped out a generation of speculators.

See also EXPORT-IMPORT BANK; HOMEOWNERSHIP; KEYNES, JOHN MAYNARD; PECORA COMMISSION; PERKINS, FRANCES; RECESSION OF 2008–2009; ROOSEVELT, FRANKLIN DELANO; STANDARD & POOR'S; THIRD DEPRESSION; WORKS PROGRESS ADMINISTRATION (WPA).

Cf. RECESSION.

GREAT MODERATION. A period of low inflation and shallow recession in the United States lasting twenty-six years, from 1982 until 2008.

GREAT RECESSION I. In general, between 2008 and 2009 the government fought back by stimulating the economy, thus ending the recession. Caused in considerable part by a rapid withdrawal of credit from the economy. The recovery followed when credit conditions recovered. The lack of availability of credit caused a fall in world trade volumes not seen since the Great Depression of the 1930s.

Synonymous with RECESSION OF 2007–2010.

Cf. GREAT RECESSION II.

GREAT RECESSION II. When the U.S. government argued over how much to reduce spending. A new bill in August 2011 forced a reduction in spending over the coming decade. Began when the usual government strategies to fight economic weakness were unavailable. Another recession on the back of the first would be deeper to overcome. With weak job growth, little opportunity exists.

Synonymous with DOUBLE-DIP RECESSION.

Cf. GREAT RECESSION I.

GREECE. Real GDP contracted in 2009 as the effects of the global crisis gradually spread to the Greek economy. Economic activity is projected to contract somewhat further in the last quarter of 2009 and early 2010, as domestic demand continues to decelerate in the face of tight credit conditions and weak sentiment. The recent improvement in the external environment should help activity to pick up slowly, and growth could gather momentum in 2011. The unemployment rate is set to reach a double-digit level over the projection period. The current account deficit is likely to remain high. A credible commitment to reducing fiscal imbalances on a sustainable basis is essential for restoring market confidence, creating room for future budgetary maneuver, and meeting the rising costs of an aging population. To achieve this, strict control of spending and curbing widespread tax evasion are vital. Long-term fiscal viability also calls for further pension and health care reforms. Increasing labor and product market flexibility will be important to achieve rates of growth.

By the end of summer 2009, recession was present and the nation's economy was projected to fall for the remaining months of the year. Tourist receipts were down by 15–20 percent. Greece's budget deficit hit 6–7 percent of GDP for the year. On November 13, 2009, data indicated that the nation's economy contracted by 0.3 percent; GDP in the January–March period declined 0.5 percent. The country's 2009 budget deficit was 12.7 percent of GDP and its debt was estimated to be about $440 billion, more than 110 percent of the country's GDP. The president declared on December 14 that it would reduce its budget deficit radically over the coming four years, from nearly 13 percent of GDP to 3 percent in 2013. Greece suffered another blow to its economy when its debt rating was downgraded a second time.

On April 6, 2010, Greece's financial crisis increased as doubts about a rescue plan would evolve, sending the nation's bonds tumbling to their lowest levels since the problems first surfaced. The result was to drive interest rates on Greek debt higher. By the middle of the month, Greece sold a block of three-month securities at a lower interest rate than originally forecast. The nation's long-term prospects worsened amid skepticism that the country could pull itself out of a financial hole without outside assistance. Greece had the highest borrowing costs in the sixteen-nation eurozone.

With real GDP falling by 9.9 percent between 2007 and 2009, and 2010 unemployment averaging 13.7 percent, on May 7, 2010, eurozone representatives approved a support package for Greece. Leaders of the sixteen countries supporting the euro agreed to provide 80 billion euros in a joint package with the International Monetary Fund totaling $140 billion. By summer 2010, the economic crisis in Greece encouraged the young to emigrate. Unemployment among fifteen to twenty-four-years-olds was 29.8 percent in June, compared with about 20 percent across the EU. For Greeks ages twenty-five to thirty-four, the figure was 16.2 percent, up from 11.8 percent in 2009. Overall unemployment was 11.6 percent, up from 8.6 percent. About 600,000 college graduates entered the labor market over the past fifteen years, but only 250,000 jobs were created, primarily in the public sector. By summer's end, the jobless rate rose to a record 12.2 percent, with joblessness increasing by 40,406.

The government's reduction of its budget deficit was expected to narrow to 7.8 percent of GDP in 2010, down from 13.8 percent in 2009. On October 12, Greece held a successful bond sale in order to repay the international bailout loans that had saved the nation from bankruptcy. Greece sold $1.62 billion of six-month treasury bills, more than the 900 million euros it had expected. The government on December 23 passed its 2011 austerity budget, which included fresh austerity measures to narrow the deficit to 7.4 percent of GDP in 2011 from a projected gap in 2010. The nation's GDP growth was -3.5 percent, with a GDP of $290 billion, an inflation of 0.9 percent, and a GDP per head of $26,350.

On February 11, 2011, the IMF and the EU recommended that Greece receive its fourth round of bailout financing of about $20.3 billion. Unemployment surged to 15.9 percent in March, compared with 14.2 percent the previous quarter. The first-quarter jobless rate was the highest since the nation began reporting quarterly rates in 1998. EU finance ministers prevented an imminent Greek default on July 2, agreeing to release a about $12.6 billion of financial assistance while stalling a deal on a second large rescue for the country probably until September 2011. On July 22, the eurozone leaders agreed to a new bailout plan of $157 billion to hopefully terminate the nation's debt crisis.

Analysts concluded that Greece was at risk for a fourth year of recession into 2012, with its economy shrinking 2 percent or more in 2012 following a contraction in 2010 of 4.5 percent and an expected 3.9 percent in 2011. Unemployment had reached almost 17 percent. Three-quarters of the GDP decline was due to budget cutbacks. Consumer spending, accounting for two-thirds of its economy, fell 7 percent in 2011. Eighty thousand businesses had fallen to bankruptcy since the crisis began in early 2010, with another 200,000 to fold by the end of the year. On September 2, talks over new bailout funds for Greece were suspended over disagreement about how to fill a government-deficit gap.

Three steps were needed to keep aid money flowing into Greece: complete a debt-restructuring plan with creditors, resolve a dispute over collateral for rescue loans, and plug a larger-than-expected budget shortfall. Larger deficits, lower deferments from private credits, and lower receipts from the privatization program all have the same consequence: either more aid is required or Greece must slash its budget further. Then, on September 21, the government decided to lower pensions, tax low-income earners, and put thousands of public employees in a special labor reserve in 2011.

Tourism by Greeks in 2011 fell about 20 percent, but the number of foreign tourists was expected to reach 16.5 million in 2011, up 12 percent from the year before. Then, on September 23, Moody's Investors Service downgraded the credit rating of eight Greek banks by two notches. Awaiting further bailout funds, by mid-September the government was preparing to put 30,000 workers on reduced pay and lower pensions again for nearly half a million public-sector retirees. A solidarity tax had already been imposed, ranging from 1 to 4 percent of income on all workers and a further tax on self-employed workers, who comprise the bulk of the economy. The government has also raised its value-added tax on many goods and services, including food, from 13 percent to 23 percent. The consequences are staggering. Unemployment is about 16 percent, emigration is increasing, the birth rate is falling, and the rate of suicide is climbing.

On September 27, the Greek Parliament voted to support an unpopular property tax. It is the first of its type and would raise about $2.7 billion in 2011. Then, on October 2, the government announced that it would miss its deficit target for the year set at 8.5 percent of GDP, as it prepared to cut thousands of public-sector positions to fulfill the demands of international creditors. Greece remains committed to a deficit of 6.8 percent of GDP.

See also INTERNATIONAL MONETARY FUND; WORLD BANK.

Cf. ASIA; IRELAND; PORTUGAL.

GREENBERG, MAURICE RAYMOND "HANK." Joined what is today AIG in 1960 and became president in 1968. AIG conducted business in 130 countries. In 2005, he was forced to resign as the result of a major accounting scandal. The New York attorney general threatened to bring criminal charges against Greenberg.

See also AMERICAN INTERNATIONAL GROUP.

GREEN ENVIRONMENT. With the global economic downturn in 2008, the ensuing cheap prices for oil and coal threatened to upend future environmental regulations and programs. Almost all green energy projects rely on heavy public spending, subsidies, and loans for their success. Cheap fossil fuels undercut their appeal.

GREEN JOBS PROGRAM. As part of President Obama's plan in 2009 to revive the U.S. economy, he proposed pouring billions of dollars into a green jobs program both to advance the economy and lay the groundwork for a more energy-efficient nation. It would include weatherizing hundreds of thousands of homes, installing of smart meters to monitor and reduce home energy use, and putting billions of dollars in grants to state and local governments for mass transit and infrastructure projects.

In 2009, he planned to devote $150 billion over ten years to energy efficiency and alternative energy projects to wean the nation from the fuels that were the main causes of the heating in the atmosphere.

GREENSPAN, ALAN. A life-long libertarian and supporter of free markets, he was chairman of the Federal Reserve for the better part of two decades.

See also FEDERAL RESERVE; LONG-TERM CAPITAL MANAGEMENT.

GRIMSSON, OLAFUR. *See* ICELAND.

GROCERY BILLS. *See* FOOD COSTS.

GROSS DOMESTIC INCOME (GDI) (U.S.). Indicates income received by U.S. households and businesses. It climbed 0.4 percent in the third quarter 2011. In theory, equal to GDP, which rose 2 percent. The discrepancy suggests that third-quarter growth was much slower than GDP numbers reveal.

Cf. GROSS DOMESTIC PRODUCT (GDP) (U.S).

GROSS DOMESTIC PRODUCT (GDP) (U.S.). The total goods and services produced in a nation over a given time period, usually one year. The market value of a country's output attributable to factors of production located in the country's territory.

The U.S. Commerce Department announced on December 23, 2008, that the GDP, the broadest measure of economic activity, declined at an annual rate of 0.5 percent in the July–September quarter. Corporate profits fell 1.2 percent in that quarter. The decline in corporate profits was slightly larger than the 0.9 percent fall estimated a month earlier.

The Commerce Department stated on March 26, 2009, that the nation's economy dropped by 6.3 percent at the end of 2008, the worst showing in a quarter of a century. The U.S. economy shrank significantly in the first quarter 2009 with its worst six-month performance in fifty-one years. The GDP declined at an inflation-adjusted 6.1 percent annual rate, nearly matching the 6.3 percent drop in the fourth quarter 2008. Business investment plunged, as did exports. This recession marked the first time since 1975 that the U.S. economy had contracted for three quarters in a row.

The government was becoming more hopeful when it announced on April 29 that there was a large drop in inventories and an upsurge in consumer spending, both suggesting that the economy might be closer to a turnaround. On June 25, it was reported that the U.S. GDP fell at a revised 5.5 percent annual rate from January to March. This was a revision from an earlier statement. Overall, the 5.5 percent drop marked a modest but important improvement from the fourth-quarter fall of 6.3 percent, which appeared to be the low point of the 2008–2009 recession. GDP shrank by 3.8 percent during the Great Recession, the worst fall since the Second World War.

By the end of January 2011, the nation's GDP grew at a 3.2 percent annual rate, up from 2.6 percent the quarter before. Officially, economic output returned to the 2007 level at $13.38 trillion, a seasonally adjusted annual rate measured in 2005 dollars. Then, on March 25, the Commerce Department revised its increase in U.S. GDP for the fourth-quarter from 2.8 percent to 3.1 percent. It announced that for all of 2010, the economy expanded 2.9 percent, the most in five years, after shrinking 2.6 percent in 2009. Consumer spending, about 70 percent of the economy, climbed at a 4 percent pace in the past quarter, the most since the same three months in 2006, compared with 4.1 percent earlier estimate and a 2.4 percent rate in the third quarter. Third-quarter figures indicated that the GDP grew at an annual rate of 2 percent in the July to September months, instead of the initially reported 2.5 percent. Corporate profits climbed 2.1 percent from the earlier quarter and 7.9 percent for the year.

At the end of January 2012, the government released figures showing that during those four years following the beginning of the Great Recession, real GDP per person was down $1,112. Had our economy grown and generated work at the average rate achieved following the ten previous postwar recessions, GDP per person would be $4,528 higher with 13.7 million more people working today, contrasted to the 5.8 million fewer Americans working than when the recession began.

Cf. GROSS DOMESTIC INCOME (GDI) (U.S.).

"GROSS UP." Payments that cover the taxes owed by executive for employer-provided benefits.

GROUP OF EIGHT. *See* G-8.

GROUP OF FIVE. *See* G-5.

GROUP OF SEVEN. *See* G-7.

GROUP OF TWENTY. *See* BASEL COMMITTEE ON BANKING SUPERVISION; G-20.

GROUP OF TWO. *See* G-2.

GROUPO MEXICANA. *See* MEXICO.

GSE. *See* FINANCIAL CRISIS INQUIRY REPORT; GOVERNMENT-SPONSORED ENTERPRISE.

GUESS. The apparel maker's second-quarter profit fell 9.1 percent. For the quarter ending July 30, 2011, it reported a profit of $60.7 million and a rise of revenue of 17 percent to $677.2 million.

GUINNESS. The Irish beer maker announced in mid-January 2009 that it would alter or abandon plans to reform production in Ireland and open a new state-of-the-art brewery because of the struggling global economy.

In February 2011, Guinness announced that its sales fell 8 percent. Pubs in Ireland have also suffered. Pub licenses dropped to 7,616 in 2010 from 8,922 in 2005.

GULF ARAB STATES. *See* MIDDLE EAST.

GULF CO-OPERATION COUNCIL. Composed of Bahrain, Kuwait, Oman, Qatar, Saudi Arabia, and the United Arab Emirates, it had economies that tripled between 2003 and 2008 to an overall GDP of close to $1 trillion. Unemployment since 2008 was expected to rise as thousands more young people, many of them graduates with high expectations, entered the job market. Social unrest could occur.

A proposed Gulf Cooperation Council monetary union has been in the making for thirty years, with a central bank and other financial institutions. In mid-May, the United Arab Emirates withdrew from negotiations, a blow to integration of the region. In 2011, Jordan was considering membership in the Gulf Cooperation Council.

See also ARAB SPRING; DUBAI; JORDAN; MIDDLE EAST; UNITED ARAB EMIRATES.

H

HACKING. The economic fall made firms more vulnerable to computer attacks as they reduced spending on security software. Businesses need to regularly upgrade computer security systems because criminals are constantly exploiting new vulnerabilities and developing new methods to avoid detection.

"HAIL MARY" PASS. *See* FEDERAL RESERVE.

HAIRCUT. The difference between the value of an asset and the amount borrowed against it.

HALLIBURTON. The oil field provider reported on April 20 that its 2009 first-quarter profit fell 35 percent following a drop in crude oil prices and lower exploration and spending by its customers. Its revenue declined 3 percent to $3.91 billion from $4.03 billion a year earlier. In October 2009, Halliburton reported its first significant quarterly revenue increase for the year. The company showed a third-quarter profit of $262 million, down 61 percent from $672 million a year before. Revenue, however, fell 26 percent to $3.59 billion. Halliburton's revenue climbed 3 percent sequentially.

The firm's first-quarter 2010 earnings fell 45 percent, and it reported a profit of $206 million. Revenue declined 3.8 percent to $3.76 billion. Halliburton's second-quarter 2010 earnings rose 83 percent to $4.39 billion, with a profit of $480 million. The firm's third-quarter earnings doubled, with a profit of $544 million; revenue climbed 30 percent to $4.67 billion following a 26 percent fall from the year before. The firm's earnings more than doubled and revenue surged 83 percent from the year before. Its fourth-quarter profit was $605 million, up from $243 million the year earlier.

On July 18, 2011, management reported a profit of $739 million, with quarterly revenue up 35 percent to $5.94 billion.

HAMILTON SUNDSTRAND. *See* UNITED TECHNOLOGIES.

HAMP. *See* HOME AFFORDABLE MODIFICATION PROGRAM.

HAMPTONS, THE. *See* WEALTH.

HANOI. *See* VIETNAM.

HANDICAPPED WORKERS. *See* DISABLED WORKERS.

HARDEST HIT FUND. Created by the U.S. Treasury in February 2010 and expanded in March, funds go to housing finance agencies in various states to create local aid programs. In early August, the administration pumped $3 billion in additional funds into these programs intended to stop the unemployed, about 400,000 people, from losing their homes.

HARLEY-DAVIDSON. In January 2009, the motorcycle manufacturer announced that it would cut 1,100 jobs over two years, close some facilities, and consolidate others as it grappled with the meltdown and slowdown in motorcycle sales. Its fourth-quarter profit for 2008 fell nearly 60 percent. On July 16, the management of Harley-Davidson announced plans to eliminate 700 hourly jobs and 300 nonproduction, mostly salaried workers, in addition to the 1,400 previous reductions.

The firm's second-quarter 2009 profit fell 91 percent. Revenue dropped 27 percent to $1.15 billion as retail motorcycle sales fell 30 percent. Retail sales declined 35 percent in the United States and eighteen countries overseas. Harley-Davidson reported on October 15, 2009, an 84 percent fall in third-quarter profit. Operating losses for the financing arm of the business totaled $110.8 million for the first nine months of the year.

In April 2010, Harley-Davidson reported a 72 percent fall in its first-quarter earnings. For its second quarter, Harley-Davidson returned to profitability of $60.8 million and earnings of $71.2 million. Revenue was flat at $1.14 billion. Even with a fall of sales, the firm's profit more than tripled in the third quarter 2010. Net income was $88.8 million, up from $26.5 million the year before. Revenue totaled $1.09 billion, up from $1.11 billion the year earlier. Retail sales fell 7.7 percent to 58,849 motorcycles. Its fourth-quarter revenue climbed 20 percent.

Management stated in the second quarter 2011 that its earnings more than doubled, with sales jumping 8 to 12 percent from the previous year. Income for the quarter was $190.6 million, with sales increasing 18 percent to $1.34 billion.

HARP. *See* HOME AFFORDABLE REFINANCE PROGRAM.

HARVARD UNIVERSITY. The wealthiest university in the world announced that it would freeze salaries for some professors and nonunion employees in the 2010 fiscal year as the university braced for a drop its endowment. On September 10, 2009, Harvard announced that its endowment shrank to $26 billion, a 27 percent decline.

By summer 2010, Harvard's endowment fund reported an 11 percent rate of return, making its value $27.4 billion, up from $26 billion the year before. The endowment for Harvard posted a 21.4 percent gain in summer 2011.

See also ENDOWMENTS.
Cf. COLUMBIA UNIVERSITY; YALE UNIVERSITY.

HASBRO. Fourth-quarter 2010 profit fell 15 percent, with revenue falling 22 percent from the year before. Revenue for this game and puzzle company dropped 20 percent to $604.8 million. The cost of sales climbed to 43.2 percent of revenue from 40.9 percent in the fourth quarter 2009. Its quarter profit was $140 million, falling from $165.6 million the year before.

On July 18, 2011, management reported that sales surged 43 percent to $374.5 million in the second quarter; earnings were up to $58.1 million.

HEAD START. *See* EDUCATION.

HEALTH AND HUMAN SERVICES. *See* U.S. DEPARTMENT OF HEALTH AND HUMAN SERVICES.

HEALTH CARE. Under the economic stimulus plan of 2009, researchers would receive $1.1 billion to study the effectiveness of doctors' treatments.

With states struggling with budget deficits into 2010, some are demanding greater contributions from their state workers. Retiree health care and other noncompensation benefits represent a $587 billion long-term liability for state governments, with less than 6 percent of that amount funded as of fiscal year 2008. As health care costs climbed during the meltdown period, firms continued to pass on high-premium costs to their workers, rising about 14 percent, an increase of about $500 each year. Employees were now paying nearly $4,000 for family coverage. The number of U.S. residents without health insurance jumped to 51 million in 2009 from 46 million in 2008.

See also AMERICAN RECOVERY AND REINVESTMENT ACT (OF 2009); AUTOMOBILE INDUSTRY; CHILDREN IN POVERTY; COBRA; JOHNSON & JOHNSON; MEDICAID; POVERTY; STATES (U.S.); UNEMPLOYMENT; UNINSURED.

HEALTH INFORMATION TECHNOLOGY. *See* AMERICAN RECOVERY AND REINVESTMENT ACT (OF 2009); ELECTRONIC HEALTH RECORDS.

HEALTH INSURANCE. By mid-summer 2011, 49.9 million U.S. citizens were without health insurance.

HEALTH INSURERS. The nation's largest health insurers reported their first-quarter 2009 earnings and most showed that they lost subscribers due to unemployment, increasing the number of uninsured citizens. The country's largest insurer, WellPoint, with nearly 35 million medical plan members, reported a 1.3 percent drop in first-quarter net members. It has lost 500,000 net members since the end of December 2008.

See also WELLPOINT.

HEARST CORPORATION. Announced on February 24, 2009, that it might close its *San Francisco Chronicle* newspaper unless it could quickly slash costs. The loss of the *Chronicle* would shutter the twelfth-largest U.S. paper and Northern California's largest daily. Hearst purchased the paper in 2000 for $660 million, sinking more than $1 billion into it, including the purchase price and its operating losses over the past ten years. Since 2001 it has lost about one-third of its readers, with a weekday circulation currently averaging about 340,000 copies.

HEAVILY INDEBTED INDUSTRIALIZED COUNTRIES (HIIC). The currencies of the United States, Europe, the United Kingdom, and Japan, where developed markets behave as if they were just emerging economies. Data indicate that people in HIIC nations are saving more, while in emerging nations they are spending more.

HEDGE. A trade that reduces the risk of the individual's or firm's current position. A person attempts to "hedge" against inflation by the purchase of securities whose values should increase proportionally in response to inflationary developments. Similarly, someone who holds a large amount of debt issued by one company might seek to short that company's stock under the belief that if their debt lost value, the company stock price would also fall, and the short stock position would compensate the investment losses suffered by the debt. Stock prices and bond values do not move in an exact inverse lockstep, so shorting stock while holding bonds or vice versa does not provide a true and complete hedge against price moves. Credit default swaps were designed to overcome this problem, conceived as a tool to hedge the counterparty risk of holding a company's debt, though in turn they spawned further problems of their own.

Hedges are rarely perfectly aligned. Many of the massive losses experienced by the financial industry in 2008 and 2009 were hedged but past a certain point of losses or due to a lack of direct correlation between the hedging investments, and the products that experienced the losses, the hedges became ineffective.

See also CREDIT DEFAULT SWAPS; HEDGE FUNDS.

HEDGE FUNDS. Coined by Alfred Winslow Jones in 1949, the term describes an investment vehicle that simultaneously buys and sells short shares, thereby lowering sensitivity to overall movements in the market. It is an aggressively managed portfolio of investments that uses advanced investment techniques, such as leveraged, long, short, and derivative positions in both domestic and international markets, with the goal of generating high returns (either in an absolute sense or over a specified benchmark). Legally, hedge funds are most often set up as private investment partnerships with a limited number of investors and requiring a very large initial minimum investment.

In December 2008, investors pulled a net $32 billion from hedge funds, making 2008 the first year the funds had significant outflows and ending the industry's eighteen years of asset growth. Hedge funds had a major shakeout in 2008, with the average fund losing almost 20 percent of its value. The year 2009 started with little more than half the nearly $2 trillion in investors' money that was held in 2008. Hedge funds globally lost about 18 percent of their value in 2008. The unregulated industry dropped by about a fifth to $1.55 trillion in November 2008.

Hedge funds were expected to eliminate 20,000 positions worldwide in 2009, a record 14 percent of the industry's workforce, as investment losses and client withdrawals eroded fees. This number was on top of the 10,000 jobs lost in 2008. Hedge fund assets rose by $100 billion in the second quarter 2009, the first quarterly increase in a year. By summer 2010, some of the globe's most prominent hedge funds posted their biggest monthly gains of the year. As of September, the average hedge fund was up just 1.19 percent for the year. For 2010, hedge funds gained 10.4 percent.

In January 2011, hedge funds posted further gains, climbing 1.96 percent. By April, hedge fund assets approached $2 trillion, drawing in new funds of $55.5 billion in 2010, the most since 2007. For most of the year, hedge funds fell by around 9 percent. For the year, hedge funds lost 5 percent. Hedge fund performance lagged behind that of stock markets for the third straight year in 2011.

See also CONVERTIBLE ARBITRAGE FUNDS; EXECUTIVE PAY; FINANCIAL OVERHAUL PLAN; FINANCIAL REGULATION PLAN (2009); G-20; HEDGE; HOUSE (U.S.); LONG-TERM CAPITAL MANAGEMENT; "SHADOW BANKS"; WALL STREET REFORM ACT (2010). *Cf.* EXCHANGE-TRADED FUND.

HEINZ. *See* H. J. HEINZ COMPANY.

HENNES & MAURITZ. *See* H&M.

HERMES. The luxury goods manufacturer reported modestly higher first-half revenue in August 2009.

Hermes first-quarter 2010 sales jumped 19 percent. The company doubled its sales-growth target in 2010 as it reported a 27 percent jump in second-quarter sales to $734 million. On November 9, 2010, Hermes raised its earnings targets and saw its shares climb 8 percent to close at $232.43, with sales rising to about 15 percent.

On March 4, 2011, Hermes management reported a 46 percent surge in profit to $589.1 million, with a 25 percent increase in sales. Then, in May, management posted a 26 percent climb in first-quarter sales to $917 million.

On August 31, management reported that the firm's first-half profit surged 22 percent to $1.89 billion. Net profit also rose 50 percent

See also LUXURY GOODS.

Cf. TIFFANY.

HERSHEY. Hershey's first-quarter 2010 earnings nearly doubled, posting earnings of $147.4 million. Net sales rose 14 percent to $1.41 billion. Its second-quarter earnings fell 34 percent, posting earnings of $46.7 million.

In February 2012, management reported that its sales came in at $1.57 billion, and for the last quarter 2011, there was a profit of $142.1 million.

HERTZ. The second-largest U.S. rental-car company cut in January 2009 more than 4,000 jobs to reduce costs as business and consumer travel slowed because of the global recession. Twelve percent of its workforce would be lost, resulting in a savings of $150–170 million in 2009. In February, Hertz reported a net loss of $1.21 billion, compared with a year-earlier profit of $80.7 million. Revenue fell 16 percent to $1.78 billion from $2.14 billion. Hertz reported at the end of July that its profit fell 92 percent.

The car rental firm announced on August 2, 2011, that its second-quarter 2011 net income was $55 million, with revenue climbing 10.3 percent to $2.07.

Cf. AVIS; ENTERPRISE.

HEWLETT-PACKARD COMPANY (HP) (H-P). On February 18, 2009, the technology giant posted a 13 percent drop in quarterly profit as sales in its computer and printing divisions plunged 19 percent from a year earlier. On February 22, Hewlett-Packard, which had already cut 24,000 jobs, announced that it would reduce salaries by 2.5–20 percent and lower contributions to employee 401(K) plans. HP had a 17 percent profit drop and announced in May that it would cut an additional 2 percent of its workforce, or more than 6,000 jobs. In August 2009, it posted a 19 percent drop in quarterly profit as sales fell sharply. HP's overall revenue fell 2 percent to $27.45 billion. Results for the second quarter 2009 ending in July were mixed. PC shipments rose 2 percent from the year before, but revenue fell 18 percent. On November 23, HP posted a 14 percent increase in quarterly 2009 profit despite an 8 percent fall in revenue. Sales of PC units climbed 8 percent.

HP reported on May 18, 2010, that its profit rose 28 percent in its latest quarter. Revenue in this period, the second quarter of the firm's fiscal year, rose 13 percent to $30.8 billion. By early June 2010, HP announced that it would shed about 9,000 workers in order to lower costs. Ultimately, about 3 percent of the firm's overall workforce would be reduced from its 304,000 people. On August 19, 2010, management reported an 11 percent revenue increase and a 6 percent profit rise for its third quarter. Income was $1.77 billion and revenue was $30.7 billion, an increase from $27.6 billion.

Management reported on November 22 that net income rose 5 percent to $2.54 billion. Revenue rose 8 percent to $33.28 billion from $30.78 billion. The firm's operating profit margin expanded to 12 percent.

Quarterly earnings rose 16 percent, with sales falling. Net income was $2.61 billion, with revenue in the period ending January 31, 2011, climbing 4 percent to $32.30 billion. On November 21, HP reported a significant fall in quarterly profit of 91 percent as the firm was shutting down its mobile-software business. Net income dropped to $239 million, and revenue fell to $32.1 billion from $33.3 billion.

Cf. DELL; INTEL.

HIDE PRICES. Cattle hide prices were at their highest point in ten years, climbing 24 percent in 2010 to $82 a piece. The government put the value of cattle hide exports in 2010 to $1.373 billion, up 68 percent from the previous year.

HIGHBALLING. Considered a fraudulent swap method. The customer's holdings can be purchased by a dealer above the current market value so that the dealer does not have a loss. The customer swaps for a new holding above its market value and the dealer accepts the loss on the purchase so as to build in a present gain on the sale.

HIGHER EDUCATION. *See* EDUCATION; STATES (U.S.).

HIGHER-MILEAGE CARS. *See* ENERGY EFFICIENCY.

HIGH-FREQUENCY TRADING. Using supercomputers, companies make trades in a matter of microseconds, or one-millionth of a second. Goals vary. Some trading firms try to catch fleeting moves in everything from stocks to currencies to commodities. They search for signals, such as the movement of interest rates, indicating which way parts of the market can shift in short periods. Some try to find ways to take advantage of subtle quirks in the infra-structure of trading. Other companies are market makers, providing securities on each side of a buy and sell order. Some firms trade on signals and make markets. Tends to lower price volatility on normal trading days.

See also FLASH ORDERS (TRADING).

HIGH-GRADE BONDS. *See* MOODY'S.

HIGH-NET-WORTH INDIVIDUALS. *See* WEALTH.

HIGH SCHOOL GRADUATES. Reflecting the weak job market, new high school graduates are enrolling in colleges at a record high level. More than 70 percent of the 2.9 million high school graduates headed to schools of higher education in 2010. In 2008, it was 68.6 percent.

See also EDUCATION.

HIGH-SPEED TRADING. *See* "FLASH CRASH"; HIGH-FREQUENCY TRADING; NAKED SHORT-SELLING.

HIGHWAY CONSTRUCTION. *See* OBAMA, BARACK; ROOSEVELT, FRANKLIN DELANO.

HIIC. *See* HEAVILY INDEBTED INDUSTRIALIZED COUNTRIES.

HIRE. *See* HIRING INCENTIVES TO RESTORE EMPLOYMENT.

HIRING. In August 2010, 4.14 million workers were hired, down from 4.28 million in July and less than the total of 4.20 million who were laid off or left their jobs for other reasons, such as quitting or retiring. In contrast, an average of 5.27 million people were hired each month in 2007. By December, U.S. job postings on the Internet climbed to 4.7 million, up from 2.7 million the year before. Hirings in 2011 were expected to increase dramatically.

At the end of the first week in January 2011, the unemployment rate stood at its lowest point in nineteen months, but the 103,000 jobs created were considered inadequate. At the December rate, it would take seventy months, or until late 2016, to make up for the rest of the jobs lost. On February 7, 2011, the president informed business leaders that they should stop hoarding cash (their $2 trillion in cash on their balance sheets) and start hiring in return for tax breaks and other government support for exports and innovation. By mid-April, 52 percent of firms announced that they planned to hire workers over the next six months, while 11 percent said they expected to reduce employment. In March 2011, the number of available jobs climbed to 3.1 million, the most since late 2008. This is far below the average of 4.4 million recorded in the three years before the recession began. By August, the U.S. economy had failed to add any jobs for the first time in one year. The $15 trillion U.S. economy created not a single net new job for the month. Meanwhile, by September, 41 percent of small firms said that they would expand their payrolls, compared with 38 percent that said they would not and 21 percent that were uncertain. Of those planning to hire, 48 percent said sales and marketing recruits were in greatest demand, with 42 percent wanting skilled laborers and 39 percent stating that customer and other service providers were the most sought.

See also HIRING RATE; JOBLESSNESS; JOB OPENINGS; UNEMPLOYMENT.

HIRING INCENTIVES TO RESTORE EMPLOYMENT (HIRE). Would have exempted wages paid to qualifying workers from the employers' 6.2 percent share of Social Security payroll taxes for the remainder of 2010 and give an additional $1,000 tax credit to employers for every worker retained for fifty-two weeks. About 4.5 million workers were estimated to be eligible for the payroll tax exemption. The proposal was never implemented.

HIRING RATE. Although the hiring rate continued to fall, by May 2009, indications were that the bottom might soon arrive. Firms continued to be skittish about hiring and employees were less willing to quit. By the end of October, when the unofficial close of the recession was announced, most employers had not resumed hiring. The United States had shed 7.2 million jobs since December 2007 when the recession began. Were the job market to evolve jobs as fast as it did during the 1990s boom, adding 2.15 million private-sector jobs each year, the United States wouldn't return to a 5 percent unemployment rate until late 2017.

Most of the job losses in 2009–2010 took place at the smallest firms. Companies with fewer than fifty workers accounted for 61.8 percent of all jobs cuts in the private sector in 2010, while they created 54.1 percent of new jobs. Small firms made up half of all jobs lost at the end of 2008 but also accounted for 53.9 percent of job gains. Larger firms, those with 1,000 or more workers, hired a larger share of workers than they let go. These companies, which employ about 38 percent of all workers, accounted for 18.3 percent of all job gains versus 17.7 percent of job losses. December private-sector hiring added 297,000 jobs, indicating new growth.

See also HIRING; JOBLESSNESS; JOB OPENINGS.

HISPANICS. By October 2009, the unemployment rate for Hispanics was 13.1 percent.

In July 2011, the government reported that the recession had hit Hispanic homes more than white domiciles. A third of Hispanics had zero or negative net worth in 2009, up from 23 percent in 2005. In addition, the government stated that the median wealth of whites was eighteen times greater than that of Hispanics.

See also CHILDREN IN POVERTY; IMMIGRATION; LIVING STANDARDS; MEXICO; REMITTANCES; UNEMPLOYMENT.

Cf. AFRICAN AMERICANS.

HITACHI. In January 2009, announced that it would post a full-year net loss of $7.8 billion. It would eliminate 7,000 jobs and freeze capital spending.

Hitachi's management reported in November 2010 that it had a profit of $893 million, compared with a net loss in the previous yearly quarter. Revenue climbed 5 percent.

In May 2011, the firm's net profit in the fiscal fourth quarter quadrupled.

H. J. HEINZ COMPANY. Earnings slid 9.8 percent for its fiscal fourth quarter 2008. For the quarter ending April 29, 2009, profit fell to $175.1 million and revenue dropped 5.6 percent to $2.54 billion.

On May 26, 2011, management reported a 16 percent increase in fiscal fourth-quarter earnings, at the same time reducing its workforce by 3 percent. Profit was $223.9 million, with revenue increasing 6 percent to $2.89 billion. Management reported a 5.7 percent fall in fiscal second-quarter earnings, with a profit of $237 million, while sales increased 8.3 percent to $2.83 billion.

H&M (HENNES & MAURITZ). With over 1,700 stores worldwide, the company reported poor sales in October 2009, falling 3 percent, the firm's sixth straight month of declining sales.

Sales in July 2010 were up 10 percent.

On August 15, 2011, management reported its worst monthly same-store sales since April of 2010, with a fall of 6 percent. Total sales increased 3 percent.

HNWIS (HIGH-NET-WORTH INDIVIDUALS). *See* WEALTH.

HOARDING. *See* HOOVER, HERBERT.

HOCKEY STICK RECESSION. *See* RECESSION.

HOEPA. *See* HOME OWNERSHIP AND EQUITY PROTECTION ACT.

HOLDER, ERIC H. U.S. attorney general in Obama's administration. Upon settlement of discrimination charges against the Bank of America on December 21, 2011, he said that the Justice Department would "vigorously pursue those who would take advantage of certain Americans because of their rate, national origin, gender or disability."

See also BANK OF AMERICA.

HOLDING COMPANY. A corporation that owns the securities of another, in most cases with voting control.

HOLDING COMPANY (MULTIPLE-BANK). A bank holding company, however defined, that owns or controls two or more banks.

HOME AFFORDABLE MODIFICATION PROGRAM (HAMP). Provides homeowners with loans owned or guaranteed by Fannie Mae or Freddie Mac an opportunity to refinance into more affordable monthly payments. The program commits $75 billion to keep 3 to 4 million Americans in their homes by preventing avoidable foreclosures.

HAMP works well when two things occur: first, if a large proportion of mortgages in trial relief qualify for permanent modification; second, its major shortcoming is that it failed to meet its aim to reduce homeowner payments while not creating further big losses for the banks or hitting the taxpayers for even greater cash.

By 2010, a mere 170,000 borrowers received permanent loan modifications, far below the 3–4 million hoped for. By year's end 2010, about 470,000 homeowners received loan assistance in the quarter either from banks or HAMP. That was a reduction of 17 percent from the second quarter and down 32 percent from the same quarter the year before. HAMP by the beginning of 2011 aided between 700,000 to 800,000 borrowers, compared with the 3 to 4 million it had aimed to assist.

On Monday January 31, 2011, it was announced that HAMP had provided permanent assistance to 521,630 homeowners since the beginning of the program in spring 2009. According to Neil M. Barofsky, until March 30, 2011, the special inspector general for the Troubled Asset Relief Program, "That program [HAMP] has been a colossal failure, with far fewer permanent modifications [540,000] than modifications that have failed and been canceled [over 800,000]. As the program flounders, foreclosures continue to mount, with 8 million to 13 million filings forecast over the program's lifetime."

See also AMERICAN RECOVERY AND REINVESTMENT ACT; BAIR, SHEILA; BAROFSKY, NEIL; EMERGENCY HOMEOWNERS' LOAN PROGRAM; FORECLOSURE; HOME EQUITY LOANS; TROUBLED ASSET RELIEF PROGRAM.

HOME AFFORDABLE REFINANCE PROGRAM (HARP). Led to refinancing of 894,000 loans in two years. On October 24, 2011, the president announced an overhaul of HARP that now permits borrowers whose mortgages are backed by Fannie Mae and Freddie Mac to refinance regardless of how far their homes' values had fallen, thus eliminating a previous limit.

HOME APPRAISALS. *See* APPRAISALS; HOME VALUATION CODE OF CONDUCT.

HOME ASSISTANCE MODIFICATION PROGRAM. By 2011, the primary program to aid the jobless in paying their mortgages until they could find work again was in jeopardy. U.S. foreclosure prevention fell short, and the program is fading away.

HOME BUILDING. *See* HOME CONSTRUCTION.

HOMEBUYER TAX CREDIT. *See* HOME SALES; UNEMPLOYMENT BENEFITS.

HOME CONSTRUCTION. New-home construction fell to record lows in 2008. It declined 15.5 percent from November to December to an annual pace of 550,000 homes, the slowest pace since the Commerce Department started compiling the data in 1959. The pace of new-home construction in December was 45 percent below its levels from a year earlier. In 2008, 904,300 housing units were started, a drop of 33 percent from 2007. Thus, 2008 became the worst year for housing starts on record.

Home construction surged in June 2009. New homes rose in June by 3.6 percent from the month before to a seasonally adjusted annual rate of 582,000. It was the third consecutive monthly gain, although significantly below the pace of 1.1 million in June 2008. Overall, the gain was led by a 14.4 percent increase in construction of single-family homes—the largest monthly increase in four years and the fourth consecutive improvement in 2009. However, reversals would follow. On November 18, 2009, the government reported that home construction again slowed unexpectedly to the lowest level in six years since April. The rate of single- and multiple-family home building indicated an overall decrease of 10.6 percent in housing starts from September to only 529,000 units.

In April 2010, home building increased to 672,000 houses up 5.8 percent. It was the highest number of housing starts since October 2008. September's home construction on single-family homes rose 4.4 percent to a seasonally adjusted annual rate of 452,000, by earlier standards still low. December's new-home construction reached its lowest level in more than a year, falling 4.3 percent from the month before to a seasonally adjusted annual rate of 529,000, the lowest level of housing starts since October 2009.

By 2011, a major gauge of confidence in home building was held at 16 for three consecutive months. The last time the home builders' confidence was above 50 (indicating good conditions) was April 2006. Housing starts declined the most in twenty-seven years in February, while building permits fell to their lowest level on record. Groundbreaking on new construction fell 22.5 percent in the month to an annual rate of 479,000 units, just above the record low set in April 2009.

See also APPRAISALS; D.R. HORTON; FIRST-TIME HOMEBUYER CREDIT; HOME SALES; PULTE; TOLL BROTHERS.

HOME DEPOT. The home-supply chain said in early 2009 that it would cut 7,000 jobs, or 2 percent of its workers, and close more than thirty-four of its stores. On February 24, the company announced a fourth-quarter loss. It had a 9.2 percent drop in same-store sales, which was less than rival Lowe's posting of a 9.9 percent loss; gross profit margin declined 0.2 percent in the quarter, compared to a drop of 1.15 percent for Lowe's. Home Depot forecast in June that it expected its fiscal-year earnings per share to fall 20 percent to 26 percent from a year earlier. On August 18, Home Depot posted a 7 percent fall in quarterly profit on a 9 percent decline in sales. About one-fourth of the fall came from declines in big-ticket items such as kitchen models. Home Depot's fiscal third-quarter 2009 profit also fell. Earnings were $689 million, down from $756 million the year before. Revenue declined 8 percent to $16.36 billion as same-store sales fell 6.9 percent.

The largest home improvement retailer, Home Depot's fiscal first-quarter 2010 earnings climbed 41 percent, with a profit increase of 6.8 percent to $725 million, up from $514 million one year before. Revenue rose 4.3 percent to $16.86 billion. On November 16, management posted a 21 percent increase in third-quarter earnings, with a profit of $834 million and revenue climbing 1.4 percent to $16.6 billion.

On February 22, 2011, Home Depot reported a 72 percent surge in quarterly profit and a 3.9 percent increase in sales.

See also RETAILING.

Cf. LOWE'S COMPANIES.

HOME EQUITY. Owners' equity in home real estate fell to $6.3 trillion in 2009, bringing the homeowners' share of equity in real estate to 38.5 percent in 2010, down from 39.5 percent. In 2005, the level was 59.7 percent before house prices were hit by significant declines.

HOME EQUITY LOANS. During the housing boom before 2007, homeowners borrowed a trillion dollars from banks, employing the soaring value of their homes as security. Now, unable to pay these loans back, the delinquency rate on home equity loans is higher than all other types of consumer loans, including auto loans, boat loans, personal loans, and even bank cards.

Lenders wrote off as uncollectable $11.1 billion in home equity loans and $19.9 billion in home equity lines of credit in 2009—more than they wrote off on primary mortgages.

HOME FLIPPING. Investors seeking bargains at foreclosure auctions in order to quickly resell for a profit. Often there is no opportunity to inspect the property or even determine if tenants are still residing in the home. The bank, upon the sale, gets money for the property right away, even if it isn't sufficient to cover the loan balance due.

HOME INVENTORY. By December 2011, the inventory of new homes remained at 162,000, the lowest level on records going back to 1963. At the October sales pace, it would take six months to exhaust that supply. In 2005, it would have taken less than two months.

See also HOME SALES.

HOMELAND SECURITY. *See* U.S. DEPARTMENT OF HOMELAND SECURITY.

HOMELESSNESS. The number of homeless families during the 2008–2009 period increased by 30 percent. Throughout the school year 2008–2009, U.S. public schools reported more than 956,000 homeless students, a 20 percent increase from the previous year. Nearly 650,000 people sought shelters each night of the year.

See also CHILDREN IN POVERTY; POVERTY.

HOME MORTGAGES. By March 2009, more than a tenth of American households with home mortgages were overdue on payments or were in foreclosure. Eleven percent of mortgages on one- to four-family homes were at least one month overdue at the end of 2008. On September 23, the Federal Reserve, in order to keep interest rates low for home purchasers through early 2010, extended and decided to gradually phase out its purchase of mortgage-backed securities. About 3.4 percent of households, or about 1.9 million homeowners, were 120 days or more overdue on their payments by November 2009.

The president's 2010 proposed budget sought to raise $318 billion over ten years by lowering the value of itemized tax deductions for the wealthy—including interest paid on home mortgages. Households that paid income taxes at the 33 percent and 35 percent rates would only be able to claim deductions at the 28 percent rate, meaning that for every $1,000 in deductions, a household in the top tax bracket would realize a tax savings of $280, down from the current $350. The proposal didn't take effect until 2011.

See also APPRAISALS; BUDGET (U.S.) (FISCAL YEAR 2010); CITIGROUP; FEDERAL HOUSING FINANCE AGENCY; FEDERAL RESERVE; HOME EQUITY LOANS.

HOMEOWNERSHIP. Fell in the first quarter 2009 to its lowest level since 2000, with the largest decline among younger buyers, who at one time benefited from easier credit that helped fuel the housing boom.

By summer 2010, the lure of homeownership had dimmed. The number of people who consider housing a safe investment continued to fall to 67 percent in July from 70 percent in January and 83 percent in 2003. The number of households that say they are more likely to rent than to purchase climbed to 33 percent from 30 percent in January 2010.

By mid-year 2011, the rate of homeownership had slipped in the past ten years by the largest amount since the Great Depression, although the percentage of citizens who own their home remains the second highest on record.

See also FORECLOSURE; HOME PRICES; HOUSING; MORTGAGES; SPAIN; UNITED KINGDOM.

HOME OWNERSHIP AND EQUITY PROTECTION ACT (HOEPA). 1994 federal law that gave the Federal Reserve new responsibility to address abusive and predatory mortgage lending practices.

HOME PRICES. Prices in twenty of America's biggest metropolitan areas fell lower in November 2008, dropping 18.2 percent from a year earlier.

Prices in eleven of those twenty areas fell at record rates, and fourteen areas reported double-digit declines from November 2007.

U.S. home prices declined 3.4 percent on a seasonally adjusted basis during the fourth quarter of 2008. The drop surpassed the 2 percent decline reported for the third quarter and was the largest decrease in the index's eighteen-year history of the Federal Housing Finance Agency.

Sales of previously owned homes fell 5.3 percent in January 2009 from December 2008. Existing sales fell to an annual rate of 4.49 million in January, the slowest rate in more than a decade. Sales were down 8.6 percent from January 2008.

The median home price fell to $170,300, its lowest point since March 2003. The median price in January was down 26 percent from its peak of $230,000 in July 2006. New home sales fell 10.2 percent in January to a seasonally adjusted annual rate of $309,000. That was the lowest since at least 1963, when the data was first tracked.

The federal government's gauge of home prices climbed in January for the first time in ten months. In February, home prices declined sharply, by 18.6 percent, but for the first time in sixteen months the annual pace of decline slowed. The Federal Housing Finance Agency reported on March 24 that home prices increased 1.7 percent from December 2008, though they were still down from about 10 percent from their April 2007 peak. By May, the downturn in home prices had left nearly 30 percent of U.S. homeowners owing more on a mortgage than their homes were worth. The increase in the number of such underwater borrowers was staggering, making it more difficult for owners who get into financial trouble to refinance or sell their homes. On July 28, 2009, it was announced that home prices in major U.S. cities registered the first monthly gain in nearly three years. Prices in twenty cities rose 0.5 percent for the three-month period ending in May compared with the three months ending in April. Nevertheless, home prices remained down about 17 percent from a year earlier.

Home prices increased for the fourth consecutive month in October 2009. However, some analysts warned that these increases were being propped up by the government and that they could resume falling in the coming months as that support disappeared. By November 2009, home prices continued to fall as sales of heavily discounted foreclosed properties dragged the market down. Median prices of existing homes fell in 123 of 153 metropolitan areas during the third quarter compared to a year before. The national median price was $177,900, down 11.2 percent from the third quarter 2008. It was expected, as the surge in foreclosures continued, that home prices would continue to fall in 2010.

Home prices fell for the fifth straight month in February 2010. A federal tax credit of up to $8,000 drew homebuyers into the market, as prices for homes continued to fall. Home prices slipped in August 2010, falling 0.1 percent in ten select cities. Then, on November 11, it was announced that home prices fell in nearly half of U.S. metropolitan areas in the third quarter, showing that the market was losing steam without government tax credits. The median price for house resale fell compared with last year in 76 out of 155 areas. It was $177,900 in the quarter, down 0.2 percent from the year before.

The housing price slump continued in the third quarter 2010, down 1.5 percent from the year before. This drop reflected the sharp fall in home sales following the expiration of government home-purchasing tax credits earlier in the year. In December, home prices fell 1 percent to new lows in eleven major U.S. cities. Then, in January, home prices continued to fall 0.3 percent for the third straight month. To a great extent, this drop was because of distressed properties hitting the market. The median sales price was now $156,100, the lowest since February 2002. In twenty large cities, home prices were down 31.8 percent since 2006. By early July, homes price were almost back to their long-term trend. Adjusting for inflation, U.S. home prices were 40 percent lower in the first quarter 2011 than at their peak five years before, just 7.5 percent above their average level from the mid 1940s through the 1990s.

Home prices were predicted to fall 2.5 percent in 2011 and climb just 1.1 percent each year through 2015. Meanwhile, prices have fallen 31.6 percent from their 2005 peak. One in five people with a mortgage owes more than their home is worth, and $7 trillion of homeowners' equity has been lost. Homeowners' equity as a share of home values fell from 59.7 percent in 2005 to 38.6 percent in 2011. Home prices were expected to fall 2.5 percent in 2011 and climb just 1.1 percent annually into 2015. Home prices fell in almost three-quarters of city areas in the third quarter 2011 and the national median price fell 4.7 percent. In twenty major metropolitan areas, prices dropped 3.4 percent; for example, in Las Vegas about 61 percent of its mortgages are underwater. Home prices were expected to be down 2.7 percent in 2011 and up slightly in 2012.

See also FORECLOSURES; HOME MORTGAGES; HOME SALES; RENTERS; UNDERWATER.

HOME REPOSSESSIONS. *See* FORECLOSURE; HOUSING; MORTGAGES; UNITED KINGDOM.

HOME SALES. In March 2009, throughout the country 19 million houses and apartments, nearly one out of every seven, were vacant, the highest percentage since the 1960s. However, only about 6 million of those homes were for sale or rent. Before March, new home sales began to rise by 4.7 percent for the first time in seven months, attributed to low mortgage rates and the significant drop in prices. The median sales price for a new home was $200,900 compared to $251,000 in February 2008. As the figures arrived,

March home sales continued their slide, falling 3 percent to a seasonally adjusted annual rate of 4.57 million units. Both high inventories and distressed sales pushed down prices. The median existing home price was $175,200, down 12.4 percent from a year earlier.

Existing home sales rose 2.9 percent in April compared to March to an annual rate of 4.68 million. The increase nearly reversed March's decline, though the sales were 3.5 percent below the level in April 2008. Sales of distressed properties, such as homes in foreclosure, accounted for 45 percent of the April total. Existing home sales rose in May, climbing to the highest level in seven months. Sales of previously owned homes increased 2.4 percent compared with April to a seasonally adjusted annual rate of 4.77 million. Sales were now two-thirds of the peak levels they reached in 2005. At this current rate, it would take nearly ten months to clear the 3.8 million homes on the market. The median price for a house was $173,000 in May, up 3.8 percent from April but down 16.8 percent from a year earlier.

Sales of new homes in the United States posted their largest monthly gain in nearly eight years in June 2009. On July 27, the government reported that sales of new single-family homes rose 11 percent, adjusted to a rate of 384,000 a year, the highest level since November 2008. Sales of existing homes in July jumped at the fastest rate in ten years. For single-family houses, sales increased 7.2 percent for the month to a seasonally adjusted annual rate of 5.24 million. Then, in August, existing home sales fell 2.7 percent to a seasonally adjusted annual rate of 5.10 million units following four straight months of increases. This was a reversal from July, when sales rose at the fastest rate in ten years to a pace of 5.24 million. Sales of new homes rose 0.7 percent in August 2009 from the previous month to a seasonally adjusted annual rate of 429,000. The supply of unsold houses also eased, dropping to 7.3 months in August from 7.6 months in July. The median price for new homes was $195,000 in August, down 11.7 percent from a year before.

In September, with the $8,000 first-time homebuyer tax credit scheduled to end November 30, 2009, and prices for homes still low, sales of existing homes rose 9.4 percent from the level in August. Then, in early November, the president signed a law extending through spring 2010 a temporary tax credit of up to $8,000 for some first-time home buyers. The law also added a new tax credit of up to $6,500 for certain repeat homebuyers. The government estimated that this new law would cost a total of $11 billion. Existing home sales for October 2009 rose to the highest level in more than two years. Sales increased 10.1 percent to an annual rate of 6.1 million. That level was last achieved in February 2007, prior to the collapse of the housing sector. A significant contributor to this increase was the $8,000 first-time homebuyer tax credit. Sales of existing homes rose 7.4 percent in November from the previous month to a seasonally adjusted annual rate of 6.54 million units—the highest rate since February 2007. Sales were 44 percent higher than a year before, with the median sales price for the month at $172,600, up from $172,200 in October, the first monthly rise since June. Sales of newly built homes fell 11.3 percent in November to a seventeen-month low.

By May 2010, sales of newly built homes fell 32.7 percent from April to a record-low seasonally adjusted annual rate of 300,000. The significant fall came after homebuyers rushed to the market before tax credits expired at the end of April. In June, sales of existing homes continued to decline as prices fell and the buyers' tax credit ended. Home sales in June 2010 continued to decline 2.6 percent tied to the expiration of a tax credit for home purchasers. The worst was in the Northeast, dropping 12.2 percent, in the Midwest, to 9.5 percent; and the West fell 0.2 percent. In the South sales rose 3.7 percent. As reported in August 2010, sales of previously owned homes fell 27.2 percent from June to a seasonally adjusted annual rate of 3.83 million, the lowest level since the industry group started to gather this information in 1999.

With the halt in foreclosure processing by banks in October 2010, home sales fell 4.43 million units, down 2.2 percent from September. Foreclosed homes made up about one-third of all home sales, but with questions about foreclosure documents, these potential sales were kept in limbo. Sales for the year were close to their lowest level in thirteen years. Foreclosures and other distressed sales made up 34 percent of all sales for the month. Sales of existing homes climbed in November 2010 to 5.6 percent to an adjusted annual rate of 4.68 million units. Nevertheless, it was 28 percent below the 6.49 million in November 2009. For December, bargains and low interest rates resulted in a gain of 12.3 percent in sales, hitting a seven-month high. Sales volume for the year was at 4.9 million, the lowest since 1997. New home sales surged in December by 17.5 percent, but 2010 remains the worst year on record for the home-building industry. Total sales in 2010 were 14.2 percent lower than in 2009. In December 2011, a confession by experts was made that the housing slump was far deeper than initially estimated by 14.3 percent between 2007 and 2010. This meant that 2.9 million fewer homes were sold during those years than believed earlier.

By January 2011, 28 percent of all homes bought were all-cash transactions. In October 2010, it was 14 percent and indicated a significant jump in some of the country's most battered housing markets. By the first two months of 2011, rising mortgage interest rates slowed home sales. Mortgage applications fell 12 percent as the average rate on a thirty-year fixed-rate mortgage rose from 4.66 percent to 5.23 percent, the highest rate since April 2010. In January, there were 5.36 million previously owned homes sold, up from

5.22 million the previous month. The rate is far lower than the six million homes a year that represents a healthy market. And the number of first-time homebuyers shrunk to 29 percent of the market. Foreclosures represented 37 percent of sales in January, and all-cash transactions accounted for 32 percent of home sales, double the rate from two years before. On March 21, 2011, it was reported that existing home sales continued their slide, with prices falling 9.6 percent and a median price of $156,000, the lowest since February 2002. In June, existing-home sales fell to a seven-month low, decreasing by 0.8 percent to a seasonally adjusted annual rate of 4.77 million. The median sales price was $184,300, up 0.8 percent from the year before. By August, home sales rose to their highest level in five months but remained weak. Sales increased 7.7 percent to a seasonally adjusted annual rate of 5.03 million.

August sales of new homes fell to 295,000 at a seasonally adjusted annual rate, down from 302,000 a month before. The inventory of new homes fell to 162,000, the lowest it has been on record since 1963. By the end of September, there were more than 2.19 million homes listed for sale, down 20 percent from the year before. By October, previously owned home sales improved by 1.4 percent. That suggests that sales could beat last year's level of 4.91 million units, which was the lowest level in thirteen years. Median prices dropped to $162,500 in October, down 4.7 percent from the year before. Sales for previously owned homes in December climbed 5 percent for the third straight month, bringing the supply of homes listed for sale to the lowest level since 2006.

HOME VALUES. In the first quarter 2011, home values fell 3 percent, the largest decline since late 2008.

See also APARTMENT VACANCIES; APPRAISALS; FORECLO-SURE; HOME PRICES; PROPERTY (2011).

HONDA. Cut its full-year forecast for net profit by 62 percent. For the fiscal year ending March 31, 2008, Honda lowered its net profit forecast to $2.08 billion, a continuing sign of the drop in demand that has hammered the global car industry. It was the carmaker's third profit warning of the year, highlighting how tough the market had become. Honda's U.S. sales dropped 31.6 percent in 2008 following a decline of 35 percent in December.

Honda said in January 2009 that it would reduce its domestic output by an additional 56,000 units and expected its Japanese production to total 1.17 million units in its business year, against its original target of 1.31 million. Honda announced a 90 percent drop in net profit for the December quarter. Honda Motor Company, the second-largest automaker in Japan, made 77,224 vehicles in January, 23 percent less than at the same time the year before. In April, Honda had a net loss of $1.92 billion in the quarter ending in March.

Sales declined 42 percent. It was Honda's first net loss on a quarterly basis in more than fifteen years. The company announced in July 2009 that its net profit for the first fiscal quarter ending June 30 tumbled 96 percent from a year before. Honda Motor Company reported that its fiscal second-quarter 2009 profit fell 56 percent. Profit for the period ending September 30 was $586.1 million. Sales tumbled 27 percent.

Honda's sales rose 62 percent in March 2010 with 349,425 cars. Even though its global production fell 7.5 percent, its full-year domestic output dropped 22 percent. Honda's June 2010 sales rose 6 percent from the year before. Then, at the end of July, management announced that its revenue climbed 18 percent from the year before. Honda Motor Company at the end of November posted its first domestic production fall in one year and ten months. November's car sales were 89,617 for an increase of 21 percent over the previous year.

In mid-March 2011, as a result of the three disasters in Japan, Honda suspended car and motorcycle operations in Japan for several days. About 30 percent of its 110 suppliers for its four- and two-wheeled vehicles were affected. In mid-June, management forecast a 31 percent fall in profit for the fiscal year. October saw a drop of 0.5 percent in sales of 98,333 cars. A net fall of 41 percent in profit occurred in the fiscal third quarter. It had a net profit of $624.3 million in the last three months of 2011.

See also AUTOMOBILE INDUSTRY; JAPAN.

HONEYWELL. Reported a 38 percent decline in first-quarter profit 2009. Its net income fell to $399 million from $647 million the previous year. On July 27, Honeywell reported that its second-quarter earnings fell 38 percent. Revenue dropped 22 percent to $7.56 billion from $9.67 billion one year earlier. Honeywell's third-quarter 2009 earnings fell 15 percent. The company posted a third-quarter profit of $608 million, down from $719 million a year before. Net sales fell 17 percent to $7.7 billion. Fourth-quarter 2010 earnings more than doubled, with a profit of $369 million, up from $150 million from a year before. Revenue increased 12 percent to $9.04 billion.

In April 2011, Honeywell's earnings climbed 44 percent. In the summer, Honeywell's management reported a 43 percent profit increase.

HONG KONG. Hong Kong climbed out of the recession in the second quarter 2009 with a 3.3 percent growth in the second quarter from the first quarter. To prevent a real estate bubble, bankers increased the down payment on luxury homes to 40 percent from the 30 percent.

Hong Kong's GDP would grow by 4.4 percent in 2011, down from 5.8 percent in 2010, with a GDP of $220 billion, an inflation rate of 2.5 percent, and a GDP per head of $30,820. Hong Kong's economy grew by 6.2 percent in the year to the fourth quarter 2010. Inflation jumped to 3.7 percent in February, a thirty-month high and a tenth of a percentage point higher than January's rate. Inflation jumped to a thirty-four-month high of 5.2 percent in May from 4.6 percent in April. Food prices surged 7 percent.

Exports increased to 10.1 percent in the year to May 2011 and imports climbed by 13 percent. The monthly trade deficit was about $4.6 billion. Shipments to China increased by 8.8 percent, the nation's largest market. Lower demand for exports and a growing weakness in financial sectors contributed to a 11.1 percent fall in exports from the first quarter, a significant reversal from a 14.4 percent surge in the earlier quarter. This caused the GDP for the three months ending June 30 to fall 0.5 percent from the first quarter.

See also CHINA; TAX HAVENS.

HOOVER, HERBERT. President Hoover was far more active than he gets credit for in the post-1929 crash. His primary method of combating the crisis was having the government make large loans to big banks in the hope that they would restore confidence. It didn't work. He also established the Reconstruction Finance Corporation to make loans to tax-starved state governments, among other entities. Hoarding was a problem in the 1930s because dollar bills (or in many cases, gold) stuffed under a mattress didn't help the banking system.

See also PECORA COMMISSION; RECONSTRUCTION FINANCE CORPORATION; ROOSEVELT, FRANKLIN DELANO.

HOSPITALS. Many hospitals are closing as a result of the shortage of state tax revenues during the Great Recession. More than a fifth of the nation's 5,000 hospitals are owned by the government and many are succumbing to the increase in their debt. In the beginning of 2010, twenty-five arrangements involved fifty-three hospitals that merged or were bought.

HOTEL GEITHNER. *Synonymous with* TROUBLED ASSET RELIEF PROGRAM.

HOTELS. Hotel occupancy indicated that revenue was down 16.1 percent in 2009. The forecast for all of 2009 was a decline of 17.1 percent, and in 2010 another 4 percent. Hotel per-room revenue continued to decline in December 2009. The average revenue per available hotel room was $54.58 in October, down 16.8 percent from the same month a year before.

Hotel per-room revenue increased in May 2011 for the ninth consecutive month. The average revenue per available hotel room was $58.37, up 8.7 percent from the year before. At the end of the year, hotel occupancy rose by 8 percent, filling 37 percent of their rooms. Revenue per room climbed 11 percent in 2011, still down 14 percent from 2007.

See also ACCOR; MARRIOTT; MGM RESORTS INTERNATIONAL; STARWOOD; TRAVEL AND TOURISM (2011).

HOTEL WORK. *See* STARWOOD; UNEMPLOYMENT.

HOUSEHOLD DEBT. U.S. families had a smaller debt burden in 2010 than any year in its previous six years. Household debt, including mortgages and credit cards, dropped for the second straight year in 2010 to $13.4 trillion. It was down from a peak debt burden of 130 percent in 2007 and was the lowest level since the fourth quarter of 2004.

From July to September 2011, household debt fell by 0.6 percent from the previous quarter to $11.66 trillion. The value of new mortgages dropped 17 percent from the earlier quarter and 24.7 percent from the year before.

HOUSEHOLDS. *See* HOUSING.

HOUSEHOLD WEALTH. Since 2007 decreased by $12 trillion, or 18 percent.

HOUSE (U.S.) FINANCIAL OVERHAUL PLAN. On December 11, 2009, the U.S. House of Representatives passed a sweeping measure putting new brakes on financial institutions. Provisions included the following:

a. Consumer Protection
   • Consolidate authority for protecting consumers into one agency. The agency would set and enforce rules on a variety of financial items, including credit cards, mortgages, and loans. Retailers and auto dealers are among the few who would be exempt from the agency's oversight.
   • Preserve the federal government's ability to preempt tougher state consumer protection laws under certain conditions.
   • Allow consumers to sue credit-rating agencies for flawed evaluations of financial products.
b. Executive Compensation
   • Give shareholders the right to vote on compensation and "golden parachute" severance packages and require that independent directors sit on compensation committees.
   • Allow regulators to ban "inappropriate or imprudently risky" compensation practices for banks and other financial institutions.
c. Federal Regulatory Powers
   • Establish a council of federal regulators to monitor the market.
   • Impose stricter standards and regulations on firms that are large enough or interconnected enough to put the entire economy at risk. The government would set up a $150 billion fund—financed by as-

sessments on large financial firms—to dissolve any "large and highly complex" financial companies that it deemed too risky.

- Merge the Office of the Comptroller, which supervised federally chartered banks, with the Office of Thrift Supervision, which supervised savings and loans.

d. Regulation of Derivatives
- Impose tighter restrictions on the largely unregulated derivates market and require many derivatives to be traded through clearinghouses where they could be monitored by the Securities and Exchange Commission and the Commodity Futures Trade Commission.

e. Other
- Require hedge funds and private equity companies with more than $150 million in assets to be registered with the SEC and to disclose financial information. Venture capital companies and small business investment companies would be exempt.
- Redirect $4 billion from the bank bailout fund to provide low-interest loans to the unemployed and homeowners struggling to keep their residences and to purchase and repair abandoned and foreclosed homes.

See also FEDERAL RESERVE; WALL STREET REFORM ACT (2010).

HOUSING. Housing starts, which were still soaring as recently as 2005, hit a new twenty-year low in 2008. Meanwhile, residential-property prices were falling in twenty-three of forty-five nations. Housing sales dropped sharply in November. Sales of existing homes declined to a seasonally adjusted rate of 4.49 million in November, down 8.6 percent from October and 10.6 percent from November 2007. The median price of a home was $181,300 in November, down 13 percent from 2007 and the lowest level since February 2004.

Housing values had plummeted since the peak of the market in July 2006, when the median home price in the United States was $230,200. In November, the median price of a new home was $220,400, down 11.5 percent from a year earlier. It was the biggest year-over-year price decline since a 12.7 percent drop in March. Housing starts in December fell by a steep 18.9 percent from the previous month to a seasonally adjusted rate of 625,000.

The median price for a single-family house fell 14 percent to $169,000 in the first quarter from a year earlier. That median price was down 26 percent from a peak of $227,000 in the third quarter of 2005. The net worth of U.S. households rose 5 percent in the third quarter 2009, with a gain to $53.4 trillion marking the second straight quarterly increase.

The good news was that year-over-year declines eased steadily and dramatically in 2009. The average drop in home prices for twenty major cities in October versus a year before was 7.3 percent, down from 9.4 percent in September and 19 percent in January. From September to October, housing prices across twenty major metropolitan areas dropped 1.3 percent, the third straight month-over-month fall. Most economists expected the declines to continue for the first half of 2011. Only in four metropolitan regions were prices higher: Washington, D.C., Los Angeles, San Diego, and San Francisco. Households retained $6.4 trillion of home equity at the end of the third quarter 2010, alongside $12.2 trillion in stocks and mutual-fund shares. In April, new-home construction fell 10.6 percent to a seasonally adjusted annual rate of 523,000. Single-family-home building fell 5.1 percent to an annual rate of 394,000.

By mid-June 2010, housing resale had fallen 3.8 percent. The national median existing-home price was $166,500 in May, falling 4.6 percent from May 2010. Sales of homes priced between $100,000 and $500,000, the largest portion of the market, fell nearly 19 percent. The ailing housing market will unlikely return to its prerecession health before 2016.

See also APARTMENT VACANCIES; BERNANKE, BEN; CHINA; DISTRESSED SALES; FORECLOSURE; FREDDIE MAC; HIGH MORTGAGE RATES; HOME SALES; HOUSING BAILOUT PLAN; LAND SPECULATION; MORTGAGE-REPLACEMENT LOANS; PROPERTY (2011); TROUBLED ASSET RELIEF PROGRAM; UNITED KINGDOM.

HOUSING AGENCIES. *See* HOUSING FINANCE AGENCIES.

HOUSING AND ECONOMIC RECOVERY ACT OF 2008. *See* FEDERAL HOUSING FINANCE AGENCY.

HOUSING AND URBAN DEVELOPMENT. *See* U.S. DEPARTMENT OF HOUSING AND URBAN DEVELOPMENT.

HOUSING BAILOUT PLAN. To reduce foreclosures, a program was announced by President Obama on February 18, 2009, in Phoenix, Arizona. Two groups were primarily affected by the president's plan. People who couldn't afford their mortgages and had fallen behind in their monthly payments, which included about 3 million households, made up the first group. The second group consisted of more than 10 million households that could afford their monthly payments but whose houses were worth less than what was owed on their mortgages. For the first group, $50 billion would be spent to entice banks to lower the monthly payments of people who otherwise couldn't afford to stay in their homes. The money came from the funds already allocated from the financial system bailout. By early March, details of this mortgage bailout plan to aid one in nine U.S. homeowners were presented. It called for reduction payments for distressed borrowers through modifications of loan terms.

The plan also involved refinancing mortgages for some people who were current on their payments but had little or no equity in their homes. "Loan moods" are modifications of loan terms. This modification plan terminates December 31, 2012.

On July 1, 2009, the government expanded the number of borrowers who could refinance home loans. Borrowers with mortgages worth up to 125 percent of their homes' value were eligible to refinance under the program, up from a 105 percent limit. The problem continued to pull down the housing market as nearly 30 percent of homeowners with mortgages owe more than their homes are worth.

See also FORECLOSURE; HOUSING; MODIFYING MORTGAGES; MORTGAGE BAILOUT; UNDERWATER.

HOUSING FINANCE AGENCIES. Those agencies operated by state government that, catering to first-time homeowners, either originate mortgage loans to state residents or guarantee loans made by lenders. In 2007, state housing agencies issued $17 billion in bonds that funded 126,611 mortgages. By September 2008, these credit markets were frozen.

HOUSING INVENTORIES. The number of homes listed for sale. In twenty-seven major cities at the end of November 2009 inventory was down 2.4 percent compared with a month before. The inventory for that month was down 28 percent.

HOUSING PLAN. *See* FANNIE MAE; FREDDIE MAC; GINNIE MAE; HOUSING BAILOUT PLAN; MODIFYING MORTGAGES.

HOUSING PRICES. *See* HOME PRICES.

HOUSING RECOVERY. *See* HOUSING.

HOUSING RESALES. *See* HOUSING.

HOUSING STARTS. Plunged to new lows in January 2009 as a large number of vacant homes, tight mortgage financing, and a deepening recession created the worst housing market in a half-century. Starts fell 16.8 percent in January from a month earlier. In March, housing starts tumbled 10.8 percent to an annual rate of 510,000 units. Starts of single-family homes remained flat from February at 358,000, marking the third straight month around that low level. Housing construction climbed in August 2009 to the highest level in nine months, rising 1.5 percent to an annual rate of 598,000 units. The increase pushed building activity to the highest level since November 2008 and left home construction 24.8 percent above the record low hit in April. Housing starts increased 0.5 percent in September to a seasonally adjusted annual rate of 590,000.

Housing starts surged in November 2011 at a seasonally adjusted annual rate of 685,000 units, the highest level in nineteen months. Starts were up 9.3 percent from October and 24.3 percent ahead of the November 2010 numbers.

See also HOME CONSTRUCTION; HOUSING; LAND SPECULATION; MORTGAGE RATES; WEYERHAEUSER.

HRYVNIA. See UKRAINE.

HSBC. Based in London, the largest bank in Europe, by December 2008, faced a sharp slowdown in emerging markets, where it had previously earned the bulk of its profits. HSBC shares dropped 17 percent.

HSBC announced on March 2, 2009, a plan to draw a line under its troubled subprime mortgage lender and asked investors for $18 billion of new capital to prepare for a further drop in the global economy. HSBC would close most of its finance branches and cut 6,100 jobs.

By August 2010, HSBC had earned $6.8 billion in the six months that ended June 30, beating the bank's combined $5.8 billion in profit over the previous year. By year's end, HSBC holdings more than doubled its profit to $13.2 billion, up from $5.83 billion the year before.

HSBC Holdings announced in early August 2011 that it would eliminate about 30,000 positions globally over the coming two years. At the same time, management reported flat first-half revenue of $35.69 billion, with net profit rising 35 percent to $8.93 billion from $6.63 billion a year before. Then, on October 9, management reported that in the third quarter the bank earned $1.95 billion. It planned to cut costs by $2.5 billion to $3.5 billion by the end of 2013, in part by eliminating 30,000 positions.

See also FEDERAL HOUSING FINANCE AGENCY; TRANSPARENCY.

HUE/DA NANG. See VIETNAM.

HUMMER. On October 9, 2009, General Motors completed an arrangement to sell its Hummer brand to Sichuan Tangshan Heavy Industrial Machinery Company, marking China's first major entry into the U.S. auto market. It was sold for $150 million, with GM manufacturing the vehicles until no later than 2012. Hummer sales were down 64 percent by October 2009 from a year before.

See also AUTOMOBILE INDUSTRY.

Cf. TATA MOTORS.

HUNGARY. After a sizeable contraction in 2009, GDP growth should progressively resume in 2010 and gather pace in 2011 on the back of strengthening foreign demand and easing credit conditions. Unless the upcoming election year repeats past electoral profligacy, planned fiscal austerity should curb domestic demand. The unemployment rate will peak at over 10 percent in 2010 before falling slightly. The significant output gap and the recent appreciation of the exchange rate have dampened inflationary pressures, which should not increase before the recovery gains momentum. A tight macroeconomic policy under the program of the International Monetary Fund and the initial success in reining in expenditure growth have boosted investor confidence, strengthened the exchange rate, and provided room for a series of interest rate cuts since mid-2009. Scope for further easing will be determined by the credibility of continued fiscal consolidation and conditions in global financial markets. To maintain investor confidence, it is crucial that the government sticks to the newly adopted medium-term fiscal framework and supports the efforts of the new fiscal council.

Hungary's public debt in November 2008 was more than 60 percent of GDP. Hungary's current-account deficit in 2008 amounted to 5.5 percent of GDP. The weak forint meant higher interest payments. Had that trend increased, Hungary risked bankruptcy. Hungary received $15.7 billion from the International Monetary Fund in October. Its central bank cut its interest rates by half a point from the 11.5 percent rate that it set in October as part of a $25 billion international bailout.

The national bank reduced its key interest rate to 9.5 percent from 10 percent in mid-January 2009 and forecast a lower-than-expected point cut in less than two months as it sought to shore up its ailing economy. Hungary's currency, the forint, plunged to a new low against the euro on March 4, declining more than 20 percent against the euro since the beginning of 2009. Then, on March 6, as its currency slipped further, Hungary attempted to assure depositors that their funds were safe to avoid a run on the banks, but the effort failed to stabilize the currency.

The central bank's plan was to intervene in foreign-exchange markets, using funds it gets from the European Union to do so. By mid-September 2009, the government cut public spending by 3.8 percent of GDP and reduced the budget deficit from 9.2 percent of GDP in 2006 to just 3.4 percent in 2008. Hungary's central bank slashed its key interest rate to a three-year low of 7 percent from 7.5 percent. In September 2009, annual consumer-price inflation was 4.9 percent.

The forint lost 4.8 percent against the euro and 7.3 percent against the Swiss franc in early June 2010. Since Hungary's public debt is denominated in foreign currency, the crisis in the nation was growing. Then, on July 17, 2010, the IMF and EU walked away from talks with Hungary stating that the government needed to do more to shrink its budget deficit prior to receiving further bailout funds. The central bank of Hungary raised interest rates to 5.75 percent on December 20 for the second month in a row. Fearing that inflation was advancing too quickly at 4.2 percent in November, the government protested the bank's move.

It was expected that after growing in 2010, the nation's economy would expand by a respectable 2.5 percent in 2011. The nation's GDP growth is 2.5 percent, its GDP at $127 billion, with an inflation rate of 3.0 percent, and a GDP per head at $12,910. GDP grew 1.5 percent from April to June 2011 but was down from the first quarter at 2.1 percent. The National Bank of Hungary warned that with a fall in its currency risked the rise of inflation. On November 29, the nation's central bank raised interest rates half a percentage point to 6.5 percent. The heavily indebted government had to pay an average yield of 7.32 percent on three-month treasury bills, a much higher rate than the roughly 5.75 percent it paid at the outset of 2011. Then, on December 16, the EU and the IMF officially terminated preliminary talks with Hungary over fears that the government was trying to limit central bank independence and lock in fiscal policies.

On January 4, 2012, investors pushed Hungary's currency to new lows, at one point hitting 321.67 forints to the euro.

See also EASTERN EUROPE.

HUNTSMAN. In mid-January 2009, the chemical manufacturer would begin cutting more than 9 percent of its workforce and close a titanium dioxide plant as it continued to scale back operations.

HYBRID. A collateralized debt obligation backed by collateral found in both cash and synthetic CDOs.

HYBRID PENSIONS. By summer 2010, a cost-cutting measure used by several U.S. states to pare back guaranteed-retirement payments. Under this concept, state workers could receive part of their retirement benefits from a 401(k)-type plan, which shifted more responsibility for funding retirement benefits to employees.

See also STATES (U.S.).

HYPO GROUP ALPE ADRIA. *See* AUSTRIA.

HYUNDAI MOTOR COMPANY. South Korea's largest carmaker by sales announced that its fourth-quarter net profits in 2008 declined 28 percent as the weaker Korean won failed to cushion the impact of the global economic downturn. The firm postponed a $600 million investment to start production in Brazil at a plant in the first half of 2011. Additionally, it adjusted plans to build a $394.2 million plant in Russia by January 2011.

First-quarter 2009 net profit fell 43 percent. Hyundai's second-quarter net profit jumped 48 percent to a record high. Through November 2009, the automaker sold 401,267 cars and light trucks in the United States, up 6.2 percent from 2008, while the overall market fell 24 percent. Its sales represented 4.3 percent of the U.S. market, up 1.2 points from the year before.

Hyundai Motor Company's management reported a 71 percent increase in its second-quarter 2010 net profit, climbing by $1.2 billion. Hyundai Motor Company posted a 38 percent rise in its third-quarter 2010 net profit.

The carmaker posted gains in June 2011 with sales soaring 20.7 percent. In October, 52,402 cars were sold for a 23 percent gain.

See also AUTOMOBILE INDUSTRY.

I

IBERIA AIRLINES (IBERIA LINEAS AEREAS DE ESPANA). Spain's largest airline by sales in March 2009 posted a net loss of $24 million, or €19 million, for the three months that ended December 31, 2008, compared with a net profit of €105 million one year before. The airline saw its 2008 net profit plunge 90 percent.

Higher fuel costs and plummeting demand during the meltdown period indicated greater bumps ahead. On November 12, 2009, the airline agreed to merge with British Airways. The new firm is called International Airlines, with both carriers retaining separate brands.

See also BRITISH AIRWAYS.

IBM. *See* INTERNATIONAL BUSINESS MACHINES CORPORATION.

ICELAND. The recession into which the Icelandic economy fell following the failure of the country's three main banks in October 2008 continues. Domestic demand has fallen sharply, and the economy is projected to continue shrinking until early 2010. Thereafter, growth is projected to return, boosted initially by the expected normalization of financial conditions and subsequently by investment in large energy-related projects. The unemployment rate is likely to rise to around 7 percent by mid-2010 and edge down thereafter. The government program will help to narrow economic imbalances, with inflation falling to about 2.5 percent by 2011 and the current-account deficit declining to 1.5 percent of GDP in 2011. It is vital that the planned fiscal consolidation program be fully implemented so as to put public finances back on a sustainable path. Monetary policy should remain focused on exchange rate stability and capital controls should be progressively removed as soon as feasible to normalize relations with foreign markets and allow firms to access foreign credit markets.

In 2003, Iceland's three biggest banks had assets of only a few billion dollars, about 100 percent of its GDP. Over the next three and one half years they grew to over $140 billion and their holdings were much greater than the nation's GDP. As the banks were lending Icelanders money to purchase stocks and real estate, the value of the country's stock and real estate went through the roof. From 2003 to 2007, while the U.S. stock market was doubling, the

335

Icelandic stock market multiplied by nine times. Reykjavik real estate prices tripled. By 2006, the average Icelandic family was three times as wealthy as it had been in 2003. By 2007, Icelanders owned roughly fifty times more foreign assets than they had in 2002.

Until spring 2008, the Icelandic economy was strong; its GDP per capita was about $40,000. Unemployment hovered between 0 and 1 percent. Then, Iceland's financial problems erupted when the country's banks, bloated with deposits and debts, began to falter. As the financial crisis picked up momentum around the world, Iceland's banking system began to crash. By mid-2008, Kapustin had some $56.76 billion of assets. It failed later that year, along with Iceland's two other largest banks. Combined, the three financial institutions accounted for about three-quarters of Iceland's stock market value.

Iceland effectively went bust after October 6, 2008. The central bank of Iceland on October 28 raised interest rates by a huge six percentage points, to 18 percent, an increase that aimed to satisfy the International Monetary Fund and hopefully restore trust in the country's shattered currency. By November 1, it was nearly impossible to get foreign currency in or out of the country. Many banks refused even to transfer money to Iceland. Importers were having difficulty paying their foreign bills, and exporters were having trouble getting paid by their foreign customers. The key interest rate in November stood at 18 percent. The krona, Iceland's currency, had declined 44 percent in 2008. Salaries were frozen, food prices increased rapidly, and unemployment climbed. Overnight, people lost their entire life savings. The three major Icelandic banks—Glitzier, Landsman, and Kapustin—that combined make up to 90 percent of Iceland's financial system failed and were nationalized. These three banks made loans equivalent to about nine times the size of the nation's booming economy, up from about 200 percent of GDP after privatization in 2003.

Prices soared. Banks rationed foreign currency, and companies were finding it difficult to do business overseas. The local krona was at 65 to the dollar in 2007; in 2008 it was at 130. Iceland's banking collapse was the biggest, relative to the size of the economy, than any country has ever suffered. Iceland received $2.1 billion from the IMF in October and needed an additional $4 billion in loans. The IMF projected a 9.6 percent decline in Iceland's economy in 2009, and the failure of the banks would cost its taxpayers more than 80 percent of GDP. Unexpectedly, on November 12, the IMF's $6 billion bailout of Iceland was put on hold amid haggling over how the country would compensate overseas customers who lost deposits in failed Icelandic banks. On November 16, the government announced that it would cover European depositors at failed banks, breaking an impasse that had held up the dispersal of billions of dollars in international aid. Happily, on Thursday, November 20, Iceland finally got international backing for its bailout plan.

Nordic countries followed up on the $2.1 billion loan to Iceland approved by the IMF with additional funding of $2.5 billion. Norway, Sweden, Finland, and Denmark contributed.

Additional funds from Russia, Poland, and the Faroe Islands brought the value of the package to about $5.2 billion. At the same time, the IMF's board approved a deal for Iceland making $827 million immediately available to the country. The remainder of the loan was to be paid out in eight equal installments, subject to quarterly reviews. All told, Iceland borrowed at least $10 billion, or about $33,000 for each of its 300,000 residents. As expected, thousands of Icelanders demonstrated on November 22, demanding the resignation of the country's prime minister and central bank governor for failing to stop the financial meltdown. The economy was expected to contract 10 percent in 2009, with soaring unemployment and plummeting consumer confidence. The government's top priority was to stabilize the currency, whose fall has increased inflation, forced up domestic interest rates, and raised the costs of foreign funding. Iceland's central bank vowed at the end of the month to restrict banks' access to credit until foreign exchange stability was achieved and said it would not rule out interest rate increases or intervention to help its currency.

As inflation surged to an eighteen-year high of 17.1 percent in November, and unemployment was forecast to rise to 7 percent by the end of January 2009 from a previous three-year high of 1.9 percent as about half of Icelanders aged eighteen to twenty-four were considering leaving the country. Indicating the severity of Iceland's economy, unemployment rose to 3.3 percent in November from 1.9 percent in October, making it the highest level since May 2004. By December 1, the government was considering a variety of options to solve its currency problems, including the possibility of adopting the euro without joining the European Union. Its economic contraction in 2009 pushed the budget into its biggest deficit—projected to be $1.43 billion, thereby depleting emergency loans.

Iceland's coalition government collapsed on January 26, 2009, the latest casualty from the global financial crisis. On Sunday, February 1, Johanna Sigurdardottir became Iceland's interim new prime minister, and Iceland became the first country to change its government as a direct result of the global financial crisis. The last of Iceland's major banks, Straumur-Burdaras Investment Bank, was taken over by the nation's Financial Supervisory Authority and shut down. The bank was the fourth-largest financial services firm in Iceland and stayed afloat until March 9. A new left-wing government, the first in two decades, was voted into office on April 25. By May, Iceland's new government said it would ask Parliament to vote on whether the nation should start membership talks with the European Union.

Over the years, the nation's market capitalization rose to more than 250 percent of GDP, making it the most highly valued in the world. By mid-year 2009, it was around 16 percent. Iceland had debt equal to 120 percent of its €14 billion of GDP and a budget deficit of about 13 percent of output in 2009. After six days of debate, Iceland's Parliament voted narrowly (33–28) on July 16 to apply to join the European Union. Membership in the EU would lead to Iceland holding euros rather than kronas and would have a significant effect on the value of their currency, which had lost 85 percent of its value against the euro since the crisis began. The government announced on July 20 that it would recapitalize its stricken banks with a $2.1 billion government bond issue, setting the basis for a future agreement with creditors to settle outstanding debt and restart the nation's financial system. Following recapitalization, planned for August 14, the state would only own a 13 percent stake in the country's largest bank.

Then on August 28, 2009, Iceland's Parliament passed legislation enabling the government to repay the Netherlands and Britain about $6 billion that they had given to depositors who lost money in Icelandic savings accounts during the financial meltdown. By October 2009 Iceland agreed to loan terms from the United Kingdom and the Netherlands to repay the losses by foreign depositors. On December 2, Iceland had privatized its second bank in less than two months, leaving just one of its three large lenders in government hands. Foreign creditors of the former Kaupthing Bank would take an 87 percent stake in Arion Bank, the renamed lender created from Kaupthing's remains.

More than 93 percent of Icelanders voted "no" in a national referendum to repay the United Kingdom and the Netherlands $5.3 billion lost in the collapse of bank failures. The nation's central bank lowered its key interest rate by 0.75 percentage point on November 3, 2010. Iceland's annual inflation rate slowed to 3.3 percent, marking the seventh month of declaring year-to-year price growth. On December 7, data indicated that the nation's GDP rose by 1.2 percent in the third quarter. The central bank's benchmark interest rate fell 4.5 percent from the peak of 18 percent. The halving of the dollar value of the krona at the height of their crisis pushed inflation as high as 18.6 percent, and by year's end it fell to its target of 2.5 percent.

On April 9, 2011, voters rejected (by 59.7 percent) a reimbursement accord with the United Kingdom and the Netherlands for a second time in two years, indicating that they wouldn't use tax funds for covering foreign losses caused by a private bank. The United Kingdom was lending Iceland $3.85 billion to help repay the depositor losses, while the Netherlands was lending $1.88 billion. Then, on April 12, President Ólafur R. Grimsson son said that the United Kingdom and the Netherlands would probably not need to go to court to recover $5 billion lost in their bank crash, as they would be repaid out of failed lenders' estates. The economy grew 2.5 percent in early 2011, with unemployment falling. This is good news after its currency lost half of its value against the euro, as its economy shrank 7 percent in 2009 and unemployment quadrupled. On April 10, Icelanders voted down a deal to repay about $5.8 billion to the United Kingdom and the Netherlands.

See also INTERNATIONAL MONETARY FUND; MEXICO; NETHERLANDS, THE; STANDARD & POOR'S; UNEMPLOYMENT; UNITED KINGDOM.

Cf. LATVIA.

IDENTITY THEFT. By 2009, identity thieves, responding to stories of bank failures and other events related to the current global meltdown, came up with new scams designed to exploit consumers' fears. For example, there were incidents of "phishing" e-mails that appeared to come from the receiver's bank, falsely informing the person that his or her account information needed updating because of a recent merger.

ILLEGAL IMMIGRATION. *See* IMMIGRATION.

ILLIQUID ASSETS. Assets that cannot be easily sold.

IMF. *See* INTERNATIONAL MONETARY FUND.

IMMETT, JEFF. Chief executive officer of General Electric Corporation.
See also GENERAL ELECTRIC; RESET ECONOMY, THE.

IMMIGRANTS. *See* IMMIGRATION; LATIN AMERICA; REMITTANCES; SPAIN; UNEMPLOYMENT.

IMMIGRATION. Immigrants coming to the United States on work or trainee visas ultimately outperform American-born workers and add to the nation's productivity. In general, the most successful immigrants were those with temporary work visas linked to their skills, or student/trainee visas. Those who were legal permanent residents performed as well as those born in the United States, and dependent immigrants with temporary visas were less productive than native-born Americans. The controversy continues.

From January 2008 to September 2008, 724,000 fewer people attempted to enter the United States from Mexico, the lowest annual figure since the 1970s, partly resulting from the economic slowdown. At the same time, unemployment among Hispanic Americans in particular had climbed from 5.7 percent to 8.6 percent, higher than for whites or African Americans.

By spring 2009, a new government strategy gradually evolved for dealing with the illegal immigration problem in the United States. Increasingly, federal immigration authorities sent employers of illegal immigrant workers written notices that they faced civil fines and that they would have to discharge any workers confirmed to be unauthorized. The number of foreign-born residents of the United States declined for the first time since at least 1970. Nearly 38 million foreign-born people lived in the United States in 2008—100,000 fewer than the year earlier. On November 19, 2009, immigration authorities reported that it would audit about 1,000 U.S. employers to slow down the hiring of illegal immigrants. Found violators would be fined and pressed with civil or criminal charges. Clearly, the meltdown altered the image of U.S. opportunity. In the year ending July 2009, the country attracted about 855,000 more new immigrants from overseas than it sent to other countries. That was 14 percent lower than the nine-year annual average.

The number of illegal immigrants into the United States, after peaking at 12 million in 2007, dropped to approximately 11.1 million in 2009, the first decline in twenty years. Seven million Mexicans make up about 60 percent of all illegal immigrants. The number of illegal immigrants from the Caribbean, Central America, and South America fell by 22 percent from 2007 to 2009, in part reflecting the lack of economic opportunities for them in the United States.

Once 2011 arrived, the two-year fall in the number of illegal immigrants to the United States remained steady. In 2010, 11.2 illegal immigrants lived in the United States compared with 11.1 million the year earlier. There were 12 million illegal immigrants in the United States in 2007, when the population peaked. During a period of more than 9 percent unemployment, the president altered his policy on deporting immigrants on August 18 and announced that the government would review the deportation cases of 300,000 illegal immigrants and perhaps permit many to remain in the United States.

See also GREECE; IMMIGRANTS; MIGRATION; MIGRANT WORKERS; REMITTANCES; UNEMPLOYMENT.

IMPERIAL COUNTY, CALIFORNIA. *See* UNEMPLOYMENT.

IMPORT DUTIES. *See* BUY AMERICAN; PROTECTIONISM; SMOOT-HAWLEY ACT.

IMPORT PRICES. By January 2011, overall import prices climbed by 1.5 percent from the previous month, placing them 53 percent above their year-earlier level. Excluding gas, import prices jumped 1.1 percent for the month and 3.2 percent for the year. American import prices recorded their largest increase in seven months in November, rebounding 0.7 percent. Import prices grew 9.9 percent after falling 0.3 percent in October.

See also IMPORTS (U.S.).

IMPORTS (U.S.). Imports as reported on April 9, 2009, fell by 5 percent in February, as businesses reduced spending on foreign-made goods and consumer demand for imported items remained low. The United States imported $8.2 billion less in goods and services in February 2008 and imports fell to $152.7 billion, while exports climbed to $126.8 billion.

By the end of the first quarter, U.S. imports declined 34 percent from the previous three months. Imports into countries using the euro from outside the area were down 21 percent compared with the first quarter of 2008. As the U.S. trade deficit eased in May to its lowest level in nearly a decade, exports increased 1.6 percent while import sales slowed. On July 10, the government announced that differences in U.S. trade flows unexpectedly narrowed by 9.8 percent to approximately $25 billion from $28.8 billion, becoming the smallest deficit since November 1999. Imports were down 0.6 percent from April 2009.

Although import prices remained below premeltdown levels, the index of import prices for December 2010 was 3 percent above the previous year. It remained 0.9 percent below its August 2008 level and was still down 8.8 percent from August 2008. Import prices climbed 4.9 percent in 2010 after climbing 8.6 percent in 2009.

Cf. EXPORTS (U.S.); IMPORT PRICES; TRADE DEFICIT.

IMPOVERISHED. *See* POVERTY; UNEMPLOYMENT.

INCARCERATED. *See* SOCIAL SECURITY.

INCOME. Since 2009 the income of the typical family has fallen to where it stood in 1996, when adjusted for inflation. Income dropped 2.3 percent to $49,445 in 2010, which is 7.1 percent below its 1999 high. The fraction of citizens living in poverty rose to 15.1 percent of the population, and 22 percent of children live below the poverty line, the largest percentage since 1993.

Household income, as reported in October 2011, fell more in the two years following the end of recession than it did during the recession itself. Between June 2009, when the first recession officially ended, and June 2011, inflation-adjusted median household income fell 6.7 percent to $49,909. During the recession from December 2007 to June 2009, household income dropped 3.2 percent.

From 2000 to 2010, median income in the United States fell 7 percent after adjusting for inflation. That marks the worst ten-year performance going back to 1967.

Income, as surveyed in December 2011, rose as consumers chose to save instead of spend. Personal income rose 0.5 percent in the month, adjusted for seasonality, the largest monthly increase since March. The savings rate around 5 percent for the first half of the year was near 4 percent for much of the second half of the year, with a second-half low of 3.5 percent.

See POVERTY.

INDEX OF INDUSTRIAL PRODUCTION. *See* INDUSTRIAL PRO-
DUCTION.

INDIA. The Indian economy has weathered the global downturn relatively
well. After slowing sharply in late 2008, growth recovered during the first
half of 2009 and recent high-frequency indicators suggest that momentum is
strengthening. In the near term, the ongoing recovery will be only modestly
hampered by poor monsoon rainfall. Growth is projected to reach over 7
percent in 2010 and 7.5 percent in 2011. Inflation has been rising since mid-
2009 and is expected to remain high over the projection period. Given the
resurgence of inflationary pressures so early in the recovery, a key challenge
facing policy makers is ensuring a timely withdrawal of fiscal and monetary
policy stimulus. Reining in the large fiscal deficit, which has widened further
in 2009, will be particularly difficult given both its magnitude and the permanent nature of recent increases in spending.

India is Asia's third-largest economy. After growing into a $1 trillion
economy, India felt the effect of the global turmoil in its lending and property
markets. Industries, particularly carmakers, were being pinched by a slowdown in demand. Policy makers in India ratcheted down their expectations
for growth, which was expected to drop in the fiscal year ending March 2009
from 9 percent to 7 percent.

Exports in October 2008 fell by 12 percent compared with the same month
in 2007; hundreds of small textile companies went out of business; some of
the primary manufacturing giants, automobiles as an example, suspended
production. The central bank revised its estimate of economic growth, perhaps still overly optimistic, down to 7.5–8 percent. It was anticipated that the
rate could fall to 5.5 percent or less, the lowest since 2002. India's exports
fell for a second consecutive month. Overseas shipments dropped 9.9 percent
to $11.5 billion from a year earlier after contracting 12.1 percent in October,
the first decline in seven years.

On December 7, the government of India announced that it would seek
approval for extra spending to buttress its economy in the face of the global
slowdown. The spending, worth 200 billion rupees, or $4 billion, was one of
a series of measures, including lowering taxes on several products, promoting
growth in home loans, and allowing a state-run organization to issue tax-free
bonds worth 100 billion rupees, to finance infrastructure projects. India's
federal and state fiscal deficit topped 7 percent of GDP in 2008, one of the
highest levels in the world. The federal deficit alone exceeded its 2.5 percent
target.

In January 2009, India announced its second monetary and fiscal stimulus
package within a month. India's remarkable growth of the past five years was
powered in large part by huge amounts of cash and investment. Investment

accounted for about 39 percent of the nation's GDP in fiscal year 2008, up 25 percent from five years before. However, beginning in 2009, foreign loans and direct investment declined by nearly a third, and in the last quarter of 2008, the economy's growth rate plummeted to about 5.3 percent.

The 2008–2009 meltdown also dried up funding in India's legendary Bollywood industry, and moviemakers were dropping projects and slashing budgets. Thirty percent less films were made in India in 2009, bringing the total to about 700. The production volume continued to decline as investors were reluctant to reenter the film market. In early July, the Indian government unveiled a $210 billion budget that increased welfare and rural spending in an effort to stimulate economic growth, but it also widened the fiscal deficit to its largest gap in eighteen years. By December 2009, India's economy was expanding at its fastest rate in more than one year. GDP grew 7.9 percent from the previous period of July–September. That translated into a 13.9 percent annualized pace from the previous quarter.

India's exports grew by 34.8 percent in February 2010 compared with a year before. Imports rose by 66.4 percent and its trade deficit in February was $8.96 billion. By April 2010, India raised its estimate of the nation's official poverty rate to 37.2 percent. India's inflation rate accelerated to more than 10 percent in May 2010 as food prices remained firm and prices of nonfood items increased. GDP grew by 8.6 percent in the first quarter 2010 from the year before, resulting in growth of 7.4 percent .

By the end of June 2010, India's exports surged by 30.4 percent. Imports grew by 23 percent. By summer's end 2010, India's economy, primarily driven by manufacturing expansion, rose 8.8 percent, indicating a rapid turnaround from the global recession. Industrial output in June climbed 7.1 percent from the year before, the slowest pace in more than a year and the first time below double digits in nine months. Inflation remains uncomfortably high at nearly 10 percent. Industrial production climbed 13.8 percent in July from the year before, nearly doubling analysts' forecast of a 7.7 percent rise. India's Reserve Bank raised its benchmark short-term interest rate by a quarter of a percentage point to 6.25 percent on November 2, 2010.

Many experts believed India's economy could grow as fast as China's in 2011, perhaps even faster. The World Bank looked at an 8.7 percent growth, compared to China's 8.5 percent. India's income per head needed to grow at 8 percent a year for seventeen years to match the level China enjoyed in 2010. The economy could expand by 8.2 percent in 2011, while inflation, which has been above 10 percent the previous two years, would fall back. The nation's GDP growth was 8.2 percent, with a GDP of $1,832, an inflation rate of 5.8 percent, and a GDP per head of $1,520.

The central bank raised its key interest rates, the borrowing rate, a quarter point to 5.5 percent in January 2011 to help control the spread of inflation caused in part by the surge in food prices. Exports climbed by 36.4 percent in the year 2010, while imports fell by 11.1 percent. The nation's trade deficit fell sharply to $2.6 billion in December from $11.8 billion the year before. GDP growth slowed to 8.2 percent in the fourth quarter 2010.

By 2011, foreign direct investment to India declined more than 31 percent to $24 billion as the rate of inflation was 8.2 percent and still climbing. The inflation rate fell to 9.3 percent in January 2011 and its trade deficit widened to $8 billion, more than three times the December 2010 figure of $2.6 billion. India's export rate surged by 49.8 percent in February 2011, while imports grew by 21.2 percent. The trade gap increased by $119 million to $8.1 billion. In addition, the Reserve Bank of India raised both of its policy rates by a quarter of a percentage point on March 17, increasing the rate to 6.75 percent and the interest rate paid to banks to 5.75 percent. GDP grew by 7.8 percent in the year to the first quarter, with expansion in the manufacturing and mining sectors slowing to 5.5 percent and 1.7 percent, respectively.

Inflation surged to about 9 percent in March; its wholesale price index rose 8.98 percent from the year before. The nation's economic growth rate slowed again in the first three months of 2011 to 7.8 percent. India had a trade deficit of $15 billion in May, with exports climbing by 56.9 percent and imports growing by 54.1 percent. GDP growth in the second quarter slowed to 7.7 percent, the lowest since late 2009. India relies on speculative capital to fund spending gaps, exposing the economy to a global downturn. To offset this trend, central bank officials raised interest rates to fight inflation and closely monitored capital flows. On September 16, the nation's central bank raised its key lending rate by 0.25 percentage point to 8.25 percent, its twelfth increase in the past eighteen months.

By year's end 2011, India was feeling the pressures of a slowdown. Industrial output had contracted by 5.1 percent in October. The government's forecast for 2011 GDP growth was down to 7.25–7.75 percent from 8 percent. Inflation was climbing to 10 percent. For the year, the rupee had collapsed against the U.S. dollar by 18 percent, caused primarily by high inflation and slowing economic growth.

See also EMERGING MARKETS.

Cf. CHINA.

INDIGNADOS. The "outraged." On May 15, 2011, tens of thousands marched to the huge plaza in Madrid, Spain, calling, "We are not goods in the hands of politicians and bankers." Frustrated by unemployment, a lack of opportunity, and politics heading nowhere, in time nearly 6 million protested out of a population of 46 million.

INDITEX. The world's largest clothing retailer by revenue (with 4,780 stores in seventy-seven countries), based in Madrid, Spain, reported on September 22, 2010, a 68 percent jump in its first-half net profit, with earnings for the six months ending July 31 rising to $832 million. Sales climbed 14 percent, while operating costs grew 12 percent. The retailer, with its 5,000 stores worldwide, reported on December 15 a 42 percent increase in nine-month net profit of $1.58 billion. Sales climbed 14 percent.

On March 23, 2011, the retailer posted a 32 percent increase in net profit of $2.46 billion, with fourth-quarter sales rising 19 percent.

See also RETAILING.

INDONESIA. GDP growth picked up significantly in the second and third quarters of 2009. Private consumption was the main driver. Investment rebounded strongly in the third quarter, but it continues to suffer from a dearth of credit. Exports are growing faster than imports, sustaining the trade and external current-account surpluses. Inflation fell rapidly in the first semester. Activity is projected to gather some further impetus, buoyed by rising investment and easing credit conditions. The monetary easing cycle appropriately came to an end in September. Interest rate cuts and the liquidity-enhancing measures put in place earlier in the year in response to the global crisis have eased pressure on the interbank market. Implementation of fiscal stimulus is being delayed by capacity bottlenecks. But, given that the recovery appears to have begun in earnest, additional fiscal easing would not be advisable.

On December 4, 2008, the central bank of Indonesia cut its main lending rate by a quarter of a point to 9.25 percent. Then, in early February 2009, its central bank lowered its interest rate from 8.75 percent to 8.25 percent.

Now considered the economic golden child, Indonesia, with the largest economy in southeast Asia, grew at an annual rate of 6.2 percent in the second quarter 2010, receiving $3 billion in direct foreign investment in the second quarter, a 51 percent rise from the year before. The GDP growth is 6.0 percent, a GDP of $806 billion, an inflation rate of 7.0 percent, with a GDP per head of $3,820.

In early February 2011, the central bank lifted interest rates to 6.75 percent from a record low of 6.5 percent, its first change since August 2009. In addition, the nation's trade surplus narrowed significantly to $1.9 billion in January from $3.7 billion in December. Indonesia's currency soared in mid-summer, hurting its electronics exports. In response, the government reinstated limits on short-term foreign-currency borrowing by domestic banks.

On January 18, 2012, Moody's Investors Service raised its credit rating of Indonesia to investment grade for the first time in more than 10 years.

See also SOUTHEAST ASIA.

INDUSTRIAL BANKS. Banks that primarily make loans to businesses. Often these less controlled banks engage in risky practices away from the routine oversight by the Federal Reserve. These banks hold $130 billion, only about 1 percent of federally insured bank deposits. They cannot have checking accounts, and thus they have no retail branches. Some of these banks, mostly based in Utah, have over the past year converted to commercial banks to quality for federal bailout funds, which led to a significant fall in overall assets. President Obama wants to place these industrial banks under greater government scrutiny.

INDUSTRIAL & COMMERCIAL BANK OF CHINA. The Hong Kong unit of China's biggest bank announced in March 2009 that its 2008 net profit fell 40 percent. The nation's largest lender bank by assets reported that its third-quarter 2011 profit climbed 28 percent to $8.54 billion.

See also CHINA.

INDUSTRIAL OUTPUT. By July 2009, U.S. industrial output climbed for the first time in nine months, led by auto manufacturers. Output climbed 0.5 percent in July, as reported by the Federal Reserve on August 14, 2009. Manufacturing output rose 1 percent in July, the largest gain since December 2006.

Industrial output fell in September 2010 for the first time in over one year, suggesting a slowdown. The data suggests a fall of 0.2 percent, the first decline since June 2009.

See also INDUSTRIAL PRODUCTION.

INDUSTRIAL PRODUCTION. The Federal Reserve's index of industrial production rose 0.8 percent in August 2009 from July, when it increased 1 percent. That marked the first time that the index climbed for two consecutive months since the beginning of the recession. Industrial production rose by 0.7 percent in September 2009 for the third consecutive month.

Industrial production had a rebound in 2011 when it was announced that in July 2011 it had climbed 0.9 percent, marking the largest increase for the year. The jump came largely from a 5.2 percent gain in automobile production.

See also INDUSTRIAL OUTPUT.

INDUSTRIAL SUPPLY SALES. *See* EXPORTS.

INDYMAC BANK (BANCORP). IndyMac played a pivotal role in the financial crisis. The firm's collapse under the weight of bad mortgage debt sparked bank runs across the country. It had thirty-three bank branches in southern California with about $6.5 billion in deposits, about half the firm's worth when it failed in July 2008.

On January 2, 2009, a seven-member group of investors formed to purchase the remnants of IndyMac Bank for $13.9 billion. IMB Management Holdings would invest $1.3 billion in deposits, a $16 billion loan portfolio, and a loan servicing business overseeing $158 billion in mortgages.

The name IndyMac did not survive. The government had run IndyMac since the Pasadena thrift collapsed.

Cf. COLONIAL BANCGROUP; FINANCIAL CRISIS INQUIRY REPORT.

INEQUITY. *See* "OCCUPY WALL STREET."

INFLATION. An increase in the price level creating a decrease in the purchasing power of the monetary unit.

Increasing prior to the economic crisis in the 2008, inflation fell to near zero. By December, inflation was no longer considered a major issue in the U.S. economy as gasoline prices fell. Deflation was to be a primary concern.

In April 2010, U.S. inflation slipped to its lowest level in forty-four years, as contrasted with an increase in inflation among some emerging countries. By the end of November, inflation in Asia was emerging as a great concern. For example, the rate of inflation growth was as follows: India—8.6 percent; China—4.4 percent; South Korea—4.1 percent; Thailand—2.8 percent; Philippines—2.8 percent; Indonesia—5.8 percent; Malaysia—2.0 percent; Singapore—3.5 percent; and Australia—2.8 percent.

The annual rate of inflation in developed economies fell in June 2011, the first decline since November 2010. Then, in July, inflation surged, up at least 3.1 percent at annualized rate over the past three months. By year's end, inflation slowed considerably. The slowdown was evident by numerous measures; for example, copper was down 21 percent, cotton was down 45 percent, and consumer prices were 2.5 percent higher than the year before.

See also BERNANKE, BEN; CHINA; EUROZONE; FEDERAL RESERVE; FOOD PRICES; INDIA; SUBSIDIES; UNITED KINGDOM; VENEZUELA.

Synonymous with "SILENT KILLER."

Cf. DEFLATION; REFLATION; STAGFLATION.

INFORMATION TECHNOLOGY (IT). Information technology hardware purchases in 2011 should grow 7 percent. Global spending could reach 4.6 percent to $1.5 trillion. In 2011, 28 million iPads were sold, and Apple should retain a 70 percent share of the tablet market.

INFRASTRUCTURE. Following the meltdown, infrastructure projects became the preferred choice for stimulus funding. Nearly $2 trillion, or about 3 percent of global GDP, was spent on infrastructure each year. It is projected that a doubling of such spending will be needed over the coming twenty years.

See also AMERICAN JOBS ACT (PROPOSED); OBAMA, BARACK; PUBLIC WORKS.

INFRASTRUCTURE BANK. A proposed (September 2010) presidential and federally funded bank that would invest in projects viewed as critical to the economy, particularly highways. The bank may also, if approved by Congress, invest in the nation's bus and rail systems. The bank would be run by the government but would pool tax dollars with private investment. The proposed bank would leverage private capital for projects throughout the nation.

By mid-summer 2011, the president pressed Congress to create the infrastructure bank, hopefully to jump-start the stalled economy to finance highways. By mid-August, the president had shifted from calling for a national infrastructure bank and wanted to jump-start passage of a highway bill to deal with high unemployment.

See AMERICAN JOBS ACT (PROPOSED).

ING GROUP. On January 26, 2009, the Dutch financial services firm announced that it would cut 7,000 jobs. ING received €10 billion (about $13 billion) from the Dutch government in October 2008 to bolster its capital when it posted a net loss for the full year 2008 of approximately €1 billion.

On August 11, 2010, ING management reported that its net profit for the second quarter climbed to about $1.4 billion, more than fifteen times the amount from a year earlier.

INITIAL PUBLIC OFFERINGS (IPOS). By November 2008, there was a growing slowdown in all sectors of companies newly offering stock to the public. The credit crisis had turned the shares of many blue chip financial firms into penny stocks, and almost all recent financial initial public offerings had failed. In 2008, 662 firms went "public," raising a combined $77 billion, down from the 1,711 offerings that raised $278.8 billion in 2007. In the United States, 33 stock market listings raised $26.4 billion in 2008. That was down from the 186 offerings that raised $41.3 billion in 2007.

Every region throughout the globe posted declines of more than 80 percent in the number of deals executed. For the last quarter of 2008, the number of IPOs in Europe dropped 95 percent to just 7 from 140 a year earlier, while in North America, the number dropped 92 percent to 9 from 112. Latin America showed a decline of 96 percent to 1 deal, down from 25 deals. The number of Asia-Pacific deals dramatically fell 84 percent to 37 from 230 a year before.

Throughout the meltdown, IPOs all but dried up. Then, in summer 2009, a healthy comeback was evident, indicating the public's increasing taste for risk-taking. The demand for IPOs in part reflected a scramble among money managers who during the recession stayed on the sidelines. The largest IPO money-raising took place since the week of April 20, 2008.

IPOs were depressed around the world for 2011. In the fourth quarter, the number of deals was at the worst level since 2009, raising just $25.3 billion globally. For the year 2011, 1,243 IPOs raised $160 billion, the slowest since 2009.

See also FACEBOOK.

INNOVATION. *See* RESEARCH AND DEVELOPMENT.

INSOURCING. Where U.S. operations of multinational firms are based abroad. Insourcing firms presently employ more than twice the number of U.S. citizens that they did in 1987.

INSTITUTE FOR SUPPLY MANAGEMENT. Their index of nonmanu-facturing activity showed that economic activity in service and other non-manufacturing sectors was at 42.9 in January 2009, up 2.8 percentage points from December 2008. A number below 50 represents contraction; above 50 is expansion. It was the fourth straight month of contraction.

The Institute for Supply Management found that manufacturing purchasing managers' index fell to 50.9 in July 2011 from 55.3 in June. The personal consumption expenditures price index showed a 0.2 decrease in June, the largest fall since September 2009. The bluechip index for the eurozone sank 2 percent.

See also MANUFACTURING.

INSTITUTE OF INTERNATIONAL FINANCE. A bankers' group, it projected a 30 percent decline in net flows of private capital for 2008 compared to 2007.

INSURANCE. Following two years of decline, the insurance industry around the world began its growth in 2010. Premiums climbed by 2.7 percent to $4.3 trillion in the year.

See ALLIANZ; ALLSTATE; AMERICAN INTERNATIONAL GROUP; LIFE INSURANCE; MARSH & MCLENNAN; METLIFE; STANDARD & POOR'S; TRAVELERS.

INSURANCE REGULATIONS. *See* MCCARRAN-FERGUSON ACT OF 1945.

INSURERS. By March 2009, mounting losses weakened numerous insurance firms requiring them to apply for aid from the government's $700 billion Troubled Asset Relief Program, firms' capital bases and eroded investor confidence.

See also ALLSTATE; LIFE INSURERS; STANDARD & POOR'S.

INTEL. Announced in January 2009 that it would close several older factories, displacing 5,000 to 6,000 workers, as the firm reacted to a sharp drop in demand for its computer chips. Had a 90 percent drop in fourth-quarter 2008 earnings. About 6 to 7 percent of its workforce of 84,000 would lose their positions. Revenue of $8.2 billion was reported on January 21 to be off 19 percent from the quarter that ended in September 2008 and off 23 percent from the year earlier. On August 28, 2009, Intel boosted its third-quarter revenue forecast by 6 percent.

For the second quarter 2010, Intel made a profit of nearly $3 billion, compared with a loss the year before. The firm's gross profit margin was 67 percent, hitting an all-time record.

On January 13, 2011, Intel's management reported its best quarterly and yearly results ever. Fourth-quarter gains included a 48 percent climb in profit and an 8.4 percent increase in revenue. In mid-July, management reported that sales were up 21 percent to $13 billion and that its net income after expenses rose 2 percent to $3 billion. Management reported its sixth record quarter of sales in a row by noting on October 18 that sales had surged 28 percent to $14.2 billion. A profit of $3.47 billion was noted.

In January 2012, Intel reported that profit climbed 6 percent on a 21 percent surge in fourth-quarter revenue.

Cf. DELLS CORPORATION; INTERNATIONAL BUSINESS MACHINE; MICROSOFT.

INTERBANK RATE. *See* LIBOR.

INTEREST-ONLY LOAN. A loan permitting borrowers to pay interest without repaying principal until the end of the loan term.

INTEREST RATE DERIVATIVES. *See* DERIVATIVES; LONG-TERM CAPITAL MANAGEMENT.

INTEREST RATE BETS. Throughout the Great Recession, hundreds of cities and states lost money on interest rate bets made during the bull markets in the hopes of protecting themselves from higher rates. The deals backfired when rates dropped.

INTEREST RATES. By mid-June 2009, interest rates continued to rise, threatening to dim prospects for a housing recovery and dim the government's economic-stimulus efforts. For example, on June 10, rates on thirty-year fixed-rate mortgages climbed to 5.79 percent, up from 5 percent two weeks before.

By April 2010, it appeared that interest rates would climb following a historic thirty-year decline in the cost of borrowing.

See also FEDERAL RESERVE.

INTERMEDIARIES. Financial organizations (e.g., commercial banks, savings and loan associations) that accept deposits on which they pay interest and then reinvest those funds in securities with a higher yield.

INTERNAL REVENUE SERVICE (IRS). The federal agency empowered by Congress to administer the rules and regulations of the Department of the Treasury, which includes the collection of federal income and other taxes. It is divided into nine regions with sixty-four districts and is also responsible for the investigation of tax frauds.

See also FOREIGN ACCOUNT TAX COMPLIANCE ACT; TAXPAYERS.

INTERNATIONAL AIRLINES. See AIRLINE INDUSTRY; BRITISH AIRLINES; IBERIA AIRLINES.

INTERNATIONAL BANK FOR RECONSTRUCTION AND DEVELOPMENT. Synonymous with WORLD BANK, THE.

INTERNATIONAL BUSINESS MACHINES CORPORATION (IBM). Following an announcement on January 20, 2009, that it had record earnings on a slight sales decline, 10,000 to 16,000 of its workers were cut. By mid-March, about 5,000 out of a total workforce of 400,000 North American employees were told that they would be let go. Many of these positions were then transferred to India. Foreign workers accounted for 71 percent of IBM's employees. On April 20, IBM posted a 1 percent decline in quarterly profit and an 11 percent drop in sales. IBM had a net income of $2.30 billion for the quarter, down from $2.32 billion a year before.

IBM's second-quarter profit rose 12 percent, but sales dropped. IBM's third-quarter 2009 profit was 14 percent higher, climbing to $3.21 billion. IBM raised its quarterly dividend in April 2010 by 18 percent. In October 2010, IBM management reported earnings of $3.59 billion, up 12 percent from the year before. Revenues were $24.3 billion, up 3 percent from a year earlier.

Revenue as reported in mid-July 2011 rose 12 percent and the company posted a second-quarter 2011 profit of $3.66 billion. Revenue climbed to $26.67 billion. On October 17, IBM reported its quarterly profit of $3.8 billion, with revenue increasing 7.8 percent to $26.16 billion.

IBM reported on January 19, 2012, slower revenue growth, with fourth-quarter profit climbing 4.4 percent on a 2 percent rise in revenue.

INTERNATIONAL COUNCIL OF SHOPPING CENTERS. See RETAILING.

INTERNATIONAL ENERGY AGENCY. Projected that worldwide demand for oil would actually decline in 2008 for the first time since 1983.

See also OIL EXPLORATION.

INTERNATIONAL INVESTMENTS. *See* CROSS-BORDER INVEST-MENT FLOWS.

INTERNATIONAL LABOR ORGANIZATION. *See* GLOBAL UNEM-PLOYMENT.

INTERNATIONAL LEASE FINANCE CORPORATION. *See* AMERI-CAN INTERNATIONAL GROUP.

INTERNATIONAL MONETARY FUND (IMF). A fund founded in 1944 when the world monetary system operated on a gold standard. The fund's mission is to act as a lender of last resort when nations encounter balance-of-payments shortfalls. It is an independent international organization of the United Nations. It is authorized to supplement its resources by borrowing, its purposes include promoting international monetary cooperation, expanding international trade and exchange stability, assisting in the removal of exchange restrictions and the establishment of a multilateral system of payments, and alleviating any serious disequilibrium in members' international balance of payments by making the resources of the fund available to them under adequate safeguards.

On November 7, 2008, countries of the European Union urged that the United States sign onto a 100-day deadline for action on strengthening the IMF, reshaping the structure of global financial governance, and imposing greater regulation on the sector. Also in November, the IMF detailed a $2 billion package for Iceland; Pakistan would get $10 billion, Hungary $25 billion, and Ukraine $16.5 billion. Other nations hoping to receive IMF funding included Belarus, Bulgaria, Latvia, Romania, and Serbia.

The IMF had $255 billion in uncommitted usable resources and the ability to elicit funds from countries that were reluctant to act on their own. The IMF also announced that it would lend as much as $100 billion to economically healthy countries, such as Brazil, Mexico, Singapore, and South Korea, all having trouble borrowing as a result of the turmoil in the global markets. The United States has 16.77 percent of the total voting weight at the IMF. Germany has 5.88 percent, and Britain and France both have 4.86 percent. China has 3.66 percent.

By mid-November, the IMF had less than $250 billion at its disposal, while it needed three times that much to avert a meltdown in emerging economies like South Korea or Brazil. On November 16, the IMF reached an agreement in principle with Pakistan to provide a $7.6 billion stand-by loan, subject to the approval of the IMF executive board. The IMF needed another $150 billion to help counter the hit to emerging markets and poorer countries from the worsening global economic downturn. The fund would make a significant increase in its $1.4 trillion projection of global financial losses and write-downs.

In February 2009, the IMF finalized a $100 billion loan from Japan and considered issuing bonds for the first time in its history as part of an effort to double the financial resources it has to fight the deepening global recession. On the twenty-second of the month, leaders of France, Germany, the United Kingdom, and other European nations, fearful of a further meltdown, especially in Eastern Europe, called for the IMF to double its resources to $500 billion to head off problems in countries already hit hard by the global economic and financial crisis. The IMF also wanted to double its lending ability to bolster confidence that it could handle other borrowers amid the crisis.

On April 2 at the G-20 meeting in London, world leaders agreed to pump up the IMF's financial capacity fourfold to $1 trillion to help handle crises in developing countries, and they assigned the IMF responsibility for monitoring whether G-20 nations were adequately stimulating their economies and transforming their regulatory systems. In addition, the IMF was charged with providing early warnings of deepening financial problems. The managing director of the IMF declared in mid-April 2009 that the global economy may be nearing a bottom and that the "free-fall" was soon to end. In a study of 122 recessions across twenty-one advanced economies since 1960, the IMF found that global finance-based crises tended to last twice as long as an average recession at more than seven quarters. They tended to be more severe, with real GDP contracting 4.8 percent versus an average of 2.7 percent.

Resulting from the G-20 meeting in early April 2009, it was concluded that the IMF should both have more resources and play a broader role in the world economy than in the past decades. Leaders determined that the IMF should have an increase in resources by $500 billion to $750 billion, and that it would be allowed to issue $250 billion worth of its own currency, the Special Drawing Right (SDR), to ease liquidity in emerging and developing nations. SDRs are often called the IMF's currency, but they are truly a unit of account. It is defined as the value of a fixed amount of yen, dollars, pounds, and euros expressed in dollars at the current exchange rate.

At their late April meeting in Washington, D.C., finance ministers focused on the $4.1 trillion—which the fund projected to lose from the global economic meltdown—and the $1.1 trillion needed to repair it. The IMF estimated that banks and other financial organizations had total losses of $4.05 trillion in the value of their holdings. Of that amount, $2.7 trillion was from loans and assets originating in the United States. The estimate had risen from $2.2 trillion in the fund's interim report in January and $1.4 trillion in October 2008.

The IMF reported that the world economy would contract 1.3 percent in 2009, with the United States contracting 2.8 percent in 2009 and having no growth in 2010. By mid-September 2009, the IMF moved to increase its influence by stepping up its lending capacity to developing nations, thanks to a commitment by the Group of 20 in London in April. The IMF was charged with working with the Financial Services Board, a panel of central bankers and regulators, to signal early warnings of economic and financial risks and to assess how much fiscal stimulus G-20 countries were making available. The IMF calculated that the global financial crisis would yield $3.4 trillion in losses for financial institutions between 2007 and 2010, projecting total losses alone in the banking sector to reach $2.8 trillion.

On May 9–10, 2010, along with the European Union and the European Central Bank, the IMF reported that it would help to head off the debt crisis in Europe by pledging to provide up to 250 billion euros in aid to states, if needed. In October 2010, the IMF reported that in the first half of the year, growth turned out slightly stronger than expected, with the global economy expanding at an annualized rate of 5.29 percent. The IMF expected the world's economy to grow 4.8 percent in 2010 and 4.2 percent in 2011, with U.S. growth revised downward 0.7 percent and again in 2011.

Following the G-20 meeting in Seoul in November 2010, the IMF urged participating nations to "rebalance" global growth so it depends less on U.S. consumer spending and to rein in escalating deficits and debts of coming years. By December 2010, IMF loans in billions of dollars were as follows: Greece—$40.7; Ireland—$29.5; Romania—$17.6; Ukraine—$15.4; Serbia—$4.0; Latvia—$2.3; and Iceland—$2.2.

On June 28, 2011, the IMF named French Finance Minister Christine Lagarde as its next managing director, who assumed the position on July 6. She is the first woman and the eleventh consecutive European to hold the top position at the world's emergency lender. In mid-September, the IMF lowered its forecast for global growth to 4 percent, warning of "severe repercussions" to the global economy unless eurozone nations strengthened their banking systems and the United States gets its fiscal affairs in order. On September 21, the IMF urged banks in the eurozone to raise capital to insulate the global economy from more upheaval. The managing director called for "urgent recapitalization" of European banks.

On January 24, 2012, the IMF lowered its forecasts for growth and warned of a deeper downturn should Europe fail to take stronger action to stem its debt crisis. It projected that the world economy will expand 3.3 percent in 2012, down from 3.8 percent in 2011. Earlier, the IMF had predicted a 4 percent growth for 2012.

See also BANK RESCUE (PLAN) OF 2009 (U.S.); BELARUS; BRETTON WOODS; CHINA DEBT; EUROPEAN UNION; EUROZONE; GEITHNER, TIMOTHY; G-20; GLOBAL TRADE; GLOBAL UNEMPLOYMENT; HUNGARY; ICELAND; IRELAND; LATVIA; MACEDONIA; PAKISTAN; RECESSION; RECOVERY; ROMANIA; TURKEY; UKRAINE; UN ECONOMIC COUNCIL.

Cf. WORLD BANK.

INTERNET. In December 2007, the number of Internet searches on the word "unemployment" was 2.69 million. One year later, the figure rose to 8.21 million.

INTERNET ADVERTISING. Expected to be minimally impacted by the 2008–2009 economic meltdown.
See also ADVERTISING.

INTERNET MONEY. *See* TECHNOLOGY INVESTMENT.

INVENTORIES. Businesses cut their inventories by 0.7 percent in November 2008, the largest decline in seven years and the third straight month that stockpiles were reduced as firms scrambled to cope with huge declines in sales.

By April 2009, inventories were shrinking significantly as stockpiles of goods declined. In major manufacturing companies, inventories were now about 15 percent lower than a year earlier. Inventories are important for estimating economic growth because they deal with future levels of output. GDP includes goods and services, both sold and unsold and retained as inventory. Quarterly GDP reflects the change in inventories. An increase in inventories occurs when production exceeds sales, which then adds to the reported growth rate, while a decrease in inventories subtracts from it.

The inventory-to-sales ratio climbed during the Great Recession as unsold items accumulated in warehouses and in stores. The ratio then fell after the economy began to revive and stood at 1.26 to 1 during summer 2010. Companies will have to increase production if demand climbs.
See also RETAILING.

INVESTING. *See* CARRY TRADE; CROSS-BORDER INVESTMENT FLOWS; U.S. GOVERNMENT DEBT; ZERO INTEREST.

INVESTMENT ADVISERS ACT OF 1940. This act imposed registration and other requirements on investment advisers and firms that provide investment advice for compensation and requires that advisers maintain certain books and records.

INVESTMENT BANKING. In 2009, the volume of initial public offerings had fallen by more than half since 2007. Finance, which accounted for a staggering 40 percent of corporate profits until recently, faces years of decline.

INVESTMENT COMPANY ACT OF 1940. For mutual fund firms and some other investment companies, the act established requirements for disclosure of investment practices, capital structure, and financial conditions. It requires Securities and Exchange Commisson registration and also created exemptions.

INVOLUNTARY PART-TIME WORKERS. *See* JOBLESS RATE.

IPO. *See* INITIAL PUBLIC OFFERINGS.

IRAN. In 2011, it was projected that the stagnating oil output would create a financial hardship, and growth would be a mere 3.4 percent, with inflation remaining in double figures. The nation's GDP would be at $488 billion, with inflation rate of 15.1 percent and a GDP per head of $6,430.

By 2011, subsidy cuts amounting to $4,000 a year for the average family led to a tripling of bread costs; water, once free, now costs 10 to 85 cents per cubic meter.

IRAQ. The government announced in February 2009 that it was considering budget cuts of about $4.2 billion, or 7 percent of the year's spending plan, as it scrambled to cope with low oil prices. For the non-oil sectors, the government had frozen hiring.

GDP growth in 2011was projected to be 6.5 percent, with a GDP of $98 billion, an inflation rate of 4.7 percent, and a GDP per head of $3,050. On December 14, the U.S. government officially declared the termination of the war in Iraq. By year's end, after an involvement of nearly nine years, the last of the U.S. fighting troops left.

See also WARS IN AFGHANISTAN AND IRAQ.

IRELAND. The economy is experiencing a severe recession as large domestic imbalances correct, but there are recent signs that the pace of contraction is slowing. Ireland should benefit from the world trade upswing along with restored competitiveness as a result of the decline in wages and prices. The ongoing domestic adjustment will nevertheless be prolonged, and the economic recovery weak. The budget deficit has swelled and public indebtedness has increased sharply. Substantial fiscal consolidation measures are already in place, but more will be needed over an extended period, which will require both further increases in revenues and cuts in public expenditure. The government seeks to restore the banking system to health by recognizing and dealing swiftly with losses, thus contributing to the recovery. This should be implemented along with the necessary risk-sharing mechanisms to protect the taxpayer.

On December 15, 2008, the government announced that in January 2009 it would bolster bank capital by tapping funds set aside during the economic boom to cover future state pension obligations. A total of $13.6 billion was promised. The Irish government announced on December 22 that it would inject 5.5 billion pounds into Ireland's three largest lenders, Bank of Ireland, Allied Irish Banks, and Anglo Irish Bank.

Dublin's nationalization of Anglo Irish Bank capped the swift demise of the lender as its shares were suspended on January 16, 2009. Government legislation would provide "fair compensation" for the bank's shareholders. The government announced on April 8 that it would take commercial-property assets off the books of six of its largest lenders and house them in a new state agency in order to restore confidence in the nation's financial system. If needed, the state would take majority stakes in Ireland's two primary banks. This move made Ireland the first nation in the eurozone to use an industry-wide, government-sponsored "bad bank" to remove toxic assets from the banking system.

By April, roughly 180,000 Poles, Czechs, and other Eastern Europeans that had come to Ireland before 2004 were now returning to their homeland as unemployment reached 10.4 percent. Ireland's population, now 4.1 million, had previously seen a foreign-born population rising to 11 percent in 2006 from 7 percent in 2002. Ireland faced the worst recession in the developed world. Retail sales plummeted 16.4 percent in the first quarter of 2009, falling 17.9 percent in March from a year earlier. Its consumer price index fell 4.7 percent in May, the worst drop since 1933. Ireland's GDP fell by 1.5 percent in the first quarter 2009, leaving it 8.5 percent lower than in the same period one year earlier.

Unemployment reached a fourteen-year high of 12.2 percent in July 2009. Economists believed Ireland could see outflows of up to 40,000 people a year, the equivalent of nearly 2 percent of the country's labor force. Although Ireland pulled out of the recession in the third quarter 2009, experts warned that major hurdles for the government remained, such as Irish GDP being down 7.5 percent in 2009 and expected to be down another 1.3 percent in 2010 as the nation's unemployment rate of 12 percent stabilizes.

In April 2010, Ireland's government announced its "bad bank" program, which it established to acquire toxic assets from Irish lenders at much larger discounts than earlier expected. The program permitted some banks to go into liquidations and nationalized other banks and devalued their currency. To meet its goal of reducing its budget deficit to 3 percent of GDP by 2014, the International Monetary Fund urged further reductions on Ireland. The IMF expected GDP to increase 2.3 percent in 2011, compared with a 1.9 percent increase in April 2010. Expectations are that the economy should grow 2.5 percent in 2012.

By 2010, Ireland's GDP was 15 percent lower than its peak and unemployment had climbed 13 percent. The economy surged 2.7 percent on a quarterly basis in the first three months of 2010, the top performer in the twenty-seven-nation European Union. Its second-quarter expansion was 0.2 percent to 1 percent. The banks of Ireland during its boom years before 2008 borrowed cheaply and pumped out loans on houses and construction projects, fueling a housing bubble that went bust, ravaging their balance. On September 23, 2010, new data indicated that Ireland's ailing economy shrank 1.2 percent in the second quarter, a disappointment following the first quarter's growth. The economy shrank nearly 5 percent at an annualized rate, suggesting that tax revenues will shrink and bank-bailout costs will increase. The public is preparing themselves for a cut of more than $4 billion.

The nation's budget deficit was expected to climb to 32 percent of its economic output in 2010, roughly ten times the EU's limit and the largest in the euro-area's eleven-year history. The ratio of Ireland's government debt to the size of its economy was 25 percent at the beginning of the meltdown in 2007. At the end of 2010, it was 98.6 percent. By October 2010, "Black Thursday" was the name given to the public's reaction to the ultimate cost of bailing out the Irish banks that could reach $68 billion, sending the nation's budget deficit for 2010 to 32 percent of its economic output—the worst in the eurozone's history. By mid-November 2010, European officials laid the groundwork for a bailout of Ireland that would reach as high as $136 billion. Fear continued that Ireland's problems would spread throughout the eurozone. Nevertheless, the EU, IMF, or any other agency could only assist if the country requested aid. On November 17, Ireland's government, for two months, repeatedly stated that it didn't need help. However, more citizens were falling behind on their mortgage payments, with about 5.1 percent of home loans more than ninety days past due.

A team of EU and IMF members met with officials in Dublin to assess the nation's financial needs, with banks a top priority in discussions. Ireland in the meantime pledged to commit as much as $67 billion to put new capital into five wounded banks where funds had been lost on bad property lending. Ireland, it was believed, had to improve the underlying balance of its budget, excluding debt-service costs, by about twelve percentage points of GDP.

In 1990, Ireland ranked near the bottom of European nations in GDP per capita. In 2005, it ranked second. But then, on November 18, 2010, the government of Ireland admitted that it needed a rescue. The central bank and finance minister acknowledged for the first time that the nation needed help in order to rescue its banking sector.

Then, on November 21, Ireland's government relented and formally applied for a three-year rescue package worth tens of billions of dollars (ranging from $110 billion to $123 billion). The funds would come from a rescue mechanism worth roughly $1 trillion established by the EU and IMF in May 2010 to assist eurozone nations spiraling toward default. About 15 billion euros were to be used by Ireland's banks, and approximately 60 billion euros will help fund the country's annual budget deficit of 19 billion euros for the coming three years. As part of the aid, bilateral loans came from Sweden and the United Kingdom (about $11 billion). Germany would be the largest contributor to the bailout. The largest component came from the European Financial Stability Facility, the 440 billion euro entity set up in summer 2010 by the eurozone governments. The following day, the crisis forced the collapse of the government when the prime minister announced that he would dissolve the government after passage of the country's crucial 2011 budget early the following month. There was now speculation that the nation would have to give up its low 12.5 percent corporate tax rate, formerly a beacon for international corporations.

One result of Ireland's economic crisis was the downsizing of its banking sector. Should the nation have to borrow excessive funds for its banks, it could push its sovereign debt to 125 percent of GDP by 2013, making it improbable that its debt could be stabilized.

The nation, under austerity measures, would have to slash public spending by $20 billion over four years. Cuts of nearly 15 percent would be applied to the country's social welfare budget, saving $4 billion each year. Nearly 25,000 public jobs were to be eliminated, saving about $1.6 billion a year. Child benefits and other social welfare payments were reduced and the minimum wage, in November $11.59 an hour, was cut by $1.34. Health care spending would be reduced by more than $1.9 billion.

By mid-November, Ireland had implemented cuts approximating 10 percent of its GDP. Public-sector employees saw their salaries fall by 13 percent over the past three years, with plans to eliminate nearly 25,000 additional jobs, slash welfare spending, and lower the minimum wage. A new property tax would be introduced, water charges imposed, and the tax base expanded to bring in lower-income earners. Following a strenuous weekend session ending November 28, the EU sealed a 67 billion euro (about $90 billion) bailout of Ireland. It will also replace, in 2013, the 440 billion (euros) fund created in May 2010 that was used to help Ireland. As debt relief is excluded before 2013, the nation faces several years of mounting debt and budget austerity.

On December 7, Ireland unveiled sweeping budget cuts on its projected four-year road to financial recovery. A total of $7.99 billion in cuts were made, allowing the financial aid packages from the International Monetary Fund and the European Union to follow. Leaders defended the 12.5 percent corporation tax rate. Taxes would increase for workers to approximately 60 percent from 45 percent. The 2011 budget widened tax brackets, reduced tax credits, and cut social welfare payments. Irish lawmakers voted on December 15 to accept $90.4 billion in loans from the EU and the IMF, utilizing the funds to stabilize Ireland's banks and provide its exchequer with funds while high borrowing costs kept the nation locked out of capital markets.

In 2011, housing prices were expected to hit bottom, with a low likely at about half the 2007 peak. Its economy should grow a bit in 2011. At the same time, the citizens are furious that the cost of bailing out their banks, which, at anywhere between 25 percent and 50 percent of GDP, are enormous. It was projected that Ireland's economy would only grow by 0.2 percent in 2011. The nation's GDP growth was 0.2 percent, with a GDP of $194 billion, an inflation rate of 0.6 percent, and a GDP per head at $46,750.

By year's end, the government was forced to take over another of the country's ailing banks (the Allied Irish Banks—the fourth Irish lender to be taken over by the government). In 2009, the bank received aid and in December another $4.85 billion was invested, leaving the government with a 90 percent ownership stake. Not since the emigration wave of the 1980s has the nation experienced an exodus of young people seeking employment elsewhere. It is expected to lose 100,000 people from April 2010 to April 2012, or about 1,000 people per week (2 percent of the population).

The Allied Irish Banks announced on April 12, 2011, a record annual loss of $15.1 billion for 2010 and that would reduce its workforce by 13 percent. On July 12, Moody's Investors Service demoted Ireland's bonds to junk status. It reduced Ireland's debt rating by one notch to BAl, from BAA3, its lowest investment-grade level. The Bank of Ireland, the only Irish lender to escape effective nationalization, reported sharply reduced first-half losses. For the six months through June 30, 2011, the bank reported an underlying loss of $1.04 billion.

By December, Ireland had some small success in bringing in new tax revenue, pulled out of recession, and its bill for bank bailouts was lower than originally thought. Its economy was expected to expand 1.1 percent in 2011, ending a three-year slump. Unemployment remains at 14 percent.

See also EUROPEAN UNION, EUROZONE; GREECE; INTERNATIONAL MONETARY FUND; PORTUGAL.

IRON CHANCELLOR. See MERKEL, ANGELA.

IRS. See INTERNAL REVENUE SERVICE.

ISRAEL. Positive growth in the second quarter of 2009, albeit slight, has marked the start of recovery. Expectation of indirect tax increases prompted a burst in car sales. Also, government spending increased rapidly, reflecting a pick-up from previously constrained expenditure. Growth rates of nondurable consumption, investment, and exports all turned positive. Economic activity is expected to pick up throughout the projection period. Underlying inflationary pressures are likely to remain muted, but the risks are on the upside. The latest government budget limited the rise in the deficit but relies excessively on short-term measures to achieve deficit and spending goals, and scheduled cuts in corporate and personal taxation for 2010 are untimely. The Bank of Israel has moved early toward a less expansionary stance, but its continued foreign-exchange interventions risk bringing additional inflationary pressures and damaging policy credibility and coherence.

As a nation increasingly dependent on exporting high-tech equipment, Israel's economy has suffered since the meltdown began. On August 24, 2009, Israel's central bank raised its key interest rate to 0.75 percent from 0.5 percent. The Bank of Israel became the first central bank to raise its key interest rate, showing that the global economy was emerging from the Great Recession. In mid-November 2009, Israel's central bank raised its key interest rate to 1 percent after the bank pegged the nation's inflation in October at 2.9 percent. The government reported that the economy grew for the second consecutive quarter, with third-quarter growth at 2.2 percent.

Israel's economy had grown at least 4 percent a year from 2004 to 2008, with only a 7.8 percent unemployment rate. Then, in the second quarter 2010, the economy grew at an annualized rate of 4.7 percent, with inflation falling in July from 2.4 percent to 1.8 percent, the lowest level in nearly three years.

In 2011, the government promised to lower the corporate tax by 1 percent to 24 percent. The nation's GDP was projected to grow by 3.4 percent, with a GDP of $227 billion, an inflation rate of 2.4 percent, and a GDP per head of $29,410. By the summer, protestors from around the country marched over issues dealing with inequality between rich and poor, inadequate middle-class housing, subsidies, military investments, and so forth.

ISSUES OF STOCKS AND BONDS. In 2008, tumbled 38 percent to $4.71 trillion.

IT. *See* INFORMATION TECHNOLOGY

ITALY. The severe recession in Italy started earlier than elsewhere but activity rebounded in the third quarter. Improved financial conditions have helped rebuild confidence and bolster domestic demand. The saving ratio, estimated to have risen substantially in 2009, is projected to fall back only slightly; consumption will be a more significant factor in growth during 2011. Further support to exports will come from the recovery in world trade. Higher unit labor costs, despite some falls in wage costs, and the oil price upturn will moderate the decline in inflation, even as unemployment rises somewhat further. Given high public debt, Italy did not introduce a large-scale fiscal stimulus. Nonetheless, with cyclically weak revenues, the deficit exceeds 5 percent of GDP and debt is set to increase to 120 percent of GDP by 2011. Significant fiscal consolidation efforts will thus be required from 2011 onward as growth picks up.

At the end of November 2008, Italy presented an economic stimulus package totaling €80 billion, or $103 billion. The government would also make a one-time cash payment to Italy's poorest families, freeze tolls on highways, and require banks to limit mortgage rates as part of its plan. Italian industrial production fell in the final month of 2008, dropping 2.5 percent from November, adjusted for the season and for the number of working days, as output of intermediate and investment goods plunged.

Italy's economy contracted 2.4 percent in the first quarter of 2009 from the previous quarter, the largest decline since data was collected in 1980. On December 7, the Italian Parliament approved $33.3 billion in budget cuts over two years. With one of Europe's highest levels of debt, equivalent to 118 percent of GDP, budget reductions were required. The nation's productivity was 24 percent less than that of the United States and 10 percent less than the average of the fifteen core countries of the European Union. Over the past decade, GDP increased at a small annual average of 0.54 percent and forecasts are for just a 1 percent rise in 2010 after a 5.1 percent fall in 2009. The nation's GDP growth was 0.6 percent, with a GDP of $1,888 billion, an inflation rate of 1.2 percent, and a GDP per head of $31,320. By year's end, the Parliament gave final approval to an overhaul of its university system, with a $1.3 billion funding cut for the nation's state-run universities. Then, on June 30, the government released a plan purporting to balance its budget by 2014 with at least $57.5 billion in fiscal savings. Public debt is 120 percent of GDP.

By mid-July 2011, Italy showed a low budget deficit of 4.6 percent and without a need to shore up its banks. But, its economy hadn't expanded in ten years and its debt-to-GDP ratio of 119 percent in 2010 was second only to that of Greece. Italy was expected to remain well above 100 percent of GDP for years, with its interest bill more than 10 percent of government revenue. On July 13, the upper house of Parliament approved a $56 billion package of austerity measured to balance the nation's budget by 2014. Then, on Friday, July 15, the lower house of Parliament approved the government's $56 billion deficit-reduction package.

By August, Prime Minister Berlusconi announced his plan for austerity:

- Make it a constitutional duty to balance budget.
- Balance its budget in 2013 rather than in 2014 as previously planned.
- Loosen labor-market regulations to encourage investment.
- Liberalize economic activities.

On August 12, the prime minister unveiled measures to balance the nation's budget by 2013, one year before originally planned. He would cut about $64 billion in public spending. By mid-August, there were two million young Italians without work. Nearly 28 percent of Italians between fifteen and twenty-four were unemployed. Around 13 percent of young Italians who had jobs before 2008 have lost them because of the downturn, compared with only 3 percent in France and Germany. Then, on August 29, the government announced its plans to alter its austerity package of $65.4 billion with proposals to cut layers of local government and require some citizens to delay their retirement. On September 7, the government moved to change its austerity package. Proposals included a mix of tax increases (value-added tax to 21 percent from 20 percent), a rise of retirement age for women in the private sector to sixty-five from sixty years of age in 2014, and pension overhauls that were part of the $64.15 billion austerity package. With its national debt at about $2.7 trillion, or 120 percent of GDP, the highest rate of debt in the seventeen-member eurozone after Greece, new measures were needed. This latest effort was intended to avoid a sovereign-debt crisis and shore up the euro. By early September 2011, Italy's Finance Ministry held discussion, with China's sovereign-wealth fund to purchase large amounts of Italian bonds. Standard & Poor's Rating Services on September 19 lowered Italy's sovereign-debt rating by one notch to A, five steps above junk territory though still considered an investment grade. Fitch and Moody's downgraded Italy in October to A+.

Following the resignation of Berlusconi, the new prime minister, Mario Monti, in early November urged the reinvigorating of the country's anemic economy and preventing the collapse of the euro. He urged further measures to supplement the austerity package of $81 billion approved in September and to deal with Italy's ability to service its 1.9 trillion euro public debt. Almost 57 percent of Italian debt is retained by Italian banks, insurance firms, and individuals. Those holdings ensured the slowing of capital from the country. Italy's ten-year bond yield climbed again to nearly 6.8 percent.

In early December, Prime Minister Monti outlined his first steps in his austerity program to include:

a. A one-time 1.5 percent tax on funds repatriated under Italy's tax amnesty.
b. A 2 percent rise in value-added tax.
c. A rise in the retirement age for women working in the private sector.
d. As much as 2 billion euros in annual tax breaks for companies that boost hiring.

On December 14, 2011, Italy's borrowing costs climbed to a euro-era record following an auction of five-year debt, paying 6.47 percent. On December 16, the Parliament approved the prime minister's multibillion euro-austerity package, which purports to generate $26 billion in cost savings through a combination of tax increases and spending cuts. Then, on December 22, the Italian Senate passed a new budget plan calling for $40 billion of cuts and combining austerity measured, such as a property tax on first homes and the increase of retirement ages, with efforts to stimulate the economy and stabilize the euro. The goal is to eliminate Italy's deficit by 2013.

On December 29, the prime minister allowed the government to pay a sharply lower yield of 5.2 percent for borrowings due in 2014, but the yield investors demand for ten-year bonds was 6.98 percent, somewhat financially unsuitable.

See also CHINA; FERRE, FIAT.

J

JAGUAR. *See* TATA MOTORS.

JAL. *See* JAPAN AIRLINES.

JANUS CAPITAL GROUP. Fourth-quarter 2010 profit climbed 78 percent. Assets increased $167.3 billion from 2009 and were ahead of third-quarter total of $155.2 billion. Profit was posted at $65.9 million.

JAPAN. The severe recession triggered by the global crisis has bottomed out, thanks in part to a rebound in exports, although production remains well below capacity. In addition, fiscal stimulus is partially offsetting the impact of falling unemployment and wages on domestic demand. Growth is projected to pick up gradually to around 2 percent in 2011, due in part to the new government's plan to increase public spending. Nevertheless, the unemployment rate is likely to stay around 5.5 percent through 2011 and deflation will persist. The Bank of Japan should fight deflation through a strong commitment to keeping interest rates at their very low current levels and to implementing quantitative measures effectively until underlying inflation is firmly positive. Additional fiscal stimulus is not warranted given the expected pick-up in output growth, as well as Japan's large budget deficit and high public debt ratio. The government should thus finance its planned rise in public expenditure through cuts in other spending programs. It is essential to develop a credible and detailed medium-term fiscal consolidation program and to implement it once a recovery is firmly in place. Such a program should include fundamental tax reform, accompanied by structural reforms, particularly in the service sector, to improve living standards in the face of a shrinking working-age population.

On August 31, 2008, Japan unveiled a $106 billion economic-stimulus package that included tax cuts and loan guarantees. The Nikkei—Japan's stock market—plunged on October 27 to its lowest level in twenty-six years and overall fell by half in 2008. In early November, the Japanese central bank cut its benchmark interest rate for the first time in seven years. The overnight lending rate between banks was lowered from 0.5 to 0.3 percent, reducing borrowing costs in order to rekindle growth in the country. It was also aimed at easing a growing credit crunch in Japan. The world's second-largest economy officially slipped into recession on November 17, hurt by weak export growth and steep cuts in corporate spending during the deepening global slowdown. Japan's GDP shrank at an annual rate of 0.4 percent from July to September after declining a revised 3.7 percent in the previous quarter.

Exports fell for the first time in nearly seven years, dashing hopes that Japan and the Southeast Asian region would be able to help the global economy during the credit crisis. Exports declined 7.7 percent in October, with exports to China alone falling 4 percent, the first decline since 2002. The Bank of Japan announced on December 2 that it took emergency measures to ease an acute squeeze in corporate financing that threatened to push the largest Asian economy deeper into recession. Steps included a program that allowed commercial banks to borrow unlimited funds at low interest rates from the central bank, provided that they had sufficient collateral to guarantee the loans. China's slowdown was also having considerable impact on Japan's economy, as Japan's economy shrank at an annualized rate of 1.8 percent in the three months prior to September, far worse than expected. On December 11, Japan's prime minister announced an emergency stimulus package to jolt the economy by spending trillions of yen to create jobs, increase business loans, and help laid-off workers. The value of the package was approximately $250 billion, which included tax cuts for homeowners and companies that build or purchase new factories and equipment, as well as grants to local governments to support job creation. Manufacturing in Japan continued to decline as the country suffered its sharpest fall in decades, and total manufacturing output was at its lowest level in seven years.

Industrial output plunged 8.1 percent in November, the nation's largest decline on record. Manufacturing output, as reported on December 25, indicated an expected drop of 11.1 percent. Exports in November had dropped 26.7 percent from a year earlier, indicating the worsening condition of Japan's battered economy. Exports tumbled by a record 35 percent for December 2008. Japan posted a trade deficit of $3.56 billion in December, wider than the 225-billion-yen deficit from the previous month. Overall exports totaled 4.83 trillion yen in December, down from 7.43 trillion yen in 2007. For all of 2008, Japan's trade surplus shrank 80 percent to 2.16 trillion yen, as exports fell 3.4 percent and imports grew 7.9 percent.

In this downturn, Japan's unemployment was rapidly rising. Projections were for 1.5 million job losses by the end of 2010, lifting the unemployment rate from 4 percent in 2008 to over 6 percent projected for 2009. The world's second-largest economy deteriorated at its worst pace since the oil crisis of the 1970s, damaged by declining exports and anemic home spending. The nation's real GDP shrank at an annual rate of 12.7 percent from October to December 2008 after contracting for the two final quarters of the year. When compared with the third quarter of 2008, the economy plummeted 3.3 percent. The fourth-quarter results were Japan's worst quarterly drop since its economy contracted at an annual pace of 13.1 percent in the first three months of 1974.

Japan, the largest holder of U.S. treasury bonds, was in the midst of its worst recession in fifty years. Exports dropped, industrial production was plummeting 30 percent from a year before, and its GDP was falling 12 percent in 2009. Industrial output plunged by a record 10 percent in January 2009, further evidence that the country's worst recession in decades was intensifying. The government called for another round of public spending to aid its ailing economy, putting the government in conflict with Europe, which was resisting additional deficit spending programs to help pull the global economy out of its meltdown.

Japan's exports fell at a record rate in February. Demand for Japanese goods continued to shrink in overseas markets, including the United States and China, with overall exports falling a record 49 percent, the fifth straight month of decline. That, along with a 43 percent drop in imports, gave Japan a trade surplus for the first time in five months. Japan's GDP grew at an annual rate of 4.9 percent in the three months ending in March, with industrial expansion of 1.2 percent. At the end of March, Japan's parliament enacted a record $897.16 billion budget for its next fiscal year, paving the way for the government to carry out its third stimulus package and accelerate work on its next steps to revive growth. On March 30, the government announced that it was prepared to implement new stimulus steps that would exceed 2 percent of its GDP. Greater concern existed that without further efforts of economic input from the government, Japan's GDP would shrink by 5.8 percent in 2009, far worse than contractions of 2.6 percent in the United States and 3.2 percent for the eurozone.

A new stimulus package was introduced by the government on April 10, with spending of at least $100 billion as the nation grappled with the worst recession since World War II. The package would work in five areas: creating a safety net for workers who do not have the status of "permanent" staff, aiding corporate financing, increasing spending on solar-power systems, lowering public anxiety over medical and nursing care services, and revitalizing regional economics. By early April, Japan's prime minister ordered the nation's largest supplemental budget, containing more than $100 billion of fresh spending, to boost the world's second-largest economy. It would exceed 2 percent of its GDP. On April 27, the government said that the economy was expected to contract by a record 3.3 percent in the current fiscal year. The new projection was much more negative than the 1.5 percent decline reported a month earlier, which at the time was the worst performance since the government began measuring growth in 1955. Japan was expected to face declining prices for the next two fiscal years and will face a protracted stretch of deflation.

Its GDP shrank 4 percent in the first quarter from the previous one. The latest reading translates into an annualized contraction of 15.2 percent, the worst performance since 1955. At the end of May, Japan enacted a record $143.73 billion extra budget, enabling the government to execute new stimulus steps to support an economy that improved mildly after six months of shrinking at a double-digit pace. The package contained spending and tax cuts valued at 3 percent of Japan's annual economic output. Unemployment in Japan rose to 5.2 percent in May from 5 percent in April. Japan's economy grew for the first time in five quarters, pulling the economy out of its longest recession since World War II. The nation's real GDP grew 0.9 percent in the second quarter from the first quarter, an annual pace of expansion of 3.7 percent.

Despite a 1.9 percent increase in industrial output in July 2009, deflation and job losses had become a twin blow for Japan. Deflation worsened while the jobless rate rose to a record 5.7 percent that month, a 0.3 percent increase from the previous month. As prices dropped, companies laid off workers, up 830,000 workers from the year before. On August 31, 2009, Japan's opposition party won an overwhelming victory and promised to do away with American-style, pro-market reforms in order to lead the nation out of its long slump. Japan was determined to avoid using market forces to raise productivity.

On September 11, the government announced that its economy grew a revised 0.6 percent in the second quarter 2009. Gross public debt mushroomed in Japan during years of stimulus spending, and in 2009 it passed 187 percent of the Japanese economy. That debt could soon reach twice the size of the $5 trillion economy, the largest, in real terms, the world has ever seen. (Japan's outstanding debt is as big as the economies of Britain, France, and Germany combined.)

Deflation continued to worry the government. Consumer prices fell for three consecutive years. The country's central bank projected a decline of 1.5 percent for the current fiscal year and 1 percent for 2010. The country's central bank predicted the economy would remain in deflation over the next two fiscal years. On October 30, 2009, the government indicated that its core consumer price index fell 2.3 percent on year in September, the seventh straight fall. It predicted real GDP to climb by 1.2 percent in fiscal year 2010 and grow by 2.1 percent in 2011.

Japan's economy rebounded in the third quarter 2009. The government reported that its GDP growth was 1.2 percent over the previous quarter, a 4.8 percent annualized pace. It was the country's second consecutive quarter of expansion, the fastest growth since early 2007. The official end to the recession in Japan was declared. During the third quarter 2009, the domestic demand deflator—a measure of changes in prices of goods and services except for exports and imports—fell 2.6 percent, its fastest pace since 1958. It was expected that Japan's national debt could rise to more than 200 percent of its GNP in 2011 from 170 percent in 2007, the highest among rich nations. On December 1, Japan's central bank announced that it would inject as much as $115.68 billion into its economy already facing deflation and a soaring currency. The following day, the government planned to raise a stimulus effort that could total more than $80 billion. The program would finance measures such as loan guarantees for small firms and incentives for consumers to purchase more energy-efficient electronics. Not willing to tolerate zero inflation or falling prices, on December 18, 2009, the Bank of Japan left its interest rate near zero. On December 30, the government released a draft economic strategy that targeted an average annual growth rate of more than 2 percent over the coming ten years. Japan's economy grew at an annualized rate of 4.6 percent in the final quarter of 2009 as a rebound in her exports helped alleviate continuing concerns over a prolonged recession.

Unemployment rose to 5 percent in March 2010 from 4.9 percent the month before. Consumer prices fell by 1.1 percent, which was Japan's fourteenth consecutive month of deflation. By May, Japan's economy was expanding its exports to rapidly growing Asian neighbors. GDP, adjusted for prices, grew at an annualized rate of 4.9 percent during the first quarter 2010. Japan was showing an enormous recovery from the recession. By summer 2010, profits at the nation's 559 major listed firms surged by 46 percent to $44 billion. This was a fourfold increase from 2009. In August, it was reported that China's economy, $1,339 trillion for the last three months ending in June, surpassed Japan's GDP of $1,288 trillion for the same period. Therefore, China became the world's second-largest economy after the United States. The Bank of Japan launched a bond-buying program on October 5 to spend about $60 billion to purchase government bonds, corporate IOUs, real estate investment trust funds, and exchange-traded funds.

Before the Great Recession of 2007, Japan commenced a period of deflation and reversal of economic fortune. The country fell into a relentless decline and was trapped with low growth and a spiral of price reductions. In 2009, the public had been suffering from a crisis of confidence and appeared during the meltdown period to be preparing for a slow withdrawal from the global stage. By 2010, Japan faced the world's largest government debt, around 200 percent of GDP, a shrinking population, and rising rates of poverty and suicide.

Japan's auto sales for October 2010 were down 23 percent. Japan's economy grew at a revised 1.1 percent in the third quarter 2010. The revised GDP translated into annualized growth of 4.5 percent. In mid-December, the government announced that it would cut its corporate income tax rate by five percentage to forty percentage points in order to shore up its economy. It was expected that this action would increase the GDP by 2.6 percentage points, or $172 billion. Growth would fall back to 1.3 percent in 2011 from 2.9 percent in 2010. The nation's GDP growth was 1.3 percent, with a GDP of $5,621 billion, an inflation rate of 0.3 percent, and a GDP per head of $44,440.

On January 25, 2011, the Bank of Japan decided to keep its easy monetary policy unchanged, leaving the unsecured overnight call night rate in a 0.0–0.1 percent range. Dramatically, on February 14, Japan reported that its economy shrank at a 1.1 percent annual rate for the last quarter of 2010, while China's GDP surged 9.8 percent from the year before. Japan's full-year GDP was $5.47 trillion, about 7 percent smaller than the $5.88 trillion GDP in China. Combined with China, Japan's GDP was less than the 2010 U.S. GDP at $14.66 trillion. Overtaking Germany in 1967 as the second largest economy in the world, Japan is now the third largest, after the United States. February 2011 automobile sales fell 14 percent, marking the sixth straight month of decline in Japan.

Following the March 2011 earthquake, tsunami, and nuclear fallout, Japan's economic ties with the world, especially with Asia would be strained. In addition, Japan is the largest source of foreign direct investment for many Asian nations, the generator of tourist revenue, and a primary source of remittance revenue for some countries. Within five days of these disasters, Japan's stock index fell about 17.5 percent. With rolling power cuts, many manufacturing plants closed, with significant production losses; for example, Toyota in the first five days lost output of 40,000 vehicles. In addition, Japan is a key supplier of advanced components, especially to Asian nations, that specialize in the final assembly phase of manufacturing. China depends on Japan for 13 percent of its imports, largely capital goods such as machine tools and electronic parts for manufacturing. On March 21, it was estimated that the cost of damage from the earthquake and tsunami would lead to economic losses as high as $300 billion. It was estimated that at least half of Japan's auto production would still be closed by early May. With the world's third-largest economy, Japan's share of exports by selected categories are as follows:

Japan exports, in billions		Japan's share of world exports
Automotive products	$171.011	3.9 percent
Integrated circuits	$44.61	10.7 percent
Other machinery	$166.04	8.5 percent
Iron and steel	$44.11	7.7 percent
Scientific, optical instruments	$21.51	7.0 percent
Total merchandise	**$781.41**	**5.0 percent**

On April 13, the government acknowledged that its economy would be significantly impacted by the earthquake and tsunami in March, at about $300 billion. Other projections showed a falling from 1.6 percent growth to 1.4 percent in 2011. Industrial recovery climbed by 5.7 percent in July. The government planned to spend about $167 billion over five years in expectations of a swift recovery from the recession. Japan's bond credit rating was cut by Moody's on August 23 to AA3 from AA2. By November, Japan's economy had significantly recovered. Its GDP surged 6 percent in the third quarter. However, exports fell 3.7 percent to a trade deficit of $3.56 billion. By year's end 2011, Japan reported an $8.8 billion trade deficit, the largest-ever shortfall for that month as exports continued to drop.

In mid-January 2012, the Japanese government announced that the country recorded its first annual trade deficit since 1980, with prolonged deficits to grow over the coming years. For the first eleven months of 2011, Japan noted a trade deficit of $30 billion compared to a surplus for all of 2010. Exports fell 2.7 percent in 2011, the first contraction in two years. Imported rose 12.0 percent, marking the second straight year of gain. Industrial production climbed 4 percent in December from November.

See also ASIA; CANON; CHINA; DEBT; DOUBLE-DECKER FUNDS; GENERAL MOTORS; HONDA; INTERNATIONAL MONETARY FUND; JAPAN AIRLINES; MANUFACTURING; MERGERS AND ACQUISITIONS; MITSUBISHI; NIKKEI; PLAZA ACCORD; PROPERTY (2011); RENAULT; TOSHIBA; TOYOTA; WORLD TRADE; YEN; ZOMBIES.

JAPAN AIRLINES (JAL). On September 15, 2009, Japan Airlines announced that it would slash its workforce by 14 percent by the end of 2011. The company was planning to reduce its 48,000-strong workforce (at one time it had 54,000 workers) by 6,800 employees. The airline needed as much as $1.65 billion in new funds. In its fiscal first quarter ending in June 2009, the airline lost more than $1 billion. Management predicted a net loss of $691 million for the full business year.

On October 29, the government set the stage for a large bailout of the airline, urging the company to seek state support. The airline posted a loss of $357 million in the quarter. This compared to a $448 million profit in 2008. In the quarter reported in November 2009, sales declined by 26 percent to $4.8 billion. At the end of November 2009, Japan Airlines had obtained government approval to receive up to $1.1 billion in emergency loans aimed at preventing the firm from grounding flights. By year's end 2009, JAL was still considering an out-of-court restructuring with a bankruptcy protection filing on the horizon should it fail to persuade more than two-thirds of about 8,800 retirees to accept a benefits-reduction plan.

The airline, which filed for bankruptcy protection in January 2010, announced in June that it would require an additional $1.1 billion in financial aid. The carrier in September announced cuts to be greater than earlier stated, with refinancing of $3.5 billion in debt by the end of March 2011. It planned to lower its workforce by about 16,000 people to approximately 32,000. Japan Airlines announced on March 28, 2011, that it had ended its bankruptcy protection, paid off its creditors, and secured more than $3 billion in new loans and capital. Japan's third-quarter output was lowered to 1.4 percent as announced on December 9, 2011.

See also AMERICAN AIRLINES; JAPAN.

JAPAN EARTHQUAKE, TSUNAMI, AND NUCLEAR CRISES. *See* JAPAN.

JAPANESE YEN. *See* PLAZA ACCORD; YEN.

J.C. PENNEY. By January 2009, same-store sales within its department store division had fallen 8.1 percent from the previous year. On February 20, the company reported a 51 percent drop in fourth-quarter profits as customers reduced spending on clothing and other discretionary items. Sales fell almost 10 percent to $5.76 billion from $6.39 billion, with sales at stores open at least a year falling 10.8 percent. J.C. Penney had a flat, no-growth fiscal second quarter 2009 and posted a loss of $1 million. The retailer reduced inventories by 12 percent in the second quarter. On November 13, 2009, the company reported a 78 percent drop in fiscal third-quarter profit, posting a profit of $27 million compared with $124 million the year before. Sales declined 3.2 percent to $4.12 billion.

The Plano, Texas, firm reported that earnings more than doubled in its fiscal first quarter 2010, with a profit of $60 million Gross margin, or profit after deducting merchandise cost, increased to 41.4 percent of sales from 40.5 percent. The retailer posted a 1.9 percent fall in sales in November 2010.

For January 2011, the retailer reported a 1.2 percent decline in sales. Then, in February, the retailer reported a 6.4 percent growth. In mid-August, management reported a flat second-quarter profit, with net income of $14 million. Revenue dropped to $3.91 billion from $3.94 billion. The retailer by year's end reported a 2 percent decline.

See also RETAILING.

JEWELRY. About 1,500 mostly small jewelry stores closed in 2008, with larger stores also shutting hundred of branches. The recession as reported in February 2009 pummeled jewelers. The Christmas sales season usually accounted for an average of 30 percent of their annual revenue. Sales of luxury items, including jewelry, fell 34 percent during Christmas 2008 compared to a year earlier.

By the end of the holiday shopping season in 2010, jewelry sales increased 8.4 percent from the previous year and improved further in 2011.

See also BULGARI; LUXURY GOODS; RETAILING; SWATCH GROUP; TIFFANY; ZALE.

JIABAO, WEN. *See* CHINA.

"JINGLE MAIL." When home values fall far below the mortgage amounts and developers give up on properties and opt to default because they believe it makes good business sense.

JOB BANKS. The era when factory workers from General Motors and Chrysler could collect nearly their full salaries after they lost their jobs ended in February 2009. Both automakers announced the end of their job bank program. Ford Motor Company, which had not borrowed money from the government, did not announce changes to its job bank.

JOB CREATION. On December 8, 2009, President Obama pressed for a job creation program to place an additional $50 billion toward infrastructure spending, utilizing unspent Troubled Asset Relief Program funds. U.S. House of Representatives leaders unveiled a $75 billion job creation package on December 14, 2009.

See also AMERICAN JOBS ACT (PROPOSED); U.S. CENSUS.

JOB FOOTPRINT. What an employee is expected to do. Tasks have increased by a third since the beginning of the Great Recession. Two-thirds of workers report they are putting in unpaid overtime, claiming that this pace is unsustainable.

JOB GROWTH. *See* HIRING; UNEMPLOYMENT.

JOBLESS (BENEFITS) CLAIMS. On September 22, 2009, the House of Representatives voted to extend unemployment insurance benefits for jobless citizens in two dozen states by thirteen weeks. On October 8, the government noted that first-time claims for unemployment insurance fell to a seasonally adjusted 521,000 from the previous week's upwardly revised total of 554,000. For the week ending December 12, 2009, jobless benefits claims rose 7,000 to a seasonally adjusted 480,000. The four-week average of new claims, which purported to smooth volatility in the data, dropped 5,250 to 467,000—its fifteenth consecutive fall.

The number of U.S. workers filing new claims for benefits surprisingly increased and in early April 2010 rose 18,000 to 460,000 for the week ending April 3. The number of people filing new claims for unemployment benefits rose in early May 2010 the largest amount in three months. Applications for benefits rose to 471,000 in the week, up by 25,000 from the previous week.

The total number of new claims was the highest since claims stood at 480,000 on April 10. In the third week of August, jobless claims climbed to the highest level in nine months by 12,000 from the week before to 500,000 in the week ending August 14. In mid-September, the jobless claims fell by 3,000 to 450,000, the lowest level in two months.

Not surprisingly, as jobless benefits increase, unemployment rises. Unemployment at the end of 2009 would have been nearly half a percentage point lower—9.6 percent instead of 10 percent—if jobless benefits hadn't been extended beyond their usual twenty-six weeks to as much as ninety-nine weeks. With the signing by the president on December 17 of the tax-cuts bill, he won a thirteen-month extension of federal jobless benefits. At year's end 2010, jobless claims hit a 2.5 year low. New weekly claims fell 34,000 to a seasonally adjusted rate of 388,000, the lowest since July 2008.

At the end of the first week in January 2011, jobless claims rose slightly. Initial unemployment claims rose by 18,000 to 409,000 for the week ending January 1. Over the past seven weeks, jobless claims fell seven times. Then, in mid-January, there was a fall by 37,000 to a seasonally adjusted rate of 404,000 jobless claims. New jobless claims in the last week of February fell to the lowest level since early 2008, dropping 20,000 to 368,000. However, in mid-May, new jobless claims had eased, with a decrease of 29,000 new filings to a seasonally adjusted 409,000. In the first week of August, jobless claims for benefits fell to a four-month low. State unemployment benefit requests fell 7,000 to a seasonally adjusted 395,000.

By mid-December 2011, the number of U.S. workers filing for jobless benefits fell to its lowest point since May 2008, suggesting that the labor market may finally be gaining strength. Initial claims for unemployment insurance fell by 19,000 to 366,000. By year's end, the jobless claims rate fell by 15,000 to a seasonally adjusted 372,000. Private employers added 325,000 in December.

See also OVERTIME; TAX CUTS; TROUBLED ASSET RELIEF PROGRAM; UNEMPLOYMENT.

JOBLESSNESS. *See* UNEMPLOYMENT.

JOBLESS RATE. By May 2010, the jobless rate in thirty-four U.S. states and the capital fell. Six states reported that unemployment had increased, while the rate remained unchanged in ten states.

The black teen jobless rate jumped to 46.5 percent from 39.2 percent in August 2011. The increase of 400,000 in "involuntary part-time workers," or those who would work full time if they could find a job, was the biggest since 2009. The number of citizens filing for initial jobless claims fell by 5,000 in mid-November to 388,000, the third consecutive week of declines, and a slowdown in layoffs was also reported.

See also AMERICAN JOBS ACT (PROPOSED); DIET; JOBLESS CLAIMS; UNEMPLOYMENT.

JOB LOSS. *See* UNEMPLOYMENT.

JOB OPENINGS. In August 2008, there were 4.65 million job openings in the country. The number of U.S. job openings sank below 3 million in January 2009, the lowest level since its series began in late 2000 and a key reason why the unemployment rate had risen sharply to 8.1 percent. By comparison, new job openings averaged more than 4 million per month from 2005 through 2007. The number of U.S. job openings shrank to a seasonally adjusted 2.5 million in October from about 2.6 million the prior month, while the number of hires fell to 3.9 million, falling below the 4 million mark for the first time since June 2009. There were 3.2 million private-sector job openings at the end of the month, up from 2.3 million a year earlier but well below the 3.7 million in October 2007, just before the Great Recession began.

By mid-2011, competition for new jobs was huge. There were 4.7 people seeking work for each job opening. One year prior, there were more than five applicants per opening. Throughout 2007 before the Great Recession, there were fewer than two unemployed people per job listing. Government figures released on October 11 indicated that job openings fell in August for the first time in four months to approximately 3.1 million, with unemployed people climbing to nearly 14 million. There were 4.6 job seekers for each opening in the month, up from 4.3 in July. By 2012, 200,000 new job openings were filled.

See also HIRING; TAX CREDITS.

JOB PRESERVATION. *See* SOUTH KOREA.

JOBS BILL. On October 11, 2011, the Senate blocked the president's $447 billion jobs bill, with forty-eight voting against it. Then, on October 16, following overwhelming Senate approval, the House of Representatives approved a measure that would repeal a tax-withholding requirement on government contractors and provide tax incentives for firms that hire veterans, providing the president his first jobs bill.

JOBS DOWNTURN. *See* JOBLESS (BENEFITS) CLAIMS; UNEMPLOYMENT.

JOBS PLAN. *See* AMERICAN JOBS ACT (PROPOSED).

JOBS PROGRAM. *See* TROUBLED ASSET RELIEF PROGRAM.

JOB STARTS. *See* AMERICAN JOBS ACT (PROPOSED); JOB CREATION.

JOBS, STEVE. On August 24, 2011, Apple's chief executive quit. "I have always said if there ever came a day when I could no longer meet my duties and expectations as Apple's CEO, I would be the first to let you know. Unfortunately, that day has come."

See also APPLE.

JOHNSON & JOHNSON (J&J). The weak economy continued to hurt the health care company's results in 2009. First-quarter 2009 profit declined 2.5 percent and net income was $3.5 billion, or $1.26 a share, compared with $3.6 billion, or $1.26 a share, a year earlier. Sales had dropped 7.2 percent to $15.02 billion from $16.19 billion the year before. Johnson & Johnson's second-quarter 2009 profit fell 3.6 percent, with sales harmed by unfavorable currency rates, competition from generic drugs, and tighter consumer spending. Sales fell 7.4 percent to $15.24 billion from $16.45 billion. Net income of $3.21 billion fell from $3.33 billion one year earlier. On November 1, 2009, Johnson & Johnson announced that it would eliminate as many as 8,200 jobs, or 7 percent of its workforce. On April 20, J&J reported an increase in first-quarter profit by 29 percent to $4.53 billion. International sales rose 14.4 percent.

In April 2010, J&J reported a 29 percent increase in first-quarter profit. First-quarter earnings were $4.5 billion, up from $3.5 billion the year before. J&J management reported on July 20 that its second-quarter revenue was flat, with a 7.5 percent increase in net income to $3.45 billion, up from $3.21 billion a year earlier. J&J's second-quarter profit climbed 7.5 percent, with its net income rising to $3.45 billion. On October 19, management noted a third-quarter profit of $3.42 billion, up 2.2 percent from $3.35 billion. J&J reported on October 18 a 6.3 percent fall in third-quarter profit, earning $3.2 billion, with sales climbing 6.8 percent to $16 billion.

On January 24, 2012, J&J reported an 89 percent fall in fourth-quarter profit of $218 million. Sales climbed 3.9 percent to $16.26 billion.

JOINT SELECT COMMITTEE ON DEFICIT REDUCTION. *See* DEBT DEAL; DEFICIT-REDUCTION COMMITTEE.

JONES, ALFRED WINSLOW. *See* HEDGE FUNDS.

JONES APPAREL GROUP. Announced a detailed cost-cutting plan to deal with slumping retail sales. Had a fourth-quarter 2008 loss and an $840 million goodwill write-down. Cut its quarterly dividend 64 percent to five cents a share while also reducing a capital spending program from $70 million in 2008 to $45 million for 2009.

See also RETAILING.

JORDAN. In 2010, real economic growth was 3.5 percent, with forecasts for 2011 at over 4 percent. Inflation was 5 percent in 2010 and forecast at over

6 percent for 2011. Unemployment averaged 13 percent in 2010, with youth joblessness above 30 percent and still on the verge of exploding. During the Arab uprising in spring 2011, the king moved fast, ordering the government to approve a special package of measures reducing prices of basic fuels and foods, increasing the salaries of government workers and security forces creating new jobs, and appointed a new prime minister. The king and government are considering membership in the Gulf Cooperation Council of six nations. The GCC has become the most important market for Jordanian exports.

See also MIDDLE EAST.

JOURNAL REGISTER CO. The owner of the *New Haven Register* and nineteen other daily newspapers filed for Chapter 11 protection on February 22, 2009.

JP MORGAN CHASE (JP MORGAN). Includes corporations, institutional investors, hedge funds, governments, and affluent individuals in more than 100 countries. JP Morgan is part of JP Morgan Chase & Company, a leading global financial services firm with assets of nearly $2 trillion.

JP Morgan survived the meltdown and proceeded to purchase other banks, including Washington Mutual and Bear Stearns. After repaying $25 billion in federal money, it reported on July 16 strong quarterly earnings of $2.7 billion. JP Morgan Chase's profits were up 36 percent from $2 billion a year earlier. Revenue climbed 39 percent from the year before to a record $27.7 billion.

Third-quarter 2009 earnings rose sevenfold to $3.59 billion for JP Morgan Chase. Profits jumped to $3.59 billion. It had a first-quarter 2010 profit of 55 percent, surging in the opening quarter of 2010. JP Morgan then announced on July 15, 2010, that it had its highest-ever quarterly profit, a 76 percent rise in net income from the year before. Nevertheless, at about the same time, as many as fifty people were terminated. On September 29, 2010, JP Morgan Chase suspended many foreclosures as it reviewed its legal procedures, halting 56,000 foreclosures. It was determined that some of its workers had improperly signed court documents. All of the suspensions were in the twenty-three states where foreclosures had to be approved by a court. GMAC Mortgage had also suspended some foreclosures. JP Morgan Chase earned $4.4 billion in the third quarter 2010, in part because it released $1.7 billion from the bank's loan-loss reserves.

On January 14, 2011, the bank posted a profit of $17.4 billion for the year 2010, up 48 percent from $11.7 billion a year earlier. The bank earned $4.8 billion in the final three months of the year. Its profit was $3.3 billion on revenue of $25.2 billion. Its mortgage banking quarterly profits rose 117 percent to $577 million. On April 15, management reported that its first-quarter profit jumped 67 percent to $5.6 billion. However, its revenue dropped to $25.8 billion in the first quarter, down 8 percent from the year before.

Its quarterly profit rose 67 percent when announced on April 13, climbing to $5.6 billion from $3.3 billion the year before. Revenue declined 9 percent to $25.2 billion. On July 14, 2011, management posted strong quarterly results as both profits in the second quarter were up 13 percent to $5.4 billion and revenue surged 7 percent to $27.4 billion from $25.6 billion the year before. On October 13, management reported that its first year-on-year fall in quarterly profits occurred since the height of the Great Recession. The bank had a 4 percent profit fall. JP Morgan's latest quarter profit of $4.3 billion was down from $4.4 billion from the year before.

On January 13, 2012, management announced that its fourth-quarter profit fell 23 percent from the year before. Earnings were $3.73 billion, down from $4.83 billion the year before. Revenue fell 17 percent to $22.2 billion.

See also BEAR STEARNS; FEDERAL HOUSING FINANCE AGENCY; FORECLOSURE; INVESTMENT BANKING; PROPRIETARY TRADING; "TOO BIG TO FAIL"; WASHINGTON MUTUAL.

Cf. GOLDMAN SACHS.

JP MORGAN CHASE & CO. The parent entity of JP Morgan Chase. *See also* JP MORGAN CHASE.

JUNK. The average junk-bond yield in February 2011 dropped below 7 percent for the first time in seven years.

See also MOODY'S; STANDARD & POOR'S.

JUNK RATINGS. *See* FALLEN ANGELS.

JUSTICE. *See* U.S. DEPARTMENT OF JUSTICE.

K

KAUPTHING BANK. *See* ICELAND.

KAZAKHSTAN. In November 2008, with oil prices falling and investors fleeing high-risk markets, Kazakhstan's economy fell by 50 percent to 5 percent from an average of 10 percent since 2000. Average wages dropped 1.1 percent.

On February 2, 2009, the government declared that it would take controlling stakes in two private banks as a condition of keeping them from a possible bankruptcy filing. Two days later, the central bank allowed a 25 percent devaluation of its national currency to protect its foreign exchange and gold reserves and boost the country's manufacturing competitiveness. Kazakhstan's largest bank stated on April 24 that it would no longer repay $11 billion in foreign debt but would pay only interest to foreign creditors.

Some of the world's largest banks funneled more than $10 billion in loans into Kasakhstan's largest bank, Bank Turalem (BTA). By fall 2009, the bank loaned billions of dollars to finance mostly real estate programs in Russia and the Ukraine. Now most of the loans have gone bad. The nation's GDP growth is 5.5 percent, with a GDP of $151 billion, an inflation rate of 6.6 percent, and a GDP per head of $9,250.

The country is already the world's largest producer of uranium and will soon join the word's top ten oil-producing nations. Average income in 2011 was $11,000 a year, with GDP growth averaging 8 percent a year for the past ten years.

See also CENTRAL ASIA.

KBC. A Belgian banking and insurance group received in January 2009 a €2 billion, or $2.59 billion, cash injection from the Flemish government.

KELLOGG COMPANY. The nation's largest cereal maker saw its third-quarter 2009 profit increase 5.6 percent by cutting costs and having lower commodities prices. The company posted a profit of $361 million, and its gross margin improved to 43.9 percent from 42.7 percent. Revenue fell 0.3 percent to $3.28 billion.

Its second-quarter 2010 profit fell 15 percent to $302 million. Revenue declined 5 percent to $3.06 billion. Kellogg's third-quarter 2010 earnings dropped 6.4 percent.

The firm's first-quarter 2011 earnings fell 12 percent.

Management reported on February 2, 2012, that its fourth-quarter earnings were up 23 percent to $232 million, with a 5.4 percent sales growth to $3.02 billion.

Cf. PROCTER & GAMBLE.

KENYA. In 2011, it was projected that economic growth would reach 5.4 percent, up from 4 percent the previous year. Its GDP is $33 billion, with an inflation rate of 5.4 percent and a GDP per head of $786.

KEYNESIAN MULTIPLIER. *See* KEYNES, JOHN MAYNARD.

KEYNES, JOHN MAYNARD. An influential British economist whose analysis of the Great Depression redefined economics in the 1930s, asserting that increased government spending during a downturn could revive the economy. His 1936 book *The General Theory of Employment, Interest, and Money* expected that general employment was always positively correlated with the aggregate demand for consumer goods. Keynes argued that government should intervene in the economy to maintain aggregate demand and full employment, with the goal of smoothing out business cycles. During recessions, he believed, government should borrow money and spend it. To this day, his departure from classical economics is debated. Critics argue that government action to stimulate aggregate demand is wrong. They in turn argued that the boom and bust of the business cycle is primarily a monetary phenomenon created by governments' artificial inflation of money and credit.

The theory beneath the American Recovery and Reinvestment Act of 2009 is called the Keynesian Multiplier, which was first posited around 1931.

See also AGGREGATE DEMAND; AMERICAN RECOVERY AND REINVESTMENT ACT (OF 2009); FISHER, IRVING; GREAT DEPRESSION (OF THE 1930S); SMOOT-HAWLEY ACT.

KIMBERLY-CLARK. The firm's third-quarter 2010 earnings for 2010 dropped 19 percent. There was a third-quarter profit of $469 million, with revenue rising 1.3 percent to $4.98 billion. It first cut production in the fourth quarter.

The firm's second-quarter 2011 earnings fell 18 percent, with a profit of $408 million. Sales climbed 8.3 percent to $5.26 billion.

KMART. *See* SEARS HOLDING CORPORATION.

KNIGHT CAPITAL GROUP. On August 4, 2011, announced plans to cut 6 percent of its global workforce of 1,465 full-time employees.

KODAK. *See* EASTMAN KODAK.

KOENIGSEGG. Swedish sports carmaker received about $600 million from the European Investment Bank in October 2009 to help finance the acquisition of GM's Saab unit. By November, the GM acquisition had collapsed. *See also* GENERAL MOTORS; SAAB.

KOHL'S CORPORATION. In mid-August 2010, Kohl's management reported a 14 percent climb in fiscal second-quarter profit of $260 million. In early November, Kohl's management reported a 2.5 percent decline in store sales.

By 2011, Kohl's posted a 5 percent rise in same-stores sales. The firm's fourth-quarter profit of $211 million climbed 6 percent. Total sales rose 3.1 percent to $4.16 billion on a 1.3 percent increase in same-store sales. On August 11, management reported that profits rose 16.5 percent to $303 million, with sales climbing 3.6 percent to $4.2 billion.

KOREA. Following the severe contraction in late 2008, Korea has achieved one of the earliest and strongest recoveries in the Organisation for Economic Co-operation and Development area, led by exports and expansionary fiscal policy. While the impact of fiscal stimulus will fade in 2010, a sustained pick-up in exports is projected to help boost output growth to 4 to 4.5 percent in both 2010 and 2011, with a rebound in domestic demand and a marked fall in unemployment. As the recovery takes hold, the growth of government spending should be scaled back to bring the budget back into balance and in line with the mid-term fiscal management plan. Other exceptional measures to stabilize the economy, such as the expanded support to small and medium-sized enterprises, should be phased out. Structural reforms to enhance productivity, notably in the nonmanufacturing sector, are needed to sustain growth over the medium term.

In December 2008, the Bank of Korea cut its benchmark interest rate by a full percentage point, its biggest cut ever, to 3 percent.

By the beginning of 2009, the Bank of Korea cut its benchmark interest rate to 2 percent, a record low, to aid the plunging South Korean economy.

On January 13, 2011, the Bank of Korea raised its benchmark interest rate by 0.25 percent to 2.75 percent to stabilize consumer prices. Its policy rate was raised by 0.25 percent to 2.75 percent. Korean's consumer inflation remained above 3 percent, with expectations that it would climb to 3.5 percent during the year.

KO SAMUI. *See* THAILAND.

KOTA KINABALU. *See* MALAYSIA.

KPS. *See* WATERFORD WEDGWOOD.

KRAFT. On August 5, 2010, Kraft reported that its second-quarter 2010 income grew 13.3 percent, earning $937 million. Its fourth-quarter sales then surged 30 percent.

Kraft Food's in May 2011 reported an 11 percent sales increase, with a $799 million first-quarter profit. Kraft's third-quarter profit surged 22 percent to $922 million. Its revenue climbed 12 percent to $13.2 billion.

In early January 2012, management announced plans to eliminate about 1,600 positions.

KROGER'S COMPANY. The nation's largest supermarket chain reported quarterly of $280.8 million on September 8, 2011. Sales climbed 11.5 percent to $20.9 billion from $18.8 billion the year before.

KRONA. See ICELAND.

KRUEGER, ALAN. Chosen in August 2011 to be the president's new head of the White House Council of Economic Advisers, helped to design the "cash for clunkers" program. Professor of economics at Princeton University. The Senate unanimously confirmed him on November 3.

See also COUNCIL OF ECONOMIC ADVISERS.

KRUGMAN, PAUL. An East Coast liberal establishment member, an economics columnist for the *New York Times*, an economics professor at Princeton University, and a Nobel Prize winner in economics. He is considered President Obama's toughest liberal critic. One of his timely statements was "it was debt what did it," not grammatical on the lingering recession.

On March 23, 2009, he said, "Tim Geithner the Treasury secretary has persuaded President Obama to recycle Bush administration policy—specifically, the "cash for trash" plan proposed, then abandoned, six months ago by then–Treasury secretary Henry Paulson. This is more than disappointing. In fact, it fills me with a sense of despair." Then, on March 9, he said, "So here's the picture that scares me. It's September 2009, the unemployment rate has passed 9 percent, and despite the early round of stimulus spending it's still headed up. Mr. Obama finally concedes that a bigger stimulus is needed. But he can't get his new plan through Congress because approval for his economic policies has plummeted, partly because his policies are seen to have failed, partly because job-creation policies are conflated in the public mind with deeply unpopular bank bailouts. And as a result, the recession rages on, unchecked."

He said on February 6, 2010, "Somehow, Washington has lost any sense of what's at stake—of the reality that we may well be falling into an economic abyss, and that if we do, it will be very hard to get out again." During the debate over George W. Bush's decade-old tax cuts clearly helping out the nation's wealthiest by keeping their taxes low, Krugman on December 6 argued: "Yes, letting taxes go up would be politically risky. But giving in would be risky, too—especially for a president whom voters are starting to write off as a man too timid to take a stand. Now is the time for him to prove them wrong."

By March 2011, he argued that the austerity strategy to save a nation's economy was wrong. He remained convinced that cutting spending in the face of high unemployment was an error. As 2011 ended, Krugman noted that the current situation showed that we were in a "depression, not a full replay of the Great Depression, but that's cold comfort. . . . The crisis of the euro is killing the European dream. The shared currency, which was supposed to bind nations together, has instead created an atmosphere of bitter acrimony."

See also THIRD DEPRESSION.

KUWAIT. In October 2008, Kuwait's Gulf Bank disclosed a $1 billion loss stemming from bad foreign-exchange bets. In January 2009, the government took a 16 percent stake in the bank to keep it from collapsing.

In February 2009, with falling oil prices, plummeting stocks, and a softening real estate market, Kuwait faced a banking crisis. In response, the government announced a $5.4 billion package to prop up banks—the only bailout plan thus far among all Persian Gulf states. In mid-April, Kuwait's central bank cut its discount rate by a quarter of a percentage point to 3.5 percent as the oil-rich nation sought to stimulate bank lending.

Cf. DUBAI.

L

LABOR UNDERUTILIZATION. *See* U6.

LAFARGE. The French basic-materials firm had a net debt of $23 billion and a market capitalization of $12 billion. Lafarge had sufficient liquidity in 2010.

LAGARDE, CHRISTINE. In early July 2011 it was announced that she would become the head of the International Monetary Fund. At the end of August at a meeting in Wyoming she called for "rebalancing global trade by stimulating demand in developing countries with big export surpluses; more aggressive mortgage relied in the U.S.; and giving job creation priority over deficit reducing in the U.S. and Europe." One week following the eurozone summit, Managing Director Laggard said: "It's not a crisis that will be resolved by one group of countries taking action. . . . It's going to be hopefully resolved by all countries, all regions, and all categories of countries actually taking action."
See also INTERNATIONAL MONETARY FUND.

LAGOS. *See* AFRICA.

LAND ROVER. *See* TATA MOTORS.

LANDSBANKI. *See* ICELAND.

LAND SPECULATION. With the housing sector falling in 2010, the land-speculation market continued to weaken into the fall.

LARGE FIRM HIRING. *See* HIRING RATE.

LAS VEGAS. *See* HOME PRICES; UNDERWATER.

LATIN AMERICA. From 2004 to fall 2008, Latin America's economy grew at an annual average rate of over 5 percent, inflation remained low, credit was expanded, and exports boomed. The proportion of people living in poverty fell from 44 percent in 2002 to 33 percent in 2008. Since September 2008, Latin America has seen many of its stock markets crash, currencies shaken, and credit drying up.

In 2009, it was projected that the meltdown in the United States would not be felt severely in Latin America. It was predicted that there would be a 2.5 percent growth in Latin America in 2009, down from earlier predictions of 3.2 percent.

By spring/summer 2010, Latin America had a rapid rebound from the Great Recession. The International Monetary Fund expected Latin America to post economic growth of 5.7 percent in 2010, compared with the 2.7 percent growth for the world's advanced economies and 4.8 percent for global growth as a whole. Latin America's economies grew by an average of 6 percent.

Latin America posted a current-account surplus of 1.6 percent of GDP in 2006; in 2011, it expected to post a deficit of a similar amount. The region's nearly 200 largest cities, those with more than 200,000 people, accounted for 60 percent of the nation's economic output, with the ten largest alone generating half of that. Poverty rates in Latin America by the close of 2011 had dropped sharply from twenty years earlier. From 1990 to 2010, the poverty rate fell by 17 percentage points to 31.4 percent from 48.4 percent. There were now 174 million Latin Americans who lived in poverty compared to 225 million in 2002. The region's population by the end of 2011 revealed that 30.4 percent was living below the national poverty lines, a fall from 48.4 percent in 1990.

See also ARGENTINA; AUTOMOBILE INDUSTRY; BRAZIL; MEXICO; PANAMA; PUERTO RICO; "THIRD WORLD"; WORLD TRADE.

LATVIA. In October 2008, the jobless rate was 5.6 percent. Unemployment in 2009 was projected by the government to reach 10 percent and then 10.8 percent in 2010 before falling to 8.4 percent in 2011. The International Monetary Fund bailed out Latvia with more than €7 billion in mid-December. The arrangement did not require Latvia to devalue its currency. The country faced a 5 percent or larger contraction of its GDP in 2009. Tax rises and spending cuts were worth a full 7 percent of GDP, and public-sector salaries declined by 15 percent. As foreign capital dried up, GDP fell by 4.6 percent.

Latvia's center-right coalition government collapsed on February 20, a victim of the country's growing economic and political turmoil. (It was the second government to fall, following Iceland's collapse during the financial crisis.) Latvia's GDP shrank at an annual rate of 10.5 percent in January, and by the end of 2009 the economy was projected to shrink by 12 percent or more. Less than three months after securing $10.5 billion in emergency funding, Latvia, considered the weakest country of among the East European economies, backtracked on a deal that the IMF hoped would lower the risk of a regional meltdown. On July 2, the European Commission announced that it would release $1.7 billion to Latvia to help the nation head off a collapse of its economy and maintain its currency link to the euro.

The IMF and the European Union agreed on July 28 to give Latvia a $2 billion loan to help its economy during the recession. Latvia's economy fell during the year and was less than $25 billion GDP. The IMF approved on August 27 the disbursement of $278.5 million to Latvia. These funds were critical, as the nation's economy shrank 20 percent in the second quarter 2009. The nation's second-quarter current account displayed a surplus of 14.2 percent of GDP compared to 15.1 percent the previous year. The economy decreased 18.7 percent year on year.

The government was attempting to keep its 2010 budget down to 8.5 percent, a condition for the continuation of an $11 billion IMF bailout package. Latvia's GDP contracted by 25 percent and the unemployment rate in 2010 soared to double digits. The prime minister's austerity program also pushed through a fiscal adjustment worth 8.5 percent of GDP in 2009 and 4 percent in 2010.

Latvia was in an economic crisis. However, the nation didn't devalue but worked to regain its competitiveness. The IMF determined that Latvia's cumulative 2008–2009 contraction was 25 percent, the sharpest of any country. Unemployment reached 20 percent and wages dropped 19 percent from their 2008 peak. By mid-year 2010, the economy was expanding at 2.7 percent a year, with joblessness falling to 19.4 percent. Her exports climbed 38 percent, with the IMF forecasting growth of 3.3 percent in 2011.

In 2011, deflation was expected to set in as the economy struggles out of recession. Economic expansion was expected to reach 3 percent in 2011. The nation's GDP growth was 3.0 percent, with a GDP of $22 billion, an inflation rate of 0.5 percent, and a GDP per head of $9,780.

See also EASTERN EUROPE.

Cf. BALTICS; ESTONIA; ICELAND.

LAW FIRMS. The economic slowdown triggered layoffs in law firms across the nation. In 2008, profits on average were down 8 percent to 12 percent after fifteen years of growth.

By 2009, the largest U.S. law firms were firing attorneys and delaying new hires. More than 3,000 lawyers lost their jobs in the first three months of 2009. Partner profits were down an average of 4 percent in 2008 at the highest-grossing firms. According to government figures, the number of unemployed lawyers jumped 66 percent in 2008 to a ten-year high of 20,000.

One of the changes resulting from the recession was how companies were pushing law firms for flat-fee contracts instead of hourly billings. Critics of the hourly schedule argued that this billing practice encourages the incentive to rack up larger bills. In 2009, 50 percent of corporate legal matters were billed on a contract basis. Some companies claim that flat-fee billing can lower legal costs by 15 to 20 percent. Funds spent on alternative billing arrangements totaled $13.1 billion in 2009 versus $8.6 billion in the same time frame in 2008.

By year's end 2010, law firms held back in raising their bonuses for attorneys, especially those at the junior levels. In part this was caused by a pull-back in fees and from the slower pace of mergers, acquisitions, and private-equity transactions. Bonuses, especially with large Wall Street law firms in 2009, were roughly $35,000, the same as for 2010.

See also BONUSES.

LAWYERS. *See* LAW FIRMS.

LAYAWAY PAYMENT PLANS. *See* WAL-MART.

LAYOFFS. *See* UNEMPLOYMENT.

LAZARD. Had a first-quarter 2009 loss accompanied by its shares falling 9.8 percent, or $53.5 million, compared with a net income of $7.8 million in the previous year. Revenue fell 19 percent to $4.25 billion. Lazard's third-quarter 2009 profit was $37.4 million, with revenue rising to a record $119.1 million in the quarter. Revenue rose 1.5 percent to $411.7 million.

The firm's second-quarter 2010 profit was $44.6 million, a rise of 58 percent from $28.2 million the year before. Revenue climbed 12 percent to $19 million. Lazard's third-quarter 2010 profit climbed 71 percent, with a profit of $64.1 million. Revenue rose 9.7 percent to $473.2 million. It earned $104.5 million in the fourth-quarter, with $594.9 million in net revenue.

Lazard's posted in October 2011 a 2.2 percent profit fall in its third quarter at $62.7 million. Net revenue was down 2 percent to $462.4 million.

LEASING. *See* GENERAL MOTORS.

LEBANON. The nation's GDP growth was 5.8 percent, with a GDP of $41 billion, an inflation rate of 3.2 percent, and a GDP per head of $9,440.

LEGACY ASSETS. Often used interchangeably with *toxic assets.*
See also PUBLIC-PRIVATE INVESTMENT FUND; TOXIC ASSETS.

LEGACY LOANS PROGRAM. *See* PUBLIC-PRIVATE INVESTMENT FUND; TOXIC ASSETS.

LEGACY SECURITIES PROGRAM. *See* PUBLIC-PRIVATE INVESTMENT FUND; TOXIC ASSETS.

LEHMAN BROTHERS. Lehman Brothers announced on June 17, 2008, that it would post a $2.8 billion quarterly loss. Then, on July 1, Lehman's shares tumbled to their lowest level since 2000 with expectations that the firm might have to sell itself. On September 15, Lehman Brothers filed for bankruptcy, the largest casualty to date of the global credit crisis. It was the biggest investment bank to collapse since 1990. In the days before it was allowed to fail, U.S. Treasury officials made it clear that they did not think the bank's collapse would have a major impact on the nation's economy. How wrong they were.

Lehman's fall was intimately tied to myriad derivatives and complex mortgage securities, which held billions of dollars in securities backed by home loans and other assets of uncertain worth. The result of Lehman's subsequent failure was for banks across the globe, fearing for their own solvency, to stop lending. In addition, issuance of corporate bonds, commercial paper, and a wide variety of other financial products largely ceased. Credit-financed economic activity was brought to a virtual standstill. Under Chapter 11 of the federal bankruptcy code, firms receiving protection from creditors have a chance to reorganize. Although Lehman filed for Chapter 11 protection, the company was not expected to emerge from its proceedings. But, there were advantages to Lehman if its bankruptcy was well managed. It could find buyers for Lehman's businesses so long as they were willing to continue employing its workers.

In one twenty-four-hour period, Lehman lost $1.6 billion when the Chicago Mercantile Exchange closed out all of Lehman's positions. U.S. Treasury experts argued that bailing Lehman out would have wrongly rewarded it for bad behavior and excessive risk-taking, and thereby would have given the U.S. financial sector a green light for future bad behavior. Lehman had assets of $639 billion at the end of May. It owed about $110.5 billion on account of senior unsecured notes, $12.6 billion on account of subordinated unsecured notes, and $5 billion on account of junior subordinated notes. By the end of August, Lehman had $600 billion of assets financed with just $30 billion of equity.

Lehman's real estate holdings were part of its huge problems for survival. As of September 12, 2007, Lehman's valuation of its commercial and residential real estate holdings was $22.9 billion. As of December 31, 2008, it had fallen to $15.9 billion, valued by the firm overseeing the bankruptcy. The number of properties on which Lehman's loans were restructured was 900. The filing represented the end of a 158-year-old company that employed nearly 26,000 people. Possessing so little capital meant that a 5 percent decline in assets would have wiped out the value of the firm.

The bankruptcy filing of what was once the fourth-largest investment bank in the United States came after a weekend of heated negotiations among regulators and Wall Street firms about Lehman's fate. The U.S. government refused to backstop Lehman's worst assets the way it had backstopped Bear Stearns's earlier sales to JP Morgan. Prospective bidders refused to buy

Lehman without government support. In the end, Lehman was allowed to fail. Part of the controversy was whether the federal government should have stepped in to save Lehman, or whether allowing it to fail was in the best interests of the national economy. In the end, Barclays Bank of Britain negotiated a deal to buy most of Lehman's businesses out of bankruptcy. Barclays agreed to take over the Federal Reserve's lending role and the transfer was made. Barclays acquired the majority of Lehman's North American and European business lines.

Lehman's demise has been rationalized by those responsible for its failure: "Lehman Brothers had to die for the rest of Wall Street to live." In mid-September 2009, the bankruptcy estate of Lehman Brothers Holdings accused some former executives of working with Barclays PLC of the United Kingdom to provide a "windfall" of at least $8.2 billion when it purchased Lehman's broker-dealer business in fall 2008. This happened when Barclays gave $45 billion to Lehman in exchange for $50 billion in securities. Instead of permitting Lehman to later purchase back the securities for $45 billion, executives of both firms decided to leave the securities with the U.K. bank, resulting in the "windfall."

Six weeks before it went bankrupt, Lehman Brothers was effectively out of securities that could have been used as collateral to back the short-term loans it needed to survive. One year after Lehman's demise and bankruptcy—the largest Chapter 11 case in American history—the firm continued to be involved in the future of its clients. As of September 11, 2009, 9,763 claims had been filed in federal bankruptcy court in Manhattan. For example, Lehman by September 2009 had 1.2 million outstanding derivates transactions with 6,500 trading partners. The cash that was recovered from Lehman's U.S. derivates business would be a major source of funds for the bankruptcy estate to be used for paying out on credit claims. It will take years to sort everything out.

With over $600 billion of assets, Lehman was America's largest and most complex corporate failure. By summer 2010, there were 65,000 claims from clients, counterparties, and other creditors against Lehman. It was envisaged that $260 billion of claims will be fulfilled, or about 25 percent of those requested.

See also BEAR STEARNS; CREDIT DEFAULT SWAPS; DOW JONES INDUSTRIAL AVERAGE; ERNST & YOUNG; EXPORTS (U.S.); FINANCIAL CRISIS INQUIRY REPORT; FORTIS BANQUE; GEITHNER, TIMOTHY; MONEY-MARKET MUTUAL FUNDS; PAULSON, HENRY; SECURITIES AND EXCHANGE COMMISSION; "TOO BIG TO FAIL."
Cf. CIT GROUP.

LEHMAN BROTHERS HOLDINGS INCORPORATED. On August 30, 2011, a judge said that creditors can vote on Lehman Brothers Holdings' historic $65 billion creditor payback plan nearly three years following the investment bank's filings for Chapter 11, in the largest bankruptcy case in U.S. history.

See also LEHMAN BROTHERS.

LEMON SOCIALISM. Where taxpayers bear the cost if things go wrong, but stockholders and executives get the benefits if things go right.

See also STRESS TESTS (U.S.); ZOMBIES.

LENDING. Top beneficiaries of federal cash from the Troubled Asset Relief Program saw outstanding loans decline 1.4 percent in the fourth quarter 2008. Ten of the thirteen big beneficiaries of the Troubled Asset Relief Program saw their outstanding loan balances decline by a total of $46 billion.

Those thirteen banks had collected the majority of the roughly $200 billion that the government had given out. By mid-April 2009, bank lending had fallen at a sharper rate than earlier realized despite government efforts to pump billions of dollars into the financial sector specifically to spur lending. The total dollar amount of new loans declined in three of the four months the government had reported this data. All but three of the nineteen largest TARP recipients originated fewer loans in February than they did at the time they received federal infusions.

The Treasury measured the monthly lending change at the top twenty-one TARP recipient banks by calculating the median change, which some experts say understated the decline. Between January and February, the median fell 2.2 percent, but total lending declined 4.7 percent.

Lending by banks continued to slow into mid-2009 as bankers and borrowers were cautious about taking risks. The total amount of loans held by fifteen large U.S. banks shrank by 2.8 percent in the second quarter 2009, and more than half of the loan volume in April and May came from refinancing mortgages and renewing credit to businesses, not new loans. Financial institutions were clamping down on lending to conserve capital as a cushion against mounting loan losses. Loan demand fell as firms sidelined expansion plans and consumers were spending less. By September 2010, bank lending following the meltdown began to return to normal. Commercial and industrial loans by banks, although down by 25 percent from the 2008 peak, inched up from $1.234 trillion in June 2010 to $1,242 trillion in early September.

By the end of 2010, U.S. banks increased their lending to businesses. Lending in the fourth quarter grew 0.2 percent from the third quarter to $1.22 trillion, the first quarterly increase in two years.

See also EUROZONE LENDING; LENDING; "TOO BIG TO FAIL"; TROUBLED ASSET RELIEF PROGRAM.

LENOVO. China's biggest personal-computer maker cut about 2,500 jobs, or 11 percent of its workforce, in early 2009.

On February 17, 2011, the company showed its largest profit in more than two years, with 46 percent coming from its domestic sales. Its fiscal third-quarter net profit climbed 25 percent to $99.65 million on $5.81 billion in revenue.

See also CHINA.

LEVERAGE. A measure of how much debt is used to purchase assets; for example, a leverage ratio of 5:1 means that $5 of assets was purchased with $4 of debt and $1 of capital.

LEVERAGED BUYOUT FIRMS. In 2008, the leveraged buyout business nearly stopped. Deal volume fell around 70 percent from 2007 as buyout firms sold companies worth only around $6 billion in the last quarter, a small fraction of the $110 billion in sales in the second quarter of 2007. Things did not look any better for the foreseeable future.

See also EQUITY BUYOUTS.

LEVERAGE RATIO. An attempt to require banks to hold reserves against all their money at risk with no leeway to manipulate accounting rules.

LEVI STRAUSS. On April 13, 2009, the denim manufacturer announced a 50 percent decline in fiscal first-quarter net income and a 12 percent slide in revenue. Profits fell to $48 million in the quarter ending March 1 from $97 million in the same period one year before. Sales slipped to $951 million from $1.1 billion a year earlier. Sales dropped 3 percent in its fiscal second quarter 2009, but Levi Strauss continued to add stores.

The firm's third-quarter profit reported on October 11, 2011, climbed 14 percent, with profits jumping to $32.2 million from $28.2 million the year before. Net sales increased 8.6 percent to $1.2 billion, with revenue increasing 4 percent.

LEW, JACOB. Nominated by President Obama on July 13, 2010, to replace Peter Orszag, the administration's first budget chief. Lew was a top State Department official overseeing the agency's budget and economic operations. The U.S. Senate voted on November 18 to support the president's proposed budget chief.

LEWIS, KENNETH D. Chairman, chief executive, and president of Bank of America.

See also BANK OF AMERICA.

LG. A Korean maker of flat-screen televisions, it posted a record loss in the fourth quarter 2008, its first loss in seven quarters. LG reported a net loss of 684 billion won, or $506 million, for the quarter. A year earlier, it had a net profit of 760 billion won, and it posted a profit of 295 billion won in the third quarter of 2008.

LG Electronics, South Korea's second-largest electronics maker by revenue, cut its expenses by $2.19 billion in early February 2009 by reducing manufacturing costs and unnecessary expenses. The firm hoped to avoid cutting jobs or capital investment. LG's display management stated that its second-quarter 2009 profit fell 60 percent from a year earlier. LG's third-quarter 2010 net profit fell 99 percent from the previous year.

LIBOR (LONDON INTERBANK OFFERED RATE). A measure of what major international banks charge each other for large-volume loans of eurodollars, or dollars on deposit outside the United States.

The common benchmark interest rate has crept up from 1.1 percent in mid-January 2009 to 1.3 percent in early March 2009.

By summer 2011, the low demand for overnight loans left LIBOR's status as a measure of banks' health in question.

LIBRARIES. As states, cities, and towns were forced to shuffle their budgets around, by mid-summer 2011 belt-tightening threatened to force the closing of libraries and the firing numerous librarians in order to salvage full-time students and teachers. In New York City, 53 of the 365 licensed librarians were threatened.

See also EDUCATION.

LIBYA. It was projected that for 2011 the economy would grow by 4 percent. The nation's GDP was $83 billion, with an inflation rate of 4.7 percent and a GDP per head of $12,450.

Then, in mid-February 2011, Libya's descent into violence during the Arab Spring rattled global financial markets, sending oil prices surging to their highest level in more than two years and driving world stock markets sharply lower. Libya exported 44 billion barrels of proven reserves representing more than 3 percent of the global total. U.S. crude oil prices soared 8.5 percent to $93.57 a barrel, while the Dow Jones Industrial Average fell 1.4 percent to 12,212.79. The chaos in Libya by March had a role to play in the sharp surge in U.S. gasoline and oil prices and could slow down recovery from the Great Recession. The country's 1.6 million barrels a day of production had fallen by about two-thirds. By March, the retail price for gasoline in the United States had climbed more than 4 percent to an average of $3.52 per gallon, the highest since September 2008.

Following liberation at the end of August, it was expected that the country would rapidly return to its rich oil market, where 95 percent of its exports are in oil. It was expected that production would quickly return to 600,000 barrels a day. Home to the largest oil reserves in Africa, Libya was producing

1.6 million barrels a day but fell to 60,000 barrels during the uprisings. On September 1, 2011, the United States released $1.5 billion of Libyan assets, of which $700 million had already been delivered. France released $2.2 billion, with a global total varying from $50 billion to $150 billion.

LIECHTENSTEIN. *See* TAX HAVENS.

LIFE INSURANCE. By summer 2010, in reaction to the fears and realities brought about by the Great Recession, nearly a third of U.S. households had no life insurance coverage, the highest percentage in more than forty years. Approximately 35 million households neither own life insurance policies nor are covered under employer-sponsored plans, up from 24 million, or 22 percent, in 2004.

LIFE INSURANCE COMPANIES. *See* LIFE INSURERS; METLIFE.

LIFE INSURERS. The U.S. Treasury decided in early April 2009 to extend bailout funds to a number of struggling life insurance firms. The Troubled Asset Relief Program would be used to provide assistance. Shares of life insurers had already fallen more than 40 percent in 2009 and had trouble raising funds.

Only insurers that owned federally chartered banks would qualify for the extended program, and they would have access to the Treasury's Capital Purchase Program, which injected funds into banks. Any life insurer receiving TARP funds would have to comply with strict executive compensation rules set by Congress.

See also METLIFE.

LILLIAN VERNON. Filed for Chapter 11 bankruptcy on February 21, 2008.

LIMITED BRANDS. Posted a fiscal second-quarter 2009 loss of 27 percent. Earnings were $74.3 million, down from $102 million a year earlier.

In early November 2010, the retailer posted its fiscal third-quarter profit, with sales climbing 9 percent.

In January 2011, Limited reported that its net sales were $772.6 million at month's end, compared with $622.6 million in 2010. By February, the retailer posted a 12 percent rise in sales. By year's end, Limited Brands showed a 7 percent increase in sales.

LIMITLESS AGE. *See* NATIONAL COMMISSION ON FISCAL RESPONSIBILITY AND REFORM.

LINENS 'N THINGS. On May 3, 2008, filed for Chapter 11 protection from creditors, with plans to close 120 stores.

LINKEDIN CORPORATION. In early August 2011, LinkedIn Corporation boasted a strong profit and revenue in its first earnings report as a public company. Revenue doubled and posted a 5.1 percent profit increase for the second-quarter ending June 30.

LIQUIDITY. Holding cash and/or assets that can be quickly and easily converted to cash.

LIQUIDITY PUT. A contract allowing one party to compel the other to buy an asset under certain circumstances. It ensures that there will be a buyer for otherwise illiquid assets.

LIQUIDITY TRAP. When banks don't lend funds and firms don't invest. Appeared during the 1930s and reappeared in Japan in the 1990s. Characterized by an economy where interest rates are so low that consumers, business, and investors don't care if funds are in cash or in interest-paying investments.

LITHUANIA. Lithuania's GDP fell at a double-digit rate in the first quarter 2009. GDP declined 12.6 percent from the year earlier. A slump of 10 percent was predicted.

Economic extraction turned to expansion in 2011, with a GDP growth of 2.9 percent. The government will work hard to lower the deficit and will prepare a number of state-run enterprises for divestment to private hands. The nation's GDP growth rate was 2.9 percent, with a GDP of $33 billion, an inflation rate of 0.9 percent, and a GDP per head of $9,960.
See also BALTICS.

LIVING STANDARDS. On September 10, 2009, the government announced that the Great Recession of 2007–2010 slashed families' earnings, increased poverty, and left more people without health insurance. Median household income, adjusted for inflation, fell 3.6 percent in 2008 to $50,303, the sharpest year-over-year fall in forty years. The poverty rate, at 13.2 percent, was the highest since 1997, and about 700,000 more people didn't have health insurance in 2008 than the year earlier.

The fall in medium income affected all races. The largest decline, 5.6 percent, was among Hispanics. The median income for Asians fell 4.4 percent, while black incomes fell 2.8 percent and non-Hispanic/white fell 2.6 percent. About 54 million people were living below the poverty line, about 3 million more than in 2007.
See also UNEMPLOYMENT.

LIZ CLAIBORNE. The apparel company said on February 3, 2009, that it would cut 725 jobs, or 8 percent of its workforce, as it tried to endure a consumer spending slowdown that had been particularly brutal for apparel retailers. On August 12, 2009, the company reported a loss of $82.1 million, its seventh consecutive quarterly loss. Sales fell 29 percent to $683.8 million.

LLOYDS. Lloyds Banking Group and the government of the United Kingdom struck a deal in early March 2009 in which the government would insure more than $353.2 billion in Lloyds' assets and increased its stake in the bank to as much as 75 percent. On June 30, 2009, Lloyds said it would cut an additional 2,100 jobs as part of its reorganization.

Lloyds made a first-quarter 2010 pre-tax profit, the first time the institution returned to the black since its bailout. The partially stated-owned Lloyds posted its first profit in nearly two years for the first half of 2010, with a pre-tax profit of $2.6 billion compared with a loss the year prior. On November 2, 2010, management announced that it made a profit in the third-quarter. At the beginning of July, Lloyds' management reported that it planned to eliminate 15,000 positions by the end of 2014. A lender owned 41 percent by the U.K. government reported it would save $2.4 billion a year by the end of 2014. Lloyds reported a net loss of 2.4 billion pounds for the first quarter. On August 4, Lloyd's management reported a net first half loss of $3.78 billion.

Cf. ROYAL BANK OF SCOTLAND; TRANSPARENCY.

LOAN MODIFICATIONS. On October 8, 2009, the government announced that it had met its goal of beginning trial loan modifications for half a million financially troubled homeowners. The $8,000 tax credit for first-time homebuyers was recommended to be extended, indicating that the housing market still required assistance from the federal government.

See also MAKING HOME AFFORDABLE PROGRAM.

LOAN MODS. *See* HOUSING BAILOUT PLAN; LOAN MODIFICATIONS; MAKING HOME AFFORDABLE PROGRAM.

LOAN REDEFAULT. *See* MORTGAGE MODIFICATION.

LOAN-TO-VALUE RATIO (LTV). The ratio of the amount of a mortgage to the value of the house, typically expressed as a percentage. "Combined" loan-to-value includes all debt secured by the house, including second mortgages.

LOBBYISTS. The number of active lobbyists declined 2 percent in 2008 to 15,900, recording its first yearly drop in seven years.

LOCAL TAXES. *See* STATES (U.S.).

LOCKE, GARY. President Obama's commerce secretary. He was formerly a two-term governor of the state of Washington.

LOCKHEED MARTIN CORPORATION. Second-quarter 2009 profit fell 17 percent, with sales slightly up. In August 2009, Lockheed Martin announced that it would cut nearly 5 percent of its space-operations workforce, or 800 jobs. Lockheed Martin's management reported a 1.9 percent increase in third-quarter 2009 profit.

The company reported an 18 percent fall in its first-quarter 2010 profit. Profit declined to $547 million from $666 million the year before. Sales climbed 3 percent to $10.6 billion. The firm's third-quarter 2010 profit fell 28 percent despite higher revenue. A profit of $571 million was declared, with revenue climbing 5.6 percent to $11.38 billion. On October 19, 2010, management lowered its earnings forecast for the year noting that its third-quarter profit fell 28 percent to $571 million, compared with $797 million the year earlier. Earnings were $565 million, with sales climbing 6 percent to $11.38 billion from $10.77 billion.

In mid-June 2011, the space-systems company said it would lay off about 1,200 employees, 7.5 percent of its workforce, out of a total of 16,000 people in the United States. At the same time, management announced plans to cut about 1,500 positions out of its 28,000.

LONDON INTERBANK OFFERED RATE. *See* LIBOR.

LONG-TERM CAPITAL MANAGEMENT. Not allowing Long-Term Capital Management to collapse in 1998 laid the foundation for the current crisis. Had regulators been less concerned with protecting the hedge fund's creditors, things might have been better today. Advised by "quants" (quantitative analysts), unsound, unfounded bets were made including investments in interest rate derivatives. With their bailout as a precedent, creditors came to believe that their loans to unsound financial institutions would be made good by the Federal Reserve.

Under Alan Greenspan's watch, the Federal Reserve organized a consortium of firms to purchase out Long-Term Capital Management and cover their debts.

See also QUANTS.

LONG-TERM JOBLESSNESS. *See* UNEMPLOYMENT.

LONG-TERM DEBT. *See* MORTGAGE CREDIT.

LOOTING. The concept of investors borrowing huge amounts of money, making considerable profits when times were good, and then leaving the government holding the bag for their eventual (and predictable) losses. Because the government was unwilling to let big, interconnected financial firms fail, and because people at those companies knew it, they engaged in excessive risk-taking.

L'OREAL. On July 12, 2011, management reported that the French cosmetics firm had second-quarter sales climbing 0.9 percent. Sales rose to $7 billion for the three months ending in June. The firm's first-half net profit climbed 12 percent, with sales climbing 5 percent.

LOS ANGELES TIMES. *See* NEWPAPERS.

LOSS SHARES. *See* LOSS SHARING.

LOSS SHARING. Provides healthy banks with an incentive to take on troubled assets of a failed institution, with the government agreeing to assume the majority of future losses. The buyer usually takes the failed bank's deposits, leaving most of the assets to be managed and sold by the Federal Deposit Insurance Corporation.

The practice is largely a response to the number of bank failures of the past two years stretching the FDIC's financial resources. The FDIC had just $10.4 billion in its deposit-insurance fund at the end of June 2009, down from more than $50 billion one year earlier. The FDIC agreed to absorb these losses.

See also FEDERAL DEPOSIT INSURANCE CORPORATION; "TOO BIG TO FAIL."

"LOST YEAR." *See* EUROPEAN COMMISSION.

LOUISIANA-PACIFIC CORPORATION. A major provider of lumber for homes and a housing developer itself, sales fell 38 percent to $1.28 billion from $2.04 billion a year earlier.

Cf. WEYERHAEUSER.

LOWE'S COMPANIES. The second-largest home improvement retailer in the United States announced on February 20, 2009, that its fourth-quarter profit fell 60 percent, with forecasts for 2009 also downward. Revenues fell 4 percent to $9.98 billion from $10.4 billion a year earlier. Lowe's posted a 9.9 percent decline in same-store sales. Gross profit margin declined 1.15 percentage points. On August 17, 2009, Lowe's reported a 19 percent fall in quarterly earnings. Sales fell 9.5 percent from a year before. It was the firm's twelfth consecutive quarter of same-store sales declines.

By May 2010, Lowe's reported a 2.7 percent increase in profit from its first quarterly sales increase in nearly four years. Profit climbed to $849 million and revenue increased 4.7 percent to $12.39 billion. Management reported on August 16 a 9.6 percent increase in quarterly profit of $832 million for the quarter, with third-quarter revenue up 3 to 5 percent. The company reported that its third-quarter 2010 profit rose 17 percent, with net income climbing to $404 million. Sales rose 1.9 percent to $11.59 billion.

Lowe's, on February 23, 2011, reported a strong 39 percent gain in its fourth-quarter profit, with profit climbing to $285 million and net sales increasing 3.1 percent to $10.5 billion. Its first-quarter profit ending April 29 fell to $461 million from $489 million the previous year. Net sales dropped 1.6 percent to $12.19 billion and were down 3.3 percent on a same-store basis. On August 15, management reported that it earned $830 million in second-quarter earnings, down 0.2 percent. Revenue rose 1 percent to $14.54 billion. By mid-October management stated that it would close twenty of its stores. Announced in November, management reported that its quarterly earnings fell 44 percent, with a profit of $225 million.

See also RETAILING.

Cf. HOME DEPOT.

L-SHAPED RECESSION. *See* RECESSION.

LTV RATIO. *See* LOAN-TO-VALUE RATIO.

LUFTHANSA. The airline posted on April 29, 2009, that it had a net loss of €256 million, compared with a profit of €44 million one year earlier. On September 3, 2009, Lufthansa took over Austrian Airlines. Prior to this takeover, Austrian Airlines was 42 percent owned by the government.

LUKOIL. Russia's largest oil producer announced at the end of November 2011 that its net profit for the third quarter fell 20 percent, with a profit of $2.24 billion compared with $2.82 billion the year before. Revenue surged 30 percent to $34.56 billion from $26.52 billion. Overall production fell 5.3 percent from the year before to 2.11 million barrels of oil equivalent a day.

See also RUSSIA.

LUXEMBOURG. The economy has been hit severely by the international financial crisis through its exposure to financial services and trade. The number of people on active labor market programs has risen. However, the fall in output has been partially absorbed by an increase in the number of workers on reduced work time from near zero before the crisis to 2.8 percent of the labor force in August. There are signs that activity has bottomed out, however, thanks to stronger equity markets and policy support. Further ahead, gradual recovery will be sustained by improving financial conditions and growth in world trade. Further fiscal stimulus of around 1.5 percent of GDP has been put in place for 2010. The authorities should lay out a credible path for medium-term fiscal consolidation. Luxembourg remains highly exposed to uncertainty about international financial conditions and the improvement to world trade. The main uncertainty, however, is about the impact of the financial crisis on potential output and the long-term prospects of the economy, given its narrow specialization in certain financial activities and types of industrial production.

See also TAX HAVENS.

LUXURY AUTOMOBILES. *See* AUTOMOBILE INDUSTRY.

LUXURY GOODS. Luxury goods sales soared until 2008. By year's end, luxury brands were suffering. In October 2008, sales in such items dropped 20.1 percent. Advertising pages at the top U.S. luxury magazines fell 22 percent from a year earlier. Demand for luxury goods was expected to drop from 3 to 7 percent in 2009. For example, Bulgari, an upscale jeweler based in Rome, saw profits in 2008 plunge 44 percent in the third quarter of 2008. Shares closed in December at €4.76, less than half of what they had closed at a year earlier.

Luxury goods had a decline over the 2008 Christmas season of 21.2 percent compared with a rise of 7.5 percent in 2007. For 2009, it was projected that the sales of luxury goods, including clothing, jewelry, and fashion accessories, would be down 8 percent to about $227 billion.

By summer 2011, wealthy consumers were shifting away from up-scale retailers. With the fall in the stock market, sales continued to slip, with high-end retailers reporting that their shares had fall between 16 and 18 percent on average. Luxury shoppers make up 48 percent of total expenditures.

See also AUTOMOBILE INDUSTRY; BULGARI; COACH; ESCADA; FERRE; JEWELRY; LVMH; MORGAN; NIEMAN MARCUS; NORDSTROM; RETAILING; SWATCH GROUP; TIFFANY; WINE MARKET.

LVMH (LVMH MOET HENNESSY LOUIS VUITTON SA). The world's largest luxury goods group by revenue posted on July 27, 2009, a 23 percent drop in first-half profit resulting from the global recession.

On April 13, 2010, LVMH management reported an 11 percent surge in first-quarter revenue. Sales for the first quarter climbed to $6.07 billion, with sales up 8 percent from 2009. Management reported on July 27 that its first half of the year 2010 profit was 53 percent higher than the year before. Its net profit was $1.36 billion for half of the year, with revenue during this period up 17 percent. The firm reported in mid-October 2010 a 24 percent jump in third-quarter sales, climbing to $7.13 billion. The luxury company reported a large climb in 2010 profit of 73 percent to $4.13 billion.

In March 2011, LVMH paid $6 billion to buy the Italian jeweler Bulgari, including its debt. It would double the firm's watch and jewelry sales, the fastest-expanding division. The firm's third-quarter sales rose 18 percent as reported on October 18, with revenue climbing to $8.26 billion.

On February 2, 2012, LVMH reported a profit of $4.04 billion in 2011, with sales climbing 16 percent to 23.66 billion euros.

See also BULGARI; LUXURY GOODS.

M

MAASTRICHT TREATY. *See* EUROPEAN UNION.

MACEDONIA. On January 19, 2011, the International Monetary Fund approved a $641 million, two-year arrangement with Macedonia to be used to prevent any future crisis.

MACRO-PRUDENTIAL PHILOSOPHY. A regulation that seeks to take account of the whole system's vulnerabilities, as well as the health of individual banks by, for example, adjusting capital charges over the economic cycle. *Cf.* MICRO-PRUDENTIAL PHILOSOPHY.

MACY'S. In January 2009, the retailer announced that it would close eleven underperforming stores in nine states, affecting 960 employees. On February 2, it estimated that 7,000 jobs, or 4 percent, of its workforce would be eliminated and announced that it was taking other steps to cut costs. The Cincinnati-based operator of 840 department stores also cut its dividend by 62 percent, ended pay increases for executives, and slashed its 2009 capital-spending budget by another $100 to $150 million, down to around $450 million. The original budget was $1 billion. On February 24, Macy's reported that its profits declined 59 percent. It earned 73 cents a share in the fiscal fourth quarter ending January 31, compared with $1.73 a share a year earlier. Macy's reported on August 12 that its sales continued to decline, with earnings falling 90 percent to $7 million in its second quarter 2009, compared with $73 million the year before. Sales in the quarter dropped 9.7 percent to $5.16 billion. Macy's third-quarter 2009 loss was $35 million on a 3.9 percent sales decline. Sales fell to $5.3 billion; sales at stores open for at least one year declined 3.9 percent, with online sales increasing 21 percent. The store's stock by mid-November 2009 was down 16 percent from the October high, trading at less than twelve times consensus earnings for the year ending January 2011.

Macy's raised its sales and profit outlook for 2010 with expectations of a 5 percent increase in sales. The retailer posted strong figures and raised its first-quarter 2010 earnings estimate for the second time in a week. Then, in August, the store reported a surge in profit for the second quarter and a net income of $147 million. Sales rose 4.9 percent. On November 10, Macy's management reported that its total sales had increased 6.6 percent to $5.62 billion as same-store sales grew 3.9 percent. Robust sales in November and December combined rose 4.6 percent. The company's fiscal fourth-quarter profit grew 50 percent, posting a profit of $667 million, up from $445 million the year before. Sales climbed 5.4 percent to $8.27 billion.

In January 2011, Macy's had a 2.6 percent increase in same-store sales. By February, same-stores sales rose 5.8 percent. The retailer's first-quarter earnings climbed sharply as reported on May 11, with a profit of $131 million rising sales of 5.7 percent at $5.89 billion. The retailer's second-quarter earnings climbed 64 percent. A profit of $241 million was reported, along with revenue climbing 7.3 percent to $5.94 billion. Third-quarter earnings showed a profit of $139 million. Macy's year-end sales rose 4.8 percent.

See also RETAILING.

MAERSK. *See* MOLLER-MAERSK.

MAGAZINES. Newsstand sales of magazines fell at their fastest rate in decades during the second half of 2008. The downward trend accelerated from a 6.3 percent drop-off in the first half of 2008.

By the end of the first quarter 2009, magazine advertising pages dropped nearly 26 percent. Only fifteen magazines had more ad pages in this quarter than they did one year earlier.

By August 2010, newsstand sales of magazines had fallen 5.6 percent, with total circulation down 2.3 percent. Expectations were that the bottom had been felt. Sales of consumer magazines fell 9.2 percent in the first six months of 2011, with total circulation off 1.3 percent.

In the fourth quarter 2011, the number of ad pages in monthly publications fell 6.8 percent. The number of advertisement pages in magazines fell 8 percent in the quarter.

Cf. ADVERTISING; NEWSPAPERS.

MAGNA. The huge Canadian auto supplier won a bid to buy GM Europe from General Motors. By the end of August 2009, Germany pressed GM to complete the sale, which included Opel and Vauxhall. On September 10, GM agreed to sell a majority stake in its European operations to Magna International. GM would not be paid anything for the stake in its money-losing Opel and Vauxhall business, while Magna agreed to invest in the operations and the government of Germany pledged to finance the plan and help fund Opel with about $6 billion in loans. GM's 55 percent sale of its Opel unit would make Magna one of the world's biggest car parts makers, with $23.7 billion in revenue and 71,000 employees worldwide. Then, on November 1, 2009, GM backed out of the deal to sell both Opel and Vauxhall to Magna International.

North America's largest auto-parts maker by sales reported that second-quarter 2011 earnings fell 4 percent, with a 24 percent increase in sales. For the quarter, Magna earned $282 million.

See also GENERAL MOTORS.

MAKING HOME AFFORDABLE PROGRAM. The government program initiated in spring 2009 uses a series of incentives, one of which is $1,000 to the servicers for every mortgage they modify, to help keep people in their homes and prevent foreclosures. And yet, by summer 2009, the rising tide of foreclosures remained the single largest threat to economic recovery. Congress passed a law immunizing the servicers from lawsuits that could arise from modifying mortgages.

The loan modification program had by May 2010 helped roughly 300,000 defaulting households to get permanent new loans. However, that yield was a small amount of the estimated four million households in danger of foreclosure and of the 1.7 million households that the government believed would qualify for the program. In spring 2010, more than 637,000 households were in the trial phase of the program in which borrowers were required to consistently make their payments. The number of failed trials, 278,000, was almost as great as the number of successful ones.

On August 20, 2010, the government announced that the dropout rate from this program was high; 96,000 trial modifications were canceled by lenders in July. The number of canceled trials exceeded 616,000. The initiative originally was intended to shield 3 million households from foreclosure, but it appeared to help only about one-sixth of that number.

See also FORECLOSURE; MORTGAGE MODIFICATION; MORTGAGES; MORTGAGE SERVICERS.

MAKING WORK PAY. A credit concept of President Obama's economic platform making available a tax credit of $500 for individuals and up to $1,000 for families to be received through a temporary reduction in payroll tax withholdings to households with annual incomes as high as $200,000.

The economic stimulus package originally gave a Making Work Pay tax credit for two years. In its final version, it was scaled back. The package set the value of the benefit at $400 for individual workers, down from $500, and at $800 for couples, down from $1,000. The benefit phased out funds for workers making $75,000 a year and for couples earning $140,000.

See also AMERICAN RECOVERY AND REINVESTMENT ACT (OF 2009).

MALAYSIA. Malaysia left the Great Recession in 2010, and in 2011 the pace of its economic growth would fall to 4.2 percent. Inflation climbed to 2.4 percent in January 2011 from 2.2 percent in December 2010.

See also SOUTHEAST ASIA.

MALL PROPERTIES. Vacancy rates at malls in the largest seventy-six U.S. markets rose to 8.6 percent in third quarter 2009, a rise from 8.4 percent. In the second quarter 2011, vacancy rates in malls rose 9.3 percent from 9.1 percent in the first quarter. The average lease rates remained unchanged at $16.54 per square foot per year.

See also GENERAL GROWTH PROPERTIES.

MANUFACTURING. Converting raw materials into a completed product by a mechanical, electrical, or chemical (i.e., not manual) process.

February 2008 figures showed that manufacturing activity was at a five-year low amid slowing demand and rising prices. By December 2008, global manufacturing was shrinking rapidly. In the United States, the Institute for Supply Management's index plunged from 38.9 percent to 36.2 percent, the lowest level since 1982. A reading below 50 indicates that activity is dropping.

The manufacturing index in the eurozone fell to 35.6, a low for the eleven-year survey. Britain's index dropped to 34.4, and in Japan it fell to 36.7. The Institute for Supply Management reported that their manufacturing index for the United States was 32.4 in December, down from 36.2 in November. In Europe, the index dropped to 33.9 from 35.6.

By 2009, it was evident that manufacturing had slumped around the world with a 17 percent annualized global contraction. Output declined 4 percent in the last three months of 2008 compared to the previous quarter, reflecting lower spending and a lack of available financing for autos, housing, and capital equipment. After eighteen months of layoffs, the manufacturing sector grew in August 2009 as new evidence emerged that the economy was pulling out of recession. On November 17, 2009, the government reported a sharp slowdown in manufacturing activity in October. Although production climbed 0.1 percent for the month, growth is weak. Capacity utilization was flat across the manufacturing areas at a combined level of 67.6 percent. Ultimately, more than 2 million U.S. manufacturing jobs were lost in the Great Recession.

By mid-January 2011, manufacturing began creating more jobs than it eliminated for the first time in more than ten years. In 2010, the number of manufacturing positions in the United States grew 1.2 percent, or 136,000, the first increase since 1997. For 2011, it was projected to increase to about 2.5 percent, or 330,000, positions. Manufacturing rose to its highest level since May 2004. In July, the manufacturing sector minimally expanded. By September, manufacturing sectors across the globe slowed down. In October, factory orders fell for a second straight month by 0.4 percent to $450.03 billion. While manufacturing continued to expand in December 2011, this was not the case outside the United States.

By January 2012, U.S. manufacturing was directed upward.

See also INSTITUTE FOR SUPPLY MANAGEMENT.

MARCHIONNE, SERGIO. The chief executive of Italy's Fiat. Since Chrysler was placed in bankruptcy at the end of April 2009, Fiat will provide the U.S. firm with technology for small, fuel-efficient models and access to its dealerships in Europe and Latin America. By 2012, the Fiat was available for sale in the United States.

See also CHRYSLER.

MARGIN DEBT. In February 2011, margin debt surged 7.2 percent, rising to a new high since the 2008 financial meltdown. At month's end, it totaled $310.27 billion, up from $289.55 at the end of January and the highest level since July 2008.

MARKET CAPITALIZATION. At the stock market's peak, the market capitalization of twenty-nine of the largest financial firms on October 9, 2007, was $1.86 trillion. The breakdown in billions of U.S. dollars was as follows:

Citigroup—$236.7

Bank of America—$236.5

American International Corporation—$179.8 (To prevent a global financial panic, the government took over the company and provided more than $180 billion in financing. It may take years to unwind AIG's bad investments.)

JP Morgan Chase—$161.0

Wells Fargo—$124.1

Wachovia—$98.3 (Failed and was bought by Wells Fargo in January 2009.)

Goldman Sachs—$97.7

American Express—$74.8 (Has repaid its TARP investment and bought the warrants held by the government, but its revenue and profits have fallen, a victim of the weak economy.)

Morgan Stanley—$73.1

Fannie Mae—$64.8 (Failed along with Freddie Mac in August 2008; both were taken over by the government. Their futures are bleak as they continue to lose money.)

Merrill Lynch—$63.9 (Acquired by Bank of America in September 2008.)

U.S. Bancorp—$57.8

Bank of New York Mellon—$51.8

Freddie Mac—$41.5

Lehman Brothers—$34.4 (Failed and liquidated in September 2008.)

Washington Mutual—$31.1 (Bought by JP Morgan Chase in 2008.)

Capital One Financial—$29.9

State Street—$27.5

SunTrust Banks—$27.0
BB&T—$23.2
Fifth Third Bancorp—$18.8
National City Corp.—$16.4
Northern Trust—$15.8
Bear Stearns—$14.8
Keycorp—$13.2
Marshall & Lisley—$11.6
Legg Mason—$11.4
Countrywide Financial—$11.1
Comerica—$8.3

One year after Lehman declared bankruptcy, seven financial giants disappeared—Lehman Brothers, Bear Stearns, Merrill Lynch, Wachovia, National City, Washington Mutual, and Countrywide. The remaining twenty-two firms that still publicly traded on September 11, 2009, were now $947 billion. Their market capitalization was as follows:

JP Morgan Chase—$167.1
Bank of America—$146.8 (It has been hurt by its acquisition of Merrill Lynch and massive layoffs in its consumer banking businesses.)
Wells Fargo—$128.1 (Government stress tests found that the bank needed almost $14 billion, but it was able to raise the money quickly from private investors. It continues to have a large portfolio of troubled loans.)
Citigroup—$105.5 (The hardest hit of the large institutions, it still had huge amounts of bad loans. However, a plan to split up the bank appeared by mid-September.)
Goldman Sachs—$91.8 (Converted from an investment bank to a commercial bank in order to qualify for FDIC insurance. Recently had its most profitable quarter ever.)
U.S. Bancorp—$41.8
American Express—$40.6
Morgan Stanley—$39.2 (Converted from an investment bank to a commercial bank.)
Bank of New York Mellon—$34.5
American International Group—$26.2
State Street—$26.1
BB&T—$18.4
Capital One Financial—$17.3
Northern Trust—$14.1
SunTrust Banks—$10.9

Fannie Mae—$9.1
Fifth Third Bancorp—$7.8
Freddie Mac—$6.1
Keycorp—$5.2

The financial sector's share of the stock market shrank for these institutions, as well as their share of the overall stock market. At their peak on October 9, 2007, the total market value was $19.1 trillion, with the financial sector representing 20.4 percent. One year following the collapse of Lehman Brothers, it was down to $12.4 trillion, representing 16.6 percent of the financial sector.

MARKET REFORM. *See* JAPAN.

MARKETS (2010). At year's end 2010, markets around the world reflected the volatility of the economy. Stocks (the Dow Jones Industrial Average) rose 11 percent, gold futures were up 28 percent, oil futures climbed 13 percent, cotton future rose 89 percent, and ten-year treasury was up 8 percent. The losers included the euros against the U.S. dollar, down 7 percent, natural gas futures were down 22 percent, coffee prices were up 73.8 percent for a thirteen-year high, sugar was up to a thirty-year high, and corn and soybeans rose 48.6 percent.

MARKS & SPENCER. In January 2009, announced 1,230 job cuts and the closing of twenty-seven of its stores. It suffered its worst quarterly revenue drop in a decade, with sales falling by 7.1 percent in the quarter ending December 27, 2008. The retailer eliminated 450 jobs at its head office in London and from closing the stores. Sales fell 7.1 percent in the third quarter 2008; clothing and furniture sales fell 8.9 percent and food fell 5.2 percent. For its fiscal first quarter 2009, Marks & Spencer posted a 1.4 percent sales drop. Second-quarter 2009 group sales rose 2.7 percent due in great part to a 9.6 percent rise in international sales and a 30 percent increase in online sales.

On April 8, 2010, management announced that sales grew in the fourth quarter by 5.1 percent. By the end of May 2010, the company reported that it had posted higher earnings and sales for its fiscal year, a 3.6 percent rise in profit for the fiscal year ending March 27. Profit prior to taxes and exceptional items rose 4.6 percent. Total sales, with its 650 stores in Britain and about 300 worldwide, rose 3.2 percent.

See also RETAILING.

MARK-TO-MARKET RULES. The Financial Accounting Standards Board announced on April 2, 2009, that they were making it easier for banks to limit losses by pushing for steps to aid banks weighed down by troubled assets. The proposed changes would lessen the need for banks to take an earnings hit when assets ran into trouble. Banks had argued that mark-to-market rules required them to value their securities at current market prices, which restricted their capital unfairly by forcing them to report huge paper losses on securities that they claimed would regain value when the financial crisis eased. Opponents argued that substituting wishful thinking for real-world prices would just make investors distrust banks even more than they already did.

See also "TOO BIG TO FAIL."

MARRIAGE. For most people, the meltdown appears to be solidifying marriage relationships, not, as some would believe, leading to an increase in the divorce rate, which continues to fall—16.9 divorces per 1,000 married women in 2008 from 17.5 divorces in 2007, a decrease of 3 percent. It is assumed that debt increases the tension in marriage, but savings and/or spending less of one's assets is constructive and strengthening for a marriage.

For the first time since records have been kept, Americans have remained single, outnumbering married couples by summer 2010 at 46.3 percent versus 44.9 percent.

MARRIOTT. The hotel chain posted a first-quarter 2009 loss on restructuring charges as revenue per room tumbled by 20 percent globally and 16 percent domestically. On July 16, Marriott reported that its second-quarter 2009 earnings fell 76 percent. Its fiscal third-quarter loss resulted in part from its write-down of its time-share business. For the quarter ending September 11, Marriott posted a loss of $466 million. Revenue fell 17 percent to $2.47 billion.

The hotel chain reported on October 6, 2010, that its fiscal third-quarter profit increased. Management stated that it had a profit of $83 million, with revenue climbing 7.2 percent to $2.65 billion. The company swung to a profit in the third quarter.

Management report in July 2011 that North American revenue increased 5.8 percent from the year before, and it looked for a 6 percent to 8 percent increase in the second quarter. The hotel posted a 13 percent climb in the second quarter. Marriott swung to a loss in the third quarter 2011 with a loss of $179 million compared to a profit of $83 million the year before. Revenue climbed 8.5 percent to $2.87 billion. The loss was attributed to its time-share unit.

Cf. ACCOR.

MARSH & MCLENNAN. Posted in November 2010, the insurance conglomerate's third-quarter profit fell 24 percent, with revenue climbing. Profit was $168 million, down from $221 million the year before. Fourth-quarter 2010 earnings soared and profit climbed to $203 million from $23 million the year before. Revenue climbed 8.6 percent to $2.79 billion.

MASKING. In banking and investment terminology, preventing financial firms from masking the risks they take by temporarily lowering their debt levels before quarterly reports to the public are due. Resulting from a report that eighteen large banks had repeatedly lowered one type of debt at the end of each of the past five quarters, lowering it on average by 42 percent from quarterly peaks. If done deliberately, considered a violation of Securities and Exchange Commission regulations.

At the end of each of the past five quarters, large banks reduced their net short-term borrowings in the repo market, lowering risk profiles they release to the public before boosting their borrowings in the middle of the successive quarter.

MASS TRANSIT. The public took 10.7 billion trips on public transportation in 2008, a 4 percent increase over 2007.

The economic stimulus package of 2009 provided $17.7 billion for mass transit, Amtrak, and high-speed rail, nearly a 70 percent increase over present spending levels.

See also INFRASTRUCTURE BANK.

MASTERCARD. Reported a third-quarter 2009 profit, with earnings of $452.2 million compared with a year-earlier loss of $193.6 million. Revenue increased 2 percent to $1.36 billion. At the same time, cost-cutting operations were 13 percent.

MasterCard posted a second-quarter 2010 net income of $458 million. Its third-quarter profit climbed 15 percent with a profit of $518 million, with revenue jumping 4.7 percent to $143 billion. MasterCard's fourth-quarter profit surged 41 percent, with a profit of $415 million, up from $294 million the year before. Revenue climbed nearly 11 percent to $1.44 billion.

MasterCard's second-quarter 2011 profit surged 33 percent, with income up to $608 million from $458 million the year before. Revenue increased 22 percent to $1.7 billion. A third-quarter profit at 38 percent with a 27 percent increase in net revenue was reported. By year's end, shares of MasterCard were up 50 percent from the previous twelve months.

Cf. VISA.

MATTEL. The major toy-making firm had a sharp 46 percent drop in profits as announced in February 2009. Mattel reported net income of $176.4 million, or 49 cents a share, compared with $328.5 million, or 89 cents a share, a year before.

In mid-July, Mattel reported an 82 percent jump in its second-quarter earnings as cost-cutting offset disappointing sales. The world's largest toy maker reported a profit of $21.5 million, up from $11.8 million from a year before. However, revenue decline 19 percent to $898.2 million. Mattel's third-quarter 2009 earnings declined 3.5 percent. Earnings in the quarter were $229.8

million, down from $238 million a year before. Revenue dropped 8 percent to $1.79 billion.

The firm swung to a first-quarter 2010 profit of $24.8 million. Revenue increased 12 percent to $880.1 million. Mattel's second-quarter 2010 profit was small, with revenue rising 13.6 percent to $1.02 billion and sales climbing 17 percent. On October 15, 2010, Mattel's management reported a 23 percent gain in quarterly profit of $283.3 million from $229.9 million the year before. Revenue increased 2.3 percent to $1.83 billion.

On July 15, 2011, management reported a second-quarter profit of $80.5 million.

MAZDA MOTOR CORP. Posted a net loss of $226.6 million in the three months ending June 30, 2009; sales dropped 4 percent.

On July 30, 2010, management reported that its fiscal first-quarter loss had been lowered, promising a profit. Revenue increased 35 percent.

MBS. *See* MORTGAGE-BACKED SECURITY.

MCCAIN, JOHN. U.S. Senator and Republican Party candidate for president of the United States in 2008; lost to Barack Obama.

See also OBAMA, BARACK.

MCCARRAN-FERGUSON ACT OF 1945. The Supreme Court in 1869 held that under the commerce clause of the Constitution, the federal government can't regulate insurance, setting the background for state insurance regulation.

The high court in 1944 overturned its 1869 decision, holding that insurance is "interstate commerce" and thus subject to federal regulation. The McCarran-Ferguson Act of 1945 returned regulatory jurisdiction over insurance to the states.

MCDONALD'S. The burger giant reported second-quarter 2009 profit of $1.09 billion, down 8.4 percent from $1.19 billion a year earlier. This was seen as a result of the recession, job losses around the country, and more people staying in and cooking at home.

McDonald's first-quarter 2010 earnings increased 11 percent, with sales growing 4.2 percent in March. Global sales rose 4.2 percent, with a profit of $1.09 billion. Revenue climbed 10 percent to $5.61 billion, or 4 percent. On July 23, 2010, McDonald's management announced that earnings rose 12 percent, reporting a profit of $1.23 billion, with revenue of $5.95 billion, up from $5.65 billion one year before. Then, on September 23, 2010, it was reported that the firm boosted its quarterly dividend by 11 percent. Sales in November climbed 4.8 percent. McDonald's fourth-quarter earnings rose 2.1 percent. Revenue increased 4 percent to $6.21 billion.

For January 2011, McDonald's same-store sales climbed 5.3 percent. In February, same-store sales rose 3.9 percent. Globally, the company's sales rose 6 percent in April. In July, sales climbed 5.1 percent worldwide and 4.4 percent in the United States. August sales rose 3.5 percent globally, with a 2.7 percent climb in Europe. In November, its global sales surged 7.4 percent. Earnings in the third quarter increased 8.6 percent, with a 14 percent surge in revenue.

See also STOCK MARKET.

MCGRAW-HILL. The publisher's first-quarter 2009 net income declined 22 percent to $66 million, down from $84.6 million a year earlier. Management predicted that revenue for 2009 would fall by between 4 and 5 percent. McGraw-Hill planned to combine some of its educational publishing businesses and would trim, as announced in mid-July 2009, 550 jobs. The firm said it would restructure other parts of the business, which would make up 38 percent of the job reductions. McGraw-Hill employed 21,649 people. In July, McGraw-Hill reported a 23 percent drop in second-quarter earnings of $164.1 million, down from $212.3 million a year earlier.

At the end of October 2009, McGraw-Hill posted a third-quarter profit of $336.1 million, down from $390.2 million a year before. Revenue fell 8.4 percent to $1.88 billion. The company reported a 14 percent decline in its third-quarter 2009 earnings after announcing it had sold its *Business Week* magazine.

See also STANDARD & POOR'S.

MEALS. *See* CHILDREN IN POVERTY.

MEDIA. *See* ADVERTISING.

MEDIAN HOUSEHOLD INCOME. By mid-summer 2011, the median household income (where half the population makes more, and half less) was down 8 percent from its peak in 1999.

MEDIAN INCOME. *See* INCOME.

MEDICAID. Medicaid rolls surged as the recession tightened its grip on the economy and Americans lost their employer-sponsored health coverage along with their jobs.

In some states, Medicaid populations grew by 5 to 10 percent in 2008. In many states, the growth rates were at least double what they had been in 2007. One result of the Great Recession is the pressure put on states to protect their overburdened budgets. With the growth of Medicaid eligibility, which primarily covers low-income children and disabled adults, support is slashed.

Under growing threat from the political and fiscal arguments over the U.S. deficit, Medicaid was supported with $102 billion in stimulus funds between

2008 and 2011. These monies ran out in June 2011. Sixty-eight million U.S. citizens are dependent on Medicaid.

See also AMERICAN RECOVERY AND REINVESTMENT ACT (OF 2009); DEFICIT (BUDGET, U.S.); OBAMA, BARACK; POVERTY; STATES (U.S.).

MEDICAL CARE. By August 2010, 26.5 percent of Americans reported reducing their use of routine medical care since the start of the Great Recession in 2007. Reductions occurred mostly among young people, those with lower incomes, and those who had lost large proportion of their wealth in the latest economic meltdown.

The federal government pays 57 percent on average of states' Medicaid costs, with states finding it difficult to pay the remaining 43 percent. Enrollment climbed to 47.8 million people in 2009 from 42.6 million in 2008, the highest since 1987.

See also HOSPITALS.

MEDICAL RECORDS. *See* AMERICAN RECOVERY AND REINVESTMENT ACT (OF 2009).

MEDICARE. *See* BALANCED BUDGET ACT (1997); OBAMA, BARACK; PAYROLL TAX CUTS.

MEN'S WAGES. *See* WOMEN'S WAGES.

MEN UNEMPLOYED. The percentage of men ages sixteen and over who were working in December 2008 was at its lowest level since the government began keeping statistics in the 1940s.

The 2.3 percentage-point gap between men's June 2009 unemployment rate of 10.6 percent and women's of 8.3 percent was near the highest it has ever been since records started in 1948. A gap of 2.5 percent is the highest on record.

By summer 2009, new figures indicated a worsening situation. Only 65 of 100 men aged twenty through twenty-four years old were working on any given day in the first six months of 2009. In the twenty-five through thirty-four age group, just 81 out of 100 men were working. For male teenagers, the numbers were even worse—only 28 of every 100 males were working among sixteen- through nineteen-year-olds. For teenagers minorities, the figures were far worse.

See also MEN WORKFORCE; OVERTIME; UNEMPLOYMENT; WOMEN UNEMPLOYMENT.

MEN WORKFORCE. In 1954, about 96 percent of American men between the ages of twenty-five and fifty-four worked. Of the people losing their jobs in the Great Recession, 78 percent were men. By October 2009, 10.7 percent of men had lost their jobs.

By 2011, about 80 percent of the people losing their jobs were men. One-fifth of all men in their prime years are not getting up and going off to work. *See also* WOMEN WORKFORCE.

MERCEDES-BENZ. November 2008 sales were down 25 percent.

By year's end 2011, management reported that its sales were up 11.8 percent from the year before. *See also* AUTOMOBILE INDUSTRY; GERMANY.

MERCHANDISE (MERCHANDISING). *See* RETAILING.

MERCK & CO. Reported on July 30, 2010, that it had a 52 percent fall in second-quarter profit of $752.4 million compared with $1.56 billion the year before. However, sales climbed 92 percent to $11.235 billion. The company's profit fell 90 percent. Its third-quarter profit declined to $342 million, with sales climbing 84 percent to $11.1 billion.

Its first-quarter 2011 profit tripled from the year before, earning $1 billion in the quarter compared to $299 million the year before. Sales climbed 1 percent to $11.6 billion. Management in July reported that it would cut about 13,000 positions by the end of 2015, of which 35 to 40 percent would be in the United States.

Third-quarter 2011 revenue rose 8 percent, with net income up to $1.69 billion. Sales also climbed 8 percent to $12.02 billion

MERGERS AND ACQUISITIONS. The volume of mergers and acquisitions fell about 35 percent in 2009 from an expected volume of $3.1 trillion in 2008, less than half of the previous year's record in deals.

Fees from mergers and acquisitions, a major source of revenue for investment banks, were down by one-third in 2008 after plunging globally. Merger and acquisition fee totals were down 40 percent in the United States, 34 percent in Europe, and 11 percent in Asia, excluding Japan. Projections for the first half of 2009 were equally dismal.

The value of global mergers and acquisitions fell 35 percent in the first six months of 2009 to $1,140 billion. The number of deals in the three months through June fell by more than 15 percent. By summer 2009, the number of mergers and acquisitions began to rise slowly.

For the year 2010, mergers and acquisitions grew 25 percent, with expectations of at least a 15 percent growth in 2011. Global mergers and acquisitions for the year were $2.74 trillion compared to $2.2 trillion in 2009. U.S. firms were targets in 9,676 deals worth $894.7 billion in 2010, up from 7,338 deals worth $797.1 billion in 2009.

MERKEL, ANGELA. During the eurozone crisis, at the Brussels Summit of 2011 the Chancellor of Germany stated the following:

a. March 24–25: "The political course has been charted." The Brussels deal created a bigger rescue fund, and shortly thereafterward, European Union leaders agreed to bail out Portugal. The euro rose 4.2 percent in April.

b. July 21: "The euro is part of Germany's economic success, and a Europe without the euro is unthinkable." Leaders agree to an additional $155 billion package to save Greece. But, the crisis spreads to Italy and Spain. Italy's borrowing costs rise to a record, increasing 5.6 percent.

c. October 26–27: "We have done what needed doing." Leaders agree to boost the eurozone's bailout fund to $1.4 trillion, but they fail to decide where funding will come from. The euro fell 3.8 percent in five days.

d. December 8–9: "By beginning a fiscal union, we've taken good steps forward." The deal tightens budget rules and adds $200 billion to the euro war chest, but Europe's central bank demurs on more bond buying. The euro fell 3.0 percent in two days.

The major force in the eurozone, she continued to oppose so-called eurobonds backed by all seventeen members of the currency union, calling this idea "unthinkable." Often referred to as the "Iron Chancellor."

At a historic session on December 8–9, 2011, the chancellor's visions of a new European Union emerged. She said, "It's interesting to note that twenty years later we have realized—we have succeeded—in creating a more stable foundation for that economic and monetary union . . . and in so doing we've advanced political union and have attended to weaknesses that were included in the system." The chancellor stated that the financial crisis provided important new lessons for how to restructure Europe: "We will use the crisis as a chance for a new beginning."

Noting that there was no quick fix to the euro crisis, she added: "This process won't last weeks, it won't last months. It will take years. This process will also be accompanied by setbacks. It is not the duration of the process that is decisive. What is decisive is whether we have the necessary patience and endurance, if we do not let reversals get us down." Perhaps her most famous quote made during the height of the euro-crisis was: "Europe is in perhaps the toughest hour since World War II."

See also EURO; EUROPEAN UNION; GERMANY; SARKOZY, NICOLAS; UN ECONOMIC COUNCIL.

"MERKOZY." An increasingly heard term for the relationship between German Chancellor Angela Merkel and French President Nicolas Sarkozy.
See also MERKEL, ANGELA; SARKOZY, NICOLAS.

MERRILL LYNCH. By April 2008, Merrill Lynch had posted a $1.96 billion loss on $6.6 billion in write-downs and announced that it was cutting 4,000 positions. As subprime lenders began toppling after record waves of homeowners defaulted on their mortgages, Merrill Lynch was left with $71 billion of eroding exotic mortgage loans on its books and billions in losses. In mid-September 2008, torn apart by its collateralized debt obligation venture, Merrill Lynch was taken over by Bank of America. Its 16,090 brokers continued to worry about their employment destiny. Fourth-quarter 2008 losses disclosed on February 24, 2009, totaled $15.84 billion, more than $500 million higher than a prior estimate of $15.31 billion from its new owner. Larger-than-expected losses at Merrill Lynch forced Bank of America to accept an additional $20 billion in U.S. aid, bringing the total government assistance to Bank of America to $45 billion.

See also BANK OF AMERICA; BERNANKE, BEN; "TOO BIG TO FAIL"; UNEMPLOYMENT.

Cf. AMERICAN INTERNATIONAL GROUP; CITIGROUP.

MERS (MORTGAGE ELECTRONIC REGISTRATION SYSTEMS). The nation's largest electronic mortgage tracking system, closely involved in the scandalous mortgage-foreclosure debacle. Led to a widespread half of foreclosures and to investigations by state attorneys general. State inquiries were focusing on signed affidavits that mortgage loan services had filed with the court documents that were incomplete and not accurate.

See also FORECLOSURE; ROBO-SIGNERS.

METALS AND MINING (2011). Copper prices were projected to climb 7 percent in 2011 and the aluminum market would shift from surplus to deficit, with prices rising by 1 percent. Steel prices are expected to fall by 17 percent.

METLIFE. The huge life insurance firm announced on April 12, 2009, that it wouldn't accept federal bailout funds, an indication of its strong position in an industry struggling with huge losses and shaky balance sheets. MetLife had a second-quarter 2009 loss as the company recorded $3.83 billion in pretax investment losses. The firm lost $1.3 billion compared with one year before.

In its second quarter 2010, management reported that the firm had a profit of $1.56 billion, with revenue climbing 72 percent to $14.25 billion. Its fourth-quarter profit fell 74 percent, and the company posted an operating earnings loss of about 5 percent. Its profit was $82 million, with operating revenue climbing 6.7 percent to $14.21 billion.

Third-quarter 2011 profit jumped to $3.58 billion, with investment income rising 17 percent.

Cf. INSURERS; PRUDENTIAL FINANCIAL; TRAVELERS.

METRO. The largest retailer in Germany, it announced in January 2009 that it would eliminate as many as 15,000 jobs as part of a plan to increase profit by €1.5 billion over four years. The reduction accounted for about 5 percent of its workforce.

METROPOLITAN OPERA. To offset its growing problems resulting from the economic meltdown and loss of revenue and contributions, the giant Marc Chagall tapestries in its lobby were placed as collateral on a bank loan. These works would remain in the opera's lobby unless the Met defaulted on the loan.

See also ARTS, THE.

MEXICANA AIRLINE. *See* MEXICO.

MEXICO. Mexico suffered its most severe crisis since the 1994 currency crisis. Real GDP fell by 9.7 percent year on year in the second quarter of 2009, reflecting lower oil prices and exports, the outbreak of influenza, and declining tourism revenues and worker remittances. Supported by the rebound in oil prices and increasing exports to the United States, the fall in activity slowed down and started to recover. As monetary and fiscal stimulus are gaining traction, the recession is projected to bottom out in the third quarter of 2009 and GDP growth should rise gradually in 2010. The central bank has reduced the policy rate from 8.25 to 4.5 percent since February 2009 and the government implemented a fiscal stimulus package amounting to around 1.6 percent of GDP. Going forward, the central bank will have little room for further monetary easing as inflation is projected to remain close to the upper bound of its inflation target range. The automatic fiscal stabilizers should be allowed to work freely in 2010, but the fiscal stimulus should be gradually withdrawn if the recovery takes hold as projected. Consolidation measures proposed by the government to contain revenue shortfalls are necessary to avoid adverse financial market reactions.

On January 1, 2009, the North American Free Trade Agreement arrived at its fifteenth anniversary, with all of its positive and negative aspects. By July, Mexican unemployment was at its highest level in eight years. The peso fell 25 percent. Exports, industrial production, and retail sales had fallen 17.3 percent. Growth forecasts for 2009 were for 1.8 percent or less. The government would run its first budget deficit in five years as it increased spending to give the economy a push forward.

Its state oil monopoly, Pemex, saw its production fall 9.3 percent for the year through November 2008. Oil production fell to its lowest level in thirteen years. Mexico pumped an average of 2.7 million barrels a day in 2008, down 9.2 percent from 2007 and the lowest annual average rate of production since 1995.

Mexican consumer prices rose at their fastest pace since 2001 in 2008, complicated by the effect of the global economic crisis on the country. The government pledged $150 million in spending to prevent layoffs, slashed household gas and electricity rates for some industries by as much as 20 percent, and froze gasoline prices until the end of 2009.

Mexico sends about 80 percent of its exports to the United States. The peso slipped more than 2 percent against the U.S. dollar to its weakest level since November 2001 as less export income entered Mexico. The central bank auctioned off $400 million in reserve in January 2009 to slow the slide. To boost the country's slowing economy, Mexico's central bank cut interest rates for the first time since 2006 in mid-January as it inched toward recession. The bank lowered its benchmark lending rate fifty additional basis points to 7.75 percent. Unemployment in 2009 was at its highest level in eight years. The peso had fallen 25 percent, leading to a spike in the price of imports and hurting consumers and businesses that depended on imported goods. Exports, industrial production, and retail sales had all fallen.

The recession of 2008 and 2009 was hitting Hispanic immigrants especially hard. The number of people trying to sneak into the United States was at its lowest level since the mid-1970s. The unemployment rate for foreign-born Hispanics, estimated to be 1 million, was 8 percent in the fourth quarter 2008.

On March 16, due to its continuing arguments with the United States, Mexico announced that it would slap tariffs on ninety U.S. industrial and agricultural products, affecting some $2.4 billion in goods across forty U.S. states. Mexico argued that the tariffs were in retaliation for the cancellation of a pilot program allowing Mexican trucks to transport cargo throughout the United States. The tariffs are based mostly on imported duties of 10 to 20 percent of their value. Fresh grapes would face a 45 percent tariff, the highest. Some of the U.S. items facing imports tariffs into Mexico included a 20 percent tariff on cherries, Christmas trees, coffee makers, curtain rods, mineral water, pears, peeled onions, potatoes, soy sauce, and statuettes, and a 15 percent tariff on manicure/pedicure products, sunglasses, sunflower seeds, shampoo, and toothpaste.

The Mexican economy took another beating as Mexico's stocks fell sharply, 3.3 percent, and businesses shut down following the impact of the H1N1 virus scare at the end of April. Mexico saw exports collapse almost 29 percent in the first quarter 2009, while the Mexican economy contracted 21.5 percent at an annual rate, more than three times the rate of decline in the United States. The amount of money sent back to Mexico in April by Mexicans working in the United States fell by almost one-fifth compared with a year earlier. By the end of November 2009, Mexico finally pulled out of its recession, though its GDP shrank by 9.7 percent from January 1 to June 30, a shocking number. Nevertheless, Mexico's economic output fell about 7 percent in 2009.

By 2010, the country's GDP grew by 4.3 percent, with industrial production climbing by 7.6 percent. It was projected to grow by only 2.7 percent in 2011. On August 27, 2010, Group Mexicana, the country's largest airline group, announced it would suspend all operations after investors failed to support management's demand to cut costs during the recession period. Since 2010, has the Mexican peso rapidly risen against the U.S. dollar, resulting in the nation's export prices climbing nearly 10 percent. Mexico's exports rose almost 30 percent in 2010, with their automobile sector exports surging 52 percent. For the entire year, the economy grew 5.5 percent, its fastest pace in a decade, with projections for 2011 at 4.5 percent. Foreign investment was $17.7 billion.

For 2011, Mexico's economy, the second largest in Latin America, was projected to slow in sympathy with the United States, and growth rate could drop to 3 percent from 4.6 percent. The nation's GDP growth was 3.0 percent, with a GDP of about $1,119, an inflation rate of 4.0 percent, and a GDP per head of $9,830. In January, Mexico's manufacturing sector rose 8.2 percent to $1.8 million, driven by the country regaining health in the electronics and automobile industries. GDP rose by 3.3 percent in the second quarter from the year before, slowing from 4.6 percent in the first quarter. Its economy grew 1.34 percent during the third quarter 2011 at an annual pace of 5.5 percent, with projections for the year to be at about 4 percent growth. $20 billion in foreign direct investment was expected for the year.

See also IMMIGRANTS; NORTH AMERICAN FREE TRADE AGREEMENT; REMITTANCES.

MGM RESORTS INTERNATIONAL. Reported on August 8, 2011, a profit of $3.44 billion compared with a prior-year loss of $883.5 million during the second quarter. Revenue climbed 17 percent to $1.81 billion.

See also HOTELS.

MICHELIN. France's tire maker announced at the end of December 2008 that there would be a reduction in production at most plants as demand declined in all markets. Michelin shares closed 3.13 percent lower. With falling demand, Michelin announced that it would eliminate about 2,900 jobs in three years.

In the first half of 2009, the tire maker had a net loss of €119 million but generated an operating profit of €282 million on sales of more expensive tires. Revenue dropped 13 percent to €7.13 billion.

At the end of July 2010, management reported that the company had swung to a profit of $657.5 million in the first half of the year, with sales rising 17 percent.

MICHIGAN. *See* STATES (U.S.).

MICROLENDING. The granting of very small loans, mostly to poor people, originating in developing nations. With present tight credit and the meltdown, more and more people are turning to sources as few banks will loan funds under $50,000.

MICRO-PRUDENTIAL PHILOSOPHY. When banks had numerous subsidiaries, regulators short of money, and time tended to worry only about their own piece of the jigsaw.
  Cf. MACRO-PRUDENTIAL PHILOSOPHY.

MICROSOFT. In mid-January 2009, Microsoft posted an unexpected 11 percent drop in quarterly profit and disclosed plans to slash 5,000 jobs. The job losses would occur over the next eighteen months, representing about 5 percent of its total workforce of roughly 96,000. On April 23, Microsoft reported the first year-over-year quarterly revenue decline since it became a public company in 1986. In its quarter, which ended March 31, its revenues fell 6 percent to $13.65 billion from $14.45 billion. Microsoft posted a 32 percent drop in profit. Microsoft posted on July 23 a 29 percent fall in quarterly profit and weak sales across all of its departments. The quarter results ending June 30 showed income of $3.05 billion compared with $4.3 billion the year before. Revenue fell to $3.11 billion from the year before. By the end of October 2009, the company's third-quarter profit was down 18 percent. Microsoft reported that fiscal first-quarter profit fell to $3.57 billion from $4.37 billion a year before. Revenue declined 14 percent to $12.92 billion from $15.06 billion. On November 4, Microsoft announced that it was releasing another 800 workers. About 6.3 percent of its 91,000 employees would lose their jobs. Microsoft management reported on April 22, 2010, that its income had risen 35 percent, and within its third quarter, sales rose 6 percent to $14.50 billion. Revenue for the fourth quarter ending June 30, 2010, was $16 billion, with net income rising for the quarter to $4.52 billion. In total, its quarterly profit rose by 48 percent. Management posted a 51 percent profit, with revenue in its fiscal first quarter 2010 ending September 2010 of $16.2 billion, up 25 percent from the year before.

Microsoft's quarterly 2011 profit climbed significantly, with its Windows operation sales falling 4 percent from the previous-year quarter of $4.45 billion, even as it reported a 31 percent increase in total profit and a 13 percent climb in total revenue. Management reported that its net income in the fiscal fourth quarter, which ended in June, climbed 30 percent to $5.87 billion from $4.52 billion the year before. Revenue rose 8.5 percent to $17.37 billion. On October 20, Microsoft announced that its profit climbed 6.1 percent, with sales up 8 percent to $5.62 billion. Earnings were $5.41 billion, and revenue was $17.37 billion.

In January 2012, Microsoft reported that net income fell 0.2 percent on a 4.7 percent increase in revenue.

See also CHINA; INTEL; INTERNATIONAL BUSINESS MACHINES CORPORATION.

Cf. FACEBOOK; GOOGLE; YAHOO!.

MIDDLE-AGED JOB SEEKERS. At the expense of those between ages thirty-five and fifty-four years, these job seekers in summer 2011 were suffering significantly. Middle-aged workers held 919,000 fewer jobs than they did eighteen months ago, a 1.4 percent fall.

See also UNEMPLOYMENT.

MIDDLE CLASS. In the past two decades, a growing middle-class population has evolved, especially in emerging market nations. These people now have about one-third of their income set aside for discretionary purchases. No longer are they simply limited only to search for food and shelter in order to survive. Within this short period, the traditionally defined middle class had grown from one-third of the world's population to about one-half, or approximately 2.5 billion people. The developing nations are no longer primarily poor. The 2008–2009 meltdown may have suddenly reversed their ambitions and goals of getting out of poverty. Their economic future and expectations are fogged by the turmoil in the present economy. Their reaction will likewise be unpredictable.

By summer 2010, middle-class U.S. citizens made their largest cuts in more than twenty years in areas such as restaurant attendance and alcohol. The middle fifth of the population averaged their spending to $41,150 in 2009, down 3.1 percent from 2007 and 3.5 percent from 2008, the steepest one-year fall since records began in 1984. With the Great Recession, the middle class was showing signs of downscaling their purchases from higher priced items to those in the lower area of buying.

See also TAX CUTS.

MIDDLE EAST. The year 2008 was an uneven one for the region. During the first half of the year, oil and other commodity prices rose rapidly, leading to huge increases in the revenue of oil- and gas-exporting countries. At the same time, all Arab and Muslim Middle Eastern states had to cope with rapidly rising food and raw material prices that threatened their economies and social stability. Then, in August 2008, as the economic clouds thickened around the world, oil prices started to fall. Between August and December 2008, they dropped by over 70 percent, and the income of the oil-producing states returned to their 2007 levels. With the meltdown, a shrinking of export markets for Middle East oil producers and non-oil producers alike became a reality.

Middle Eastern banks were not overly exposed to the U.S. mortgage or derivatives markets, but sovereign wealth funds and other holders of equities suffered significant losses. Moreover, a regional housing boom and bust contributed to local financial woes. Gulf Arab states extended assistance to banks that had particular problems, such as those hurt by the bursting of the real estate bubble in Dubai. In the twelve-month period ending in February 2009, the Saudi stock market fell by 49 percent, Dubai's by 72 percent, Egypt's by 61 percent, Qatar's by 29 percent, and Morocco's by 26 percent. These losses reduced consumption and discouraged investment in both financial and real assets.

Foreign investment, tourism revenues, and remittances had all declined. These are vital for Egypt, Jordan, Morocco, and other regional nations. The most important challenge facing Middle East countries in 2009–2010 was to reduce unemployment. The number of people joining the labor market is huge and is increasing at a much faster rate than the population as a whole. The slowdown in growth that is being experienced is expected to last at least a year and will likely further reduce the level of employment. Greater socioeconomic and even political pressures in the region can be expected. Throughout 2011, the Arab Spring spread across the region, having severe social and political impact.

See also AUTOMOBILE INDUSTRY; individual listed nations of the Middle East.

MID-TERM ELECTIONS (2010). In November 2010, mid-term elections brought the Republicans back in control of the House of Representatives. Nationally, the economy indicated a continuing hangover from the 2008–2009 recession. Home prices had fallen on average 6.3 percent, the poverty rate jumped up 1.1 percentage points to 14.3 percent, and the share of adults who weren't working climbed 3.3 percentage points to 33.1 percent. More than half of the congressional districts (282) fared better than average; 153 did worse.

See also OBAMA, BARACK; TAX CUTS.

MIGRATION. Migration to industrialized nations was slowest after the start of the Great Recession, falling approximately 7 percent in 2009 from the year before to 4.3 million people.

See AFRICAN AMERICANS; IMMIGRATION; IRELAND; MIGRANT WORKERS.

MIGRANT WORKERS. Migration tends to be slow during a recession—fewer people leave the urban cores to go to the suburbs. Migration throughout the United States barely happened in 2008, as a weak housing market and job insecurity forced many citizens to stay put. The global recession was hitting immigrants around the world harder than native-born workers. In the United States, unemployment for immigrant workers in summer 2009 was about 10 percent compared to 9.4 percent for the overall population. Prior to the recession, immigrant unemployment was lower than nonimmigrant employment.

The Great Recession has had a profound impact on migration patterns. Until July 2006, Florida and Nevada attracted net inflows of 141,448 and 41,640 people, respectively. By mid-July 2009, Florida, at one time a great attractor of migrant workers, lost more than 31,000 residents to other states; Nevada lost nearly 4,000. Specifically, the Great Recession had a significant impact on migration creating large losses of population in the Sun Belt.

See also CZECH REPUBLIC; IMMIGRATION; IRELAND; REMITTANCES.

MILITARY CUTBACKS. *See* UNITED KINGDOM.

MILLIONAIRES. *See* WEALTH.

MINIMUM WAGE. In 2008, only 1.1 percent of Americans who worked forty hours a week or more even earned the minimum wage. Therefore, 98.9 percent of forty-hour-a-week workers earn more than the minimum.

At the beginning of 2009, the 70-cent-per-hour increase in the minimum wage cost 300,000 jobs. Then, the mandated increase to $7.25 in July also led to a rapid disappearance of jobs for teenagers. The unemployment rate for teenagers reached 25.9 percent in September 2009.

In 2011, California became the first state in the United States to raise the minimum wage to $10/hour.

See also UNEMPLOYMENT.

MINING. International mining companies have postponed or canceled projects and locked the gates to mines as consumers have cut spending on cars, jewelry, and housing.

In 2010, mining firms posted record profits of more than $50 billion.

See also METALS AND MINING; RIO TINTO.

MINNEAPOLIS STAR TRIBUNE. On January 15, 2009, the newspaper filed for bankruptcy protection.

MISERY INDEX. By adding together the unemployment rate and the budget deficit as a percentage of GDP an index is revealed. A high index indicates that a nation badly needs fiscal stimulus to spur economic growth but may be in no condition to pay for it. For 2010, the nations with an overwhelming misery index are, in descending order, Czech Republic, Italy, Germany, Hungary Portugal, Estonia, France, United States, Iceland, Britain, Greece, Ireland, Lithuania, Latvia, and Spain.

MITSUBISHI (BANK). Japan's biggest bank by assets announced on March 23, 2009, that its main banking unit planned to close about fifty branches and cut 1,000 jobs over three years. Seventy branches had already been closed. On April 27, Mitsubishi announced weaker results for the latest fiscal year, posting a net loss of $565 million, a significant decline from its net profit a year earlier.

Its net profit more than doubled to $6.77 billion for the nine-month April–December 2010 period.

See also JAPAN.

MITSUBISHI MOTORS. Reported a net loss of 26.64 billion yen in the second quarter 2009, compared with a net profit of 10.3 billion yen of a year-earlier.

By the end of June 2010, the automobile company reported a narrower net loss than the year before, with revenue climbing 56 percent.

MOBILITY. The number of people who changed residences declined to 35 million from March 2007 to March 2008, the lowest number since 1962, when the population had 120 million fewer citizens. It suggested that people were unable or unwilling to follow job positions around the nation. On average, it took a homeowner 10.5 months to sell a house in 2008 compared with 8.9 months in 2007. The impact was that it could further slow the U.S. economy or any subsequent recovery.

MODIFICATION PROGRAM. *See* HOME ASSISTANCE MODIFICATION PROGRAM.

MODIFYING MORTGAGES. The nation's fourteen largest banks reported that more than half of the loans they modified in 2008 became delinquent again after just six months. Although banks and investors absorbed significant losses in foreclosures, some mortgage firms viewed foreclosures as more profitable and expedient than modifications because they could levy extra charges and did not have to wait to see if the homeowner would continue on the payments.

The history of modifying mortgages was not positive. The number of loans modified in the first quarter that were thirty days delinquent was 37 percent after three months and 55 percent after six months. The number of loans modified in the first quarter that were sixty or more days delinquent was 19 percent at three months and nearly 37 percent after six months.

On March 5, the House of Representatives passed a bill that would allow bankrupt homeowners to have their loans modified in bankruptcy court, where the common solution was to reduce the principal. By August 2009, 235,247 mortgages had been modified on a trial basis. That was not even 9 percent of the 2.7 million troubled loans deemed eligible.

See also CRAMDOWN; HOUSING PLAN; MAKING HOME AFFORDABLE PROGRAM; MORTGAGE MODIFICATION.

MOET HENNESSY LOUIS VUITTON. *See* LVMH.

MOLLER-MAERSK (A.P. MOLLER-MAERSK). In the first nine months of 2009, the world's largest container-shipping company posted a loss of $1 billion in the year after posting a profit in 2008. Prices fell on average 32 percent from 2008, along with volume at 3 percent.

In April 2010, A.P. Moller Maersk reported its first full-year loss since its founding in 1904. In 2009, losses amounted to $1.31 billion following a $3.33 billion profit the previous year.

On February 23, 2011, the company, based in Copenhagen and with 243 ships, returned to profit of $4.84 billion, with revenue climbing 21 percent. In May, the firm reported an 85 percent increase in first-quarter profit. Revenue rose 10 percent to $14.5 billion. The firm's first-half net profit fell in 2011. The world's largest container shipper by volume announced its intention in December 2011 to cut its capacity on Asia-to-Europe routes, indicating that the eurozone debt crisis was disrupting global trade.

See also SHIPPING.

MOLSON COORS BREWING COMPANY. Posted a 44 percent drop in fourth-quarter net income on February 10, 2009, reflecting sluggish demand in the economic downturn period.

Its second-quarter 2010 profit rose 27 percent to $237.2 million.

MOMENT OF TRUTH, THE. *See* NATIONAL COMMISSION ON FISCAL RESPONSIBILITY AND REFORM.

MONACO. *See* TAX HAVENS; WEALTH.

MONETARY BASE. The notes and coins in the hands of consumers and corporate entities, plus the cash reserves that commercial banks hold with their central banks.

MONEY MARKET MUTUAL FUNDS. Funds that were usually low-risk investments in short-term debt, they have been troubled since the collapse of

Lehman Brothers in September 2008. Around $500 billion was withdrawn from the market, which invested in commercial paper, certificates of deposit, and other financial instruments. The Federal Reserve facility created five "special-purpose vehicles" that would purchase instruments held by the funds. The Federal Reserve Bank, in order to boost liquidity, provided up to $540 billion to support these money market mutual funds.

New proposed regulations not requiring legislative approval would require money market funds to retain a larger share of their assets in highly liquid investments like stocks, reduce their exposure to long-term debt, and limit their investments to securities with high credit ratings. By mid-September, the Securities and Exchange Commission had proposed the changes with expectations for them to go into effect in 2009.

See also FEDERAL RESERVE; FINANCIAL REGULATION PLAN (2009); WALL STREET REFORM ACT (2010).

MONOLINE. An insurance firm whose single line of business is to guarantee financial products.

MONSANTO. The world's largest seed producer said that its third-quarter 2008 profit fell 14 percent and it planned to cut 900 jobs, or about 4 percent of its workforce.

On September 10, 2009, Monsanto announced that it would double previously stated job cuts to about 8 percent of its global workforce, some 1,800 jobs, from its earlier predicted positions.

Management reported on June 30, 2010, that the firm's third-quarter profit fell 45 percent, with sales slipping 6.3 percent to $2.96 billion. On October 6, management reported that earnings would grow in 2011, noting that the net income for the year ending August 31 had fallen by nearly half to $1.1 billion from $2.1 billion the year before. Sales dropped for the year by 10 percent to $10.5 billion from $11.7 billion. Quarterly sales were $1.95 billion, an increase from $1.88 billion the year earlier. For the quarter ending November 30, the firm reported a profit of $6 million compared to a loss of $19 million the year before. Revenue increased 7.8 percent to $1.83 billion after declining 36 percent the year prior.

For its fiscal third quarter ending May 31, 2011, the firm reported a profit of $680 million, up 77 percent from the year before. Revenue jumped 21 percent to $3.59 billion. The firm's fourth-quarter loss narrowed to $222 million, compared to the previous year loss of $143 million. Revenue was $2.25 billion.

Quarterly earnings reported on January 5, 2012, sales climbing 46 percent to $895 million and a profit of $126 million. Total net sales climbed 33 percent to $2.44 billion.

MONTENEGRO. Economy grew by 8.6 percent in 2007. In 2008, the government forecast 8 percent growth, but the actual figure was lower. In

2009, the government projected growth of 5 percent, while the International Monetary Fund estimated only a 2 percent growth rate.

MONTI, MARIO. Early in November 2011, he became the Italian Prime Minister. On November 25, he declared that an Italian collapse would mean "the end of the euro." His "Save Italy" program includes a package of fiscal adjustments worth $40 billion over three years.
See also ITALY.

MOODY'S. A company that rates the creditworthiness of bond issuers. By 2009, the public and government were questioning the objectivity and reliability of rating services.

By the end of July 2010, Moody's second-quarter earnings had risen 11 percent, with U.S. revenue climbing 10 percent and overseas revenues up 1 percent. Revenue from its investors service, which accounts for 70 percent of its profits, rose 5.9 percent. Fourth-quarter profit climbed 35 percent to $137.4 million, up from $101.9 million the year before. Revenue rose 16 percent to $564.3 million.

Moody's first-quarter 2011 profit rose 37 percent. By mid-September, Moody's downgraded France's Société Générale long-term debt by one notch to AA3, and Credit Agricola's rating to AA2, one notch higher.
See also BANK OF AMERICA; BUFFETT, WARREN E.; CITIGROUP; CREDIT-RATING AGENCIES; FINANCIAL CRISIS INQUIRY REPORT; GENERAL ELECTRIC; INDONESIA; IRELAND; RATING AGENCIES; WELLS FARGO.
Cf. FITCH RATINGS; ITALY; PORTUGAL; SPAIN; STANDARD & POOR'S.

MOORE, GEOFFREY H. *See* ECONOMIC CYCLE RESEARCH INSTITUTE.

MOORE, MICHAEL. Just as the Great Recession neared its end in September 2009, the film director and writer released *Capitalism: A Love Story.* Its purpose was to entertain while at the same time inform the public of the growing debate about the nation's motivating principles of capitalism and free markets. The story accused Washington politicians of favoring corporate decision makers over the welfare of the general public. Moore urges change as he examines a system that he calls "immoral" and "undemocratic."
See also CAPITALISM.

MORGAN. The fashion brand founded forty years ago by two Parisian sisters became the first French retailer to fall victim to the credit crisis after being forced in late December 2008 to file for bankruptcy protection.
See also RETAILING.

MORGAN BANK. *See* JP MORGAN CHASE.

MORGAN, J. P. *See* PECORA COMMISSION.

MORGAN STANLEY. On December 17, 2008, Morgan Stanley reported a quarterly loss of $2.36 billion, or $2.34 a share, Morgan's first for the fiscal year. Nevertheless, the company reported a full-year profit of $1.59 billion, or $1.54 a share, down 49 percent from 2007.

In February 2009, it announced that 1,500 to 1,800 employees, or about 3 to 4 percent of its workforce, would lose their jobs. Morgan Stanley had previously announced in 2008 that it would cut 7,000 positions. Morgan Stanley suffered its second consecutive quarterly loss in the first quarter of 2009 as it posted a net loss of $177 million compared with quarterly profits of $1.41 billion one year earlier. This was the first back-to-back quarterly loss for the bank since it went public. The company reported a $159 million second-quarter loss. It was the firm's third quarterly loss in a row. On August 6, Morgan Stanley agreed to pay $950 million to buy back a warrant it issued to the government.

Profit for the second quarter 2010 fell 22 percent from the first quarter to $1.4 billion. A year before, the loss was $138 million. By mid-summer, total revenue was $7.95 billion, down 12 percent from the first quarter but a 53 percent rise from the year before. On October 20, 2010, Morgan Stanley reported a net loss of $91 million in the third quarter, with its trading revenue falling 58 percent to $1.44 billion in the quarter from the year before. In December 2010, Morgan Stanley told its executives to expect a 10 to 25 percent reduction of bonuses for the year. The executive pay cuts affected traders, back-office staff, and other major employee groups. Nevertheless, Morgan Stanley showed a 35 percent jump in fourth-quarter profit, which rose to $836 million from $617 million in the same period one year earlier.

On April 21, 2011, management reported that first-quarter earnings fell 45 percent to $968 million and revenue fell 16 percent to $7.64 billion. Then, on September 30, shares of the bank fell 10 percent over concerns of its European exposure to Europe's troubled debt. On November 10, the bank agreed to end its "Robo-Signing" program. On December 15, management declared that it would eliminate 1,600 positions, or 2.6 percent of its workforce, by the first quarter 2012.

Morgan Stanley posted a loss of $250 million in the fourth quarter 2011, with revenue of $5.7 billion.

See also CHINA; FEDERAL HOUSING FINANCE AGENCY; FINANCIAL CRISIS INQUIRY REPORT; "TOO BIG TO FAIL."

Cf. GOLDMAN SACHS.

MOROCCO. With large subsidies and state investment, in 2011 the economy was expected to grow to 3.8 percent. The nation's GDP was $99 billion, with an inflation rate of 2.6 percent and a GDP per head of $3,020. On November 25, 2011, the king granted a parliamentary election to help select a new prime minister.

See also MIDDLE EAST.

MORTGAGE. A written conveyance of title to property, but not possession, to obtain the payment of a debt or the performance of some obligation, under the condition that the conveyance is to be void upon final payment; property pledged as security for payment of a debt.

By the beginning of 2009, 13.6 million Americans owed more on their mortgages than their homes were worth.

See also BUYING DOWN A MORTGAGE; FORECLOSURES; HOUSING PLAN; MAKING HOME AFFORDABLE PROGRAM; MODIFYING MORTGAGES; MORTGAGE SCAMS; UNDERWATER.

MORTGAGE AID. *See* HOME AFFORDABLE MODIFICATION PROGRAM.

MORTGAGE-BACKED CERTIFICATES. Certificates covering pools of conventional mortgages insured by private mortgage insurance companies. These certificates are issued in big denominations, so the market is limited mainly to institutions.

MORTGAGE-BACKED DEBT. *See* FEDERAL RESERVE.

MORTGAGE-BACKED SECURITY (SECURITIES) (MBS). A type of asset-backed security that is secured by a collection of mortgages; bond-type investment securities representing an interest in a pool of mortgages or trust deeds. Income from the underlying mortgages is used to make investor payments. By mid-September 2009, the Federal Reserve had bought $850 million of mortgage-backed securities.

Mortgage securities backed by Fannie Mae, Freddie Mac, and Ginnie Mae rose to their highest level for the year on November 25, 2009.

The president released his plan on February 1, 2012, and was received with mixed reviews by members of Congress. Funds are available since the administration has spent only about $3 billion of the nearly $46 billion available for housing through the Troubled Asset Relief Program of 2008.

See also ASSET-BACKED SECURITY; BOND BUYING; FEDERAL HOME BANK; FEDERAL OPEN MARKET COMMITTEE; HOME MORTGAGES; MARK-TO-MARKET RULE; SECURITIZATION.

MORTGAGE BAILOUT. A program designed to assist one in nine homeowners who owe more than their homes are worth. President Obama announced details of the housing bailout plan on March 4, 2009. By the end of November, the government wanted banks and loan-servicing firms to amend hundreds of thousands of mortgages so they would be easier for borrowers to pay, usually without reducing the principal owed.

See also HOME AFFORDABLE MODIFICATION PROGRAM; HOUS-ING BAILOUT PLAN; MAKING HOME AFFORDABLE PROGRAM; MORTGAGE LEGISLATION; RESIDENTIAL MORTGAGE-BACKED SECURITIES WORKING GROUP; UNDERWATER.

MORTGAGE BANKER. A banker who specializes in mortgage financing; an operator of a mortgage financing firm. Mortgage-financing companies are mortgagees themselves, as well as being mortgage agents for other large mortgages.

See also MORTGAGE BANKING.

MORTGAGE BANKING. The packaging of mortgage loans secured by real property to be sold to a permanent investor with servicing retained by the seller for the life of the loan in exchange for a fee. Activities include the origination, sale, and servicing of mortgage loans by a firm or individual.

See also MORTGAGE BANKER; MORTGAGE BROKER.

MORTGAGE BROKER. A firm or individual that brings the borrower and lender together, receiving a commission; does not retain servicing.

See also MORTGAGE BANKING.

MORTGAGE CERTIFICATE. An interest in a mortgage evidenced by the instrument, generally a fractional portion of the mortgage, which certifies as to the agreement between the mortgagees who hold the certificate and the mortgagor as to such as terms as principal, amount, date of payment, and place of payment. Such certificates are not obligations to pay money, as in a bond or note, but are merely a certification by the holder of the mortgage, generally a corporate depository, that he or she holds such mortgage for the beneficial and undivided interest of all the certificate holders. The certificate itself generally sets forth a full agreement between the holder and the depository, although in some cases a lengthier document, known as a depository agreement, is executed.

MORTGAGE CHATTEL. A mortgage on personal property.

MORTGAGE CREDIT. Money that is owed for the acquisition of land or buildings (frequently of a home) and that is paid back over an extended period of time; hence, long-term debt.

MORTGAGE DEBENTURE. A mortgage bond.

MORTGAGE DEBT. An indebtedness created by a mortgage and secured by the property mortgaged; it is made evident by a note or bond.

See also FINANCIAL CRISIS INQUIRY REPORT.

MORTGAGE-DELINQUENCY RATE. By November 2009, one in ten borrowers were at least a month behind on their monthly mortgage payments, translating into about 5 million households. This figure was up from about one in fourteen mortgage holders in the third quarter of 2008.

The mortgage delinquency rate fell during the fourth quarter 2010 to the lowest level in two years. The number of loans where the borrower missed just one payment dropped to its lowest level since the end of 2007. In total, some 12.9 percent of home loans were thirty days or more past due or were in foreclosure at the end of December. That was down from 14 percent at the end of 2009 but still up from 11 percent at the end of 2008.

See also SUBPRIME; UNDERWATER.

MORTGAGEE. The lender of funds used to purchase a house and/or property. The mortgagor retains possession and use of the property during the term of the mortgage (e.g., a bank—mortgagee—may hold the mortgage on your house, of which you are the mortgagor.)

See also MORTGAGE LOAN.

MORTGAGE ELECTRONIC REGISTRATION SYSTEM. *See* MERS.

MORTGAGE FINANCING. *See* MORTGAGE BANKER; MORTGAGE LENDING.

MORTGAGE FORECLOSURES. The October 2010 controversy could have cost the banking industry $6 billion to $10 billion. Delays in foreclosing each month would have resulted in an approximate cost to banks of $1,000 per home loan. A three-month delay on the near 2 million homes in foreclosure would have resulted in a $6 billion loss. Lawsuits resulting from faulty foreclosure procedures could have resulted in another $3 billion to $4 billion. On October 20, several banks chose to proceed with foreclosures, supported by President Obama.

See also BANK STOCKS; EMERGENCY HOMEOWNERS' LOAN PROGRAM; RESIDENTIAL MORTGAGE-BACKED SECURITIES WORKING GROUP; SECURITIES LENDING; STOCK MARKET.

MORTGAGE FRAUD. Ranging from falsified credit reports to identity theft, mortgage fraud climbed 17 percent in 2009 after falling 57 percent in 2006–2008. In 2009, $14 billion in loans, or about 0.7 percent of all mortgage loans originating in the United States, contained fraudulent application data.

See also FINANCIAL CRISIS INQUIRY REPORT.

MORTGAGE GUARANTEE POLICY. A policy issued on a guaranteed mortgage.

MORTGAGE IN POSSESSION. A mortgagee creditor who takes over the income from the mortgaged property upon default of the mortgage by the debtor.

MORTGAGE INSURANCE POLICY. Issued by a title insurance firm to a mortgage holder, resulting in a title policy.
See also TITLE INSURANCE.

MORTGAGE INVESTMENT TRUST. A specialized form of real estate investment trust that invests in long-term mortgages and makes short-term construction and development loans.

MORTGAGE LEGISLATION. In mid-September 2009, one year after the collapse of Lehman Brothers, various proposals were being deliberated in Congress. They would require lenders to make sure customers could repay loans, essentially banning loans that required little or no documentation and sharply restricting subprime and other exotic mortgages. Proposals would also ban "steering" of customers into subprime loans and certain hidden broker fees like "yield spread premiums."

By mid-September, the House passed a predatory lending bill that incorporated the proposals and required lenders to keep 5 percent of mortgages they originate so they would be less likely to make bad loans. The Federal Reserve adopted regulations in 2008 that sharply restricted subprime mortgages.
See also RESIDENTIAL MORTGAGE-BACKED SECURITIES WORKING GROUP.

MORTGAGE LENDING. Effective January 1, 2010, federal regulations required mortgage lenders and brokers to give consumers better estimates of the barrage of costs they incurred when taking out home loans. Announced in November 2008, it was created to clarify the cost of mortgages.
See also FINANCIAL CRISIS INQUIRY REPORT.

MORTGAGE LIEN. A mortgage given as security for a debt, serving as a lien on the property after the mortgage is recorded.

MORTGAGE LIFE INSURANCE. Insurance on the life of the borrower that pays off a specified debt if he or she dies.

MORTGAGE-LINKED SECURITIES. *See* FEDERAL HOUSING FINANCE AGENCY.

MORTGAGE LOAN. A loan made by a lender, called the mortgagee, to a borrower, called the mortgagor, for the financing of a parcel of real estate. The loan is evidenced by a mortgage. The mortgage sets forth the conditions of the loan, specifies the manner of repayment or liquidation of the loan, and reserves the right of foreclosure or repossession to the mortgagee. In case the mortgagor defaults in the payment of interest and principal or if he or she permits a lien to be placed against the real estate mortgaged due to failure to pay the taxes and assessments levied against the property, the right of foreclosure can be exercised.

At the end of the first quarter 2010, 4.63 percent of loans on one- to four-unit residential properties were in the foreclosure process, up from 4.58 percent in the fourth quarter 2009 and 1.08 percent five years ago. An additional 9.38 percent of mortgages were past due.

See also FINANCIAL CRISIS INQUIRY REPORT; FORECLOSURE; UNDERWATER.

MORTGAGE MODIFICATION. The federal government had by November 2009 enrolled one in five eligible homeowners in a program to modify their mortgages to prevent foreclosure.

On May 17, 2010, the Treasury Department reported that nearly one in four homeowners who were offered lower payments under the program had been weeded out. Many were deleted from the trials because they had failed to make payments, didn't provide all the financial documents needed to qualify, or were found to be ineligible. If borrowers made the payments and satisfied other criteria, those trials became permanent, ensuring a cut in payments for five years.

Loan redefault rates six and twelve months after modification were as follows:

	6 months	**12 months**
Fannie Mae	27.6 percent	52.5 percent
Freddie Mac	28.7 percent	55.8 percent
Government Guaranteed	42.9 percent	62.3 percent
Private	42.1 percent	58.2 percent
Portfolio Loans	18.2 percent	30.1 percent
Overall	33.8 percent	51.4 percent

See also FINANCIAL CRISIS INQUIRY REPORT; FORECLOSURE; MAKING HOME AFFORDABLE PROGRAM; MODIFYING MORTGAGES; MORTGAGE LEGISLATION; PUBLIC-PRIVATE INVESTMENT FUND.

MORTGAGE NOTE. A note that offers a mortgage as proof of indebtedness and describes the manner in which the mortgage is to be paid. This note is the actual amount of debt that the mortgage obtains, and it renders the mortgagor personally responsible for repayment.

MORTGAGE PREMIUM. An additional bank fee charged for the issuance of a mortgage when the legal interest rate is less than the prevailing mortgage market rate and there is a shortage of mortgage money.

MORTGAGE-PURCHASE PROGRAM. *See* HOME MORTGAGES.

MORTGAGER. *Synonymous with* MORTGAGOR.

MORTGAGE RATES. Rates on a thirty-year fixed-rate mortgage fell to a record low for the second straight week at the end of December 2008. This caused refinancing applications to surge to the highest level in more than five years a month after the Federal Reserve pledged to channel billions to prop up the sinking U.S. housing market.

On October 7, 2010, average mortgage rates continued their slide, falling with the average rate on a thirty-year fixed and two other loans setting a record low. The thirty-year fixed-rate mortgage averaged 4.27 percent for the week and the fifteen-year fixed mortgage averaged 3.72 percent.

By August 2011, mortgage rates were approaching 4 percent. A thirty-year fixed-rate loan averaged 4.32 percent. About 58 percent of borrowers with a thirty-year fixed-rate mortgage could lower their mortgage rate by one percentage point but a majority of them didn't qualify for a new loan because of tight credit standards.

Average fixed mortgage rates by January 2012 were at or near record lows. The rate for a thirty-year fixed-rate mortgage was for the fifth week in a row below 4 percent at 3.91 percent and for a 15-year fixed-rate mortgage, 3.23 percent.

See also FEDERAL RESERVE; FREDDIE MAC; HOME SALES; REFINANCING; RENTERS.

MORTGAGE-REPLACEMENT LOANS. Concept of loans to prevent distressed homeowners from walking away from their debts. Under a plan in 2008, the government would provide low-cost loans to all mortgage holders worth 20 percent of their outstanding mortgage debt. Homeowners would secure lower interest costs.

See also TROUBLED ASSET RELIEF PROGRAM.

MORTGAGE SCAMS. On June 17, 2010, the U.S. Justice Department announced the arrests of nearly 500 people involved in a nationwide "takedown" of mortgage scams, many of them homeowners in financial distress. More than $200 million had been recovered, with losses of $2.3 billion stemming from mortgage-fraud cases.

MORTGAGE SECURITIES. *See* FEDERAL RESERVE; LEHMAN BROTHERS; MARK-TO-MARKET RULE; PUBLIC-PRIVATE INVESTMENT FUND.

MORTGAGE SERVICER. A company that acts as an agent for mortgage holders, collecting and distributing payments from borrowers and handling defaults, modifications, settlements, and foreclosure proceedings.

MORTGAGE SERVICERS. *See* FORECLOSURE; MERS; OFFICE OF THE COMPROLLER OF THE CURRENCY.

MORTGAGE SERVICES. On July 28, 2009, the Treasury Department met with twenty-five mortgage servicer representatives, in part to order that more home loans be modified.
See also MAKING HOME AFFORDABLE PROGRAM.

MORTGAGE UNDERWRITING. Process of evaluating the credit characteristics of a mortgage and borrower.

MORTGAGOR. A debtor or borrower who gives or makes a mortgage to a lender on property owned by the mortgagor.
Synonymous with MORTGAGER.

MOTOROLA. Motorola had 6,7000 employee layoffs in 2008, as the economic downturn and a slump in cell phone demand increased pressure on the firm, which was already losing market share.

It announced in January 2009 that it would eliminate another 4,000 jobs, or an estimated 6 percent of its workforce, and showed a fourth-quarter loss because sales of cell phones were weaker than expected. The plan would bring its cost cuts to $1.5 billion for 2009 and $700 million in new savings on top of a previously announced plan for $800 million in expense cuts. On February 3, Motorola reported that sales of its troubled cell phone unit plummeted in the fourth quarter 2008. Motorola announced at the end of April that its total cash on hand had dropped to $6.1 billion from $7.4 billion at the end of 2008. The company posted a first-quarter net loss of $228 million compared with a loss of $190 million a year before. Cell phone shipments worldwide dropped 13 percent in the first quarter of 2009. The company had a third-quarter 2009 profit of $12 million compared with a loss of $397 million a year before. Revenue fell 27 percent to $5.45 billion. Four years ago, its stock touched $55 billion; by 2010, it was just over $20 billion. Sales continued to fall 27 percent in the third quarter 2009 to $5.5 billion, reporting $12 million in earnings.

Second-quarter 2010 earnings were $162 million, with revenue falling to $5.41 billion from $5.50 billion.

At the beginning of 2011, the company split itself up with two specialized companies—Motorola Mobility and Motorola Solutions. Motorola had a loss in the second quarter 2011 of $56 million, with revenue climbing to $3.3 billion.
Cf. NOKIA; VODAFONE.

MOYNIHAN, BRIAN. *See* BANK OF AMERICA.

MOZILO, ANGELO. *See* COUNTRYWIDE FINANCIAL.

MUNI BONDS. *See* MUNICIPAL BONDS.

MUNICH RE. The world's largest reinsurer in February 2011 fell to a $725 million net loss compared with a $394 million profit the year before. Its net profit in the fourth quarter 2010 fell 39 percent from the year before to $649.3 million. The reinsurer said it was targeting an after-tax profit in 2011 of $2.4 billion euros.

MUNICIPAL BONDS (MUNI BONDS). In the United States, bonds that made up this market of $2.7 trillion were issued by local-government borrowers. By 2011, credit-rating agencies, such as Standard & Poor's, stated that downgrades of bonds worth about $2.9 trillion issued by state and local governments could be on the increase. Fears of default on debt could lead to a downgrade, lowering the price of its bonds.

MUNICIPALITIES. *See* INTEREST-RATE BETS; STATES (U.S.).

MUTUAL FUND ASSETS. For 2008, these assets had declined by $2.4 trillion, a fifth of their value, in the United States alone. In the United Kingdom, the drop was more than one-quarter, or almost $195 billion.
See also EUROPEAN PARLIAMENT; UNITED KINGDOM.

MUTUAL FUNDS. On July 21, 2010, the Securities and Exchange Commission proposed new limits on the sales fees that mutual fund firms could charge investors on shares that are sold via brokers. The proposal would cap the amount that investors could pay to compensate fund brokers and sales forces over the lifetime of their investment.
See also SECURITIES AND EXCHANGE COMMISSION; STOCK MARKET (U.S.).

MUZAK. The maker of background music heard in elevators and offices filed for Chapter 11 bankruptcy protection on February 10, 2009. The firm listed its total debt at $100 million to $500 million, with assets of less than $50,000.

N

NAKED SHORT-SELLING. A controversial trading practice using high-speed traders and accounting for nearly 40 percent of U.S. stock-trading volume today. Trading firms are usually unidentified, thereby reducing accountability.

See also SHORT-SELLING.

NAME AND SHAME. As part of his program to restrict executive compensation for executives whose firms received bailout funds, President Obama on February 4, 2009, introduced the name and shame provision, designed to make companies think twice about indulgent outlays. The intent was not to reward "executives for failure, especially when those rewards are subsidized by U.S. taxpayers."

See also CLAWBACKS; EXECUTIVE PAY; GOLDEN PARACHUTES.

NAMING RIGHTS. As states attempt to bridge huge budget gaps, they are increasingly turning to corporate or private donors to have their public properties named after the giver.

NASDAQ COMPOSITE INDEX. A major American stock exchange with 3,700 companies and corporations. For 2008, it fell 40.5 percent, the worst percentage decline in its thirty-eight-year history, surpassing its 39.3 percent plunge in 2000 after the tech-stock bubble burst.

On February 3, 2012, the NASDAQ Composite Index surged 1.61 percent to 2,905.66, its highest close since December 2000.

See also STOCK MARKET.

NATIONAL BANK ACT OF 1863. Created a national banking system and established the Office of the Comptroller of the Currency, which charters, regulates, and examines all national banks.

NATIONAL BANK SUPERVISOR. Proposal that would eliminate savings and loans and close the Office of Thrift Supervision. Its responsibilities would fall under the new regulator, which would replace the Comptroller of the Currency and oversee all banks. By mid-September 2009, the Obama administration had submitted a draft bill to Congress. There have been no votes in the House or the Senate.

See also FINANCIAL REGULATION PLAN (2009).

NATIONAL BUREAU OF ECONOMIC RESEARCH (NBER). A U.S. government data-collecting agency responsible for determining, among other matters, the official end of the recession of 2008–2009. The group spent a year examining statistics before declaring that the recession had begun in December 2007. Its Business Cycle Dating Committee looks at output as well as other indicators such as employment to finalize their decision. It is the responsibility of this nonprofit research group to declare the beginning and end of U.S. recessions. The bureau defines recession as "a significant decline in economic activity spread across the economy lasting more than a few months."

Why didn't the bureau declare the end of the recession when it met in April 2010 even though most indicators had turned up? Their response was, "The Business Cycle Dating Committee of the National Bureau of Economic Research reviewed the most recent data for all indicators to the determination of a possible date of the trough in economic activity marking the end of the recession that began in December 2007. The trough date would identify the end of contraction and the beginning of expansion. Although most indicators have turned up, the committee decided that the determination of the trough date on the basis of current data would be premature. The committee acts only on the basis of actual indicators and does not rely on forecasts in making its determination of the dates of peaks and troughs in economic activity. The committee did review data relating to the date of the peak, previously determined to have occurred in December 2007, marking the onset of the recent recession. The committee reaffirmed that peak date."

On September 20, 2010, the bureau announced the end of the recession in June 2009, nineteen months after the economy began sliding into a downturn in December 2007. The recession wiped out 7.3 million jobs, cut 4.1 percent from economic output, and cost Americans 21 percent of their net worth.

By November 2011, the bureau had chosen not to make any assertion on a double-dip recession.

See also RECESSION OF 2007–2012.

NATIONAL COMMISSION ON FISCAL RESPONSIBILITY AND REFORM. On February 18, 2010, President Obama signed an executive order establishing this new bipartisan commission to address the nation's fiscal challenges. Social Security was likely to be its major target of inquiry. The commission wanted to reduce the federal deficit to 3 percent of the GDP by 2015, an unlikely goal. On November 10, 2010, the commission reported its sweeping proposal to cut the federal budget deficit by hundreds of billions by targeting U.S. tax and spending policies, such as Social Security benefits, middle-class tax breaks, and defense spending. Home-mortgage interest would be eliminated. It would tax capital gains and dividends at the higher rates, low levies on wage income, and would lower and simplify individual rates to 9 percent, 15 percent, and 24 percent. The title of the report was "The Moment of Truth."

Since the Industrial Age in the United States and between World War II and the oil crisis of the 1970s, reality was supreme for the country. Wages and profits climbed, the social safety net and the nation's military reach expanded, and Washington lived within its means. College education seemed available to all who qualified and Medicare and Medicaid, along with Social Security, were solid. No longer true. The commission's primary point was that the limitless age is at an end.

Overall, the plan would restrain the growth of the federal debt by roughly $3.8 trillion by 2020, or about half of the $7.7 trillion by which the debt would have otherwise grown by that year. It would:

- Cut $100 billion in defense spending.
- Rise the Social Security age to sixty-nine.
- Raise the gas tax by 15 cents.
- Lower corporate tax rate to 26 percent.
- Repeal the alternative minimum tax.
- Scrap deductions on mortgages over $500 thousand.
- Cut federal work force by 10 percent.
- Cut farm subsidies by $3 billion.

Recommendations were aimed at a deficit reduction of $3.8 trillion, with spending cuts of $2.2 trillion (cut discretionary spending, pay doctors and other providers less, limit Medicare cost increases, and raise retirement age by 2075; higher incomes would be subject to payroll taxes and cost-of-living increases would be smaller; allocate $0.2 trillion for new revenue and $0.8 trillion of other tax changes, such as eliminating mortgage interest deduction, child tax credit, and the earned income tax credit; and $0.7 trillion for interest savings.)

The debt-panel proposed changes to U.S. spending and tax policy to hold growth of the federal debt down by roughly $3.8 trillion by 2020. The current national debt was about $13.8 trillion. The plan before the commission was a 75 percent spending cut and a 25 percent revenue increase. On Friday, December 3, the bipartisan debt commission voted 11–7 to approve a controversial plan to shave deficits by nearly $4 trillion over the next ten years. That fell short of the fourteen votes needed to formalize its recommendations and send them to Congress for an up or down vote. The final package would overhaul the tax code, reducing both tax rates and tax breaks. It would cut back spending on Social Security, Medicare, Medicaid, the military, and many other domestic programs. Nevertheless, there was considerable support for much of the plan, and it might lead to a solution to the nation's crushing debt.

Synonymous with DEFICIT COMMISSION.

See also BIPARTISAN POLICY CENTER DEBT REDUCTION TASK FORCE.

NATIONAL CREDIT UNION ADMINISTRATION. *See* CREDIT UNIONS.

NATIONAL DEBT. The debt at about 40 percent of GDP in 2008 was expected to rise to 60 percent by 2010 as a result of the recession and spending tied to the federal bank bailout and stimulus program.

See also TAX CUTS.

NATIONAL ECONOMIC COUNCIL. *See* SPERLING, GENE; SUMMERS, LAWRENCE.

NATIONAL EXPORT INITIATIVE. Launched by President Obama in March 2010 with a goal of doubling U.S. exports in five years.

NATIONAL INFRASTRUCTURE BANK. *See* AMERICAN JOBS ACT (PROPOSED).

NATIONAL INSTITUTES OF HEALTH. *See* AMERICAN RECOVERY AND REINVESTMENT ACT (2009).

NATIONALIZATION. The governmental takeover of a private firm. Nationalization usually means that the government buys big stakes in banks or other institutions/organizations to help them survive; other times it involves federal seizure of an insolvent institution. The government doesn't need to have 100 percent ownership. It is risky for a government to run the private sector—the government's record as a corporate manager is poor, and should the effort fail, taxpayers may lose billions of dollars they have spent; it also violates the spirit of its concept of free markets. The biggest problem for the government in nationalizing banks is that it is impractical and expensive to take over all 8,000 banks or even the 314 institutions that described themselves as "banks" in order to receive government aid. It also would not solve the pressing problem of potential bank failures. Most specialists believe that nationalization should be used as an emergency method to prop up banks during difficult times. However, there is evidence that nationalization can cause market distortions. The longer banks remain in government hands, the more likely they will be used to further government policies. Assuredly, should banks lose large amounts of deposits or access to credit, they will need to be seized.

See also AUTOMOBILE INDUSTRY; "BAD BANKS"; ECONOMIC NATIONALISM; OBAMA, BARACK; TRUMAN, HARRY S.

NATIONAL SEMICONDUCTOR. Announced in mid-March 2009 its intent to eliminate 26 percent of its workforce, or more than 1,700 jobs, in one of the most severe cutbacks by a Silicon Valley firm during the current recession. National Semiconductor's fiscal first-quarter profit 2009 dropped 63 percent as revenue fell by a third. For the quarter ending August 30, it reported a profit of $29.8 million, down from $79.6 million a year earlier.

NATURAL GAS. Prices were bolstered by the approaching summer 2010. Gas for June delivery rose 2 percent to $4.398 per million BTUs.

NAV. *See* NET ASSET VALUE.

NAVISTAR. Reported on December 22 lower quarterly 2010 earnings, with a profit of $39 million.

The firm reported on June 7, 2011, that its second-quarter profit rose 72 percent from the year before, but earnings were below expectations. A profit of $74 million was made, with revenue climbing 22 percent to $3.36 billion. On September 7, management warned that the truck manufacturer could shift production from Mexico. A profit for the third quarter was reported at $1.4 billion, up from $117 million the year before. For its quarter ending October 31, the firm noted a profit of $255 million. Revenue climbed 28 percent to $4.32 billion.

NBER. *See* NATIONAL BUREAU OF ECONOMIC RESEARCH.

NEC CORPORATION. The international information technology company announced at the end of January 2009 that it would cut 20,000 jobs worldwide in response to mounting losses in the deepening global downturn. NEC's net loss for the October–December 2008 quarter swelled to $1.46 billion. The job cuts, which included nearly 7 percent of the firm's permanent workforce, would be completed by March 2010.

NEGATIVE AMORTIZATION LOAN. A loan that permits a borrower to make monthly payments that do not fully cover the interest payment, with the unpaid interest added to the principal of the loan.

NEGATIVE INFLATION RATE. *See* DEFLATION; SPAIN.

NEIMAN MARCUS. In January 2009, the upscale retailer announced it would cut about 375 jobs, or 2.3 percent of its workers. Then, in mid-February, it cut an additional 450 positions, its second round of layoffs in two months. In mid-March, the company posted a $509.2 million quarterly loss compared with a loss of $44.3 million a year earlier. For its fourth quarter ending August 1, Neiman Marcus posted a loss of $168.5 million compared with a $35.6 million loss one year earlier. Sales declined 25 percent to $768 million from $1.03 billion in the previous-year quarter.

Neiman Marcus sales were 11 percent higher in April 2010 than the previous year, making a rebound from a 22.5 percent fall in the year to April 2009. Neiman Marcus enlisted designs in cost-cutting plans. The firm's gross margin climbed to 30.9 percent from 24.1 percent. For the quarter ending July 31, 2010, its loss was narrowed to $32.8 million from $168.5 million from the year before. Revenue climbed 14 percent in the fourth quarter to $826.3, with sales climbing 6.5 percent following the drop in 2009 of 23 percent.

The retailer posted on May 30, 2011, sharply higher earnings in its fiscal third quarter, with a profit of $46.2 million and revenue for the quarter climbing 9.9 percent to $984 million. Sales increased by 8.6 percent.

See also RETAILING.

NESTLE. Its net profit more than tripled in 2010, as the world's largest food company reported sales of $114.35 billion in 2010, up 2 percent from the previous year.

Sales rose 7.5 percent in August 2011. First-half year sales climbed 7.5 percent, with a profit of 4.7 billion francs, down 14 percent.

NET ASSET VALUE (NAV). Value of an asset minus any associated costs; for financial assets, typically changes each trading day.

NET CHARGE-OFF RATE. A ratio of loan losses to total loans.

NETFLIX. Posted a 52 percent profit surge and a 34 percent revenue increase for its fourth quarter 2010.

In late July 2011, Netflix management reported a 57 percent increase in quarterly profit, with income for the second quarter of $682 million. Revenue increased to $788.6 million from $519.8 million the previous year. In the fourth quarter, Netflix proved its management skills by recovering many of its former subscribers. It added 610,000 U.S. subscribers to end 2011 with 24.59 million members. Revenue surged 47 percent to $876 million, but its profit dropped 13 percent.

NETHERLANDS, THE. After a sharp recession, the economy looks set to grow again on the back of a recovery in world trade, fiscal stimulus, and easier monetary conditions. However, growth will be too weak to prevent further increases in the unemployment rate, one of the lowest in the Organisation for Economic Co-operation and Development, until the end of 2010. As companies need to restore profitability they will continue to shed workers throughout 2010. The resulting improvements in profitability should lay the foundation for renewed investment growth and hence a more durable recovery in 2011. The fiscal stimulus has contributed to a budget deficit around

4.5 percent of GDP in 2009. To restore fiscal sustainability, the government should pursue its consolidation plan set to start in 2011. The planned two-step increase in the retirement age will help meet this objective but would be more effective with a phased-in implementation. Further focus on active labor market policies and easing of labor protection legislation would help stimulate employment growth.

The Dutch economy contracted starting in the third quarter of 2008 into the first three months of 2009, resulting in its first recession since 1982.

In 2011, the budget gap will take most of the government's attention. Fiscal policy will become restrictive throughout the year, holding GDP growth to a small 1.1 percent. The nation's GDP growth was 1.1 percent, with a GDP of $743 billion, an inflation rate of 1.0 percent, and a GDP per head of $44,630.

See also FORTIS BANQUE; ICELAND.

NET WORTH. *See* WEALTH.

NEVADA. By March 2011, Nevada remained the state with the highest jobless rate at 14.2 percent. The lowest was North Dakota at 3.8 percent.

"NEW BANKS." Not saving bad banks, but creating and/or supporting existing banks to become good banks would be a major means for solving the banking crisis and bringing other, usually smaller banks to provide the new lending that the economy needs. With a minimum of $350 billion in assets, the government encouraged these institutions to enter the market.

Cf. AGGREGATOR BANK; "BAD BANKS"; "GOOD BANKS."

NEW COMPANIES. These business start-ups are crucial to any economic recovery. In their first ninety days of life, businesses accounted for 14 percent of hiring in the United States between 1993 and 2008. New companies fell 9 percent between the third quarter of 2000 and the first quarter of 2003. Business starts fell 14 percent from the third quarter of 2007 to the third quarter of 2008. The 187,000 businesses created in that quarter were the fewest in a quarter since 1995.

NEW DEAL. *See* G-20; PERKINS, FRANCES; ROOSEVELT, FRANKLIN DELANO.

NEW EUROPEAN TREATY. *See* CAMERON, DAVID; EUROPEAN UNION.

NEW EURO, THE (NEW EURO PACKAGE, THE). *See* EURO.

NEW FISCAL COMPACT. *See* CAMERON, DAVID; EUROPEAN UNION.

NEW FOUNDATION. President Obama's approach to curb financial "risks built on piles of sand."

See also REGULATORS; WALL STREET REFORM ACT (2010).

NEW HAVEN REGISTER. See JOURNAL REGISTER CO.

NEW HOME CONSTRUCTION. *See* HOME CONSTRUCTION.

NEW HOME SALES. *See* HOME SALES.

NEW JOB OPENINGS. *See* JOB OPENINGS.

NEW MONEY. Since September 2008, the Federal Reserve's balance sheet had ballooned to more than $2 trillion from about $900 billion as the central bank created new money and loaned it out through all of its new programs. By the time the Federal Reserve completed its plans to purchase up mortgage-backed debt and consumer debt, the balance sheet was up to about $3 trillion.
See also FEDERAL RESERVE.

"NEW NORMAL." As summer 2010 arrived, it was clear from the high rate of nearly 15 million unemployed, excluding those who have ceased searching for full-time work, this concept spread among specialists and economists. It was a pattern of joblessness that refused to budge down. It envisions an economy in which growth is too slow to bring down the unemployment rate, while the government is forced to intervene ever more forcefully in a struggling private sector. Not only are more people out of work longer, but their options are narrowing. Roughly 1.4 million people have been jobless for more than ninety-nine weeks. Many believe that the "new normal" will be with us for three to five years.
See also UNEMPLOYMENT.

NEW PECORA COMMISSION. *See* FINANCIAL CRISIS INQUIRY COMMISSION.

NEW POOR. People long accustomed to the comforts of the middle-class life that are now relying on public assistance for the first time in their lives, potentially for years to come.

NEW REGULATORY AGENCIES. Proposed agencies will require legislative approval.
See also CONSUMER FINANCIAL PROTECTION AGENCY; NATIONAL BANK SUPERVISOR.

NEWS CORPORATION. Owners of the *Wall Street Journal* took a large write-down on the value of its assets, pushing it to a $6.4 billion loss for the fiscal second quarter 2009. The company's net income climbed 11 percent in the third quarter 2009. News Corporation reported a net income of $581 million.

In August 2010, net income totaled $875 million compared to a loss of $203 million the previous year. In early November, News Corporation posted a 36 percent increase in first-quarter profit to $775 million. Revenue increased 3.2 percent to $7.43 billion for the quarter.

In May 2011, profit fell by 24 percent, with net income of $639 million. On August 10, management reported a fourth-quarter small profit, with operating earnings climbing 8.9 percent for the quarter. Revenue climbed 11 percent to $8.96 billion. In early November, News Corporation management reported a 7 percent increase in revenue to $7.96 billion, but net income dropped 4.8 percent to $738 million.

NEWSPAPER ADVERTISING. *See* NEWSPAPERS.

NEWSPAPERS. Newspaper advertising, already in its worst slump since the 1930s Great Depression, suffered its sharpest drop during the first quarter of 2009, down 30 percent for many papers. New figures released at the end of April indicated that U.S. newspapers continued their downward trend with a 7 percent drop from the previous year. Of the most widely circulated twenty-five newspapers, all had declines, except for the *Wall Street Journal*, with a tiny 0.6 percent gain. For the others, the declines ranged from 20.6 percent to a slight 0.4 percent. Average U.S. weekly newspaper circulation for the six months ending September 30, 2009, fell nearly 11 percent. Nearly two-thirds of the twenty-five largest newspapers posted circulation declines of 10 percent or more. On October 26, 2009, the Audit Bureau of Circulations revealed that the *Los Angeles Times* had lost 11 percent of its paying readers in 2009. Circulation at the *Boston Globe* fell by 18 percent and at the *San Francisco Chronicle* it declined by 26 percent. Circulation at the *Wall Street Journal* climbed to 2 million, making it America's best-selling newspaper. Daily sales of the *New York Times* declined by 7 percent and *USA Today* saw circulation fall by 17 percent.

Newspaper circulation by April 2010 among the twenty-five largest newspapers had fallen nearly 9 percent. In the six-month period ending March 31, 2010, sales dropped 6.5 percent and weekday sales 8.7 percent compared with the same six-month period one year earlier. Nevertheless, 13,500 newsroom jobs have been lost in the United States since 2007. Spending on newspaper ads declined 5.6 percent in the second quarter 2010, narrowing the decrease of the past. After falling 29 percent in the second quarter 2009 and 27.9 percent in the third quarter, the decline in the first quarter 2010 was only 9.7 percent. Problems in the industry would continue into 2012.

See also ADVERTISING; *BALTIMORE SUN*; *FINANCIAL TIMES*; GANNETT; HEARST CORPORATION; JOURNAL REGISTER CO.; *MINNEAPOLIS STAR TRIBUNE*; NEWS CORPORATION; NEWSPAPER WEBSITES; *NEW YORK TIMES*; *ROCKY MOUNTAIN NEWS; SUN-TIMES*; TRIBUNE; *WASHINGTON POST*.

NEWSPAPER WEBSITES. In the first quarter 2009, newspaper websites attracted more than 73 million hits, or visitors, every month on average. That was a 10.5 percent increase the first quarter 2008.

See also NEWSPAPERS.

NEW YORK TIMES (NY TIMES). Revenues from print and online operations fell nearly 22 percent in November 2008 from the previous year. Its newspaper ad revenue declined 14.2 percent for a drop of 19.5 percent in the last two years.

The Times Company had $1.1 billion in debt, $46 million in cash, and a substantial amount of debt maturing over the next couple of years. It continued to seek outside investors. In January 2009, the company sold a portion of its midtown Manhattan headquarters. On February 19, it announced that it would suspend dividend payments to shareholders for the first time in four decades as a publicly traded company. In mid-month, the company announced that it had raised $225 million in a sale of some of its assets. Pay was cut in March by 5 percent for editors, and 100 workers on the business side were dismissed, representing a cut of about 5 percent of its 2,000-person staff. The newspaper posted a steep first-quarter 2009 loss amid worse-than-expected advertising results. Total revenue fell 19 percent to $609 million. It posted a loss of $74.5 million and a 28.4 percent decline in advertising revenue.

The New York Times Company sold its New York City radio station to Univision Communications in an arrangement that netted the publisher $45 million as it sought to stabilize its finances. WQXR-FM is among 275 of the nation's 13,000 radio stations carrying classical music. On July 23, 2009, the New York Times Company reported a second-quarter profit of $39.1 million. Ad sales had fallen more than 30 percent in the quarter. On October 14, the company scrapped efforts to sell the *Boston Globe.* The company announced on October 19 its intention to shed another 100 jobs from its nearly 1,300-person newsroom by year's end. Buyouts were offered.

The New York Times Company reported on April 22, 2010, a net income of $12.8 million for the first quarter compared with a loss of $74.5 million. Revenue decreased 3.2 percent in the quarter to $588 million and advertising income rose 18 percent. Its second-quarter profit fell 18 percent and the company reported a profit of $32 million. Management announced on September 22 that circulation revenue in the third quarter 2010 fell about 5 percent, wiping out most of the 6.7 percent increase a year before that flowed from June 2009 price increases. Circulation revenue was up 1.4 percent over the 2008 period. The firm reported on October 19 a third-quarter loss, with declines in print advertising and circulation revenue; at the same time, costs increased for the first time in three years. A net loss of $4.3 million was noted, with total revenue of $554.3 million, down 2.7 percent. Fourth-quarter net income fell

26.2 percent to $67.1 million, with revenue falling 3 percent to $662 million. For the year, the paper earned $107.7 million versus $19.9 million in 2009. The company ended 2010 with about $597 million in net debt and $400 million in cash and short-term investments.

The company reported on April 21, 2011, a 58 percent fall in first-quarter profit. It had a net income of $5.42 million, with total revenue falling 3.6 percent to $566.5 million. In mid-September, management reported that it expected third-quarter advertising revenue to fall 8 percent and envisioned that circulation revenue would increase 4 percent in the present quarter. Its third-quarter profit had a net income of $15.7 million. Revenue fell 3.1 percent to $537.2 million.

Reported on February 2, 2012, the newspaper's fourth-quarter profit fell 12.2 percent, with net income totaling $58.9 million.

See also NEWSPAPERS; OBAMA, BARACK.

Cf. TRIBUNE.

NEW ZEALAND. New Zealand is finally emerging from its five-quarter-long recession as the beneficiary of strong domestic and global policy stimulus. Recent indicators, notably improving business production expectations and retail sales, suggest that the third quarter is on track to register modest positive growth. But, the recovery could be hampered by the overhang of high private-sector indebtedness, ongoing credit contraction, the currency's recent strength, and rising unemployment. Unemployment is rising markedly and, as a lagging indicator, will continue to do so. This may hold down incomes and, along with the need to unwind the burden of household debt, raise the propensity to save. Given weak and fragile private demand, it is appropriate that monetary and fiscal policies remain expansionary for the time being. However, if the recovery takes hold as projected, stimulus should start to be withdrawn by mid-2010 in order to reinforce balance-sheet restructuring and, in conjunction with structural reforms, to steer activity toward tradable production rather than housing investment as the main generator of income and wealth.

New Zealand's central bank cut rates by 1.5 points to 5 percent on December 4, 2008. The nation's unemployment rate fell to 6.4 percent in the three months prior to September 2010 from 6.9 percent in the earlier quarter. Economic growth should reach 3.4 percent, up from 2.6 percent in 2010. The nation's GDP growth was 3.4 percent, GDP at $148 billion, an inflation rate of 3.9 percent, and a GDP per head of $33,490.

NEXTEL. *See* SPRINT NEXTEL CORP.

NICHE BANKS. *See* INDUSTRIAL BANKS.

NIGERIA. In 2011, oil revenue will continue to buoy the economy and a strong performance by non-oil industries will help keep growth up to 5.8 percent. The nation's GDP is $248 billion, with an inflation rate of 11.2 percent and a GDP per head of $1,600. With 2012, unrest came back to Nigeria.

See also AFRICA.

NIKE. The world's largest maker of sportswear by sales announced on February 10, 2009, a 4 percent reduction in its workforce, affecting about 1,400 employees, as it realigned its operations amid the difficult economic times. It announced on May 14 that it would cut another 1,750 jobs in its worldwide operations, comprising about 5 percent of its workforce. Nike's fiscal second-quarter 2009 profit fell 4 percent on lower sales, with a profit of $375 million, and revenue fell 4 percent to $4.41 billion. Fourth-quarter profits dropped 30 percent, with revenue declining 7.4 percent to $4.71 billion.

The firm's fiscal fourth-quarter profit then climbed 53 percent following restructuring. For the quarter ending May 31, 2010, Nike posted a profit of $521.9 million, with sales rising 4 percent in North America. On December 21, Nike posted a 22 percent increase in quarterly income. Profit climbed to $457 million, with sales rising 10 percent to $4.84 billion.

By 2011, Nike had posted a 5.2 percent increase in its fiscal third-quarter earnings and a profit of $523 million, up from $497 million the year before. Revenue climbed 7.3 percent to $5.08 billion. The firm's stock price fell by 9.5 percent in March as it reported that its gross margins fell 1.1 percentage points. Management reported on June 27 that its fiscal fourth-quarter earnings had risen 14 percent. Revenue increased 21 percent in North America, 16 percent in China, and 19 percent in emerging markets. The company had a $594 million profit in the quarter, with revenue increasing across the board by 14 percent to $2.55 billion. The firm on September 22 reported its fiscal first-quarter earnings had climbed 15 percent. In North America alone, sales climbed 15 percent. A profit of $645 million was shown, with revenue increasing 18 percent to $6.08 billion. With a 31 percent surge in sales to China, Nike earned in its quarter ending November 30, 2011, $469 million, with revenue jumping 18 percent to $5.73 billion.

NIKKEI. A stock market index for the Tokyo Stock Exchange. Its 225-company index ended 2008 by recording a 42.1 percent fall, well above its last greatest annual loss of 38.7 percent in 1990.

See also JAPAN.

NINETY-NINE PERCENT VS. ONE PERCENT. *See* "OCCUPY WALL STREET."

NINTENDO. In January 2009, the videogame maker cut its full-year earnings estimate by 33 percent. The company said its net profit fell 18 percent to 212.5 billion yen ($2.35 billion) in the first nine months of its fiscal year ending March 31.

At the end of July 2010, Nintendo reported its first quarter loss in more than two years. Management noted a net loss of about $290 million for its fiscal first quarter.

The firm lost $327 million in the three months ending June 30, 2011. Sales plunged 50 percent from the year before.

NISSAN. Japan's third-largest carmaker by sales, it posted a December 2008 drop in car sales of 31 percent. Then, on February 9, 2009, it announced plans to slash more than 20,000 jobs worldwide (it had 240,000 employees in March 2008), shift production out of Japan, and seek government assistance in Japan, the United States, and elsewhere. The firm reduced monthly domestic production 59 percent in January 2009 to 47,477 vehicles. It was its lowest monthly output volume since at least 1971. Nissan announced on May 12 that it had its first annual net loss in its history. Nissan reported a loss of 16.53 billion yen in the three months ending in June compared with a profit of 52.80 billion yen a year earlier.

Nissan's production in March 2010 climbed an amazing 85 percent to 318,827 cars, with its domestic output gaining 61 percent to 99,903 vehicles. Worldwide production rose 7.8 percent to 3.146 million cars. Management reported that its sales climbed 11 percent in spring 2010. At the end of July 2010, Nissan's management reported that the firm posted a net profit of $1.22 billion. Nissan logged a 21 percent drop in production to 87,215 cars in November 2010. Car sales were 71,366 for a 27 percent increase over the previous year. Total sales were 4.08 million vehicles, up nearly 22 percent from 3.36 million one year earlier. Nissan's sales grew 18 percent in the United States.

Nissan had a profit in its fiscal fourth quarter 2011, with 4.19 million vehicles sold worldwide, up 19 percent. October sales with 82,346 cars saw an increase of 18 percent.

See also AUTOMOBILE INDUSTRY.

NOBEL PEACE PRIZE. *See* OBAMA, BARACK.

"NO FIRING" PLAN. *See* GERMANY.

NOKIA CORPORATION. On January 22, 2009, Nokia posted a worse-than-expected 69 percent drop in fourth-quarter net profit, saying that the market would contract further in 2009 than what was earlier forecast. The world's largest mobile phone maker noted that the economic downturn had led to a rapid decline in consumer demand for electronic goods. Nokia's shares fell 9 percent, with net profits for the quarter dropping to $749.8 million and sales declining 19 percent. On February 24, Nokia announced a range of new job-cutting measures to lower costs and adapt to a weak market condition, including voluntary buyout packages for 1,000 workers, as well as wider use of short-term unpaid leaves and sabbaticals. Nokia employs nearly 130,000 workers worldwide. The company announced on March 17 that it would eliminate as many as 1,700 jobs in order to reduce operating expenses by about $900 million in 2009. Nokia faced a 69 percent decline in its fourth-quarter net profit. Nokia posted a smaller-than-expected decline in second-quarter 2009 net profit. Sales and market share were down 15 percent. Nokia reported a worse-than-expected third-quarter 2009 net loss. It expected industry volumes to fall 7 percent in 2009.

On April 22, 2010, Nokia's management posted a first-quarter profit, with net income rising to about $465.6 million. Nokia reported on June 16 that its sales and profitability were lower than expected. Its profit fell to $291 million for the three months ending June 30, 2010, as sales climbed slightly. Its fourth-quarter profit for the three months ending December 31 was $1.02 billion, down 21 percent from the year before. By then, Nokia's overall sales around the globe fell to 31 percent in the quarter.

Nokia's second-quarter results were reported on July 18, 2011, as their phone market share fell to 24.3 percent in the first quarter of 2011 from 38.8 percent one year before. On September 29, Nokia said it would eliminate 3,500 jobs, or 6 percent of its workforce. On October 20, Nokia reported a second successive quarterly net loss. Cost cuts came from shedding positions, general cost cuts, and selling of real estate.

See also FINLAND; NOKIA SIEMENS NETWORKS.
Cf. MOTOROLA; VODAFONE.

NOKIA SIEMENS NETWORKS. Created in 2006, the equipment joint venture of Nokia and Siemens announced on November 23, 2011, that it planned to cut nearly a quarter of its workforce, 17,000 positions, by the end of 2013. The reductions would lower the workforce by 23 percent from its current level of 74,000.
See also NOKIA CORPORATION; SIEMENS.

NON-AGENCY MORTGAGE-BACKED SECURITIES. Mortgage-backed securities sponsored by private companies other than a government-sponsored enterprise, such as Fannie Mae or Freddie Mac.
Synonymous with PRIVATE-LABEL MORTGAGE-BACKED SECURITIES.

"NO NEW BAILOUT." *See* GEITHNER, TIMOTHY.

NON-FARM UNEMPLOYMENT. *See* UNEMPLOYMENT.

NON-INVESTMENT GRADE. *Synonymous with* JUNK BONDS.

NON-MANUFACTURING. *See* INSTITUTE FOR SUPPLY MANAGE-MENT.

NONPRIME MORTGAGE SECURITIZATION. *See* FINANCIAL CRISIS INQUIRY REPORT.

NONPROFIT ORGANIZATIONS. State and local governments, devoid of income from taxes during the recession, are increasingly being told in 2010 and 2011 that they must start paying for some or more of the local services that were once free. Civil functions, such as roads and bridges, wastewater, schools, and energy dams have long been services that nonprofit institutions have not paid into. Now, in a growing number of local governments, services that were once free are now requiring fees.

NONRESIDENTIAL CONSTRUCTION. *See* NONRESIDENTIAL PROPERTIES.

NONRESIDENTIAL PROPERTIES. Includes everything from hotels to factories; activity significantly declined at the end of October 2008. The U.S. commercial real estate bust reinforced the credit crunch, put added strain on taxpayers, and deepened the recession.
Cf. RESIDENTIAL PROPERTIES.

NORDSTROM. The upscale department store chain reported a 68 percent drop in fourth-quarter profit, hurt by falling sales and a lower profit margin. Income in the quarter fell to $68 million, or 31 cents a share, from $212 million, or 92 cents a share, in the same quarter of 2007.

Nordstrom posted a better-than-expected 7.5 percent rise in April 2010 sales. Then, on August 12, Nordstrom showed a profit of $146 million, up from $105 million the year before, with earnings increasing 39 percent. Nordstrom's fiscal third-quarter earnings surged 43 percent on sales and margin gains. The upscale retailer posted a profit of $119 million, with total revenue increasing 11 percent to $2.18 billion.

In January 2011, the retailer reported a 4.8 percent gain in sales. By February, the retailer posted a 7.3 percent rise in sales. The retailer then noted a 25 percent increase in fiscal first-quarter earnings, with a profit of $145 million. Total revenue climbed 11 percent to $2.32 billion. Nordstrom's profit announced in August climbed 20 percent to $175 million, with sales rising 12.4 percent to $2.72 billion. By year's end, Nordstrom showed rising sales of 5.6 percent.
See also RETAILING.

NORMURA. *See* FEDERAL HOUSING FINANCE AGENCY.

NORTEL NETWORKS. Toronto-based company, the one-time huge telecommunications equipment maker filed for bankruptcy protection in the United States and Canada on January 14, 2009, becoming the first major technology firm to take steps in the global meltdown. The filing came a day before Nortel was due to make a debt payment of $107 million. At the time of filing, Nortel had $4.5 billion in debt and $2.4 billion in cash. During the 1990s telecom and Internet boom, Nortel had more than 95,000 employees and a market capitalization of $297 billion. In 2000, it accounted for one-third of the market value of the Toronto stock exchange.

By January 2009, its market value was just $155 million, with about 26,000 employees. Then, in February, it was announced that Nortel would cut an additional 3,200 jobs. Once valued at $250 billion, Nortel sought Chapter 11 protection in January.

The firm raised its fiscal 2010 earnings forecast after reporting a first-quarter profit of 44 percent.

NORTH AMERICAN FREE TRADE AGREEMENT (NAFTA). Effective January 1, 1994, a trade accord that created international marketing opportunities among the United States, Mexico, and Canada. Supplemental or side agreements on environmental cooperation and labor cooperation were signed in September 1993. Congress debated NAFTA in the fall of 1993; approval by a simple majority of both houses was needed for passage. On November 17, 1993, the House of Representatives, followed by the Senate on November 20, voted approval to the trade pact. NAFTA went into effect on January 1, 1994.

On January 1, 2009, NAFTA celebrated its fifteenth year of existence. Over this time period, exports accounted for almost a third of Mexico's GDP. More than 80 percent of Mexican exports went to the United States. In mid-April, the government concluded that it wasn't necessary to renegotiate NAFTA despite a campaign promise by President Obama to strengthen the pact's labor and environmental provisions.

See also MEXICO; PROTECTIONISM.

NORTH CAROLINA. *See* STATES (U.S.).

NORTH DAKOTA. *See* UNEMPLOYMENT.

NORTHERN ROCK. *See* UNITED KINGDOM.

NORWAY. Economic recovery has already started in Norway, with the largest fiscal and monetary stimulus boosting consumption and sustaining employment. The rebound in house prices is a sign that this stimulus is encouraging households to spend rather than to consolidate their balance sheets.

Growth in private investment will resume next year, once consumption growth is well established and credit markets return to normal. Unemployment has barely increased, partly thanks to specific government measures, but also because of a reversal of migration flows, though the size of the latter is not known with certainty. Given the large deviation from the "4 percent rule" in 2009 and 2010, sizeable subsequent tightening of the fiscal stance is desirable for both macroeconomic management and medium-term fiscal sustainability. Monetary policy tightening has already started and should continue for some time as the economy recovers, the labor market tightens, and inflation expectations edge up. Policies to improve public spending efficiency should be pursued further, helping fiscal consolidation for the years to come.

The jobless rate rose to 1.8 percent in October 2008 from 1.7 percent the previous month. Economic growth more than halved in November 2008 to 0.2 percent. Unemployment was expected to stay below 3 percent from 2009 to 2010. The central bank in mid-December cut its benchmark interest rate by a larger-than-expected 1.75 percentage points, lowering the overnight deposit rate to 3 percent; two months later, the central bank cut its main interest rate from 3 percent to 2.5 percent.

In early February 2009, the government unveiled a $14.8 billion plan to inject capital into the country's banks and lend directly to banks and other businesses by buying corporate bonds. At the end of October, Norway raised its main interest rate by twenty-five basis points to 1.5 percent, the first country in Europe to raise rates since the height of the global meltdown.

The central bank of Norway raised its policy rate by twenty-five basis points in May 2010 to 2 percent.

Oil provides a buffer against economic weakness, and Norway plans to return to monetary policy in 2011–2012. The nation's GDP growth was 1.3 percent, with a GDP of $431 billion, an inflation rate of 2.1 percent, and a GDP per head at $86,740. Norway had a current-account surplus of $15.7 billion in the three months up to June, the highest since 2008.

See also ICELAND.

NOTARY BILL. *See* FORECLOSURE.

NOTIONAL AMOUNT. A. measure of the outstanding amount of over-the-counter derivates contracts based on the amount of the underlying referenced assets.

NO TROUGH. *See* NATIONAL BUREAU OF ECONOMIC RESEARCH.

NOVARTIS. Announced on January 13, 2012, that it would cut 1,960 jobs to save about $450 million by 2013.

NOVATION. A process by which counterparties can transfer derivative positions.

NOVEMBER 15, 2008, SUMMIT. *See* SUMMIT OF NOVEMBER 15, 2008.

NY TIMES. See NEW YORK TIMES.

O

OBAMA, BARACK. On November 4, 2008, Barack Obama won the presidential election, beating John McCain by 52 percent to 46 percent, subsequently declaring that "change has come to America." From a campaign of promises to restore peace, Barack Obama became consumed by the need to restore the nation's prosperity.

Upon his becoming president on January 20, 2009, he pushed his economic agenda forward immediately. At the outset, he sought an economic stimulus package; direct mortgage relief to aid homeowners; new government regulations, including tightening reins on Wall Street; and automobile industry assistance and development.

Prior to his inauguration he had spoken of a recovery that would generate 2.5 million jobs in the first two years of his administration. That would require not just zero economic growth but a fairly robust expansion, a swing, in effect, from the present 4 percent contraction to a growth rate of 2.5 percent, or 3 percent a year. This achievement would mean adding nearly $1 trillion in annual output to the economy. Shortly before taking office he called for the creation of an additional half million jobs, taking the total target to 3 million.

Obama planned to present a recovery plan soon after taking office that might cost $500 to $700 billion, soon raised to between $675 and $775 billion. Besides new spending, he would provide tax relief for low-wage and middle-income workers of about $150 billion. The government would also lower the withholding of income or payroll taxes so that more employees received larger paychecks as soon as possible in 2009. Over a two-day period, December 6 and 7, 2008, President-Elect Obama pledged a recovery program "equal to the task ahead," with a vast public works plan built around bridge and highway projects and the creation of green jobs and the spread of new technologies. He called for the largest infrastructure program since the federal highway system was built in the 1950s during the Eisenhower administration under the Federal Aid Highway Act of 1956. He planned to stimulate the economy through large direct government spending on infrastructure projects as well as through business and individual tax cuts.

Prior to becoming president he proposed a plan that would permit those who lost jobs that did not come with insurance benefits to apply for Medicaid.

He would also review existing programs, such as the Trade Adjustment Assistance Act and the Workforce Investment Act. On February 26, 2009, the president proposed $634 billion in new taxes on upper-income Americans and reductions in government spending over the coming decade. One day before the G-20 summit on April 1, the president conceded U.S. culpability in starting the global financial crisis. The president, in his warning of April 14 that tough months were ahead for the economy, laid out his five "Pillars" to build a lasting recovery: new regulations for Wall Street; education spending focusing on strengthening the workforce; renewable energy investments to create jobs and lessen the nation's dependence on imported oil; health care containment; and long-term deficit reduction based on controlling the growth of Medicare, Medicaid, and Social Security.

President Obama's first 100 days showed dramatic shifts in the economic conditions of the nation. In summary, the major events of his first 100 days in office include the following:

January 26—Timothy Geithner becomes Treasury secretary following a confirmation delayed over problems with his personal tax payments.

January 28—House of Representatives passes $819 billion stimulus bill without a single Republican vote; regulators guarantee $80 billion in uninsured deposits at the financial institutions that service credit unions.

February 5–6—A bipartisan group works to craft a lower-cost stimulus plan after Senate amendments swell package to $920 billion.

February 10—Treasury secretary outlines plan to examine banks and get credit flowing; Dow declines nearly 5 percent.

February 11—Congress and White House reach a stimulus deal.

February 17—President signs $787 billion stimulus bill.

February 18—President pledges as much as $275 billion in programs for homeowners.

February 26—President releases budget blueprint, signaling shift in U.S. policy by expanding government activism and raising taxes on the rich.

March 6—Labor Department announces 651,000 job losses in February and an unemployment rate of 8.1 percent.

March 19—House passes bill to recoup bonuses paid by American International Group.

March 30—President announces restructuring measures for General Motors and Chrysler, including the ousting of GM's chief executive, Rick Wagoner.

April 2—G-20 leaders conclude summit by agreeing to pump up the International Monetary Fund's financial capacity to $1 trillion to help handle crises in developing countries.

April 10—President says economy shows "glimmers of hope."

April 23—President steps up pressure on banks and credit card issuers that are boosting fees and tightening lending.

The president lost his first big legislative fight on April 30, 2009, when his measure that would have allowed bankruptcy-court judges to reduce the value of some mortgages, called cramdowns, was defeated. On September 14, at Federal Hall on Wall Street, commemorating the first anniversary of the demise of Lehman Brothers, President Obama sternly admonished the financial industry and members of Congress to accept his proposals to reshape financial regulations. Expectations of passage of most of his suggestions remained doubtful as the markets slowly recovered.

At the G-20 summit in Pittsburgh, Pennsylvania, President Obama urged a reshaping of the global economy: "We have achieved a level of intangible, global economic cooperation that we've never seen before. Our financial system will be far different and more secure than the one that failed so dramatically this year."

On October 9, 2009, President Obama won the 2009 Nobel Peace Prize.

Meeting with top executives from the twelve biggest banks on December 14, 2009, the president pressured them to "take extraordinary" steps to revive lending from small businesses and homeowners. He declared that it was their obligation, considering that the taxpayers were behind the bailout. It was becoming increasingly clear that with these banks paying off their government obligation, they now had a stronger hand to do as they wish.

The Republicans on November 2, 2010, won control of the House of Representatives following the mid-term national elections. The result had a significant impact on the president's goals for income and estate tax cuts, spending, the federal debt ceiling (currently $14.3 trillion), health care, and the stimulus proposal in which the administration wanted business tax breaks and an infrastructure bank to spur investment. On December 6, nearly two years into his presidency, Obama chose to extend all the Bush-era income tax cuts for another two years, a great disappointment to many Democratic leaders. His argument was to compromise and win an extension of unemployment benefits for another thirteen months for millions of out-of-work Americans. Some media writers called Obama's decision "capitulation" to Republican obstructionism. In his counterargument, President Obama said that "we cannot play politics at a time when the American people are looking for us to solve problems."

On January 25, 2011, the president delivered his State of the Union speech with the theme "Win the Future," shifting his remaining first-term two years from focusing on the past to focusing on the future. On Monday, April 4, Barack Obama confirmed that he would seek another four years in the White

House. At this time, his approval ratings were about 50 percent. The unemployment rate, while still high, had dropped to its lowest level in two years. On September 8, the president proposed before a joint session of Congress an American Jobs Act. At year's end, the president asked Congress for $1.2 trillion in additional borrowing authority that would increase the U.S. federal debt limit to $16.4 trillion and would avoid the need for additional increases before the 2012 elections.

In late January 2012, the president announced that he would create a task force—the Residential Mortgage-Backed Securities Working Group—to investigate the abusive practices in the mortgage industry.

See also AMERICAN JOBS ACT; AMERICAN RECOVERY AND REINVESTMENT ACT (2009); AUTOMOBILE INDUSTRY; BUDGET (U.S.) (FISCAL YEAR 2010); BUDGET (FISCAL 2011) (PROPOSED); BUDGET (FISCAL 2012) (PROPOSED); FEDERAL AID HIGHWAY ACT; G-20; GREEN JOBS PROGRAM; HOME AFFORDABLE REFINANCE PROGRAM; JOBS BILL; KRUGMAN, PAUL; MAKING WORK PAY; MCCAIN, JOHN; MID-TERM ELECTIONS (2010); NATIONAL COMMISSION ON FISCAL RESPONSIBILITY AND REFORM; NEW FOUNDATION; ONE-HUNDRED ELEVENTH CONGRESS (111TH); PELOSI, NANCY; PUBLIC WORKS; RESIDENTIAL MORTGAGE-BACKED SECURITIES WORKING GROUP; "SHOVEL READY"; TARP 2.0; TAX BREAKS; TAX CUTS; TRADE ADJUSTMENT ASSISTANCE ACT; WALL STREET REFORM ACT (2010); "WIN THE FUTURE"; WORKFORCE INVESTMENT ACT.

OCC. *See* OFFICE OF THE COMPTROLLER OF THE CURRENCY.

OCCIDENTAL PETROLEUM. For 2009, when overall chief executive pay fell, the head of Occidental Petroleum was awarded total compensation of $52.2 million, leading the chief executive pay survey.

Occidental's third-quarter 2010 earnings climbed 28 percent, with a profit of $1.19 billion and revenue climbing 19 percent to $4.9 billion.

Occidental reported on April 28, 2011, that its profit jumped 46 percent to $1.55 billion. By October, Occidental Petroleum reported earnings of $1.77 billion, up 49 percent.

"OCCUPY WALL STREET." In mid-September 2011, several hundred people, most in their teens and twenties, demonstrated in the Wall Street area of New York City expressing discontentment with what they felt was an inequitable financial system. Sometimes referred to as the American Autumn. No particular political dimension was present. With police arrests of several hundred, by October 1, "Occupy Wall Street" had spread across the country, starting with protests in Los Angeles, Boston, and Washington, D.C. An edition of *Occupied Wall Street Journal*, a four-page broadsheet, was published on October 8.

Inequality between the wealthy and the average citizen, translated into "one percent vs. ninety-nine percent," that control the wealth of the country is in the hands of 1 percent of the people.

OECD. *See* ORGANISATION FOR ECONOMIC CO-OPERATION AND DEVELOPMENT.

OFFICE DEPOT. Showed a $1.5 billion net loss for the fourth quarter of 2008 as sales fell 15 percent to $3.3 billion.

In April 2009, Office Depot announced a first-quarter net loss of $55.3 million amid $120 million of restructuring charges. Office Depot's second-quarter 2009 loss widened, with a sales decline of 22 percent to $2.82 billion. The company had by now closed five stores, opened three, and relocated one.

OFFICE MARKET. *See* COMMERCIAL REAL ESTATE.

OFFICE OF CREDIT RATINGS. *See* WALL STREET REFORM ACT (2010).

OFFICE OF FEDERAL HOUSING ENTERPRISE OVERSIGHT (OFHEO). A government agency created in 1923 to oversee financial soundness of lending firms; responsible for regulating Fannie Mae and Freddie Mac. Assumed by its successor, the Federal Housing Finance Agency.

See also FANNIE MAE; FEDERAL HOUSING FINANCE AGENCY; FINANCIAL CRISIS INQUIRY REPORT; FREDDIE MAC.

OFFICE OF FINANCIAL RESEARCH. *See* U.S. TREASURY; WALL STREET REFORM ACT (2010).

OFFICE OF INFORMATION AND REGULATORY AFFAIRS (OIRA). Reviews major regulations written by federal agencies (on matters such as the environment, the financial system, Medicare and Medicaid, and public health and safety). Cass Sunstein, appointed by President Obama, heads OIRA, which requires that federal agencies express the costs and benefits of their proposed rules in dollars.

OFFICE OF MANAGEMENT AND BUDGET. *See* DEFICIT (BUDGET, U.S.).

OFFICE OF NATIONAL INSURANCE. One of three regulators under the Wall Street Reform Act.

OFFICE OF THE COMPTROLLER (OF THE CURRENCY) (OCC). By October 2010, began to examine big mortgage servicers' foreclosure practices. The OCC has final say over the examination of foreclosure and loss procedures at big banks.

See also FINANCIAL CRISIS INQURIY REPORT; FORECLOSURE; HOUSE (U.S.) FINANCIAL OVERHAUL PLAN; NATIONAL BANK ACT OF 1863; NATIONAL BANK SUPERVISOR; WALL STREET REFORM ACT (2010).

OFFICE OF THRIFT SUPERVISION (OTS). U.S. Thrifts reported a slight quarterly profit of $4 million in the second quarter 2009, the first positive result since mid-2007. This profit compared with a first-quarter loss of $1.62 billion. With passage of the financial reform bill in July 2010, the Office of Thrift Supervision went out of business.

See also BANKING; FINANCIAL CRISIS INQUIRY REPORT; FINANCIAL INSTITUTIONS REFORM, RECOVERY, AND ENFORCEMENT ACT OF 1994; FINANCIAL REGULATION PLAN (2009); HOUSE (U.S.) FINANCIAL OVERHAUL PLAN; NATIONAL BANK SUPERVISOR; WALL STREET REFORM ACT (2010).

OFFICE RENTS. Office rents fell 2.7 percent in the second quarter 2009 from a year before, the largest single-quarter decline since the first quarter 2002. Rents continued to decline. By October 2009, rent for office space fell 8.5 percent, the fastest pace in more than a decade. The fall came as companies returned a net 19.6 million square feet of space to landlords in the third quarter, slightly more than in the second quarter. The vacancy rate hit 16.5 percent, a five-year high.

See also OFFICE VACANCY.

OFFICE VACANCY. By mid-summer 2010, vacant office space continued to accumulate. Office buildings across the country lost 1.8 million square feet in the second quarter, pushing the office vacancy rate to 17.4 percent, the highest since 1993.

See also DOWNTOWN; OFFICE RENTS.

OFFSHORE-BANKING HAVENS. *See* TAX CURBS; TAX HAVENS.

OFFSHORE TAX HAVENS. *See* TAX CURBS; TAX HAVENS.

OFHEO. *See* OFFICE OF FEDERAL HOUSING ENTERPRISE OVERSIGHT.

OIL. Oil briefly reached $100 a barrel on January 3, 2008, for the first time. Prices of oil then reached a peak in July at $147 a barrel before turning downward again. By the end of October, oil had dropped to $62 a barrel. In 2008, following a quarter century of growth, global oil consumption had its first annual drop since 1983. In the United States, oil demand fell 5 percent in 2008. The demand for oil declined by 1.1 million barrels per day, or 5.4

percent—the first time annual oil consumption declined by more than a million barrels since 1980.

For 2009, U.S. oil demand was projected to decline by another 250,000 barrels per day, or 1.3 percent. On December 2, the price of a barrel of oil slipped below $47, the lowest level since May 2005 and less than a third of the peak reached in July 2008. Oil prices continued to decline in December, sliding to $38.85 per barrel, as the widening global recession showed no sign of relenting soon. The demand for oil was expected to fall 1.2 percent in 2009, the biggest annual drop in twenty-seven years. On October 21, oil prices went above $81 a barrel for the first time in twelve months; by December 28, it was above $79 a barrel.

By 2010, oil imports had dropped by 10 percent in the United States. In addition, crude-oil futures fell on July 2, 2010, for a fifth consecutive day, capping their worst weekly fall since early May 2010. Crude-oil prices fell 2.8 percent, the largest one-day drop since early July 2010, with the price of crude-oil futures contracts for September delivery falling $2.23 to $78.02 a barrel. By September 22, crude-oil prices fell to $74.71 a barrel. Crude-oil futures reached a five-month high on October 6, 2010, at $83.23 a barrel, a 0.5 percent increase. At the same time, gasoline inventories dropped by 2.6 million barrels. On October 19, in part a reaction to China's rate rise, oil prices suffered their biggest fall in eight months, losing more than 4 percent to $79.49. Oil prices reached a two-year high on December 26, with futures up 0.5 percent to $91.00 a barrel.

On February 7, 2011, crude-oil futures for March delivery fell $1.55 or 1.7 percent, to end at $87.48 a barrel, in part reflecting the continuing crisis in Egypt. On February 23, crude-oil prices reached $100 a barrel, the highest price in more than two years. Fueled by the turmoil in the Middle East and North Africa, light, sweet crude for May 2011 delivery rose to a 2.5-year high at $105.75 a barrel, the highest since September 2008. By April 6, crude oil was trading for May delivery at $121.70 a barrel. On June 23, the United States and twenty-seven other nations agreed to release 60 million barrels of oil from strategic reserves to booster the world's weak economy. For the United States, it was only the third time in its history that this had happened. Then, on August 4, oil closed at $86.63 a barrel, the biggest one-day fall in three months.

In summary, crude hit a 2011 settlement high in late April at $113.93 a barrel, up 25 percent for the year, and ended the year at $98.93, up $7.45, or 8.2 percent, for the year and up 45 percent from the 2010 low in 2010.

Most experts predict that in 2012 oil prices will remain above $100 a barrel, with a range reaching $120 a barrel. Uncertainty remains the hidden catalyst in the pricing of crude oil. Crude-oil prices tumbled to a six-week low of below $97.

See also BRITISH PETROLEUM; CHEVRON; CHINA; CONOCOPHIL-LIPS; EXXON; GASOLINE PRICES; HALLIBURTON; LIBYA; OIL EXPLORATION; OPEC; REFINERS; ROYAL DUTCH SHELL; SCHLUMBERGER; TOTAL.

OIL COMPANIES. In July 2009, oil firms reported lower profits because of falling prices and weaker demand. Royal Dutch Shell's net profit fell by 67 percent to $3.8 billion. ConocoPhillips's profit fell by 76 percent and British Petroleum by 53 percent.

OIL EXPLORATION. By December 2008, oil exploration had been meaningfully reduced; dozens of major oil and natural gas projects had been put on hold or canceled as firms scrambled to adjust to the collapse in energy markets. Such postponements would likely lower future energy supplies and could set the stage for another rapid climb in prices once the global economy recovers. Oil demand growth had weakened throughout the industrial world. The International Energy Agency projected that worldwide demand would actually drop in 2008 for the first time since 1983.

See also OIL.

OIRA. *See* OFFICE OF INFORMATION AND REGULATORY AFFAIRS.

OLDER PEOPLE. *See* RETIREMENT.

OLYMPIC GAMES. *See* UNITED KINGDOM.

100 DAYS. *See* OBAMA, BARACK.

111TH CONGRESS. Ending on December 2010, the 111th Congress was among the most prolific in decades. Key bills passed relating to the Great Recession include the following:

- *Economic Stimulus*: Congress began pumping hundreds of billions of dollars into the U.S. economy in 2009 through infrastructure projects, energy investments, and tax breaks, along with other projects.
- *Wall Street Regulations*: Lawmakers passed a 2,300-page bill touching every corner of finance. The measure created a consumer bureau and a council of regulators to watch for risks to the financial system, and set new standards for derivatives trading.
- *Credit Cards*: New rules on credit card issuers include a ban on certain fees and requirements for clearer disclosure in bills.
- *Cash for Clunkers*: The $3 billion program offered consumers vouchers of as much as $4,500 if they swapped their old cars for more fuel-efficient new models. Discarded automobiles were destroyed rather than sent to a used-car lot.

- *Tax Deal*: Following a compromise between the White House and Senate Republicans, lawmakers extended Bush's income and investment tax cuts for two years, temporarily cut the payroll tax for most workers and set the estate tax at 35 percent with a $5 million exemption.

ONE PERCENT VS. NINETY-NINE PERCENT. *See* "OCCUPY WALL STREET."

ONLINE. *See* ADVERTISING; RETAILING; WOOLWORTHS.

OPEC (ORGANIZATION OF PETROLEUM EXPORTING COUNTRIES). A group comprising thirteen members concentrated in the Middle East but also including countries in Africa, South America, and the Far East. By virtue of their large exports, Saudi Arabia and Iran have been the most powerful influences.

During summer 2008, the OPEC cartel could not prevent oil prices from surging to record levels. At the end of the year, the producers seemed equally unable to stop prices from collapsing as the global economy cooled down. Accounting for 40 percent of the world's oil exports, OPEC officials were also puzzled by how oil topped $147 a barrel in July and then rapidly dropped by more than $90, ostensibly due to lower economic growth around the world. Prices could keep falling in 2009, analysts said, with some predicting new lows of around $30 a barrel. OPEC members need prices of $60 to $90 a barrel to balance their budgets, so the prospect of lower prices and crimped revenues is daunting for them. At the December 18 OPEC meeting, members agreed to the largest ever production cut—2.2 million barrels a day—in an effort to put a floor on falling oil prices as demand waned. It was the third time OPEC had reduced its output in three months. The new target set OPEC's production at 24.85 million barrels a day starting on January 1, 2009. The cartel had not faced such a situation since the early 1980s. Oil consumption had declined for the first time in twenty-five years because of the economic crisis. Indicative of the meltdown, OPEC collectively postponed thirty-five oil-drilling projects in various stages of development.

On October 14, 2010, the twelve ministers of OPEC decided to retain their production quotas at the same level since December 2008 as a result of concerns about the health of the economic recovery and the weak U.S. dollar. OPEC resisted pressure for higher prices. For the year, the average OPEC oil price rose 26.5 percent.

In mid-December 2011, OPEC agreed to increase its production target to 30 million barrels for the first time in three years. The largest one-day drop in oil prices of 5 percent occurred in almost three months below $95 per barrel.

See also MIDDLE EAST; OIL; OIL EXPLORATION.

OPEL. General Motors, which owns Opel and Vauxhall operations in Europe, reconsidered whether to sell these units in August 2009. Then, on November 1, 2009, General Motors reversed its earlier decision and backed out of the deal to sell the automobile makers to Magna International.

See also MAGNA.

"OPERATION TWIST." *See* FEDERAL RESERVE BANK.

OPTION ADJUSTABLE-RATE MORTGAGES (OPTION ARMS). Nearly $750 billion in these mortgages were issued from 2004 to 2007. Option ARMS were usually made to borrowers with higher credit scores than those getting subprime mortgages. But, many of these borrowers were stretched thin by the global economic decline and rising unemployment. Borrowers faced payment shock when they had to begin making payments of full interest and principal.

See also WELLS FARGO.

ORACLE CORPORATION. At the beginning of 2009, posted a revenue decline for the first time since 2002. Profits dropped 7.2 percent to $1.89 billion and revenue fell 5.2 percent to $6.86 billion. Oracle's first-quarter 2009 profit climbed 12 percent. Revenues rose 4 percent from the year before, which followed two straight periods of revenue declines amid a greater slowdown in tech spending.

In June 2010, the firm's quarterly profit climbed 25 percent, with a profit in the fourth quarter totaling $2.36 billion, up from $1.89 billion the year before. The firm's first-quarter 2010 profit climbed 20 percent, with income totaling $1.4 billion, up from $1.1 billion the year earlier. Revenue climbed 48 percent to $7.5 billion, up from $5.05 billion the year before. Revenue climbed 47 percent to $8.6 billion from $5.9 billion, and profit rose 28 percent in its second quarter. Net income rose to $1.9 billion from the year-ago quarter of $1.45 billion.

On March 24, 2011, Oracle reported that its fiscal third quarter profit was up 78 percent. Its income for its overall business was $2.12 billion, with revenue increasing 37 percent to $8.76 billion. By mid-September, Oracle's sales increased 12 percent. Net income in the quarter ending August 31 rose 36 percent to $1.8 billion, with revenue climbing to $8.4 billion from $7.5 billion the year before.

ORGANISATION FOR ECONOMIC CO-OPERATION AND DEVELOPMENT (OECD). Created in 1948, an organization of seventeen European nations (including the German Federal Republic) known until 1960 as the Organisation for European Economic Co-operation (OEEC). Initially, the group developed and implemented economic recovery programs following

World War II. It was enlarged to twenty-one members with the change of its name to OECD. Headquartered in Paris, France, it promotes the economic growth of member nations, the expansion of world investment and trade, and the economic development of emerging countries.

By the end of November 2008, the OECD called for aggressive economic stimulus measures. The OECD claimed the number of unemployed people in their now thirty member nations could climb to 42 million over two years from the current 34 million.

At the same time, they said the U.S. economy would shrink 0.9 percent in 2009, after posting growth of 1.8 percent in 2008. The OECD concluded in March that large emerging economies were being dragged down by the recession in richer countries. The OECD had set standards on transparency and information exchange in tax matters and demanded cooperation from tax haven nations. In an updated forecast at the end of March, the OECD predicted that 2009 GDP would drop 4.2 percent in their thirty countries. This dramatic deterioration from its forecast in November, when they predicted contraction of just 0.4 percent, indicated the huge shift in decline.

The combined GDP of the OECD nations fell 2.1 percent in the January–March period from the previous year. It was the largest drop since 1960, when the organization began collecting such data. The GDP of member countries fell 2 percent in the final quarter 2008. The OECD nation economies, which accounted for 71 percent of the world GDP in 2007, shrank 4.2 percent in the first quarter 2009 from a year earlier.

At the end of June 2009, the OECD revised upward its assessment of the world's economy, saying that the worst would soon be over in the current recession. The OECD forecasted that the combined output of its member nations would contract 4.1 percent in 2009 and expand 0.7 percent in 2010. The OECD showed in mid-November that economic output from its members in the third period was up 0.8 percent from the second quarter, although it was 3.3 percent lower in annual terms. The combined GDP of the OECD nations, accounting for 61.3 percent of world GDP, increased for the first time since 2008 first quarter.

By the end of May 2010, the OECD raised its forecast for economic growth in 2010 and 2011. It forecast the global economy to rise 4.6 percent in 2010 and 4.5 percent the following year. By mid-November, the OECD of thirty-three members projected growth for 2011 to be 2.7 percent. The OECD projected that world growth would fall to 4.2 percent in 2011 from 4.6 percent in 2009. In early December, the OECD projected that cross-border investment in would fall in 2010, with foreign direct investment dropping 8 percent after falling 43 percent in 2009 and 19 percent in 2008. In 2009, global flows totaled $1.1 trillion.

For the second-quarter 2011, the OECD indicated that the world's largest economies slowed to 0.2 percent from 0.3 percent in the first three months of the year. On September 8, the OECD argued that "the sovereign debt crisis in the euro area could intensify again." The Paris think-tank announced that its leading indicator of economic activity in its thirty-four members dropped to 101.6 in July from 102.1 in June. In August, the OECD indicated that consumer prices in their thirty-four member nations had climbed 3.2 percent in the year, after rising 3.1 percent in the year to July. Food prices were primarily to blame.

By December 2011, the OECD reported that the global outlook had significantly deteriorated. The growth forecasts for the world's largest economies fell, and they warned that the eurozone was heading for a mild recession. The OECD cut its forecast among its thirty-four members to 1.9 percent in 2011 and 1.6 percent in 2012. For 2012, it predicted that the seventeen-country bloc's economy would grow by 0.2 percent. By year's end 2011, the OECD warned that financial stresses were likely to continue with the "animal spirits" of the markets becoming a threat to the stability of many governments that required refinancing of their debt. The organization noted that its members were expected to reach gross borrowing needs of $10.4 trillion in 2011 and projected to be $10.5 trillion in 2012, a $1 trillion increase from 2007.

The OECD's chief economist declared, "The euro area is so important in sheer size that if it slows down or contracts, it is going to be felt everywhere."

See also G-20; PENSION FUNDS; TAX HAVENS; UNEMPLOYMENT; and OECD listings by country.

ORGANIZATION OF PETROLEUM EXPORTING COUNTRIES. *See* OPEC.

ORGANIZED LABOR. *See* UNIONS.

ORIGINATE-TO-DISTRIBUTE. When lenders make loans with the intention of selling them to other financial institutions or investors, as opposed to holding the loans through maturity.
Cf. ORIGINATE-TO-HOLD.

ORIGINATE-TO-HOLD. When lenders make loans with the intention of holding them through maturity, as opposed to selling them to other financial institutions or investors.
Cf. ORIGINATE-TO-DISTRIBUTE.

ORIGINATION. The process of making a loan, including underwriting, closing, and providing the funds.

ORSZAG, PETER. President Obama's White House budget director. He had been director of the Congressional Budget Office for nearly two years. He resigned as budget director in summer 2010.
See also LEW, JACOB.

OTIS ELEVATORS. *See* UNITED TECHNOLOGIES.

OTS. *See* OFFICE OF THRIFT SUPERVISION.

OUTPUT PER HOUR. *Synonymous with* PRODUCTIVITY.

OVERSEAS MONEY. *See* SCAMS.

OVERSEEING. *See* REGULATORS.

OVERSIGHT. *See* TIER 1 FINANCIAL HOLDING COMPANIES; TRANSPARENCY.

OVERSIGHT OF EXECUTIVE PAY. *See* EXECUTIVE PAY.

OVER-THE-COUNTER DERIVATIVES. *See* FINANCIAL CRISIS INQUIRY REPORT; FINANCIAL REGULATION PLAN (2009); WALL STREET REFORM ACT (2010).

OVERTIME. Enables firms to increase productivity to meet rising customer orders without adding fixed costs such as health care benefits for new hires. Should business suddenly slow, firms choosing increased overtime expenses can withdraw workers without having to make costly layoffs. For example, during the gradual recovery in the economy in fall 2009, overtime increased 6.5 percent to 3.2 hours per week in October over September's level of 3 hours and 14 percent from the 2.8 hours of overtime averaged in the second quarter. The downside of using overtime is that the process does not create new jobs. Also, it helps provide a middle-class lifestyle for many hourly workers.

See also UNEMPLOYMENT.

P

PACE. *See* PROMOTE AMERICA'S COMPETITIVE EDGE.

PACIFIC INVESTMENT MANAGEMENT COMPANY. The world's biggest bond fund.

PAKISTAN. In August 2009, the International Monetary Fund added $3.2 billion to a loan it extended to Pakistan in 2008, bringing the total value of aid offered the country to $11.3 billion. Pakistan's central bank cut its benchmark rate by half a percentage point to 12.5 percent in November 2009.

Economic growth dropped to 3.2 percent from 4.4 percent in 2010. The nation's GDP growth was 3.2 percent, with GDP at $188 billion, an inflation rate of 9.9 percent, and a GDP per head of $992. At the end of December 2010, the IMF warned Pakistan to take further steps to reduce its spiraling budget deficit of 6 percent. The IMF had withheld $3.5 billion in 2010 from its total $11.3 billion loan package to pressure the country. The aid agency was to end its support on December 31 but extended the loan by nine months to give Pakistan more time to implement needed reforms. In addition, inflation has been over 15 percent, and Pakistani remittances, those living abroad, surged by 16.8 percent in the second half of 2010.

Industrial production to April fell by 8.6 percent in 2011 after climbing by 6.7 percent in the year to March.

See also INTERNATIONAL MONETARY FUND; REMITTANCES.

PANAMA. Latin America's fastest growing economy. Canal revenues were 7.5 percent of its GDP ($2 billion); import tariffs are among the lowest in Latin American and foreign direct investment equals nearly 9 percent of GDP.

PANASONIC. Reported on February 4, 2009, that it was shedding 15,000 jobs, the second significant layoff in Japan's electronics industry in less than one week. The company projected a net loss of 380 billion yen, or $4.2 billion, for the year ending March 31, 2008. On August 3, 2009, Panasonic posted a fiscal first-quarter loss of about $460 million for the April–June period. Revenue during this period fell 26 percent from a year earlier. By the end of October, the company announced that it had a decline in revenue and would be eliminating 15,000 jobs in a turnaround effort.

In June 2011, management reported that its net profit fell 59 percent, greatly due to the earthquake in Japan.
See also SANYO.

PANDIT, VIKRIM. *See* CITIGROUP.

PANG DA AUTOMOBILE TRADE CO. *See* SAAB.

PAR. The face value of a bond.

PARAGUAY. Growth was projected into 2011 at 4.5 percent following a bumper harvest that put the economy at an 8.6 percent growth in 2011. The nation's GDP growth was 4.5 percent, with GDP at $18 billion, an inflation rate of 5.7 percent, and a GDP per head at $2,690.

PARTNERING. *See* PUBLIC-PRIVATE INVESTMENT FUND.

PART-TIME WORKERS. Under the Economic Stimulus Plan of 2009, $7 billion was made available to states for workers such as part-timers and people in training programs. While the vast majority of workers contributed directly or indirectly to the unemployment insurance pot, just 36 percent of people out of work actually collected benefits. By February 2009, the number of people working part time because they couldn't secure full-time work or their hours had been cut back rose by 787,000 to 8.6 million, up 3.7 million over the previous year.
See also PRIVATE-SECTOR PAYROLLS; SPENDING; UNDEREMPLOYMENT RATE.

"PATCH." *See* TAX CUTS.

PAULSON, HENRY (HANK). President George W. Bush's Treasury secretary. Criticized on February 28, 2008, for his promoted rescue plans for homeowners, branded by many as bailouts for reckless lenders and speculators; predicted the administration's market-based approach would keep a foreclosure crisis under control.

Attended Harvard University and, after a brief stint in Washington, worked at Goldman Sachs and in 1982 became a partner and then co-chief executive in June 1998. He became sole chief executive and was the highest-paid CEO on Wall Street in 2005, with $38.3 million in compensation. After thirty-two years of Goldman service, he returned to Washington, D.C.

Hank Paulson's $700 billion plan in October created quite a stir. Many on the left accused him of ripping off taxpayers to save banking inefficiencies and mismanagement, while those on the right argued that it was approaching socialism. Paulson misread the severity of the economic meltdown and problems in the housing sector. He was seen as a hero for taking decisive action to back up the U.S. banking system but was criticized for confusing markets.

On July 23, 2007, he said that the housing slump appeared to be "at or near the bottom."

See also BANK BAILOUT; EMERGENCY ECONOMIC STABILIZA-TION ACT OF 2008; "TOO BIG TO FAIL"; TROUBLED ASSET RELIEF PROGRAM.

PAULSON, JOHN A. *See* GOLDMAN SACHS.

PAY. By December 2008, pay across the United States hadn't significantly fallen, as had been projected by many experts. For the year, the weekly salary of rank-and-file workers, who make up roughly 80 percent of the workforce, had risen 2.8 percent.

The meltdown kept salary growth to a minimum in 2009, and predictions for 2010 weren't better. Employers increased salaries in 2009 by the smallest percentage in decades. Median pay increases ranged between 2 and 3 percent. The government announced that pay for the average worker increased 2.2 percent in the first quarter 2009, down from 3.2 percent in the year before. Firms were projecting an average 3 percent increase in 2010, making it the smallest forecast increase in the twenty-nine years that these figures have been collected. By mid-September, the Federal Reserve and the U.S. Treasury were preparing broad new rules to force banks to rein in practices that made multimillionaires. Under the proposal, banks would have wide leeway in how they structure their rewards, and it would not prohibit million-dollar pay packages or address issues of fairness. The Federal Reserve's program would affect roughly 5,000 bank holding companies as well as state-chartered banks.

By summer 2010, there was an increasing climb in the percentage of workers receiving pay cuts. At the outset of the meltdown, organizations were considering forcing furloughs on workers, but little materialized as pay reductions began to take hold. As reported in May 2010, chief executives of large firms saw their pay increase sharply in 2010, surging on average 11 percent to $9.3 million.

It was expected that Wall Street employees would receive an annual compensation at the end of 2011 from 27 to 30 percent lower than the year before. Bonuses were expected to fall 35 to 40 percent on average.

See also G-20; OVERTIME; PAY CZAR; TROUBLED ASSET RELIEF PROGRAM.

PAY CUTS. *See* PAY; PAYROLL TAX CUTS.

PAY CZAR. Kenneth Feinberg, who oversaw the federal government's compensation fund for victims of September 11, 2001, was appointed to serve as the pay czar for the Treasury Department. Feinberg would focus on pay restrictions related to firms receiving bailout funds from the Troubled Asset

Relief Program, aiding them in interpreting the rules and ensuring that they were being followed. The pay czar would review, reject, and even set pay levels, with no appeal.

By October 2009, Feinberg was planning to clamp down on compensation at firms receiving significant sums of government stimulus funding by reducing annual cash salaries for many of the top employees, expected to be 175 people at the firms he oversaw. He wanted to shift a portion of an employee's annual salary into stock that couldn't be touched for several years, thus reducing take-home pay.

Kenneth Feinberg oversaw seven firms that accepted bailout packages: American International Group, Citigroup, Bank of America, General Motors, GMAC Financial Services, Chrysler Group, and Chrysler Financial. The Treasury Department gave him the responsibility of tying more compensation at these firms to long-term performance and cutting pay deemed "excessive." By the end of October 2009, Feinberg cut total compensations by half and, at the same time, increased regular salaries. According to some legal experts, one of the lingering issues is the constitutionality of having Feinberg make these decisions as he was never properly appointed an officer of the United States.

The U.S. Treasury Department's pay czar worked to cap salaries of top employees under his jurisdiction. He also planned to expand the $500,000 salary cap.

See also AMERICAN INTERNATIONAL GROUP.

PAY FOR SUCCESS. *See* HOUSING PLAN.

PAY FREEZE (FEDERAL). *See* FEDERAL PAY FREEZE.

PAYMENT-OPTION ADJUSTABLE-RATE MORTGAGE. Mortgages that permit borrowers to pick the amount of payment each month, possibly low enough to increase the principal balance.

PAYROLLS. *See* PRIVATE-SECTOR PAYROLLS.

PAYROLL TAX CUTS. By the end of February 2009, the Treasury Department had begun to direct its employees to lower taxes withheld from the paychecks of workers, effective April 1; this increased take-home pay for an average family by at least $65 a month.

Then, on December 17, 2011, the Senate voted overwhelmingly to extend a payroll tax cut until February 2012. The $33 billion package would also extend unemployment benefits and avoid cuts in payments to doctors who accept Medicare. It also required that the president make a final decision on an oil pipeline across the heart of the country by the end of February.

On December 22, Speaker of the House John Boehner, bowing to pressure from fellow Republications, agreed to a two-month extension of a payroll tax break that forestalled a January 1, 2012, tax increase on 160 million workers. As part of the deal, employees' share of the Social Security payroll tax would remain at the current level, 4.2 percent of wages, through February 29, 2012, instead of the usual 6.2 percent. In addition, the government would continue paying unemployment insurance benefits under the existing policy until February. Without this action, many of the long-term unemployed would have lost benefits by January.

See also AMERICAN JOBS ACT (PROPOSED); AMERICAN RECOVERY AND REINVESTMENT ACT (OF 2009); BOEHNER, JOHN; TAX CUTS.

PC MARKET. *See* DELL; INTERNATIONAL BUSINESS MACHINES CORPORATION; PERSONAL COMPUTER MARKET.

PDCF. *See* PRIMARY DEALER CREDIT FACILITY.

PECORA COMMISSION. The Pecora inquiry was begun on March 4, 1932, by the U.S. Senate Committee on Banking and Currency. These Depression-era hearings sought to expose banking practices deemed "detrimental to the public welfare" and to reveal "unsavory and unethical methods" used in the sale of securities. Ferdinand Pecora served as chief counsel. The hearings ended on May 4, 1934, after which Pecora was appointed as one of the first commissioners of the Securities and Exchange Commission.

Pecora was a Sicilian immigrant and a former assistant district attorney for New York County before President Herbert Hoover appointed him in 1929 to the Senate committee. During the hearings he met with President Roosevelt and was instrumental in helping the president enact sweeping changes to the law. Pecora's fame spread during the hearings, and he had his photograph on the cover of *Time* magazine in May 1933, with the accompanying article "Wealth on Trial."

The Pecora Commission was intended to lay the foundation for remedial legislation. The investigation uncovered a wide range of abusive practices on the part of banks and bank affiliates. During the inquiry, J. P. Morgan stated that he had not paid personal income taxes in 1930, 1931, and 1932. Several National City Bank executives cushioned their stock losses by tapping interest-free loans from a special bank fund, while others made millions selling short bank shares. While the investigation proceeded, Congress enacted the Glass-Steagall Banking Act of 1933, the Banking Act of 1933, the Securities Act of 1933, and the Securities Exchange Act of 1934.

Pecora ended his autobiography with, "Laws aren't a panacea and they're not self-executing."

Cf. FINANCIAL CRISIS INQUIRY COMMISSION; GREAT DEPRESSION.

PEE-PIPS. *See* PUBLIC-PRIVATE INVESTMENT PARTNERSHIPS.

PELL GRANTS. About 9 million students currently have these grants, which assist low-income students with paying for college. These grants were spared spending reductions in the August 2011 signing of the debt deal. Instead, $17 billion was added to the Pell Grants, while at the same time federal subsidies for graduate student loans were ended.

See also AMERICAN RECOVERY AND REINVESTMENT ACT (OF 2009); BUDGET (U.S.); DEBT DEAL; STUDENT LOANS.

PELOSI, NANCY. One-time U.S. House of Representatives Speaker, she differed from Barack Obama on at least two issues—tax increases and investigating the Bush administration. After Obama's inauguration, the speaker wanted Congress to consider repealing President Bush's tax cuts for those who make more than $250,000 well before they expired at the end of 2010. The president had promised to repeal the tax cuts but then backed off that pledge, signaling that he would be willing to simply let them expire in 2010. A key figure in the passage of legislation in the House of Representatives.

See also OBAMA, BARACK.

PENSION BENEFIT GUARANTY CORPORATION. *See* DELPHI CORPORATION.

PENSION FUNDS. The meltdown of 2008 significantly affected pension funds. By October 2008, total assets had dropped by nearly 20 percent since the beginning of 2008. In the United States, these funds accounted for two-thirds of the $3.3 trillion in losses. In countries of the Organisation for Economic Co-operation and Development, pension funds lost over 20 percent of their values during the Great Recession.

In early 2010, a bipartisan coalition of Colorado state legislators passed a pension overhaul bill that included reducing the raise that people who are already retired get in their pension checks each year. This would be challenged but is also being considered by other states across the nation.

Unfunded public pensions could well be the coming financial disaster for the United States. Some are proposing that the government bail out these public institutions and primarily state governments. The total unfounded liabilities of the fifty states' pension funds amounted to about $ 1 trillion in 2008, while some believe it to be closer to $3 trillion. Pension obligations are threatened for both future and existing retirees. By summer 2010, several states realized that they had overfunded pensions, creating debt to communities.

By 2010, the need to preserve and fund state pensions pushed property and other taxes higher. To make up for staggering investment losses from the financial meltdown, property taxes are rising at an unprecedented rate. Tax increases and budget reductions are raising pressure on state politicians to tame growing pension costs.

See also HYBRID PENSIONS; STOCK MARKET.

PENTAGON. In early 2011, the White House ordered the Pentagon to rein in its budget, designed to reduce the military budget over five years by $78 billion.

PEOPLE'S BANK OF CHINA. *See* CHINA.

PEPSICO. On October 7, 2010, reported that its quarterly profit rose 12 percent, with the company earning $1.92 billion. Revenue rose 40 percent to $15.51 billion from $112.08 billion.

PERKINS, FRANCES. Secretary of Labor in President F. D. Roosevelt's administration. First woman secretary in a president's cabinet who forged most of the New Deal programs. Ended her career in the 1960s as a visiting faculty member at the New York State School of Industrial and Labor Relations.

See also GREAT DEPRESSION.

PERKS. *See* "GROSS UP."

PERSIAN GULF. *See* KUWAIT.

PERSONAL BANKRUPTCY. *See* BANKRUPTCY FILINGS.

PERSONAL COMPUTERS. Worldwide shipment of personal computers dropped 4.5 percent in 2009 as the economy continued to deteriorate. Shipments in the fourth quarter 2008 fell 1.9 percent and during the first half of the year declined by more than 8 percent.

PERSONAL INCOME. Before adjusting for inflation, it climbed 0.5 percent in October 2010, mostly coming from strong wage and salary growth.

PERSONAL SAVING RATE. *See* SAVING RATE.

PERU. Following economic growth into double figures in 2010, the 2011 national GDP growth was 4.5 percent, with GDP at $167 billion, an inflation rate of 2.7 percent, and a GDP per head at $5,490.

PESO. *See* MEXICO.

PETERSON, DOUGLAS. *See* STANDARD & POOR'S.

PEUGEOT-CITROEN. On June 23, 2009, the French carmaker announced that it would lose as much as $2.75 billion in 2009. Peugeot-Citroen announced at the end of July 2009 that its sales plunged into the red in the first half of the year, with a net loss of €962 million, down from net profit of €733 million a year before.

See also FRANCE.

PFIZER. The world's largest drug organization announced it was laying off up to 800 scientists in 2009, reducing its global research staff of about 10,000 by 5 to 8 percent. The company also announced that it planned to lay off nearly a third of its 8,000 salespeople.

Sales reported on July 22 were $2.26 billion for the second quarter, down from $2.78 billion. Revenue declined 9.4 percent to $10.98 billion. Pfizer's second-quarter profit dropped 19 percent. Pfizer's third-quarter 2009 profit rose 26 percent despite a drop in sales, with revenue falling 2.9 percent to $11.62 billion. Pfizer planned to eliminate a total of 19,500 jobs. By mid-December 2009, Pfizer raised its quarterly dividend 13 percent. Its first-quarter 2010 earnings fell 26 percent, with sales increasing 54 percent to $16.5 billion.

On May 18, 2010, management announced that it would cease work at eight manufacturing facilities, curb production at six others, and cut 6,000 jobs in the company. Fifteen percent of its workforce would be let go and $4 billion would be saved in the process. Its second-quarter 2010 profit was up 9.5 percent, with earnings of $2.48 billion. Pfizer's third-quarter 2010 profit fell 70 percent, but revenue increased 39 percent. The company announced that it would slash as much as 5 percent of its 110,600 workers.

The firm reported in early August 2011 a second-quarter income profit of $2.61 billion, rising 5.2 percent. Revenue fell 0.9 percent to $16.98 billion.

Reporting on January 31, 2012, Pfizer's profit fell 50 percent to $1.4 billion, with U.S. sales falling 12 percent. Sales outside the United States rose 3 percent.

PG&E. The California-based utility gas pipeline company reported a 22 percent fall in third-quarter 2011 profit on November 3, 2011. Net income was $203 million on revenue of $$3.86 billion.

PHILIPPINES, THE. The Philippines' economy contracted in the first quarter 2009 for the first time since 2001. GDP shrank a seasonally adjusted 2.3 percent in the first quarter from the fourth quarter 2008. In 2009, the nation's 10 million overseas workers sent back about $18 billion in remittances, roughly 5 percent more than in 2008. Remittances were up 8 percent for the first ten months of 2010.

The economy was expected to grow 4.3 percent in 2011. The nation's GDP growth was 4.3 percent, with a GDP of $224 billion, an inflation rate of 4.8

percent, and a GDP per head of $2,200. The government's revenues amounted to 13.4 percent of GDP and collected less than a fifth of the value-added taxes it was owed.

See also SOUTHEAST ASIA.

PHILIPS ELECTRONICS. Its first-quarter 2010 net profit was $270.2 million compared with a net loss from a year before. On October 18, 2010, the company reported a better-than-expected third-quarter net profit of $746.3 million.

On July 18, 2011, management reported a second-quarter net loss of $1.9 billion.

On January 30, 2012, Philips reported a fourth-quarter 2011 loss of $214 million. Sales climbed 3.2 percent

PHILLIPS-VAN HEUSEN. Announced in January 2009 that it would cut jobs and close 175 stores over the coming two to three years. It planned to cut 250 salaried positions and about 150 hourly neckwear-manufacturing positions.

See also RETAILING.

PHISHING. *See* IDENTITY THEFT.

PICK-A-PAYMENT MORTGAGES. *See* WELLS FARGO.

"PILLARS" OF RECOVERY. *See* OBAMA, BARACK.

"PLAIN VANILLA." Mortgages and credit cards with simple standard terms. Products without specifying what these might be as part of the consumer protection program.

PLATINUM. Briefly, on August 7, 2011, platinum's price dropped below that of gold for the first time since 2008. Platinum is thirty times rarer than gold and known as an industrial metal, with car catalytic converters accounting for almost half of its demand. Then, on September 22, platinum fell 4.3 percent.

The high for platinum was on August 22, 2011, reaching a three-year peak of $1,905.70 an ounce. Within a month, platinum fell 19 percent.

See also GOLD; SILVER.

PLEDGED-ACCOUNT MORTGAGE. A variation on graduated-payment mortgages in which a portion of the borrower's down payment is used to fund a pledged savings account, which is drawn on to supplement the monthly payment during the first years of the loan. The net effect to the borrower is lower payments, at first. Payments gradually rise to slightly above those on conventional mortgages.

See also GRADUATED-PAYMENT MORTGAGE.

PLS. *See* PRIVATE-LABEL MORTGAGE-BACKED SECURITIES.

POLAND. Despite the deep recession throughout the Organisation for Economic Co-operation and Development, the Polish economy continued to grow in 2009 due to several factors, including monetary easing, exchange rate depreciation, relatively limited dependence on international trade, a sound banking sector and unleveraged private sector; tax cuts and other fiscal measures, and infrastructure investments linked to European Union transfers and the 2012 football championship. Activity is projected to pick up, mainly driven by fixed investment, but to remain well below potential rates for some time. While headline inflation was, until recently, above the official target, it is expected to diminish steadily as economic slack increases. The general government deficit is projected to reach levels that are unprecedented since the beginning of the transition process, but no fiscal consolidation measures have been announced for 2010 by the authorities. The constitutional public debt limit of 60 percent of GDP is being dealt with mainly through an ambitious privatization program. This will nevertheless only delay the much needed consolidation of public finances until 2011. The monetary authorities should refrain from any interest rate increases unless circumstances change.

In November 2008, the European Central Bank opened a €10 million credit line to Poland, which saw its currency fall sharply at the beginning of the month. On November 30, the government of Poland was prepared to spend about $31 billion to help the country weather the global economic crisis. It also lowered its 2009 economic forecast to 3.7 percent growth from 4.8 percent. For the month of November, unemployment increased to 9.1 percent, rising 0.3 percentage point from October, the first increase after five years of steady declines. Poland's jobless rate had previously peaked at 20.7 percent in February 2003.

The International Monetary Fund set up a $20.5 billion credit line with Poland in April 2009. The zloty had fallen by 30 percent since its peak; the central bank reduced interest rate from 6 percent in October 2008 to 3.75 percent in April 2009.

The government of Poland projected a 2010 budget with a growing deficit and heavy borrowing. Its treasury needed to raise $12.8 billion by year's end through the sale of state-owned assets. Poland avoided formal recession, with a GDP increase of 0.8 percent in the first quarter from a year before, and 1.1 percent in the second quarter. Poland's economic growth rose in the second quarter 2010 with the economy expanding by 3.5 percent. In early November, Poland's central bank held its benchmark interest rate at 3.5 percent. At the end of 2010, Poland announced that it would seek an expanded credit line from the IMF for $29 billion. The nation's GDP was up 1.3 percent.

Output was projected to increase 4 percent in 2011 following a 3.6 percent growth in 2010. Commercial real estate prices rose 10 percent for the year, with foreign direct investment up 28 percent. Poland raised interest rates on January 19, 2011. It was the first rate increase since June 2008. Worried over inflation and increases in consumer prices at 3.1 percent, the decision was made to better control the economy with wages climbing 5.4 percent. Poland's GDP climbed by 4.4 percent in the year to fourth quarter 2010, up from 4.2 percent for the previous quarter.

Inflation rose to 5 percent in May 2011 from 4.5 percent the previous month. In the second quarter 2011, Poland's economy surged, with output rising 4.3 percent. GDP climbed 1.1 percent. As a reminder, Poland was the only nation in the European Union not to fall into recession in 2008–2009. Projections for 2012, according to the OECD, indicated a GDP growth of 2.5 percent following its 2011 growth of 4 percent. Expectations are that the government will sign on to the eurozone in 2015.

Strong foreign trade supported Poland throughout the Great Recession. In 2011 it was expected that the nation's growth would reach 3.4 percent. The nation's GDP growth was 3.4 percent, its GDP at $469 billion, inflation at 2.4 percent, and a GDP per head of $12,310. Its fiscal first-quarter earnings grew 52 percent.

See also EUROPEAN BANK FOR RECONSTRUCTION AND DEVELOPMENT.

POLO RALPH LAUREN. Net income fell 6.6 percent for its fiscal third quarter 2008 on slumping sales and margin. For the period ending December 31, the company posted net income of $105.3 million, with retail sales declining 71 percent. Profits in August fell 19 percent in its fiscal first quarter 2009. Sales fell 9 percent in the quarter.

The firm's fiscal second-quarter 2010 earnings rose a bigger-than-expected 16 percent, with an 8 percent growth to $1.35 billion. Revenue climbed 11 percent to $1.53 billion.

See also RETAILING.

POOLING. Combining and packaging a group of loans to be held by a single entity.

POOR CHILDREN. *See* POVERTY.

POOR, THE. *See* FOOD STAMPS; POVERTY; WEALTH.
  Cf. MIDDLE CLASS.

POPULATION. U.S. population grew by 2.2 million between July 2010 and July 2011 to a total of 311.6 million. It was the slowest growth rate since the 1940s due to lower immigration, the economic downturn, and a large fall in the national birthrate. The Great Recession and slowness in its recovery had prompted many people to put off having families.

PORSCHE. Porsche and Volkswagen agreed on May 3, 2009, to merge corporations, uniting ten auto brands, including Porsche's sports cars, into a single company. At that point, Porsche had already owned a 51 percent stake in Volkswagen. On May 17, Porsche indefinitely postponed talks with Volkswagen. Almost as suddenly, a few days later Volkswagen and Porsche agreed to continue discussions toward a potential merger. By mid-June, Porsche announced that its vehicle sales had fallen nearly 30 percent in the first nine months of its fiscal year. From August 2008 to April 2009, Porsche sold 53,635 cars, down 28 percent from the year before. Revenue fell 15 percent to $6.44 billion.

Porsche's request for a $2.5 billion loan from a state-controlled German bank was rejected. The carmaker continued to seek an "alternative financing possibility," which included an investment from Qatar. Porsche garnered nearly $13 billion in debt when it accumulated a stake in Volkswagen. On December 18, 2009, Porsche reported that revenue fell 31 percent in its fiscal first quarter. Revenue was $1.6 billion and sales fell 40 percent from a year before to 11,385 cars in the three months ending October 31.

The automaker reported on November 29, 2010, that it had a profit of $205.3 million in the first three months of its fiscal year.

On October 28, 2011, management posted an operating profit increase of 25 percent to 1.51 billion euros, with revenue climbing 20 percent to 7.93 billion euros.

See also AUTOMOBILE INDUSTRY; VOLKSWAGEN.

PORTUGAL. Growth resumed in the second quarter 2009 but will remain subdued as private-sector deleveraging constrains the recovery. As a result, unemployment is likely to increase to around 10 percent in 2010. The budget deficit is set to rise further in 2010 and 2011, following a substantial increase in 2009 due to the combined impact of the fiscal stimulus and the recession. Core inflation, after dropping to near zero, may increase rather slowly over the projection period. Long-standing current-account imbalances, translated into rising indebtedness, limit the pace of recovery, which may be somewhat weaker than that of the euro area. Despite anemic growth, designing and gradually implementing fiscal consolidation is a major priority. Structural reforms to promote competitiveness are central to achieving higher growth through more dynamic exports, while the pursuit of education reform should help foster longer-term potential.

Unemployment in Portugal in the second quarter 2009 was 9.2 percent, and the economy shrank by 3.7 percent in 2009. The government cut its budget deficit from 6.1 percent of GDP in 2005 to 2.8 percent by 2008.

Public-sector jobs were reduced by 10 percent and a 2006 reform limited real increases in pensions to when the economy would grow rapidly. Portugal's goal was to reduce the percentage of GDP to 7.3 percent in 2010 and 4.6 percent in 2011.

On May 13, 2010, Portugal announced new austerity measures to shore up investor confidence. The government approved a value-added tax increase of one percentage point across all categories, 6 percent for necessities, 13 percent for restaurants, and 21 percent for most other goods and services. Firms with profits of more than $3.6 million would pay an extra 2.5 percent tax on their profits. The government expected to cut the nation's deficit to 7.3 percent of GDP in 2010 and 4.6 percent in 2011. The Portuguese parliament on November 26, 2010, approved $4 billion in spending cuts with further tax increases. The following day, the parliament passed a budget for 2011 aiming to lower the nation's deficit from 9.3 percent of GDP in 2009 to less than 3 percent by 2013. At the end of the month, lawmakers approved a tough 2011 budget to help to reduce the deficit to 4.6 percent of GDP in 2011, down from 9.3 percent in 2009.

With soaring borrowing costs straining the national accounts, in 2011 the focus was firmly on narrowing the fiscal gap, hoping the economy would return to recession after a brief rally in 2010. The nation's GDP is -1.0 percent, with a GDP of $211 billion, an inflation rate of 0.8 percent, and a GDP per head of $19,810. On January 28, 2011, the central bank of Portugal asked the nation's banks to suspend paying dividends to conserve capital. In February Portugal sold $4.76 billion in five-year notes through a syndicate of banks. On March 23, Portugal's parliament rejected a new government austerity plan forcing them to reach out for a euro bailout. That made Portugal the third of seventeen nations using the euro to seek aid from other members of the European Union and the International Monetary Fund. Paying an interest rate of 7.8 percent on ten-year government bonds in March indicated that investors remained unconvinced that an inconclusive strategy for bailing out troubled nations in the eurozone wasn't working. For Portugal, the bailout would be about $113 billion.

On April 1, the government successfully staged a bond auction of $2.3 billion in short-term government bonds. Then, on April 5, Portugal's bond ratings were downgraded for the second time in two months. The country had about $13 billion of bond debt due in April and June. The following day, April 6, the nation's finance minister said for the first time that the country would require help from the European Union to solve its debt crisis. On April 7, the European Commission received Portugal's formal request for aid, which was valued at $116 billion. Domestic public debt represented 3.4 percent of banking assets compared with an average of 5 percent across the EU banking sector.

Questions remained demanding data to show that bailouts work. Many question the wisdom of funds being wasted. Escaping from the "debt trap" requires devaluation of currency, which cannot happen among nations that use the euro as their common currency or have strong economic growth, which troubled countries do not have. The government then asked the EU for its third financial bailout. On May 5, Portugal imposed new austerity measures, with a package valued at $115.5 billion.

For the first quarter 2011, the nation's deficit was 8.7 percent of its GDP, greater than the 5.9 percent that was needed before the end of the year. Under the IMF agreement, Portugal was to cut its budget deficit to 3 percent of GDP by 2013. Under the bailout plan of $108 billion from the EU and IMF, Portugal was required to reduce its deficit to 5.9 percent of GDP in 2011, 4.5 percent in 2012, and 3 percent in 2013. By December, Fitch Ratings, as did Moody's Investor's Service in July, had downgraded Portugal's debt rating to junk status at BB-plus from BBB-minus.

In 2012, the nation faces a difficult economy, expected to contract by 3 percent with increased austerity. The 2012 budget, with wage and job cuts, received 90 percent approval in its parliament.

See also EUROPE (BAILOUT); EUROZONE; INTERNATIONAL MONETARY FUND.

POUND (BRITISH). In July 2008, the British pound was trading around $2 against the U.S. dollar, and dropped to around $1.80 by September and $1.55 on October 27. It fell in late October 2008 to a five-year low against the dollar. Most specialists argued that the sterling had been overvalued at $2.

The pound tumbled on January 21, 2009, to a twenty-three-year low against the U.S. dollar. Debt was expected to exceed 80 percent of GDP. The United Kingdom had a large fiscal deficit of 7.3 percent of GDP as its goal for 2010, with strong possibilities of a recession in 2011.

See also DOLLAR (U.S.); UNITED KINGDOM.

POVERTY. In 2005, just over a quarter of the world's population, or 1.4 billion people, was living in extreme poverty, according to the World Bank. That compared with 42 percent in 1990. In China, the share of people below the threshold of $1.25 a day fell from 60.2 percent to 15.9 percent between 1990 and 2005. But, the poverty rate fell much more slowly in India, to 41.6 percent in 2005 from 51.3 percent in 1990. South Asia has the most very poor people of any region in the world. The fraction of the population that lived in extreme poverty is highest at 50.9 percent in sub-Saharan Africa, though it had fallen from 57.6 percent in 1990.

In 2009, the United Nations calculated that the 500 richest people in the world earned more than the 416 million poorest people. As many as 222 million workers run the risk of joining the ranks of the working poor, earning less than $1.25 a day. In addition, remittance flows, which reached $328 billion in 2008, dropped by 7.3 percent in 2009. In the United States, the poverty rate rose to 13.2 percent in 2008, the highest level since 1997 and a significant increase from 12.5 percent in 2007, suggesting that some 40 million U.S. citizens were living below the poverty line, defined as an income of $22,205 for a family of four. Median household income fell in 2008 to $50,300 from $52,200 in 2007, the steepest year-to-year decline in forty years. The recession's impact on low-income families brought more children into poverty as family incomes shrank. On September 29, 2009, the government reported an increase in poverty across the United States, especially among children. The percentage of children living in poverty increased in twenty-six states, compared with seventeen states in 2007. The highest concentration of poor was in southern states, with a 21.2 percent poverty rate in Mississippi, while Kentucky, West Virginia, and Arkansas each had poverty rates of about 17 percent. About one out of seven Americans was living in poverty. Four million additional citizens were in poverty in 2009, with the total reaching 44 million (millions more survived only because of expanded unemployment insurance and other assistance). The number of poor people in the suburbs jumped by 37.4 percent to 13.7 million, compared to 12.1 million people below the poverty line in cities. For a single adult in 2009, the poverty line was $10,830 in pretax cash income; for a family of four it was $22,050. The poverty rate for non-Hispanic whites was 9.4 percent, for African Americans 25.8 percent, and for Hispanics 25.3 percent. The rate for Asians was unchanged at 12.5 million.

By summer 2011, 46.2 million Americans were living in poverty. The breakdown was: 25.2 million women and girls, 13.2 million Hispanics, 31.7 million whites, 3.5 million ages 65 or older, 10.7 million blacks, 1.7 million Asians, 21 million men and boys, and 16.4 million ages 17 or younger. The official poverty line was $22,314 in 2010 for a family of four (including Social Security and other cash benefits). By mid-September, more than one in three young families with children was living in poverty. At 37 percent, it was the highest level on record, surpassing the previous peak of 36 percent in 1993. In 2000, the rate was about 25 percent.

By September, for the first time the single largest group of poor children were Latino. Of 6.1 million Hispanic children in 2010, 37.3 percent were non-white Latino, 30.5 percent were white, and 26.6 percent were black. By the beginning of November, it was shown that the ranks of America's poorest had climbed to a record-high one in fifteen people. Roughly 20.5 million citizens, or 6.7 percent of the population, made up the poorest, defined as those at 50 percent or less of the official poverty level. The 6.7 percent represented the highest in the thirty-five years that the government had maintained such records. In 2010, the poorest poor meant an income of $5,570 or less for an individual and $11,157 for a family of four. The District of Columbia had the highest at 10.7 percent, followed by Mississippi and New Mexico.

See also CHILD CARE; CHILDREN IN POVERTY; FOOD AID; FOOD STAMPS; HEALTH CARE; HOMELESSNESS; INCOME; LIVING STANDARDS; MEDICAID; SCHOOLS IN POVERTY; TEMPORARY ASSISTANCE FOR NEEDY FAMILIES; UNEMPLOYMENT; UNEMPLOYMENT BENEFITS.

PPIP. *See* PUBLIC-PRIVATE INVESTMENT PARTNERSHIP.

PPP. *See* PURCHASING-POWER PARITY.

PRADA. Its net profit and sales surged in the fiscal year ending January 31, 2011. Its net profit more than doubled to $353 million and sales climbed 31 percent to 2.05 billion euros. On September 19, management reported a 74 percent surge in first-half year profit to $264.4 million, with a 21 percent climb in sales. By December 2011, Prada reported a 75 percent climb in third-quarter net profit. Net profit climbed to $124.7 million, with revenue rising 33 percent.

PRATT & WHITNEY. *See* UNITED TECHNOLOGIES.

PREFORECLOSURE SALE. *Synonymous with* REAL ESTATE OWNED.

PREP SCHOOLS. Along with most institutions of education, prep schools faced significant losses in their endowments, resulting in large cutbacks in student aid during the meltdown. Many endowments fell 20–21 percent at many independent private schools.
See also EDUCATION.

PRESIDENTIAL TASK FORCE ON AUTOS. A government committee that oversaw the reorganization of General Motors and Chrysler in 2009.
See also AUTO TASK FORCE; CAR CZAR.

PRESIDENT'S COUNCIL ON JOBS AND COMPETITIVENESS. *See* COUNCIL ON JOBS AND COMPETITIVENESS.

PRICES. *See* CONSUMER PRICES.

PRIMARY DEALER CREDIT FACILITY (PDCF). The Federal Reserve's overnight-lending facility. Loans were made during the financial crisis to institutions desperate to raise cash and to struggling foreign banks in 2008 and 2009. $3.3 trillion was funneled to different parts of the economy and financial system, with foreign banks receiving hundreds of billions of dollars in short-term loans.
See also FEDERAL RESERVE.

PRINCE, CHARLES O. Speaking before the Financial Crisis Inquiry Commission on April 8, 2010, the former chairman and chief executive at

Citigroup said, "I'm sorry that the financial crisis has had such a devastating impact on our country. I'm sorry for the millions of people, average Americans, who have lost their homes. And I'm sorry that our management team, starting with me, like so many others, could not see the unprecedented market collapse that lay before us."

Left Citigroup and became a senior counselor to Albright Stonebridge Advisors.

See also CITIGROUP; FINANCIAL CRISIS INQUIRY COMMISSION.

PRINCETON UNIVERSITY. One of the nation's wealthiest colleges reported on September 29, 2009, that its endowment shrank 23 percent over the past year, losing $3.7 billion.

On October 15, 2010, the university declared that its endowment had returned a 14.7 percent profit in 2009, bringing its total to $14.4 billion.

Cf. HARVARD UNIVERSITY; STANFORD UNIVERSITY; YALE UNIVERSITY.

PRINCIPAL. The amount borrowed.

PRINCIPAL STRATEGIES UNIT. *See* PROPRIETARY TRADING.

PRISON. Resulting from huge budget deficits and the 2007 recession, many states across the country are trimming their prison populations by expanding parole programs and early releases.

By January 2011, a by-product of state budget cuts for prisons had led to the release of inmates and at the same time a boost probation and parole. States spend a total of $50 billion a year, or 7 percent of discretionary budgets.

PRISONERS. *See* PRISON.

PRISON TIME (EU). On December 8, 2010, the European Union urged mandatory prison terms for insider trading and other abuses as part of measures aimed at supporting confidence and attempting to strengthen laws on banking, insurance, and trades.

PRIVATE EQUITY FIRMS. By 2009, private equity companies saw declines of 15 to 50 percent amid the deep economic recession.

See also BUYOUT FIRMS.

PRIVATE EQUITY FUNDS. *See* FINANCIAL REGULATION PLAN (2009).

PRIVATE-LABEL MORTGAGE-BACKED SECURITIES (PLS). *Synonymous with* NON-AGENCY MORTGAGE-BACKED SECURITIES.

PRIVATE MORTGAGE INSURANCE. Insurance on the payment of a mortgage provided by a private firm at an additional cost to the borrower to protect the lender.

PRIVATE-SECTOR PAYROLLS. Since the beginning of the meltdown in 2007, the country has lost nearly 7.3 million private-sector jobs. By the end of 2010, there were 108 million private-sector jobs, the same number the United States had in April 1999.

January's 2011 payrolls in the private sector rose by 36,000, a disappointing number as 200,000 is considered the minimum growth needed to absorb the increase in population. The private sector added 50,000 jobs, while government lost 14,000, and 13.9 million people remained out of work.

See also EMPLOYMENT; SPENDING; UNEMPLOYMENT.

PROBLEM BANKS. Banks with the highest risk of failure. In 2010, this represented one in nine lenders.

PROCTER & GAMBLE. The world's largest consumer goods firm reported in August 2009 that its profit of $2.5 billion was down 18 percent and that sales of its paper towels and detergents were down 11 percent. On October 29, 2009, the company reported that the quarter ending September 30 had a profit of $3.31 billion, down from $3.35 billion a year earlier, with sales falling 6 percent to $19.81 billion.

In August 2010, management announced that its sales climbed nearly 5 percent, with its profit falling 12 percent. For the fourth quarter, Procter & Gamble posted a profit of $3.33 billion, down 28 percent from the year before. Revenue reached $21.35 billion, up 1.5 percent.

Procter & Gamble's fiscal third-quarter 2011 earnings rose 11 percent. On August 5, management reported that its earnings were up 15 percent, with a profit of $2.51 billion. Revenue increased 10 percent to $20.86 billion. In October, management reported a 1.9 percent fall in profit to $3.02 billion. Net sales climbed 8.9 percent to $21.9 billion. Fourth-quarter profit fell by 49 percent as net sales climbed 3.7 percent to $22.14 billion.

Cf. COLGATE-PALMOLIVE COMPANY.

PRO-CYCLICALITY. The tendency of banks and the regulations that govern them to exacerbate the cycle, both the ups and the downs. To prevent this from happening, banks should arrange capital in good times that can be tapped in times of stress.

PRODUCER PRICE INDEX. In February 2011, producer prices surged at their fastest pace in eighteen months, rising the core producer prices 0.2

percent in January, retreating from a 0.5 percent climb. In the twelve months prior to February, the core Producer Price Index climbed 1.8 percent, the largest increase since August 2009, following a 1.6 percent increase in January.

See also WHOLESALE PRICES.

PRODUCTIVITY. Output per hour jumped in the fourth quarter 2008, rising at a 3.2 percent seasonally adjusted annual rate. American worker productivity grew in the second quarter 2009 at the fastest rate in almost six years, as employers slashed payrolls to bolster profits. Productivity rose at an annual rate of 6.4 percent.

Productivity surged in the third quarter 2009 as the economy resumed growing. When taken together with the second quarter's 6.9 percent rise, it was the strongest productivity growth rate over a six-month period since 1961. November production figures rose 0.8 percent, the largest increase since August, outpacing expectations.

Productivity in the fourth quarter 2010 increased at a 2.6 percent annual rate, up from 2.4 percent in the third quarter.

By 2011, the stalled economy had cut sharply into the productivity of companies. As measured in output per hour of work, it fell at a 0.3 percent annual rate in the second quarter 2011 from the first quarter. After dropping in the first half of the year, productivity output per hour was 2.3 percent higher in the third quarter. The great recession has made U.S. companies leaner and more muscular.

Synonymous with OUTPUT PER HOUR.

PROFITS. Corporate profits posted their third consecutive gain in the third quarter 2009 as the U.S. economy grew by 2.8 percent. There was a 10.6 percent annualized gain over the second quarter to a seasonally adjusted $1.3 trillion coming at the expense of employees.

By mid-November 2010, corporate profits grew $44.4 billion in the third quarter over the previous three months to a $1.66 trillion seasonally adjusted rate. After-tax earnings climbed by 3.2 percent compared with the second quarter's gain of 0.9 percent. Year-over-year profits were $28.2 trillion for the year. The annualized 2.3 percent profit growth in the fourth quarter was driven by financial firms. Nonfinancial firms saw profits fall $10 billion to an annual rate of $879 billion.

Strong earnings appeared for the second quarter 2011, indicating the disparity between corporation performance and the overall health of the U.S. economy. Standard & Poor's believed that corporation earnings would rise 13 percent from a year before. Profits were up 47 percent over the first twenty-one months of the recovery.

By the end of the second quarter 2011, corporation profits climbed 3 percent—better than the 1 percent improvement in the first quarter of the year. Profit increased more than 8 percent from 2010's second quarter. Experts predicted a growth at a 2.3 percent pace in the last six months of the year and 2.8 percent in 2012.

PRO-GROWTH TRADE. A strategy based on the view that global economies would recover strongly and included bets that commodities, high-yielding currencies, and stocks would continue to climb, while safer investments such as the U.S. Treasury's, would fall.

PROJECT MERLIN. *See* UNITED KINGDOM.

PROMOTE AMERICA'S COMPETITIVE EDGE (PACE). A coalition of business associations and corporations founded in spring 2009 to confront the government's advancing new rules on the conduct of business. Specifically, this not-for-profit organization confronted President Osama's program to curb corporations' ability to park their overseas business earnings indefinitely outside the United States and avoid U.S. taxes, a practice known as *deferral.*

In addition, PACE looks to confront the government's plan to right an imbalance created by U.S. tax policy between multinationals and the small businesses that generate the bulk of American jobs but generally don't qualify for these tax breaks.

PROPERTY (2011). Following a 4 percent fall in 2010, house prices in the United States slipped another 2 percent in 2011. Other projections included the gloomy forecast for commercial property, with loan rates continuing to climb throughout the year. Commercial rents also fell further.

China surpassed the United Kingdom and Japan to become the world's second-largest market in 2011 for commercial real estate investments, after the United States.

PROPERTY TAXES. *See* FORECLOSURE.

PROPRIETARY TRADERS. People who basically trade company money in hopes of increasing bank profits and their own paychecks. Usually, these traders work primarily on helping big bank clients, including firms, buy and sell derivates in an attempt to hedge, or limit, losses from exposure to some commodities or other markets. Under the Volcker rule and the financial reform legislation of July 2010, federal officials will disallow most proprietary trading at banks unless the trades are meant to serve near-term client demand or reduce risk.

See PROPRIETARY TRADING; VOLCKER RULE.

Synonymous with "PROP" TRADERS.

PROPRIETARY TRADING. Involves putting a company's own capital at risk in trades.

"PROP" TRADERS. *Synonymous with* PROPRIETARY TRADERS.

PROP-TRADING. *See* PROPRIETARY TRADING.

PROTECTIONISM. The imposition of high tariffs and quotas on imports that are presumed to compete with domestic items, with the objective of giving the domestic manufacturer an advantage.

Advancing protectionism threatened the global economy in concert with the current recession. Following the Group of Twenty's meeting in mid-November 2008, when the signers to the meeting said they would not create barriers to trade, several countries turned around and raised tariffs to protect domestic industries.

The belief appeared to be that this style of protectionism, reminiscent of the Smoot-Hawley Act of the 1930s, would be an antidote to the current recession. The Smoot-Hawley Act raised duties on more than 20,000 items imported into the United States. The result was that U.S. international trade declined by 42 percent, while world trade fell 60 percent, measured in dollars. Needless to say, it was a disaster. An often unnoticed part of the 2009 stimulus package is one provision that discourages federal bailout companies from hiring skilled foreign workers.

By 2009, in response to the economic meltdown, nations around the globe were involved in more trade disputes and were pondering protectionist policies in response to the deepest global downturn since World War II. In fact, in early March, seventeen members of the Group of Twenty had adopted forty-seven measures aimed at restricting cross-border trade. Increasingly, protectionist policies would only hurt the economy of U.S. citizens and curtail exports to the world.

See also BUY AMERICAN; BUY LOCAL; FINANCIAL PROTECTIONISM; GENERAL AGREEMENT ON TARIFFS AND TRADE; G-20; GLOBAL UNEMPLOYMENT; MEXICO; SMOOT-HAWLEY ACT; WORLD TRADE ORGANIZATION.

PROTESTORS. *See* G-20; INDIGNADOS; "OCCUPY WALL STREET."

PRUDENTIAL FINANCIAL. Reported a sharp quarter 2010 fall in net income, while its profit climbed 75 percent.
Cf. METLIFE.

PUBLIC COMPANY ACCOUNTING OVERSIGHT BOARD. *See* SARBANES-OXLEY ACT OF 2002.

PUBLIC DEBT (U.S.). *See* CHINA; DEBT, FEDERAL (U.S.).

PUBLIC-PRIVATE INVESTMENT FUND. The Treasury secretary on February 10, 2009, called for an investment fund to "provide government capital and government financing to help leverage private capital to help get private markets working again." With this fund, the government was trying to help private investors buy toxic bank assets.

The U.S. Treasury's public-private effort to rid banks of toxic assets was built on existing financial rescue plans and included:

a. Stress tests for major banks, with new capital requirements for those in need of it.
b. A Treasury/Federal Reserve program to spur auto, credit card, and other consumer lending.
c. Government purchasing of securities backed by small business administration loans to encourage lending.
d. A mortgage-loan modification plan to reduce foreclosures.

The Public-Private Investment Program (PPIP) aimed to spur purchases of soured loans and real-estate-related securities. The two-part plan used up to $100 billion of bank rescue funds from the Treasury, as well as financial guarantees from the Federal Reserve and Federal Deposit Insurance Corporation. Funds were established to purchase and manage mortgage securities, and the government provided financing to private investors to purchase the loans.

TALF (Term Asset-Backed Securities Loan Facility), which sought to jump-start the market for newly issued securities by a range of consumer and small-business loans, would also be expanded. The expansion extended TALF to existing securities, not only new ones. "PEE-pips" is the insider's name for public-private investment partnerships.

The Legacy Loans Program purported to clear bank balance sheets of distressed loans. A bank holding a mortgage loan with face value of $100 informs the FDIC that it wants to rid itself of the loan and faces the following steps:

a. The bank will take a loss on a portion of the original value.
b. The FDIC will decide how much it is willing to guarantee in financing for a purchaser. The amount of financing could be more than half the loan's face value.
c. The highest bidder at auction purchases the loan and pays for half the equity position. This private owner services the loan using asset managers approved by the FDIC.
d. The Treasury finances the other half of the equity.

Under the Legacy Securities Program, one of the aims is to set prices for hard-to-value securities backed by commercial and residential mortgages. Up to five managers will assist the government with managing pools of assets that will be created by the plan.

a. Asset managers raise private funds and present a plan to purchase eligible securities from banks and financial firms.
b. The Treasury approves plans and matches the amount raised privately.
c. The Treasury provides a loan of 100–200 percent of the private financing, turning that $100 into a potentially $400 fund. Banks can accept or reject bids for their securities.

By mid-October 2009, five investment funds that raised $1.94 billion in private capital to purchase troubled assets began buying. With the PPIP, the Treasury pledged to match the funds raised by approved money-management firms. It would also provide leverage, or loans to the fund, equal to the full amount of the fund, doubling its spending power.

See also BAILOUT RESCUE PLAN (OF 2009) (U.S.); BUFFETT, WARREN E.; HEDGE FUNDS; STRESS TESTS (U.S.); TOXIC ASSETS; TROUBLED ASSET RELIEF PROGRAM.

PUBLIC-PRIVATE INVESTMENT PROGRAM (PPIP). *See* PUBLIC-PRIVATE INVESTMENT FUND.

PUBLIC WORKS. Upon being sworn in on January 20, 2009, President Obama urged the spending of $500 billion to $700 billion over two years to help pull the country out of its economic downslide. His plan included funds for infrastructure rebuilding around the nation, including rebuilding new hospitals and schools, with more to come.

PUB, THE. *See* GUINNESS.

PUERTO RICO. At the beginning of January 2009, the governor of Puerto Rico declared a fiscal emergency, forecasting a towering deficit of $3.2 billion. "The present deficit is the greatest, in percentage terms, of all the U.S. states." More than 30,000 government workers, about 14 percent of the public workforce in Puerto Rico, would be fired, according to a March 2009 report.

See also LATIN AMERICA.

PULTE. One of the two largest home builders in the United States reported in August 2009 that its second-quarter loss widened to $189.5 million. Revenue dropped 58 percent to $678.6 million. New orders fell 34 percent to 3,367 homes.

On August 4, 2010, management reported that the firm returned to a quarterly profit for the first time in more than three years, with net income totaling $76.3 million, compared to a loss in 2009 of $189.5 million. Revenue climbed 92 percent to $1.31 billion. The largest home builder in the nation reported a fourth-quarter loss of $165.4 million verus the previous year's loss of $116.9 million.

Cf. D.R. HORTON.

PURCHASING-POWER PARITY (PPP). The concept that in the long run, exchange rates should equalize prices across nations.

Q

QATAR. Qatar's permanent residents, 250,000 (out of 1.7 million people), are the richest in the world. Qatari shares soared on March 9, 2009, after the government said it would purchase investment funds from banks to help shield the financial system from the global credit crisis.

The economy of Qatar grew by more than 23 percent in the first half of 2010 after a 10 percent climb in 2009 and a 13 percent climb in 2008. The nation's GDP per head was nearly $84,000, the world's highest.

See also BARCLAYS; MIDDLE EAST; PORSCHE.

QE. *See* QUANTITATIVE EASING.

QUANTAS AIRWAYS. Australia's largest airline posted a 66 percent decline in profit for the fiscal first half of 2008. Its net profit for the first half fell to AZ$210 million from AZ$617.7 million a year earlier.

Management forecast in April 2009 that it would need to cut as many as 1,750 jobs as it extended efforts to reduce costs. Quantas said its fiscal-year net profit fell 88 percent to $96.2 million as revenue continued to slide. On December 21, 2009, airline management reported that it expected to return to profitability shortly as passenger listings increased.

In 2010, the airline saw if first-half profit climb to $242 million from the year before.

On November 29, 2011, management forecast a steep fall in its fiscal first-half profit, with a pretax profit of $136 million for the six months ending December 30. Traffic volume fell 1.8 percent.

QUANT FIRMS. Firms specializing in quantitative investment.

QUANT FUNDS. Investment funds with securities selected by quantitative analysis.

QUANTITATIVE ANALYSTS. People employing mathematical models in quantitative finance. They apply quantitative investment techniques.

In 2010, the combined assets of quantitative funds specializing in U.S. stocks plunged to $467 billion from $1.2 trillion in 2007, a 61 percent fall. One in four quant hedge funds had been terminated since 2007.

See also LONG-TERM CAPITAL MANAGEMENT.
Synonymous with QUANTS.

QUANTITATIVE EASING (QE). Buying bonds with newly created money. Incorporates various measures for pumping money into the economy. It is considered an unconventional monetary policy because its effect is felt through the quantity rather than the costs of credit. The newly printed money is used to buy assets. It is a way of making monetary policy effective when interest rates are close to zero. Some argue that it leads to inflationary money printing, while others complain that too little attention is paid to the flow of credit.

The Federal Reserve's program ended in June 2010. Under this strategy, the Federal Reserve purchased $600 billion of U.S. Treasury securities between November 2009 and June 2010, pumping funds into the financial system. Its impact remains under debate.

See also FEDERAL RESERVE (U.S.).

QUANTS. *Synonymous with* QUANTITATIVE ANALYSTS.

R

RACE TO THE TOP PROGRAM. The federal government's attempt to overhaul school systems with stimulus funding of $4.35 billion in education grants serving as an incentive. Under this program, states were rewarded for promoting one of the federal government's top aims—the adoption of common educational standards and testing assessments. Under a point system, the government intended to reward states that band together in adopting the same testing standards.

See also EDUCATION.

RADIO SHACK. The electronics retailer's profits dropped 39 percent in its fourth-quarter earnings for 2008 as reported on February 24, 2009. In the fourth quarter 2008, sales at stores open at least one year dropped 9.2 percent compared with a year earlier. Profits fell $62 million from $101 million a year before.

Third-quarter 2009 earnings plummeted 24 percent. The company reported a profit of $37.4 million compared with $491 million a year earlier. Revenue fell 3.1 percent to $990 million as same-store sales declined 2.9 percent.

Radio Shack's second-quarter 2010 profit climbed 8.6 percent, with earnings of $3 million. Revenue increased 4.7 percent to $1.01 billion.

Radio Shack's first-quarter 2011 earnings fell 30 percent. For its fourth quarter, shares were down 20 percent, with sales of $1.39 billion and growth of about 2 percent.

RAIL HAULERS. *See* FREIGHT HAULERS.

RAIL INVESTMENTS. *See* ECONOMIC STIMULUS PLAN.

RAIL SERVICE. On April 16, 2009, the government announced that it planned to spend $8 billion in stimulus funds on high-speed passenger-rail service.

U.S. railroads hauled more in the fourth quarter 2010, leading to new hires and a return to service of once-idle rail cars and locomotives.

RAIL TRAFFIC. *See* FREIGHT HAULERS.

RAT BOARD. Charged with sniffing out waste, fraud, and abuse in the $787 billion stimulus plan.

Synonymous with RECOVERY ACCOUNTABILITY AND TRANSPARENCY BOARD.

RATERS. The Securities and Exchange Commission was given authority over credit-rating firms in 2006, then naming ten of them as "nationally recognized." On August 28, 2009, the Commission indicated serious concerns about one firm. Some rating firms have been accused of exacerbating the meltdown by giving overly positive ratings to certain types of debt, including some backed by subprime mortgages.

See also FITCH RATINGS; MOODY'S; SECURITIES AND EXCHANGE COMMISSION; STANDARD & POOR'S.

RATING AGENCIES. By mid-May 2010, the U.S. Senate approved a provision to rate complex bond deals in a move to end alleged conflicts of interest. The change aimed to resolve what's considered a problem in financial markets where bond issuers choose rating agencies and pay for ratings, meaning raters' revenues depend on the very firms whose bond they are asked to judge. If approved, a powerful credit-rating board is urged.

See also CREDIT RATINGS; FITCH RATINGS; MOODY'S; STANDARD & POOR'S.

RATTNER, STEVEN. President Obama's top auto industry troubleshooter; one of fourteen people on a committee that was charged with orchestrating the rescue of the giant U.S. automakers. Rattner, the chief architect of the General Motors and Chrysler bailouts, left the administration after less than six months on the job and just days after completion of the GM return from bankruptcy.

In mid-October 2010, Rattner finalized a deal with the Securities and Exchange Commission to resolve his role in a "pay to play" scandal involving New York State's public pension fund. He would pay roughly $6 million and agreed to a two-year ban from the securities industry. On November 18, the very day that General Motors began its stock market initial public offering, the New York State attorney general sought to ban Mr. Rattner from the securities industry in New York for the rest of his life and seeking to collect $26 million for using special favors to win a $150 million investment from the state pension fund.

As 2010 ended, Rattner settled his dispute with the Office of the New York State Attorney General for $10 million to end lawsuits alleging he traded favors for business from the state's $125 billion public pension fund. Rattner would pay restitutions to the state pension fund and be barred from appearing in any capacity before a public pension fund within the state for five years. He did not admit to any wrongdoing.

See also AUTO TASK FORCE; CHRYSLER; GENERAL MOTORS.

RAW MATERIALS. *See* RIO TINTO.

RBS. *See* ROYAL BANK OF SCOTLAND.

R&D. *See* RESEARCH AND DEVELOPMENT.

READER'S DIGEST. Announced on January 29, 2009, that it would lay off close to 300 people, about 8 percent of its workforce, putting employees on unpaid furloughs and suspending contributions to their 401(k) plan. On August 17, *Reader's Digest* declared that it would seek bankruptcy protection to restructure $2.2 billion in debt.

On July 17, 2011, having emerged from bankruptcy protection in early 2010, the firm put itself up for sale for roughly $1 billion.

"READY TO GO" PROJECTS. Under the economic stimulus plan, federal funds would flow quickest to identifiable projects that could start within a couple of months.

Cf. "SHOVEL READY."

REAL ESTATE. *See* COMMERCIAL REAL ESTATE; COMMERCIAL REAL ESTATE LOANS; FARM REAL ESTATE.

REAL ESTATE OWNED. *See* REO.

REBALANCING. *See* INTERNATIONAL MONETARY FUND.

REBATES. *See* AMERICAN RECOVERY AND REINVESTMENT ACT OF 2009.

RECESSION. The International Monetary Fund (IMF) defines a global recession as growth below 3 percent because that is far too weak to keep up with the demands of a growing population in emerging markets for jobs. The National Bureau of Economic Research defines recession as "a significant decline in economic activity spread across the economy, lasting more than a few months."

Likewise, recovery from a recession can take many shapes. Major ones are:

1. *A V-shaped recession*: Cases when the economy snaps back as quickly and steeply as it fell. Few economists are predicting a V shape now since consumers and job seekers are still facing difficulties.
2. *A W-shaped recession*: Downturns that become upturns but then revert to downturns again. Some economists fear that this type of recession may be ahead for the nation.
3. *An L-shaped recession*: Probably the most worrisome of all. It suggests that once the economy plunges, it stays down for a long period. Because the current meltdown was triggered by an asset bubble, this form of recession is likely. Sometimes called a hockey stick recession.
4. *A U-shaped recession*: Somewhere between a V and an L shape.

See also DOUBLE DIP-RECESSION; NATIONAL BUREAU OF ECO-NOMIC RESEARCH.

RECESSION OF 1972. Several months of a stagnant labor market were followed by a violent contraction over the next year. After the worst month, December 1974, the job market turned around.

Cf. RECESSION OF 1982; RECESSION OF 2007–2012.

RECESSION OF 1982. Employment suffered a major contraction in December 1981 and January 1982, and workers did not see a stable market for about ten months, including another big round of layoffs in July 1982. The first big blow to the economy was the 1979 revolution in Iran, which sent oil prices skyrocketing. The larger blow was a series of sharp interest rate increases by the Federal Reserve, meant to snap inflation. Home sales plummeted. At their worst, they were 30 percent lower than in 2008. Nationwide, the unemployment rate rose above 10 percent in 1982.

See also RECESSION; UNDEREMPLOYED; UNEMPLOYED.

Cf. RECESSION OF 1972; RECESSION OF 2007–2012.

RECESSION OF 2001. *See* RECESSION OF 2007–2012.

RECESSION OF 2007–2012. The U.S. economy went into a recession in December 2007, although it wasn't announced by the National Bureau of Economic Research until December 2008. This was the first recession in the United States since 2001, when the economy suffered after the bursting of the technology bubble and the economic repercussions of the 9/11 attacks on the World Trade Center. The period of expansion lasted seventy-three months, from November 2001 to December 2007. The 2008–2009 meltdown was the worst since 1982. Unofficially, the Great Recession ended on October 29, 2009, awaiting an official declaration from the National Bureau of Economic Research.

Evidence of a downturn had been widespread for months, with slower production, stagnant wages, and hundreds of thousands of lost jobs. The current recession had become the second worst in the last half century and was close to surpassing the severe 1973–1975 downturn. The Conference Board's March figures indicated a decline of 5.6 percent from the high set in November 2007. The drop in the 1970s recession was 6 percent.

In April 2009, the U.S. recession became the longest since the Great Depression. It marked the seventeenth month of the recession beginning in December 2007. On July 15, a commission was created to examine the causes of the financial crisis. The panel was to issue its report no later than the end of 2010 (changed to January 2011).The Commerce Department announced on July 31 that the current recession turned out to be worse than previously thought, while the 2001 recession was milder than earlier reported. Revisions indicated that from the fourth quarter 2007 to the first quarter 2009, inflation-adjusted GDP fell at a 2.8 percent annual rate compared with the 1.8 percent drop earlier reported. The decline continued in the second quarter 2009, producing the worst recession since World War II.

A comparison of the recessions for the past eighty years indicates the following:

2007–2009: duration, eighteen months; decline in real GDP, 3.8 percent; decline in industrial production, 16.9 percent; unemployment, 9.5 percent

1937–1938: duration, thirteen months; decline in real GDP, 18.2 percent; decline in industrial production, 32.4 percent; unemployment, 20 percent

1973–1975: duration, sixteen months; decline in real GDP, 4.9 percent; decline in industrial production, 15.3 percent; unemployment, 9 percent

1981–1982: duration, sixteen months; decline in real GDP, 3 percent; decline in industrial production, 12.3 percent; unemployment, 10.8 percent

By the end of September 2009, most economists believed that, statistically, the Great Recession had come to an end. Then, on October 29, 2009, the government announced that the country's GDP had grown at an annual rate of 3.5 percent in the quarter ending in September, matching its average growth rate of the last eighty years. Unofficially, the United States had emerged from the longest economic contraction since World War II. The stock market reacted favorably, as the people remained gloomy over a projected sluggish growth and the near 10 percent workforce unemployment. (After the 2001 recession, output rose for six quarters before the economy added jobs.)

By mid-summer 2010, government figures indicated that the recovery of the Great Recession was slower than originally estimated and that the recession was worse than thought. The Commerce Department declared that GDP had to be revised down in seven of the twelve quarters of 2007, 2008, and 2009 because consumer spending grew more slowly and home building dropped more sharply than originally thought. The overall depth of the meltdown period surpassed that of any other downturn since the late 1940s. GDP fell by 4.1 percent from the fourth quarter 2007 to the second quarter 2009. The earlier estimate for the peak-to-trough decline was 3.7 percent.

New Commerce Department data indicated that the worst of the Great Recession came in the last quarter 2008 not the first quarter 2009. Then, surprisingly, in August 2010, the Commerce Department acknowledged that the Great Recession was even worse than anyone had thought. Economic activity declined by 4.1 percent from its peak, outstripping the 3.7 percent dip shown in the downturn of 1957–1958 (in 1981 the fall was just under 3 percent). The decline in real GDP in 2009 was the worst annual performance since 1946.

On September 20, 2010, the National Bureau of Economic Research (based in Massachusetts), a group of academic economists responsible for determining the benchmarks for U.S. recessions, officially declared that the 2007 recession was over. Marking the longest slump since the Great Depression, it was the next-longest postwar decline compared to the ones of the early 1970s and early 1980s, each lasting sixteen months. It eliminated 7.3 million jobs, cut 4.1 percent from economic output, and cost Americans 21 percent of their net worth.

Some 6.2 million unemployed workers had been out of a job for at least twenty-seven weeks. In addition, real GDP by summer 2010 had made up only 2.9 percentage points of the 4.1 percent lost during the recession, while household net worth had recovered only 4 percentage points of the 21 percent lost. By summer 2011, GDP increased at a minimal 1.3 percent annual rate. First-quarter revisions, down to 0.4 percent from 1.9 percent, indicated an economy at a near standstill. Weak demand was the primary cause.

See also ACCOUNTANTS; CONFERENCE BOARD; DOUBLE-DIP RECESSION; ECONOMIC CYCLE RESEARCH INSTITUTE; ECONOMIC RECOVERY; ECONOMY (U.S.); FEDERAL RESERVE; FINANCIAL CRISIS INQUIRY COMMISSION; "FLASH CRASH"; NATIONAL BUREAU OF ECONOMIC RESEARCH; RECOVERY; WALL STREET REFORM ACT (2010).

Cf. DOUBLE-DIP RECESSION; GREAT DEPRESSION; RECESSION OF 1972; RECESSION OF 1982; THIRD DEPRESSION.

Synonymous with GREAT RECESSION; GREAT RECESSION I.

RECONSTRUCTION FINANCE CORPORATION (RFC). A former U.S. government agency created in 1932 by the administration of Herbert Hoover. Its purpose was to facilitate economic activity by lending money during the depression. At first, it lent money only to financial, industrial, and agricultural institutions, but the scope was widened during President Roosevelt's administration. It financed the construction and operation of war plants, made loans to foreign governments, provided protection against war and disaster damages, among other activities.

In 1939, the RFC merged with other agencies to form the Federal Loan Agency. The Federal Loan Agency was abolished in 1947, and RFC was abolished as an independent agency by an act of Congress in 1953 and was transferred to the Department of the Treasury to wind up its affairs, effective June 1954. It was totally disbanded in 1957, after having made loans of approximately $50 billion since its creation.

See also HOOVER, HERBERT.

RECOVERY. Recovery from the Great Recession is expected to take years. The evidence was abundant. From the 2001 recession to the present, the economy advanced at an average annual rate of 2.5 percent. That would amount to roughly $350 billion a year, demanding three years to restore the $1 trillion in lost capacity.

The stimulus package of $787 billion would be consumed in two years. Therefore, should every dollar of spending restore a dollar of output, more than three years could be needed before output approaches the level achieved just before the start of the recession in December 2007.

Examining 122 recessions in rich economies since 1960, the International Monetary Fund found that in the aftermath of a financial bust, private investment tends to fall even after the downturn approaches stability, whereas private consumption grows more slowly than in other recoveries. Recoveries from global recessions take 50 percent longer than other recoveries.

The initial step to recovery is for output to stop shrinking. Then, one of three types of recovery may occur—V, U, or W. A V-shaped recovery is strong and vigorous, with significant demand released. A U-shaped recovery is flatter and tends to be weaker. A W-shaped recovery has a return of growth for a few quarters, only to return to another slump.

By February 2010, for the twenty-fifth time in twenty-six months jobs were lost. By September, the National Bureau of Economic Research declared that the official termination of the Great Recession, which began in December 2007 was over in June 2009. By the end of summer 2010, it was becoming obvious that an economic upturn involved the following:

1. At the current rate of job creation, the country would need nine more years to recapture the jobs lost during the recession.
2. Median house prices had dropped 20 percent since 2005. Given an inflation rate of about 2 percent, it would take thirteen years for housing prices to climb back to their peak.
3. Commercial vacancies, which continue to soar, could take a decade to absorb the excess in many of the nation's cities.

See also ECONOMIC RECOVERY; RECESSION OF 2007–2012; WALL STREET REFORM ACT (2010).

RECOVERY ACCOUNTABILITY AND TRANSPARENCY BOARD. Monitors the way the $787 billion in the stimulus package was spent.
See also FRAUD.
Synonymous with RAT BOARD.

RECOVERY ACT. *Synonymous with* AMERICAN RECOVERY AND REINVESTMENT ACT.

RECOVERY SUMMER 2010. It never happened.

REDBACK. *Synonymous with* RENMINBI; YUAN.

REDCORP VENTURES. A Canadian gold and silver mining firm that filed for bankruptcy in March 2009 in the United States and Canada, citing cost overruns and a lack of financing.

RED ZONE. Term used in 2011 to describe fears that the European Union's persistent debt woes will lead to a broader financial crisis and economic slowdown.

REFI. Short for refinancing, as in mortgage refinancing.
See REFINANCING MORTGAGES.

REFINANCE. *Synonymous with* DEBT PAYBACK.

REFINANCING MORTGAGES. Six of ten homeowners at the end of December 2009 with mortgages had rates that exceeded the 4.8 percent rate currently available on thirty-year fixed mortgages. However, only half as many refinancing applications were reported in the month than were reported in January 2009. The total volume of refinancing activity in 2009 was about $1 trillion. In 2003, it was $2.8 trillion. Mortgage rates were at their lowest since the end of World War II, but banks continued to balk at refinancing and the shortage of credit continued to slow the nation's economic recovery.
See also HOUSE (U.S.) FINANCIAL OVERHAUL PLAN; HOUSING PLAN.

REFINERS. On February 11, 2009, U.S. gasoline refiners announced that they would cut production to the lowest level since 2003 as higher prices and fears of recession decreased demand.
See also OIL.

REFLATION. The expectation that the world's economy will rebound, driving up interest rates and commodities prices.
Cf. DEFLATION; INFLATION; STAGFLATION.

REGIONAL BANKS. *See* STANDARD & POOR'S; STRESS TESTS (U.S.).

REGIONAL ECONOMICS. *See* BEIGE BOOK.

REGULATION. Under President Obama's proposed 2010 budget, enforcement was high on his agenda. Closer government scrutiny was called for and specially allocated funds were to be available to hire regulators to discharge responsibilities of transparency, accountability, and fulfilling the laws of the nation. For example:

a. *Department of Agriculture*—$26 billion to improve food-safety monitoring and nutrition education and promotion.

b. *Army Corps of Engineers*—Management reforms to lower project costs, improve accountability, and maximize returns on waterway projects.

c. *Internal Revenue Service*—Nearly $890 million to fight fraud and improve enforcement, resulting in "a $5 return for every $1 spent."

d. *Department of Defense*—Money to monitor military contracting through improved reporting and scrutiny of no-bid contracts.

e. *Securities and Exchange Commission*—Budget increase of more than 13 percent for "risk-based, efficient regulatory structure that will better detect fraud and strengthen markets."

f. *Commodity Futures Trading Commission*—A 44 percent increase in part for "filling gaps in regulatory oversight of energy and over-the-counter derivative trading," as well as foreign exchange.

By the end of August 2009, new financial and banking regulations were few. Changes that were adopted include:

a. *Credit cards*—Legislation passed required card companies to inform consumers before raising rates, limited credit card fees, and restricted card ownership among people under twenty-one years old. Few changes have resulted.

b. *Short-selling*—Legislation prohibited "naked" short-selling—that is, selling shares of stock without borrowing them first—and required short-selling trades to be reported daily. The SEC instituted a temporary ban in April 2009 that was made permanent in July 2009.

See also ACCOUNTABILITY; CONSUMER FINANCIAL PROTECTION BUREAU; EUROPEAN UNION; FINANCIAL REGULATORY STRUCTURE; FINANCIAL STABILITY OVERSIGHT COUNCIL; OFFICE OF INFORMATION AND REGULATORY AFFAIRS; OFFICE OF NATIONAL INSURANCE; REGULATORS; TRANSPARENCY; WALL STREET REFORM ACT (2010); "WINDOW DRESSING."

REGULATORS. Regulators in 2009 were to play an increasing role in the future of the banking industry. The Financial Stability Forum (FSF) brought together central banks, financial regulators, and treasuries from the big Western economies. They were charged with and have successfully closed loopholes that banks previously took advantage of. The issue of violations and enforcement was left to other global agencies. Beginning in 2009, changes would be forthcoming.

In 2009, the primary financial regulators in the federal government were:

a. *Securities and Exchange Commission*—regulates financial markets, sets disclosure rules, and oversees accounting rules for corporations that trade on U.S. exchanges.

b. *Federal Reserve*—the central banking entity, which oversees monetary policy, bank holding companies, and some state-chartered banks.
c. *Federal Deposit Insurance Corporation*—insures bank deposits at more than 8,000 banks nationwide. It also supervises most state-chartered banks.
d. *Office of the Comptroller of the Currency*—division of the Treasury Department that oversees and charters all national banks.
e. *Office of Thrift Supervision*—division of the Treasury Department that regulates and oversees federal thrifts and thrift holding companies.
f. *Commodity Futures Trading Commission*—oversees commodity futures and options markets in the United States.
g. *Federal Housing Finance Agency*—oversees Fannie Mae, Freddie Mac, and the twelve Federal Home Loan Banks.
h. *National Credit Union Administration*—charters and supervises federal credit unions.

See also BANK BUYOUTS; CONSUMER FINANCIAL PROTECTION AGENCY; DODD, CHRISTOPHER J.; FEDERAL DEPOSIT INSURANCE CORPORATION; FINANCIAL CRISIS INQUIRY REPORT; FINANCIAL REGULATION PLAN (2009); FINANCIAL STABILITY OVERSIGHT COUNCIL; "FLASH CRASH"; HOUSE (U.S.) FINANCIAL OVERHAUL PLAN; NATIONAL BANK SUPERVISOR; OFFICE OF INFORMATION AND REGULATORY AFFAIRS; OFFICE OF NATIONAL INSURANCE; REGULATION; SECURITIES AND EXCHANGE COMMISSION; STRESS TESTS (U.S.); TRANSPARENCY; WALL STREET REFORM ACT (2010); "WINDOW DRESSING."

REINSURER. *See* MUNICH RE; SWISS RE.

RELOCATING. *See* MOBILITY.

REMITTANCES. Funds sent back to one's native country from another nation where there is employment. The U.S. government started tracking cross-border flows of money from migrants after the September 11, 2001, terrorist attacks. The World Bank estimated that foreign workers sent $328 billion from developed and richer nations to poor and developing ones in 2008. For example, $52 billion was sent by Indian foreign workers back to India.

Since the meltdown in 2008, remittances from Latin America, and primarily from Mexico, fell by 4.2 percent between January and August 2008 compared with the same period in 2007. In the poor, rural communities, remittances from migrant workers would often account for 12 percent or more of local income. Migrant workers, initially lured by the building boom and other opportunities for work, were losing jobs and struggling to send cash home.

The amount of money that Mexicans working in the United States sent back home dropped 3.6 percent in 2008 as the rising U.S. jobless rate took a toll on immigrants. It was the first decline in remittances recorded since Mexico began tracking money flows from abroad thirteen years before. The drop to $25 billion from $26 billion was twice what the government forecast. Migrant workers in the United States sent home a record $69.2 billion in 2008, nearly 1 percent more than in 2007. That would change during the meltdown. Mexico had a 12 percent drop in remittances in January 2008; Colombia suffered a 16 percent decline, Brazil saw a 14 percent drop, and Ecuador, the hardest hit, had a drop of 22 percent on remittances in the fourth quarter 2008.

By mid-2009, remittances by Mexicans had fallen 8.7 percent over the first four months in 2008. Migrants sent $1.8 billion in April 2009, 18.7 percent less than in April 2008. By the end of summer 2009, remittances to Mexico fell by 11 percent to $62 billion in 2009 from $69 billion in 2008. This was the first decline in global remittances to the region since records were kept. While remittances reached $328 billion in 2008, they fell by 7.3 percent in 2009. With the fall in 2009, unemployment among Mexicans in the United States was sharply increasing.

By mid-March 2011, immigrants sent more money to their homeland than they did one year before. From Central American nations, remittances were up nearly 16 percent from the year earlier. Between 2008 and 2009, there had been a fall of 15 percent. Remittances to Mexico climbed 5.8 percent. For all of 2010, Mexico had a 0.1 percent increase in remittances over 2009.

See also ARMENIA; IMMIGRANTS; IMMIGRATION; JAPAN; MEXICO; PAKISTAN; SOUTHEAST ASIA.

RENAULT. The French carmaker's first-quarter 2009 revenue slid 31 percent from a year earlier to $9.3 billion, with unit sales declining 22 percent.

Renault's management reported a net profit of $1.02 billion at the end of July 2010, with sales increasing in the first half of the year.

One week after the three disasters in Japan, Renault announced on March 18, 2011, that it was trimming production of its high-end sedans at a South Korean plant, reducing its production between 15 and 20 percent because the plant was running low on stocks of engines and gearboxes.

See also AUTOMOBILE INDUSTRY; FRANCE; JAPAN.

RENEGOTIABLE-RATE MORTGAGE. Authorized by the Federal Home Loan Bank Board, it requires homebuyers to renegotiate the terms of the loan every three to five years, a distinct advantage if interest rates drop but a poor hedge against inflation if they go up.

See also CONVERTIBLE WRAPAROUND MORTGAGE; FLEXIBLE MORTGAGE; FLEXIBLE-PAYMENT MORTGAGE; VARIABLE-RATE MORTGAGE.

RENEGOTIATING MORTGAGES. *See* HOUSING PLAN.

RENEWABLE ENERGY SOURCES. *See* ENERGY EFFICIENCY.

RENMINBI. *See* CHINA. *Synonymous with* REDBACK; YUAN.

RENTAL CARS. *See* AVIS; ENTERPRISE; HERTZ.

RENTERS. By December 2011, with low mortgage rates and the fall of home prices, the monthly cost of owning a home was more affordable than at any point in the past sixteen years and remained less costly than renting in a growing number of communities.

See also APARTMENT VACANCIES; HOMEOWNERSHIP.

REO (REAL ESTATE OWNED). Distressed or foreclosed properties purchased through a preclusive sale. With an REO, the bank typically clears any title issues before it puts the house on the market. Most are sold as is, so buyers can make their offers contingent on a home inspection and buyers who pay in cash do best. Often all short sales in which homeowners, under pressure, sold a property for less than their mortgage.

Repo 105 was a method to help a firm flatten its numbers by temporarily moving assets off its balance sheet at the end of each reported quarter. As an attempt to deceive, it allowed financial institutions to lower their reported leverage substantially and thereby avoid ruinous rating downgrades in their fight to survive.

See also FORECLOSURE; REPO MARKET; SHORT SALE.

Synonymous with PREFORECLOSURE SALE.

REPAYMENT OF BAILOUT FUNDS. *See* "TOO BIG TO FAIL"; TROUBLED ASSET RELIEF PROGRAM.

REPO. *See* REO; REPO MARKET; REPURCHASE AGREEMENT.

REPO 105. *See* REPO.

REPO MARKET. Funds that banks have lent and borrowed on the repurchase in which short-term loans are made in exchange for collateral such as treasury bonds and mortgage-backed securities.

See also FINANCIAL CRISIS INQUIRY REPORT; LEHMAN BROTHERS; MASKING; REO.

REPOSSESSIONS. *See* UNITED KINGDOM.

REPURCHASE AGREEMENT (REPO). A method of secured lending where the borrower sells securities to the lender as collateral and agrees to repurchase them at a higher price within a short period, often within one day.

RESEARCH AND DEVELOPMENT (R&D). By 2012, it was apparent that the United States was rapidly losing high-technology positions in China and throughout Asia. In six years since 2009, about 85 percent of the expansion in R&D has been overseas. The ten largest economies in Asia now spend roughly $400 billion a year on R&D, as much as the United States and well ahead of Europe's $300 billion. China's investment in R&D jumped 28 percent in one year and past Japan to become the world's second-largest spender. The U.S. share of global R&D spending is slipping. Throughout the first decade of the millennium, it dropped from 38 percent to 31 percent, whereas Asia's climbed from 24 percent to 35 percent.

RESEE ECONOMY. Term coined by the chief executive of General Electric, suggesting the concept that business needs to adjust its expectations and behavior to a new, postrecession world.

RESIDENTIAL MORTGAGE-BACKED SECURITIES WORKING GROUP. Proposed by President Obama in late January 2012 to investigate the abusive practices in the mortgage industry. Both lending and the practice of bundling loans into securities will come under its scrutiny. The president said, "This new unit will hold accountable those who broke the law, speed assistance to homeowners, and help turn the page on an era of recklessness that hurt so many Americans."

RESIDENTIAL PROPERTIES. Improved real property used or intended to be used for residential purposes, including single-family homes, dwellings for two to four families, and individual units of condominiums and cooperatives.

See also NONRESIDENTIAL PROPERTIES.

RESIDENTIAL SPENDING. *See* CONSUMER SPENDING.

RESIDUAL. *Synonymous with* TRANCHE.

RESOLUTION TRUST CORPORATION (RTC). As part of the savings and loan bailout of the 1990s, this U.S. government agency administered the last federal bailout. The Resolution Trust Corporation was set up by the government in 1989 to sell off what ultimately grew to $450 billion worth of real estate and other assets assembled from 747 collapsed savings banks.

As a model for the 2008–2009 bank crisis, the U.S. government had rejected the creation of a new RTC. Instead, it was relying on financial institutions to find their own ways to sell off bad debts or assets that they ended up with as a result of foreclosures. New regulations would soon be forthcoming.

See also BANK BAILOUT; EMERGENCY ECONOMIC STABILITY ACT OF 2008.

RESPONSIBLE HOMEOWNERS. *See* HOUSING PLAN.

RESTAURANTS. *See* EATING OUT; FRIENDLY'S ICE CREAM CORPORATION.

RESTAURANT WORK. *See* UNEMPLOYMENT.

RETAILING. The activity of purchasing for resale to a customer, including all activities undertaken by intermediaries. The primary function is to sell goods and services to ultimate consumers. The four functions of retailing are (a) buying and storing merchandise; (b) transferring title of those items; (c) providing information on the nature and uses of those goods; and (d) in some situations, extending credit to buyers.

On February 8, 2008, figures indicated the worst monthly sales in five years as big retail chains prepared for a prolonged slowdown with plans to close stores and cut jobs. American consumers clearly had lost their appetite to shop starting in October 2008. Numerous retailers witnessed an approximate 50 to 80 percent drop in their stock value. November sales through December 4, the days following Thanksgiving, were dismal. Discount stores also suffered. November sales were down by about 2 percent from 2007. Many department stores had double-digit declines. Major sectors like apparel, luxury goods, and electronics all suffered steeper declines in November than in September and October. Sales in November tumbled to the weakest level in more than thirty-five years. For 2008, electronic equipment and appliances fell a combined 26.7 percent versus a 2.7 percent gain in 2007. Women's apparel slid 22.7 percent compared with a 2.4 percent drop a year before. The International Council of Shopping Centers estimated that 148,000 stores closed in 2008, the most since 2001. It predicted that there would be an additional 73,000 closures in the first six months of 2009. Customer traffic during the week of Christmas 2008 fell 4.9 percent compared to 2007, and for the entire holiday season it plummeted 16 percent. Total retail sales sank 2.3 percent. For the entire 2008 year, retail sales were down 0.1 percent, a sharp decline after a 4.1 percent gain in 2007. It was the first time the annual retail sales figures had fallen based on government records going back to 1992.

Retail sales took another monthly tumble of 1.1 percent in March 2009 as job losses and tight credit left consumers cautious and constrained. It would dampen hopes for a rapid economic turnaround as consumer spending represented 70 percent of the U.S. economy. Retail sales were down more than 9 percent from the same month a year earlier. In June, retail sales climbed 0.6 percent from a month earlier on a seasonally adjusted basis to $342.1 billion. July 2009 was the worst month since January for retailers, with a decline of 5.1 percent.

Retailers had their worst sales performance of school items in more than a decade. One analyst found that summer sales of school supplies fell 3 to 4 percent compared to a 1 percent increase one year earlier. Overall shopping center sales were off 8.3 percent. Another firm found that clothing purchases for school were down 5.4 percent, footwear was down 4.4 percent, and electronics were down 1.8 percent. In stores that specialized in selling only clothing, sales peaked in 2007. In the summer of that year, stores sold $13 billion worth of goods. In July and August 2009, sales fell to $11.9 billion. Specialty clothing sales were back to 2005 levels. There were signs of shoppers beginning to return to retailing operations as stores, especially in malls, reported a 2.9 percent sales decline in August 2009, small by comparison with past months.

Department store sales had dropped an average of 8.9 percent each month since the start of 2009. September 2009 store sales indicated the first monthly gain in more than a year, climbing 0.6 percent. These results compared to a 0.9 percent drop in September 2008. Retail sales declined 1.5 percent in September with the termination of the Cash for Clunkers program. On November 16, the government reported that retailers saw sales improve, climbing 1.4 percent from the prior month to a seasonally adjusted $347.5 billion. At the end of November 2009, on Cyber Monday, the Monday following Thanksgiving, online shopping sites reported a surge in sales and traffic. Web shoppers spent, in total, 11 percent more than they did a year before, although the average size of each sales ticket fell nearly 14 percent from the previous year. Sales grew about 5 percent, with shoppers spending $887 million online.

Holiday sales in 2009 were sluggish at retailers, encouraging larger price discounts. While most experts expected a 2.2 percent increase during this holiday period, sales were up less than 1 percent from last year. Retailers added 321,000 jobs in November. That was more than a year earlier but far below 465,000 from November 2007. Sales for the week ending December 5, 2009, declined 18 percent from the prior week. For the same period in 2008, these sales fell only 14 percent. Nine of ten people waited to complete their holiday 2009 shopping to get discounts of at least 50 percent. A third were holding off purchases until they could receive a 70 percent discount. November sales climbed 1.3 percent from October. Excluding autos, auto parts, and gasoline, retail sales were up 0.4 percent, the first gain in thirteen months. However, such sales were 3.7 percent lower than those of November 2007, just prior to the official beginning of the Great Recession. By year's end 2009, sales at traditional stores were about flat compared with 2008. Online retailing grew 4 percent from the beginning of November through December 18, 2009, to $24.8 billion. The good news appeared on December 27, 2009. Holiday shoppers spent a little more in 2009 than the previous year. Retail sales rose 3.6 percent from November 1 to December 24 compared with a 3.2 percent decline in 2008.

In February 2010, retail sales in the seventeen nations using the euro fell at their fastest pace in thirteen months; sales volume tumbled 0.6 percent, the largest fall since December 2008. In the United States in March 2010, retailers posted a 0.5 percent increase in sales. The following month, the industry suffered a 2.7 percent fall. By the end of summer 2010, retailers surprised many with sales doing better than predicted. Sales at stores open more than one year rose 3.3 percent. The result followed a 2.9 percent fall from a year ago. Twenty-seven large retailers reported on December 2, 2010, that their November sales collectively climbed 6 percent. Online sales increased more than 15 percent during the Christmas season 2010, with retailers bringing in $36.4 billion compared with $31.5 billion from the previous year. Thanksgiving spurred a 34.5 percent increase in online sales to $597 million. By year's end 2010, holiday shoppers spent more money than even before the Great Recession. Following a drop of 6 percent in 2008 and a 4 percent increase in 2009, retail spending rose 5.5 percent in the fifty days prior to Christmas. Apparel sales increased 11.2 percent. Jewelry rose 8.4 percent and luxury goods and expensive clothes increased 6.7 percent.

By January 2011, retail sales increases crept forward, rising 0.3 percent for the month to $381.57 billion. In part, this slow rise was due to the storms in the country throughout January. In February, most of nation's retailers reported improved sales. Overall, for stores open at least one year, sales rose 4.2 percent for the month. By February, retail sales jumped another 1 percent from January. Twenty-five retailers surveyed showed an 8.9 percent gain, the best performance since March 2010. Retail sales climbed for the tenth straight month in April at $389.4 billion, up 0.5 percent. Earlier in 2011, retail sales showed monthly gains of about 0.8 percent in June, they were a disappointing 0.1 percent increase. June 2011 retail sales at twenty-five major stores climbed 6.5 percent. During July, retail sales grew 0.5 percent, the strongest yield since March. Electronics and appliance sales were up 1.4 percent, auto sales were up by 0.4 percent, and spending by wealthier consumers climbed 11.6 percent in July. In August, retail sales remained flat, revised down to a 0.3 percent gain. By October, sales at chain stores in the United States climbed 3.4 percent, below the expected 4.5 to 5.1 percent in September. Sales did well in November 2011, rising about 3.2 percent for the month. Christmas sales were up but not overly impressive.

Holiday 2011 retail sales reported in January 2012 showed that it was far less robust than expected, with many stores falling below the returns of 2010, indicating a weak Christmas. At twenty-two retailers there was a 3.4 percent gain in December sales compared with 4.3 percent in 2010.

By the end of January 2012, retail sales for the quarter were as follows:

Costco—up 8 percent to $7 billion
Target—up 4.3 percent to $4.6 billion
TJX—up 7 percent to $1.4 billion
Macy's—up 2.4 percent to $1.3 billion
Kohl's—up 0.6 percent to $0.8 billion
Gap—down 1 percent to $0.8 billion
Limited Brands—up 9 percent to $0.8 billion
Nordstrom—up 5.0 percent to $0.7 billion

See also ABERCROMBIE & FITCH COMPANY; ADVERTISING; BEST BUY; BURBERRY; CARREFOUR; CASH FOR CLUNKERS; CHICO'S FAS; CHRISTMAS SALES; CONSUMER SPENDING (2011); COSTCO WHOLESALE; DOLLAR GENERAL; DOLLAR STORES; EDDIE BAUER HOLDINGS; ESCADA; ESPRIT; FAMILY DOLLAR STORES; FUR INDUSTRY; GENERAL GROWTH PROPERTIES; GOODY'S FAMILY CLOTHING; HOME DEPOT; INDITEX; INVEN-TORIES; IRELAND; J.C. PENNEY; JONES APPAREL GROUP; LIM-ITED BRANDS; LIZ CLAIBORNE; LOWE'S COMPANIES; LUXURY GOODS; MACY'S; MARKS & SPENCER; METRO; NEIMAN MARCUS; NORDSTROM; PHILLIPS-VAN HEUSEN; POLO RALPH LAUREN; RADIO SHACK; SAKS; SEARS HOLDING CORPORATION; SHOP-LIFTING; TARGET; TIFFANY; TJMAXX; UNEMPLOYMENT; UNITED KINGDOM; WILLIAMS-SONOMA; WOOLWORTHS.

RETAIL SALES. *See* RETAILING.

RETENTION BONUS. A corporate bonus given or promised to pay certain executives for staying in their jobs. The payments, in the form of cash, stock, or both, are usually given over a period of a few years, in some cases regardless of how the executives or their firms perform.
    See also BONUSES; CITIGROUP.

RETIREES. *See* RETIREMENT.

RETIREES (STATE AND CITY). *See* STATES (U.S.).

RETIREMENT. The percentage of workers who claimed that they were confident about having sufficient funds to retire comfortably declined to 13 percent in 2009, down from 18 percent in 2008 and from its all-time high of 27 percent in 2007. Confidence was particularly low among households with annual incomes of $75,000 or higher, in large part because these people had more money at risk in the stock market.

With the Great Recession, retirement appeared to be out of the question with new debt and seeing savings evaporate. Also, people are living longer and firms are hiring older workers. Between 2007 and 2010, the number of working Americans over sixty-five years old jumped 16 percent; the number of working Americans under sixty-five years old in the labor force was reduced. The number of people over sixty-five in the labor force went from 10.8 percent in 1985, to 12.1 percent in 1995, to 15.1 percent in 2005, and to 17.4 percent in 2010. From the 1940s to the 1980s, the percentage of men who were sixty-five and older in the labor force dropped from 47 percent in 1949 to 15.6 percent in 1993, while 36.5 percent of fifty- to sixty-year-old men remain in the labor pool. For working women, the numbers are slightly less.

Current retirees, 20 percent as contrasted to 41 percent in 2007, were very confident of being able to afford a financially secure retirement. Twenty-five percent of workers indicated that they planned to postpone retirement, with the median age of retirement rising from an expected sixty-two in 1991 to sixty-five since 2004.

One of the primary reasons that firms weren't hiring by summer's end 2009 was due to many older workers being unable, reluctant, or fearful of retiring. The contrast is impressive: in the United States in 2008, almost a third of people aged sixty-five to sixty-nine were still in the labor force; in France, just 4 percent in this bracket were still working or seeking employment.

By summer 2010, at least 10 percent of U.S. state governments required new civil servants to work longer before retiring with full pension or face increased penalties for early retirement.

By 2011, more Americans in their senior years or above sixty had so much debt that they couldn't or wouldn't retire. With climbing prices and greater debt, many lived beyond their means. Many of them are trying or succeeding in postponing retirement, reducing their living standards, or perhaps both. Today, four out of five households with residents in their early sixties and with mortgages have too little savings to pay off debts without dipping into retirement accounts.

See also BABY-BOOMERS; CONSUMER CONFIDENCE; FRANCE; STATES (U.S.); UNITED KINGDOM.

RETIREMENT BENEFITS. U.S. firms needing to conserve cash began to trim their contributions to workers' retirement plans, especially the so-called 401(k) plans, placing a new strain on a workers' safety net at the same time that many were seeing their accounts fall along with the stock market.

Retirement plans such as 401(k) accounts allow employees to opt in or out and require them to invest their own funds, bearing the market risk on their own. By contrast, employers had greater freedom to stop making matching contributions to the plans, especially during difficult financial times. Baby boomers that are retiring often turn to their 401(k)-retirement savings plan. Approximately 60 percent of households nearing retirement age have 401(k) type accounts.

By 2012, less than one-quarter of what is needed to maintain a standard of living in retirement is available. Assuming that retirees require about 85 percent of their working income when they retire has not become the reality and most participants appear to have adequate savings.

RETIREMENT SAVINGS. As of February 2009, U.S. citizens' retirement savings were down more than $2 trillion in about one year's time.

See also RETIREMENT BENEFITS.

REVLON. In mid-February 2011, the cosmetic firm announced that its profit surged to $296.2 million, with total sales increasing 7.1 percent.

REVULSION STAGE. Indiscriminate and contagious selling of distressed assets that leads banks to stop lending on the collateral of such assets.

See also EMERGENCY ECONOMIC STABILIZATION ACT OF 2008; SUBPRIME.

RICH, THE. *See* WEALTH.

RIEGLE-NEAL INTERSTATE BANKING AND BRANCHING EF-FICIENCY ACT OF 1994. Repealed the ban on interstate banking in the United States.

RIO HEDGE. The idea of a trader who is facing financial or legal troubles to hedge his or her position with a ticket to a tropical location (such as Rio de Janeiro). If the investment goes bad (either legally or through financial loss), the investor will use the ticket to escape, preferably to a nonextraditing country, depending on the circumstances.

RIO TINTO. On December 10, 2008, the Anglo-Australian mining company announced that it would cut 14,000 jobs and sharply lower spending as demand for raw materials slowed dramatically. Rio Tinto would release 12.5 percent of its workforce of 112,000.

The company had a net debt of $39 billion and a market capitalization of $32 billion, with record debts since its acquisition of Alcan. Rio Tinto abandoned plans to raise $10 billion from asset sales in 2008. Rio Tinto announced that iron ore production, used to make steel, tumbled 18 percent in the fourth quarter 2008, and that its aluminum subsidiary would double previously announced production costs.

In mid-August 2009, Rio Tinto posted a 65 percent fall in first-half profit. First-half net profit fell to $2.4 billion from $6.95 a year earlier.

On April 15, 2010, Rio Tinto reported disappointing first-quarter production results but predicted a 7.8 percent increase in iron ore output for the year.

The firm's first-half profit more than tripled, with earnings of $5.85 billion for the six months ending June 30, 2010; sales climbed 37 percent to $26.77 billion from $19.52 billion.

On February 10, 2011, management reported that it nearly tripled its annual net profit to $14.32 billion for 2010 from $4.87 billion the year before. On August 4, Rio Tinto's management reported that its first half net profit rose 30 percent to a record. Net profit surged to $7.6 billion from $5.8 billion the year before. Sales climbed 21 percent to $31.76 billion.

See also MINING.

RISK. *See* SYSTEMATIC RISK.

RITE AID. Its fiscal first-quarter 2011 loss fell 2.3 percent. Sales remained flat at $6.36 billion, with same-store sales climbing 0.8 percent.

RIVLIN, ALICE. *See* BIPARTISAN POLICY CENTER DEBT REDUCTION TASK FORCE.

ROAD BUILDING. *See* AMERICAN RECOVERY AND REINVESTMENT ACT (OF 2009).

ROBO-SIGNERS. *See* FORECLOSURES; MERS; MORGAN STANLEY.

ROCHE HOLDING. The Swiss drug maker saw profits decline, with projected slow sales growth in 2009. Profits announced on February 4, 2009, were 8 percent lower than in 2008.

On July 22, 2010, the company reported a sharp rise in first-half net profit to about $5.2 billion, with sales climbing 3 percent. On September 1, 2010, Roche launched a cost-cutting plan. As part of its strategy to cut costs, in November 2010 management decided to restructure its operations and shed 4,800 jobs over two years, or about 6 percent of its staff.

ROCKWELL AUTOMATION. A maker of industrial-automation products. On February 2, 2009, it reported a 24 percent slump in its fiscal first-quarter profit and lowered its 2009 forecast as customers closed factories and reduced capital outlays. Its stock fell 11 percent.

ROCKY MOUNTAIN NEWS. On February 27, 2009, this 150-year-old Denver, Colorado, newspaper printed its last edition. Falling revenues, lower advertising, and big debts caused the paper's downfall.

See also NEWSPAPERS.

ROLLING BROWNOUTS. The closing of fire department stations on differing days as the economic meltdown forced communities to make deep cuts that lower the trucks' response rate to fires and other emergencies.

ROLLOVER RISK. The threat of a nation not being able to refinance or rollover its debt, encouraging the country to seek emergency bailouts.

ROMANIA. Had a current-account deficit of only 14 percent of GDP in 2009, a floating currency that gave it more flexibility, and was less dependent on exports to the slowing eurozone.

However, its projected growth rate in 2009 was just 0.9 percent and its banking system was minimally profitable. Its interbank rates had nearly doubled in 2008 to 15 percent. Foreign reserves were minimal and the International Monetary Fund believed that its currency was overvalued by 19 percent. By mid-March 2009, Romania sought aid from the European Union and the IMF to save it from a possible financial crisis. By March 25, Romania reached an agreement with the IMF for a financial aid package valued at about $25.9 billion. Two-thirds of the package would come from the IMF in the form of a standby loan. The funds would be used to support Romania's central bank reserves and its ability to manage local liquidity, while the other funds would be used to cover public financing and other needs.

A top Romanian court declared at the end of June 2010 that many of the sweeping austerity measures proposed by the government were unconstitutional, a decision unless reversed would delay a major loan of $24.6 billion from the International Monetary Fund.

The IMF program to Romania would hold any government to a tight economic policy. It projected that after a jobless recovery and two years of contraction, a jobless recovery would occur in 2011. The nation's GDP growth stood at 2.7 percent, with a GDP of $166 billion, an inflation rate of 5.0 percent, and a GDP per head at $7,740.

By April 2011, the Romanian economy led growth among the ten emerging economies in the European Union's east. The World Bank reported on April 19, 2011, that average growth in the ten former communist states would climb 1 percent to 3.8 percent on 2012. GDP growth slowed to 1.4 percent from 1.7 percent in the first three months of 2011. At year's end, the economy grew by 4.4 percent. Projections into 2010 include lowering its budget deficit to 1.9 percent of GDP from 4.4 percent in 2011. Others forecast growth in 2012 to be from 1.1 to 3.8 percent.

See also EASTERN EUROPE.

ROMER, CHRISTINA. First chair of President Obama's Council of Economic Advisers. On August 5, 2010, she announced her intent to leave government and return to her teaching post at the University of California at Berkeley.

See also GOOLSBEE, AUSTAN D.

ROMERO, CHRISTY. *See* BAROFSKY, NEIL.

ROMPUY, HERMAN VAN. European Council president who was recommended in August 2011 to become the eurozone's chief executive.

See also EUROZONE.

ROOSEVELT, FRANKLIN DELANO. In 1933, when Roosevelt became president, unemployment stood at a staggering 26 percent and the Dow Jones Industrial Average was down 75 percent from its 1929 peak. There were many more bank failures and many more devastating foreclosures, especially among farmers, than in the 2008 meltdown. To this day, experts argue that his economic policies were too cautious. However, his New Deal placed millions of Americans on the public payroll via the Works Progress Administration and the Civilian Conservation Corps.

After winning a smashing election victory in 1936, the Roosevelt administration cut spending and raised taxes, precipitating an economic relapse that drove the unemployment rate back into double digits. What saved the New Deal was the enormous effort and activity of World War II, which finally provided a fiscal stimulus adequate to the economy's needs. The single biggest cause of the depression of the 1930s was that the Federal Reserve let the money supply fall by one-third, causing deflation. Banks were allowed to fail, causing a credit crisis. The worst years of the New Deal were 1937–1938, immediately after the Federal Reserve increased reserve requirements for banks, thus curbing lending and moving the economy back to dangerous deflationary pressures. The president instituted a disastrous legacy of agricultural subsidies and sought to cartelize industry, backed by force of law. Neither helped the economy to recover. Government spending increased significantly, but taxes also climbed.

New Deal fiscal policy didn't do much to promote recovery. World War II did help the American economy, especially before the U.S. entry in 1941. Expansionary monetary policies and wartime orders from Europe, not the policies of the New Deal, did more to drive the U.S. recovery and bring it out of the depression. Roosevelt was inaugurated on March 4, 1933. The next day, he declared a national bank holiday and set the Federal Reserve and the Treasury to work on a phased program to sort good banks from bad ones, provide finance, and restore confidence in the banking system.

Real government spending, measured in 1937 dollars, declined by less than 0.7 percent of GDP between 1936 and 1937 and rebounded in 1938. However, the president won a tax on corporate profits, with a sliding scale tax beginning at 7 percent if a firm retained 1 percent of its net income and going to 27 percent if the company retained 70 percent of net income. It significantly raised the costs of investment.

See also BANKING ACT OF 1933; DEPRESSION (OF THE 1930S); DOUBLE-DIP RECESSION; GREAT DEPRESSION; HOOVER, HERBERT; PERKINS, FRANCES; RECONSTRUCTION FINANCE CORPORATION.

ROYAL BANK OF CANADA. On August 26, 2010, the Royal Bank of Canada reported that its third-quarter 2010 earnings declined 18 percent, with net income falling to US $121 billion.

The Royal Bank of Canada posted its second quarterly 2011 loss in eighteen years. Its revenue climbed 2 percent.

ROYAL BANK OF SCOTLAND (RBS). On January 20, 2009, the British government took an almost 70 percent stake in the bank, the second major British bank bailout in two months. It also offered to insure other banks against large-scale losses on risky assets in exchange for binding agreements to lend out more money. Royal Bank of Scotland's 2008 losses reached $41.3 billion, the biggest ever for a British corporation. This arrangement would save the bank about $862 million a year in interest charges, but it ignited fear in the market that the bank would soon be fully nationalized. On February 26, the British government moved toward nationalization by agreeing to place as much as $36.64 billion and insure 300 billion pounds in the bank's assets as Royal Bank of Scotland reported the largest loss in British corporate history. The move gave the United Kingdom a stake of as much as 95 percent in the bank, up from 70 percent, and also indicated the lack of other bailout options available. Following the government's claim to a stake of 70.3 percent ownership of the bank, it announced on April 7 that it would trim its staff by 9,000. Some 4,500 jobs were in the United Kingdom. On August 7, Royal Bank of Scotland posted a $1.7 billion loss for the first half of 2009, with forecasts for improvement in 2011.

Management announced on September 2, 2010, its intension to cut an additional 3,500 jobs and close ten offices in Britain to reduce costs.

See also ASSET PROTECTION SCHEME; BARCLAYS; FEDERAL HOUSING FINANCE AGENCY; UNITED KINGDOM.

Cf. LLOYDS.

ROYAL CARIBBEAN CRUISES. In July 2009, the company swung to a second-quarter loss. The cruise company reported a 44 percent decline in third-quarter 2009 earnings. Net yields, or revenue per available passenger cruise days, fell 17 percent. The firm showed a profit of $230.4 million, down 15 percent from the year before.

Its third-quarter 2010 earnings soared 55 percent.

Cf. CARNIVAL CRUISES.

ROYAL DUTCH SHELL. Europe's largest oil firm announced that its second-quarter 2009 profit tumbled by 67 percent to $3.82 billion from the previous year. Since July, it cut 20 percent of its top management positions, reducing them to 600 from 750. It expected further reductions of 24,000 out of its total workforce of 102,000.

By mid-March 2010, management said it would produce 3.5 million barrels of oil a day, 11 percent more than it did in 2009.

By June 2011, Royal Dutch Shell posted a profit of $6.29 billion, up 30 percent. The largest European oil firm posted profits of $8.7 billion, up from

$4.4 billion the year before. In October, management reported earnings of $1.77 billion, up 49 percent.

See also OIL COMPANIES.

RTC. *See* RESOLUTION TRUST CORPORATION.

RUBIN, ROBERT E. Speaking before the Financial Crisis Inquiry Commission on April 8, 2010, the former U.S. Treasury secretary and former director at Citigroup said, "We all bear responsibility for not recognizing this, and I deeply regret that."

Left Citigroup to become counselor for Centerview Partners.

See also CITIGROUP; FINANCIAL CRISIS INQUIRY COMMISSION.

RUBLE. *See* BELARUS; RUSSIA.

RUSSIA (RUSSIAN FEDERATION). After an initial sharp rebound from the deep recession of the past year, real GDP is projected to converge toward its potential. The decline in inflation seen since early 2009 is expected to continue into 2010 before flattening out. The current account surplus will increase in 2010 as a result of terms of trade gains, but it will decline in 2011 as import growth strengthens again. Net private capital flows should strengthen, allowing a rebuilding of reserves. Although recovery is in prospect, the large output gap and subdued inflation suggest that policy stimulus should not be removed too hastily. Fiscal policy should be managed to avoid dissociative demand effects from a surge of expenditures in late 2009 followed by a tightening in 2010. Discriminatory anti-crisis measures to protect domestic industries are counterproductive and should be unwound as quickly as possible.

In October 2008, the Russian stock market plunged by two-thirds from its peak in May. With $1.3 trillion in oil and gas reserves from the past eight years, Russia had a pile of cash and liquid assets in excess of $500 billion. With plummeting oil prices in November, a 70 percent drop in stock markets, a global credit crunch, and a slow-motion run on private banks, Russia had to spend its reserves faster than anybody imagined. On August 8, reserves peaked at just under $600 billion; by November, they had dropped to $484 billion. Russian investment banks cut jobs as a deepening crisis threatened to stall a ten-year economic boom. Russian banks in November had seen trading, investment banking, and asset management revenues plunge, and bonuses were cut.

On November 18, the World Bank halved its forecast for Russian economic growth in 2009 as the global financial crisis pushed down the price of oil and companies cut investments. Predictions were also that inflation would reach 13.5 percent. On November 24, Russia's central bank allowed the ruble to weaken by widening its trading bank against other currencies, the second time it had done so in two weeks. The central bank allowed the ruble to weaken about 1 percent against the dollar and the euro while raising interest rates by a full percentage point on November 28. The central bank raised its refinancing rate to 13 percent, an increase of one percentage point.

Russia's chief macroeconomic planner announced on December 11 that a recession had started in the country. Growth in the third quarter 2008 was the slowest in three years, and the October trade surplus hit a thirteen-month low. The central bank devalued the ruble again on December 15 for the second time in one week as signs appeared that despite spending $161 billion defending its currency, it would be forced to let it decline even further. The central bank supported the ruble that was 45 percent euros and 55 percent dollars, but the bank had been allowing it to notch down by about 1 percent a week in six devaluations starting in November. The bank spent $17.9 billion defending the ruble in the week that ended on December 5, when it had $437 billion remaining. Still, the ruble had declined 16 percent against the dollar since oil prices peaked in summer 2008. Russian industrial output shrank 10.8 percent in November from the previous month and wage arrears doubled, raising the fear of recession for the once-buoyant economy. Economic growth, which had averaged 7 percent a year, came to an abrupt halt.

On the first trading day in 2009, Russia had its thirteenth ruble devaluation in two months. The ruble had weakened around 1.5 percent with a euro/dollar basket trading at thirty-five/thirty rubles. The dollar rose to thirty rubles for the first time in more than five years. Russian authorities announced in February that they would slash spending and expand bank bailouts as their economic troubles prompted a new cut to its debt rating. The government pledged more than $1 billion in state support in March to aid its ailing car industry in order to avoid heavy job losses and potential social unrest as the once-booming industry contracted 60 percent in 2009. On April 6, the prime minister presented his economic recovery program to generate domestic consumer demand as a substitute for decreasing oil exports. The program offered $90 billion in stimulus spending, including $17.6 billion in new spending emphasizing tax reductions and social welfare spending for the elderly and young families. Soon after, the central bank cut its key lending rate by half a percentage point and increased its reserve requirements.

The World Bank projected that Russia's recession would run deeper and longer than originally estimated. The bank indicated that the Russian economy would shrink by 7.9 percent in 2009 and not recover to precrisis levels until 2012. Russian consumer prices were flat at the end of December 2009, up 8.8 percent since January compared with a rise of 13.3 percent in the year before. Inflation was projected to be below 9 percent in 2009, one of the lowest readings in the nation's post-Soviet history. A 6 percent growth in 2010 was predicted. Russia's economy fell at an annual rate of 3.8 percent in the fourth quarter 2009 after contracting by 7.7 percent in the third quarter. In 2009, its economy shrank by 7.9 percent, putting its economic performance 206 out of 213 nations.

In mid-April, the country's central bank cut its key interest rates by a quarter of 1 percent to 8.5 percent for the first time in 2010 in order to stimulate bank lending. Inflation in the nation eased to 6.1 percent in April 2010 from 6.5 percent in March. Then, in July, it slowed to 5.5 percent.

It was expected in 2011, now that the recession was gone from Russia, that growth would run at a steady 4 percent for the next decade. The nation's GDP growth was 4.0 percent, with a GDP of $1,737 billion and a GDP per head of $12,280. Inflation slowed slightly to 9.4 percent from 9.6 percent in May. Unemployment in Russia reached 6.5 percent in July, up from 6.1 percent the previous month, while the nation's trade surplus rose to $18.3 billion. By the summer, Russia was the only large emerging market economy where more capital was flowing out than in, reflecting concerns about slowing growth, future spending, and political risks ahead of the 2012 presidential elections.

See also HYUNDAI MOTOR COMPANY; LUKOIL; RUSSIAN TRADING SYSTEM (RTS) INDEX.

RUSSIAN TRADING SYSTEM (RTS) INDEX. An index of Russian stocks trading on the Russian Trading System. For 2008, it fell 72 percent.

RYANAIR HOLDINGS. On May 19, 2011, posted a 23 percent increase in fiscal-year profit of $530.3 million, with revenue climbing 21 percent.

S

SAAB. The Swedish automaker filed for bankruptcy protection on February 20, 2009. It was owned by General Motors. GM had taken a 50 percent stake in Saab in 1990 and full control in 2000. In a Swedish court, Saab sought protection from its creditors and said it would, with Swedish government help, reorganize to pave the way for private investors to purchase all or part of the firm. Saab was General Motors' smallest brand in the United States, selling 21,383 cars in 2008, down 34.7 percent from 2007. Saab had lost about $343 million in 2008.

On March 12, 2009, Saab management announced that it would lay off nearly one-fifth of its workforce, giving notice to 750 staff people. It had employed 4,100 workers prior to this announcement. The government of Sweden, in response to pleas for assistance from Saab, said no. Reports from Saab management noted that the firm sold just 93,295 vehicles worldwide in 2008. In mid-June, Saab's creditors approved the proposal for settling its debts by paying a quarter of what it originally owed.

General Motors subsequently sold its Saab division to Koenigsegg, a small, quality carmaker based in Sweden. The firm received a $600 million loan from the European Investment Bank, guaranteed by the Swedish government, and approximately $500 million from General Motors. With a workforce of forty-five people, Koenigsegg presently sells fewer than twenty cars a year, at a cost of more that $1.2 million per automobile. Saab declared the Swedish equivalent of Chapter 11 bankruptcy on August 21, 2009, one day after General Motors formally agreed to sell the carmaker to Koenigsegg. Koenigsegg declared on November 24, 2009, that it was withdrawing from the GM deal, citing costly delays with no promise of high-volume sales. The future of nearly 4,000 workers was in question. Beijing Automotive Industry Holding Company, in mid-December 2009, reached a tentative deal to acquire some of the assets of GM's Saab unit. This would allow the Chinese firm to integrate the Saab technology into its own vehicles. Then, on December 18, GM, with little choice left, announced that it would shut down Saab. A potential buyer, Spyker Cars, a small Dutch maker of high-end sports cars, failed to bail out Saab. If closed, Saab's 3,500 workers would lose their jobs and it would have a significant impact on Sweden's economic base.

By April 2011, Saab's production line was idled after the automaker failed to pay some of its suppliers' bills, indicating a possible risk to its survival. On September 7, awaiting investments from firms in China, Saab sought court protection from creditors, avoiding, perhaps temporarily, a breakup of the company. In Sweden, this protection is referred to as "voluntary reorganization." Then, on September 8, a Swedish court rejected the carmaker's application for protection from creditors.

After a two-year struggle to turn itself around, Saab, the sixty-year-old carmaker, agreed on October 28 to sell out to two Chinese firms, Pang Ad Automobile Trade Company and Zhejiang Youngman Lotus Automobile Company, for $141.9 million.

By year's end 2011, following months of trying to salvage Saab, the owner filed for bankruptcy. Three thousand workers would lose their jobs.

See also GENERAL MOTORS; SWEDEN.

Cf. VOLVO.

SABMILLER. The brewer of several global beers, SABMiller reported in January 2009 that its underlying volume fell 1 percent with signs that drinkers in emerging markets, which accounted for more than 80 percent of its profits, were cutting back amid the economic slowdown.

On May 20, 2010, SABMiller posted a 1.6 percent rise in fiscal-year profit to $1.91 billion, up slightly from $1.88 billion the year before. Sales climbed 4 percent to $26.4 billion. Its second-quarter 2010 profit rose 28 percent.

The maker of Grolsch, Peroni Nastro Assuro, and Miller Lite reported on May 19, 2011, that its net profit for the year rose 26 percent to $2.41 billion, up from $1.91 billion the year earlier. Sales climbed 7 percent to $28.3 billion.

"SACRIFICE." *See* NATIONAL COMMISSION ON FISCAL RESPONSIBILITY AND REFORM.

"SADDLE POINT." When the unemployment rate after having flattened out moves either lower or higher, with a preference for the downward shift.

SAFETY NET. *See* STATES (U.S.).

SAIGON. *See* VIETNAM.

SAKS. An up-scale retailer, Saks said in February 2009 that it would cut 1,100 jobs, or about 9 percent of its workers. Saks announced that it had a fourth-quarter 2008 loss. The company reported a fiscal first-quarter 2009 net loss of $5.1 million. Saks reported a 15.5 percent drop in same-store sales in the quarter ending August 1, 2009.

Saks reported a 3.2 percent growth in sales in early 2010. By May, the chain posted a profit of $18.8 million in contrast to a $5.1 million loss the year before. After reporting a $32.2 million loss in summer 2010, Saks announced that it was closing several of its stores. Sales increased 5.1 percent to $593 million. In early November, Saks management posted an 8.1 percent increase in same-store sales. Then, in the middle of the month, Saks reported a sharply higher fiscal third-quarter profit of $36.3 million, with net sales growing 4.3 percent to $658.8 million. The year before, it posted declines of 8.5 percent in net sales.

Saks noted a 4.4 percent increase in January 2011. By February, the retailer reported a 15 percent surge in same-store sales. For the quarter ending July 30, 2011, Saks management showed a loss of $8.37 million, with sales climbing 13 percent to $670.2 million. Sales at $1.4 billion for the first half of 2011 were up 11 percent over the first half of 2010, with a profit of $20 million from a $13.4 loss in 2010. By the end of the year, sales had risen 9.3 percent.

See also RETAILING.

SALARIES. *See* PAY.

SALARY CAPS. *See* TROUBLED ASSET RELIEF PROGRAM.

SALES. *See* CONSUMER CONFIDENCE.

SALES TAX REVENUES. *See* STATES (U.S.).

SAMSONITE CORPORATION. The luggage maker filed for bankruptcy court protection on September 2, 2009. The company planned to close as many as 84 of its 173 stores. As of July 31, it had $233 million in assets and $1.5 billion in debt.

SAMSUNG (ELECTRONICS). In mid-January 2009, Samsung announced a major restructuring, consolidating business operations into two divisions as South Korea's most powerful and iconic corporation dealt with the slowing global economy. The world's largest manufacturer of flat-screen televisions, memory chips, and liquid crystal displays posted its first-ever quarterly loss as the global economic slump hit both prices and demand for mainstay products. Samsung lost $14.4 million in the three months ending December 31, 2008.

Samsung's first-quarter 2009 net profit fell 72 percent to $460 million. Samsung's second-quarter profit climbed 5.1 percent, with a net profit of $1.8 billion. The company's third-quarter 2009 profit more than tripled from a year before to $3.14 billion, its highest quarterly profit ever. Revenue was $20.9 billion.

The firm's fourth-quarter 2010 operating profit was about $2.7 billion, with a net profit of $3.06 billion, a 12.5 percent increase from the year earlier. Revenue was up 6.7 percent.

In April 2011, Samsung Electronics reported that its first-quarter profit dropped 30 percent to about $2.6 billion. Revenue climbed nearly 7 percent from the year before. Its second-quarter profit fell 18 percent, earned $3.33 billion, and had a revenue increase of 4 percent. The firm's fourth-quarter 2011 profit rose 17 percent, or $3.55 billion.

SAN FRANCISCO CHRONICLE. *See* NEWPAPERS.

SANYA DECLARATION. *See* BRICS.

SANYO ELECTRIC. Set to be acquired by Panasonic in 2009, the company cut its annual net profit outlook as losses climbed in its chip business and announced that it would eliminate 1,200 jobs. Sanyo was the world's top producer of rechargeable batteries. Sanyo announced a fiscal full-year net loss in 2009. The company posted a net loss of $978.5 million for the year ending March 31, 2009, compared with a year-earlier net profit. Sales fell 12 percent. By the end of October, Sanyo reported that its profit tripled to $3.14 billion from a year before. The firm's fiscal-fourth quarter loss narrowed, and in December 2009 management reported a loss of $427 million in the January–March quarter.

See also PANASONIC.

SARBANES-OXLEY ACT OF 2002. Created a new regulator in 2002 for the auditing profession, the Public Company Accounting Oversight Board. It required greater disclosure, heightened standards for auditor independence, and increased penalties for certain white-collar crimes.

See also REGULATORS.

SARKOZY, NICOLAS. President of France. Working closely with Chancellor Merkel of Germany, salvation of the eurozone debt crisis was the big issue for 2011. At Brussels Summits, he said the following:

a. March 25–25: A euro pact "will reinforce convergence of economic policies and competitiveness." The Brussels deal created a bigger rescue fund, and shortly afterward, European Union leaders agreed to bail out Portugal. The euro climbed 4.2 percent in April.

b. July 21: "Our ambition is to seize the Greek crisis to make a quantum leap in eurozone government." Leaders agreed to an additional $155 billion package to save Greece. But, the crisis spread to Italy and Spain. Italy's borrowing costs rose to a record 5.8 percent in July.

c. October 26–27: "If there had not been an agreement last night, it was not just Europe that would have sunk into catastrophe. It was the whole world." Leaders agreed to boost the eurozone's bailout fund to $1.4

trillion, but they failed to decide where funding would come from. The euro fell 3.8 percent in five days.

d. December 8–9: "We're doing everything we can to save the euro." The deal tightened budget rules and added $200 billion to the euro war chest, but Europe's central bank demurred on more bond buying. Euro dropped 3.0 percent in two days.

See also EUROZONE; FRANCE; MERKEL, ANGELA.

SAS. *See* SCANDINAVIAN AIRLINES.

SAUDI ARABIA. Oil continues to drive the economy. In 2011, the nation had a GDP growth of 3.7 percent, with a GDP of $481 billion, an inflation rate of 6.0 percent, and a GDP per head of $17,250.
See also MIDDLE EAST.

SAVINGS AND LOAN HOLDING COMPANY ACT OF 1967. Authorized the Federal Reserve to monitor non-depository-related businesses of savings and loan holding companies.

SAVING(S) RATE. On average, U.S. consumers from 1950 to 1985 saved 9 percent of their disposable income. That rate then steadily declined to around zero early in 2008.

As the recession deepened, American consumers and businesses were embarking on an era of thrift, saving money as they cut spending on purchases. The personal savings rate, which indicates what we collectively spend from what we make expressed as a percentage, in the last three months of 2008 rose to its highest level in six years. This rate of 2.9 percent was the highest since early 2002. One concern, should this trend continue, was that it would increase the worries of deflation spreading throughout the global economy.

Savings jumped to 5 percent of disposable income in January 2009, the highest level in fourteen years. Then, in March, the national savings rate was at 4.2 percent from 4 percent in February. The savings rate climbed to 6.9 percent in May 2009, its highest level in fifteen years, as consumers tried to build a buffer against the threat of job losses and more economic instability. By June, Americans were saving more of their paychecks than at any time since February 1995. In October 2009, the savings rate for U.S. citizens was 4.4 percent.

By summer 2010, Americans were setting aside 6.2 percent of their disposable income in the second quarter and 5.5 percent in the first quarter. The personal savings rate fell in October 2010, for the fourth consecutive month, to below 5.3 percent. This meant that consumers were spending more of their incomes and saving less.

By the end of September 2011, with falling incomes and rising prices, people pulled more from their savings as the weak economy further strained household budgets. Personal income was down 0.1 percent, and spending climbed 0.2 percent. By then, Americans saved 4.5 percent of their income in August, down from 4.7 percent in July and 5.6 percent a year before. The personal saving rate, the share of income left after spending and taxes, increased to 3.5 percent in October 2011 from 3.3 percent in the month before. Savings had been falling steadily from 5.2 percent in January as consumers increased their spending. By December, people put away more of their disposable income, 4 percent, into savings, up from 3.5 percent in the previous month.

SCAMS. The Great Recession has led to a growing number of financial scams where victims are tempted to invest their funds on the false promise of large returns, often from supposed caches of overseas funds.

See also MORTGAGE SCAMS.

SCANDINAVIAN AIRLINES (SAS). Announced on August 12, 2009, that it would cut as many as 1,500 more jobs and reduce salaries as it posted a wider second-quarter net loss. In total, about 9,000 workers would lose their jobs. The carrier's net loss was $143 million from a year earlier.

See also AIRLINES.

SCANIA. This Swedish truck maker reported a 93 percent decline in its first-quarter 2009 profit. Net profits fell $22.1 million, while revenue fell 28 percent. Orders for its trucks and buses declined 70 percent to 6,061.

See also VOLVO.

SCHAPIRO, MARY L. President Obama's head of the Securities and Exchange Commission. She called for tighter regulation of hedge funds and credit-rating agencies. She proposed greater federal oversight of insurance companies and the credit default swap markets.

SCHLUMBERGER. In January 2009, the oilfield services giant painted a bleak picture of the oil patch, reporting a 17 percent drop in fourth-quarter earnings for 2008 and announcing that it planned to cut 5,000 jobs worldwide. These reductions amounted to about 5 percent of its global staffing.

Schlumberger's first-quarter 2009 net income fell 30 percent, with net income falling to $940.4 million compared to $1.34 billion the year before. Revenue dropped 4.5 percent to $6 billion.

Schlumberger's first-quarter 2010 earnings dropped 28 percent. The firm had a profit of $672 million, though revenue fell 6.7 percent to $5.6 billion. The firm's fourth-quarter profit climbed 31 percent $1.04 billion, up from $795 million a year before.

See also OIL.

SCHOOL LAYOFFS. *See* EDUCATION.

SCHOOL SALES. *See* RETAILING.

SCHULARICK, MORITZ. *See* CHIMERICA.

SDRS (SPECIAL DRAWING RIGHTS). *See* INTERNATIONAL MONETARY FUND.

SEARS HOLDINGS CORPORATION. Sears and Kmart merged in 2005. Sears posted a $94 million loss on August 20, 2009, dropping $94 million. The company's third-quarter 2009 loss narrowed to $127 million compared to the year before, when its losses were $146 million. Revenue declined 4.4 percent to $10.19 billion.

On May 20, 2010, Sears reported a quarterly net income drop to $16 million. Revenue was off slightly at $10.05 billion. The company's revenue dropped more than 10 percent from 2005 through 2009, and sales were about 1.9 percent less compared to the previous year.

For the fourth quarter ending January 31, 2011, Sears' earnings dropped 13 percent, with a profit of $374 million. Gross margin fell to 27.9 percent from 28.5 percent. On May 19, Sears posted a first-quarter loss at $170 million, with revenue dropping 3.4 percent to $9.71 billion. At the same time, inventory rose 6 percent to $9.88 billion. For the quarter ending July 30, Sears reported a loss of $146 million compared to the $39 million loss the year before. Revenue fell 1.2 percent to $10.33 billion. Management posted its fiscal third quarter with a loss of 7.8 percent, or $421 million. Revenue fell 1.2 percent to $9.56 billion. Gross margin fell $110 million to $2.4 billion.

On December 27, 2011, Sears Holdings announced intentions to close up to 120 of its locations following a major fall in sales during the holiday season. During the post-Thanksgiving period to Christmas, Sears reported that same-store sales were down 5.2 percent. This was contrasted with an expected national rise in retailing by 3.8 percent. The closings were expected to generate up to $170 million as the firm sold inventory. Then, on December 29, management identified seventy-nine of its stores to be closed, with nearly half being Kmart locations.

SEBELIUS, KATHLEEN. President Obama's secretary of health and human services, sworn in on April 28, 2009.

SEC. *See* SECURITIES AND EXCHANGE COMMISSION.

SECONDARY BUYOUTS. Passing a company from one private equity firm to another.

SECOND MORTGAGES. *See* MORTGAGES.

SECTION 13 (3). A section of the Federal Reserve Act under which the Federal Reserve may make secured loans to nondepository institutions, such as investment banks, under "unusual and exigent" circumstances.

SECURITIES ACT OF 1933. The first major federal securities law, still in effect, that prohibits securities fraud and requires registration or an exemption of registration of securities offered for public sale. It also requires that investors receive financial and other significant information.

See also PECORA COMMISSION.

SECURITIES AND EXCHANGE COMMISSION (SEC). Agency of the U.S. government created by the Securities Exchange Act of 1934 charged with protecting the interests of the public and investors in connection with the public issuance and sale of corporate securities. The five members of the SEC are appointed by the president and confirmed by the Senate for five years.

By 2008, the U.S. Treasury secretary had convinced Christopher Cox, chairman of the SEC, to begin a crackdown on improper short-selling in the shares of Fannie Mae and Freddie Mac, as well as seventeen other financial companies, including Lehman Brothers. Cox would be present at the Lehman collapse meeting and its eventual bankruptcy. The SEC chairman was directly involved, along with the U.S. Treasury, in attempting to get Barclays Bank in Britain to take over Lehman. All attempts failed.

On December 16, 2009, the SEC voted 4–1 to expand the disclosure requirements for public firms. The SEC also changed a formula that critics say permitted firms to understate how much their senior executives were paid. The new requirements included information on how a firm's pay policies might encourage too much risk-taking.

By the end of May 2010, the SEC was determined to eliminate "stub quotes"—placeholder prices that tended to be far from the actual market price. "Stub quotes" are used by companies when they don't wish to trade. When a firm wants to pull away and ensure that no trades happen, it offers quotes that are widely out of bounds, such as an offer to purchase for one penny a share or sell for $100,000. On November 3, the SEC moved to encourage corporate whistleblowers to report any wrongdoing they uncover internally, and to bar lawyers and compliance personnel from whistleblower payouts. The rules purported to ease concerns among firms about a new bounty program created by the Dodd-Frank law that offers large rewards to people who tip off the agency to fraud. If passed, the program would reward people reporting frauds by as much as 30 percent of the penalties and recovered funds collected by the SEC. Rewards to whistleblowers can be from 10 percent to 30 percent of fines and settlement extracted in enforcement actions triggered by a whistleblower's claim. The SEC forecast that it will get 30,000 tips each year, of which about half will lead to formal money claims.

See also DERIVATIVES LEGISLATION; EXPAND REGULATORY LEGISLATION; FINANCIAL CRISIS INQUIRY REPORT; FINANCIAL REGULATION PLAN (2009); "FLASH CRASH"; FLASH ORDERS (TRADING); FRAUD; GOLDMAN SACHS; MASKING; MONEY MARKET FUNDS; RATERS; SECURITIES EXCHANGE ACT OF 1934; SHORT-SELLING; SHORT-TERM BORROWING; WACHOVIA; WALL STREET REFORM ACT (2010).

SECURITIES EXCHANGE ACT OF 1934. Created the Securities and Exchange Commission and granted it broad authority over the nation's securities markets, brokerage firms, transfer agents, clearing agencies, and self-regulatory organizations.

See also PECORA COMMISSION; SECURITIES AND EXCHANGE COMMISSION.

SECURITIES LENDING. Where funds lend some of their stocks and bonds to Wall Street firms in return for cash that a bank may invest. Should the trade perform well, the banks take a cut of the profits. If the trade does poorly, the funds absorb all of the losses—a questionable arrangement.

SECURITIES MARKET PROGRAM. An open-ended program under which the European Central Bank purchases the government bonds of the troubled eurozone member states on the secondary market.

SECURITIES REGULATIONS. *See* CREDIT RATING AGENCY REFORM ACT OF 2006; INVESTMENT ADVISERS ACT OF 1940; INVESTMENT COMPANY ACT OF 1940; SARBANES-OXLEY ACT OF 2002; SECURITIES ACT OF 1933; SECURITIES EXCHANGE ACT OF 1934; WALL STREET REFORM ACT (2010).

SECURITIZATION. The process of taking an illiquid asset or group of assets and, through financial engineering, transforming them into a security. Pooling loans with others as securities, which are then sold into a secondary market, where investors buy them. Includes the packaging and selling of bundles of debts from credit cards to mortgages. It helped fuel the massive expansion of consumer finance over the past fifteen years. A typical example is the mortgage-backed security.

Most of the tightness or lack of accessibility to credit in 2008–2009 was due to the collapse of securitization. A significant amount of taxpayers' money would be needed to overcome this huge problem.

See also BEAR STEARNS; MORTGAGE-BACKED SECURITY.

SECURITIZED LENDING. Beginning March 17, 2009, large investors, including hedge funds and private-equity firms, could secure cheap credit from the Federal Reserve and utilize these funds to purchase newly issued securities backed by such loans. It was originally designed for markets for things such as credit card debt, student loans, car loans, and loans guaranteed by the Small Business Administration.

TALF (Term Asset-Backed Securities Loan Facility) was the appropriate outlet for this program, which was announced on March 3 and set up to finance up to $1 trillion in new lending to consumers and businesses.

See also TALF; WALL STREET REFORM ACT (2010).

SEIDMAN, LESLIE. Became the full chairman on December 23, 2010, of the Financial Accounting Standards Board. She had been an FASB member since 2003 and will serve through June 2013.

See also FINANCIAL ACCOUNTING STANDARDS BOARD.

SEMICONDUCTORS. Sales fell almost 10 percent in November 2008 as the economic slowdown shook the chip sector. Sales fell to $20.8 billion in November from $23.1 billion a year earlier.

SENIOR DEBT ISSUE. *See* EMERGENCY ECONOMIC STABILIZATION ACT OF 2008.

SEQUESTER. In U.S. government practices, when the Joint Committee on Deficit Reduction failed (November 22, 2011) to produce a solution to the $1.2 trillion cut, the sequester would be implemented in 2013 across the board. The cut was split evenly between the non-exempt portion of defense, requiring an approximately $44 billion annual cut to each, and non-defense, another $55 billion annual cut. The reduction to Medicare is capped at 2 percent.

See also DEFICIT DEAL; DEFICIT-REDUCTION COMMITTEE.

SERVICEMEMBERS CIVIL RELIEF ACT. *See* FORECLOSURE.

SERVICE SECTOR. Firms remained hesitant well in mid-2010 to hire workers. The service area grew more slowly in June. Representing more than four of every five private-sector employees, service-sector growth hiring had slowed. By September 2010, the service sector expanded, arguing against a possible double-dip recession. Service-sector companies account for about two-thirds of GDP workers.

See also UNEMPLOYMENT.

SETTLEMENT SYSTEMS. *See* FINANCIAL REGULATION PLAN (2009).

"SHADOW BANKS." Finance firms, investments banks, off-balance sheet vehicles, government-sponsored enterprises, and hedge funds that fueled the credit boom and were aided by less regulation and more leverage than commercial banks.

By 2008, shadow banks moved as a herd, helping to inflate the bubble and worsen the bust. Losses at shadow banks knocked holes in the balance sheets of the ordinary banks that had lent to them.

See also FINANCIAL CRISIS INQUIRY REPORT; FINANCIAL STABILITY BOARD; HEDGE FUNDS; "TOO BIG TO FAIL."

SHADOW MARKET. *Synonymous with* DERIVATIVE MARKET.

SHANGHAI. *See* CHINA.

SHANGHAI COMPOSITE INDEX. For 2008, fell 65.4 percent.

SHARMA, DEVEN. *See* STANDARD & POOR'S

SHARP. The electronics company reported on April 27, 2009, its first annual loss in more than fifty years. Revenue declined 17 percent.

Sharp Corporation management reported for the fiscal year 2010 that it had lowered its net profit to $367.2 million from an earlier forecast. The company posted a net profit of 14.3 billion yen for the six months ending September 30. Revenue climbed 16 percent to 1.5 trillion yen.

SHARPER IMAGE. Filed for Chapter 11 bankruptcy on February 21, 2008.

SHEDDING DEBT. *See* DELEVERAGING.

SHELL. *See* ROYAL DUTCH SHELL.

SHIPPING. Container shipping firm profits fell amid softer container demand. A.P. Moller-Maersk, a Danish shipping line—the world's largest, reported a 4.8 percent decline in 2008 net profit. By mid-2009, the company announced a first-half loss as freight rates fell sharply.

Almost 10 percent of the world's merchant ships were unused during this economic meltdown. It was projected that shipping capacity would exceed the needs of the market by between 50 and 70 percent in the near future. Container shipping remains in turmoil. Since the second half of 2008, the industry has experienced a spectacular fall as charter rates fell alongside the rest of the global economy. Container shipping rates dropped to zero in January on the Asia-to-Europe route as brokers waived fees and charged only for fuel costs. Cargo shipping declined 4.5 percent in 2009 and the world's merchant fleet grew by 7 percent.

By 2011, shipping containers were bringing less cargo into the States. For example, the number of containers unloaded at California ports fell 3.6 percent from the year before. It was found that retailers were keeping their inventories tight amid a still-uncertain economy, leading to less demand for overseas goods.

See also MOLLER-MAERSK.

SHOPLIFTING. Since fall 2008, retailers have had to reduce the number of employees in their stores who were responsible for preventing the theft of merchandise. With the meltdown, shoplifting had increased, with shoplifting arrests 10 to 20 percent higher in 2008 than in 2007. More than $35 million in merchandise is stolen in the United States every day. The problem remains into 2012.

SHORTCUT FORECLOSURE. A method of foreclosure in which a power of the sale clause in the mortgage allows the lender to sell a property if it goes into default. The borrower must be informed, but the issuing of a public statement need not be carried out. Upon property foreclosure, the junior mortgage holders' positions are wiped out, unless the sale yields more than the outstanding first mortgage.

SHORT SALES. In real estate, sales involving homeowners under duress selling properties for less than their mortgages.
See also REO.

SHORT-SELLING. Borrowing a security and selling it with the intent of buying it back at a lower price to return to the lender. A proposal not requiring congressional approval was made by the Obama administration that would ban "naked" short-selling—selling shares of stock without borrowing them first—and require short-selling trades to be reported daily. In mid-September 2008, the Securities and Exchange Commission instituted a temporary ban on short-selling, but it was lifted in October.

The negative bets of financial stocks in several European countries were temporarily banned on August 11, 2011. French, Italian, and Spanish stock market regulators announced on August 25 that they would extend the temporary ban on short-selling until September 30 for the Spanish and Italian markets and until November 11 for the French market.
See also NAKED SHORT-SELLING; REGULATION; SECURITIES AND EXCHANGE COMMISSION.

SHORT-TERM BORROWING. On September 17, 2010, the Securities and Exchange Commission approved a proposal to reinstate a requirement that publicly traded firms disclose more information about their short-term borrowings. This ruling was to prevent firms from hiding liquidity problems by coloring their balance sheets at the end of a quarter. The ruling requires companies to report, each quarter, their average daily or monthly amount of outstanding short-term debt, the maximum level of these borrowings, and their weighted average interest rate.
See also SECURITIES AND EXCHANGE COMMISSION.

"SHOVEL READY." Describes projects already designed and ready to be launched within 90 to 120 days of being funded by President Obama's proposal to provide funds to states.

Cf. "READY TO GO" PROJECTS.

SHRINKING INVENTORIES. *See* INVENTORIES.

SICHUAN TENGZHONG HEAVY INDUSTRIAL MACHINERY COMPANY.
See HUMMER.

SIEMENS. Reported on July 29, 2010, that its profit for the quarter ending June 30 rose 9 percent to $1.87 billion as sales climbed 4 percent. On November 11, Siemens reported a significant jump in orders as the global economic recovery stimulated demand for its products. New orders were up 25 percent to $32.4 billion during the quarter and sales climbed 8 percent to $29.2 billion.

Siemens' net profit in the three months ending June 30, 2011, fell 65 percent to $716 million.

See also NOKIA SIEMENS NETWORKS.

SIGURDARDOTTIR, JOHANNA. *See* ICELAND.

SIKORSKY HELICOPTERS. *See* UNITED TECHNOLOGIES.

"SILENT KILLER." *Synonymous with* INFLATION.

SILVER. Silver futures on September 16, 2010, hit their highest level since October 15, 1980, settling at $20.7450 a troy ounce. Silver prices once again soared at the end of December to 51 percent. It closed on December 26 at $29.31 a troy ounce, up from $16.822 at the beginning of 2010. For the year 2010, silver was up 74 percent compared with gold, which was up 26 percent in the year.

In mid-February 2011, the spot price of silver brokered $33 a troy ounce, not seen since the mid-1980s. In mid-April, silver prices soared toward $50 an ounce. Prices in 2011 had already climbed 52 percent. Then suddenly, on May 2, silver prices tumbled 12 percent as margin requirements were tightened. On July 13, silver surged 7.1 percent, or $2.519, to settle at $38.148 an ounce, its largest one-day percentage move since March 2009 and the largest dollar gain since 1980. On September 22, silver fell 9.6 percent to $36.538. For the week ending September 24, silver plunged 18 percent, its largest single-day decline since 1987. With the close of 2011, worries about the debt crisis in Europe dragged silver lower, with futures down 12 percent for the year to date. Silver settled at its lowest levels since

January. For December, delivery silver fell $1.505, or 5.2 percent, to settle at $27.192 a troy ounce.

For the month of January 2012, silver prices climbed 19 percent.

Cf. GOLD; PLATINUM.

SIMPSON, ALAN. *See* NATIONAL COMMISSION ON FISCAL RESPONSIBILITY AND REFORM.

SINGAPORE. Plunged deeper into recession in the fourth quarter 2008 as its GDP marked its biggest quarterly decline on record, which substantially demanded a revision of its 2009 forecast. The economy contracted at a seasonally adjusted annualized pace of 12.5 percent in the fourth quarter, accelerating from a 5.4 percent decline in the third quarter.

Sharply cut its 2009 economic outlook and revised an expectation for its economy to shrink by 2 percent to 5 percent in 2009. Singapore's economy had a significant rebound in the third quarter 2009. GDP expanded 14.9 percent.

Arguably, Singapore by July 2010 had become the world's fastest growing economy, with an expansion of 15 percent. For the year until October, Singapore's exports grew by 34.5 percent.

The pace of growth in 2011 fell to 4.1 percent from 12.2 percent in 2010, and the basic fiscal gap would narrow from 2.6 percent to -1.2 percent. GDP growth was 4.1 percent, with GDP at $237 billion, an inflation rate of 2 percent, and a GDP per head of $45,200. Consumer price inflation remained unchanged at 4.5 percent in May.

See also SOUTHEAST ASIA; TAX HAVENS.

SINGLE CURRENCY. *See* EURO.

SIV. *See* STRUCTURED INVESTMENT VEHICLE.

SIX FLAGS. The U.S. amusement park company with twenty locations filed for Chapter 11 bankruptcy protection in mid-June 2009. It needed $2 billion of debt restructuring.

Six Flags swung to a second-quarter 2010 profit of $743.5 million compared with a year earlier loss of $121.6 million. Revenue climbed 8.2 percent to $321.3 million, with park attendance in the year up 7 percent from the previous year.

SKF. Based in Sweden, the world's largest maker of ball bearings said on December 10, 2008, that it would cut 2,500 jobs after a steeper-than-expected decline in demand from automakers and industrial customers. This was equal to about 6.3 percent of its total workforce.

See also SWEDEN.

SKIING. *See* SWITZERLAND.

SLOVAK REPUBLIC (SLOVAKIA). Economic activity rebounded in the second quarter after sharp falls earlier on. Notwithstanding continued positive growth in the third quarter, annual GDP is expected to fall by close to 6 percent in 2009. Activity will gradually pick up in 2010 owing to a brighter outlook for world trade growth and a resumption of inflows of foreign direct investment, and growth should reach an annual rate of above 4 percent in 2011. The strong increase in unemployment is expected to gradually level off. With substantial slack in the economy, consumer price inflation is expected to remain fairly low. The fiscal position will worsen markedly this year and next, largely due to the cyclical rise in spending on social benefits and the fall in tax revenues but also to two fiscal stimulus packages enacted earlier in 2009. In 2010, the rise in the deficit will be limited by a set of ambitious expenditure cuts. Over the medium term, further fiscal consolidation will be necessary to ensure the sustainability of public finances. While the automatic phasing-out of the stimulus measures at the end of 2010 will help in this regard, additional measures will be needed.

On October 11, 2011, lawmakers failed to support a plan to expand the euro bailout with about $10 billion in debt guarantees to the eurozone. Its government was brought down and a future vote was planned.

See EUROZONE.

SLOVENIA. Although Slovenia had already moved out of recession in the second quarter 2009, the precipitous decline in the previous two quarters was severe enough to give a year-on-year output fall in 2009 of close to 8 percent. A mild rebound has been occurring and is expected to continue through 2010, driven by external demand, before growth strengthens further in 2011 on the back of strong investment. Inflation should remain moderate due to the negative output gap and high unemployment. Private consumption will be adversely affected by rising unemployment but should progressively recover with more dynamic wage developments in the private sector at the end of the projection period. Following the strong 2009 fiscal stimulus, the fiscal stance is set to tighten in 2010 and 2011 given the need for consolidation. A new pension reform should bolster fiscal consolidation, while labor market reforms to increase flexibility should help speed up employment recovery.

The economy, which grew for sixteen straight years before falling in 2009, expanded by 2.1 percent in 2011, an increase from 1.1 percent the year before. The nation's GDP was expected to grow by 2.1 percent, with a GDP of $47 billion, an inflation rate of 2.4 percent, and a GDP per head of $23,550.

SMALL BANKS. As contrasted with the giant U.S. banks, these community banks became more visible during the meltdown. Of the more than 8,000 such banks in the United States, most have less than $10 billion in assets. By year's end 2009, 165 banks had failed. Small banks represent 95 percent of the total assets within the banking system.

Synonymous with COMMUNITY BANKS.

SMALL BUSINESS ADMINISTRATION. *See* SECURITIZED LENDING.

SMART BRIDGES. *See* SMART INFRASTRUCTURE.

SMART ELECTRIC GRIDS. *See* ENERGY EFFICIENCY; SMART INFRASTRUCTURE.

SMART INFRASTRUCTURE. With passage of the economic stimulus plan in mid-February 2009, funds would be moved into the infrastructure area. Tens of billions of dollars were poured into building or rebuilding smart roads, smart bridges, smart electric grids, etc.

SMART ROADS. *See* SMART INFRASTRUCTURE.

SMITH BARNEY. *See* CITIGROUP.

SMITH, JOSEPH A. Appointed by President Obama on November 12, 2010, to head the Federal Housing Finance Agency, which oversees mortgage giants Fannie Mae and Freddie Mac. Mr. Smith had served as North Carolina's banking commissioner since 2002.

SMOOT-HAWLEY ACT OF 1930. Had a significant impact on the creation of the Great Depression of the 1930s. The tariff act increased nearly 900 American import duties. Willis Hawley, a congressman from Oregon, and Reed Smoot, a U.S. senator from Utah, both projected an isolationist flair, which was popular at the time. What began as an agricultural program spread throughout the economies of the nation. The average rate on dutiable goods rose from 40 percent to 48 percent, with dutiable import rates down to 17–20 percent. U.S. imports dropped by 15 percent following its passage. The Tariff Act of 1930 effectively raised duties by 20 percent. The 2008–2012 recession had reinvigorated calls for greater U.S. protectionism. Some have even called for a reinvention of a new Smoot-Hawley Act.

See also BUY AMERICAN; BUY LOCAL; FISHER, IRVING; PROTECTIONISM; WORLD TRADE ORGANIZATION.

Synonymous with TARIFF ACT OF 1930.

SOCIAL SECURITY. To rein in the federal deficit, a mid-November 2010 survey found that 57 percent of respondents opposed gradually raising the

Social Security retirement age to sixty-nine over the next sixty years, while 41 percent stated that they could accept this change. Under the compromised tax cuts of December 2010, the 6.2 percent Social Security payroll tax was to be reduced for all wage earners by two percentage points for one year, putting more money in the paychecks of workers. For a family earning $50,000 a year, it would amount to a savings of $1,000. The recession also led to a surge in applications for Social Security disability benefits. There is a high correlation between people seeking Social Security disability payments when their unemployment benefits are exhausted.

Social Security cutbacks remain on the table as the government continues to find ways to reduce the deficit in 2012. On December 22, 2011, Congress supported a payroll tax cut and, at the same time, agreed that employees' share of the Social Security payroll tax would remain at its current level, 4.2 percent of wages, through February 29, 2012. In its absence, the payroll tax would have reverted to the usual 6.2 percent by January 2012.

See also NATIONAL COMMISSION ON FISCAL RESPONSIBILITY AND REFORM; OBAMA, BARACK; TAX CUTS.

SOCIETE GENERALE. France's second largest bank by market capitalization posted a second-quarter 2010 net profit more than triple that of 2009, rising to $1.43 billion, with revenue up 17 percent from the period before in 2009. On November 3, 2010, the bank reported that its third-quarter net profit doubled, rising to $1.26 billion. Revenue climbed 5.5 percent.

The bank's second-quarter 2011 net profit fell 31 percent to $1.06 billion. On August 10, shares declined more than 20 percent and recovered to end the daily coverage with a 15 percent fall. Since mid-July, the bank's stock fell 40 percent. By mid-September, nearly half of its share price had dropped since the beginning of August. Moody's Investors Service downgraded Societe General's long-term debt by one notch to AA3—three notches below AAA—with a negative outlook.

See also FEDERAL HOUSING FINANCE AGENCY; MOODY'S.

SOLIS, HILDA. President Obama's labor secretary.

SONY CORPORATION. In December 2008, the electronics maker announced cuts of 8,000 jobs, or 4 percent of its workforce. It planned to reduce investments in response to the global financial crisis and the severe drop in spending by consumers around the world. Sony was aiming to save $1.1 billion annually, which included the shutdown of several manufacturing sites. The number of production sites was reduced by about 10 percent from fifty-seven.

In mid-January 2009, Sony announced an operating loss of $29 billion—an annual loss for the first time in fourteen years—as plunging LCD television prices hit the biggest name in the consumer-electronics sector. Crippled by a global economic downturn, Sony announced that it would cut 16,000 jobs from its electronics division and close as many as six factories in order to save over $1 billion in annual costs. On July 30, Sony reported a 37.1 billion yen first-quarter net loss. Sony's net income fell to 1.6 trillion yen; revenue dropped 19.2 percent from a year earlier. The company posted its fourth consecutive quarterly loss on October 30, 2009. During this period, Sony had a net loss of $289 million. Sales for the period, which ended September 30, fell 20 percent.

In May 2010, Sony narrowed its losses from 2009 and forecast a return to profit in 2010. Its net loss for the year ending March 31, 2010, was $441 million. Sales fell 7 percent. In mid-July 2010, Sony Ericsson posted its second consecutive 2010 quarterly profit of $15.5 million. With a strong yen and falling TV prices, Sony reported that its profit fell 8.6 percent in the last quarter.

On July 28, 2011, Sony reported a quarterly loss of $199 million, with sales for the year running to $92.4 billion compared with a previous forecast of $96.3 billion. Sony expected a loss of more than $1 billion in 2011 for its fourth straight year.

SONY ERICSSON. *See* SONY.

SOTHEBY'S. The world's largest auction house swung to a fourth-quarter net loss, hurt by charges and a 52 percent drop in the auction house's sales. A net loss of $8.45 million was shown for the fourth quarter 2008 compared with the previous year's net income of $102.4 million. Revenue fell 52 percent to $166.2 million as auction sales declined 46 percent.

Sotheby's profit plunged 87 percent in the second quarter 2009, and earnings dropped to $12.2 million from $95.3 million a year before. Sotheby's reported a third-quarter 2009 loss as sales slumped; its revenue fell 41 percent to $44.9 million. The loss for the quarter was $57.8 million compared with the 2008 loss of $47 million.

The firm's first-quarter 2010 loss narrowed to $2.2 million compared to the year-before loss of $34.5 million. Revenue rose 87 percent to $101.9 million. It was believed that Sotheby's would only make about $36 million in 2010. By year's end, the auction house netted $4.3 billion, a 90 percent increase from the previous year, with Sotheby's profit rising 31 percent.

SOUTH AFRICA. Real GDP growth will be negative in 2009 but should turn positive in the fourth quarter and accelerate in the first half of 2010, boosted by the World Cup soccer tournament. Inflation should return to the target range in 2010 aided by a substantial output gap and the feed through of past rand appreciation. The current account deficit will narrow this year but should widen thereafter as imports outpace exports. Given the fragile nature of the recovery, the planned increase in public spending in 2010 should be implemented. It must, however, remain cast within a medium-term framework consistent with debt sustainability, which is likely to imply substantial spending restraint in the coming cyclical upswing. The downturn and the attendant large deficits have also made it more urgent to increase the efficiency of public expenditure.

The South African Reserve Bank cut its benchmark interest rate by a half point to 11.5 percent in the fourth quarter 2008. The move was intended to help economic growth in the global economic downturn. Its trade deficit widened to 12.1 billion rand, or $1.3 billion, in November 2008 as the global economic recession cut demand for exports of platinum and ferrochrome. South Africa's economy contracted for the first time in a decade in the final three months of 2008, with declining demand for the country's commodities exports. GDP for the largest economy in Africa shrank an annualized 1.8 percent in the fourth quarter compared with essentially flat growth of 0.2 percent in the third quarter.

Matters did not improve in 2009. Output declined by an annualized 3 percent in the second quarter, its third quarterly contraction in a row. This was, however, half the 6.4 percent decline from the first three months in the year. Nearly half a million jobs were lost in the first half of 2009 from a workforce of 17 million. By October 2009, the annual rate of inflation fell by 0.2 percentage points to 5.9 percent. South Africa, the world's twenty-fourth largest economy and Africa's biggest, accounted for 40 percent of sub-Saharan Africa's total GDP. The economy grew nearly 5 percent a year in the five years prior to 2009. In 2009, the nation's economy fell into recession for the first time in seventeen years, shrinking by 1.8 percent.

The continent's largest economy has one of the world's lowest labor-participation rates and one of its highest unemployment rates. Almost 40 percent of the country's working-age population has jobs compared with 60–75 percent in other emerging markets. One in three within the workforce, including half of young black people ages fifteen to twenty-four, was unemployed. Government figures indicated an unemployment rate of only 25 percent, but if you include those who have ceased searching for work, it was more than 35 percent.

The nation's GDP growth projected for 2011 was 3.7 percent, with a GDP of $346 billion, an inflation rate of 5.7 percent, and a GDP per head of $7,050. Consumer prices climbed 4.6 percent in May, the highest level in one year. By summer, the rand had risen around 30 percent since early 2009, hampering growth and job creation by making mining and manufacturing exports more expensive. The government made it easier for capital to leave the country and to increase central bank reserves.

See also AFRICA; BRICS.

SOUTH AMERICA. *See* ARGENTINA; BRAZIL; LATIN AMERICA; WORLD TRADE.

SOUTHEAST ASIA. By 2009, export orders throughout Southeast Asia declined. Factories slowed down as the main motor of these economies sputtered, according to government officials.

Thailand, Indonesia, the Philippines, and Vietnam depend heavily on exports to power economic growth. For Malaysia and Singapore, overseas markets are even more crucial to domestic prosperity.

See also CHINA; MALAYSIA; REMITTANCES; SINGAPORE; THAILAND; VIETNAM.

SOUTH KOREA. Economy shrank a seasonally adjusted 5.6 percent in the fourth quarter 2008 from the previous three months.

South Korean exports tumbled a record 32.8 percent in January 2009 as shipments of products, including cars and wireless communication equipment, fell. The drop in exports to $21.7 billion was the steepest since South Korea began collecting monthly tallies of exports and imports in 1980. The Bank of Korea cut its benchmark interest rate to 2 percent, a record low, to aid the plunging economy. Corporate leaders were proposing ways of avoiding layoffs by convincing workers and union officials to reduce wages, often by about 20 percent, in a strategy referred to as job preservation. Exports fell 19 percent in April, and imports declined 35.6 percent.

South Korea's economic output grew 2.9 percent in the third quarter 2009. In October, South Korea had a larger-than-expected $3.79 billion trade surplus. Exports for the month fell 8.3 percent from a year before at $34.03 billion, less than the 12 percent decline projected by market observers, while imports were down 16.3 percent at $30.23 billion versus a forecast for a 15.7 percent fall.

South Korean export growth accelerated to 35.1 percent to March 2010 from 30.5 percent in the twelve months prior to February 2010. Industrial production rose by 22.1 percent. By July 2010, industrial production climbed by 15.5 percent in one year. The nation's jobless rate dropped to 3.4 percent in August 2010 from 3.7 percent the month before.

South Korea's GDP was expected to expand by 3.9 percent in 2011. The nation's GDP growth was 3.9 percent, with GDP at $1,094 billion, an inflation rate of 3.3 percent, and a GDP per head of $22,050. The nation's unemployment rate climbed to 4 percent in February from 3.6 percent the month before.

The nation's economy grew 4.2 percent in the first quarter 2011. Unemployment fell to 3.3 percent in May, the lowest since November 2010. Consumer prices climbed by 4.7 percent. Inflation rose to 5.3 percent in August, the highest since August 2008. Capital flows helped spur inflation, even as the economy slowed. The government then placed a 14 percent tax on foreign holdings of government bonds and central bank securities placed a restriction on banks' foreign-exchange derivative positions.

See also HYUNDAI MOTOR COMPANY; LG; SAMSUNG; SOUTH-EAST ASIA.

SOUTHWEST AIRLINES. Reported in mid-January 2009 that although it had strong revenue growth, it also had a second consecutive quarterly loss after years of steady profits. The company posted a net loss on January 22 of $56 million. The airline booked its third straight quarterly loss and provided a down forecast as it laid plans to reduce its staff. In July, the airlines returned to a profit after three straight quarterly losses. Southwest's third quarter 2009 showed a slight loss of $16 million compared to a $120 million the year before. Revenue fell 7.8 percent to $2.67 billion. On July 29, 2010, management reported a second-quarter net income of $112 million, with revenue climbing 21.1 percent to $3.17 billion. In October, management reported a net profit of $205 million compared with a loss of $16 million the year earlier. Fourth-quarter earnings rose 13 percent, with a profit of $131 million and revenue of $3.11 billion.

In June 2011, traffic climbed 11 percent, with revenue rising 11 to 12 percent from the year before. On August 4, management reported a 44 percent surge in its second-quarter profit, and revenue climbed 31 percent to $4.14 billion.

See also AIRLINES.

SOVEREIGN-DEBT DOWNGRADE. *See* BELGIUM; STANDARD & POOR'S.

SOVEREIGN FUND. A portfolio of investments in foreign markets funded from current-account surpluses.

SOYBEAN PRICES. In six months, this farm commodity had plunged about 40 percent since July 2008.

S&P. *See* STANDARD AND POOR'S.

SPAIN. Output is projected to fall by 3.5 percent in 2009 and by a further 0.25 percent in 2010 before recovering at a slow rate in 2011. The unemployment rate is expected to peak at close to 20 percent in 2010. Inflation may rise temporarily in 2010, reflecting higher oil prices and projected value-added tax increases, but it is expected to fall to close to zero in 2011. The decline in housing transactions has leveled off and the fall in house prices has flattened. The planned tightening of the fiscal stand should be deferred to 2011 to allow the economy to recover more firmly. However, structural reforms, including steps to curb age-related spending increases, need to be implemented to ensure long-term fiscal sustainability. Programs to support construction of social housing should be halted; support to low-income households should be provided via means-tested cash benefits earmarked to rent payments. The effectiveness of the public employment service should be improved.

In November 2008, the number of people filing jobless claims in Spain rose 7.3 percent and was at the highest level since 1996. The jobless rate stood at 11.3 percent in October, the highest rate among the twenty-seven countries in the European Union. As a beginning strategy, the government announced a program that may have been the first of its kind to allow out-of-work homeowners to defer mortgage payments. The government announced on November 27 that a $14.3 billion stimulus package would be put in place, aimed at creating 300,000 jobs and attempting to cushion the Spanish economy from the global crisis. It would cost the equivalent of about 1 percent of the nation's GDP. It included about $10 million for public works and an additional $1 billion to help the ailing automobile industry. In addition, the government said it would buy $10 billion of debt at its second purchase of bank assets and urged the financial sector to use the proceeds from the sale to provide credit to businesses and families.

The government encouraged immigrants to return home on lump-sum welfare payments. Spain created more jobs and drew more immigrants than any country in Europe over the past decade, largely because of a construction boom. The foreign population had risen to 5.2 million in 2008, out of Spain's total population of 45 million, from a foreign population of 750,000 in 1999. As the economy shrank, firms were releasing workers at an alarming rate. Unemployment soared 11 percent in the third quarter 2008 and immigrants in low-skilled jobs were the hardest hit, with job losses estimated to be 17 percent.

The government instituted a €33 billion public works program that it hoped would lead to 25,000 new building projects by May 2009. Spain's automobile sales plummeted in 2009. Registrations fell 42 percent in January to 59,385 cars.

Nearly 50 percent of Spain's lending institutions were in the hands of un-listed savings banks largely controlled by the regional governments, and were demanding state aid. In March, Spain became the first of the sixteen countries that use the euro to record a negative inflation rate of 0.1 percent, the first time since the government began tracking inflation in 1961. Combining rising unemployment and decreasing prices, Spain may be in the early grip of deflation, resulting in a downward spiral. As unemployment in Spain, at 15.5 percent, continued to climb, consumers cut their spending.

Spain's unemployment had jumped to 17.4 percent from 13.9 percent in the previous quarter. Unemployment was predicted to reach 19.3 percent by the end of 2009. The nation's GDP climbed by 0.1 percent, lower than in the first quarter of 2009. By July, Spain's unemployment rose to 18 percent, the highest within the twenty-seven member nations of the European Union. It shed 1.2 million jobs in one year and would soon have as many jobless as Italy and France combined. Spain's budget deficit was nearly 12 percent of its GDP. On July 24, the government announced that more than 1 million households had no working members. The nation's unemployment rate more than doubled on the year to 17.92 percent in the second quarter, by far the highest rate of the thirty countries within the Organisation for Economic Co-operation and Development. Spain's economy contracted in the second quarter 2009, with GDP falling 4.1 percent. The prime minister of Spain in early September announced tax increases and spending cuts to reverse a ballooning budget deficit. With a soaring unemployment rate of 18.5 percent, the tax burden rose as much as 1.5 percent of GDP. Spain's economy shrank for the sixth quarter in a row. By December 10, Spain became the latest eurozone country to face a possible downgrade of its government debt. The nation's deficit topped 11 percent of GDP in 2009.

About 3.2 million people were on unemployment benefits in March 2010. Some 40 percent of those younger than twenty-five years old, were unemployed, double the European average. On April 28, 2010, Spain's credit rating was cut following the downgrades to Portugal and Greece, creating fears that the eurozone's debt crisis was spreading. Industrial production in Spain rose by 6.8 percent in the twelve months ending in March 2010. Unemployment rose to 19.1 percent for the three months ending March from 18.8 percent for the last quarter 2009.

The government planned to reduce the nation's budget deficit by nearly half to 6 percent of GDP in 2011 and by half again in 2013 to bring it into line with the 3 percent of GDP limit set for eurozone nations. About 125,000 firms, approximately 10 percent of Spain's total, have gone out of business since the meltdown began in 2007. This situation continued to haunt the government in mid-2010 as it tried to slash its budget deficit to the 3 percent of GDP limit set for EU nations by 2013. Spain's government had forecast a 1.3 percent growth in 2011, while the International Monetary Fund had predicted 0.7 percent. Jobless claims continued their spiral in October 2010, indicating a continuing weak recovery due in great part to the collapse of a ten-year construction boom and government efforts to cut a towering budget deficit. Registered jobless claims rose by 68,213, or 1.7 percent, to nearly 40.09 million, making it more than twice the EU average.

Following Ireland's need to borrow from the EU and IMF, it was feared in November that Spain could follow, further upsetting the eurozone. Spain accounts for roughly 10 percent of all economic activity within the eurozone of sixteen nations. On December 2, 2010, Spanish jobless claims climbed for the month by 24,318, or 0.6 percent, to 4.1 million. Its unemployment rate of 20.7 percent was twice the average of the sixteen nations of the eurozone. The nation's average deficit across its seventeen regions was 1.24 percent of GDP at the end of the third quarter, all within the 2.4 percent target for 2010. The nation's GDP growth was 0.6 percent, with a GDP of $1,337 billion, an inflation rate of 0.9 percent, and a GDP per head of $ 28,990.

The nation's unemployment rate shot up to 20.3 percent in the last three months of 2010 as more than 138,000 jobs disappeared. Fourth-quarter unemployment rose from 19.8 percent in the third quarter and was the highest level since the second quarter 1997, when it was 20.7 percent. Overall, 4.7 million people were unemployed in Spain, which has the highest unemployment rate in the developed world. In addition, there were 700,000 unsold new homes in the country.

On January 24, 2011, Spain announced that it would overhaul its bank regulations to permit the partial nationalization of its ailing savings banks and enable the injection of fresh capital into them. The fourth-quarter results indicated that the nation's GDP rose quarterly 0.2 percent after slowing down the previous quarter. Output for the year 2010 fell 0.1 percent. Following Portugal's lead in March 2011 for a bailout from the EU, attention turned to Spain. The cost of saving Spain, with its $1.56 trillion economy, would dwarf previous bailouts, thereby testing the financial strength of Europe. Industrial production climbed by 0.8 percent after falling by 4 percent from one year before. In mid-September, the government approved a tax on its wealthiest people. The wealth tax was eliminated in 2008 and would affect citizens with net assets of more than $971,000 in 2011 and 2012. Spanish land prices had fallen about 30 percent from the 2007 high, and home prices were down about 22 percent. In September, jobless claims soared, rising by 95,817, or 2.3 percent. In September, Fitch Ratings and Moody's downgraded Spain to AA–.

The jobless rate hovered above 20 percent since early 2010 and, as announced by the government on October 28, reached its highest rate in fifteen years in the third quarter at 21.5 percent. In addition, the number of households without any income also hit record levels, rising to 559,000, or 3.2 percent of the nation's families. On November 17, the Treasury paid a 7 percent yield to sell a new ten-year government bond, a euro-era high. On November 22, Spain was forced to pay a euro-era record 5.11 percent yield on a three-month bill at an auction of treasury bills, more than double the 2.29 percent rate it paid at auction the month before. It also sold six-month debt at 5.23 percent, up from 3.30 percent in October. In December, Spain's car market fell 3.6 percent, with car registration falling 18 percent to 808,059 cars, the third straight year they fell below one million. On the last trading day of 2011,

Spain missed its deficit target by a large margin. The result was spending cuts and tax increases of about $19.4 billion. The nation's economy shrank in the last three months of 2011, with GDP falling 0.3 percent in the fourth quarter from the third, the first drop in GDP since the nation pulled out of recession two years before.

On January 27, 2012, it was reported that Spain's jobless rate approached 23 percent, up from 21.52 percent the previous quarter and more than twice the average unemployment rate of 10 percent throughout the EU. Nearly 1.6 million households currently have no working members and 48.6 percent of job seekers under twenty-five years old are unemployed.

See also EUROZONE; INDIGNADOS; INTERNATIONAL MONE-TARY FUND.

SPECIAL DRAWING RIGHTS (SDRS). *See* INTERNATIONAL MONETARY FUND.

SPECIAL-PURPOSE VEHICLES (SPVS). *See* EUROPEAN COMMISSION; MONEY MARKET MUTUAL FUNDS; STRUCTURED INVESTMENT VEHICLE.

SPENDING. As the unemployment rate rose, people with jobs were increasingly fearful of spending, which only made the economy's problems worse. In the last three months of 2008, consumer purchases accounted for 69.9 percent of GDP compared with 70.5 percent in the same period a year earlier.

By summer's end 2009, transportation spending fell 1.8 percent and apparel outlay dropped 4.3 percent. Families spent 8.1 percent more on home dining, or $279 a family.

By mid-December 2011, consumers were spending more for their holidays, although their incomes hadn't increased substantially and the job market remained soft. To make these purchases, consumers were dipping more into their savings and borrowing at a higher level that continued to grow.

See also MIDDLE CLASS; PART-TIME WORKERS; SAVINGS RATE; WEALTH.

SPERLING, GENE. Veteran policy maker moved in January 2011 from his post as a senior adviser to the Treasury secretary to direct the White House's National Economic Council.

SPRINT NEXTEL CORP. Announced the cutting of 8,000 jobs, with most to be completed by March 31, 2009, as it sought to reduce labor costs by $1.2 billion.

On October 29, 2009, the company reported that during its third quarter, it lost 801,000 customers, while 991,000 customers defected in the second quarter and 1.25 million customers left in the first quarter of the year. Sprint lost $478 million in the third quarter compared with $326 million one year earlier. Revenue fell by 9 percent to $8.04 billion. At the beginning of November, the company was eliminating up to 2,500 jobs, or 6 percent of its workforce, thereby cutting expenses by at least $350 million. The firm showed a 2010 increase in customers by adding 111,000 people in the second quarter for the first time in three years.

On July 28, 2011, management reported that its second-quarter net operating revenue rose to $8.31 billion from $8.03 billion. Sprint Nextel posted a wider quarterly fall in summer 2011, with a loss of $847 million, while revenue climbed 3.6 percent to $8.31 billion. On October 7, Sprint Nextel's stock was down almost 20 percent for the day to $2.41.

SPVS. *See* SPECIAL PURPOSE VEHICLES.

SPYKER CARS. *See* SAAB.

SRI LANKA. The nation's GDP growth in 2011 was expected to be 6.6 percent, with a GDP of $53 billion, an inflation rate of 6.7 percent, and a GDP per head at $2,580.

STABILITY OVERSIGHT COUNCIL. *See* WALL STREET REFORM ACT (2010).

STABILIZATION FUND. Under the final economic stimulus package, and designed to help states avoid budget cuts, it was increased to $53.6 billion from $44 billion.

See also AMERICAN RECOVERY AND REINVESTMENT ACT (OF 2009).

STAGFLATION. Stagnation in the economy accompanied by a rise in prices. Combining high inflation and high unemployment results in stagflation. Individual earning power evaporates and the standard of living declines.

Cf. DEFLATION; INFLATION; REFLATION.

STANDARD LIFE. Net profit for this insurer was $700 million in 2010; shares fell 7.3 percent in London.

STANDARD & POOR'S (S&P). A stock index and bond rating organization, it gave a rating action on more than 8,000 residential mortgage bonds and collateralized debt obligations on January 31, 2008. It forecast financial firms' losses would reach $265 billion. Standard & Poor's stock index had fallen at the end of November 2008 by 50 percent, lower than at any point since 1997. It had lost more than a third of its value in a calendar year only twice before, both times during the Great Depression of the 1930s. It fell 41.9 percent in 1931, and 38.6 percent in 1937. The worst postdepression year until now was 1974, when the index fell 29.7 percent amid the worst postwar recession the United States had yet seen.

In 2009, the public and government were questioning the objectivity and reliability of S&P and the other rating companies in making recommendations. For example, S&P failed to predict the bankruptcy of Iceland in 2008, a nation that had a very high rating up until it suddenly collapsed. On June 17, S&P cut the credit ratings and outlooks of twenty-two banks, most of them regional ones, and downgraded five of them to junk status. Between March 9, 2009, and September 9, 2009, S&P's 500 stock index rose 53 percent. By the end of the summer, the S&P 500 remained 35 percent below its 2007 high. Some critics believed that the firm and other rating agencies were part of the cause of the global financial crisis that led to the Great Recession. Another concern was that a credit agency rating can have, and has had, a distinct effect on a truly global scale, and that the decision on these ratings were made by the firms' workers, who were not elected by the public and therefore were not accountable for their decision-making process.

On August 5, 2011, S&P officials argued that the U.S. Treasury debt no longer deserved to be considered among the safest investments in the world. For the first time, S&P pulled the triple-A (AAA) rating that the United States held for seventy years, downgrading long-term U.S. debt to AA+, one notch below the ranking of more than a dozen nations. S&P in addition placed the new grade on "negative outlook," suggesting that the United States had little chance of regaining the top rating in the near term. Only hours before the announcement was made to the public, the U.S. Treasury noticed a $2 trillion error in S&P's calculations. S&P officials argued that the downgrade "reflects our opinions that the fiscal consolidation plan that Congress and the administration recently agreed to falls short of what, in our view, would be necessary to stabilize the government's medium-term debt dynamics." S&P left the U.S. short-term credit rating unchanged, the downgrade will not have a large impact on money market funds that own U.S. Treasury bills. In response to the S&P August 5 report, the Treasury Department's representative said, "In fact, S&P's $2 trillion mistake led to a very misleading picture of debt sustainability—the foundation for their initial judgment. This mistake undermined the economic justification for S&P's credit rating decision." On August 8, S&P downgraded the stock of both Fannie Mae and Freddie Mac from AAA to AA+. The company rates borrowers on a scale from AAA to D. Five insurers also were downgraded from AAA to AA+. The insurers believed that they were downgraded solely because of an S&P regulation that no insurer can have a higher rating than the sovereign debt of its home nation. On August 17, the U.S. Department of Justice announced its investigation of S&P for improperly rating dozens of mortgage securities preceding the 2008 meltdown. On August 23, it was announced that Devin Sharma, the president of S&P during the U.S. downgrade, would resign by the end of 2011. Douglas Peterson became president of the credit-rating firm in September.

The S&P 500 stock index fell on September 30, 2011, to its largest quarterly drop since 2008. It declined 14 percent for the quarter. Then, on November 29, S&P downgraded some of the world's largest financial institutions and lowered its long-term credit ratings by one notch on fifteen banks. On December 5, S&P put France, Germany, and thirteen other eurozone nations on review for credit downgrades, highlighting the concern about the currency bloc's inability to evolve a decisive fix for its debt problems, and suggesting at least a 50 percent chance of a downgrade within three months.

By the beginning of 2012, the S&P 500 stock index ended almost right where it started, finishing down 0.003 percent. "Wall Street Ends Back Where It Started," where the S&P 500 stock index closed out 2011 at 1,257.60, down from 1,257.64 in 2010. Then, on January 13, in a shock report, S&P downgraded nine eurozone nations on their sovereign debt. S&P stripped triple-A ratings from France and Austria and downgraded seven others, retaining the triple-A rating for Germany. S&P declared: "In our view, the policy initiatives taken by European policy makers in recent weeks may be insufficient to fully address ongoing systemic stresses in the eurozone." At this time, S&P's sovereign credit ratings of the seventeen eurozone nations were as follows:

AAA	Finland, Germany, Luxembourg, and the Netherlands
AA+	Austria, France
AA	Belgium
AA-	Estonia
A+	Slovenia
A	Slovakia, Spain
A	Malta
BBB+	Ireland, Italy
BB+	Cyprus
BB	Portugal
CC	Greece

On January 16, 2012, S&P downgraded its long-term credit rating of Europe's rescue fund to AA+ from AAA. For the month of January, S&P's 500 gained 4.4 percent, the best performance to open a year since 1997. On February 3, the broader S&P's 500 stock index rose 1.46 percent to 1,344.90, up 6.9 percent for the year, its best start since 1987. Stocks in the S&P 500 are trading at around thirteen times the forecast corporate-profit levels for 2012.

See also AAA RATING; AA+ RATING; BELGIUM; CREDIT-RATING AGENCIES; DEXIA SA; DOW JONES INDUSTRIAL AVERAGE;

ITALY; MUNICIPAL BONDS; RATINGS AGENCIES; STOCK BUY-BACKS; TOYOTA; TURKEY; U.S. DEPARTMENT OF THE TREA-SURY.

Cf. FITCH RATINGS; MOODY'S.

STANDARD & POOR'S 500 STOCK INDEX. *See* STANDARD & POOR'S.

STANFORD UNIVERSITY. Laid off 412 employees by summer 2009 and planned another 60 layoffs by the year's end, attempting to offset a significant fall in the value of its endowment, which was expected to fall 30 percent for the year. In addition, the university froze salaries and faculty hiring, eliminated unfilled positions, and suspended campus construction.

In addition, following the university's loss of one-quarter of its original endowment of $12.6 billion, the administration put on the block as much as $1 billion of hard-to-sell investments ranging from private equity to real estate as it sought cash.

Cf. HARVARD UNIVERSITY; PRINCETON UNIVERSITY; YALE UNIVERSITY.

STAPLES. The office supply retailer reported a 14 percent profit decline for its fiscal fourth quarter 2008.

Staples' fiscal second-quarter 2009 earnings fell 38 percent. For the quarter ending August 1, the firm posted a profit of $92.4 million, down from $150.2 million a year before. The management reported that its fiscal third-quarter 2009 earnings rose 72 percent from a year before. Profit climbed to $269.4 million from $156.7 million the year earlier.

Staples fiscal first-quarter 2010 earnings climbed 32 percent, with a profit of $188.8 million, up from $143 million; revenue increased 4 percent to $6.1 billion.

The firm's fiscal first-quarter 2011 earnings showed a profit of $198.2 million, with an increase in sales of 1.9 percent to $6.17 billion.

STARBUCKS. Posting a 69 percent drop in quarterly 2008 profit, the company announced in January 2009 that it would close another 300 stores and cut 6,700 workers.

After reporting a 77 percent decline in first-quarter 2009 profit, the company declared on April 29 that it would adjust its pricing in some markets and lower prices on basic drinks. Starbucks posted a small profit in its fiscal third quarter 2009. Net revenue fell 6.6 percent to $2.40 billion from $2.57 billion a year before. In November, Starbucks Corporation reported a profit in its fiscal fourth quarter, earning $150 million.

On March 24, 2010, the founder and chief executive announced a first-ever dividend after two years of humbling performance. The firm's second-quarter 2010 earnings climbed to $207.9 million and revenue increased to $2.61 billion from $2.4 billion. In early November, Starbucks reported an 86 percent profit as their worldwide same-store sales rebounded from a fall in their fourth straight quarter.

Starbucks' management reported that its fiscal third-quarter profit had climbed 34 percent in summer 2011. Earnings in the quarter were $279.1 million and net revenue climbed 12 percent to $2.93 billion. Starbucks' fiscal first-quarter earnings rose 10 percent. Sales rose about 9 percent internationally.

START-UPS. *See* VENTURE CAPITAL.

STARWOOD. Operating more than 900 properties in 100 countries, it posted a 46 percent drop in fourth-quarter 2009 net income amid anemic consumer demand, offering the first detailed look at the dimming prospects for the global hotel industry. Starwood's net income declined to $79 million from $146 million in the year-earlier quarter.

First-quarter 2009 profit tumbled 82 percent, with a net income of $6 million, down from $32 million a year earlier.

Starwood had a loss of $6 million in the third quarter 2010. For the fourth quarter, revenue increased more than 10 percent from the year before. The hotel chain posted quarterly earnings of $339 million versus a loss of $107 from 2009. Revenue increased 7.5 percent to $1.34 billion from $1.25 billion.

STATE AND LOCAL REVENUES. *See* STATES (U.S.)

STATE STREET. Profits for the bank's first quarter 2009 fell 10 percent on a loan-loss provision tied to mortgages from the previous quarter 2008. Net income fell from $530 million to $476 million.

STATE SUBSIDIES. *See* EUROPEAN COMMISSION.

STATES (U.S.). Twenty of the fifty American states cut their budgets for the 2009 fiscal year. Many are having trouble paying for health care for the poor or disabled. Forty-six states were bracing for budget shortfalls by the end of 2008. These states were running deficits, forcing governors to raise taxes and trim spending while postponing urgent repairs to roads, bridges, hospitals, and ports.

Jobless rates rose in nearly every state in January 2009, indicating that no region was immune to the recession. The February American Recovery and Reinvestment Act provided $150 billion in state relief.

State tax revenues fell by $5.4 billion compared with the same period in 2007, a decline of 3.6 percent, the steepest drop since the second quarter

2002. Of forty-seven states involved in a study, thirty-five reported declines. By March 2009, the decline in tax revenues was pushing state lawmakers to reconsider increasing taxes in a bid to close widening budget gaps. While many states had managed to cope with dwindling cash by reducing spending and raising fees, it was probably insufficient to cover the needs of the public. Sales tax revenues had declined more sharply than at any other time in fifty years, and income tax and sales tax increases were considered by more states. State sales tax revenues continued to fall into 2009. The decline in tax revenue had forced cities and towns to cut back local services. State and local taxes fell 6.1 percent in the fourth quarter 2008; revenue from personal income taxes was down 1.1 percent in the fourth quarter, and corporate income taxes fell 15.5 percent, reflecting weaker profits. In the first two months of 2009, the forty-one states that had reported tax revenues saw total receipts decline 12.8 percent versus the same time a year earlier.

In March, California and North Carolina posted their highest jobless rates in at least three decades. California's unemployment rate jumped to 11.2 percent, while North Carolina's rose to 10.8 percent, the highest since records of state joblessness began in 1976. Eight states posted double-digit unemployment rates in March, with the highest level being 12.6 percent in Michigan. In nineteen states, rates were higher than the national rate. In twenty states, unemployment grew faster than the national rate since the beginning of the recession. State tax collections continued to fall in the first quarter 2009. Forty-seven states reported that first-quarter revenues dropped by 12.6 percent, about $20 billion, compared with the first three months of 2008. The steepest drops were in income taxes. Corporate income taxes declined 16.2 percent, personal income taxes fell 15.8 percent, and sales taxes were down 7.6 percent. Forty-five of the forty-seven reporting states saw revenues decline. By summer's end 2009, many states began to "shut down" to preserve cash with furloughs, leaves, and other means to save money. States with the highest budget gaps of more than $4 billion and their cost-cutting measures include the following:

California—$45.5 billion: Layoffs (some 210,000 state workers were affected by furloughs the first three Fridays of each month through June 2010)
New York—$20 billion: Layoffs
Illinois—$13.2 billion: Layoffs
New Jersey—$8.8 billion: Furloughs (the enacted budget requires ten unpaid furlough days for state workers)
Florida—$5.9 billion
Massachusetts—$5.0 billion

Pennsylvania—$4.8 billion: Layoffs
North Carolina—$4.6 billion: Layoffs
Connecticut—$4.2 billion
Oregon—$4.2 billion: Layoffs
Georgia—$4.1 billion: Furloughs
Arizona—$4.0 billion: Layoffs and furloughs (the state has implemented
  employee furloughs of one or two days per month, depending on salary)

By mid-September 2009, California's jobless rate reached a seventy-year
high of 12.2 percent (it was 14.7 percent in 1940). While the average in the
nation was 9.7 percent, other states with higher unemployment than California's were Michigan (13.2 percent) and Rhode Island (12.8 percent).

In fourteen states and the District of Columbia, at least a tenth of the
workforce was unemployed in August 2009. State tax revenues in the second
quarter 2009 fell 17 percent from a year earlier, the sharpest decline since at
least the 1960s. The largest fall was in state income taxes, down 28 percent
from a year before. Sales tax revenues fell 9 percent. About two-thirds of
state revenues came from sales and income taxes. By November 2009, states
had filled 30 to 40 percent of their budget gaps with federal stimulus money,
receiving about $250 billion of the $787 billion stimulus package, most
disbursed by the end of 2010. States still faced a combined deficit of $142
billion for 2011, up from $113 billion for 2009. By the third quarter 2009,
tax collection fell 11 percent across forty-four states, resulting in increasingly
low government revenues. All forms of tax revenue from sales and corporate
and personal income taxes declined. The largest fall was in corporate income
taxes, down 19.4 percent. Personalized income taxes fell 11.4 percent, while
sales taxes fell another 8.2 percent. Approximately 80 percent of states' total
tax collection came from state and personal income taxes.

On December 16, 2009, the House of Representatives passed a separate
$154 billion package that included $23 billion for states to pay teachers'
salaries. New reports at year's end 2009 indicated a third-quarter 7 percent
decline in state and local tax revenues. Sales taxes were down 9 percent to
$70 billion in the third quarter 2009 compared to the year before. Income
taxes fell 12 percent to about $58 billion. Together, sales and income taxes
made up roughly half of state and local tax revenue. Twenty-two states saw
third-quarter revenues fall more than 10 percent.

Then, by mid-April 2010, thirty-three states recorded sizable gains in
employment. Since August 2008, state and local governments had cut more
than 230,000 jobs, or about 1.2 percent of their payrolls. Collection of sales
and personal income and corporate taxes, which make up 80 percent of state
revenue, fell 12 percent since the recession began to $477.4 billion in 2010

from $541.4 billion in 2008. States were expected to face $127 billion in budget gaps between 2010 and 2012. States had added $23.9 billion in taxes and fees in 2010, with recommendations to raise taxes by $3.1 billion for 2011.

Briefly, the beginning of a turnaround was evident in July 2010. Tax increases boosted state governments to a year-over-year rise in collections in the first quarter 2010 for the first time since the beginning of the meltdown. State tax revenue increased 2.5 percent to $164.5 billion in the first quarter. The gain was led off by a 2.5 percent rise in personal income taxes and a 0.4 percent climb in sales taxes. U.S. states (and local governments) employed more workers—19.5 million—than manufacturing and construction together, with more than $3 trillion in retirement benefits. By the end of September, tax revenues to states and local government rose 1.7 percent to $318.2 billion (in 2005, tax collections rose 14 percent) in the second quarter. However, corporate income taxes, making up a small share of state tax collections, plunged 18.3 percent in the second quarter to $15.2 billion. By fall 2010, strapped states (and cities) found investors shifting away from the municipal bond market, as they demanded higher interest rates to buy paper from the government.

In addition, many state governments had borrowed heavily from the U.S. government to keep paying unemployment-insurance benefits, and states were raising tax payments to pay off the loans. For example, thirty-one states, their unemployment-insurance funds empty, had borrowed nearly $41 billion from the U.S. government.

There are about 90,000 local governments in the United States, mainly cities, counties, and school and utilities districts. Along with the fifty state governments, they account for 15 percent of total employment in the nation. Since local and state governments cannot legally run deficits, it is projected that up to half a million jobs will be lost in this group over the coming years.

By year's end 2010, state and local revenues continued to recover, with tax revenues increasing 5.2 percent to $284.3 billion in the third quarter 2010 from the year before. This was considerable compared to 2009 when tax revenues dropped 5.4 percent from the year before. In the fourth quarter 2010, state tax revenues grew at the fasted rate in almost five years. Collections increased 6.9 percent in forty-one states, with income tax receipts rising 10.7 percent. Fourth-quarter revenues were, however, from 0.8 percent below their level from three years earlier. Total spending of all state budgets for fiscal 2011, which began for most states on July 1, climbed 5.3 percent to $645.1 billion from the previous year. State tax collections looked better in the second half of 2010. State tax revenues in forty-eight states grew 3.9 percent in the third quarter 2010 compared to the year before.

In February 2011, the president offered in his 2012 budget to rescue states that had borrowed billions of dollars from the federal government to continue paying unemployment benefits. He proposed giving the states a two-year breather before automatic tax increases would hit employers and prior to states having to begin paying interest on the loans. If passed, it would have forced many states to raise their unemployment taxes in years ahead.

By 2011, states and cities facing huge surges in health benefits for millions of their government employees, some as much as 20 percent each year, began considering ways to lower their costs. Longer years of service and greater contributions were among the suggestions made. Sixty-eight percent of city and country officials want their retirees to assume more of their health costs, and 39 percent said they had already or plan to eliminate retiree health benefits for new hires. As private employment grew in February 2011, states and other localities lost a combined 30,000 jobs after cutting 8,000 positions in January. As spring arrived, state tax revenues were up, nearing the peak of several years before. However, to weather the Great Recession, states relied on the now-depleted federal stimulus funds, allowing them to avoid layoffs and cutbacks. Total tax receipts for state and local governments hit $1.29 trillion in 2010, just 2.3 percent less than the $1.32 trillion of 2008, not adjusted for inflation. For 2010, tax hikes boosted state revenue by $12.3 billion, or about 2 percent.

State tax collections increased by 9.1 percent in the first three months of 2011 for forty-seven states. State tax revenue nevertheless remained 3.1 percent below the 2008 level. In June, the jobless rate surged in twenty-eight states, with California, Florida, and Nevada the worst affected by the recession and unemployment well over 10 percent. By month's end in September, twenty-seven states collectively owed almost $38 billion. For example, California owed the government on loans for unemployment benefits more than $303.5 million; Michigan owed $106 million, and Pennsylvania $104.6 million. By December 2011, following four years of recession, states were "crawling" free of their financial burdens. In the third quarter 2011, states witnessed their overall tax revenue increase 5.6 percent from the year earlier. Unemployment rates fell in forty-three states and D.C. in November to 8.6 percent.

The Center on Budget and Policy Priorities showed that practically all U.S. states will spend less on vital services in 2012 than they did in 2008; at the same time, there are more children enrolled in public school and more poor people on Medicaid. State budgets for 2012 were to climb 2.9 percent to $666.6 billion, still below the $687.3 billion states spent in 2008, a peak year. States' fiscal 2012 budgets have $584.1 million less in taxes and fees. For 2012, state spending on higher education is expected to drop by $3.2 billion. Meanwhile, state tax revenue slowed its rate of growth. In the 2012 fiscal year, states will no longer have the approximately $150 billion in stimulus funds from the past two years. Job cuts were 14,000 in December 2011 compared with 24,000 in December 2010.

See also AMERICAN RECOVERY AND REINVESTMENT ACT (OF 2009); DEATH TAXES; GAMBLING; HYBRID PENSIONS; INTEREST-RATE BETS; MEDICAID; MUNICIPAL BONDS; NAMING RIGHTS; PENSIONS; PRISON; RETIREMENT; ROLLING BROWNOUTS; UN-EMPLOYMENT.

Cf. CITIES.

STEEL. Steel prices in the United States tumbled in June 2010, and mills reduced their production output. In May 2008, the peak of steel production was 121.1 million tons around the world. Its rapid decline during the Great Recession in December 2008 was 81.7 million tons.

In 2009, China produced 568 million metric tons, 16.5 times the 1979 level. By year's end 2010, China accounted for 45 percent of the global output of steel.

With rising sales of cars, farm gear, and oil-drilling equipment, steelmakers were lifting their prices and output by the end of 2011.

See also ARCELORMITTAL; CHINA; PROPERTY (2011); US STEEL.

STEEL, ROBERT K. Former president and chief executive of Wachovia who became deputy mayor for economic development in New York City.

STEERING. *See* MORTGAGE LEGISLATION.

STERLING. *See* POUND (BRITISH).

STEVENS, DAVID. Commissioner of the Federal Housing Administration announced that he would be stepping down from his position by the end of April 2011.

STIMULUS PLAN. By July 2009, the loss of an additional 467,000 jobs for the month indicated that the meltdown continued to have a significant impact on the economy as a whole. Average hours worked per week fell to thirty-three, the lowest level in at least forty years. Because people worked less, wages declined by 0.3 percent for the first half of 2009. Factories operated at only 65 percent capacity, while the overall jobless rate hit 9.5 percent. Including discouraged workers who wanted full-time work, the labor under-utilization rate climbed to 16.5 percent.

Most U.S. citizens saved their 2008 stimulus checks, and a mere one-third of consumers spent them. Most of the $96 billion that was put aside for one-time stimulus payments designed to encourage consumer spending was not used to purchase goods or services.

See also AMERICAN RECOVERY AND REINVESTMENT ACT; OVERTIME.

STIMULUS PLAN (EUROZONE). By early December 2008, a variety of substantial stimulus plans had been introduced by several European governments. In Spain, €11 billion, €31 billion in Poland, €80 billion in Italy, €32 billion in Germany, €20 billion in Britain, and €20 billion in France.

See also BAILOUT PLAN; EUROPEAN COMMISSION; EUROZONE.

STIMULUS SPENDING (G-20). *See* G-20; LENDING.

STOCK BROKERS. In April 2009, more than 2,800 people registered as brokers left the securities industry. The total number of departures from January to the end of April stood at 11,600; the loss of about 35 percent of brokers had occurred by the end of 2009.

STOCK BUYBACKS. Tumbled 66 percent in the fourth quarter 2008 from a year earlier on the benchmark S&P 500 stock index. Buybacks fell 42 percent in all of 2008 from the record $589.1 billion index members spent on buybacks in 2007.

On March 17, 2011, the Federal Reserve approved the largest six banks to raise their dividends of $8.7 billion in 2011 and buy back stock. Potential 2011 dividends of more than $12 billion paid by just ten banks would dwarf the $4.5 billion in profits the entire industry listed in 2008.

STOCK MARKET CRASH. *See* GREAT DEPRESSION; PECORA COMMISSION.

STOCK MARKET (DOW JONES). On January 18, 2008, the Dow Jones Industrial Average declined 306.95 points, or 2.5 percent, to 12,159.21 on fears of more damage from the subprime mortgage crisis. On November 4, 2008, the United States recorded its biggest election-day gain in twenty-four years. The Dow Jones Industrial Average and the NASDAQ indices both closed more than 3 percent higher. Nevertheless, the 2008 fall in the marketplace was so steep that it erased all the gains made in the rally from 2003 to 2007. Meanwhile, $30 trillion of global stock market value was wiped out in 2008. The Dow Jones Industrial Average ended 2008 at 8,776.39, down 4,488.43 points, or 33.8 percent from its high, the weakest year since 1931. Stocks lost 42 percent of their value in 2008, erasing more than $29 trillion in value and all of the gains made since 2003. The year 2008 was the stock market's third-worst year in more than a century. The only two Dow stocks to rise in 2008 were Wal-Mart Stores, with an 18 percent gain, and McDonald's, up nearly 6 percent.

On February 10, 2009, the day Treasury Secretary Geithner announced his bank rescue plan, the Dow dropped nearly 400 points, the worst performance since President Obama took office. Two weeks later, the stock market dropped to 50 percent of its peak, which was achieved only sixteen months prior. It lost 3.4 percent that day. Then, on March 2, the Dow dropped 4.2 percent to 6,763.29, its lowest close since April 1997. It had lost almost one-quarter of its value in 2009 and more than half since its high in October 2007.

By mid-March, the share prices for some prime companies had sunk to or near the level of penny stocks. For example, AIG was $0.35, Citigroup was $1.02, General Motors was $1.86, Bank of America was $3.17, and General Electric was $6.66. On March 23, the day the Treasury secretary announced plans for a public-private program to purchase up to $1 trillion in toxic assets and securities, the stock market soared 6.8 percent, or 497.48 points, to 7,775.86 in its biggest gain since October 2008. Also, bank stocks jumped sharply in the hope that the plan would rid them of much of the soured debt and securities weighing on their balance sheets.

Throughout June, the stock market kept rising based on hopes of a rapid economic recovery. By mid-month, resurgent fears about a longer downturn and an anemic recovery had a severe impact on financial markets. A World Bank report indicated that recovery would be the slowest since World War II. The World Bank predicted a 2.9 percent decline until 2010, as the world was "entering an era of slower growth." On June 22, the Dow lost 200.72 points, or 2.35 percent, to close at 8,339.01. By June 30, the stock market completed its best quarter in years, with a gain of 35 percent. Nevertheless, it was still a long way from the 14,000 mark it was at before the economic recession.

Fear that rising unemployment would prolong the recession sent stocks tumbling on July 2, pushing the broad market into the red again for the year. Then, on July 7, following a three-month rise, the Dow fell 161.27 points, or 1.94 percent, to its lowest close since April 28, 2009. Part of this fall was based on concerns about second-quarter corporate losses or gains about to be reported. The stock market completed its best six months since 1933 on September 1, 2009, and ended the year with a comeback of historic proportions. By September 2010, it was clear that investors had turned their backs on the stock market. Investors withdrew a staggering $33.12 billion from domestic stock market mutual funds in the first seven months of the year. As that rate continued, more money would be pulled out of these funds in 2010 than in any year since the 1980s. Investors withdrew $19.1 billion from domestic equity funds in May 2010, the largest outflow since October 2008. This followed the withdrawal of $151.4 billion from stock market funds for the year 2008. Even though the stock market rose 7 percent in July, the trend continued into the summer. By the end of summer 2010, worldwide, the number of stock offering was down 15 percent from the same period in 2009, with expectations that the annual revenue would fall from $56 billion in 2009 to around $42 billion in 2010, for a drop of 25 percent.

As the Great Recession officially ended, corporate pension plan managers were reducing their involvement with the stock market. Searching for less-risky bets, investors had lowered their stock exposure to 45 percent, while in the booming 1990s, almost 70 percent of their funds were in the stock market. Pension managers concluded that loading up on stocks in search of high returns was inappropriate and not as profitable as once thought. The shift to bonds had replaced a large part of the turning away from stocks. The stock market performed extremely well in the fourth quarter 2010. Stocks remain attractive due to other asset classes given cash-rich balance sheets, strong earnings, and global growth. Cash returned to the stock market in fall 2010. Investors placed $28 billion into equity funds and pulled $6 billion from bonds in November.

By the start of 2011, the Dow Jones Industrial Average had gained 93.24 points, or 0.8 percent, to close at 11,670.75, a twenty-eight-month high. The U.S. stock market closed out 2011 with an average 7.9 billion shares traded per day, about 6 percent below 2010's daily average of 8.5 billion, which was lower than 2009 levels.

See also BAILOUT RESCUE PLAN (2009); DOW JONES INDUSTRIAL AVERAGE; LIBOR; NASDAQ COMPOSITE INDEX; PUBLIC-PRIVATE INVESTMENT PROGRAM; UNEMPLOYMENT; WINDOW DRESSING; WORLD BANK.

STOCKS. *See* DOW JONES INDUSTRIAL AVERAGE.

STOCK VALUE (WORLDWIDE). *See* DOW JONES INDUSTRIAL AVERAGE.

STRATEGIC DEFAULT. The third wave of the foreclosure crisis in which borrowers, even those with stable jobs, began to see negative equity as a reason to cease making their payments.
See also FORECLOSURE.

STRAUMUR-BURDARAS INVESTMENT BANK. *See* ICELAND.

STRESS TESTS (EUROPEAN UNION). European Union governments agreed on June 17, 2010, to submit their banks to public tests of their soundness. Following pressure from the United States; the EU used stress tests to shore up global confidence in the Continent's financial soundness. These tests were modeled on the May 2009 U.S. stress tests of nineteen top U.S. banks. On July 23, 2010, European regulators provided the results of their stress tests on ninety-one banks in twenty countries and indicated that they could possibly face $730 billion in losses in a deteriorating economy. Only seven failed the tests with a short-fall in capital requirements. Bankers claimed the results indicated the stability of their institutions, while critics argued that the tests were not sufficiently tough. They had to raise their capital by $4.5 billion. Five of the troubled lenders were Spanish, one was Greek, and one was German.

In mid-July 2011, the European Banking Authority presented results of their banking stress tests. The authority reported that eight of the ninety-one banks it examined fell short of the needed amount of capital under the tests' simulations of a deep, two-year economic downturn. Five were from Spain, two were from Greece, and one was from Austria.

See also EUROPEAN BANKING AUTHORITY; STRESS TESTS (U.S.); TIER 1.

STRESS TESTS (U.S.). As part of the new bailout plan announced on February 10, 2009, many U.S. banks would be subject to rigorous examinations to see if they were sufficiently healthy to lend to before receiving further financial aid. The secretary of the Treasury used this approach to determine if the big banks were adequately capitalized; if not, new funds may or may not be provided.

The stress test would use computer-run "what if" situations to estimate what would happen to each bank under depression-like conditions—unemployment surging to 10 to 12 percent, for example, or home prices dropping by 27 percent over two years. The nineteen largest banks (those with more than $100 billion in assets) were asked to undergo the stress test to make certain that they would remain adequately capitalized even if the economic recession became substantially worse than expected. Under the rules of the stress test, a bank that could not cover a projected shortfall by raising funds from private investors would have to accept it from the government. In exchange, the government would take a potentially large ownership stake. On May 6, 2009, the Federal Reserve directed at least seven of the nation's largest banks to reinforce their capital levels by $65 billion. Six others were found to be stable.

Stress tests were being applied under the Capital Assistance Program and began on February 25, 2010. On April 24, regulators began briefing banks about how they fared in their stress tests before the results were to be made public on May 7. While the April 24 announcement of the condition of the nineteen largest banks appeared to present a strong picture, regional banks were preparing for huge losses. They were among the hardest hit by the housing collapse and remained saddled with piles of commercial real estate and corporate loans expected to sour throughout 2009. The Bank of America and Citigroup were informed by regulators on April 27 that they would probably have to raise more capital based on early results of the stress test. The stress tests revealed that many of the nineteen banks studied would need more money. The banks were expected to plug some of the shortfalls by selling assets or raising new funds from investors. But, the banks were also able to use bailout money that they had already received by converting some of the government's preferred stock into common stock, increasing the government's stake but diluting existing shareholders' stake. The Federal Reserve on November 17, 2010, issued a demand that the nineteen largest bank holding firms had to submit capital plans by early 2011 showing their ability to withstand losses under a set of conditions set by the central bank. These banks were the same as those who underwent stress tests in early 2009.

Regulators announced in November 2011 that they would publish full results in 2012 of a new, more sophisticated stress test of the thirty-one largest U.S. banks compared with nineteen tested in early 2011. The six largest banks would be asked to gauge losses from a "hypothetical global market shock."

See also CITIGROUP; EUROPEAN UNION; FEDERAL RESERVE; LEMON SOCIALISM; PUBLIC-PRIVATE INVESTMENT FUND; STRESS TESTS (EUROPEAN UNION); "TOO BIG TO FAIL."

STRUCTURED BANKRUPTCY. A procedure in which a government convenes creditors, unions, shareholders, and the firm's management and assigns a share of the hit to each of them.

STRUCTURED INVESTMENT VEHICLE. Leveraged special-purpose vehicle funded through medium-term notes and asset-backed commercial paper that invested in highly rated securities.

STUB QUOTES. *See* SECURITIES AND EXCHANGE COMMISSION.

STUDENT LOANS. President Obama's proposed 2010 fiscal budget included making the government the sole provider of federal student loans, ending the participation of private lenders in the program. Private lenders would be eliminated, and the government would use the savings, estimated at $47.5 billion over the coming ten years, to help bolster the Pell Grant program for low-income students.

By mid-April 2009, defaults on student loans were rapidly climbing. Default rates for federally guaranteed student loans reached 6.9 percent for fiscal year 2007. That was up from 4.6 percent two years earlier and was the highest rate since 1998.

By September 2010, the overall student loan default rate for 2008 was 7 percent, up from 6.7 percent the year before and 5.2 percent in the 2006 fiscal year. The default rate at public institutions increased to 6 percent from 5.9 percent. Schools with default rates of 25 percent or more for three consecutive years, or a default rate higher than 40 percent in a single year, lost their eligibility for the federal student aid that provided most of the revenues for for-profit colleges.

By September 30, 2010, 8.8 percent of federal student loans had dropped into default, up from 7 percent in fiscal 2008. Default rates in 2011 rose sharply.

See also BUDGET (U.S.) (FISCAL YEAR 2010); PELL GRANTS.

SUBARU. Subaru's U.S. sales were higher in 2008, making the Japanese firm the only major automaker with a yearly sales increase. Sales rose by 0.3 percent to 187,699 vehicles from 187,208 in 2007. The company announced on December 26, 2008, that it would reduce output by a further 10,000 vehicles in the business year ending in 2009, bringing the total reduction to 70,000. In addition, it shed 300 temporary jobs.

See also AUTOMOBILE INDUSTRY.

SUBPRIME. The designation of a loan typically having relatively unfavorable terms and made to a borrower who does not qualify for other loans because of a poor credit history.

The mortgage-delinquency rate among subprime borrowers reached 25 percent in the first quarter 2009, with the pace of delinquencies accelerating. Since prime loans account for 80 percent of U.S. bank exposure to mortgages and credit cards, these losses may ultimately exceed those from weaker borrowers.

See also BEAR STEARNS; EMERGENCY ECONOMIC STABILIZATION ACT OF 2008; FINANCIAL CRISIS INQUIRY REPORT; GOLDMAN SACHS; STOCK MARKET; WALL STREET REFORM ACT (2010).

SUBPRIME LENDING. *See* FINANCIAL CRISIS INQUIRY REPORT.

SUBPRIME MORTGAGE. *See* BANK OF AMERICA; CREDIT UNIONS; EMERGENCY ECONOMIC STABILIZATION ACT OF 2008; FEDERAL HOUSING FINANCE AGENCY; GOLDMAN SACHS; OPTION ADJUSTABLE-RATE MORTGAGES; RATERS.

SUBSIDIES. The bankruptcy of both Chrysler and General Motors has had an impact on the idea of subsidies, usually from governments. U.S. trade experts claim that the country could be accused by foreign nations of unfairly subsidizing manufacturing and production.

By 2011, many emerging nations took on their fight against inflation in an attempt to protect consumers by expanding subsidies and imposing price controls. Subsidies could include gasoline, cooking fuels, and tax rebates and cash grants for medium-sized firms.

See also AUTOMOBILE INDUSTRY; CHRYSLER; EUROPEAN COMMISSION; GENERAL MOTORS; INFLATION; UNFAIR TRADE SUBSIDIES; WALL STREET REFORM ACT (2010).

SUBURBAN POVERTY. *See* DOWNTOWN; POVERTY.

SUICIDES. Throughout the Great Recession, the number of U.S. suicides increased. Data from nineteen states indicated a total of 15,335 suicides in 2008, up about 2.3 percent from a year earlier. Traditionally, 90 percent of those committing suicide had issues beyond unemployment, job failure, or economic downturns. The suicide rate in 2007, prior to the meltdown, was 10.8 per 100,000 citizens.

See also GREECE; JAPAN.

SUMMERS, LAWRENCE. President Obama's senior economic adviser. He was director of the White House's National Economic Council. At Harvard University, he remains the Charles W. Eliot University Professor. As Treasury secretary in 2000, he championed the law that deregulated derivates, the financial instruments that had spread the financial losses from reckless lending around the globe.

Summers was on the staff of the Council of Economic Advisers from 1982 to 1986. In 1991, he left Harvard University and served as chief economist for the World Bank until 1993. He left the Treasury Department in 2001 and returned to Harvard University as its twenty-seventh president, serving from July 2001 until June 2006. Summers backed the law in 1999 that removed barriers between commercial and investment banks, and continued to back it despite recent criticism.

On September 21, 2010, the White House announced that Summers would be stepping down as head of the National Economic Council and returning to Harvard University at the end of the year.

SUMMIT OF NOVEMBER 4, 2008. The November 4 session of the twenty-seven European Union finance ministers was one of two gatherings to prepare a common European position for the G-20 summit meeting, described as a new Bretton Woods. The governments watered down a French call for speedy international agreement on a range of specific measures regarding the credit crisis, lowering expectations for the summit meeting. By convening the G-20 rather than the closed rich club of G-7, the old order had in effect acknowledged that the rest of the world had become too important to bar them from participation.

See also BRETTON WOODS II; EUROPEAN UNION; FRANCE; G-20.

SUN CAPITAL PARTNERS. See FRIENDLY'S ICE CREAM CORPORATION.

SUNSTEIN, CASS. See OFFICE OF INFORMATION AND REGULATORY AFFAIRS.

SUN-TIMES. The Chicago newspaper filed for Chapter 11 bankruptcy on April 1, 2009.

SUPER COMMITTEE. Set up by Congress in August 2011 to recommend at least $1.5 trillion of additional deficit reduction measures.

See also DEBT DEAL; DEFICIT-REDUCTION COMMITTEE.

SUPER-REGULATOR. *See* DODD, CHRISTOPHER J.

SUPER-RICH. *See* WEALTH.

SUSTAINABLE JOBS. The *Wall Street Journal*'s 2010 CEO Council recommendations included the following:

1. *Promote Rules-Based Trading*—Aggressively promote a global marketplace that benefits U.S. businesses and consumers. Emphasize free-trade agreements, equalize corporate taxes, and launch a joint public-private effort to promote trade. Remain open to imports that provide lower-priced goods to U.S. consumers, fueling job-creating spending.
2. *Overhaul Tax Policy*—Promote a territorial tax system; allow expensing of capital equipment and software; change the capital-gains tax (reduce it to zero over four years) so it applies to everyone, including nonprofits.
3. *Revise Immigration Laws*—Liberalize visa and quota allowances in the United States to attract and keep the best and brightest from the rest of the world.
4. *Invest in Infrastructure*—Create programs marrying public money with private capital to fund economically important infrastructure projects, particularly in energy policy. Leading examples: smart grid and alternative energy.
5. *Improve Financing*—Adopt policies more debt and equity capital to small businesses (could be public, private, or job effort). Create a more effective venture/microfinance market for new businesses with appropriate regulation based on company structure.

See also CEO COUNCIL.

SUZUKI. *See* VOLKSWAGEN.

SWAP. The simultaneous purchase and sale of a currency for different maturity dates that closes the gaps in the maturity structure of assets and liabilities in a currency.
See also BORN, BROOKLSEY; FOREIGN CURRENCY LIQUIDITY SWAPS.

SWAP AGREEMENTS. *See* FUTURES TRADING PRACTICES ACT OF 1992.

SWAP CONTRACT. A derivative contract that involves exchanging cash-flow streams.
See also BORN, BROOKSLEY.

SWAP FUND. A fund into which many investors put their own investments and receive a share in the pooled investment portfolio. The purpose of this exchange of investments is to obtain a diversified portfolio without selling stock and paying capital gains.

SWAP RATE. The loss rate for exchanging units of currencies at a future date.

SWATCH GROUP. Sales fell 6 percent in the second half of 2008.

By 2011, Swiss watch exporters had returned to profitability. Exports climbed nearly 15 percent.

SWEDEN. The Swedish economy has experienced a deep contraction triggered by the global economic crisis. A gradual recovery has started, but economic slack is very large and unemployment will remain high for some time. Consumer and business confidence have been improving over the past six months and retail sales have picked up. Financial market conditions have also improved, with spreads on interbank and mortgage rates reverting toward more normal levels. Lending to households has started to accelerate, although lending to firms is still slowing. The monetary policy stance is very simulative and ought to remain so for the time being. Both automatic and discretionary fiscal response will continue to support demand, as will the recent measures to limit long-term unemployment. As the recovery firms up, however, fiscal consolidation efforts will be needed to reach the medium-term budget surplus target.

The Swedish government took over the struggling investment bank Carnegie on November 10, 2008, following a series of actions that drained the bank of liquidity and prompted regulators to revoke its license. The takeover was the government's first nationalization of a major bank since the financial crisis in the early 1990s. The national debt office would own Carnegie after it extended the bank loans of up to 5 billion kronor, or $645 million, to replace loans that the central bank had previously provided to keep the bank liquid. On December 4, the Swedish central bank reduced its key-lending rate by 1.75 percentage points to 2 percent. The government introduced stimulus measures worth the equivalent of $1 billion in December. On December 11, the government said it would provide credit guarantees and emergency loans to its ailing automobile industry, but it had no plans to buy stakes in Volvo or Saab. The government said it would provide up to $2.5 billion in collateral-backed credit guarantees directed toward the manufacture of more environmentally friendly vehicles, as well as rescue loans of up to approximately $600 million.

Its benchmark interest rate dropped from 2 percent to 1 percent on February 11, 2009. Sweden's economy was expected to shrink by 1.6 percent in

2009. In 2009, Sweden's economy faltered, but by 2010 it bounced back strongly. GDP was expected to grow faster than in any other Western nations in the Organisation for Economic Co-operation and Development, with a budget surplus in 2011.

In 2011, Sweden's economy grew by 2.2 percent, above the European Union average but lower than the 3.1 percent in 2010. The nation's GDP growth was 2.2 percent, with a GDP of $449 billion, an inflation rate of 2.0 percent, and a GDP per head of $47,300. The central bank raised its key policy rate by a quarter of a percentage point to 2 percent on July 5. In the first quarter 2011, the nation's annual growth rate was about 6.4 percent, unemployment was rapidly falling, the budget had a surplus, and public debt was nearing less than 40 percent of GDP. By year's end, with its tight fiscal policy, it possessed a budget surplus of 0.1 percent of GDP and a shrinking public debt. In 2010, GDP expanded by 5.7 percent, and in 2011 it would grow by 4.4 percent, with projections in 2012 for a fall below 1 percent.

See also AUTOLIV; "BAD BANKS"; ELECTROLUX; GENERAL MOTORS; SAAB; SKF; VOLVO.

SWIPE FEES. *See* CREDIT CARDS.

SWISS FRANC. By the end of 2010, the currency of Switzerland reported record strength against the eurozone currency and British pound. The nation's $173 billion export sector may ultimately bear the brunt of the stronger franc. The strength of the Swiss franc pushed the government and private economists to cut the 2011 growth estimates to 1.5 percent from 2 percent.

The nation's Swiss franc remained strong against the U.S. dollar and the euro and would have a negative impact on economic growth. The franc rose 17 percent against the dollar since June 2010 and about 16 percent against the euro since August 2009. By early August 2011, the Swiss franc was up 52 percent against the euro from its low in 2007 and up 69 percent against the U.S. dollar from its low in 2005.

See also DOLLAR (U.S.); EXCHANGE RATES; SWITZERLAND.

SWISS RE. The world's second-largest reinsurer stated in early April 2009 that it would cut 10 percent of its global staff over the coming months.

SWITZERLAND. Positive growth is projected to resume from the end of 2009 onward, driven by growing demand from trading partners and improving activity in financial markets. Unemployment may rise to about 5 percent, while inflation is projected to be low but positive. Leading business cycle indicators have improved markedly in recent months, turning positive from low levels in the second quarter 2009. Orders in manufacturing have risen to a level indicating expansion in the fourth quarter. Growth is expected to pick up in 2011, reaching 2.1 percent at the end of the year. Once the recovery takes hold, monetary policy stimulus will need to be withdrawn, but care will need to be taken to avoid deflation risk. While fiscal stimulus should be maintained in 2010, spending reductions need to be identified from 2011 onward to adhere to budgetary rules.

On November 12, 2008, the government announced a stimulus plan of up to 1.55 billion francs, or $1.31 billion, to help the Swiss economy as the global outlook worsened. The government released about 550 million francs from a fund for small and midsize firms. In addition, an additional 1 billion francs were tapped from the federal budget to revive the stalling economy. It was clear to Switzerland's government that tourism would decline over the next two years. Overnight stays were expected to drop 3 percent the first year and 1.4 percent the following year. Ski-lift operators braced for a 6.3 percent decline in 2008 after an 18 percent increase in 2007. On Thursday, November 20, the Swiss central bank lowered its benchmark interest rate by a percentage point after the economic outlook worsened. It reduced its target for the three-month LIBOR to 1 percent and promised a "generous and flexible" supply of Swiss francs. By December 1, the Swiss market index lost 31 percent of its value. UBS, the flagship Swiss bank, amassed the biggest losses in Europe in the credit crunch, forcing the government and central bank to offer $59 billion in support. UBS shares fell 67 percent in 2008.

The Swiss economy shrank 0.2 percent in 2009 after expanding 1.9 percent in 2008. Manufacturing contracted in November, the most since at least 1995. The Swiss National Bank cut its benchmark interest rate in half to 0.5 percent on December 11, citing the worsening situation in financial markets and a deterioration of the global economy. The decision was the fourth cut by Switzerland since October.

UBS, the world's biggest manager of money for the wealthy, and the country's largest bank, had eliminated 9,000 positions companywide, or 11 percent of its workforce. Then, in early February 2009, UBS announced more staffing cuts at its investment-banking operation, cutting more than 2,000 jobs as it reported the largest annual loss ever by a Swiss firm. On March 12, 2010, the Swiss National Bank announced steps for fighting deflation by lowering interest rates and intervening to weaken the Swiss franc as it forecast a deep recession.

Inflation softened for the third consecutive month, falling by a tenth of a percentage point to 0.4 percent in July 2010. In August 2010, the Swiss National Bank revealed that the central bank reported a loss for the first half of 2010 of about $3.8 billion to check the rise of the Swiss franc against the weakening euro. The bank's foreign currency reserved mushroomed to 232 billion francs in June 2010 from less than 50 billion francs in early 2009. On

September 2, 2010, the nation's GDP accelerated in the second quarter to hit its highest rate in 2.5 years. The economy expanded 0.9 percent from the earlier quarter and 3.4 percent from the comparable period in 2009. The nation reached its strongest level of growth since the fourth quarter 2007, when the yearly rate stood at 3.9 percent.

By mid-summer 2011, the government attempted to rein in the ultrastrong Swiss franc. Banks in Switzerland sought to pull down the soaring Swiss franc, in part by raising banks' most readily available deposits. This was an attempt to flood the market with liquidity. On August 31, the government lowered its economic stimulus package by more than half. Instead of providing nearly $2.44 billion in funding, it would pay out about 870 million francs in a first installment.

GDP growth rate fell to 2.3 percent in the year to the second quarter from 2.5 percent in the year to the first. The central bank announced on September 6 that it would try to stall the flood of capital entering the country by capping the surging Swiss franc. The Swiss National Bank would buy euros in "unlimited quantities" whenever the single currency fell below 1.20 francs. The Swiss National Bank successfully weakened the Swiss franc and the currency fell 9.3 percent against the euro.

See also SWATCH GROUP; SWISS FRANC; TAX HAVENS; UBS.

SYMS CORPORATION. *See* FILENE'S BASEMENT.

SYNTHETIC CDO. A collateralized debt obligation that holds credit default swaps that reference assets (rather than holding cash assets), allowing investors to make bets for or against those referenced assets.

See also FINANCIAL CRISIS INQUIRY REPORT.

SYRIA. The regime's five-year plan, 2011–2015, envisions annual GDP growth of 5.5 percent. The nation's present GDP growth was 4.6 percent, with a GDP of $67 billion, an inflation rate of 6.8 percent, and a GDP per head of $2,870.

See also MIDDLE EAST.

SYSTEMATICALLY IMPORTANT. Banks and other financial institutions whose problems could spread throughout the financial system.

SYSTEMATIC RISK. The domino effect of one business's failure on the rest of the economy.

SYSTEMATIC RISK EXCEPTION. A clause in the Federal Deposit Insurance Corporation Improvement Act (FDICIA) under which the Federal Deposit Insurance Corporation may commit its funds to rescue a financial institution.

T

3M. After posting a 37 percent drop in quarterly net income, the company announced plans in January 2009 to reduce capital spending by about 30 percent. It reported sharply lower profit and sales for the first quarter 2009, with net falling 47 percent. Revenue fell 21 percent to $5.09 billion. Second-quarter earnings for 3M fell 17 percent to $783 million from $945 million the year before. Revenue dropped 15 percent to $5.7 billion from a year earlier.

Its first-quarter 2010 profit rose 79 percent on double-digit sales. Total sales climbed 25 percent to $6.35 billion. Management reported a 16 percent increase in third-quarter 2010 profit. Forecasts for sales growth in 2011 were 11 percent.

TAA. *See* TRADE ADJUSTMENT ASSISTANCE ACT.

TAF. *See* TERM AUCTION FACILITY.

"TAILORED" RESPONSE. *See* FORECLOSURE.

TAIL RISK. A higher-than-expected risk of an investment moving more than three standard deviations away from the mean.

TAIWAN. The government announced that its exports in January 2009 plunged a record 44 percent from the same month the previous year, pushing them down to a level unseen since 2005. By February, Taiwan ranked as the country impacted hardest by the global slump. Output plummeted by 32 percent in 2008; in the fourth quarter, it plunged at an annual rate of 62 percent.

Taiwan's exports fell by a record 44 percent over the year 2009. Average wages fell 5 percent. Taiwan's exports declined 34 percent from a year before to $14.9 billion, the eighth consecutive month of decline and steeper than the 28.2 percent forecast. The country recorded $15.5 billion in April, the first time in 2009 when exports decreased on a month-on-month basis.

Industrial output jumped by 30.7 percent in the year to the end of May 2010. Industrial production grew by 19.4 percent in the year to November, having risen by 14.5 percent in the year to October. Its GDP growth slowed to 6.5 percent in the fourth quarter from the previous quarter's 9.8 percent.

Growth slowed to 4.2 percent in 2011 following a surge the previous year. The nation's GDP growth was 4.2 percent, with GDP at $466 billion, an inflation rate of 1.4 percent, and a GDP per head of $20,040. Industrial growth slowed to 13.3 percent for the year to February 2011 from 17.4 percent in the year to the previous month. By January 2011, output rose by 17.2 percent. Industrial output rose by 3.9 percent in July, up from 3.8 percent in June.

TALBOTS. Maintained a third second-quarter loss in 2010, with sales down about 8 percent from the year before, with a loss of $37.3 million. Sales had fallen 9.9 percent to $271.1 million.

TALF (TERM ASSET-BACKED SECURITIES LOAN FACILITY). Created in November 2008, the Term Asset-Backed Securities Loan Facility lent as much as $200 billion to investors in securities backed by credit card debt, auto loans, and students loans. It provided financing to investors so they could buy new securities backed by loans.

The Federal Reserve extended TALF even as it allowed other recovery programs to expire. TALF was set to expire at the end of 2009 but was extended to March 31, 2010.

See also FEDERAL RESERVE; PUBLIC-PRIVATE INVESTMENT FUND; SECURITIZD LENDING; TROUBLED ASSET RELIEF PROGRAM.

TANF. *See* TEMPORARY ASSISTANCE FOR NEEDY FAMILIES.

TANZANIA. The nation's GDP growth for 2011 was projected to be 7.1 percent, with a GDP of $25 billion, an inflation rate of 7.4 percent, and a GDP per head at $531.

TARGET. In January 2009, the retailer announced a 4.1 percent decline in same-store sales; net income fell 41 percent in the fourth quarter 2008. Target posted a net of $609 million, or 81 cents a share, down from $1.03 billion, or $1.23 a share, a year earlier. Revenue dropped 1.6 percent to $19.56 billion. Target's fiscal first-quarter 2009 earnings fell 13 percent. Target reported that sales at stores open at least a year were down 6.2 percent from a year before in the quarter ending August 1, 2009.

Target's net income climbed nearly 29 percent in the first quarter 2010 to $61 million, with revenue climbing 5 percent to $15.59 billion from $14.83 billion the year earlier. In early November 2010, Target posted a same-store sales gain of 1.7 percent after having posted a solid rise in fiscal third-quarter net profit of $535 million, with same-store sales climbing 1.6 percent.

In January 2011, the discount retailer reported a 1.7 percent increase in sales. On February 23, Target's management report an 11 percent climb in fourth-quarter earnings, with a profit of $1.04 billion. The retailer's first-quarter profit climbed 2.7 percent, with net income rising to $689 million. Sales climbed 2.8 percent to $15.58 billion. On August 17, management reported a 3.9 percent increase in same-store sales. Earnings in the second quarter climbed 3.7 percent to $704 million, with revenue increasing 4.6 percent to $16.24 billion. Fiscal third-quarter earnings rose 3.7 percent, or $555 million. Revenue climbed 5.1 percent to $16.4 billion.

See also RETAILING.

TARIFF ACT OF 1930. *Synonymous with* SMOOT-HAWLEY ACT.

TARIFF BARRIERS. Tariff barriers can once again become the protectionist's barrier of choice, despite limits agreed upon by members of the World Trade Organization. Should all nations raise tariffs to the maximum permitted, the average global rate of duty would be doubled.

See also GLOBAL TRADE; PROTECTIONISM; WORLD TRADE ORGANIZATION.

TARP. See TROUBLED ASSET RELIEF PROGRAM.
Synonymous with TARP 1.0.

TARP 1.0. *See* TROUBLED ASSET RELIEF PROGRAM.

TARP 2.0. Use of remaining funds from the Troubled Asset Relief Program not as a stimulus plan for the rescue of financial and banking institutions but for job creation.

See also BAILOUT RESCUE PLAN (OF 2009).
Synonymous with FINANCIAL STABILITY (AND RECOVERY) PLAN.

TARP-FUNDED WARRANTS. *See* TROUBLED ASSET RELIEF PROGRAM.

TATA MOTORS LTD. India's biggest automaker by sales showed fiscal third-quarter 2008 net losses amid declining auto sales and foreign exchange losses. It reported an unconsolidated net loss of $53.8 million (2.63 billion rupees) for the quarter ending December 31, 2008, compared with a net profit of 4.99 billion rupees a year earlier. Tata Motors acquired Jaguar and Land Rover in 2008.

The company's earnings doubled in its fiscal second quarter 2009 as raw-material costs dropped and sales in India increased, marking Tata Motors' second consecutive quarter of profit growth. The company's sales declined in the quarter ending June 30, 2009, indicating a loss of $67 million compared with a profit of $147 million for the same period in 2008. The company posted profit of $156.8 million for the quarter ending September 30. Sales rose 13 percent. On November 26, 2009, Tata Motors turned to a consolidated net profit for its second quarter from a net loss a year before. The automaker posted a consolidated net profit of $4.6 million in the three months ending September 30. Net sales fell 8.5 percent.

By March 2010, Tata Motors reported a net profit of $141 million for its fiscal third quarter after a year-earlier loss thanks to a rebound in sales of its Jaguar and Land Rover premium-car models. Tata Motors' management reported on August 10, 2010, a net profit of $431.5 million for the three months ending June 30 compared with a loss a year before. Sales increased 64 percent.

Management reported on May 25, 2011, a 72 percent rise in quarterly consolidated net profit, with sales climbing 23 percent to $7.59 billion.

Cf. HUMMER.

TATA STEEL. India's Tata Steel, with a net debt of $11 billion and a market capitalization of $3 billion, was burdened by the leveraged takeover of a giant competitor. Tata had sufficient liquidity to cover maturing debt until 2010. Tata posted a 39 percent drop in fiscal third-quarter consolidated net profit. Profits in the last three months of 2008 declined to $159.6 million (8.14 billion rupees) from 13.25 billion rupees a year before. On February 9, 2009, Tata Steel shares were down 76 percent compared to a year earlier.

TAX BREAKS. The tax breaks were supposed to last for only ten years. Candidate G. W. Bush proposed to return a portion of the then budget surplus to voters Then, after 2001, the economy turned sour, and stimulus became the rationale for the cuts. The cost of the cuts over the ten years to 2011 was $1.7 trillion.

Fears of raising taxes would worsen the economic crisis in 2009, according to President Obama. However, he believed that eliminating Bush's tax cuts would make it possible to generate a much larger immediate increase in total spending. It would pay for larger temporary tax cuts for low- and middle-income families. These people tended to spend most or all of their post-tax income, roughly equal to the additional revenue from repealing the Bush tax cuts. Or, the extra revenue could be used to raise benefits, such as unemployment insurance, and extend them more broadly. That would lift total spending by almost the full amount of the additional revenue.

In early September 2010, the president proposed that companies be permitted to write off 100 percent of their new investments in plants and machinery, which would reduce business taxes by nearly $200 billion over a two-year period.

See also BUFFETT, WARREN E.; DEFICIT (BUDGET, U.S.); HIRING; INFRASTRUCTURE BANK; OBAMA, BARACK; PELOSI, NANCY; TAX CREDITS; TAX CUTS.

TAX CODE. *See* BIPARTISAN POLICY CENTER DEBT REDUCTION TASK FORCE.

TAX COLLECTIONS. *See* STATES (U.S.).

TAX CREDITS. In early October 2009, in an attempt to encourage more hiring, the government floated the idea of a tax credit for firms that create new jobs, last done in the 1970s. The proposal would give employers a two-year tax credit if they increased the size of their workforce or added significant hours of work. Employers would then receive a credit worth twice the first-year payroll tax for each new hire, amounting to several thousand dollars, depending on the new workers' incomes.

In early September 2010, the president proposed the expansion of the research and experimentation tax credit to $50 billion in additional spending on roads, railways, and airport runways. The $50 billion would come from a transportation funding bill pending in Congress.

See also HIRING INCENTIVES TO RESTORE EMPLOYMENT; HOME SALES; INFRASTRUCTURE BANK; TAX BREAKS; TAX CUTS.

TAX CURBS. President Obama detailed on May 3, 2010, a far-reaching crackdown on offshore tax avoidance, targeting U.S.-based multinational corporations and wealthy individuals. His proposal was to curb the practice of leaving foreign earnings parked in offshore tax havens indefinitely. It was estimated that as much as $700 billion or more of U.S. corporate earnings sit in overseas accounts.

The proposal also sought to curb other tax avoidances by U.S.-based firms by changing the legal treatment of offshore subsidiaries and structures they had used to avoid not only U.S. taxes but also taxes in other nations. Additionally, the president sought to tighten rules that had encouraged thousands of U.S. citizens to open offshore bank accounts in order to avoid U.S. taxes.

See also TAX HAVENS.

TAX CUTS. On July 22, 2010, the Treasury secretary said that the administration would allow tax cuts for the wealthiest to expire and therefore permit top earners to pay higher taxes in 2011 as part of an effort to bring down the budget deficit. Over the weekend of December 4–5, a compromise between Democrats and Republicans appeared close to a deal to temporarily continue the decade-long tax cuts at all income levels for all workers. It would keep the rates for higher earners for two years. By extending the tax cuts for all citizens, including those with taxable income over $250,000 for couples and $200,000 for individuals, would cost the nation about $40 billion in 2011 and about $700 billion over the coming decade. On December 7, the president reached agreement with leaders in Congress on a broad tax package extending the Bush-era income tax cuts for two years as follows:

- *All taxpayers*: Two-year extension of current tax rates, including top capital gains tax rate of 15 percent. Employee share of payroll tax reduced from 6.2 percent to 4.2 percent.

- *Upper-income taxpayers*: First $5 million of estate exempted; after that, top rate of 35 percent, down from scheduled 55 percent.
- *Middle-income taxpayers*: Extension of credit for college students to offset tuition costs. Some 22 million families exempted from alternative minimum tax.
- *Lower-income taxpayers*: Expansion of $1,000 child tax credit to more families
- *Unemployed workers*: Unemployment benefits extended for long-term jobless.
- *Businesses*: Up to 100 percent expensing of investments, including plants and equipment.

Signed by the president on December 17, tax issue provisions included the following:

- *Individual income*: Extends the Bush-era tax rates for two years for all taxpayers. Current rates will remain in place, with a top rate of 35 percent.
- *Capital gains and dividends*: Current rates will be extended, and the top rate for both long-term capital gains and qualified dividends—those from most stocks held longer than two months—will remain 15 percent for two years.
- *Payroll tax*: Employees' payroll (Federal Insurance Contributions Act) tax will be cut to 4.2 percent from 6.2 percent on the first $106,800 for 2011 only.
- *Alternative minimum tax* (AMT): A two-year "patch" for 2010 and 2011 will keep the AMT exemptions at or near current levels. Without the patch, 21 million additional taxpayers would have owed AMT for 2010.
- *Estate and gift tax*: Top rate will be 35 percent, with an exemption of $5 million per individual for 2011 and 2012.
- *Extenders*: Includes transfers of IRA assets to charities by those over age 70.5, a state and local sales tax deduction for itemizers, and a deduction for teachers' expenses for 2010 and 2011.
- *Unemployment insurance*: Federal benefits will be extended at their current level for thirteen months, through the end of 2011.
- *Select tax credits*: Extends $1,000 child credit and maintains its expanded refund ability for two years. Expanded earned income tax credit for larger families and married couples. Maintains higher-education tax credit and its partial refund ability.
- *Business investment*: Businesses will be allowed to depreciate new equipment investments at 100 percent in 2011 and 50 percent in 2012.

The provisions of December 17, 2010, with their $485 billion deal, and the two-year $139 billion extension of the high-end Bush-era tax cuts would continue to be controversial in terms of economic recovery and the impact of spending on the nation's increasing deficit.

See also NATIONAL DEBT; PELOSI, NANCY; SOCIAL SECURITY; TAX BREAKS.

TAX DATA. *See* TAX HAVENS.

TAXES. President Obama proposed on February 26, 2009, the spending of $634 billion in new taxes on upper-income Americans and cuts in government spending over the coming ten years. The tax increases were projected to raise an estimated $318 billion over ten years by lowering the value of such longstanding deductions as mortgage interest and charitable contributions for people in the highest tax brackets.

TAX GAP. The difference between taxes owed and taxes collected.

In 2008, the tax gap was $300 billion, of which more than $100 billion was believed to be collectible.

TAX HAVENS. Countries that shield the holdings of its clients, mostly rich people. Switzerland is the world's biggest offshore-banking haven with about $2 trillion of foreign assets under its management. Switzerland also announced that it would relax its bank secrecy laws to cooperate with international tax probes.

See also G-20; TAX CURBS.

TAX PACKAGE (2010). *See* TAX CUTS.

TAXPAYERS. As the nation sank deeper into recession in 2009, the Internal Revenue Service offered to waive late penalties, negotiate new payment plans, and postpone asset seizures for delinquent taxpayers who were financially strapped but made a good-faith effort to settle their tax debts.

See also BUDGET DEFICIT; BUFFETT, WARREN E.; UNEMPLOYMENT.

TAX REVENUES. *See* STATES (U.S.).

TBTF. *See* "TOO BIG TO FAIL."

TECHNOLOGY COMPANIES. By mid-November 2008, purchases of computer hardware, software, and services had been affected by the global credit crisis. Specifically, software firms and semiconductor companies, some with high debt loads, were negatively affected. Bankruptcies were climbing by the end of the year.

TECHNOLOGY INVESTMENT. Tailoring of technology systems according to what is needed and the condition under which the technology will be used. Technology investment is increasingly being used in President Obama's strategy for his economic stimulus plan. His approach is to minimize waste and the spending of huge sums of funds for "things that people don't need or can't use."

TECH STOCK BUBBLE BURST. *See* NASDAQ COMPOSITE INDEX.

TEENAGE UNEMPLOYMENT. *See* UNEMPLOYMENT.

TELECOMMUNICATIONS. Any transmission, emission, or reception of signs, signals, writing, images, and sounds or intelligence of any nature by wire, radio, optical, or other electromagnetic systems. In varying ways, both positive and negative resulted from the meltdown; some telecommunication companies providing these services have prospered, while others have suffered.

See also ALCATEL-LUCENT.

TELEVISION ADVERTISING. *See* ADVERTISING.

TEMPORARY ASSISTANCE FOR NEEDY FAMILIES (TANF). A $16.6 billion block grant to assist states in providing cash to 2 million poor families as well as child care and other services. In 2011, 700,000 recipients on TANF funds were to be significantly reduced under pressure during the U.S. deficit debate.

See also POVERTY.

TEMPORARY HIRINGS. Throughout 2010 and 2011, small and large firms remained reluctant to hire full-time workers and instead found temporary employees. Temporary workers usually receive few benefits and have no job security. In 2010, firms hired temporary help in large numbers; for example, in November they accounted for 80 percent of the 50,000 jobs added by the private sector.

Demand for temporary help fell in November 2011. Information technology was 1.1 percent below its year-earlier level. Temporary hiring often was seen as a good gauge of the labor market's overall health, but it often fell when employers assigned temporary workers on to permanent positions.

See also UNEMPLOYMENT; U.S. CENSUS.

TEMPORARY LAYOFFS. *Synonymous with* FURLOUGHS.

TEMPORARY WORK (WORKERS). Employment with hours that are usually less than full time and often short term. Temporary workers in 2009, especially in Europe, were losing jobs faster than permanent ones.

Temporary workers had risen for eleven of the past twelve months, with the sector adding jobs in September 2010. This suggested that firms were making do with a mix of more temporary and part-time help at the expense of adding permanent jobs, thus keeping the full-time employment rate high.

In 2010, 26.2 percent of all jobs added by the private sector were temporary. Traditionally, it has been 10 percent or less.
See also OVERTIME; UNDEREMPLOYMENT; UNEMPLOYMENT.

TERM ASSET-BACKED SECURITIES LOAN FACILITY. *See* TALF.

TERM AUCTION FACILITY (TAF). Intended to provide cash-short banks with funds to reduce the pressure on the banking system; created in December 2007.
See also FEDERAL RESERVE.

TERM SECURITIES LENDING FACILITY (TSLF). Permits banks to borrow money using mortgage-backed securities and other hard-to-sell assets as collateral.

TERM STRUCTURE. The difference between near-term and long-term options prices.

TEXAS INSTRUMENTS (TI). The technology firm announced in January 2009 that it would eliminate 3,400 jobs, or 12 percent of its workforce. On April 20, 2009, it announced that its first-quarter net profit declined 97 percent. The firm posted first-quarter net income of $17 million, or 1 cent a share, compared with a net profit of $662 million, or 49 cents a share, a year earlier. Revenue fell 36 percent to $2.1 billion from $3.3 billion. Texas Instruments' second-quarter 2009 profit dropped 56 percent on lower sales. Texas Instruments reported third-quarter 2009 profit declined 4.4 percent on lower sales. Profit dropped to $538 million from $563 million a year before. Revenue fell 15 percent to $2.88 billion.

On July 19, 2010, Texas Instruments reported that its profit nearly tripled on a 42 percent increase in revenue to $3.5 billion from $2.46 billion in the second quarter; net income for the period ending June 30 was $769 million, up from $260 million the year before. The company's profit surged 44 percent for the fourth quarter at $942 million, up from $655 million the year before. Revenue climbed 17 percent to $3.53 billion.

THAILAND. A contraction in Thailand's quarterly economic growth in 2009 confirmed fears that the country, until recently a brighter spot in the world economy, was sinking into a potentially deep recession. The government reported on February 23, 2009, that the GDP contracted 4.3 percent in the fourth quarter. The government's forecast for the year was 0 percent to minus 1 percent contraction, down from earlier projections of 3 to 4 percent growth. In early April, Thailand's central bank cut its benchmark interest rate by 0.25 percentage point to 1.25 percent, its lowest since June 2003, to boost its worsening economy. Thailand's economy contracted by 2.8 percent in the year to the third quarter 2009, an improvement over the 4.9 percent decline in the previous three-month period. The output of the nation's industries grew by 32.6 percent in the first quarter 2009.

By July 2010, Thailand's industrial production was 16.3 percent higher than a year before. The growth of manufacturing output slowed to 5.6 percent in the year to November from 6.0 percent in October. Exports grew by 28.5 percent in the year to November; the pace sped along from 15.7 percent in October. The nation's GDP growth was 4.0 percent, with a GDP of $336 billion, and inflation rate of 2.0 percent, and a GDP per head of $4,920. Industrial production fell by 3.9 percent in the year to May 2011.

See also SOUTHEAST ASIA.

THAIN, JOHN A. Was chairman and chief executive of Merrill Lynch; became chairman and chief executive of CIT Group.

THATCHER, MARGARET. *See* UNITED KINGDOM.

THIRD DEPRESSION. Some financial experts, including Paul Krugman, believed that by summer 2010 the United States had entered the early stages of a third depression, with millions of lost jobs. The lack of adequate policy and long-range planning to combat deflation rather than inflation was at the heart of the continuing struggle.

See also KRUGMAN, PAUL.

"THIRD WORLD." While the developed and rich countries of the world struggled to leap out of recession, nations of Asia, Africa, and South America—the so-called countries of the "third world"—were accelerating with huge contributions to the world's economy. In the 1980s, these nations accounted for 33.7 percent of global income; by 2011 it was about 43.4 percent.

THRIFTS. *See* BANKING; OFFICE OF THRIFT SUPERVISION.

TI. *See* TEXAS INSTRUMENTS.

TIER 1 FINANCIAL HOLDING FIRM. Usually, a bank that is so big and systematically important that it is subject to especially thorough scrutiny and tight controls. Under the government's proposed financial regulatory plan, certain firms would face much stricter oversight from the Federal Reserve. The Federal Reserve would have the power to examine all data from the company's domestic parent to its smallest overseas subsidiary.

See also EUROPEAN BANKING AUTHORITY; STRESS TESTS (U.S.).

TIER 2 CAPITAL. A means of taking a type of debt at the bottom of a bank's balance sheet and giving supervisors the power to write it off or convert it into equity without forcing a default, should the bank be having difficulty.

See also BASEL III ACCORD.

TIFFANY. For the 2008 holiday season, sales slid 24 percent. Total sales for the November–December period dropped 20 percent, while worldwide sales fell 21 percent to $687.4 million. This followed more than two decades of price increases and rising demand.

On May 29, 2009, Tiffany announced a 62 percent drop in fiscal first-quarter earnings as its jewelry sales plunged. Sales fell 22 percent to $523.1 million from a year earlier, as sales at its New York City flagship store dropped 42 percent. The firm reported on August 28 that its second-quarter profit fell when it earned $56.8 million, down 30 percent from $80.8 million a year before. Sales at stores open at least one year in the United States fell 27 percent. At its flagship store in New York, sales dropped 30 percent.

Then, on March 22, 2010, Tiffany reported that its fourth-quarter 2009 profit more than quadrupled. Net income climbed to $140.4 million. In its flagship store, sales climbed by 22 percent. Overall U.S. sales rose 14 percent. The firm's fiscal first-quarter 2010 earnings more than doubled. For the quarter ending April 30, Tiffany reported a profit of $64.4 million, with sales rising 22 percent to $633.6 million.

On January 11, 2011, Tiffany announced that its worldwide sales climbed 10 percent in November and December 2010. The jeweler's fourth-quarter profit climbed 29 percent. For the fiscal quarter ending January 31, the firm posted a profit of $181.2 million, up from $140.4 million, with total sales climbing 12 percent to $1.1 billion. Tiffany's fiscal first-quarter 2011 earnings rose 26 percent on double-digit sales growth. Profit was $81.1 million, with sales climbing 20 percent to $761 million. The company reported that its fiscal second-quarter earning surged 33 percent. Tiffany's fiscal third-quarter 2011 earnings surged 63 percent, a profit of $89.7 million, with sales climbing 21 percent to $821.8 million.

Management lowered its full-year earnings forecast. For its fiscal year ending January 31, Tiffany envisioned earnings in 2012 of $3.60 a share, with sales worldwide climbing 7 percent to $952 million.

See also LUXURY GOODS; RETAILING.

TIME **MAGAZINE.** *See* PECORA COMMISSION.

TIME WARNER. The media giant reported in February 2009 a $16 billion fourth-quarter loss and expected its 2009 profit to be essentially flat. On February 4, it announced that a quarterly loss of $16 billion occurred, the worst results since at least 2001. Advertising revenue fell 20 percent in the fourth quarter 2008. Time Warner's second-quarter 2009 profit fell 34 percent, with its operating income falling just 2 percent. Time Warner's third-quarter 2009 profit, fell as advertising sales continued to drop. Quarterly sales fell 22 percent, with operating income falling 40 percent. The company reported a profit of $661 million.

On May 5, 2010, Time Warner posted a 9.8 percent increase in earnings of $725 million for the first quarter, up from $660 million a year before. Revenue rose to $6.3 billion, the firm's largest gain in two years. In August, Time Warner reported a 7.3 percent increase in second-quarter profit, with earnings climbing to $562 million. Revenue increased 7.7 percent to $638 billion. In early November, Time Warner posted strong growth in third-quarter earnings as profits fell. Time Warner's fourth-quarter 2010 profit climbed 22 percent, with net income increasing to $769 million. Revenue for 2010 was $26.9 billion, 6 percent higher than in 2009.

On May 4, 2011, it was reported that revenue increased by 5.7 percent to $6.68 billion, while profit fell 9.9 percent to $653 million. On August 3, management reported a 10 percent climb in revenue to $7.03 billion, up from $6.38 billion the year before. This was the highest growth rate since 2007. Its third-quarter earnings soared 57 percent, with a profit of $822 million.

See also AOL.

TITLE. In real estate, proper and rightful ownership.

TITLE GUARANTY COMPANY. A firm that examines real estate files and conducts title searches to determine the legal status of a property and to find any evidence of encumbrances, faults, or other title defects. Once a search has been completed and the property found sound, the company receives a fee from the property purchaser who needed to determine that his or her title was clear and good. The property purchaser receives an abstract of the prepared title, and the title is verified by an attorney of the company, who gives an opinion but does not guarantee the accuracy of the title.

The company agrees to indemnify the owner against any loss that may result from a subsequent defect, with costs based on the value of the property and the risk involved determined by the condition of the title.

TITLE INSURANCE. An insurance contract from a title guarantee company presented to owners of property indemnifying them against having a defective or unsalable title while they possess the property. This contract is considered to be a true indemnity for loss actually sustained by reasons of the defects or encumbrances against which the insurer agrees to indemnify; it includes a thorough examination of the evidences of title by the insurer.

See also TITLE GUARANTY COMPANY.

TJMAXX. The retailer of low-priced merchandise enjoyed booming sales during the Great Recession. Operating more than 2,700 stores in North America and Europe, its fourth-quarter earnings climbed 58 percent to $395 million on a 12 percent increase in sales. Its revenues rose 7 percent to $20 billion in 2009.

In mid-November 2010, management reported that its fiscal third-quarter earnings climbed 7 percent, with a profit of $372.3 million. Revenue increased 5.4 percent to $5.53 billion.

See also RETAILING.

TOFAS. *See* TURKEY.

TOLL BROTHERS. The largest U.S. builder of luxury homes reported a significant loss of $472.3 million for its third quarter 2009. Toll Brothers' fiscal fourth-quarter 2009 loss of $111.4 million compared with a loss of $78.8 million a year earlier.

By third quarter 2010, Toll Brothers had its first profit in nearly three years at $27.3 million and a fall in revenue by 1.6 percent to $454.2 million. In December 2010, Toll Brothers swung to a profit for its second consecutive quarter. For the fourth quarter its profit was $50.5 million compared with a year before loss of $111.4 million. Revenue dropped 17 percent to $402.6 million.

Toll Brothers had a first-quarter profit of $3.4 million ending on January 31, 2011, compared to the year before loss of $40.8 million. It had a pre-tax profit of $8.1 million from a loss of $23.4 million, with revenue climbing 2.3 percent to $334.1 million. The firm's fiscal second-quarter loss narrowed to $20.8 million, with revenue climbing 2.7 percent to $319.7 million. The firm's fiscal third-quarter earnings climbed 54 percent. For the quarter ending July 31, Toll Brothers had a profit of $42.1 million, up from $27.3 million the year before. Revenue, however, fell 13 percent to $394.3 million.

"TOO BIG TO FAIL." A concept, still unproven, suggesting that the largest U.S. financial and banking institutions must survive in order to protect against a collapse of the economy, both domestically and internationally. The argument is that these organizations are so interconnected, so leveraged, or so complex that the government cannot let them collapse for fear of endangering the whole economic system.

By mid-September 2008, the country's financial system was in a free-fall. Lehman Brothers had filed for bankruptcy, and Merrill Lynch was forced to sell itself to Bank of America. Days later, the world's largest insurance company, AIG, would be nationalized, while Goldman Sachs and Morgan Stanley voluntarily turned themselves into highly regulated banks. The federal government in turn rushed in to save some of the most prized financial institutions to prevent the world economy from collapsing.

However, by mid-November 2010, it was clear that large banks still retained much of their financial advantage over smaller ones. U.S. banks with more than $10 billion of assets, of which there were 109, paid an average annual rate of around 0.80 percent to their depositors. The nation's 7,651 smaller banks paid on average 1.29 percent.

See also AMERICAN INTERNATIONAL GROUP; BANK OF AMERICA; BAROFSKY, NEIL; FEDERAL DEPOSIT INSURANCE CORPORATION; FINANCIAL CRISIS INQUIRY REPORT; GOLDMAN SACHS; LEHMAN BROTHERS; MERRILL LYNCH; MORGAN STANLEY; TROUBLED ASSET RELIEF PROGRAM; WALL STREET REFORM ACT (2010).

TOSHIBA. Projecting the biggest annual loss in the firm's history from a sharp decline at its computer chip division, Toshiba announced on January 29, 2009, that it planned to slash costs by 15 percent, shift semiconductor production to cheaper markets, and cut 4,500 temporary jobs in Japan.

TOTAL. France's biggest oil company by market value reported on May 6, 2009, a 36 percent drop in first-quarter net profit. Total's management said that net profit fell to $3.05 billion in the three months ending March 31.

At the end of July 2010, management reported a 43 percent increase in second-quarter net profit of $4.04 billion for the three months ending June 30.

TOURISM. Declined in 2008 and then in 2009 for the first time since the 9/11 terrorist attacks. People canceled vacations, a strong dollar kept foreigners away, and businesses slashed travel budgets. Spending declined at a 22 percent annualized rate in the October–December 2008 quarter. The decline was the greatest since the government's quarterly records began in 2001, topping the 19 percent drop after the terrorist attacks that year.

Ten million jobs would be lost over 2009–2011 as the recession led to a slump in spending on travel. The industry contracted by 3.6 percent in 2009 and was expected to expand by less than 0.3 percent in 2010.

By summer 2009, European tourism was down 10 percent or more, outpacing an already 8 percent worldwide slump. In the Mediterranean region, 10 million fewer tourists arrived for a loss of about $20 billion in income. Tourist volume in Italian airports fell by 13.4 percent in the first quarter 2009. Spain reported a 19.1 percent drop in tourist arrivals. Nice airport reported a drop of 8 percent in passengers during the first half of 2009. Tourism spending increased slightly in the third quarter 2009. Spending increased 6.4 percent to $587 billion compared to the $619 billion spent in the third quarter 2007, before the official start of the Great Recession.

The number of international tourists to the United States climbed 10 percent during the first eleven months of 2010. With 55 million tourists, $122.7 billion was spent, up 11 percent from the year before.

See also airlines by name; EGYPT; SWITZERLAND; TRAVEL AND TOURISM (2011).

TOURRE, FABRICE. A junior banker with Goldman Sachs, self-nicknamed "Fabulous Fab" in a boastful email, who was accused by the Securities and Exchange Commission and the firm with defrauding investors in a mortgage-related security. He denied the civil charges of fraud.

See also GOLDMAN SACHS.

TOXIC ASSET FUND. An investment concept of purchasing shares in closed-end funds. The fund would permit people or retail investors to buy toxic assets from banks.

TOXIC ASSETS. The federal government announced on March 23, 2009, its three-pronged program to rid the financial system of toxic assets, hoping that investors would be attracted to the combination of discount prices and government aid. It would create an entity backed by the Federal Deposit Insurance Corporation to purchase and hold loans.

In addition, the Treasury Department expanded a Federal Reserve facility to include older so-called *legacy assets*, a term used interchangeably with toxic assets. Originally, the Term-Asset Backed Securities Loan Facility was created to purchase newly issued securities backing all manner of consumer and small-business loans. Some of the most toxic assets were securities from before 2006, which TALF was now able to absorb.

The government would establish public-private investment funds to purchase mortgage-backed and other securities. These funds would be run by private investment managers but be financed with a combination of private money and capital from the government, which would share in any profit or loss. Since it has a negative connotation, the term is frequently replaced with *legacy assets* or *legacy securities* to reflect a more positive approach for the federal bank rescue plan.

See also FEDERAL DEPOSIT INSURANCE CORPORATION; FEDERAL RESERVE; PUBLIC-PRIVATE INVESTMENT FUND; TOXIC MORTGAGE ASSETS; TROUBLED ASSET RELIEF PROGRAM; U.S. TREASURY.

TOXIC MORTGAGE ASSETS. *See* "BAD BANKS"; BAILOUT RESCUE PLAN (OF 2009) (U.S.); LEGACY ASSETS; PUBLIC-PRIVATE INVESTMENT FUND; TOXIC ASSETS; TROUBLED ASSET RELIEF PROGRAM.

TOYOTA. On December 22, 2008, Toyota Motor announced that it expected its first loss in seventy years. With about $18.5 billion in cash and little debt, Toyota was still in far better shape to weather the meltdown than most other global carmakers. Losses during the fiscal year were $1.66 billion, its first operating loss since 1938, one year after the firm was founded. Toyota's sales in the United States dropped 33.9 percent in 2008. It sold 141,949 vehicles in the United States in December, down from 224,399 a year earlier. Sales of the Prius hybrid fell 45 percent as gas prices declined from their record highs in July. Toyota lowered its worldwide forecast for its fiscal year ending March 31, 2009, to 7.54 million cars, down from 8.9 million sold the previous year. For its 2008 fiscal year, Toyota expected to sell 2.17 million vehicles in the United States, down from 2.9 million the previous year. Toyota suspended production at all twelve of its Japan plants for eleven days during February and March 2009.

On January 16, 2009, the company announced cuts at North American plants where its auto sales in 2009 would be its lowest in twenty-seven years. Toyota expected a first-ever annual operating loss in 2009 as its inventory of vehicles built in North America covered eighty to ninety days of sales, having doubled in the past year. Sales were falling 30 to 40 percent each month. Toyota announced on February 12 that it would offer job buyouts to its U.S. workers for the first time and cut the workweek at some of its American plants by 10 percent. It also announced that it would eliminate bonuses or approximately 3,000 executives and salaried employees and reduce executive pay as part of an emergency cost-cutting program. The world's largest carmaker announced on February 25 that its Japanese factories now producing 40.3 percent less automobiles, its biggest drop in sales since 1988. By March, Toyota saw its worldwide production fall to about 12 percent in the fiscal year, its lowest level in seven years, from 7.08 million cars down to 6.2 million. Toyota, the world's largest carmaker by volume, planned to scale back production in Japan by 54 percent. On May 8, Toyota posted a $7.74 billion fiscal fourth-quarter net loss, leading the world's largest automaker to its first annual loss in fifty-nine years. On August 27, 2009, it was announced that Toyota topped the list for purchases made in the cash-for-clunkers program. Toyota Motor Corporation reported a quarterly profit on November 5, 2009, citing a net profit of $241.1 million in its fiscal second quarter ending September 30, down 84 percent from a year earlier. Sales fell 24 percent, leading to a net loss for the fiscal year. On November 26, Toyota announced that it was reducing bonus pay by 20 percent for 8,700 managers as it tackled an enormous recall program due to defective accelerators and deep losses for the second consecutive fiscal year.

Toyota had displaced General Motors as the world's biggest carmaker. Those glory days have faded. In the financial year that ended in March 2009, the worst sales slump in the history of the automobile took hold. Toyota had a net loss of $4.3 billion, its first since 1950, and it lost in the three months to March alone the equivalent of $2.5 billion more than GM did in the same time period. In 2007, Toyota's sales had reached almost 9 million cars, 13.1

percent of the world total, and in 2009 it fell to 11.8 percent. Toyota's sales in the United States had fallen by 23.8 percent in 2009, while Toyota's share was the lowest in Europe since 2005.

Toyota reported on April 26, 2010, that its global production in March had nearly doubled from the year before, climbing 97 percent to 773,297 cars. On May 11, 2010, following its period of global recalls, Toyota made a surprise fiscal-fourth quarter profit of 112.2 billion yen after a net loss of 765.8 billion yen one year earlier. The automaker posted an operating profit in the fourth quarter of 95.3 billion yen. May 2010 sales were 14 percent lower than the year before, but by the summer, management reported a 7 percent jump. Toyota posted its highest quarterly net profit in two years. In August 2010, it reported a $2.2 billion profit in its fiscal first quarter ending June 30. Sales rose 27 percent from April to June. On November 5, Toyota noted a lower-than-expected increase in fiscal second-quarter net profit, fourfold to 98.69 billion yen. Sales increased 5.8 percent to $59.58 billion, with an operating profit in the quarter nearly doubling. For October 2010, domestic production came to 237,089 cars, down 22 percent from the year before, as domestic sales fell 25 percent to 103,672 vehicles. Toyota's production of cars in Japan fell for the second straight month following the first fall in eleven months in September. November car sales were at 129,317 for a drop of 3.3 percent over the previous year.

In February 2011, Toyota reported that its profit had slumped 39 percent from a year before. From October to December 2010, its profit was $1.14 billion, resulting from global sales falling 11.7 percent. Then, on March 4, Standard & Poor's lowered its bond rating for the automaker, indicating a slow recovery for the car manufacturer. In May, Toyota reported a 77 percent fall in earnings for its quarter ending March 31, 2011. On June 10, Toyota projected a 31 percent fall in annual profit resulting from the earthquake and the strength of the yen against the dollar. The automaker's net profit plunged 99 percent for the fiscal first quarter 2011 to $15 million for the first quarter ending in June. On December 9, management lowered its annual profit forecast by half. It would lose its title as the world's largest carmaker in 2011, falling 54 percent to $2.3 billion. Worldwide sales for the year would fall to 7.38 million cars, down from an earlier forecast of 7.6 million. Management projects that 2012 sales will surge by a fifth.

See also AUTOMOBILE INDUSTRY; CASH FOR CLUNKERS; GENERAL MOTORS; JAPAN; STANDARD & POOR'S; VOLKSWAGEN.

TRADE. In January 2009, U.S. imports and exports slumped for the sixth month in a row, creating the biggest collapse in global trade activity since the end of World War II. Imports fell 6.7 percent to $160 billion, having plunged by nearly a third since August 2008. There was a similar drop in exports of 5.7 percent.

See also GLOBAL TRADE; PROTECTIONISM; SMOOT-HAWLEY ACT OF 1930.

TRADE ADJUSTMENT ASSISTANCE ACT (TAA). To be considered by President Obama as part of a model to assist the unemployed, the Trade Adjustment Assistance Act serves those who have lost their jobs because of changing patterns of trade, giving eligible workers counseling, training, income support, and other services. But, TAA relieves only a fraction of the displaced.

See also UNEMPLOYED; WORKFORCE INVESTMENT ACT.

TRADE BARRIERS. Were on the increase in late 2008 and more evident in 2009. For example:

- Russia raised import tariffs on dozens of products, including cars and combine harvesters.
- The European Union put anti-dumping duties on imports of Chinese screws.
- The United States announced it would increase tariffs on French cheese and Italian water.
- Egypt increased tariffs on sugar imports.
- Brazil and Argentina have asked Mercosur, the Latin-America free-trade area, for tariff increases on numerous goods.

See also PROTECTIONISM; TRADE; WORLD TRADE ORGANIZATION.

TRADE DEFICIT (U.S.). The U.S. trade deficit widened in October 2008 for the first time since July. It rose 1.1 percent to $57.2 billion from $56.6 billion in September. The trade deficit with China widened to $28 billion from $27.9 billion in September. For 2008, the trade deficit ran at an annual rate of $709.11 billion, up slightly from $700 billion in 2007. The deficit for November plunged by 28.7 percent to $40.4 billion. As of November 30, China held $682 billion in U.S. currency, a sharp rise from $459 billion a year earlier. Japan had reduced its holdings to $577 billion from $590 billion a year earlier. Government figures released in February 2009 indicated that the U.S. trade deficit shrank for the second consecutive month, to $35 billion from $40 billion in November 2008. Oil prices fell nearly 27 percent in December, pushing the dollar value of oil imports lower, while the end of a Boeing strike bolstered exports.

At the end of the first quarter 2009, the U.S. trade deficit fell to 2.4 percent, the smallest deficit in a decade and less than half of the deficit in the first quarter 2008. The deficit widened for the second consecutive month in April as exports dropped more than imports. The U.S. deficit in international trade in goods and services rose to $29.2 billion from a revised $28.5 billion in March. The drop in exports accelerated in April, falling 2.3 percent to $121.1 billion from March's $123.9 billion. Imports declined 1.4 percent to $150.3 billion. The spread between what the U.S. imports and exports grew in June 2009. On August 12, the government said that the trade deficit widened as imports rose ($3.5 billion) for the first time in nearly one year and U.S. exports increased from the month before, though not as much as imports. The gap between the import and export of goods and services grew 16.3 percent to $31.96 billion, up from $27.49 billion in June 2009. Imports surged 4.7 percent to $159.55 billion, while exports grew 2.2 percent to $127.59 billion. After widening in September, the trade deficit narrowed again in October 2009 to $32.9 billion, as exports climbed 2.6 percent—the sixth straight monthly gain. Imports rose 0.4 percent. In October, manufactured goods exports were 2.8 percent higher than in September but still 20 percent below July 2008.

The nation's trade deficit became the largest since 2008 as increased imports from China more than offset U.S. exports. The gap in trade increased 4.8 percent in May 2010 to $42.3 billion. U.S. exports increased 2.4 percent to a twenty-month high of $152.3 billion, but imports grew faster, expanding to 2.9 percent to $194.5 billion. The trade deficit with China expanded to $22.3 billion in May, the widest level since October and 15 percent larger than the previous month.

The trade gap widened 19 percent in June 2010 from the month before to $49.9 billion, the widest deficit since the financial meltdown hit. Imports climbed 3 percent. In July, the trade gap narrowed sharply by 14 percent to $42.8 billion from $49.8 billion in June. Exports increased 1.8 percent to $153.3 billion and imports fell 2.1 percent to $196.1 billion. In September 2010, the U.S. trade deficit shrank 5.3 percent to $44 billion. Exports grew to their highest level in a little over two years. Sales abroad expanded 0.3 percent to $154.1 billion, the most since August 2008 and up from $153 billion the previous month. Imports dropped 1.0 percent to $198.1 billion from $200.1 billion the month earlier. Year to date, the trade deficit was $379.1 billion, up 40 percent from the same period in 2009. In December, the trade deficit widened to its highest level in four months, climbing nearly 6 percent from the previous month to $40.6 billion. Overall imports of goods and services were at their highest since October 2008.

On March 15, 2011, it was announced that the U.S. trade deficit narrowed in the fourth quarter at $113.3 billion, down from $125.5 billion in the third quarter. This resulted in a 3.1 percent showing of GDP, not as low as the 2.4 percent when global trade dropped sharply in 2009, but well below the prevailing levels of the past decade. The U.S. trade deficit climbed to $59.8

billion, $6.1 billion higher than the previous month's gap. The trade deficit widened in March 2011, increasing 6 percent to a seasonally adjusted $48.2 billion. Exports rose 4.6 percent to a seasonally adjusted $172.7 billion, while imports increased 4.9 percent to $220.8 billion. The United States spent $40.49 billion more than it collected, with a monthly deficit smaller than April 2010's shortfall of $82.69 billion. By May, the U.S. deficit was its widest in more than 2.5 years as imports climbed and exports fell. The deficit in international trade of goods and services surged 15.1 percent to $50.2 billion in the month from $43.6 billion the month before, the largest gap since October 2008. Exports dropped 0.5 percent. For the month of June, as exports fell faster than imports, U.S. trade deficit increased to $53.1 billion from $50.8 billion the month before. The 2.3 percent drop in exports reflected the slowing down of global demand.

See also DEFICIT (BUDGET, U.S.); EXPORTS; UNEMPLOYMENT.

TRADE FINANCING. Financing of cross-border purchasing and selling. Roughly 90 percent of global trade requires financing.

In the economic meltdown of 2008–2009, trade financing became more expensive and more difficult to secure, thereby accelerating an already large downturn. Banks hesitated to allocate scarce capital to trade financing and were wary about being caught short by defaults of other banking institutions that write letters of credit or by the importers and exporters themselves.

TRADE GAP. *See* TRADE DEFICIT (U.S.).

TRADE SUBSIDIES. *See* AUTOMOBILE INDUSTRY; UNFAIR TRADE SUBSIDIES.

TRADE WAR. *See* MEXICO.

TRADING DESKS. *Synonymous with* DARK POOLS.

TRANCHE(S). French, meaning a slice. Refers to the different types of mortgage-backed securities and collateralized debt obligation bonds that provide specified priorities and amounts of return; "senior" tranches have the highest priority of returns and therefore the lowest/risk interest rate; "mezzonine" tranches have mid-levels of risk/return; and "equity" ranches typically receive any remaining cash flows.

Synonymous with FINANCIAL CRISIS INQUIRY REPORT; FIRST LOSS; RESIDUAL.

TRANSIT IMPROVEMENTS. *See* AMERICAN RECOVERY AND REINVESTMENT ACT (OF 2009); MASS TRANSIT; RAIL SERVICE.

TRANSPARENCY. The extent to which agreements and practices are open, clear, measurable, and verifiable. The Obama administration pledged to make the bank bailout program more transparent, demanding that banks report publicly how they were spending funds from the bailout. True transparency would require putting specific details of government expenditures before the public, a difficult and perhaps overwhelming challenge. The government had promised to disclose how much it gives to a state, and the state must report how the funds are distributed. But, no requirements exist to disclose where the money actually ends up.

Under the Emergency Economic Stabilization Act and the Financial Stability Oversight Board, transparency would be studied for all programs. The success of the financial regulation legislation of 2010 would parallel the evolution of how transparency was to be carried out. Transparency will be upgraded to avoid the appearance of improper relationships with lobbyists, bankers, and executives in the financial world. The Federal Reserve requires all staff personnel to keep track of every meeting with private-sector personnel. The Federal Deposit Insurance Corporation announced in August 2010 that it would publish every two weeks the names of lobbyists who met with officials dealing with legislation. The Commodity Futures Trading Commission and the Securities and Exchange Commission have similar transparency regulations and opened special e-mail accounts to take in public commentary, which it will then post on websites. In 2011, most U.K. banks started to report financial performances on a quarterly basis as opposed to the traditional two times per year.

See also ACCOUNTABILITY; EMERGENCY ECONOMIC STABILIZATION ACT; FINANCIAL CRISIS INQUIRY REPORT; FINANCIAL STABILITY OVERSIGHT BOARD; G-20; HSBC HOLDINGS; LLOYDS; REGULATION; UNITED KINGDOM.

TRANSPORTATION. *See* U.S. DEPARTMENT OF TRANSPORTATION.

TRAVEL AND TOURISM (2011). The travel industry grew 5 percent, bringing the level to its high of 2008. France could well be the largest beneficiary of this trend, followed by China. Hotel occupancy rose by 6.7 percent.

See also AIRLINES; CLUB MED; TOURISM.

TRAVELERS. The commercial and personal insurance provider's second-quarter 2009 profit fell 21 percent on lower revenue and high claims costs.

Its fourth-quarter 2010 profit fell 30 percent to $894 million.

On April 21, 2011, management reported a first-quarter profit, with net income climbing to $839 million. Its third-quarter profit fell 67 percent to $333 million.

Cf. METLIFE.

TREASURY DEPARTMENT (U.S.). *See* U.S. TREASURY DEPARTMENT.

TREASURIES. On October 1, 2011, the government announced that Treasurys had ended the quarter by posting the largest quarterly gains since the 2008 financial crisis, as growing concerns about the global economy fueled a rush into safe assets. The thirty-year bond continued to be the best performer. U.S. Treasuries yields fell broadly in 2011, with its ten-year yield at 1.9 percent for the year, down 14 percentage points.

On February 3, 2012, investors moved away from Treasury bonds, fueling the biggest one-day sell-off for the benchmark ten-year note since the previous October. The ten-year note climbed 0.12 percent for the session and hit a one-week peak of 1.956 percent.

TREATY OF MAASTRICHT. *See* EUROPEAN UNION.

TRIBUNE. The U.S. newspaper chain that owned the *Chicago Tribune* and the *Los Angeles Times* filed for bankruptcy protection on December 8, 2008. The Tribune Corporation's assets included twenty-three television stations and twelve newspapers, including two of the largest in the United States by circulation. It also owned the Chicago Cubs baseball team and Wrigley Field. The Tribune Corporation maintained a $13 billion debt.

See also NEWPAPERS.

Cf. NEW YORK TIMES.

TRICHET, JEAN-CLAUDE. President of the European Central Bank who retired at the end of October 2011 after an eight-year term.

See also EUROPEAN CENTRAL BANK.

TRILLION DOLLAR BAILOUT (EUROPE). *See* EUROPE (BAILOUT).

TROUBLED ASSET RELIEF PROGRAM (TARP) (TARP 1.0). The bailout plan of 2008 was also called TARP. It could slow the resolution of the crisis by stopping property prices and homeownership from falling to sustainable levels. Some homeowners who were up-to-date with payments but whose homes were worth less than their mortgages could cease paying, betting the federal government would be a more forgiving creditor.

The Treasury considered using TARP funds to write down mortgages to levels that squeezed homeowners could afford. If TARP assisted banks and investors established reliable prices for mortgage securities, it could restart lending and help to bring the housing crisis to an end.

However, the $700 billion government program, passed by Congress on October 3, was adding to the U.S. deficit. As of December 5, the Treasury had allocated a total of $335 billion to TARP and disbursed $195 billion to institutions under its various parts. About forty-eight employees were assigned to TARP; only five were permanent staffers, the rest coming from other Treasury offices, U.S. government agencies, and organizations providing temporary assistance. For them, critical questions remain: What are the banks' assets really worth? How much can they earn? How much capital would the banks require to operate profitably?

The decision by the U.S. Treasury not to buy toxic mortgage assets with TARP money after it said it would do so produced paper losses for the banks that held these securities. The value of those securities rose when TARP was announced but fell significantly when the mortgage-purchasing program was abandoned. The U.S. deficit for the full year would top $1 trillion.

Just over half of the Treasury Department's $700 billion TARP was committed—$379.8 billion—during the George W. Bush administration. On February 10, the new Treasury secretary unveiled some details about how the new administration would use the fund's remaining $320.2 billion.

The Congressional Budget Office in April quietly changed its estimate of the ultimate cost to taxpayers for the $700 billion TARP, concluding that the initiative would be more expensive. In January, the CBO estimated the cost to taxpayers for TARP at $189 billion; in late March, it was reassessed at $356 billion.

Banks that benefited from TARP funds included the following:

- Bank of America, $45 billion
- JP Morgan Chase, $25 billion
- Citigroup, $50 billion
- Morgan Stanley, $10 billion
- Goldman Sachs, $10 billion
- Wells Fargo, $25 billion
- PNC Financial Services, $8 billion
- American Express, $3 billion
- State Street, $2 billion

By April, the banking industry was lobbying the Treasury Department to make it less costly for them to get out of TARP. At issue were "warrants" the government received when it bought preferred stock in roughly 500 banks, permitting the government to buy common stock in the banks at a later date so taxpayers could receive more of a return on their investment. Many banks wished to return their TARP funds and wanted to expunge the warrants. To do this, the banks must either purchase them back from the government or allow the Treasury to sell them to private investors.

To buy back TARP-funded warrants, the banks had to provide the Treasury with an independent valuation of the warrants. Then, the Treasury and the banks had to agree on the price. If they could not agree, the Treasury had to try to sell the warrants in the private market. Those banks wishing to return

TARP funds had to demonstrate their ability to wean themselves off another major federal program—a guarantee of debt issuance by the Federal Deposit Insurance Corporation that allowed firms to borrow money relatively inexpensively.

The Treasury Department announced on June 8, 2010, that it received an initial payback from the nation's largest banks of at least $50 billion in bailout funds, an indication of improvement in the banking sector. These banks and the government's TARP investment, in billions, were as follows:

- American Express, $3.38
- BB&T, $3.13
- Bank of New York Mellon, $3
- Capital One, $3.55
- Goldman Sachs, $10
- JP Morgan, $25
- KeyCorp, $2.5
- State Street, $2
- U.S. Bancorp, $6.59

The government dropped its plans to cap salaries at firms receiving federal bailout funds, leaving them subject to congressionally imposed limits on bonuses. A pay czar to monitor the firms receiving the greatest government aid was announced in mid-June. Then, on June 17, the government received $68 billion from ten financial firms eager to leave the curbs that came with taxpayer-funded capital infusions. By returning these funds, the banks were to be left alone to wrestle with the recession and financial meltdown. Some of these banks announced that they planned to immediately begin the tricky task of negotiating to repurchase warrants that the government received in return for the infusions.

The special inspector general for TARP testified on July 21 before a House committee that "the total potential federal government support could reach up to $23.7 trillion." The figure was considered not realistic or plausible, but became a point of political debate. By September 1, 2009, the U.S. government, and thereby the U.S. taxpayers, began to profit from many of its largest investments; for example, Goldman Sachs received $10 billion in TARP funds, and the government had already received in return $1.418 billion plus the original investment; American Express received $3.389 billion in TARP funds, and the government had already gotten back $414 million plus the original investment. Morgan Stanley received $410 billion in TARP funds, and the government had already profited by $1.268 million plus received the original investment back. By November 2009, about $210 billion in TARP funds remained unspent, including about $70 billion returned from financial firms.

An additional $50 billion was expected to be repaid in the coming twelve to eighteen months. Also, it was found that more than twenty-seven U.S. banks that received TARP funds had been taken over by federal regulators, putting taxpayers at risk of losing as much as $5.1 billion invested in the banks since TARP was launched in October 2008. By December 2009, the government was discussing the possibility of using unspent and repaid TARP funds to help offset additional spending to create jobs and aid the long-term unemployed. TARP's long-term cost was reported to be lower by more than $200 billion and the president would use this money to pay for a new jobs program. The Treasury Department expected to recover all but $42 billion of the $370 billion it had lent to ailing financial institutions. The Treasury estimated that over the next ten years TARP would cost $141 billion at most, down from the $341 billion projected in August 2009. The government extended the $700 billion financial-sector bailout until October 2010. Citigroup and Wells Fargo announced on December 14 that they were about to pay back a total of $45 billion in aid from TARP. The Treasury Department expected $19 billion in total profits from its infusions and other investments in financial institutions, reversing the agency's initial projection of a $76 billion net loss. The top-tier banks announced by the end of 2009 that they had or were prepared to pay back TARP. However, of the other sixty-nine banks receiving TARP funds, only seventeen of the other banks that received at least $100 million from TARP had repaid the funds.

Toward the end of July 2010, TARP commitments were to be reduced to $475 billion from $535.5 billion as a result of the financial overhaul legislation. U.S. Treasury officials planned to terminate a long-delayed, never used $30 billion program for boosting small-business lending and cut the amount of funds available for a Federal Reserve ending program. In addition, the Treasury would cease creating any new programs to stabilize the financial sector. On Monday, October 4, the U.S. Treasury Department officially terminated new programs and other commitments under TARP. Originally created under President Bush's administration, the bailout fund was set at $700 billion and lowered to $475 billion by the Dodd-Frank (Wall Street Reform Act) in July 2010. One hundred firms had by the end of the summer repaid $200 billion more than $180 billion remained outstanding, mostly among 616 banks, two car dealers, and the insurance firm AIG. The government also retained the right to spend up to $46 billion on foreclosure issues—funds that would not be reclaimed. The Treasury had already profited with nearly $27 billion from interest, dividend payments, and the sale of warrants.

Five principal areas of TARP were:

- *Banks*: Commitment of $250 billion, with a $5–20 billion profit. Financial institutions were given $250 billion in capital injections and guarantees to offset losses on overvalued mortgages and securities. Ninety-one banks by summer 2010 had repaid the bulk of these funds to the government and the program was expected to generate a profit. Yet, $58 billion remained with more than 600 companies. Banks would continue to reimburse the government, which should continue to profit from interest, dividend payments, and the sale of warrants. A congressional panel overseeing TARP questioned the ability of smaller financial institutions to repay the government. The panel noted that more than 15 percent of recipient banks had missed dividend payments by summer 2010.

- *AIG*: Commitment of $70 billion, with a projected (summer 2010) loss of $50 billion to a $15 billion profit. The government extended TARP funds to AIG for a total of $183 billion. At the end of September 2010, the government announced some of the details to end support for AIG, involving converting the government's stake to common stock and selling those shares over time. The plan had risks; should the government sell its shares too rapidly, AIG's market value could be driven downward, affecting the amount of funds that would be returned to the taxpayers.

- *Automobiles*: Commitment of $82 billion, with a projected $15 billion to $34 billion loss. Both GM and Chrysler were restructured as a result of their bankruptcy with loans and other government aid. At that time, the U.S. government owned 61 percent of GM and 10 percent of Chrysler. The U.S. Treasury assisted Chrysler Financial and GMAC. About $67 billion remains with three of these firms. The government unveiled a plan to reestablish GM as an independent company. It can take two or three years before the government pulls out of this relationship. Chrysler said it would pay back its government loans by 2014.

- *Housing*: Commitment of $46 billion, with a projected $10 billion to $49 billion loss. The U.S. Treasury established a $50 billion program to aid homeowners in modifying and refinancing mortgages. Later, the program was lowered to $30.5 billion by the Wall Street Reform Act. It also evolved two new programs to assist the most troubled borrowers. Only a small share of eligible homeowners had received permanent loan modifications. The Treasury had spent only a fraction of the funds it was allocated to assist homeowners. It has the authority to spend up to $46 billion even following the expiration of TARP. These funds would not be repaid.

- *Lending*: Commitment of $27 billion, with a projected $2 billion loss to a $0.2 billion profit. The government decided to assist banks with increasing lending and removing troubled mortgage assets from their balance sheets. While the effectiveness of these efforts was widely debated, they had been downsized and were now closed to new commitments. The bulk of outstanding funds remained with the Public-Private Investment Program, intended to assist banks with removing troubled mortgage assets from their balance sheets. The program would unwind over the next few years, and minimal losses were anticipated.

With its expiration, TARP's more than 600 banks sit on about $65 billion in government bailout monies. Of the $386.4 billion invested by the government, about $199 billion had already been paid by September 2010. On October 5, 2010, the Treasury Department reported that it expected to lose $29 billion on the federal bailouts, including a $17 billion loss from its investments in GM, Chrysler, and the automobile finance firms, as well as a $46 billion loss from housing programs known as the Home Affordable Modification Program.

On January 25, 2011, Neil Barofsky, special inspector general for TARP reported continuing disappointment with the program. Designed to prevent foreclosures, he argued, "[TARP] continues to fall dramatically short of any meaningful standard of success."

See also AUTO PARTS; AVIS; BANK BAILOUT; BANK OF AMERICA; BAROFSKY, NEIL; CAPITAL PURCHASE PROGRAM; CITIGROUP; CONGRESSIONAL BUDGET OFFICE; DEBT CEILING; ENTERPRISE; EXECUTIVE PAY; FEDERAL DEPOSIT INSURANCE CORPORATION; FINANCIAL STABILITY OVERSIGHT BOARD; FOREIGN MBAS; FRAUD; GEITHNER, TIMOTHY; GOLDMAN SACHS; HARDEST HIT FUND; HERTZ; INSURERS; JOB CREATION; JP MORGAN CHASE; LENDING; LIFE INSURERS; MORGAN STANLEY; MORTGAGE-BACKED SECURITY; PAY CZAR; TOXIC ASSETS; U.S. TREASURY; WALL STREET REFORM ACT (2010); WELLS FARGO.

Synonymous with BAILOUT; BANK BAILOUT FUND; BANK FAILURES; FAILED BANKS; FINANCIAL STABILITY PLAN; HOTEL GEITHNER; TARP 1.0.

TROUBLED ASSETS. *See* "BAD BANKS"; BANK BAILOUT; TROUBLED ASSET RELIEF PROGRAM.

TRUCKING DISPUTE. *See* MEXICO.

TRUCKING INDUSTRY. Following a few years of doubling their output, truck manufacturers began to retrench. It was predicted that through 2009, the global demand for heavy trucks of more than fifteen tons would drop by 29 percent. A 24 percent decline in developed markets would accompany a 32 percent decline in emerging nations.

Prior to 2009, it seemed that the trucking industry was having difficulty recruiting new drivers. Into the New Year, the industry suddenly found that it had more applicants than positions. In January, the industry, which employed about 1.32 million people, lost 25,000 jobs. In 2008, more than 3,600 trucking firms went out of business, with roughly 7 percent of its capacity disappearing. Sales of heavy trucks in Europe fell about 40 percent in 2009, but demand for trucks globally was expected to start recovering before the end of the year. Between 180,000 and 200,000 trucks were to be sold in Europe in 2009, down from 318,000 in 2008.

See also AUTOMOBILE INDUSTRY; FREIGHT HAULERS; SCANIA; VOLVO.

TRUMAN, HARRY S. President Truman seized U.S. steel mills in 1952 rather than allow a strike to imperil the conduct of the Korean War. He was on the edge of nationalizing the industry and told his staff, "The president has the power to keep the country from going to hell."

See also NATIONALIZATION; OBAMA, BARACK.

TURKEY. Output is on track for a record year-on-year decline in 2009 of 6.5 percent. However, four quarters of negative growth ended with a strong rebound in the second quarter 2009. Inflation fell from 11.9 percent in October 2008 to 5.3 percent in September 2009, and the current-account deficit is expected to fall from 5.5 percent of GDP in 2008 to around 2 percent in 2009. After recovering more moderately in the rest of the year, GDP is projected to expand by 3.75 percent in 2010 and 4.5 percent in 2011. Policymakers should aim to preserve the improvement in investor confidence, which permitted a decline in real interest rates. Making further progress in fiscal transparency is crucial in this context and the planned fiscal rule should be backed by specific consolidation measures. Structural reforms boosting the competitiveness of the business sector would help improve the performance of the economy in the upturn.

A deal with the International Monetary Fund for $20 billion to $40 billion was announced at the end of November 2008. Foreign investors, who held as much as 70 percent of the Istanbul Stock Exchange, had been pulling out, and the Turkish lira tumbled by more than a third against the U.S. dollar in 2008. Growth of GDP had dipped sharply to below 2 percent. Turkey's huge current-account deficit made it more vulnerable than many other emerging markets. Officials released figures on December 15 indicating that the country's GDP was contracting and that unemployment was increasing.

The IMF returned to Turkey in January 2009 to assist in restoring the economy, which was plagued by a current-account deficit. The jobless rate rose to 10.3 percent in September from 9.3 percent the year earlier. At the end of December, Turkey's parliament cut the budget allocations of most ministries by as much as 16 percent as the country prepared for a loan arrangement with the IMF.

Between 2002 and the end of 2010, Turkey's national income rose by about 30 percent and GDP per capita by 20 percent in real terms, making it the world's seventeenth-largest economy.

The government reported on September 14, 2010, that its second-quarter growth was in the double digits. GDP climbed 10.3 percent in the quarter. Turkey tied China as the world's fastest-growing economy in the second quarter 2010 at 10.3 percent of GDP. On October 10, 2010, the government revised upward its GDP growth expectations to 6.8 percent for the year and 4.5 percent for 2011. Following its nearly 5 percent contraction in 2009, the economy expanded 11.7 percent in the first quarter and 10.3 percent in the second, tying with China for the fastest growth in the Group of Twenty nations.

By the end of December 2010, it was clear that Turkey had become an automobile maker's powerhouse. Togas, the nation's biggest carmaker, was the primary exporter with seven out of every ten cars made in Turkey exported. The $22 billion auto industry employs more than 230,000 workers and accounts for 20 percent of the nation's total exports. Turkey is now the largest carmaker in eastern and emerging Europe outside of Russia. Sales of cars and light trucks were 31 percent higher than the previous year with 1.05 million vehicles produced in 2010.

By 2011, with a population of 73 million, GDP was $736 billion, with a GDP per capita of $10,100, inflation at 6.4 percent, exports of goods and services of $185 billion, imports of good and services of $39 billion, and unemployment (percent of labor force) at 14.2. The nation's unemployment rate was expected to fall to 12 percent in 2011 and 11.7 percent in 2012 from 12.2 percent in 2010. It is projected that Turkey will return to prosperity in 2011, but with an economic growth slowed by internal political forces. The nation's GDP growth was 3.6 percent, with GDP of $760 billion, an inflation rate of 6.5 percent, and a GDP per head of $10,270. On January 20, despite the country's near 8 percent growth rate for 2010, the central bank cut its key interest rate to a record low of 6.25 percent. By April 2011, its GDP generated $730 billion, the seventeenth largest, and its economy grew 9 percent in 2010, with an inflation rate of 8 percent and a budget deficit a bit more than 2 percent of GDP. Turkey has an economy nearly four times that of Egypt. In mid-May 2011, consumer prices climbed 7.2 percent, with its economy expanding 8.9 percent in 2010. Despite a falling currency and a struggling stock market, Turkey's economy was booming and grew by 11 percent in the first quarter. Considered Eurasia's "rising tiger," the nation's trade deficit doubled from the previous year, with imports climbing by 42.6 percent, nearly four times faster than its exports at 11.7 percent.

Despite the nation's surging economy with $2.5 billion in annual trade, second only to China, Turkey's trade deficit widened to $10.2 billion in June 2011, nearly double that of the previous year. Imports were up 42 percent compared to a 19 percent annual increase in exports. On August 8, Turkish stocks fell 7.1 percent, the largest fall in nearly three years. Tourism, a $25 billion industry, boomed in 2011, up 11 percent in the first seven months. As indicated on September 13, Turkey's climbing economy showed a GDP expanding 8.8 percent in the second quarter after outstripping China in the first three months of the year. By mid-September 2011, Standard & Poor's upgraded Turkey's local currency credit rating to investment grade, illustrative of the country's economic strength. The upgrade of lira-denominated debt by one notch to BBB– from BB+ was driven by improvements in the nation's financial sector and the deepening of local markets.

Then, in mid-October, the government intervened strongly to stop an abrupt slide in its currency. The central bank spent $350 million in an auction to buy Turkish lira on October 7, bringing the week's intervention total to $1.64 billion. The lira had dropped around l0 percent in September and the IMF forecast that Turkey will only grow by 2.5 percent in 2012 after a spurt of 10 percent growth in the first half of 2011. Having witnessed a precipitous fall in its currency, on October 26 the central bank more than doubled the interest rates it charged banks for overnight loans to 12.5 percent from 5.75 percent. Its third quarter showed an 8.2 percent surge. In the year, the nation's economy was forecast to grow between 7 and 8 percent following a 9 percent expansion in 2010. Inflation reached its highest level in three years, with December's numbers showing that consumer prices climbed 10.45 percent, the highest figure since November 2008. By the end of December, the government had much to boast about—low public debt (42 percent in 2011) and a tightly regulated bank sector, accompanied by falling unemployment.

See also INTERNATIONAL MONETARY FUND.

TYSON FOODS. The company posted a net loss of $455 million in its fiscal fourth quarter 2009 compared to a year-earlier profit of $48 million. Revenue climbed slightly to $7.21 billion from $7.20 billion.

In August 2010, Tyson management announced that its earnings surged 89 percent, with a profit of $248 million, and revenue climbed 12 percent to $7.44 billion. On November 22, Tyson Foods reported record earnings for its fiscal fourth quarter, with a profit of $213 million. Revenue increased 3.2 percent to $7.44 billion.

In mid-February 2011, Tyson reported an 86 percent rise in its fiscal first-quarter profit.

U

U6. A larger gauge of unemployment designed to measure "labor underutilization." It includes people who are jobless and have given up seeking work as well as those working part time out of necessity rather than choice, estimated in September 2011 to be about 25 million people.

UAL. *See* UNITED AIRLINES.

UBS. The world's largest private bank agreed on February 18, 2009, to pay fines of $780 million and to hand the American authorities the names and account details of up to 300 clients accused of tax fraud. The offshore banking business of UBS gathered some $20 billion in assets from more than 20,000 U.S. clients, earning the bank huge sums of money each year. The U.S. government concluded that some 17,000 of these clients failed to mention their numbered Swiss accounts on their tax returns. With a big loss in the first quarter 2009, UBS announced 8,700 layoffs and a 15 percent cut to its operating costs. The bank employed 83,800 people at its peak in 2007, and with its latest cuts, 11 percent of its workers, the figure fell to 67,500. On August 4, 2009, UBS posted a $1.3 billion quarterly loss, its third.

UBS reported at the end of July 2010 that it had a third straight profitable quarter. Its profit was $1.92 billion in the second quarter.

The bank reported on February 8, 2011, that it had a profit of $7.5 billion. UBS last posted an annual profit in 2006. The bank also reported that it was lowering its 2010 bonus pool by 10 percent. At the end of August, UBS management announced it would lay off more than 5 percent of its workforce to save $2.53 billion annually, following a collapse in second-quarter profit by almost half. Third-quarter profit fell 39 percent to $1.16 billion.

See also SWITZERLAND.

UKRAINE. Since October 2008, Ukraine's stock market plunged by nearly 80 percent. The hryvnia, the national currency, hit a seven-year low against the dollar. Economic growth plunged, and inflation was 25 percent.

The International Monetary Fund provided an emergency loan of $16.5 billion—around a fifth of the $55 billion that the Ukraine needed to raise by 2009 in order to roll over short-term loans, pay interest on other debts, and finance the rest of its current-account deficit. The World Bank announced at the end of November that it would provide the Ukraine with a $500 million loan to battle the crippling economic crisis. The IMF reached an agreement with the Ukraine in mid-April 2009 paving the way for resuming disbursement of a $16.4 billion loan. Ukraine would receive $2.8 billion of the loan by mid-May. By then its economy was contracting at an annual rate of 9 percent. Then, on December 30, the IMF reworked a loan agreement with the government freeing up about $2 billion.

The nation's economy grew on average by 7 percent by mid-2010.

It was expected that the nation's economy would grow by 3.9 percent in 2011. The nation's GDP growth was 3.9 percent, with a GDP of $165 billion, an inflation rate of 11.6 percent, and a GDP per head of $3,630.

See also INTERNATIONAL MONETARY FUND.

UN. *See* UNITED NATIONS.

UNDERCAPITALIZED. A condition in which a business does not have enough capital to meet its needs or to meet its capital requirements if it is a regulated entity.

UNDEREMPLOYED. People working part time for lack of full-time positions; also includes so-called labor force reserve, workers who have abandoned their job searches but would work if employment became available.

In October 2008, this rate jumped to 12.5 percent from 8 percent. Most of the underemployed are people working part time, want to work full time, but cannot find positions. The 12.5 percent figure was the highest level of underemployment since the statistic was first compiled in 1994.

By 2009, this pool of underutilized labor had risen above 24 million, with expectations that it would continue to grow. The peak underemployment rate was higher in the recession of 1981–1982 than it is today, largely because the last big wave of the baby boom generation was entering the job market in the early 1980s. Those boomers who couldn't find work were officially counted as unemployed. In the first thirteen months of the 2008–2009 meltdown, the number of jobs lost was a staggering 4 million.

Nearly 2.2 million young people ages sixteen through twenty-nine lost their jobs in 2009. About 1.7 million people were working part time in January because they could not secure full-time employment, a 40 percent increase from when the recession officially began in December 2007. Even with the end of the recession, about 10 percent of the workforce will remain unemployed, unable to find gainful employment. By summer 2009, there were more than five unemployed workers for each job opening in the country. The numbers of the poor and on welfare rolls continued to rise.

In December 2007—the official start of the Great Recession—about 7 million Americans were unemployed. By mid-year 2009, it had doubled to about 14 million. One should add to this figure people who are working part time who would prefer to be working full time and those who have become disillusioned and have stopped seeking employment. It was estimated that nearly 30 million people were underutilized in May 2009, the largest number in the country's history. The overall labor underutilization rate that month rose to 18.2 percent, its highest in twenty-six years.

Cf. UNEMPLOYMENT.

UNDEREMPLOYMENT RATE. *See* UNDEREMPLOYED.

UNDERFUNDED PENSION PLANS. *See* PENSION FUNDS.

UNDERUTILIZATION. *See* UNEMPLOYED.

UNDERWATER. The condition of a home being worth less than the mortgage taken out on it due to declining prices. This creates an incentive for the mortgage borrower to walk away and allow the home to be foreclosed on. At the end of 1991, 6.4 percent of households were underwater and were eventually foreclosed on.

In February 2009, it was estimated that 10 million households fit into this category. By mid-November 2009, the proportion of homeowners owing more on their mortgages than their properties were worth jumped to 23 percent. Nearly 10.7 million households had negative equity in their homes in the third quarter 2009. Thus, one out of four borrowers was underwater. Roughly 588,000 borrowers defaulted on mortgages in 2008, more than double the number in 2007.

Underwater mortgages fell to 10.8 million at the end of September 2010, down from a peak of 11.3 million at the beginning of the year. This total accounted for nearly 22.5 percent of U.S. homeowners with a mortgage. The number of homeowners who owed more on their mortgages than their homes were worth dropped in the third quarter 2010. Las Vegas had about 61 percent of its mortgages underwater.

At the start of 2011, nearly 27 percent of homeowners with a mortgage were underwater, up from 23.2 percent in the previous quarter. The increase resulted from a 2.6 percent fall in home values during the quarter and the fact that fewer homes went through foreclosure following banks halting foreclosures to correct document-handling errors. By June, nearly 40 percent of homeowners who took out second mortgages were underwater on their loans, more than twice the rate of owners who didn't take out such loans.

See also FORECLOSURE; HOME PRICES; HOUSING PLAN; MODIFYING MORTGAGES.

UNDERWATER MORTGAGES. *See* UNDERWATER.

UN ECONOMIC COUNCIL. A proposal made by German Chancellor Angela Merkel in February 2009 to form an internationally funded institution within the United Nations as a possible replacement for the International Monetary Fund. Was never adopted.

See also GERMANY; INTERNATIONAL MONETARY FUND.

UNEMPLOYMENT BENEFITS. U.S. unemployment benefit rolls rose to a twenty-six-year high in the last week of December 2008. Extending unemployment benefits through 2010 would cost about $100 billion. The number of people still on jobless rolls after drawing an initial week of aid jumped 101,000 to 4.61 million, the highest since November 1982 and higher than analysts' expectations of 4.5 million.

By the end of September 2009, there was a push by Democrats in Congress to extend unemployment coverage that would provide four more weeks of benefits to all states, while states over the 8.5 percent threshold would get twelve additional weeks. On October 29, the Labor Department reported that initial claims for unemployment insurance fell by 1,000 to a seasonally adjusted rate. In Europe, unemployment benefits provide a better cushion against financial collapse than in the United States. For example, Belgian and Norwegian workers took home almost three-quarters of what they earned when employed. France and Sweden both paid unemployed workers around two-thirds of their previous income in the first year of joblessness. Such benefits were less generous in the United States and usually expired after one year.

The government reported that the jobless rate hit 10.2 percent in October 2009. If statistics were available, the measure would be at its highest level since the Great Depression. More than one out of every six workers, 17.5 percent, was unemployed or underemployed. The previous high of 17.1 percent in December 1982. On November 6, the president signed the Worker, Homeownership and Business Assistance Act (2009) into law, extending unemployment benefits by twenty weeks and renewing the first-time homebuyer tax credit until April 2010. About 1 million laid-off workers would see their unemployment benefits extended for another fourteen weeks. This federally paid aid was extended to unemployed people who had exhausted state and federal limited benefits that already lasted up to seventy-nine weeks in many states. For the majority of states with especially high unemployment, it added six more weeks of payments, bringing the total to ninety-nine weeks. By November, the unemployment rate had fallen in thirty-six states, while only eight states saw a rise in unemployment rates.

The number of workers making new claims for jobless benefits rose in the last week of July to the highest level in nearly four months, climbing by 19,000 to 479,000. Most economists don't expect unemployment to fall below 6 percent until 2013. In mid-summer 2011, the issues dealing with the U.S. deficit threatened the nation's unemployed. In 2010, the U.S. Congress allocated $56.5 billion to renew expiring federal jobless benefits through 2011 but dropped a $25-a-week supplement that would have been added under the stimulus. That reduction could push an estimated 175,000 people into poverty in late 2011. Unemployment insurance claims fell to 364,000 in mid-December, the lowest reading since April 2008.

As part of the agreed-on payroll tax cuts on December 22, 2011, the government decided to continue paying unemployment insurance benefits under the current policy through February 2012. Without congressional action, many of the long-term unemployed would have begun losing benefits on January 1, 2012.

In late January 2012, it was reported that fewer workers were laid off than in previous months. New claims for unemployment benefits dropped by 12,000 for the last week of the month to a seasonally adjusted 367,000, well below the 400,000-plus new claims filed weekly throughout the summer and early fall.

See also AMERICAN JOBS ACT (PROPOSED); DEFICIT (BUDGET, U.S.); EMPLOYMENT; GREECE; HIRINGS; JOBLESS BENEFITS; JOBLESS CLAIMS POVERTY; "SADDLE POINT"; UNEMPLOYMENT.

UNEMPLOYMENT CLAIM FRAUD. Nearly $3 billion was lost to unemployment insurance fraud nationwide in 2009, more than double the 2008 figures. Although the rate of fraud fell to 2.14 percent in 2009 from 2.8 percent in 2008, unemployment payments in the nation overall increased to $140 billion in 2009 from $48.6 billion in 2008.

UNEMPLOYMENT COVERAGE. *See* UNEMPLOYMENT BENEFITS.

UNEMPLOYMENT INSURANCE. *See* TAX CUTS.

UNEMPLOYMENT (U.S.). At the end of 2007—the official beginning of the Great Recession—the jobless rate reached 5 percent, its highest level in more than two years.

By March 2008, 63,000 jobs were lost, the most in five years, adding to January's unexpected decline of 17,000 jobs. The U.S. economy lost an additional 240,000 jobs in October 2008. The unemployment rate jumped 6.5 percent from 6.1 percent, the highest level since 1994. The economy had shed 1.2 million jobs since the beginning of the year. By the end of November, new claims for unemployment benefits stood at a sixteen-year high. Losses cut across all industries, but they appeared to begin within the financial and banking communities and then rapidly spread to other industries. About

90,000 jobs were cut at major global banks since September 2008. Of these, more than 50,000 had been at Citigroup. Bank of America, which acquired Merrill Lynch, cut about 10,000 investment jobs at the combined banks. On December 4, Credit Suisse announced plans to eliminate 5,300 of its jobs, or 11 percent of its workforce. Commerzbank announced plans to eliminate 1,200 jobs in London.

AT&T, the biggest telephone company in the United States, announced plans to cut 12,000 jobs, or 4 percent of its workforce. DuPont, the chemical company, said it would lay off 2,500 employees, equaling about 4 percent of its workforce, and Viacom, the media/film firm, eliminated 850 jobs. While financial firms had the most job cuts in November with a 91,356 reduction, the retail industry showed the second-worst performance with 11,073 losses, and this was before the Christmas season. Headlines of newspapers around the country on December 6–7 revealed that November's job losses were the worst in thirty-four years, reaching more than 1.5 million, which at 0.4 percent of the workforce was the worst showing since 1980. The unemployment rate rose to 6.7 percent in what was the eleventh consecutive monthly fall in employment, arguably making the recession the longest since the Great Depression.

In addition, 70 percent of the jobs lost were in the service sector, notably in retailing, temporary work, and hotel and restaurant employment. The only sectors adding jobs in November 2008 were health care and education. The manufacturing sector had been particularly hard hit, losing more than 600,000 jobs in 2008. The nation lost 524,000 jobs in December 2008. The unemployment rate jumped to a sixteen-year high of 7.2 percent, nearly 50 percent larger than at the start of the recession in December 2007. There were 1.9 million U.S. layoffs in 2008.

There were 3.3 unemployed individuals for every vacancy, a ratio that worsened in 2009. Job hunting took on average about four months before finding a position, which often carried a 20 to 30 percent cut in salary. In mid-January 2009, the Labor Department reported that first-time requests for unemployment insurance jumped to a seasonally adjusted 524,000 in the week ending January 10 from an upwardly revised figure of 470,000 the previous week. By the start of 2009, unemployment had risen in every state. The Labor Department announced on February 6 that 598,000 jobs were lost in January. The contraction in jobs was steeper than in any other recession since at least the early 1980s. The unemployment rate rose from 7.2 percent in December to 7.6 percent, which worked out to 11.6 million unemployed workers. If the rate had included part-time workers who needed full-time jobs and jobless workers who had given up seeking because their prospects were so poor, the figure would have reached 13.9 percent, or 21.7 million workers, up from 13.5 percent in December. As reported on February 26, the number of Americans filing new claims for unemployment insurance rose to 667,000. In February alone, the economy shed 651,000 jobs, and the government revised some recent months to include more losses than previously thought for a total of 4.4 million jobs lost since December 2007.

During the current downturn, more jobs have been lost faster than in any period since 1974, as measured from peak employment. The economy had now lost 3.2 percent of its jobs since December 2007. It dropped 3.1 percent between summer 1981 and the end of 1982. The losses pushed the unemployment rate to 8.1 percent, its highest level since March 1983, but this did not take into account those who had given up looking for work or those who were working part time but wanted full-time work.

Manufacturing and overtime hours declined, leading to more job cuts in the future. A quarter of a million construction and manufacturing jobs disappeared; the service sector lost 375,000 positions. (Only health services and government showed a slight increase.) Claims for jobless benefits added 12,000 to reach 669,000 in the last week of March, hitting a new high for the current recession. Claims for unemployment benefits rose to a record 5.7 million as of March 21. March figures indicated that the unemployment rate was at its highest level since 1983 with job losses at 5.1 million, with two-thirds of the cuts coming since November 2008. The jobless rate climbed to 8.5 percent from 8.1 percent a month earlier. The number of jobs lost in March was 663,000. Almost one in twelve adult males was now jobless. Almost every private industry lost jobs—construction, 126,000; manufacturing, 161,000; business services, 133,000; and retailing, 48,000.

Workers ages forty-five and older had a disproportionate share of the long-term unemployment, those out of work for six months or longer. On average, laid-off workers in this group were out of work 22.2 weeks in 2008 compared with 16.2 weeks for younger workers. The unemployment rate for workers ages forty-five and older was 6.4 percent, the highest since at least 1948.

Initial jobless claims tumbled 53,000 to 610,000 in the week ending April 11. The decline brought the four-week average for claims down 8,500 to 651,000, the first decline since the beginning of 2009. Continuing claims for unemployment benefits jumped 172,000 to 6.02 million in the week ending April 4, underscoring the difficulty in finding new work. Initial jobless claims fell 14,000 to 631,000 in the week ending April 25. That raised hopes that job losses could moderate over the coming months. Unemployment in April, although reaching 8.9 percent, showed signs of a slowdown. The month's figure was 539,000 people without full-time work. This jobless number indicated that those receiving benefits would rise to 6.35 million. Nonfarm payrolls fell by 345,000 in May, less than April's 504,000 drop and the smallest decline since September. Yet, more jobs were lost in May than in any month of the prior three recessions, and the economy had now lost 6 million jobs since the recession began in December 2007. The unemployment rate rose half a point to 9.4 percent, its highest level since February 1983.

The jobless rate in June continued to inflict damage, reaching its highest level in twenty-six years. Challenging visions of an economic recovery, the Labor Department released its May unemployment figures on July 2. The U.S. economy had lost 467,000 more jobs in June, and the unemployment rate edged up to 9.5 percent. These numbers made a compelling case for further government stimulus funds. The economy fell short by some 8.8 million jobs since the recession began; 6.5 million jobs had been lost and 2.3 million new jobs that were needed just to keep up with population growth never materialized. New figures confirmed that unemployment was highest for teenagers (24 percent), African Americans (14.7 percent), and Hispanics (12.2 percent). Of the 14.7 million jobless workers, 4.4 million, or nearly 30 percent, had been out of work for twenty-seven weeks or more. Unemployment benefits began to expire in September for nearly 650,000 jobless workers. On July 16, the government reported that claims for unemployment benefits fell sharply for the second consecutive week. Newly filed jobless claims fell 47,000 in one week on a seasonally adjusted 522,000, the lowest level since January.

In the one and a half years since the meltdown began, the unemployment rate had doubled and one out of six construction workers was out of work. Labor hoarding sometimes occurs during recessions, as companies retain their workers even as business declines, a form of stockpiling for the future, but this recession appeared to be working inversely, where hoarding had reversed its course and layoffs continued in greater number. This suggested that companies were not optimistic about their future growth. At the same time, wages were also declining. By the end of the first half of the year, overall wage growth was zero. The U.S. unemployment rate fell in July to deliver the labor market's best performance in a year. Nonfarm payrolls fell by 247,000 jobs in July, far fewer than the 443,000 shed in June. The jobless rate slipped to 9.4 percent from 9.5 percent one month before, the first decline since April 2008. Unemployment of people sixteen to nineteen fell to 23.8 percent, the highest since record-keeping began in 1954. Among African American teens, it was 35.7 percent, nearly four times the national average of 9.4 percent. By summer 2009, the national employment population ratio was 59.4 percent. For teenagers, it was 28.9 percent, the lowest on record. Jobless benefit claims climbed in mid-August, rising 15,000 to 576,000, the highest level in three weeks. The El Centro metropolitan area in Imperial County, California, had America's worst unemployment, 27.5 percent as of June

2009, almost three times the then national rate of 9.7 percent. Throughout the summer, unemployment rates in 372 U.S. cities continued to climb. Nineteen metropolitan areas had unemployment rates above 15 percent, with eight in California. Detroit's unemployment rates were the highest in the country at 17.7 percent. Job losses in August 2009 indicated a small improvement. Employment declined by 146,000 in the month, while goods-producing jobs, including construction and manufacturing, fell by 152,000. This combined loss of 298,000 positions was an improvement from July's revised drop of 300,000 and was less than half the pace of decline seen at the beginning of the year. Even though August 2009 job cuts were at their slowest rate for the year, a climb in unemployment to a twenty-six-year high of 9.7 percent does not forecast the recession end. Nonfarm payrolls dropped by 216,000 in August, fewer than the 276,000 of July according to a government announcement on September 4. The construction and manufacturing sectors together accounted for more than half of August's losses, while retail and business services narrowed. The largest gain was in health care with nearly 28,000 new positions. Teenage unemployment rose to 25.9 percent, the highest since government records began in 1948 and up from 23.8 percent in July. The jobless rate for men rose to 10.1 percent, well above the 7.6 percent rate for women. People who have stopped looking for employment and those working part time but desire full-time positions rose half a percentage point to 16.8 percent. In August, temporary payrolls fell by 6,500, far fewer than the average monthly drop of 51,000 during the first half of 2009. Since December 2007, the official beginning of the recession, temporary employees fell from 2.6 million to 1.7 million. One of every eight jobs lost during the meltdown had been a temporary position. In addition, the proportion of people who had been searching for work for longer than six months climbed to 35.6 percent of the unemployed from a third of the workforce in August. With a poor job market, there was a drop of 571,000 people in the labor force.

The International Monetary Fund predicted that U.S. unemployment would average 10.1 percent in 2010 and forecast that the jobless rate would not drop to 5 percent until 2014. As the recession was bottoming out, job losses continued to slow in September 2009 as the private sector shed fewer jobs than in August. GDP decreased at a 0.7 percent annual rate in the second quarter, better than the 6.4 percent fall in the first quarter. September's unemployment was the smallest since July 2008. Nevertheless, employers laid off another 263,000 people in the month, and the unemployment rate climbed to a twenty-six-year high of 9.8 percent. The nation was facing twenty-one consecutive months of job losses. The 15.1 million unemployed was greater than the population of all but four states. On October 2, 2009, the government stated that the jobs picture was far worse than it had previously claimed. It was found that during the twelve months ending in March 2009, the economy lost 5.6 million jobs, 824,000 more than the 4.8 million given earlier. During the first half of 2008, job losses averaged 146,000 per month. That was three times the average of 49,000 jobs indicated in the initial estimates.

Private-sector employment declined 203,000 in October 2009, the seventh-straight month of moderating job losses and the smallest decline since July 2008. Job cuts declined for the third straight month, down 16 percent from September 2009 to 55,679. The government reported that the jobless rate in October 2009 hit 10.2 percent. More than one out of every six workers, 17.5 percent, was unemployed or underemployed that month, probably the highest since the Great Depression of the 1930s. In October, nearly 16 million people were unemployed and more than 7 million jobs had been lost since the start of the Great Recession in December 2007. By mid-November 2009, the jobless rate was up in twenty-nine states, hitting records in four of them. The unemployment rate fell in thirteen states. Then, by early December, the government reported that after a two-year climb the jobless rate had dropped to 10 percent in November from 10.2 percent earlier. Employers shed 11,000 jobs, the fewest since December 2007. Temporary hiring picked up 52,400 jobs in November, and workers received more hours in November, 33.2 per week, or 0.2 percent.

The number of Americans unemployed for some period of time shot higher in 2009. There were 26.1 million people experiencing some unemployment in 2009, roughly one out of every nine citizens age sixteen or older. That was up from 21.2 million in 2008 and 15.1 million in 2007. The 2009 median spell of unemployment was 19.7 weeks, up from 15.7 weeks in 2008. The number of workers who had been without work for more than twenty-six weeks rose to 5.9 million in November, the highest ever and more than double the number in January. The median duration of unemployment was up to 20.2 weeks.

At the beginning of 2010, employment in residential construction and car-making was down by almost a third, and in retailing and banking, by 8 percent. By May 2010, the unemployment rate climbed to 9.9 percent from 9.7 percent in March, mostly because of a significant rise in the number of people who had previously given up hope but now decided to look ahead to secure work. This was accomplished with employment increasing to 290,000 jobs, the largest gain in four years. The economy lost 131,000 jobs in July 2010 as 143,000 temporary census workers left their government jobs. Private-sector work increased by 71,000, and government jobs, excluding census workers, fell by 59,000. The unemployment rate held steady at 9.5 percent, with 14.6 million people seeking positions remaining unemployed. Roughly 6.6 million were jobless for more than twenty-seven weeks in July. The summer 2010 picture was a gloomy 9.5 percent unemployment rate, as indicated below:

DEMOGRAPHICS

July	One month change	One year change
White, 8.6%	unchanged	0.1 pt
Black, 15.6%	+ 0.2 pt	+ 0.9 pt
Hispanic, 12.1%	– 0.3 pt	– 0.3 pt
Asian, 8.2%	+/–5 pt	– 0.1 pt

DURATION OF UNEMPLOYMENT
In weeks

Average, 34.2	– 2.8%	+ 35.2%
Median, 22.2	– 12.9%	+ 39.6%

SHARE OF POPULATION
June

Employed, 58.4%	– 0.1 pt	– 0.9 pt
Labor Force, 64.6%	– 0.1 pt	– 0.8 pt

HIDDEN UNEMPLOYMENT (in millions)
Workers and unemployed

Working part time, 8.5	– 1.1%	– 3.2%

Want full-time work

People who currently want a job, 6.1	– 4.9%	– 1.6%

UNEMPLOYMENT BY EDUCATION LEVEL

Less than high school, 13.8 %	– 0.3 pt	–1.5 pt
High school, 10.1%	– 0.7 pt	+ 0.7 pt
Some college, 8.3%	+ 0.1 pt	+ 0.3 pt
Bachelor's or higher, 4.5%	+ 0.1 pt	– 0.2 pt

TYPE OF WORK (in millions)

Nonfarm, 130.2	– 0/1%	unchanged
Goods, 18.0	+ 0.2%	– 1.9%
Services, 112.2	– 0.1%	+ 0.3%
Agriculture, 2.2	+ 3.4%	+ 2.5%

AVERAGE WEEKLY EARNINGS
Rank and file workers

$772.58	+ 0.5%	+ 3.0%

The unemployment rate rose to 9.6 percent from 9.5 percent in July partly because more people entered the workforce. With 14.9 million remaining jobless, the unemployment number marked the sixteenth straight month above 9 percent, the longest period in twenty-five years. The number of workers filing new claims for jobless benefits rose by 2,000 in early August 2010 to the highest level in close to six months at 484,000 people. The U.S. economy lost jobs for the third month in a row. Fortunately, private-sector employers added 67,000 positions. Overall, nonfarm payrolls fell by 54,000 as the United States lost 114,000 temporary census workers and state governments reduced employment.

Youth unemployment in the thirty-three nations of the Organisation for Economic Co-operation and Development climbed 18.8 percent from 2007 to 2009, or by about 4 million people. The percentage of people out of work for 12 months or more remained fixed at 24 percent in 2009. Following the meltdown, 210 million people were seeking work throughout the world, an increase of more than 30 million since 2007. Three-fourths of the increase had been in the most developed economies. In the coming decade, 440 million jobs will have to be created.

Firms cut jobs in September 2010 by 39,000 from August. Service-sector positions rose by 6,000 in September, but factory jobs fell by 17,000. Businesses with 500 or more workers trimmed 11,000 jobs. Those with 50 to 499 workers cut 14,000 positions and small businesses with fewer than 50 workers shed 14,000. U.S. payrolls fell by 95,000 in September as private employers added 64,000 workers, while government lost 159,000 half-temporary census workers and local (state and city) governments released 83,000 workers. More than 58,000 teachers and other education people were not called back for the 2010 school year, and some 3.5 million people had either quit seeking work or not entered the labor force during the meltdown. The 9.6 percent unemployment, the last quote before the November mid-term election, would be up to 2 percentage points higher with the stimulus plan of 2009. The unemployment figure was almost 27 million citizens, including underemployment. In October, 6.2 million people were listed as having been out of work for more than six months, and the average duration of unemployment stood at thirty-four weeks. The economy was running 7.5 million jobs short of its earlier peak, and a growing number of people were exhausting their unemployment benefits.

By mid-November, the number of workers filing new claims for unemployment insurance increased 2,000 to 439,000. It was reported that the nation's unemployment rate climbed to 9.8 percent in November, a seven-month high, as hiring slowed. The jobless rate topped 9 percent for nineteen straight months, the longest stretch on record. Only 39,000 jobs were created in the month, a sharp decline from the 172,000 created in October. Private firms, the backbone of the economy, created only 50,000 positions, down from the 160,000 private-sector jobs created in October and the smallest gain since January. The country's unemployment rate was 15.1 million in November. At the end of 2010, the government said it was changing its surveys to permit unemployed workers to report length of jobless spells of up to five years. Prior to this change, the jobless would only be counted for up to two years.

By February 2011, the unemployment rate had fallen below 9 percent for the first time in nearly two years. As 192,000 new jobs (nonfarm) were added, the rate dropped to 8.9 percent, the lowest since April 2009. Unfortunately, there was a rise in people dropping out of the labor force. By mid-March, the number of workers filing for unemployment insurance fell 5,000 to 382,000 from the previous week. That brought the four-week moving average, used to smooth the volatile figures, down to 385,250—the lowest level since July 2008. On April 1, it was reported that 216,000 jobs were added and unemployment fell to 8.8 percent. June figures created a new aura of disappointment. The country added only 18,000 jobs in the month. Private-sector hiring fell to its slowest pace in more than one year, and governments continued shedding jobs. The unemployment rate climbed to 9.2 percent from 9.1 percent the previous month. Shockingly, more workers dropped out of the job market. In June and July, the United States recorded an average of only 21,500 new jobs, far below the level required to bring down unemployment.

In July 2011, employers added 117,000 new jobs and the unemployment rate fell to 9.1 percent from 9.2 percent the month earlier. Manufacturing, which added 240,000 workers in the month, had been a driver of the economic recovery. By mid-summer 2011, unemployment touched 14 million people, who were both jobless and seeking work. As subgroups, the breakdown was as follows: 6.6 million were women, 2.6 million were Hispanic, 14 million were totally jobless, 3.1 million were black, 0.5 million were Asian, and 7.4 million were men. September figures showed that employers added 103,000 workers, falling short of the pace needed to get 14 million jobless working. By the end of summer 2011, 4.5 million workers had been unemployed for fifty weeks or longer and were still searching for work, of which 1.6 percent of the people had been unemployed for at least one year. Unemployment remained at 9.1 percent. It was felt that 125,000 new jobs were needed to keep up with population growth and 200,000 new positions would be needed to have a significant impact on the unemployment impact rate. In October, unemployment rates fell in almost three-quarters of U.S. states, with nine showing no change and five indicating increases.

November's unemployment figures reflected a sharp fall to 8.6 percent, its lowest level in thirty-two months the first time it has fallen below 9 percent since March. A total of 120,000 jobs were added. However, half of the figures reflected that people had increasingly dropped out of the labor force, suggesting that they no longer could be counted and unemployed. At 5.7 million, the number of long-term unemployed barely had shifted. Private-sector growth was 140,000, but that was less than half the 300,000 needed for monthly job creation to suggest any expansion. Since 2009, more than 2 million people had withdrawn from the workforce.

2012 would begin with an 8.5 percent unemployment rate. The unemployment rate fell to its lowest level in nearly three years with 200,000 jobs added in December 2011, double the previous month's rate. On February 3, the government announced that the economy added more jobs for the previous month since early 2011. With 243,000 additional positions mostly from the service sector, it was the fastest pace of job growth since April, bringing the unemployment rate down to 8.3 percent, the fifth consecutive monthly decline. Should the economy add 200,000 or more jobs each month, the unemployment rate would likely continue to drop.

See also APARTMENT VACANCIES; AUTOMATIC STABILIZERS; BABY-BOOMERS; COBRA; COLLEGE GRADUATES; CRIME; DIET; ELDERLY; EMPLOYMENT; EUROPEAN UNION YOUTH; EURO-ZONE; FLEXICURITY; FOOD AID; FOOD BANKS; FOOD STAMPS; FURLOUGHS; GLOBAL UNEMPLOYMENT; GREECE; HIRINGS; ICELAND; IMMIGRATION; JOB CREATION; JOBLESS CLAIMS; JOB OPENINGS; KEYNES, JOHN MAYNARD; MEN UNEMPLOYED; MINIMUM WAGE; MISERY INDEX; "NEW NORMAL"; OBAMA, BARACK; OVERTIME; POVERTY; PRIVATE-SECTOR PAYROLLS; ROOSEVELT, FRANKLIN DELANO; "SADDLE POINT"; SERVICE SECTOR; SPAIN; SPENDING; STATES (U.S.); SUICIDES; TAX CREDITS; TEMPORARY WORK(ERS); TRADE ADJUSTMENT ASSISTANCE ACT; UNDEREMPLOYMENT; UNEMPLOYMENT BENEFITS; UNEMPLOYMENT (WORLDWIDE); U.S. CENSUS; U6; VETERANS; WALL STREET; WALL STREET REFORM ACT (2010); WELFARE; WOMEN UNEMPLOYED; WORKFORCE INVESTMENT ACT.

Cf. AMERICAN JOBS ACT (PROPOSED); EMPLOYMENT; JOBLESS BENEFITS; JOBLESS RATE; UNDEREMPLOYED; UNEMPLOYMENT (WORLDWIDE); YOUTH.

UNEMPLOYMENT (WORLDWIDE). Global unemployment showed considerable differences. The percent of labor force (extreme) without jobs included the following:

Percent	Date	Percent	Date
Monaco 0	2005	Afghanistan 35	2008
Azerbaijan 0.9	2010	Kenya 40	2008
Uzbekistan 1.1	2010	Haiti 40.6	2010
Thailand 1.1	2010	Bosnia/Herzeg. 43.1	2010
Cuba 1.6	2010	Senegal 48	2007

| Kuwait 2.2 | 2004 | Namibia 51.2 | 2008 |
| Singapore 2.2 | 2010 | Zimbabwe 95 | 2009 |

See also UNEMPLOYMENT (U.S.).

UNFAIR TRADE SUBSIDIES. The discriminatory commercial exchange activities of goods that are either unfairly subsidized or dumped or are otherwise illegitimate, as with counterfeit items.

A huge debate ensued following George W. Bush's announcement in the fall 2008 of the use of $17.4 billion of taxpayers' money to prevent the collapse of General Motors and Chrysler. European and Asian carmakers had been hard pressed to refrain from using their government funds to assist failing companies but now chose to reexamine their positions.

See also AUTOMOBILE INDUSTRY.

UNILEVER. The Anglo-Dutch consumer goods company reported that its first-quarter 2009 sales volume dropped 1.8 percent, with revenue falling to $974.5 million. That was down 45 percent from the year before. The world's third-largest consumer goods firm by sales reported in August that its profits in the second quarter were down 17 percent. Unilever's third-quarter 2009 profit fell. Revenue fell 2 percent.

Unilever's third-quarter 2011 sales rose 4.9 percent, or $16.66 billion, from the year before, with an increase of 19 percent in volume.

UNINSURED. The number of uninsured citizens climbed by 4.4 million to 50.7 million in 2009, the largest annual jump since the government started gathering data in 1987. The percentage of citizens covered by private insurance in 2009 was 63.9 percent, the lowest since 1987, while the percentage of those covered by government programs, 30.6 percent, was the highest. Overall, the number of people with any form of health coverage fell in 2009, for the first time since 1987, to 253.6 million from 255.1 million in 2008. The total number of citizens with private insurance fell to 194.5 million from 201 million. In September, the Census Bureau noted that the number of uninsured people rose to 49.9 million in 2010, up from 49 million the year before. The percentage of Americans covered by private health insurance continued its decade-long fall, and the percentage covered by employment-based policies, the heart of the insurance system for working people, fell to 55 percent.

UNIONS. Union membership has been falling for decades both in the public and private sectors, accounting for only 11.9 percent of the workforce in 2010. This was down from 12.3 percent in 2009 and well below the peak of 28.3 percent in 1954. In 2010, 7.6 million government workers in unions made up more than half of the 14.7 million workers in the United States. Union membership in 2010 slipped to 36.2 percent in the public sector.

See also AUTO TASK FORCE; EMPLOYEE FREE CHOICE ACT.

UNITED AIRLINES (UAL). The airline planned to reduce its mainline capacity by as much as 9.5 percent in 2009, on top of a 4.2 percent reduction in 2008. United Airlines reported a net loss of $1.3 billion for the fourth quarter 2008, for an annual net loss of $5.35 billion. There were plans to cut another 1,000 salaried and management positions by the end of 2009, bringing the reduction in ranks to 30 percent, after previous cuts of 1,500 positions. On June 17, 2009, UAL declared that the second-quarter traffic was to fall as much as 10.5 percent. In September 2009, UAL reported a 5.8 percent decline in its mainline service, with capacity down 8.9 percent.

UAL posted sharply higher second-quarter 2010 earnings of $273 million following its $28 million profit one year earlier. Revenue climbed 28 percent to $5.2 billion.

See also AIRLINES; UNITED CONTINENTAL HOLDINGS.

UNITED ARAB EMIRATES. In mid-May 2009, the United Arab Emirates, the second-largest Arab Gulf economy, informed the Gulf Cooperation Council that it was withdrawing from plans to join a monetary union with the GCC, damaging hopes for economic integration planned for thirty years. The program was intended to improve relations between oil-rich Arab states straddling the Persian Gulf. A projected central bank for five GCC nations also was put on hold. The collapse in November 2009 in Dubai has put considerable pressure on the government of the United Arab Emirates to step in with fresh financial support.

The nation's GDP growth projected into 2011was 3.5 percent, with a GDP of $312 billion, an inflation rate of 3.2 percent, and a GDP per head at $44,450.

See also DUBAI; MIDDLE EAST.

UNITED AUTO WORKERS. *See* AUTOMOBILE INDUSTRY; CHRYSLER; FIAT; FORD; VEBA.

UNITED CONTINENTAL HOLDINGS. Their pro forma combined results for the period indicated earnings climbing to $885 million from $28 million the year before. The company posted a fourth-quarter 2010 loss following its merger but witnessed strong revenue gains. The loss was $325 million and revenue was $8.4 billion, up 15 percent from the year before.

UNITED KINGDOM. The economy is set for recovery supported by improving financial conditions, an expansionary monetary policy, and stronger international growth. However, the pick-up will be slow, with GDP projected to grow by slightly more than 1 percent in 2010, reflecting strong headwinds from balance sheet adjustments, a still weakening labor market, and fiscal tightening. In 2011, the recovery will gain momentum, but resource utilization will remain low and the unemployment rate is projected to reach 9.5 percent. Inflation is likely to remain below the 2 percent target for an extended period. Financial sector support, monetary easing, and fiscal stimulus have cushioned the downturn. While monetary policy should remain expansionary over the projection period, normalization of interest rates will probably need to start in 2011. The weak fiscal position makes further consolidation necessary; an announcement of concrete and comprehensive consolidation plans up front would enhance macroeconomic stability. Strengthening financial regulation and supervision would also support stability and hinder a build-up of new imbalances at historically low interest rates.

In 2001, large British banks lent about the same amount to their corporate and consumer clients as they took in deposits, but by the end of June 2008, they were lending out $1.16 trillion. The British economy contracted by 0.5 percent in the three months through September 2008, ending a string of sixteen years without a negative quarter. On September 3, Prime Minister Gordon Brown unveiled the first in a series of measures to prop up the collapsing housing market.

The number of people in Britain receiving jobless payments increased at the fastest pace in sixteen years in October, reaching 980,000. The Bank of England predicted that the economy was likely to shrink through much of 2009, and the total unemployment rate for the third quarter rose to 5.8 percent, the highest in eleven years. On November 24, the British government announced a large sales tax cut as part of a package of measures to stimulate the struggling national economy. The government attempted to spend its way out of its first recession in seventeen years by cutting taxes and increasing public spending despite a budget deficit that was already among the largest of any developed nation. As part of the $30 billion fiscal package presented to Parliament, the government planned to reduce the value-added tax to 15 percent from 17.5 percent for a year, help homeowners struggling with mortgage payments, and further support retirees and small businesses.

As a result, Britain's budget deficit was projected to climb to 8 percent of GDP in 2010. To cover for the tax cuts, the government increased national insurance payroll deductions and raised income taxes for those earning more than 150,000 pounds a year. The tax rate rose to 45 percent from 40 percent, which was the highest bracket for the past twenty years, to take effect beginning in 2011. Only 32,000 mortgages were approved for house purchases in October. The number matched the record low from August and was almost two-thirds below the level of a year earlier. Housing prices in England registered their largest decline in sixteen years during November. This drop, the tenth in a row, was the largest since 1992 when house prices fell a monthly

3 percent. As banks pulled in mortgage lending and buyers were deterred by the economic slowdown, house prices were projected to decrease 10 percent in 2009 and 3 percent in 2010 after a 9 percent decline in 2008. Repossessions were expected to reach a near record high of 70,000 in 2009. That number would be up from 45,000 in 2008 and close to the highest level ever recorded, 75,500 in 1991, when the United Kingdom was last in a recession.

The United Kingdom's bank rescue plan, considered the global model of what to do right, ran into trouble by mid-December. Domestic banks were resisting pressure to lend more as they sought to protect themselves in the harsh meltdown. In October, when Gordon Brown presented the plan to inject capital into banks in exchange for a substantial shareholding, he promised he would not only attempt to stabilize the British banking system but to jump-start the stalled lending markets. British retail sales posted a 0.6 percent drop for November following October's 0.1 percent dip. On December 15, the government increased the amount that it would make available for lending to first-time home buyers by a third in an effort to help the struggling construction industry. The funds were lent to first-time homebuyers, were interest free for five years, and could be used as a deposit for up to a third of the price of a home. This increase brought the total to about $600 million. The Exchequer sought support of the biggest British banks for a 1 billion pound mortgage program aimed at preventing home repossessions.

In the third quarter of 2008, the British economy shrank by more than previously thought as Britain headed into a deep recession. GDP fell 0.6 percent in the quarter compared with a 0.5 percent decline earlier. The drop was the steepest since 1990. Manufacturing shrank 1.6 percent, the largest decline since 2001, while the distribution, hotels, and catering sector contracted 2.1 percent, the biggest decline since 1980.

The British economy officially sank into recession in January 2009, with output falling 1.5 percent in the fourth quarter 2008 as the financial crisis ravaged banks, retail, and manufacturing. Britain was officially in recession, based on the standard definition of a recession of two consecutive quarters of negative growth. It was the biggest decline since the early days of Margaret Thatcher's government nearly thirty years ago and prompted a further bout of selling of the pound, which slumped to a new twenty-three-year low against the dollar.

The government released $642 million in public funds to bail out two key venues for the 2012 London Olympics in the face of the global economic downturn. The United Kingdom lost a record number of jobs in the closing months of 2008, with unemployment claims rising for the eleventh straight month, increasing 77,900.

In January 2009, Prime Minister Brown pledged to create 100,000 jobs through a public works program and announced that he would press banks to resume normal lending. On January 27, Britain declared a $3.2 billion aid package loan guaranteed from the European Investment Bank and another 1 billion pounds from its Treasury. By January 2009, luxury home prices fell 3.7 percent. In the year, the average price of homes that cost more than $1.4 million slumped 21 percent. The declining British pound pushed up prices for food and other imported items. Consumer price inflation rose to 3.2 percent in February on an annualized basis, up from 3 percent in January. The 26 percent decline of the pound against the U.S. dollar and 16 percent decline against the euro over a twelve-month period failed to encourage demand for British exports. The United Kingdom's fourth-quarter GDP contracted 1.6 percent in 2008, more than the 1.5 percent reported in January. In early April, the Bank of England's Monetary Policy Committee kept its key interest rate at 0.5 percent and agreed to pump $110 billion in new money into the economy through June 2009. By mid-April, Britain's budget deficit was 11 percent of its GDP compared with the 13 percent forecast for the United States in 2009. Without large spending cuts, it would jump to 80 percent of the overall economy in coming years from today's level of about 40 percent.

A drop in U.K. retail prices, their first fall in nearly half a century, fueled fears that shook up the government's forecasts. By the end of April, it was feared that the country's economy would contract by 3 to 3.5 percent in 2009. On April 22, the government laid out plans for more than $1 trillion in deficit spending over the next five years and ordered a five-percentage-point increase, to 50 percent, in the top marginal rate of income tax for the nation's highest earners. By the end of April, the government stated that it would run its largest peacetime budget deficit on record—about 12 percent of GDP in both of the next two years. Should the economy return quickly to growth after shrinking by 3.5 percent in 2009, the deficit would remain above 5 percent of GDP in 2013. That would push the government's debts up to more than 75 percent of GDP from about the present 43 percent.

The U.K. economy took its worst drop in three decades, shrinking by 1.9 percent in the first quarter 2009 from the previous quarter. By June, Britain's unemployment rate rose to 7.2 percent in the three months prior to April from 6.5 percent in the previous quarter. The number of claimants for unemployment benefits more than doubled in the twelve months ending in May to 1.54 million, the highest level since 1997. By the end of June, weak lending was predicted to contribute to a 4.3 percent fall in the United Kingdom's GDP, more pessimistic than an earlier forecast for a 3.7 percent decline. The GDP fell by 0.8 percent in the second quarter from the first and dropped 5.6 percent year over year, the largest annual decline since quarterly records began in 1955. On August 28, the government reported that the nation's GDP contracted 0.7 percent from April to June 2009. Many experts expected economic growth to resume in the third quarter after bottoming out in a 2.4

percent contraction in the first three months. Any return to expansion in the third quarter would be the first quarterly rise since early 2008 and would be the official end of the 2008–2009 meltdown.

The nation's manufacturing output rose in July 2009, the best monthly manufacturing data in three years, with output climbing 0.9 percent. The country's GDP edged up 0.2 percent over the period following a 0.3 percent decline in the three months to July 2009. Unemployment in the United Kingdom jumped to 7.9 percent in the three months through July 2009, lowering hopes of a speedy economic recovery. The British economy remained in recession during the third quarter 2009. GDP contracted by 0.4 percent from July to September from the earlier three months, and it shrank by 5.2 percent compared to a year before. The British economy contracted for six successive quarters, making this the longest downturn since 1955, lagging behind other European Union nations. By October 2009, housing prices rose for the third straight month as a low supply of suitable properties continued to push prices upward. House prices increased 0.2 percent from September, though they fell 4.2 percent for the year. To offset the recent gloomy news on the U.K. economy, the European Commission announced on November 1, 2009, that the United Kingdom's GDP would expand 0.9 percent in 2010 and 1.9 percent in 2011, outpacing growth of 0.7 percent in 2010 and 1.5 percent in 2011 for the sixteen nations of the eurozone. On December 9, 2009, the government said that it would return money from banks to taxpayers by placing a 50 percent tax on banker bonuses of more than $40,700.

By mid-April 2010, the U.K. economy was recovering but still delicate. Output rose by a mere 0.2 percent in the first quarter of the year. In the three months ending in February, unemployment increased by 43,000. The number of people seeking work was 2.5 million, and the joblessness rate reached 8 percent. Consumer price inflation rose to 3.4 percent. With a new coalition government in place, tough choices were to be made by the end of May 2010. Cuts came to $8.9 billion. The budget deficit was 11.1 percent of GDP, setting a peacetime record. The burden of the cuts fell on departmental budgets responsible for public services. The government aimed to deliver a huge fiscal retrenchment equal to 6.3 percent of GDP by 2014–2015.

By summer 2010, new studies indicated that Britain's recession was deeper than estimated, as the economy grew by only 0.3 percent in the first three months of 2010. GDP fell during the meltdown by 6.4 percent, not the 6.2 percent originally presented to the public. In addition, the unemployment rate remained at 7.8 percent for the three months ending in July. On October 19, in order to lower its daunting levels of national debt, the government announced plans to lower it military personnel by 10 percent, scrap 40 percent of the army's artillery and tanks, withdraw all of its troops from Germany within a decade, and eliminate 25,000 civilian jobs in its Defense Ministry. Then, as expected, the government detailed on the following day sweeping budget cuts that would have an impact on every citizen from welfare recipients to the queen as a strategy that chose austerity over stimulus to repair the economy.

By 2020, the retirement age was expected to reach sixty-six years. Over four years, $127 billion, or 19 percent, will help to pare a budget deficit of 155 million euros. On October 21, the government stated that it would introduce a new bank levy on the United Kingdom's largest banks to raise nearly $4 billion in annual tax revenue from 2012. Then, on October 26, the government announced that its GDP rose 0.8 percent, or a seasonally adjusted annual growth rate of 3.2 percent. The nation's GDP growth was strong in the third quarter 2010, with output climbing by 0.8 percent for the quarter and 2.8 percent for the year. By the end of November 2010, the country's leadership planned a 40 percent cut in government spending for higher education from 2011 to 2015. To fill this gap, expectations were for a significant tuition increase. On December 9, it was reported that the United Kingdom's five major banks will each pay hundreds of millions of pounds to the government each year as a charge to offset the risks they pose to the economy, raising about $4 billion a year beginning in 2012. The GDP growth in 2011 was 1.3 percent, with a GDP of $2,403 billion, an inflation of 3.1 percent, and a GDP per head of $38,360.

In early January 2011, the U.K. financial sector cut more jobs in the last three months of 2010 than at any time in the past seventeen years. Thirty thousand positions were lost in financial services in the fourth quarter, with another 15,000 lost in the first three months of 2011. The nation's economy shrank for the first time in more than one year during the fourth quarter, with GDP dropping 0.5 percent in October through December after expanding by 0.7 percent in the third quarter. The fall in the fourth quarter indicated that the U.K. economy grew by 1.4 percent for 2010 after contractions of 4.9 percent in 2009 and 0.1 percent in 2008. By the start of 2011, consumer confidence in the United Kingdom crashed, reaching its lowest level in twenty-two months. In addition, retail sales slowed and were expected to continue their decline. On February 9, the government announced an agreement with the nation's major banks to increase their lending to businesses, at the same time lowering bonuses and increasing transparency in pay practices. The program was called Project Merlin.

In March, the unemployment rate rose to 8 percent in the three months to January from 7.9 percent in the quarter ending in December. In addition, inflation began to climb as consumer prices jumped 4.4 percent in February from the previous year. Then, in March, inflation fell to 4 percent, the first time since the summer, as food prices dropped. With retail sales falling 3.5 percent in March, the sharpest monthly downturn in fifteen years, economic concerns grew. In addition, real household incomes were predicted to decline

2 percent in 2011, making the United Kingdom's income squeeze the worst for two years in a row since the 1930s. The number of people claiming unemployment benefits climbed in May by 19,600 to 1.49 million, the largest count since July 2009. The output of the nation's service industries, which accounted for almost three-quarters of its GDP, climbed by 0.8 percent from January to April. The nation's inflation hit a greater-than-expected 5.2 percent rise in September.

On November 17, Northern Rock became the first bailed-out bank in the United Kingdom to be sold back to the private sector, suggesting that the government had given up on turning a profit on the bank stakes it retained and was now focused on shedding its ownership stakes instead. Four years after Northern Rock collapsed, it was sold to Virgin Money, a unit of Virgin Group, for $1.18 billion. The U.K. taxpayers therefore lost at least $600 million on their investment. Then, on November 29, the government announced that it was falling behind with its deficit reduction plan and that it would be another two years before a turnaround would occur. The United Kingdom would now have to borrow an additional $172 billion through 2015, with the nation's economy expected to grow 0.9 percent in 2011, less than the original 1.7 percent predicted, and 0.7 percent in 2012. The economy was predicted to grow 2.1 percent in 2013.

In mid-2010, the new government announced its intention to slash deficits and energize economic expansion with radical fiscal austerity. It failed. For 2012, the government plans for further austerity measures (until 2017) as the economy continues to falter. So far, 2.6 million people have lost their jobs, the highest in seventeen years. Unemployment continues to climb, growth is flat, and the ratio of national debt to GDP continues to rise faster than originally expected. The budget deficit was expected to fall to 8.4 percent of GDP in fiscal 2011.

Then, on January 25, 2012, it was reported that the U.K. economy had contracted 0.2 percent in the 2011 fourth quarter.

See also ASSET PROTECTION SCHEME; BANK OF ENGLAND; BARCLAYS; BBC; EUROPEAN CENTRAL BANK; FTSE; ICELAND; KEYNES, JOHN MAYNARD; LLOYDS; MANUFACTURING; PROPERTY (2011); ROYAL BANK OF SCOTLAND; WATERFORD WEDGWOOD; WINDFALL TAX; WOOLWORTHS.

UNITED NATIONS (UN). *See* POVERTY.

UNITED PARCEL SERVICE (UPS). UPS's second-quarter 2009 income fell 49 percent, with its export volume falling 7.3 percent. Profits in the third quarter 2009 fell 43 percent from a year earlier. UPS's second-quarter 2010 profit climbed 90 percent to $845 million, up from $445 million the year before.

On October 21, 2010, UPS posted an 81 percent surge in third-quarter profit of $991 million. Revenue climbed 9.3 percent to $12.19 billion. UPS forecast that its package shipments would climb 7.5 percent in the 2010 Christmas season.

UPS reported a 5.1 percent increase in third-quarter earnings on October 25, 2011. It posted a profit of $1.04 billion, with revenue of $13.17 billion.

Cf. FEDERAL EXPRESS.

UNITED STATES. The economy is gradually coming out of a severe recession in 2010. The decline of output has ceased since the summer, though significant trouble spots remain. The risk of new large bankruptcies in the banking system has diminished, but equity capital will need to be replenished to offset financial losses. The household sector is also undergoing significant adjustment, with a sharp reduction of debt and rebuilding of assets. Sizeable macroeconomic stimulus and easing financial conditions will support growth, though it will be somewhat weaker than during past recoveries. Unemployment will decline slowly. The Federal Reserve and the administration must begin to withdraw economic support as economic growth becomes self-sustaining. Gauging the appropriate timing will not be a simple task, but prolonged stimulus risks unanchoring inflation expectations and destabilizing asset markets. While the need to be flexible in the face of changing economic conditions is desirable, exit strategies should nonetheless be communicated clearly.

In 2011, it was projected that the lack of jobs and unemployment would remain high. Economic growth would weaken as policy stimulus faded and the inventory cycle topped out. Households and banks were still repairing their balance sheets following the meltdown, and growth could stay below trend for several years.

See also STATES (U.S.); U.S. DEPARTMENTS.

UNITED STATES STEEL CORPORATION. *See* US STEEL.

UNITED TECHNOLOGIES. Maker of Otis elevators, Carrier air conditioners, Pratt & Whitney jet engines, Sikorsky helicopters, Hamilton Sundstrand aerospace components, and various fire and security products. Hard hit by a simultaneous downturn in the building and aerospace industries, it cut 5 percent of its workforce, or 11,600 jobs, in early 2009. Their first-quarter net income announced on April 21 slid 26 percent as the firm moved to cut costs because of slipping demand. Its net income of $499 million dropped from $1.08 billion a year before.

The company reported a decline of 17 percent in its third-quarter sales profit. The company's third-quarter 2010 earnings rose 13 percent to $1.2 billion, up from $1.06 billion in 2009. Revenue climbed 1.1 percent to $13.53 billion. In 2009, revenue fell 11 percent.

Its third quarter 2011 showed a profit of $1.32 billion, up from $1.2 billion the year before. Revenue increased 8.7 percent to $14.8 billion.

UNIVERSITY ENDOWMENTS. *See* HARVARD UNIVERSITY; STANFORD UNIVERSITY; YALE UNIVERSITY.

UNIVISION COMMUNICATIONS. *See NEW YORK TIMES.*

UNPAID FURLOUGHS. *See* FURLOUGHS.

UPS. *See* UNITED PARCEL SERVICE.

URUGUAY. Following a grand economic growth in 2010, Uruguay expansion as projected would slow to 4.4 percent in 2011 from 6.0 percent the year before. The nation's GDP growth was 4.4 percent, with GDP at $40 billion, an inflation rate of 7.2 percent, and a GDP per head of $11,850.

U.S. *See* UNITED STATES; STATES (U.S.).

US AIRWAYS. Reported second-quarter 2009 profit of $58 million compared to a $568 million loss a year earlier. In early September 2009, US Airways reported that its August passenger traffic fell 3.9 percent, about in line with the airline's 3.8 percent reduction in capacity. On October 28, 2009, the airlines disclosed its retrenchment program, cutting back on a number of routes so it could focus on its main hubs and losing 1,000 jobs.

In March 2010, traffic was flat, with a 1.7 percent reduction in capacity. However, its revenue, the sum it takes in for each seat flown per mile, rose about 18 percent from the year before. US Airways reported that its profit climbed to $279 million and revenue for the second quarter 2010 rose 19 percent to $3.17 billion. Its fourth-quarter profit, the first since 2006, was the second best in its history. Income was $28 million, with revenue climbing 6.1 percent.

In January 2012, US Airways was exploring the possibilities of acquiring American Airlines. The country's fifth airline by traffic posted a profit of $18 million on record revenue of $3.2 billion.

See also AIRLINES.

USA TODAY. See NEWSPAPERS.

U.S. BANCORP. Posted a 65 percent drop in fourth-quarter 2008 net income as it took a $253 million securities write-down and boosted credit-loss provisions. It had received $6.6 billion in November 2008 from the U.S. Treasury under the Troubled Asset Relief Program. It reported a net income of $330 million, or 15 cents a share, compared with $942 million, or 53 cents a share, the year before.

Bancorp's third-quarter 2010 profit rose 51 percent of $908 million, with a profit of $908 million. Net revenue climbed 7.9 percent to $4.59 billion. U.S. Bancorp reported fourth-quarter earnings surging 62 percent to $974 million.

U.S. CENSUS. Preparing for the 2010 census would employ 1.2 million people and inject $2.3 billion into the job market. For the 2010 census count, the government hired 700,000 citizens, leading to a fall in unemployed people. By mid-July 2010, about 225,000 were released from their work, increasing the percentage of unemployed.

U.S.–CHINA TRADE. China and the United States were each other's second-largest trading partner, with the value of the two-way trade in goods exceeding $300 billion. Since 2003, U.S. exports to China have doubled. The U.S. trade surplus with China in services grew 36 percent each year and the overall value of American export services to China exceeded $16 billion in 2008.

U.S. businesses invested more than $60 billion in 57,000 projects in China. In 2007, American-funded companies in China enjoyed a 17 percent profit, while domestically the profit of U.S. businesses dropped by 3 percent on average. A possible new trade war between China and the United States began in September 2009, with the United States placing tariffs on imported Chinese tires, and China in response imposing tariffs on U.S. chickens and auto parts.

See also CHINA; G-2.

U.S. COMMERCE DEPARTMENT. A federal agency established in 1913 to promote domestic and foreign trade. The agency has a $19 million annual budget and fewer than twenty grant officers. Under the stimulus plan of 2009, the department is now in charge of $7 billion in grants to expand Internet access in rural areas. In mid-summer 2010, the Commerce Department revised major figures on the Great Recession, which began in December 2007.

See also RECESSION OF 2007–2012; U.S.–CHINA TRADE.

U.S. DEFICIT. In the 2008 fiscal year, the budget deficit approached $1 trillion, roughly equal to the combined budgets of the U.S. military and Medicare, the government health care program for the elderly and disabled.

See also CHIMERICA; DEFICIT (BUDGET, U.S.); NATIONAL COMMISSION ON FISCAL RESPONSIBILITY AND REFORM; TAX CUTS.

U.S. DEPARTMENT OF COMMERCE. By mid-summer 2010, with the stimulus funds of $862 billion detailed, the Commerce Department used most of the money to help with the census count and for consumers converting their television sets from analog to digital. Other programs funding scientific research and facilities were proceeding slowly.

U.S. DEPARTMENT OF EDUCATION. By mid-summer 2010, with the stimulus funds of $862 billion detailed, the Education Department gave states a $53 billion fund, administered by the department, to help balance their budgets. Most of that money is now gone. States received another $10 billion from the aid bill signed in August 2010. Infrastructure projects were worth around $27.26 billion.

U.S. DEPARTMENT OF ENERGY. A federal agency established in 1977 to control oil prices and allocations, coordinate energy research and development efforts, set rates for oil and oil-product appliances, and design conservation standards.

In 2009, the Energy Department's annual budget was approximately $25 billion. With $40 billion in new funds from the stimulus plan of 2009, some programs would grow.

By mid-summer 2010, with the stimulus funds of $862 billion detailed, the Energy Department had more than 100 clean energy manufacturing facilities built, and $6 billion was used to increase the pace of clean-up work at former nuclear sites.

U.S. DEPARTMENT OF HEALTH AND HUMAN RESOURCES. By mid-summer 2010, with the stimulus funds of $862 billion detailed, the Health and Human Services Department paid out almost all of the $87 billion included in the stimulus package to assist states balance their Medicaid budgets. Then, in August, the president signed a bill that gave the states another $16 billion to 2011.

U.S. DEPARTMENT OF HOMELAND SECURITY. By mid-summer 2010, with the stimulus funds of $862 billion detailed, the Homeland Security Department's projects included installing new explosive detection systems at ten airports and modernizing ten land ports of entry.

U.S. DEPARTMENT OF HOUSING AND URBAN DEVELOPMENT. By mid-summer 2010, with the stimulus funds of $862 billion detailed, the Housing and Urban Development Department used its fund to help public-housing authorities build or rehabilitate more than 150,000 low-income housing units. The department had made almost all of its funds available and was paying the funds out as work was completed.

U.S. DEPARTMENT OF JUSTICE. By mid-summer 2010, with the stimulus funds of $862 billion detailed, the Justice Department awarded grants for the hiring of local police officers and anti-crime programs. More than 99 percent of its funds had been made available and were paid out over time.

See also STANDARD & POORS.

U.S. DEPARTMENT OF LABOR. A federal agency created in 1913 to advance workers' welfare, working conditions, and employment opportunities in general.

See also UNEMPLOYMENT.

U.S. DEPARTMENT OF THE TREASURY. A federal agency created in 1789 to impose and collect taxes and customs duties, enforce revenue and fiscal laws, disburse federal funds, manage the public debt, and coin and print money.

The Treasury was and remains a central player in the meltdown. The Treasury led the way for the $700 billion bank bailout plan passed during the George W. Bush administration.

On September 8, the Treasury announced plans to replace the chief executives of both Fannie Mae and Freddie Mac and buy $1 billion of preferred shares in each without providing immediate cash. The Treasury initially turned down a request by General Motors for as much as $10 billion to help finance a merger with Chrysler. On December 31, the Treasury drafted broad guidelines for aid to the auto industry that would allow them to provide bailout funds to any firm they deemed important to making or financing cars.

The Treasury laid out details of its proposal on May 26, 2009, for dealing with bank stock warrants it received in return for cash injections into troubled banks.

With passage of the Wall Street Reform Act (2010), the U.S. Treasury received funds for an Office of Financial Research to track looming problems.

In March 2011, the Treasury expected profit from the bailouts to approach $24 billion.

See also ASSET GUARANTEE PROGRAM; AUDITORS; AUTOMOBILE INDUSTRY; BANK BAILOUT; ECONOMIC STIMULUS PLAN; EMERGENCY ECONOMIC STABILIZATION ACT OF 2008; FINANCIAL REGULATION PLAN (2009); FINANCIALSTABILITY.GOV; GEITHNER, TIMOTHY; GENERAL MOTORS; GMAC; INTERNAL REVENUE SERVICE; LEHMAN BROTHERS; LIFE INSURERS; OFFICE OF FINANCIAL RESEARCH; PAULSON, HENRY; PAY; TOXIC ASSETS; TROUBLED ASSET RELIEF PROGRAM; VEBA; WALL STREET REFORM ACT (2010).

U.S. DEPARTMENT OF TRANSPORTATION. By mid-summer 2010, with the stimulus funds of $862 billion detailed, the Transportation Department made available most of its funds for smaller projects, though less of the money had been paid out. Around 11,000 highway projects and hundreds of airport and rail projects were under way.

U.S. DOLLAR INDEX. Measures the dollar's performance against a basket of currencies; climbed 1.5 percent in 2011.

U.S. GOVERNMENT DEBT. The world's safest investment, it lowers the cost of borrowing for the U.S. government but slows down the recovery. Investors remaining reluctant to put money into stocks and corporate bonds could choke off funds that businesses require to keep financing day-to-day activities.

See also CHINA; CHIMERICA; ZERO INTEREST.

U-SHAPED RECESSION. *See* RECESSION.

US STEEL. Had a $439 million first-quarter 2009 loss. US Steel reported at the end of April that its sales fell 47 percent to $2.75 billion from $5.20 billion one year earlier.

At the end of July 2009, US Steel reported a second-quarter loss of $392 million. Nevertheless, it recalled about 800 workers at its huge flat-rolling mill, suggesting a forecast by them of a brighter future. The company swung to third-quarter 2009 losses. US Steel narrowed its third-quarter 2010 losses to $51 million from $303 million the year before. Management reported its ninth straight quarterly loss. Revenue climbed 25 percent to $4.86 billion.

Cf. ARCELORMITTAL.

U.S. SUPREME COURT. *See* CHRYSLER.

U.S. THRIFTS. *See* BANKING.

UTILITY CUTOFFS. During the Great Recession, utility shutoffs rose 5 percent in 2009 and 4.3 million households were disconnected for nonpayment.

UZBEKISTAN. The economy was expected to grow by 8.5 percent in 2011. The nation's GDP growth was 8.5 percent, with a GDP of $44 billion, an inflation rate of 14 percent, and a GDP per head of $1,510.

V

VACANCIES. *See* APARTMENT VACANCIES; OFFICE RENTS.

VARIABLE-RATE MORTGAGE. A type of mortgage that permits the interest rate on the loan to rise or fall automatically in accordance with a predetermined index, for instance, an index of banks' cost of funds, such as the London Inter-Bank Offer Rate (LIBOR). The interest rate can fluctuate every six months but cannot be raised by more than 2.5 percentage points over the life of the mortgage. In addition, banks must offer customers a choice between variable-rate and other conventional mortgages.

See also CONVERTIBLE WRAPAROUND MORTGAGE; FLEXIBLE MORTGAGE; FLEXIBLE-PAYMENT MORTGAGE; LIBOR; RENEGO-TIABLE-RATE MORTGAGE.

VAUXHALL. *See* MAGNA; OPEL.

VEBA (VOLUNTARY EMPLOYEE BENEFICIARY ASSOCIATION). U.S. Treasury Department protection for the United Auto Workers union pension fund that controls 55 percent of the equity in the new Chrysler Corporation since it emerged from bankruptcy. The Treasury's contribution was a $4.6 billion note, payable over thirteen years at a 9 percent interest rate, helping to fund roughly $10 billion in liabilities.

See also CHRYSLER.

VENEZUELA. In the winter of 2007–2008, $100 million of free heating oil was supplied to poor people throughout the United States by the government of Venezuela. Then, on January 5, 2009, President Chavez announced that he was suspending the program. This temporary action resulted from the sharp drop in oil prices, which forced the country to reduce government spending.

Oil accounts for 93 percent of the government's export income and about 50 percent of its overall income. Venezuela also sold 15,000 barrels a day of subsidized oil to Central American nations. The government provided nearly 100,000 barrels a day of oil and oil products to Cuba, a close ally, free of charge. On March 21, President Chavez announced a lowering of 2009's federal budget, offsetting a drop in the government's oil revenues. Growth slowed to its most sluggish rate in five years. The new measures included a plan to expand the government's domestic debt by roughly $10 billion. The budget would be lowered by 6.7 percent, while the minimum wage would rise in 2009 by 20 percent from about $372 per month. An annual inflation rate of 29.5 percent in the capital was a major reason for the wage adjustment.

As most emerging nations of the world were improving their economies by fall 2009, Venezuela's third-quarter output declined 4.5 percent compared with the year before. This fall followed a second-quarter drop of 2.4 percent, the second consecutive quarter of economic decline, which officially placed the nation into recession. Imports were down 29 percent and retail sales fell 11.5 percent. Inflation remained high at nearly 30 percent for 2009. By December 2009, the president of Venezuela threatened to nationalize the nation's entire private banking system even though its ten largest banks, which control about 70 percent of deposits, were in good shape. By mid-month, with its economy shrinking and inflation soaring, Venezuela began nationalizing its banks, stroking fears that a full-blown banking crisis was fast approaching. Venezuela's economy was falling deeper into recession even as the rest of the region recovered.

For 2011, it was projected that the economy would continue to shrink for a third year running. The nation's GDP growth was -2.5 percent, with GDP at $215 billion, an inflation rate of 40.3 percent, and a GDP per head of $7,370. On January 1, 2011, the government devalued its currency for the second time within the year. During the year it would add to inflation by raising the costs of imported items. The nation's annual inflation rate was already 26.9 percent, among the world's highest.

By January 2011, the nation's inflation rate rose to 28.9 percent from 27.4 percent the month before. In March, the nation's currency had been devalued two times in 2010. By summer, Venezuela had the world's highest inflation rate. In the third quarter, the economy grew by 4.1 percent.

VENTURE CAPITAL. Venture capitalists had a dismal 2009 resulting from the decline in investment activity. They invested just $14.6 billion into start-ups through the first three quarters of 2009, down from more than $25 billion the year before. It does not appear that the venture industry in 2010 will match the $31 billion invested for all of 2008.

By September 2011, venture-capital groups raised $21 billion in 80 funds, matching the total for 2009 gathered by 190 funds. The amount collected and the number of funds are still only half what they were before the meltdown.

VERIZON. As businesses cut back and unemployed people no longer needed cell phones and laptop data cards, the company announced on July 27, 2009, a 21 percent decline. Management announced that it would eliminate 8,000 jobs in the landline unit by the end of 2009. Verizon Communications posted a 30 percent drop in its third-quarter 2009 profit. The company added 1.3 million new wireless subscribers in the quarter, down from 2.1 million a year before.

VETERANS. While the 8.4 percent unemployment rate for veterans in 2010 was lower than the 9.5 percent rate for the general population, the jobless rate for veterans who served since 9/11 climbed to 11.8 percent in July 2010. Those aged twenty-five to twenty-nine years, who made up 39 percent of the total, had an unemployment rate of 14.9 percent.

By year's end 2011, with the ending of U.S. involvement in Iraq and a slowdown in Afghanistan, returning veterans were facing a difficult homecoming. About 800,000 veterans were jobless, 1.4 million lived below the poverty line, and one in every three homeless adult men in the United States was a veteran. For veterans of these two wars, unemployment was 11.1 percent. For veterans between ages eighteen and twenty-four, it was 37.9 percent, up from 30.4 percent in November.

VETO (PRESIDENTIAL). *See* FORECLOSURE.

VIACOM. By February 2009, Viacom reported a 69 percent drop in quarterly profit resulting from the recession. On April 30, Viacom posted a 34 percent slide in first-quarter net income to $177 million.

Viacom reported a 37 percent gain in its first-quarter profit on April 29, 2010. Viacom witnessed a 12 percent fall in earnings for the fourth quarter. Profit for the quarter was $610 million, with revenue falling 4.8 percent to $3.83 billion. Revenue in the last quarter of the year fell 5 percent to $3.8 billion, with net earnings declining to $610 million.

In August 2011, Viacom reported a 37 percent quarterly profit of $574 million, up from $420 million the year before. Revenue climbed 15 percent to $3.77 billion. Net earnings increased in September by 33 percent. Total revenue climbed 22 percent to $4.05 billion. Revenue for the year grew 12 percent to $14.91 billion.

On February 2, 2012, management reported a $212 million profit for the fourth quarter 2011, with revenue climbing 3 percent to $3.95 billion.

See also UNEMPLOYMENT.

VIETNAM. Vietnam's central bank devalued the dong by 5.4 percent against the U.S. dollar and raised its benchmark interest rate by one percentage point to 8 percent. In the first seven months of 2010, exports of clothing and textiles rose by 17 percent to $5.8 billion. In 1990, GDP per person was below $100, and by 2010 it was well over $1,000. Inflation marched above 8 percent. Cheap labor is the primary catalyst for its huge growth over the past decade.

The nation's GDP growth was projected for 2011 to be 7.0 percent at $110 billion, with an inflation rate of 8.0 percent and a GDP per head of $1,240. Vietnam's economy by year's end 2010 remained burdened by inflation at 11.75 percent in December. The nation had a trade deficit that reached $13.235 billion for the year. In 2010, Vietnam imploded with debts of $4.5 billion and the fiscal deficit rose to 7.4 percent of GDP, breaching the target of 6.2 percent.

In 2011, Vietnam devalued its currency 8.5 percent, driving up prices of basic commodities. Consumer prices rose more than 12 percent in January, having an impact on the nation's growing inflation. In mid-April, the government lowered its 2011 GDP growth target to 6 percent from 6.5 percent and raised its inflation forecast to 15 percent from 11.75 percent.

See also SOUTHEAST ASIA.

VIOLENT CRIME. *See* CRIME.

VIRGIN GROUP. *See* UNITED KINGDOM.

VIRGIN MONEY. *See* UNITED KINGDOM.

VISA. Reported fourth-quarter 2009 earnings of $514 million.

For the quarter ending March 31, 2010, Visa reported a profit of $713 million compared with the year earlier profit of $536 million. On July 28, 2010, management reported that its third-quarter 2010 profit fell 1.8 percent from the year before. For the quarter ending June 30, Visa showed a profit of $716 million, and revenue climbed 23 percent to $2 billion. Visa's fiscal fourth-quarter 2010 profit rose 51 percent, with a profit of $774 million. The number of transactions processed on Visa's network increased 16 percent.

Visa's fiscal second-quarter 2011 earnings surged 40 percent. A profit of $1.01 billion, with revenue climbing 14 percent to $2.32 billion, was posted. In its fiscal fourth quarter, Visa's profit rose 14 percent. Net income in the quarter was $880 million, with an operating revenue in the quarter climbing 13 percent to $2.38 billion. By year's end, Visa had a fiscal fourth-quarter profit of 14 percent

Cf. MASTERCARD.

VIX. What traders refer to as a "fear index," a gauge tracked by the Chicago Board Options Exchange measuring investor use of options to guard against market fall. On August 8, 2011, the VIX surged to 48, the highest close since March 2009 when the bear market was terminating and registered its largest single-session percentage gain since 2007.

VODAFONE. A giant telecommunications firm, it declared in February 2009 that it would cut 500 jobs in the United Kingdom as part of a $1.45 billion cost-reduction program.

Cf. MOTOROLA; NOKIA.

VOLCKER, PAUL. He was the chairman of the Federal Reserve under presidents Carter and Reagan from August 1979 to August 1987. In 1952, he joined the staff of the Federal Reserve Bank of New York as a full-time economist. In 1962, he returned to become the director of financial analysis within the U.S. Treasury Department. In 1963, he became deputy undersecretary for monetary affairs, and from 1969 to 1974, he served as undersecretary of the Treasury for international monetary affairs.

Volcker is credited with ending the U.S. stagflation crisis of the 1970s. Inflation, which peaked at 13.5 percent, was lowered to 3.2 percent by 1983.

President Obama appointed him as the chairman of the White House's Economic Recovery Advisory Board. On September 16, 2009, Volcker said that banks should operate in a much less risky fashion, including not making trading bets with their own capital. He also believed that banks should be restricted to trading on their client's behalf instead of making bets with their own funds through internal units that often act like hedge funds.

VOLCKER RULE. Limits banks' investments with their own capital; goes into effect in 2012, with two years to comply.

See also PROPRIETARY TRADERS; VOLCKER, PAUL; WALL STREET REFORM ACT (2010).

VOLKSWAGEN. By December 2009, Volkswagen made public its application for financial assistance from Germany's $650 billion bank bailout program. The carmaker's affiliated bank and financial services units both wanted state loan guarantees. Volkswagen said that it would put about two-thirds of its employees in Germany, about 60,000 workers, on shorter hours for five days in the last week of February.

Following a 20 percent fall in fourth-quarter 2008 profit, the automaker forecast lower earnings and vehicle sales in 2009. In the first quarter 2009, Volkswagen sold 1.39 million cars worldwide. It reported a 74 percent drop in first-quarter net profit, which was $314.4 million. Revenue fell 11 percent from one year earlier. Volkswagen announced on May 17 that it was indefinitely postponing talks over a possible merger with Porsche. Days later, Porsche and Volkswagen confirmed that they would continue talks. On August 13, 2009, Volkswagen reported that it had reached a broad agreement to merge the premium sports carmaker Porsche into Volkswagen, paying as much as $4.7 billion. Volkswagen would take a 42 percent stake in Porsche's business by the end of 2009, with a full merger projected for 2011. The company reported an 86 percent fall in third-quarter 2009 profit. Net income at Europe's largest carmaker fell $253 million, as sales slumped 10 percent from a year earlier. On December 9, 2009, Volkswagen reported that it would purchase a 20 percent stake in Suzuki Motor for $2.5 billion.

June 2010, U.S. sales climbed 11 percent over June 2009. Management stated on July 30 that Volkswagen had posted a high net profit of $1.62 billion.

On February 25, 2011, management reported that its profit surged sevenfold for 2010, climbing to $9.41 billion. Full-year revenue climbed 21 percent. It placed Volkswagen's earnings above those of Ford and GM. Volkswagen sold 7.28 million cars and trucks in 2010, up 15 percent from 6.31 million in 2009, placing Volkswagen third in global sales behind Toyota's 8.42 million and GM's 8.39 million. Volkswagen doubled its 2010 profit to $3.16 billion. In February, Volkswagen posted a sevenfold increase in 2010 profit. Global sales climbed 17.5 percent to 1.2 billion cars. Profit in the second quarter more than tripled to $6.9 billion. October had sales of 28,028 cars, up 39.6 percent from the year before.

See also AUTOMOBILE INDUSTRY; GERMANY; PORSCHE.
Cf. FORD; GENERAL MOTORS; TOYOTA.

VOLUNTARY EMPLOYEE BENEFICIARY ASSOCIATION. *See* VEBA.

VOLVO. New truck deliveries fell by more than half in January 2009 to 10,232 vehicles, down 51 percent from 20,856 in 2008. Deliveries to Eastern Europe and North America were hardest hit, down 78 percent and 67 percent, respectively. Volvo made trucks under the Mack, Renault, Eicher, and Nissan Diesel brands, as well as their own. On March 12, Volvo management announced that it was freezing salaries and scaling back production. To avoid further layoffs, Volvo signed a deal with its unions to lower personnel costs. Truck deliveries fell 51 percent globally and 63 percent in Europe from a year before. By April, it swung to a first-quarter 2009 loss of $510 million. Revenue declined 27 percent. In April, truck deliveries plunged 63 percent from a year earlier. Volvo delivered 9,196 vehicles, down from 24,616 in April 2008. In Europe and North America, deliveries fell 69 percent to 4,052 and 1,128 trucks, respectively. Deliveries in Eastern Europe dropped 87 percent to 382 trucks.

On July 21, Volvo posted its worst-ever quarterly net loss as sales fell in the wake of the economic downturn. It had a net loss of $718.5 million for the three months ending June 30. Ford Motor Company announced on October 28, 2009, that it had chosen China's Zhejiang Geely Holding Group as the preferred bidder for its Volvo subsidiary. For the entire year, Volvo was expected to sell about 325,000 cars made by 20,000 employees. By year's end 2009, Ford agreed to terms for Volvo's sale, with a formal agreement to be signed in the first quarter of 2010. On March 28, 2010, Geely agreed to purchase Volvo cars for $1.8 billion in the hopes of bringing the Chinese company onto the global automotive stage.

Volvo has about one-half of its production staff in Sweden and yet laid off one-fifth of its workforce between fall 2008 and the end of 2009. For its second quarter 2011, Volvo's net debt was $14.5 billion.

See also AUTOMOBILE INDUSTRY; SWEDEN.

VOUCHERS. *See* GERMANY.

V-SHAPED RECESSION. *See* RECESSION.

W

WACHOVIA. In late October 2008, Wachovia suffered a $23.7 billion quarterly loss, the biggest ever for an American bank. Sold to the Wells Fargo Bank.

In December 2011, the Securities and Exchange Commission, the Justice Department, and other regulators agreed to a $148 million settlement from Wachovia Bank on charges that the bank received millions of dollars in profits by rigging bids in the municipal securities market. The settlement also included an injunction against future violations of the antifraud provisons of federal securities laws.

See also FINANCIAL CRISIS INQUIRY REPORT; WELLS FARGO BANK.

WAGE GROWTH. *See* UNEMPLOYMENT.

WAGES. By December 2009, the average weekly wage for most of U.S. workers rose by nearly two-thirds of a percentage point in a single month to $622. The recession of 2007 led to a considerable fall in the growth of real wages in the West in 2009. Growth in average monthly wages worldwide (115 countries and territories) was 1.6 percent in 2009 and 1.5 percent in 2008 compared with 2.8 percent in 2007. In advanced nations, real wages fell 0.5 percent at the onset of the meltdown in 2008 before growing 0.6 percent in 2009. In 2007, they rose 0.8 percent. In Asia, real wages grew 8 percent in 2009; in Eastern Europe and Central Asia, real wage growth contracted 2.2 percent in 2009; in Latin America and the Caribbean, growth was at 2.2 percent; and for Africa, wages climbed 2.4 percent in 2009.

WAGONER, RICK. Became president of General Motors on October 5, 1998, and in June added chief executive to his title. On February 26, 2009, General Motors announced a $9.6 billion loss in the fourth quarter 2008, bringing its loss for the year to $30.9 billion and raising new concerns about its viability. On March 27, the U.S. government asked Wagoner to resign as part of an agreement for new federal aid. He accepted.

See also GENERAL MOTORS.

WALGREEN CO. Management posted that August 2010 sales rose 2.1 percent, the third straight monthly increase.

Walgreen's fiscal fourth-quarter 2011 earnings climbed 69 percent, with a profit of $792 million and sales rising 6.5 percent to $18 billion.

WALL STREET. Firms on Wall Street reported nearly $3 billion in losses in the third quarter 2011, reducing profits through September to $9.6 billion. It was estimated that Wall Street banks and smaller brokerages may lay off about 10,000 positions in New York City by the end of 2012.

***WALL STREET JOURNAL* (WSJ).** On October 14, 2009, the *Wall Street Journal* announced that its average weekday circulation rose to 2.02 million printed copies and online subscriptions, making it the nation's largest newspaper by weekday circulation.

In a December 2011 survey reported in the *Wall Street Journal*, economists expected an unemployment rate of 8.5 percent by the end of 2012.

See also CEO COUNCIL; CONFIDENCE BUILDING; ENERGY INNOVATION; GLOBAL FINANCE; NEWS CORPORATION; NEWSPAPERS; SUSTAINABLE JOBS.

WALL STREET REFORM ACT (DODD-FRANK) (2010). Signed by President Obama on July 14, 2010, it is considered the largest overhaul of the industry since legislation of the 1930s. The act created a council of regulators to monitor economic risks, established a new agency—Bureau of Consumer Financial Protection—to police consumer financial products, and set new standards for the way derivatives are traded, rules on golden parachutes for employees at public firms, policies for ATM cards, the abolishment of the Office of Thrift Supervision, and rules on hedge fund registration. The law subjected more financial companies to federal oversight. The planned timetable was as follows:

- *Summer 2010*: Federal authority to seize systematically important firms on the brink of collapse; creation of federal insurance office at the Treasury Department.
- *Fall 2010*: Financial Stability Oversight Council meets for first time.
- *Winter 2010*: Rules governing nonbonding shareholder votes on executive pay.
- *Spring 2011*: Rules setting risk-retention requirements for securitized assets; Federal Reserve writes rules on fees charged to retailers when customers use debit cards.
- *Summer 2011*: Consumer protection bureau gets authority over consumer issues; Office of Thrift Supervision merges with the Office of the Comptroller of the Currency; derivatives rules completed, including clearing and exchange trading requirements; hedge funds and investment advisers must register with the Securities Exchange Commission.

- *Fall 2011 and beyond*: Established rules limiting banks' ability to invest in hedge funds and use their own capital to trade—the so-called Volcker Rule establishes limiting the size of large institutions to no more than 10 percent of aggregated liabilities; regulators begin writing rules requiring banks to hold a new form of capital, known as contingent capital; issue new streamlined mortgage-disclosure forms.

It was expected that this financial reform program will require no fewer than 243 new rules by eleven agencies over a twelve-year period.

Synonymous with DODD-FRANK FINANCIAL REFORM.

See also BUREAU OF CONSUMER PROTECTION; CONSUMER FINANCIAL PROTECTION BUREAU; CONTINGENT CAPITAL; DERIVATIVES; EMERGENCY HOMEOWNERS' LOAN PROGRAM; FEDERAL DEPOSIT INSURANCE CORPORATION; FINANCIAL STABILITY OVERSIGHT COUNCIL; HEDGE FUNDS; OFFICE OF NATIONAL INSURANCE; OFFICE OF THE COMPTROLLER OF THE CURRENCY; OFFICE OF THRIFT SUPERVISION; "PLAIN VANILLA"; SECURITIES AND EXCHANGE COMMISSION; STABILITY OVERSIGHT COUNCIL; TROUBLED ASSET RELIEF PROGRAM; U.S. TREASURY DEPARTMENT; VOLCKER RULE.

WAL-MART STORES. The largest retailer in the United States said on February 10, 2009, that it would cut 700 to 800 jobs at its headquarters in Arkansas. Wal-Mart reported a 5.1 percent same-store sales increase in February compared with a 2.7 percent increase for the period a year before. The company's fourth-quarter profit 2009 was $3.25 billion, up 3.2 percent from $3.14 billion a year before. Net sales increased 1.1 percent to $98.67 billion.

On August 17, 2010, the company reported a 3.6 percent gain in second-quarter earnings to $3.6 billion, with sales rising 2.8 percent to $103 billion. The retailer continued to lose U.S. customers to other competitors but nevertheless reported a 9 percent increase in quarterly earnings on November 16. Sales fell 1.3 percent, the sixth straight drop.

On February 22, 2011, the world's largest retailer posted an overall 2.5 percent increase in sales and a 27 percent surge in profit for its fiscal fourth quarter ending January 31, 2011. With its $419 billion in annual revenue, sales fell 1.8 percent for thirteen straight weeks. Its total quarterly sales climbed to $115.6 billion from $112.8 billion the year before, with net income in the quarter at $6 billion, up from $4.8 billion the year before. Full-year net income amounted to $16.4 billion, up 14 percent from $14.4 billion the year earlier. In August, the firm posted a higher-than-expected profit of $3.8 billion. Revenue rose 5.4 percent to $109.3 billion. Then, on September

8, management announced that it was bringing back its layaway payment plan for the 2011 holidays as more shoppers were feeling the recession's impact. By November, Wal-Mart Stores had broken a two-year streak of decline, with a 2.9 percent fall in its fiscal third-quarter earnings. Sales climbed 1.9 percent. It had a $3.34 profit for the third quarter, with revenue increasing 8.1 percent to $110.23 billion.

See also STOCK MARKET.

WALT DISNEY COMPANY. *See* ABC.

WARREN, ELIZABETH. A Harvard law professor and authority on bank bankruptcy. On September 17, 2010, President Obama appointed her, the person who conceived the Consumer Financial Protection Bureau, to oversee its establishment as an assistant to the president. The bureau would be part of the Federal Reserve, and the central bank cannot influence its personnel or regulations. She was also a special adviser to the secretary of the Treasury for the bureau and a candidate for the U.S. Senate in 2012.

WARS IN AFGHANISTAN AND IRAQ. "A troop withdrawal may not bring budget relief. The economic payoff may be in the nation's psychology." On February 27, 2009, President Obama announced that the troops would be coming home from Iraq. The annual budget of the United States would be significantly altered.

The war had already cost an estimated $860 billion. The cost in Afghanistan and Iraq followed a simple progression in the president's budget plan: $144 billion in fiscal year 2009, $130 billion in 2010, and possibly $50 billion for 2011 and beyond.

In October 2008, a government agency estimated that in 2006 (the last year of available numbers), it cost $390,000 a year to sustain each American soldier overseas. Then, in January 2009, the Congressional Budget Office estimated that between 2010 and 2019 the costs would be based on two alternatives. In the first, the number of soldiers deployed in both nations draws down fairly quickly to about 30,000 by 2011. In the second option, levels drop to 75,000 by 2013. Both were significantly lower than the present 180,000 troops. The cost would be $388 billion for the first case or nearly double, at $867 billion, for the second option.

WASHINGTON MUTUAL. On September 26, 2008, federal regulators seized Washington Mutual and struck a deal to sell the bulk of its operations to JP Morgan in the largest bank failure in U.S. history.

See also BANK FAILURES.

WASHINGTON POST. First-quarter 2009 losses were $18.7 million compared with a profit of $39.3 million a year earlier. Revenue for the quarter dropped 0.8 percent to $1.05 billion. By August 1, 2009, the *Washington Post* showed a profit for the second quarter. Effective December 31, 2009, the newspaper closed its remaining U.S. news bureaus outside of Washington, D.C.

The newspaper reported a 3.3 percent fall in fourth-quarter 2010 profit, with net income of $79 million. Revenue was flat at $1.19 billion for the quarter.

In November 2011, management reported a small third-quarter loss of $6 million and a fall of 13 percent in revenue of $1.03 billion.

WASTE. *See* TECHNOLOGY INVESTMENT.

WATCH INDUSTRY. *See* SWATCH GROUP.

WATERFORD WEDGWOOD. Makers of classic china and crystal, the company filed for bankruptcy protection in January 2009. Founded 250 years ago, this iconic British firm succumbed to the global economic slowdown and credit squeeze.

Sales for the year that ended in April 2008 were €672 million, down 9.4 percent from the previous year. The firm posted a loss of €231 million, up from €71 million. About 1,900 workers would lose their jobs in Britain alone.

On February 27, 2009, it was announced that KPS Capital Partners would purchase the Irish and U.K. operations of Waterford Wedgwood.

WATER INFRASTRUCTURE. *See* AMERICAN RECOVERY AND RE-INVESTMENT ACT (OF 2009).

WEALTH. The wealth of American families dropped nearly 18 percent in 2008, erasing years of sharp gains on housing and stocks. It was the largest loss since World War II.

The number of U.S. millionaires fell from 9.2 million to 6.7 million between 2007 and 2008, and it was also estimated that the number of global billionaires in 2008 fell to 793 from 1,125. The 400 richest people in 1982 had a combined net worth of $92 billion; by 2006, they owned $1.25 trillion. (To get on the list in 1982, you needed a net worth of $5 million; by 2006, it had to be $1 billion.) The gap between rich and poor had been widening for thirty years; now it was narrowing. For example, in 2008, Monaco was the most expensive residential property location in the world. Ending in 2007, prices for property reached £100,000 per square meter. By April 2009, it had fallen back to $50,000. Also, in New York's Hamptons, where the rich often own large estates, offers were presented at 40 percent off the peak bids from the previous year.

By the end of June, the world population of millionaires fell 15 percent, with the superrich losing the most. The number of millionaires fell to 8.6 million from 10.1 million in 2008. The wealth held by the world's millionaires plunged nearly 20 percent to $32.8 trillion from $40.7 trillion. The ultra-wealthy—those with $30 million in investable assets—saw their ranks tumble 25 percent, with their wealth declining 24 percent. There were 2.5 million millionaires in the United States at the end of 2008, down from 3 million in 2007. The wealthiest people are referred to as high-net-worth individuals (HNWIS).

After nearly two years, American households grew a bit wealthier in the second quarter 2009. Net worth grew by 3.9 percent to $53.1 trillion in the April–June period from the first quarter. Yet, it was still down almost 19 percent from the $65.3 trillion peak in the third quarter 2007.

The increasing share of national income in the United States has gone to the top 1 percent of earners since the 1970s, when their share was 8 to 9 percent. In the 1980s, it climbed to 10 to 14 percent. In the late 1990s, it was 1 to 19 percent, and in 2005 it passed 21 percent. By 2007, the richest 1 percent were taking more than 23 percent of all income. The richest one-tenth of 1 percent, presenting just 13,000 households, took in more than 11 percent of total income in 2007.

From 2003 to 2007, incomes of the rich climbed at an annualized rate of 13.9 percent compared with 1.8 percent for everyone else. Since 1982, the income of the top 1 percent of earners had been roughly 2.4 times as volatile as the average for everyone.

U.S. households' wealth fell in the second quarter 2010. The decline was 2.8 percent to $53.5 trillion, leaving the average net worth at abut $182,000 a person. The richest fifth of people by summer 2010 reacted to the meltdown, spending 2.6 percent less from 2007 to 2009.

By the third quarter 2011, attempts to reclaim wealth lost during the recession failed. Stock losses and home prices continued to fall. Worth—the value of houses, stocks, and other investments minus debts and other liabilities—fell $2.4 trillion to $57.4 trillion from the second to the third quarter. Announced on December 8, it was the greatest decline since the fourth quarter 2008.

See also TAX CUTS.

WEAPON SALES. *See* ARMS SALES.

WEATHERIZATION. *See* AMERICAN RECOVERY AND REINVESTMENT ACT (OF 2009); ENERGY EFFICIENCY.

WELFARE. By 2009, despite soaring unemployment and the worst economic crisis in decades, eighteen states had cut their welfare rolls. Nationally, the number of people receiving cash assistance remained at or near the lowest in more than forty years. Twenty-three of the thirty largest states, which accounted for more than 88 percent of the country's population, indicated on June 22 that welfare caseloads were higher than the previous year. The largest increases were in states with the worst jobless rates.

The total number of welfare recipients is climbing. Paralleling this increase, the number of Americans receiving food stamps has risen sharply from 24.9 million in September 2007 to 33.2 million in March 2009.

See also CHILD CARE; FOOD STAMPS; POVERTY; SPAIN.

WELLPOINT. The nation's largest health insurer reported a 61 percent drop in fourth-quarter profit on January 28, 2009. The insurer announced in mid-January 2009 that it would cut about 1,500 jobs, or 3.5 percent of its staff. The company's third-quarter 2009 profit declined 11 percent to $730 million. Revenue climbed 3.1 percent to $15.43 billion.

The firm's third-quarter 2010 profit rose 1.2 percent, reporting earnings of $739.1 million, although revenue fell 5.7 percent to $14.33 billion. Its fourth-quarter profit fell 80 percent. Fourth-quarter profit fell 39 percent, with a profit of $335.3 million.

See also HEALTH INSURERS.

WELLS FARGO BANK. The nation's largest consumer bank posted a $2.55 billion loss in the fourth quarter 2008, becoming the first quarterly loss for the San Francisco–based bank since 2001.

In March 2009, the bank became the latest large U.S. firm to sharply cut its dividend—by 85 percent to a nickel a share—amid growing scrutiny of its once-strong balance sheet. The move looked to save $5 billion a year. Management announced on April 9 that its profit in the first quarter 2009 rose to roughly $3 billion. This triggered a jump in shares of banks.

Wells Fargo posted a $3.2 billion profit for the second quarter 2009, up from $1.75 billion a year before. By September 2009, Wells Fargo announced its intention to return $25 billion in federal bailout funds. On December 14, 2009, Wells Fargo became the last of the big bank lenders to rush through a repayment of $25 billion before year's end. It first had to secure $10.4 billion by selling shares.

The bank reported on July 21, 2010, that its second-quarter earnings fell 3 percent to $3.06 billion and it had a $3.06 billion profit. In early October, management reported that it was paying $24 million to attorneys general in eight states to end an investigation into whether lenders acquired by the bank made risky mortgages to consumers without disclosing their perils. These loans, called "option adjustable-rate loans" or "pick-a-payment mortgages," were considered deceptive by the states in that the loans permitted borrowers to defer some interest payments and add them to the principal balance. The agreement included no admission of wrongdoing by Wells Fargo. The fourth-largest U.S. bank by assets reported on October 20, 2010, that it earned $3.3 billion, up 7 percent from one year earlier. However, revenue fell 7 percent from the year before to $20.9 billion. Wells Fargo reported fourth-quarter earnings surging 21 percent to $3.41 billion. Wells Fargo, with its number-one position in new-home mortgages, increased its profit 48 percent to $3.8 billion as reported on April 20, 2011. Then, on September 21, Moody's cut its credit rating on Wells Fargo's senior debt to A2 from A1. Its Prime-1 short-term rating was affirmed. Management reported on October 17 that its quarterly results were down, with its net interest margin falling to 3.84 percent, the fourth consecutive decline.

See also WACHOVIA.

Cf. CITIGROUP.

WEYERHAEUSER. The timber industry building products firm announced in March 2009 that it would close two lumber mills as demand for wood products continued to decline with the slump in home construction. Nearly 300 employees, or 1.5 percent of the firm's workforce, were affected. Weyerhaeuser had already closed ten plants making wood products. It had losses in the first quarter of $264 million from a loss of $148 million the year earlier. On July 31, Weyerhaeuser reported that its second-quarter 2009 loss had widened. The company lost $106 million, with sales dropping 36 percent to $1.39 billion from $217 billion a year earlier.

Cf. LOUISIANA-PACIFIC CORPORATION.

WHIRLPOOL. Fourth-quarter 2008 net income fell 76 percent by revenue for the world's largest appliance company. Management projected that its North American appliance sales would drop around 10 percent in 2009 after a 16 percent decline in the fourth quarter. They forecast sales in Europe to drop 8 percent in the same period, while sales in Asia and Latin America were projected down 5 percent.

Whirlpool's first-quarter 2009 net income declined 27 percent on lower global sales and production. The world's largest appliance maker by revenue posted a first-quarter net income of $73 million, down from $100 million. The company's third-quarter 2009 earnings fell 47 percent, with sales in North America—its largest market—slipping 9 percent from the previous year.

Whirlpool reported that its first-quarter 2010 earnings were $164 million, with sales climbing 20 percent to $4.27 billion. The firm's second-quarter earnings more than doubled, with net income of $205 million and sales increasing 8.8 percent to $4.53 billion. Whirlpool reported a 9.2 percent drop in third-quarter 2010 earnings, with sales climbing 0.5 percent to $4.52 billion.

By mid-October 2011, appliance sales had dramatically tumbled. Whirlpool announced that it would close two factories and cut 5,000 jobs, or 7 percent of its workforce. The manufacturer's profit in the third quarter was $177 million, with sales climbing 2.3 percent to $4.63 billion. Following a 20 percent climb in earnings for the fourth quarter to $205 million, sales fell 2.6 percent to $4.91 billion.

See also APPLIANCES; ELECTROLUX.

WHISTLEBLOWERS. *See* SECURITIES AND EXCHANGE COMMISSION.

WHITE-COLLAR WORKERS. Usually, those working in the service sector. Unlike most union workers, salaried workers have no safety net of health care or guaranteed income for a year.

WHOLESALE CREDIT UNIONS. *See* CREDIT UNIONS.

WHOLESALE FOOD PRICES. *See* FOOD PRICES; WHOLESALE PRICES.

WHOLESALE INVENTORIES. Wholesalers reduced their inventories in December 2008 by the largest amount in nearly seventeen years. This reduction would encourage wholesalers to order fewer new goods, leading to reduced production and potentially more job layoffs.

Wholesale inventories plunged by 1.4 percent, which was double analysts' expectations. It also was the fourth consecutive monthly decline. Inventories at the wholesale level were reduced for a record eleventh consecutive month by July 2009, more than the 1 percent decline expected.

Wholesale firms added to their stockpiles for a seventeenth consecutive month in May 2011 as sales fell for only the second time in the past eleven months, further indicating the slowdown in the U.S. economy. The government reported on July 8 that wholesale inventories climbed 1.8 percent in May, the largest increase since October 2010, with sales falling at the wholesale level by 0.2 percent.

WHOLESALE PRICES. Inflation at the wholesale level in January 2011 pressured firms to increase their prices. The producer-price index, which shows what manufacturers and wholesalers pay for finished goods, climbed 0.8 percent in the month from December 2010. By September, wholesale-prices rose sharply by 6.9 percent.

At the end of 2011, wholesale prices fell 0.1 percent from November to December. Cars and truck jumped 0.3 percent

WIA. *See* WORKFORCE INVESTMENT ACT.

WILLIAMS-SONOMA. Facing difficult sales trends, the retailer of kitchenware cut 1,400 jobs as part of an effort to trim fiscal 2009 overhead costs by $75 million before taxes. Sales plunged 24 percent over the eight-week Christmas period as consumers curbed discretionary spending. The firm's fourth-quarter 2008 net income dropped 90 percent on declining sales.

The company posted a first-quarter 2009 loss and a 22 percent decline in sales. Williams-Sonoma's fiscal fourth-quarter earnings soared. It posted a profit of $88.4 million, while revenue increased 8.1 percent to $1.09 billion.

The company's second-quarter 2010 profit climbed to $30.8 million, hitting a record for the period, as merchandising changes and lower discounting boosted sales. Revenue rose 15 percent to $775.6 million. The home décor seller's fiscal fourth-quarter profit had surged 28 percent. For the quarter ending January 30, 2011, profit was $113.4 million, up from $88.4 million the year before. Revenue increased 9.7 percent to $1.2 billion from the year earlier as sales climbed 5.2 percent.

Reporting on May 19, 2011, the company's profit climbed 62 percent for its fiscal first quarter, with a profit of $31.6 million. Revenue increased 7.4 percent to $770.8 million.

WINDFALL TAX. For significant bonuses being given, the United Kingdom slapped on a hefty windfall tax. The government expected to make nearly $1 billion from a 50 percent tax on bonuses above $40,000.

See also UNITED KINGDOM.

"WINDOW DRESSING." The act of selling the month's losers and purchasing strong performers so that those names show up on clients' quarterly statements.

On September 17, 2010, U.S. federal regulators proposed new disclosure rules targeting "window dressing," the practice undertaken by some large banks to temporarily lower their debt levels before reporting finances to the public. The practice indicated that some banks were carrying more risk than was apparent to their investments or customers, who only saw the levels recorded on the firms' quarterly balance sheets. The Securities and Exchange Commission proposed new regulations requiring greater disclosure from banks and other firms about their short-term borrowing. A group of eighteen large banks lowered debt at the end of each of the past six quarters (2010), lowering it on average by 42 percent from quarterly peaks.

WINE MARKET. In the first six months of 2009, luxury wine sellers saw both an increase in sales and lower profits as Americans continued to consume a greater amount of wine but purchased less expensive brands.

"WIN THE FUTURE." The theme of President Obama's January 25, 2011, State of the Union speech, shifting the focus of his first two years in office to the next two years delving into issues of the future. The talk spoke of the role of government, budget cuts, as the economic future of the nation.

WOMEN'S WAGES. Wages of the average woman who had a position during 2008–2009 climbed faster than those of the typical male. Over this time period, the median wages of women rose 3.2 percent after adjusting for inflation. For men, wages rose 2 percent. Minority men were especially hard hit, while minority women and highly educated women of all races did better.

By 2011, even following significant strides of education and economics, women made far less money on average than men and remained disproportionately in poverty. The share of women who are married fell to 62 percent in 2009 from 70 percent in 1970. In 2009, about 87 percent of women had graduated from high school, while in 1970 only 8 percent of women had a college degree. Today, women make on average 75 percent of what their male counterparts earn.

WOMEN UNEMPLOYED. The share of women with jobs in December 2008 had fallen almost two percentage points from the peak it reached in 2000; at no other point in the past fifty years had the share of employed women fallen so much from its peak.

By October 2009, 8.1 percent of working women became unemployed.

In the United States, female unemployment increased in winter 2011 to 8 percent even as unemployment fell to 8.7 percent for men. By April 2011, women's unemployment rate was 8.4 percent, with about 18.2 percent of them working in the public sector.

See also MEN UNEMPLOYED; OVERTIME; UNEMPLOYMENT; WOMEN'S WAGES; WOMEN WORKFORCE.

WOMEN WORKFORCE. In early 2009, U.S. women surpassed men on payrolls, capturing the majority for the first time. The proportion of working women had not significantly changed, but a full 82 percent of the job losses had been borne by men.

The Great Recession has driven women who had left the workforce to return. By September 2009, women held nearly half (49.9 percent) of all U.S. jobs, excluding farm workers and the self-employed, a rise of 1.2 percent from the 48.7 percent when the Great Recession began in December 2007 (in 1970, women held 35 percent of positions). Unemployment among women was lower than men at 8.8 percent.

See also WOMEN'S WAGES; WOMEN UNEMPLOYED.

WOOLWORTHS. In mid-December 2008, all Woolworths in the United Kingdom were shut down. It closed its 807 stores, with the last one shutting its doors on January 5, 2009, putting 27,000 people out of work. Woolworths terminated U.S. operations in 2001. Woolworths, the largest retail casualty during the British recession, was reborn on June 25, 2009, as an online brand selling children's wear, toys, and party goods.

By March 2010, Woolworths reported an 11 percent rise in its first-half net profit, with sales climbing 6 percent.

See also RETAILING.

WORKER, HOMEOWNERSHIP, AND BUSINESS ASSISTANCE ACT (2009). *See* UNEMPLOYMENT BENEFITS.

WORKFORCE INVESTMENT ACT (WIA). Enacted in 1998, the act sought to replace jumbled federal schemes with a streamlined system for workers and employers. States have some flexibility, with help for job searches, career counseling, and, for some, money for training, often at community colleges.

Its funding is confused and declining, down 10 percent since 2002 to about $3.2 billion for the whole country in 2008. Only about 40 percent of WIA money is spent on training.

WORK OPENINGS. *See* JOB OPENINGS.

WORKS PROGRESS ADMINISTRATION(WPA). Established on April 8, 1935, this job creation program led to the building of 650,000 miles of roads. The WPA absorbed 2.1 percent of the nation's GDP from 1935 to 1941. The deficit during the WPA's life averaged 3.2 percent of GDP.

See also GREAT DEPRESSION; ROOSEVELT, FRANKLIN DELANO.

WORLD BANK (THE BANK). Commenced operation in June 1946 to provide funds and technical assistance to facilitate economic development in its poorer member countries. Funds come from capital provided by member nations, sales of its own securities, sales of parts of its loans, repayments, and net earnings.

In December 2008, the World Bank declared that the global financial meltdown was a heavy burden on developing economies, forecasting 4.5 percent growth in 2009, down from 6.3 percent in 2008.

The World Bank argued that net private capital flows to emerging economies in 2009 were likely to be only half the record $1 trillion of 2007, while global trade volumes would shrink for the first time since 1982. The World Bank plans to increase lending over the next three years to $100 billion to emerging countries to help them in dealing with the 2008 2009 economic meltdown. The World Bank predicted that in 2009 global trade would shrink by 2 percent for the first time in twenty-seven years.

In mid-June 2010, the World Bank reported that developing nations' net private capital inflows fell 41 percent in 2008 and would be reduced by nearly half in 2009. The World Bank offered little hope that nations would provide the spark for the global economic engine. GDP growth in emerging nations was projected to grow only 1.2 percent in 2009, as rich countries contracted by 4.5 percent. The World Bank stated in June that global economic growth could falter significantly if the sovereign debt crisis in Europe produced a debt default or created a loss in market confidence.

In early January 2012, the World Bank revised downward its global growth for the year, forecasting it at 5.4 percent, down from 6.2 percent projected earlier.

See also BRETTON WOODS; BRETTON WOODS II; CHINA; EURO-PEAN CENTRAL BANK; G-20; GLOBAL TRADE; POVERTY; RUSSIA; TRADE; ZOELLICK, ROBERT.

Cf. INTERNATIONAL MONETARY FUND.

Synonymous with INTERNATIONAL BANK FOR RECONSTRUCTION AND DEVELOPMENT.

WORLDCOM. *See* GENERAL MOTORS.

WORLD ECONOMIC FORUM (2012). Held annually in Davis, Switzerland. Its 2012 theme focused on how the eurozone's sovereign debt crisis can be resolved.

WORLD TRADE (2011). In 2011, the world's economy shifted from stimulus to austerity, evolving a marked slowdown in growth. The global economy was expected to expand by 3.6 percent, down from 4.4 percent in 2010. Central banks would keep interest rates low throughout the year. Emerging nations would, however, expand by 6.3 percent.

Global trade should grow by 5.7 percent, a softening from the previous year when inventory restocking fueled an 11.5 percent surge.

See also EXPORTS; GLOBAL TRADE; PROTECTIONISM.

WORLD TRADE ORGANIZATION (WTO). Replacing the General Agreement on Tariffs and Trade (GATT) in 1995, its multilateral trade rules are a bulwark against protectionism. Headquarters are in Geneva, Switzerland. After two decades of unilateral tariff-cutting, most countries' tariffs have fallen below their "bound" rates, the ceilings agreed to in the trade group. In the period of meltdown and increased protectionism, nations will be able to increase, sometimes tripling their import levies, without breaking World Trade Organization rules.

On March 23, 2009, the WTO predicted that global trade would drop 9 percent or more in 2009. It issued its most negative report on global trade in its sixty-two-year history. Three days later, its 153 members were told that there was a significant slip in the global commitment to free trade, with increases in tariffs, new nontariff measures, and more resorting to trade defense measures such as antidumping actions. The WTO reported that world trade fell 12.2 percent in 2009.

On April 7, 2011, the WTO projected a 6.5 percent rise in world trade, above the average rate of 6 percent from 1990 to 2008.

See also CHINA; GENERAL AGREEMENT ON TARIFFS AND TRADE; G-20; GLOBAL TRADE; PROTECTIONISM; SMOOT-HAWLEY ACT; TRADE BARRIERS.

WORLD WAR II. *See* ROOSEVELT, FRANKLIN DELANO.

WPA. *See* WORKS PROGRESS ADMINISTRATION.

WQXR-FM. *See New York Times.*

WRITE-DOWNS. Reducing the value of an asset as it is carried on a firm's balance sheet because the market value has fallen.

W-SHAPED RECESSION. *See* RECESSION.

WSJ. *See Wall Street Journal.*

WTO. *See* WORLD TRADE ORGANIZATION.

WYNDHAM. Fourth-quarter 2010 earnings rose to 6.9 percent, overcoming a weak 2009.

X

XEROX. In April 2009, Xerox reported a small first-quarter profit as revenue fell 18 percent. On July 23, it reported a profit decline, with earnings down 35 percent to $140 million. Revenue declined 18 percent to $3.73 billion.

On April 23, 2010, management reported a first-quarter loss, with a 33 percent jump in sales. The firm's profit jumped 62 percent in the second quarter 2010 to $227 million from $140 million the year before. Revenue climbed 48 percent to $5.51 billion. On October 21, management declared that its profit more than doubled to $250 million from $123 million the year before. At the same time, it announced plans to lay off about 2 percent of its workforce.

XSTRATA. The international mining company had a net debt in 2008 of $15 billion and a market capitalization of $9 billion. It planned a 50 percent cut in jobs.

On February 8, 2011, Xstrata reported that its full-year net profit climbed nearly sevenfold. Its 2010 net profit totaled $4.69 billion, with a rise of 34 percent in revenue to $30.49 billion and operating profit increase of 75 percent to $7.65 billion.

Y

YAHOO!. Posted a 76 percent quarterly profit decline as the recession hit. The firm said on April 21, 2009, that it would eliminate about 675 more jobs, or 5 percent of its workforce. Yahoo!'s revenue fell 13 percent in the first quarter to $1.58 billion from $1.81 billion a year before. Yahoo! saw sales decline again in the second quarter 2009. The company's overall revenue fell 13 percent from a year earlier and made a profit gain of 7.6 percent.

From December 25, 2009, through January 1, 2010, Yahoo! shut down its offices, except essential functions, as one way of cutting expenses during the meltdown.

On April 20, 2010, the firm's first-quarter earnings nearly tripled as its revenue edged up for the first time in more than one year. Earnings were $310.2 million compared with $117.6 million the year before. Revenue increased 1 percent to $1.6 billion. Yahoo! reported on July 20, 2010, that its profit increased more than 50 percent in the second quarter but that its net revenue was $1.13 billion below the average analyst expectation of $1.16 billion. In October, Yahoo! posted a $396 million profit for the period ending September 2010, up from $186 million the year before. Revenue climbed 1.7 percent to $1.6 billion. Soon after, Yahoo!'s net income more than doubled to $396 million from $186 million the year before. Revenue climbed 2 percent to $1.6 billion. In mid-December, management announced its intention to cut as many as 650 jobs, almost 5 percent of its workforce, following the nearly 700 people let go during the second quarter 2009. Third-quarter revenue rose 1.6 percent while sales dropped 7 percent. Yahoo!'s quarterly profit more than doubled, with revenue falling 12 percent.

In January 2011, the firm announced that it would cut 4 percent of its payroll from the present 13,600 employees. The firm posted second-quarter 2011 income of $237 million, with revenue falling 23 percent to $1.23 billion. Its third-quarter profit fell 26 percent, with four consecutive quarterly slowdowns. Revenue dropped to $1.22 billion, with earnings of $293 million.

Management announced on January 24, 2012, that its fourth-quarter, 2011 profit fell 5 percent and revenue dropped 13 percent from the year before.

For the entire year, revenue fell about 5 percent to $4.4 billion in 2011 from $4.6 billion in 2010.

Cf. APPLE; FACEBOOK; GOOGLE.

YALE UNIVERSITY. Yale University estimated that its endowment had fallen 25 percent by mid-December 2008 to $17 billion since the end of June because of the global financial crisis, leading the university to restrict pay raises and cut spending to close a projected $100 million budget deficit. Yale's endowment fell to $16 billion on June 30 from $22.9 billion a year earlier. In 2009–2010, Yale cut staff and nonsalary expenses by 7.5 percent. The university projected an annual deficit of $150 million each year from 2010–2011 through 2013–2014.

By the end of September 2010, Yale's endowment earned 8.9 percent for the twelve months ending June 30, climbing to $16.7 billion from $16.3 billion a year earlier. The return still fell below the 13.3 percent median return of other large investments but showed an improvement over the approximately 25 percent loss from the year before. Spending from the endowment represented 38 percent of the university's net revenue for the 2010–2011 fiscal year.

The endowment posted a return of 21.9 percent for the fiscal year ending June 30, 2011.

Cf. COLUMBIA UNIVERSITY; HARVARD UNIVERSITY; PRINCETON UNIVERSITY; STANFORD UNIVERSITY.

YEN. By the end of October 2008, the Japanese yen rose up against most major currencies, surging as much as 10 percent against the dollar. This rise was another signal of weakness in the world's economy. The U.S. dollar weakened 19 percent against the yen in 2008, the biggest winner in the currency markets.

By February 2009, the yen was 23.2 percent higher than the previous year's low point against the dollar, 46.7 percent higher against the euro, and 65 percent up against the British pound.

In 2010, with a weak economy, the yen was strong. The U.S. dollar lost 12.8 percent against the currency.

On March 17, 2011, many of the world's economic powers united in an attempt to slow down the rise in the value of the yen, as it was handicapping Japan's recovery.

See also JAPAN; PLAZA ACCORD.

YIELD CURVE. The difference between short-term and long-term interest rates on government bonds. Indicating growing investor optimism, this measure hit a record on December 21, 2009, suggesting that the economic recovery was growing.

YIELD SPREAD PREMIUMS. *See* MORTGAGE LEGISLATION.

YOUTH UNEMPLOYMENT. *See* UNEMPLOYMENT.

YUAN. Launched in the United States in early January 2011 for the first time to encourage trading and investment in its currency, the state bank was now permitting customers to trade the yuan in the United States, expanding the offshore market for the currency, which began last year in Hong Kong. By mid-July, the yan soared against the U.S. dollar as the official exchange rate was set higher. Trading on July 4 strengthened to 6.4599, up 5.7 percent against the dollar in 2011.

See also CHINA. *Synonymous with* REDBACK; RENMINBI.

Z

ZALE CORPORATION. The third-largest jewelry retailer's sales declined to $658.7 million in the third quarter 2009 from $679.4 million a year before. Zales closed hundreds of its branches in 2008. On November 24, it posted a loss of $57.6 million for the fiscal first quarter ending October 31. The figures compared with a year before loss of $48.4 million. Sales fell 18.6 percent in November 2009.

In November and December 2010, sales rose 7.5 percent following a fall of 12 percent one year earlier. Overall revenue for the two months totaled $533.1 million, up 8 percent from $497.3 million in 2009.

Zales' fiscal third-quarter 2011 loss was $8.99 million, as revenue climbed 14 percent to $411.8 million. On August 31, Zales' management posted a 9.8 percent climb in sales but noted a wider loss of $32.6 million.

See also JEWELRY.

ZAMBIA. *See* AFRICA.

ZANA. *See* INDITEX.

ZERO RATE. For some people who have lost vast amounts on stocks, bonds, and real estate, making an investment that offers security but no gain is tantamount to coming out ahead. With no apparent acceptable option, a zero percent rate of return appealed to many people.

Often shortened to ZIRP, zero interest rate policy.

See also U.S. GOVERNMENT DEBT.

ZHEJIANG GEELY HOLDING GROUP. *See* VOLVO.

ZHEJIANG YOUNGMAN LOTUS AUTOMOBILE COMPANY. *See* SAAB.

ZIMBABWE. The nation's GDP growth was projected into 2011 at 4.3 percent, with a GDP of $2 billion, an inflation rate of 8.5 percent, and a GDP per head at $157.

ZIRP (ZERO INTEREST RATE POLICY). *See* ZERO RATE.

ZOELLICK, ROBERT. A former U.S. trade representative and deputy secretary of state, now World Bank president. Following the August 1–5, 2011, volatile Dow Jones Industrial Average week of huge gains and losses about the strength of the U.S. economy and Europe's deepening debt crisis, he argued, "We are entering a new danger zone, both short- and long-term to restore confidence." He believed that the European Central Bank's decision to purchase bonds from distressed eurozone nations would only solve near-term liquidity issues. He urged national leaders to endorse structural overhauls to boost productivity, job creation, and free trade in a push to get growth back on track.

See also EUROPEAN CENTRAL BANK; WORLD BANK.

ZOMBIE BANKS. Banks that are failing but allowed to linger on.

See also BANK RESCUE (PLAN) OF 2009 (U.S.); ZOMBIES.

ZOMBIES. Debtors that have little hope of recovery and manage to avoid being wiped out thanks to support from their lenders or from the government. They consume tax monies, capital, and labor that could be better used in growing companies. By lowering prices to generate sales, zombie firms can draw healthier rivals into insolvency. Zombies are financial institutions that are effectively bankrupt but are kept alive by government assistance.

Japan was confounded during its lost decade of minimal growth in the 1990s. Weak Japanese borrowers used the proceeds from new loans to pay interest on old ones, a process called *ever greening* that kept banks from having to acknowledge losses.

Protecting zombies stunts long-term growth by blocking the needed reallocation of resources from declining firms and sectors to rising ones.

Sectors that could spawn them are:

a. Finance—The government props up weak banks that may never be capable of normal lending.
b. Homeowners—Assistance for homeowners may keep them out of foreclosure but still leave them with significant debt.
c. Automakers—Assistance to U.S. carmakers could tie up billions supporting firms that are unable to compete successfully.

See LEMON SOCIALISM; ZOMBIE BANKS.

ZUCKERBERG, MARK. *See* FACEBOOK.

INDEX

ABOUT THE AUTHOR

Jerry M. Rosenberg, 2010 Distinguished Faculty Award recipient, 2008 Fulbright Specialist grant winner, and 2006 Marshall Foundation Fellow, is professor emeritus of global business and management at Rutgers University Business School, New Jersey. Acclaimed by the *New York Times* as "The Leading Business and Technical Lexicographer in the Nation."